THE ALMANAC INVESTOR

THE ALMANAC INVESTOR

Profit from Market History and Seasonal Trends

Jeffrey A. Hirsch   J. Taylor Brown

WILEY

John Wiley & Sons, Inc.

Published by John Wiley & Sons, Inc., Hoboken, New Jersey
Published simultaneously in Canada

For general information on our other products and services or for technical support, please contact our Customer Care Department within the United States at (800) 762-2974, outside the United States at (317) 572-3993 or fax (317) 572-4002.

Wiley also publishes its books in a variety of electronic formats. Some content that appears in print may not be available in electronic books. For more information about Wiley products, visit our web site at www.wiley.com.

ISBN-13: 978-0-471-65405-6
ISBN-10: 0-471-65405-1

Printed in the United States of America

10 9 8 7 6 5 4 3 2 1

The Almanac Investor is respectfully and lovingly dedicated to Yale and Davida Hirsch. Yale and Davida have been a never ending source of inspiration and guidance. Individually two of the finest people you will every meet; together they exemplify how patience, love, and understanding can overcome all obstacles.

Acknowledgment

We would like to acknowledge Christopher Mistal whose tireless commitment and keen insight made completion of this project possible. Besides his vital contribution to this book, Christopher has proven to be a software developer, database programmer, and Internet guru nonpareil and has left an indelible mark on all elements of the *Almanac Investor Platform*.

CONTENTS

Part 2: Seasonal Sector Investing

Part 3: Databank

PREFACE

Investing is an evolving art that is perpetually morphing as the world changes. Thirty-nine years ago, Yale Hirsch, legendary market guru and founder of The Hirsch Organization, used graph paper and a ruler to formulate his observations and as a result of his groundbreaking work gave birth to the concept of "Almanac Investing." He realized while pouring over his notebooks that certain patterns repeated themselves. In 1967 he first published what would grow into the world famous *Stock Trader's Almanac*.

In addition to the *Stock Trader's Almanac*, Yale went on to create numerous investment publications that were always on the cutting edge of the investing world. In the summer of 2001, as the bear gnashed some of the fiercest teeth ever to rip into the Street, we realized that people, us included, had forgotten lessons that never should have ever passed into lore. The *Almanac Investor Newsletter* was born.

We strove to create a service individual investors and professionals alike could turn to when they wanted to know what was really going on. A source of historical analysis easily understood, yet insightful. For over five years we have amassed studies, created indicators, and analyzed situations. This book is an amalgamation of the most effective indicators, patterns, and strategies expounded on in the *Stock Trader's Almanac* and *Almanac Investor Newsletter*.

There is no magic formula to make investing easy. Nothing can replace research, experience, and a healthy dose of luck. There is, however, a methodology investors can employ to mitigate losses and enhance returns. Nineteenth century philosopher George Santayana once quipped, "Those who cannot remember the past are condemned to repeat it." This is the cornerstone of the philosophy behind what we call Almanac Investing. Simply put, Almanac Investing relies on analyzing and studying the markets from an historical perspective. Whether a person is a short-term trader or a longer-term investor, being aware of historical and seasonal patterns and tendencies is helpful and valuable.

There are three key elements to becoming an *Almanac Investor*. First, you must understand how the market moves under normal conditions. Whether in a Bull market or a Bear, Wall Street moves to a predictable cadence governed by the passage of time. Recurring events such as the Presidential Election cycle, End of Quarter portfolio rebalancing, Options and Futures Expirations, Tax Deadlines and Holidays, to name a few topics addressed in this book, have a predictable influence on traders and investors.

People's day-to-day lives, such as paying bills, going on summer vacations, holiday shopping, and 401(k) contributions have a profound effect on the market. Humans are creatures of habit. Knowing the habits of your fellow investors will make market events, once dismissed as chance, unfold before you with apparent outcomes. *Almanac Investor* will help you understand that market movements are not a random walk through the woods.

Exogenous events, whether foreign or domestic, have been impacting the market since our forefathers gathered under the buttonwood tree. This undisputable reality is the second aspect of Almanac Investing. In today's geopolitical cauldron, an investor who doesn't comprehend the difference between peacetime markets and wartime markets is a sitting duck. Watergate, the Cuban Missile Crisis, presidential assassinations, oil embargos, wars, and terror attacks are but a few events that must be analyzed and comprehended. Though the market never reacts the same way every time, knowing how it performed in the past gives an Almanac Investor the edge during times of crisis. It's best to remember that the word "crisis" in Chinese is comprised of two symbols: the first is danger and second is OPPORTUNITY.

Lastly, to be an effective investor, you need access to clean data and usable investing tools that put the numbers to work. *Almanac Investor* provides you with the data you will need in the easy to understand manner that we have made famous for four decades. This book is designed not only to be an instructional "how to" book, but a valuable desk reference as well.

With the advent of powerful computers and flexible software we have been able to sort, cull, and analyze data with speed and efficiency that even the most progressive technophiles of previous generations would have thought preposterous. The Internet has become ubiquitous for all levels of investors.

This electronic revolution is both a blessing and a curse. There is a so much data and information available to investors today that many feel bombarded and overloaded. For this reason, we are inviting individuals who purchase this book to sign up for a free 60-day trial to our *Almanac Investor Platform*.

The *Almanac Investor Platform* includes many of the studies and tools detailed in this book. Instead of the reports being a static page of text, you will be able to dig deeper into the data by altering date ranges and data sets. This comprehensive platform encompasses all the Hirsch Organization has to offer. Included is a full subscription to the monthly *Almanac Investor Newsletter*, all interim Email Alerts, and full access to the Online Research Tool. To activate your free account visit *almanacinvestor.com*, click on the free-trial box and use promo code AIB1.

Seasonal Investing has become the cornerstone of our approach to the markets. The advent of exchange traded funds (ETFs) has facilitated Almanac Investing. Before the creation of this vehicle, investors would have to hand-pick a basket of stocks from a sector, thus incurring additional commission costs and risks. ETFs are funds that track an index, but can be traded like a stock. Basically, they bundle together the securities that are in an index.

Investors can do just about anything with an ETF that they can do with a normal stock, such as short selling or options trading. Because ETFs are traded on stock exchanges, they can be bought and sold at any time during the day (unlike most mutual funds). Their prices fluctuate from moment to moment, just like any other stock's price, and an investor needs a broker in order to purchase them. In this book, we illustrate on a sector-by-sector basis what ETFs you ought to hold, the returns you should expect, and easy methods to get in and out of them at the right time.

Almanac Investor is a tool to help investors gain perspective of the markets. Trading with this book as your only reference is akin to planning an outdoor wedding with the *Old Farmers Almanac*. Just because there is only a 5 percent chance of rain on your wedding day doesn't mean you shouldn't have a tent. Trading with any one trading tool, book, or advisor for that matter is, in general, a bad idea. However, once you take a long hard look back at where the stock market has been, the shroud of uncertainty covering Wall Street begins to lift.

Those who study market history are bound to profit from it!

Jeffrey A. Hirsch & J. Taylor Brown

PART 1:
INDICATORS AND PATTERNS

JANUARY INDICATORS AND PATTERNS

January Almanac

January, namesake month of the Roman god of doorways and passages, Janus, has quite a legendary reputation on Wall Street. Our January Barometer (JB), of course, garners much of the notoriety with its .806 batting average since 1938. As the opening of the New Year, January is host to many important events, indicators, and recurring market patterns. U.S. Presidents are inaugurated and present State of the Union Addresses. New Congresses convene. Financial analysts release annual forecasts. Residents of Earth return to work and school en mass after holiday celebrations. Small stocks are rumored to outperform large stocks in the nom de guerre, the "January Effect." And, the largest number of our seasonal indicators occurs in January: Day two marks the end of our "Santa Claus Rally," the "First Five Days" is our first glimpse at the trading environment for the coming year and a whole month gain or loss of the S&P 500 triggers our January Barometer. Every down January on the S&P 500 since 1938, without exception, has preceded a new or extended bear market, or a flat year.

Ranked number one on NASDAQ and the S&P 500 (second on the Dow) the last 35 years, January ends the year's best three-month span. NASDAQ averages a 4.0% gain since 1971. January's whole month performance is impressive but this dynamic month is also packed with important seasonality and telltale indicators. As the New Year commences cash flows from year-end bonuses and portfolio restructuring increases and floods the market. Analysts and market strategists try to decipher the market's tea leaves for the year ahead making January arguably the most important market month of the year.

Typical January

Based on our market probability models January has a rather distinct typical trading pattern. The first trading day of the year starts slow and is frequently down before the effects of holiday revelry fully wear off—but the Dow has been up 10 of the last 15. It can be an opportune time to jump into the market, while traders are still groggy, ahead of a much stronger day two. Arguably one of the better trading days of the year—the Dow has also been up 10 of the last 15, second trading days gain ground a large majority of the time with hefty gains as more sober traders turn over a "new leaf" of positivity and ramp-up buying in the New Year. Day one has improved recently, apparently in anticipation of day two's stellar record.

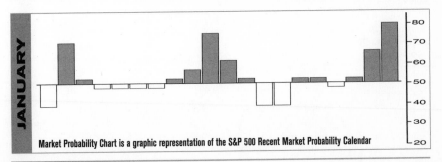

Market Probability Chart is a graphic representation of the S&P 500 Recent Market Probability Calendar

Over the next several days markets fluctuate with a slightly bearish bias. Then equities come alive around the tenth trading day of the month as the first mid-month 401(k) cash infusion is injected into the market. Buying also swells ahead of, and after, the first three-day weekend of the year, Martin Luther King Jr. Day. The Dow has been up 6 of the last 8 first days of expiration week—the day after MLK day is also an official bullish day. After this two-to-three day spurt stock prices sell off and meander until month-end. January expiration day has seen the Dow down five of the last six, but 2004 broke a 5-year losing streak. As January comes to a close stocks head higher with the last day of January being one of the strongest days of the year.

January Vital Statistics

	DJIA	S&P 500	NASDAQ	Russell 1K	Russell 2K
Rank	4	3	1	2	2
Up	37	35	24	18	16
Down	18	20	10	8	10
Avg % Change	1.4%	1.5%	3.9%	1.9%	2.7%
4-Year Presidential Election Cycle Performance					
Post-Election Year	1.3%	1.3%	3.9%	3.3%	4.5%
Mid-Term Year	-0.6	-0.9	-0.6	-1.2	-1.8
Pre-Election Year	4.5	4.7	8.6	4	4.9
Election Year	0.5	0.7	3.4	1.1	3
Best & Worst January					
	% Change	% Change	% Change	% Change	% Change
Best	1976 14.4	1987 13.2	1975 16.6	1987 12.7	1985 13.1
Worst	1960 −8.4	1790 −7.6	1990 −8.6	1990 −7.4	1990 −8.9
Best & Worst January Weeks					
Best	1/9/76 6.1	1/31/75 5.5	1/12/01 9.1	1/9/87 5.3	1/9/87 7.0
Worst	1/24/03 −5.3	1/28/00 −5.6	1/28/00 −8.2	1/28/00 −5.5	1/28/00 −5.5
Best & Worst January Days					
Best	1/17/91 4.6	1/3/01 5.0	1/3/01 14.2	1/3/01 5.3	1/3/01 4.7
Worst	1/8/88 −6.9	1/8/88 −6.8	1/2/01 −7.2	1/8/88 −6.1	1/2/01 −4.4
First Trading Day of Expiration Week 1990-2005					
Record (#Up - #Down)	10-6	7-9	8-8	6-10	8-8
Current streak	U3	U2	U2	U2	U2
Avg % Change	−0.03	0.04	0.09	0.01	0.1
Options Expiration Day 1990-2005					
Record (#Up - #Down)	9-7	8-8	10-6	8-8	9-7
Current streak	D1	D1	D1	D1	D1
Avg % Change	−0.03	0.01	−0.1	0.0	−0.1
Options Expiration Week 1990-2005					
Record (#Up - #Down)	8-8	7-9	11-5	7-9	10-6
Current streak	D1	D1	D1	D1	D1
Avg % Change	0.2	0.5	0.8	0.5	0.7
Week After Options Expiration 1990-2005					
Record (#Up - #Down)	8-8	10-6	9-7	10-6	11-5
Current streak	U1	U2	U1	U2	U2
Avg % Change	−0.6	−0.3	−0.03	−0.3	−0.02
2006 Bullish Days based on data from 1984 to 2004					
	4, 17, 18, 25, 26, 30, 31	4,17, 18, 30, 31	4, 5, 6, 13, 17, 31	4, 17, 18, 26, 30	4, 5, 6, 12, 13, 17
		18, 19, 26, 27, 31		18, 19, 26, 30, 31	
2006 Bearish Days based on data from 1984 to 2004					
	19, 20, 23, 24	3, 20, 23	20	3, 20, 23	3, 20, 25

Dow & S&P 1950-June 2005, NASDAQ 1971-June 2005, Russell 1K & 2K 1979-June 2005. Options data 1990 through August 2005. Bullish/Bearish days based on index rising or falling 60% of the time on a particular trading day 1984-2004 (see pages 68-75).

Indicators and Patterns

January's First Five Days "Early Warning System"

Two early warning indicators surface the first several days of the month, the Santa Claus Rally and January's First Five Days. The seven-day Santa Claus Rally, which averages 1.6% for the S&P 500 since 1969, ends on the second trading day of January. This brief, reliable indicator is more significant in its absence. Times when this typical end-of-year bullishness has been missing have preceded bear markets or corrections.

January's First Five Days can provide a preliminary gauge of the year to come—especially when they are up. Since 1950, 35 up First Five Days on the S&P 500 were followed by 30 full-year gains for an 85.7% accuracy ratio and a 13.8% average gain in those 35 years. The five exceptions include flat 1994 and four related to war. Vietnam military spending delayed start of 1966 bear market. Ceasefire imminence early in 1973 raised stocks temporarily. Saddam Hussein turned 1990 into a bear. The war on terrorism, instability in the Middle East, and corporate malfeasance shaped 2002 into one of the worst years on record.

The 20 down First Five Days were not indicative—up 10, down 10. In Post-Election Years however, down First Five Days can be telling. Eight of the last thirteen times the S&P 500 posted a loss for January's First Five Days—six of these eight were followed by full-year losses averaging -11.1%. Five Post-Election First Five Days showed gains and four years followed suit gaining 22.6% on average.

In Midterm Election Years this indicator has had a spotty record—almost a contrary indicator. In the last 14 Midterm Years only six full years followed the direction of the First Five Days and none did in the last seven. The full-month January Barometer (see below) has a better Midterm record of 64.3% accurate.

Pre-Election years start with a stacked deck—none have been down since 1939. Only two First Five Days were down (1955 and 1999). Both years posted S&P 500 gains of over 26%. Election Years have followed the direction of the First Five Days 12 of the last 14 times though the S&P 500 has been down only twice in Election Years since 1950.

The Incredible January Barometer

Devised by Yale Hirsch in 1972, our January Barometer has registered only five major errors since 1950 for a 90.9% accuracy ratio. This indicator adheres to propensity that as the S&P goes in January, so goes the year. Of the five major errors Vietnam affected 1966 and 1968; 1982 saw the start of a major Bull market in August; two January rate cuts and 9/11 affected 2001; and the market in January 2003 was held down by the anticipation of military action in Iraq. (*Almanac Investor* newsletter subscribers were warned at the time not to heed the January Barometer's negative reading as it was being influenced by Iraqi concerns.) Including the six flat years yields a .800 batting average. Bear markets began or continued when Januarys suffered a loss. (See Down Januarys, page 12.)

Excluding 2001, full years followed January's direction in the last 13 Post-Election years. Midterm Years tracked January's direction 9 of the last 14. With the dice loaded for Pre-Election Years as mentioned above, the JB has a 13-and-1 record,

THE FIRST-FIVE-DAYS-IN-JANUARY INDICATOR

Chronological Data

	Previous Year's Close	January 5th Day	5-Day Change	Year Change
1950	16.76	17.09	2.0%	21.8%
1951	20.41	20.88	2.3	16.5
1952	23.77	23.91	0.6	11.8
1953	26.57	26.33	−0.9	− 6.6
1954	24.81	24.93	0.5	45.0
1955	35.98	35.33	−1.8	26.4
1956	45.48	44.51	−2.1	2.6
1957	46.67	46.25	−0.9	−14.3
1958	39.99	40.99	2.5	38.1
1959	55.21	55.40	0.3	8.5
1960	59.89	59.50	−0.7	− 3.0
1961	58.11	58.81	1.2	23.1
1962	71.55	69.12	−3.4	−11.8
1963	63.10	64.74	2.6	18.9
1964	75.02	76.00	1.3	13.0
1965	84.75	85.37	0.7	9.1
1966	92.43	93.14	0.8	−13.1
1967	80.33	82.81	3.1	20.1
1968	96.47	96.62	0.2	7.7
1969	103.86	100.80	−2.9	−11.4
1970	92.06	92.68	0.7	0.1
1971	92.15	92.19	0.04	10.8
1972	102.09	103.47	1.4	15.6
1973	118.05	119.85	1.5	−17.4
1974	97.55	96.12	−1.5	−29.7
1975	68.56	70.04	2.2	31.5
1976	90.19	94.58	4.9	19.1
1977	107.46	105.01	−2.3	−11.5
1978	95.10	90.64	−4.7	1.1
1979	96.11	98.80	2.8	12.3
1980	107.94	108.95	0.9	25.8
1981	135.76	133.06	−2.0	− 9.7
1982	122.55	119.55	−2.4	14.8
1983	140.64	145.23	3.3	17.3
1984	164.93	168.90	2.4	1.4
1985	167.24	163.99	−1.9	26.3
1986	211.28	207.97	−1.6	14.6
1987	242.17	257.28	6.2	2.0
1988	247.08	243.40	−1.5	12.4
1989	277.72	280.98	1.2	27.3
1990	353.40	353.79	0.1	− 6.6
1991	330.22	314.90	−4.6	26.3
1992	417.09	418.10	0.2	4.5
1993	435.71	429.05	−1.5	7.1
1994	466.45	469.90	0.7	− 1.5
1995	459.27	460.83	0.3	34.1
1996	615.93	618.46	0.4	20.3
1997	740.74	748.41	1.0	31.0
1998	970.43	956.04	−1.5	26.7
1999	1229.23	1275.09	3.7	19.5
2000	1469.25	1441.46	−1.9	−10.1
2001	1320.28	1295.86	−1.8	−13.0
2002	1148.08	1160.71	1.1	−23.4
2003	879.82	909.93	3.4	26.4
2004	1111.92	1131.91	1.8	9.0
2005	1211.92	1186.19	−2.1	??

Ranked By Performance

Rank		5-Day Change	Year Change
1	1987	6.2%	2.0%
2	1976	4.9	19.1
3	1999	3.7	19.5
4	2003	3.4	26.4
5	1983	3.3	17.3
6	1967	3.1	20.1
7	1979	2.8	12.3
8	1963	2.6	18.9
9	1958	2.5	38.1
10	1984	2.4	1.4
11	1951	2.3	16.5
12	1975	2.2	31.5
13	1950	2.0	21.8
14	2004	1.8	9.0
15	1973	1.5	−17.4
16	1972	1.4	15.6
17	1964	1.3	13.0
18	1961	1.2	23.1
19	1989	1.2	27.3
20	2002	1.1	−23.4
21	1997	1.0	31.0
22	1980	0.9	25.8
23	1966	0.8	−13.1
24	1994	0.7	− 1.5
25	1965	0.7	9.1
26	1970	0.7	0.1
27	1952	0.6	11.8
28	1954	0.5	45.0
29	1996	0.4	20.3
30	1959	0.3	8.5
31	1995	0.3	34.1
32	1992	0.2	4.5
33	1968	0.2	7.7
34	1990	0.1	− 6.6
35	1971	0.04	10.8
36	1960	−0.7	− 3.0
37	1957	−0.9	−14.3
38	1953	−0.9	− 6.6
39	1974	−1.5	−29.7
40	1998	−1.5	26.7
41	1988	−1.5	12.4
42	1993	−1.5	7.1
43	1986	−1.6	14.6
44	2001	−1.8	−13.0
45	1955	−1.8	26.4
46	2000	−1.9	−10.1
47	1985	−1.9	26.3
48	1981	−2.0	− 9.7
49	1956	−2.1	2.6
50	2005	−2.1	??
51	1977	−2.3	−11.5
52	1982	−2.4	14.8
53	1969	−2.9	−11.4
54	1962	−3.4	−11.8
55	1991	−4.6	26.3
56	1978	−4.7	1.1

Based on S&P 500

AS JANUARY BAROMETER GOES, SO GOES THE YEAR

Market Performance In January

	Previous Year's Close	January Close	January Change	Year Change
1950	16.76	17.05	1.7%	21.8%
1951	20.41	21.66	6.1	16.5
1952	23.77	24.14	1.6	11.8
1953	26.57	26.38	—0.7	— 6.6
1954	24.81	26.08	5.1	45.0
1955	35.98	36.63	1.8	26.4
1956	45.48	43.82	—3.6	2.6
1957	46.67	44.72	—4.2	—14.3
1958	39.99	41.70	4.3	38.1
1959	55.21	55.42	0.4	8.5
1960	59.89	55.61	—7.1	— 3.0
1961	58.11	61.78	6.3	23.1
1962	71.55	68.84	—3.8	—11.8
1963	63.10	66.20	4.9	18.9
1964	75.02	77.04	2.7	13.0
1965	84.75	87.56	3.3	9.1
1966	92.43	92.88	0.5	—13.1 X
1967	80.33	86.61	7.8	20.1
1968	96.47	92.24	—4.4	7.7 X
1969	103.86	103.01	—0.8	—11.4
1970	92.06	85.02	—7.6	0.1
1971	92.15	95.88	4.0	10.8
1972	102.09	103.94	1.8	15.6
1973	118.05	116.03	—1.7	—17.4
1974	97.55	96.57	—1.0	—29.7
1975	68.56	76.98	12.3	31.5
1976	90.19	100.86	11.8	19.1
1977	107.46	102.03	—5.1	—11.5
1978	95.10	89.25	—6.2	1.1
1979	96.11	99.93	4.0	12.3
1980	107.94	114.16	5.8	25.8
1981	135.76	129.55	—4.6	— 9.7
1982	122.55	120.40	—1.8	14.8 X
1983	140.64	145.30	3.3	17.3
1984	164.93	163.41	—0.9	1.4
1985	167.24	179.63	7.4	26.3
1986	211.28	211.78	0.2	14.6
1987	242.17	274.08	13.2	2.0
1988	247.08	257.07	4.0	12.4
1989	277.72	297.47	7.1	27.3
1990	353.40	329.08	—6.9	— 6.6
1991	330.22	343.93	4.2	26.3
1992	417.09	408.79	—2.0	4.5
1993	435.71	438.78	0.7	7.1
1994	466.45	481.61	3.3	— 1.5
1995	459.27	470.42	2.4	34.1
1996	615.93	636.02	3.3	20.3
1997	740.74	786.16	6.1	31.0
1998	970.43	980.28	1.0	26.7
1999	1229.23	1279.64	4.1	19.5
2000	1469.25	1394.46	—5.1	—10.1
2001	1320.28	1366.01	3.5	—13.0 X
2002	1148.08	1130.20	—1.6	—23.4
2003	879.82	855.70	—2.7	26.4 X
2004	1111.92	1131.13	1.7	9.0
2005	1211.92	1181.27	—2.5	??

X = 5 major errors

Ranked By Performance

Rank	Year	January Change	Year Change
1	1987	13.2%	2.0%
2	1975	12.3	31.5
3	1976	11.8	19.1
4	1967	7.8	20.1
5	1985	7.4	26.3
6	1989	7.1	27.3
7	1961	6.3	23.1
8	1997	6.1	31.0
9	1951	6.1	16.5
10	1980	5.8	25.8
11	1954	5.1	45.0
12	1963	4.9	18.9
13	1958	4.3	38.1
14	1991	4.2	26.3
15	1999	4.1	19.5
16	1971	4.0	10.8
17	1988	4.0	12.4
18	1979	4.0	12.3
19	2001	3.5	—13.0 X
20	1965	3.3	9.1
21	1983	3.3	17.3
22	1996	3.3	20.3
23	1994	3.3	— 1.5 flat
24	1964	2.7	13.0
25	1995	2.4	34.1
26	1972	1.8	15.6
27	1955	1.8	26.4
28	1950	1.7	21.8
29	2004	1.7	9.0
30	1952	1.6	11.8
31	1998	1.0	26.7
32	1993	0.7	7.1
33	1966	0.5	—13.1 X
34	1959	0.4	8.5
35	1986	0.2	14.6
36	1953	—0.7	— 6.6
37	1969	—0.8	—11.4
38	1984	—0.9	1.4 flat
39	1974	—1.0	—29.7
40	2002	—1.6	—23.4
41	1973	—1.7	—17.4
42	1982	—1.8	14.8 X
43	1992	—2.0	4.5 flat
44	2005	—2.5	??
45	2003	—2.7	26.4 X
46	1956	—3.6	2.6 flat
47	1962	—3.8	—11.8
48	1957	—4.2	—14.3
49	1968	—4.4	7.7 X
50	1981	—4.6	— 9.7
51	1977	—5.1	—11.5
52	2000	—5.1	—10.1
53	1978	—6.2	— 1.1 flat
54	1990	—6.9	— 6.6
55	1960	—7.1	— 3.0
56	1970	—7.6	0.1 flat

Based on S&P 500

the only loss in 2003 due to exogenous events ahead of the military action in Iraq. Ten of the last 14 Election years have followed January's course.

1933 "Lame Duck" Amendment — Why JB Works

Passage of the Twentieth "Lame Duck" Amendment to the Constitution in 1933 created the January Barometer. Since then it has essentially been "As January goes, so goes the year." January's direction has correctly forecasted the major trend for the market in most of the subsequent years.

Prior to 1934, newly elected senators and representatives did not take office until December of the following year, 13 months later (except when new presidents were inaugurated). Defeated congressmen stayed in Congress for all of the following session. They were known as "lame ducks."

Since 1934, Congress convenes in the first week of January and includes those members newly elected the previous November. Inauguration Day was also moved up from March 4 to January 20.

January's prognostic power is attributed to the host of important events transpiring during the month: new Congresses convene; the president gives the State of the Union message, presents the annual budget, and sets national goals and priorities.

These events clearly affect our economy and Wall Street and much of the world. Add to that January's increased cash inflows, portfolio adjustments, and market strategizing and it becomes apparent how prophetic January can be. Switch these events to any other month and chances are the January Barometer would become a memory.

The table at right shows the January Barometer in odd years. In 1935 and 1937, the Democrats already had the most lopsided Congressional margins in history, so when these two Congresses convened it was anticlimactic.

JANUARY BAROMETER (ODD YEARS)

January % Change	12-Month % Change	Same	Opposite
− 4.2%	41.2%		1935
3.8	− 38.6		1937
− 6.9	− 5.4	1939	
− 4.8	− 17.9	1941	
7.2	19.4	1943	
1.4	30.7	1945	
2.4	N/C	1947	
0.1	10.3	1949	
6.1	16.5	1951	
− 0.7	− 6.6	1953	
1.8	26.4	1955	
− 4.2	− 14.3	1957	
0.4	8.5	1959	
6.3	23.1	1961	
4.9	18.9	1963	
3.3	9.1	1965	
7.8	20.1	1967	
− 0.8	− 11.4	1969	
4.0	10.8	1971	
− 1.7	− 17.4	1973	
12.3	31.5	1975	
− 5.1	− 11.5	1977	
4.0	12.3	1979	
− 4.6	− 9.7	1981	
3.3	17.3	1983	
7.4	26.3	1985	
13.2	2.0	1987	
7.1	27.3	1989	
4.1	26.3	1991	
0.7	7.1	1993	
2.4	34.1	1995	
6.1	31.0	1997	
4.1	19.5	1999	
3.5	− 13.0		2001
− 2.7	26.4		2003
− 2.5	??	2005?	2005?

12 month's % change includes January's % change
Based on S&P 500

The January Barometer in subsequent odd-numbered years had compiled a perfect record until two January interest rate cuts and 9/11 affected 2001 and the anticipation of military action in Iraq held the market down in January 2003. January is compared to prior "New Congress Barometers" below.

Almanac Investor Platform subscribers are emailed the official final results of the January Barometer after the close at the end of every January.

New Congress Barometers

Between 1901 and 1933 the market's direction in January was similar to that of the whole year 19 times and different 14 times. Comparing January to the 11 subsequent months, 16 were similar and 17 dissimilar.

New Congress Barometers
Prior to 1933 "Lame Duck" Amendment (Odd Years)
NEWLY ELECTED PRESIDENT INAUGURATED MARCH 4TH

March % Change	12 Month's % Change	Same	Opposite
5.2%	11.6%	1909	
0.7	2.4	1913	
1.0	14.0	1921	
-2.7	**-14.6**	1929	
7.8	101.3	1933	

12 month's % change includes March

NEW CONGRESS CONVENES FIRST WEEK IN DECEMBER
13 MONTHS AFTER ELECTION

November % Change	12 Month's % Change	Same	Opposite
0.9%	2.5%	1901	
-1.8	39.7		1903*
7.3	10.9	1905	
1.2	4.3	1907	
0.7	8.9	1915	
4.3	17.5	1923	
3.5	3.9	1925	
9.1	38.8	1927	
-11.0	**-41.3**	1931	

Panic of 1903 ends 11/9 as Congress convenes (off 37.7%)
12 month's % change includes November

NEW CONGRESS CONVENES IN APRIL OR MAY
EARLIER THAN USUAL, NO CHANGE IN PRESIDENCY

Month's % Change	12 Month's % Change	Same	Opposite
0.5%	6.0%	1911	
-2.3	**-19.6**	1917	
13.6	0.7	1919**	

** *Wilson in Europe 6 months; Post-Armistice surge (up 30.9% Feb to May)*
12 month's % change includes applicable month

Tables based on Dow Jones industrial average (1901-1933)

Prior to the Twentieth Amendment in the last century, we had a "March Barometer" when newly-elected presidents (Taft, Wilson, Harding, Hoover, and Roosevelt) were inaugurated on March 4. Newly elected Congresses convened in March for the occasion. Score 5 out of 5 for the "March Barometer" prior to the Twentieth Amendment.

Between 1900 and 1933, eight new Congresses convened on the first Monday in December (13 months after the election). But because of annual year-end reinvestment, it would be misleading to use December as a barometer. We used a "November Barometer" instead and the score was almost perfect. In 1903, the only time Congress actually convened in November, the barometer was in error. The Panic of 1903 took the Dow down 37.7% and the new Congress was called in one month earlier, ostensibly to "stem the tide." The Panic ended on November 9, the day Congress convened, but the month remained negative while the market moved up over the next 11 months.

Three other new Congresses were convened in other months for different reasons—April in 1911 and 1917 and May in 1919. The record is a double bulls-eye for the "April Barometer." As for the one-shot "May Barometer" a post-Armistice 30.9% surge in four months (February to May) took May up 13.6% but the 12-month period (including May) almost lost it all. President Wilson spent six months in Europe trying to win the peace.

This "New Congress Barometer" performed rather impressively until the passage of the Twentieth Amendment. Since then its successor, the January Barometer has compiled the best record in odd-numbered years of all other known indicators.

JB versus All

Over the years there has been much debate regarding the efficacy of our January Barometer. Skeptics never relent and we don't rest on our laurels. Disbelievers in the January Barometer continue to point to the fact that we include January's S&P 500 change in the full-year results and that detracts from the January Barometer's predicative power for the rest of the year.

Others attempt to discredit the January Barometer by going further back in time. A certain diligent newsletter watchdog, who does impeccable and thorough research, tested the January Barometer back to 1897. While we respect and appreciate the depth of the research, it fully misses the point and the basis for the January Barometer. (Hosts of others have gone down the same dead end street.) Almanac Investors know there would be no January Barometer without the passage of the twentieth "Lame Duck" Amendment to the constitution in 1933.

After the Lame Duck Amendment was ratified in 1934 it took a few years for the Democrat's heavy congressional margins to even out and for the impact of this tectonic governing shift to take effect. Hence our January Barometer starts in 1938. In light of all this debate and skepticism we have compared the January Barometer results along with the full year results, the following 11 months' results, and the subsequent 12 months' results to all other "Monthly Barometers" using the Dow Jones Industrials, the S&P 500, and the NASDAQ Composite.

Here's what we found going back to 1938. There were only six major errors. In addition to the five major errors mentioned above, in 1946 the market dropped sharply after the Employment Act was passed by Congress, overriding Truman's veto, and Congress authorized $12 billion for the Marshall Plan. Including these six errors, the accuracy ratio is 91.0% for the 67-year period. Including the 7 flat years the ratio is 80.6%—still effective.

For the benefit of the skeptics, the accuracy ratio calculated on the performance of the following 11 months is still solid. Including all errors—major and flat years—the ratio is still a respectable 73.1%.

Now for the even better news: In the 43 up Januarys there were only three major errors for a 93.0% accuracy ratio. These years went on to post 16.6% average full-year gains and 12.1% February-to-December gains.

Now let's compare the January Barometer to all other "Monthly Barometers." For the accompanying table we went back to 1938 for the S&P 500 and the Dow—the year in which the January Barometer came to life—and back to 1971 for NASDAQ when that index took its current form.

The accuracy ratios listed are based on whether or not the given month's move—up or down—was followed by a move in the same direction for the whole period. For example, in the 67 years of data for the S&P 500 for the January Barometer, 54 years moved in the same direction for 80.6% accuracy. (Maybe Steinbrenner can find a hitter that bats .806.)

The Calendar Year ratio is based on the month's percent change and the whole year's percent change; i.e., we compare December 2003's percent change to the change for 2003 as a whole. By contrast, the 11-month ratio compares the month's move to the move of the following eleven months. February's change is compared to the change from March to January. The 12-month change compares the month's change to the following

January Barometer versus All

Monthly S&P Barometers Accuracy Ratio
Since 1938

	Calendar Year	11-month	12-month
January	80.6%	73.1%	74.6%
February	64.2%	59.7%	59.7%
March	65.7%	55.2%	50.7%
April	70.1%	62.7%	62.7%
May	62.7%	53.7%	55.2%
June	67.2%	58.2%	55.2%
July	58.2%	50.7%	50.7%
August	62.7%	53.7%	56.1%
September	62.7%	47.0%	47.0%
October	55.2%	47.0%	48.5%
November	61.2%	54.5%	54.5%
December	70.1%	59.1%	54.5%

Monthly Dow Barometers Accuracy Ratio
Since 1938

	Calendar Year	11-month	12-month
January	82.1%	71.6%	65.7%
February	61.2%	55.2%	56.7%
March	58.2%	50.7%	50.7%
April	59.7%	50.7%	49.3%
May	58.2%	52.2%	53.7%
June	62.7%	58.2%	59.7%
July	58.2%	50.7%	52.2%
August	64.2%	52.2%	60.6%
September	58.2%	40.9%	42.4%
October	47.8%	47.0%	53.0%
November	61.2%	57.6%	56.1%
December	68.7%	50.0%	53.0%

Monthly NASDAQ Barometers Accuracy Ratio
Since 1971

	Calendar Year	11-month	12-month
January	76.5%	76.5%	70.6%
February	61.8%	58.8%	52.9%
March	67.6%	58.8%	52.9%
April	82.4%	64.7%	64.7%
May	70.6%	61.8%	64.7%
June	64.7%	61.8%	61.8%
July	58.8%	55.9%	52.9%
August	58.8%	50.0%	57.6%
September	76.5%	54.5%	51.5%
October	52.9%	45.5%	51.5%
November	73.5%	60.6%	60.6%
December	61.8%	66.7%	66.7%

twelve months. February's change is compared to the change from March to the next February.

Though the January Barometer is based on the S&P 500 we thought it would clear the air to look at the other two major averages as well. You can see for yourself in the following table that no other month comes close to January in forecasting prowess.

There are a few interesting anomalies to point out though. On a calendar year basis the Dow in January is one notch above the S&P. For NASDAQ April sticks out as well on a calendar year basis, but that is after four months have passed. Besides, you want to know how the year might pan out following January, not April. And no other month has any basis for being a barometer. January is loaded with reasons.

Being the first month of the year it is the time when people readjust their portfolios, rethink their outlook for the coming year and try to make a fresh start. There is also an increase in cash that flows into the market in January, making market direction even more important. Then there is all the information Wall Street has to digest: The State of the Union Address, FOMC meetings, fourth-quarter GDP, earnings, and the plethora of other economic and market data. We'll continue to delve deeper into the January Barometer (and other indicators) but for now we are content that its results will refute any representations to the contrary.

Down Januarys Followed by Further Declines

Though some years posted full-year and 11-month gains, every down January since 1938 was followed by a new or continuing bear market or a flat year. Excluding 1956, down Januarys were followed by substantial declines averaging –13.6%, providing excellent buying opportunities in most years.

Down Januarys are harbingers of trouble ahead, in the economic, political, or military arenas. Eisenhower's heart attack in 1955 cast doubt on whether he could run in 1956 — a flat year. The two other election years with down Januarys were also flat. Eleven bear markets began and four continued into second years with poor Januarys. 1968 started down as we were mired in Vietnam, but Johnson's "bombing halt" changed the climate. January 2003 closed down in the face of imminent military action in Iraq, and the market triple-bottomed in March just before U.S. led forces began their blitz to Baghdad. The market put three years of the bear behind it as the fall of Baghdad combined with pre-election and recovery forces to fuel 2003 into a banner year.

FROM DOWN JANUARY S&P CLOSES TO LOW NEXT 11 MONTHS

Year	January Close	% Change	11-Month Low	Date of Low	Jan Close to Low %	% Feb to Dec	Year % Change	
1939	12.30	− 6.9%	10.18	8-Apr	− 17.2%	1.5%	− 5.5	cont. bear
1940	12.05	− 3.5	8.99	10-Jun	− 25.4	− 12.2	− 15.3	cont. bear
1941	10.07	− 4.8	8.37	29-Dec	− 16.9	− 13.7	− 17.9	cont. bear
1948	14.69	− 4.0	13.84	14-Feb	− 5.8	3.5	− 0.7	FLAT
1953	26.38	− 0.7	22.71	14-Sep	− 13.9	− 6.0	− 6.6	bear
1956	43.82	− 3.6	44.10	28-May	0.9	6.5	2.6	FLAT
1957	44.72	− 4.2	38.98	22-Oct	− 12.8	− 10.6	− 14.3	bear
1960	55.61	− 7.1	52.30	25-Oct	− 6.0	4.5	− 3.0	bear
1962	68.84	− 3.8	52.32	26-Jun	− 24.0	− 8.3	− 11.8	bear
1968	92.24	− 4.4	87.72	5-Mar	− 4.9	12.6	7.7	cont. bear
1969	103.01	− 0.8	89.20	17-Dec	− 13.4	− 10.6	− 11.4	bear
1970	85.02	− 7.6	69.20	26-May	− 18.6	8.4	0.1	cont. bear
1973	116.03	− 1.7	92.16	5-Dec	− 20.6	− 15.9	− 17.4	bear
1974	96.57	− 1.0	62.28	3-Oct	− 35.5	− 29.0	− 29.7	bear
1977	102.03	− 5.1	90.71	2-Nov	− 11.1	− 6.8	− 11.5	bear
1978	89.25	− 6.2	86.90	6-Mar	− 2.6	7.7	1.1	cont. bear
1981	129.55	− 4.6	112.77	25-Sep	− 13.0	− 5.4	− 9.7	bear
1982	120.40	− 1.8	102.42	12-Aug	− 14.9	16.8	14.8	cont. bear
1984	163.42	− 0.9	147.82	24-Jul	− 9.5	2.3	1.4	FLAT
1990	329.07	− 6.9	295.46	11-Oct	− 10.2	0.4	− 6.6	bear
1992	408.79	− 2.0	394.50	8-Apr	− 3.5	6.6	4.5	FLAT
2000	1394.46	− 5.1	1264.74	20-Dec	− 9.3	− 5.3	− 10.1	bear
2002	1130.20	− 1.6	776.76	9-Oct	− 31.3	− 22.2	− 23.4	cont. bear
2003	855.70	− 2.7	800.73	11-Mar	− 6.4	29.9	26.4	cont. bear
2005	1181.27	− 2.5	1137.50	20-Apr	− 3.7	*At Presstime - not in totals or average*		
Totals					**− 325.9%**	**− 45.3%**	**− 136.3%**	
Average					**− 13.6%**	**− 1.9%**	**− 5.7%**	

The So-Called "January Effect"

Small cap stocks have generally outperformed large caps by the greatest margin in January. This market phenomenon is known as the January Effect. Anticipation of this pattern has caused much of the "effect" to occur in December and November and a reversal often takes place mid-January after which small caps resume leadership through the first quarter. Taking quick small-cap gains off the table or protecting them with trailing stops in January is advisable. This strategy can also be applied to our Free Lunch menu of year-end bargain stocks, emailed to subscribers every December.

FEBRUARY INDICATORS AND PATTERNS

February Almanac

January is a hard act to follow and the short, cold month of February is nearly forgotten on Wall Street and barely leaves a mark. Usually the weak link in the Best Six months, February tends to follow the current trend though big January gains often correct or consolidate during the month of Valentines and Presidents as Wall Street evaluates and adjusts market outlooks based on January's performance. Since 1950 significant January S&P 500 gains of 2% correct or consolidate in February 68% of the time. January losses are followed by February losses 76% of the time.

Over the years, February is up only slightly more than half the time and, depending on the index, up or down marginally on average. However, small cap stocks, benefiting from the "January Effect" carryover, outpace large cap stocks in February. The Russell 2000 index of small cap stocks turns in an average gain of 1.5% in February since 1979—the fifth best month for that benchmark.

Post-election year Februarys fare worse with the major indices posting average losses. It is the worst NASDAQ month in post-election years averaging a –4.1% loss, down seven of the last nine times. Midterm and pre-election year Februarys do not exhibit any major fluctuations from the month's overall performance. Election year Februarys on the other hand are a standout for NASDAQ and the Russell 2000. February is NASDAQ's best month in election years with an average 3.4% gain, up seven of the last nine. Election year Februarys rank second for the Russell 2000 averaging 3.4%, up five of the last seven.

Typical February

After January's usually strong finish, February opens cautiously for large cap stocks perhaps in tribute to the Romans who named the month after their month-long feast of Februalia which they celebrated in the spring as their "new year." It was a time period when sacrifices were made to atone for sins. Day one trades up about half of the time with a slight gain, followed by a second day that advances more often than not yet averages a minor net loss. Over the last ten years February's first trading day has improved dramatically—off only twice on the S&P, averaging 0.46%. This runs with the pattern in recent years of first-trading-day-of-the-month-strength. Strength builds mildly over the third day but fades

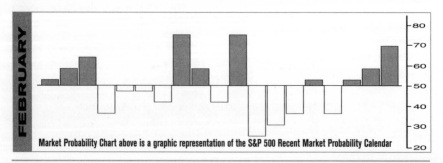

Market Probability Chart above is a graphic representation of the S&P 500 Recent Market Probability Calendar

after that until the stronger eighth and eleventh trading days. The second half of the month struggles until the last day. NASDAQ stocks are much more solid the first five days of the month and small cap Russell 2000 stocks are robust all month long. Monday of option expiration week is dramatically bullish with the S&P 500 up twelve in a row.

February Vital Statistics

	DJIA	S&P 500	NASDAQ	Russell 1K	Russell 2K
Rank	8	11	7	11	5
Up	32	30	19	16	16
Down	24	26	16	11	11
Avg % Change	0.2%	−0.02%	0.6%	0.3%	1.5%
4-Year Presidential Election Cycle Performance					
Post-Election Year	−0.9%	−1.4%	−4.1%	−1.0%	−1.0%
Mid-Term Year	0.7	0.4	0.3	0.7	1.5
Pre-Election Year					
Election Year	−0.1	0.1	3.4	0.3	3.4
Best & Worst February					
	% Change	% Change	% Change	% Change	% Change
Best	1986 8.8	1986 7.1	2000 19.2	1986 7.2	2000 16.4
Worst	2000 −7.4	2001 −9.2	2001 −22.4	2001 −9.5	1999 −8.2
Best & Worst February Weeks					
Best	2/22/74 4.4	2/8/91 4.8	2/4/00 9.2	2/8/91 4.6	2/1/91 6.6
Worst	2/11/00 −4.9	2/23/01 −4.3	2/9/01 −7.1	2/23/01 −4.4	2/10/84 −4.6
Best & Worst February Days					
Best	2/24/84 2.7	2/22/99 2.7	2/11/99 4.2	2/22/99 2.6	2/29/00 3.6
Worst	2/18/00 −2.8	2/18/00 −3.0	2/16/01 −5.0	2/18/00 −2.9	2/16/93 −3.3
First Trading Day of Expiration Week 1990-2005					
Record (#Up - #Down)	12-4	13-3	9-7	13-3	11-5
Current streak	D1	U12	U6	U12	U6
Avg % Change	0.5	0.4	0.2	0.4	0.2
Options Expiration Day 1990-2005					
Record (#Up - #Down)	7-9	6-10	6-10	6-10	6-10
Current streak	U1	U12	D2	U12	D2
Avg % Change	−0.2	−0.3	−0.6	−0.3	−0.2
Options Expiration Week 1990-2005					
Record (#Up - #Down)	8-8	6-10	6-10	5-11	8-8
Current streak	D2	D2	D2	D2	D2
Avg % Change	0.2	−0.2	−0.4	−0.2	0.00
Week After Options Expiration 1990-2005					
Record (#Up - #Down)	6-10	7-9	9-7	7-9	9-7
Current streak	U1	U2	U1	U2	U2
Avg % Change	−0.5	−0.3	−0.3	−0.3	−0.1
2006 Bullish Days based on data from 1984 to 2004					
	10, 15	3, 10, 15, 28	1, 2, 3, 6, 14 15, 28	1, 3, 10, 15, 28	1, 2, 3, 6, 7, 8, 10 14, 15, 23, 24, 27, 28
2006 Bearish Days based on data from 1984 to 2004					
	6, 8, 16, 17	6, 16, 17, 21, 23	16	6, 16, 17, 23	16, 21

Dow & S&P 1950-July 2005, NASDAQ 1971-July 2005, Russell 1K & 2K 1979-July 2005. Options data 1990 through August 2005. Bullish/Bearish days based on index rising or falling 60% of the time on a particular trading day 1984-2004 (see pages 66-73).

Market Negative Before & After Presidents' Day

Presidents' Day is the lone holiday that exhibits weakness the day before and after. Trading has turned more negative over the last sixteen years. The Friday before this mid-winter three-day break is exceptionally bad, whereas the Tuesday after is not as brutal and has shown some improvement recently. The accompanying table illustrates Friday's bearish bent.

MARKET NEGATIVE BEFORE & AFTER PRESIDENTS' DAY
Dow Jones Industrial Average

2 Days Before		Day Before		Day After	
Year	Close	Close	% Change	Close	% Change
1990	2649.55	2635.59	− 0.5%	2596.85	− 1.5%
1991	2877.23	2934.65	2.0	2932.18	− 0.1
1992	3246.65	3245.97	− 0.02	3224.73	− 0.7
1993	3422.69	3392.43	− 0.9	3309.49	− 2.4
1994	3922.64	3887.46	− 0.9	3911.66	0.6
1995	3987.52	3953.54	− 0.9	3963.97	0.3
1996	5551.37	5503.32	− 0.9	5458.53	− 0.8
1997	7022.44	6988.96	− 0.5	7067.46	1.1
1998	8369.60	8370.10	0.01	8398.50	0.3
1999	9363.46	9274.89	− 0.9	9297.03	0.2
2000	10514.57	10219.52	− 2.8	10304.84	0.8
2001	10891.02	10799.82	− 0.8	10730.88	− 0.6
2002	10001.99	9903.04	− 1.0	9745.14	− 1.6
2003	7749.87	7908.80	2.1	8041.15	1.7
2004	10694.07	10627.85	− 0.6	10714.88	0.8
2005	10754.26	10785.22	0.3	10611.20	− 1.6
	Average Since 1990		**-0.40%**		**-0.21%**
	Up		**4**		**8**
	Down		**12**		**8**
	Average Since 1994		**-0.58%**		**0.10%**
	Up		**3**		**8**
	Down		**9**		**4**

Do note that the two silver-lining years, 1991 and 2003, were both related to military action in the Persian Gulf. In 1991 the month-long punishing air war waged by coalition forces to liberate Kuwait from Saddam's August 1990 invasion began to impact Iraqi forces. On February 15, 1991, the Friday before Presidents' Day, Iraq's offer to pull out of Kuwait for the first time tied to lifting sanctions was rejected by President Bush as "cruel hoax." The following Tuesday after the holiday, General Schwartzkopf said Iraqi forces were "on the verge of collapse." These two clear signs of capitulation were celebrated on Wall Street with buying. In February 2003 the Dow had dropped 13.2% from the previous November high as the anticipation of another fray into Iraq loomed over the world. As the invasion of Iraq became imminent the market rallied the day before and after Presidents' Day before falling to its final 2003 low the week before the March 19 offensive.

MARKET NEGATIVE BEFORE & AFTER PRESIDENTS' DAY

S&P 500

2 Days Before		Day Before		Day After	
Year	Close	Close	% Change	Close	% Change
1990	334.89	332.72	− 0.6%	327.99	− 1.4%
1991	364.22	369.06	1.3	369.39	0.1
1992	413.69	412.48	− 0.3	407.38	− 1.2
1993	447.66	444.58	− 0.7	433.91	− 2.4
1994	470.34	467.69	− 0.6	471.46	0.8
1995	485.22	481.97	− 0.7	482.74	0.2
1996	651.32	647.98	− 0.5	640.65	− 1.1
1997	811.82	808.48	− 0.4	816.29	1.0
1998	1024.14	1020.09	− 0.4	1022.76	0.3
1999	1254.04	1230.13	− 1.9	1241.87	1.0
2000	1388.26	1346.09	− 3.0	1352.17	0.5
2001	1326.61	1301.53	− 1.9	1278.94	− 1.7
2002	1116.48	1104.18	− 1.1	1083.34	− 1.9
2003	817.37	834.89	2.1	851.17	1.9
2004	1152.11	1145.81	− 0.5	1156.99	1.0
2005	1200.75	1201.59	0.1	1184.16	− 1.5
	Average Since 1990		-0.57%		-0.29%
	Up		3		9
	Down		13		7
	Average Since 1994		-0.74%		0.03%
	Up		2		8
	Down		10		4

NASDAQ Composite

2 Days Before		Day Before		Day After	
Year	Close	Close	% Change	Close	% Change
1990	429.61	429.01	− 0.1%	423.83	− 1.2%
1991	444.31	448.71	1.0	450.32	0.4
1992	639.10	636.43	− 0.4	626.41	− 1.6
1993	695.88	690.54	− 0.8	665.39	− 3.6
1994	790.24	788.85	− 0.2	791.15	0.3
1995	793.31	786.97	− 0.8	784.62	− 0.3
1996	1090.54	1090.71	0.02	1083.24	− 0.7
1997	1370.81	1367.19	− 0.3	1365.79	− 0.1
1998	1714.34	1710.42	− 0.2	1703.43	− 0.4
1999	2405.55	2321.89	− 3.5	2313.87	− 0.3
2000	4548.92	4411.74	− 3.0	4382.12	− 0.7
2001	2552.91	2425.38	− 5.0	2318.35	− 4.4
2002	1843.37	1805.20	− 2.1	1750.61	− 3.0
2003	1277.44	1310.17	2.6	1346.54	2.8
2004	2073.61	2053.56	− 1.0	2080.35	1.3
2005	2061.34	2058.62	− 0.1	2030.32	− 1.4
	Average Since 1990		-0.87%		-0.81%
	Up		3		4
	Down		13		12
	Average Since 1994		-1.13%		-0.58%
	Up		2		3
	Down		10		9

MARCH INDICATORS AND PATTERNS

March Almanac

Stormy March markets tend to drive prices up early in the month and batter stocks at month end. Named after Mars, the Roman god of war, the third month of the year often serves as a battleground for bulls and bears. Julius Caesar may not have heeded the famous warning to "beware the Ides of March" but investors would be served well if they did. Stock prices have a propensity to decline, sometimes rather precipitously, around mid-March. Remember, NASDAQ topped out on March 10, 2000 and the S&P peaked March 24, 2000. Most recent March gains have been logged in the beginning and middle of the month. The second half of the month is full of red ink and the last three or four days of the month have posted net declines in eleven of the last fourteen years.

March packs a rather busy docket. It is the end of the first quarter, which brings with it Triple Witching and an abundance of portfolio maneuvers from The Street. March Triple-Witching Weeks have been quite bullish in recent years. But the week after is the exact opposite, down fourteen of the last eighteen years—and frequently down sharply for an average drop of –1.0% on the S&P 500.

The market has been much luckier the day before St. Patrick's Day (as will be dicussed later). When Good Friday occurs in March there is a bearish bias both the day before and after the Friday holiday. This has occurred ten times since 1950. On days before the S&P 500 are up five and down five, days after are up two and down eight. Both days have accumulated net losses over the period. These two March holiday phenomena are more likely due to Triple-Witching and end-of-first-quarter forces.

Normally a decent performing market month, March is much weaker in post-election years with the Dow Jones Industrials and S&P 500 off fractionally and NASDAQ averaging a –2.0% drop. In midterm years performance is above average moving up better than 60% of the time with greater than 1.0% average gains in the broad indices. Pre-election year Marches rank third or fourth, depending upon the yardstick, and boast 2.0% average gains or better across the board. But in election years March is the worst NASDAQ month, down –2.5% on average.

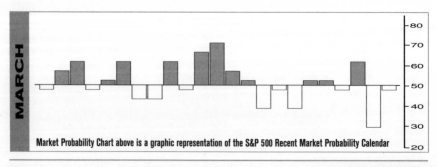

Market Probability Chart above is a graphic representation of the S&P 500 Recent Market Probability Calendar

Typical March

First days have been weaker for big cap stocks, up about half the time. NASDAQ stocks and small cap Russell 2000 stocks are much stronger in the beginning of March. By the sixth or seventh trading day things cool off until mid-month as the first Triple Witching of the year and 401k cash inflows tend to push stocks higher. After the Ides has past, market gains become scarce until the third to last day of the month. Like the beginning of the month, small stocks and techs perform best the last day with the Russell 2000 up 82% of the time while the Dow Jones Industrials are down much of the time. This is reminiscent of the end of the second quarter when big caps lose ground and small stocks shine.

March Vital Statistics

	DJIA	S&P 500	NASDAQ	Russell 1K	Russell 2K
Rank	6	5	9	8	9
Up	35	36	21	17	18
Down	21	20	14	10	96
Avg % Change	0.9%	1.0%	0.3%	0.7%	0.6%
4-Year Presidential Election Cycle Performance					
Post-Election Year	−0.4%	−0.2%	−2.0%	−0.8%	−0.3%
Mid-Term Year	1.0	1.1	1.4	1.8	2.2
Pre-Election Year	2.4	2.3	4.2	2.9	3.7
Election Year	0.5	0.8	−2.5	−1.1	−3.0
Best & Worst March					
	% Change	% Change	% Change	% Change	% Change
Best	2000 7.8	2000 9.7	1999 7.6	2000 8.9	1979 9.7
Worst	1980 −9.0	1980 −10.2	1980 −17.1	1980 −11.5	1980 −18.5
Best & Worst March Weeks					
Best	3/21/03 8.4	3/21/03 7.5	3/3/00 7.1	3/21/03 7.4	3/3/00 7.4
Worst	3/16/01 −7.7	3/16/01 −6.7	3/16/01 −7.9	3/16/01 −6.8	3/7/80 −7.6
Best & Worst March Days					
Best	3/16/00 4.9	3/16/00 4.8	3/13/03 4.8	3/16/00 4.9	3/28/80 4.8
Worst	3/12/01 −4.1	3/12/01 −4.3	3/12/01 −6.3	3/12/01 −4.4	3/27/80 −6.6
First Trading Day of Expiration Week 1990-2005					
Record (#Up - #Down)	12-4	12-4	8-8	12-4	10-6
Current streak	U1	U1	U1	U1	U1
Avg % Change	0.2	0.1	−0.3	0.1	−0.2
Options Expiration Day 1990-2005					
Record (#Up - #Down)	9-7	11-5	6-10	9-7	5-11
Current streak	U1	D2	D2	D2	D2
Avg % Change	0.2	0.1	−0.2	0.1	−0.2
Options Expiration Week 1990-2005					
Record (#Up - #Down)	11-5	11-5	8-8	10-6	7-9
Current streak	D2	D2	D2	D2	D2
Avg % Change	1.0	0.7	−0.6	0.6	−0.4
Week After Options Expiration 1990-2005					
Record (#Up - #Down)	4-12	3-13	6-10	3-13	7-9
Current streak	D1	D5	D1	D5	D1
Avg % Change	−1.0	−0.7	−0.2	−0.7	−0.3
2006 Bullish Days based on data from 1984 to 2004					
	2, 3, 16, 20, 29	3, 8, 13, 15, 16	1, 3, 13, 16,20	3, 8, 13, 15, 16	1, 2, 3, 6, 7
		29	31		13, 16, 17, 29, 31
2006 Bearish Days based on data from 1984 to 2004					
	22, 24, 31	21, 23, 30	21, 22, 27	21, 23, 30	10

Dow & S&P 1950-July 2005, NASDAQ 1971-July 2005, Russell 1K & 2K 1979-July 2005. Options data 1990 through August 2005. Bullish/Bearish days based on index rising or falling 60% of the time on a particular trading day 1984-2004 (see pages 66-73).

Luck of the Irish Hits Wall Street Day Before St. Pat's

Saint Patrick's Day is March's sole recurring cultural event. Sure Good Friday and Easter land in the vernal month from time to time, but only ten times in the last 53 years. Islam's New Year often falls in March as does the Jewish celebration

ST. PATRICK'S DAY TRADING RECORD (DAYS BEFORE AND AFTER)

Year	St. Pat's Day	% Change 2 Days Prior	% Change 1 Day Prior	S&P 500 St. Pat's Day or Next *	% Change St. Pat's Day *	% Change Day After
1953	Tue	0.19%	0.15%	26.33	0.42%	− 0.34%
1954	Wed	− 0.45	− 0.04	26.62	0.23	0.41
1955	Thu	2.15	0.76	36.12	0.39	0.17
1956	Sat	0.97	0.31	48.59	0.93	0.58
1957	Sun	0.07	− 0.05	43.85	− 0.45	0.43
1958	Mon	0.12	− 0.31	42.04	− 0.69	− 0.36
1959	Tue	0.12	− 1.08	56.52	0.82	− 0.23
1960	Thu	0.77	0.55	54.96	− 0.15	0.09
1961	Fri	0.30	1.01	64.60	0.61	0.40
1962	Sat	0.21	− 0.17	70.85	− 0.13	− 0.27
1963	Sun	− 0.47	0.50	65.61	− 0.49	− 0.21
1964	Tue	0.08	0.00	79.32	0.23	0.08
1965	Wed	0.03	− 0.13	87.02	− 0.13	− 0.24
1966	Thu	− 0.57	0.58	88.17	0.35	0.41
1967	Fri	0.95	1.01	90.25	0.18	− 0.06
1968	Sun	− 1.90	0.88	89.59	0.55	− 0.67
1969	Mon	− 0.67	− 0.40	98.25	0.26	0.24
1970	Tue	− 0.53	− 1.08	87.29	0.44	0.29
1971	Wed	1.14	0.50	101.12	− 0.09	0.07
1972	Fri	0.13	− 0.23	107.92	0.39	− 0.31
1973	Sat	− 0.75	− 0.51	112.17	− 1.21	− 0.20
1974	Sun	− 0.09	− 0.37	98.05	− 1.24	− 0.84
1975	Mon	0.18	1.22	86.01	1.47	− 1.02
1976	Wed	− 1.05	1.12	100.86	− 0.06	− 0.41
1977	Thu	0.55	0.19	102.08	− 0.09	− 0.22
1978	Fri	− 0.26	0.44	90.20	0.77	0.69
1979	Sat	0.15	0.83	101.06	0.37	− 0.55
1980	Mon	− 1.17	− 0.18	102.26	− 3.01	1.80
1981	Tue	− 0.06	1.18	133.92	− 0.56	0.22
1982	Wed	0.77	− 0.16	109.08	− 0.18	1.12
1983	Thu	0.35	− 1.03	149.59	− 0.14	0.21
1984	Sat	0.41	1.18	157.78	− 0.94	0.68
1985	Sun	− 0.20	− 0.74	176.88	0.20	1.50
1986	Mon	0.28	1.44	234.67	− 0.79	0.47
1987	Tue	− 0.46	− 0.57	292.47	1.47	0.11
1988	Thu	− 0.09	0.95	271.22	0.96	− 0.04
1989	Fri	0.52	0.93	292.69	− 2.25	− 0.95
1990	Sat	0.36	1.14	343.53	0.47	− 0.57
1991	Sun	− 0.29	0.02	372.11	− 0.40	− 1.48
1992	Tue	0.48	0.14	409.58	0.78	− 0.10
1993	Wed	0.36	− 0.01	448.31	− 0.68	0.80
1994	Thu	− 0.08	0.52	470.90	0.32	0.04
1995	Fri	− 0.20	0.72	495.52	0.02	0.13
1996	Sun	0.36	0.09	652.65	1.75	− 0.15
1997	Mon	− 1.83	0.46	795.71	0.32	− 0.76
1998	Tue	− 0.12	1.00	1080.45	0.11	0.47
1999	Wed	0.98	− 0.07	1297.82	− 0.66	1.44
2000	Fri	2.43	4.76	1464.47	0.41	− 0.54
2001	Sat	0.59	− 1.96	1170.81	1.76	− 2.41
2002	Sun	− 0.09	1.14	1165.55	− 0.05	0.41
2003	Mon	3.45	0.16	862.79	3.54	0.42
2004	Wed	− 1.43	0.56	1123.75	1.17	− 0.13
2005	Thu	− 0.75	− 0.81	1190.21	0.18	− 0.05
Average		**0.11%**	**0.31%**		**0.14%**	**0.01%**

When St. Patrick's Day falls on Saturday or Sunday, the following trading day is used. Based on S&P 500.

of Purim. But Saint Patrick's Day occurs on the same day every year in March. There is no official stock market closing or bank holiday but the festivities do hit close to Wall Street. Parades are held worldwide but the largest runs right up the center of Manhattan.

Gains the day before Saint Patrick's Day have proved to be to be greater than the day itself and the day after. Perhaps it's the anticipation of the patron saint's holiday that boosts the market and the distraction from the parade down Fifth Avenue may cause equity markets to languish. Or is it the absent, and then hung-over, traders that hold the market back? Or maybe it's the fact that Saint Pat's usually falls in Triple-Witching Week.

Whatever the case, since 1953, the S&P 500 posts a wee gain of 0.14% on Saint Patrick's Day, an almost nonexistent gain of 0.01% the day after, but the day before averages a cheerful 0.31% advance.

APRIL INDICATORS AND PATTERNS

April Almanac

April is the first and only month so far to gain 1000 points on the Dow Jones Industrials. That was 1999. But since those heady days, "Income Tax" month has been hit hard in four of the last six years. The other two years were up dramatically but nevertheless, April has been knocked down a notch, relinquishing its number-one Dow ranking since 1950 on an average monthly change basis to December. April has also showered the rest of the market with gains over the years. Most damage in April has occurred during bear markets, most recently in 2000 and 2002. The bulk of first-half declines in 2004 and 2005 also came in April. This dynamic history for the first month of the second quarter illustrates April's propensity for huge market swings in either direction.

April marks the end of our "Best Six Months" for the Dow Jones Industrials and the S&P 500. It also maintains a firm position in all of our broad index "Seasonal-Switching Strategies." When April comes around, especially if the market has recently rallied substantially, we began to look for our MACD (Moving Average Convergence Divergence) indicator seasonal sell signal for the Dow Jones Industrials and S&P 500.

The first half of April used to outperform the second half but since 1994 that has no longer been the case. The effect of April 15 Tax Deadline appears to be diminished. The market is clearly focused on first quarter earnings during April. Exceptional Q1 earnings and positive surprises tend to be anticipated with stocks and the market moving up in advance of the announcements.

In post-election years April averages respectable gains with big moves up and down. Midterm Aprils are also peppered with wild swings but with a downside bias. Pre-election Aprils are strongest for large cap stocks with the S&P 500 down only once since 1950. Election year Aprils are mediocre generating net losses on NAS-DAQ and the Russell 2000 and fractional gains for larger capitalization stocks.

Options expiration week likely impacts the market positively in April and Dow Jones Industrial stocks the most. The first trading day of expiration week is better than expiration day and the week as a whole generally is marked by sizeable gains. The week after however, is ruled by sellers.

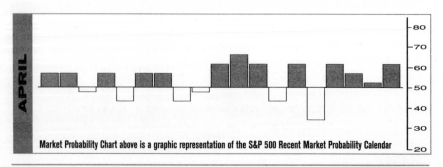

Market Probability Chart above is a graphic representation of the S&P 500 Recent Market Probability Calendar

Typical April

Over the past 23 years, since the big market-turnaround year of 1982, April has experienced a fair share of volatility throughout the month. Sizeable one-day gains and losses have been quite commonplace. April's first several days are strongest for the Dow Jones Industrials and mid-month strength exists for stocks of all varieties. After the mid-month Tax Deadline the market has been prone to weakness, but the last several days of the month exhibit more NADSAQ and Russell 2000 strength.

April Vital Statistics

	DJIA	S&P 500	NASDAQ	Russell 1K	Russell 2K
Rank	2	4	6	5	6
Up	34	37	22	16	17
Down	22	19	13	11	10
Avg % Change	1.8%	1.3%	1.1%	1.2%	1.3%
4-Year Presidential Election Cycle Performance					
Post-Election Year	1.6%	1.0%	1.3%	1.6%	0.7%
Mid-Term Year	0.6	−0.01	−0.2	−0.7	0.8
Pre-Election Year	4.2	3.6	3.7	2.9	3.8
Election Year	0.8	0.5	−0.7	0.6	−0.3
Best & Worst April					
	% Change	% Change	% Change	% Change	% Change
Best	1978 10.6	1978 8.5	2001 15	2001 8	2003 9.4
Worst	1970 −6.3	1970 −9.0	2000 −15.6	2002 −5.8	2000 −6.1
Best & Worst April Weeks					
Best	4/11/75 5.7	4/20/00 5.8	4/12/01 14	4/20/00 5.9	4/20/00 6.2
Worst	4/14/00 −7.3	4/14/00 −10.5	4/14/00 −25.3	4/14/00 −11.2	4/14/00 −16.4
Best & Worst April Days					
Best	4/5/01 4.2	4/5/01 4.4	4/5/01 8.9	4/5/01 4.6	4/18/00 5.8
Worst	4/14/00 −5.7	4/14/00 −5.8	4/14/00 −9.7	4/14/00 −6.0	4/14/00 −7.3
First Trading Day of Expiration Week 1990-2005					
Record (#Up - #Down)	12-4	11-5	10-6	10-6	6-10
Current streak	D1	U3	D1	D1	D1
Avg % Change	0.6	0.5	0.5	0.5	0.2
Options Expiration Day 1990-2005					
Record (#Up - #Down)	10-6	9-7	6-10	9-7	8-8
Current streak	D1	D1	D2	D1	D1
Avg % Change	0.2	0.03	−0.4	0.00	−0.1
Options Expiration Week 1990-2005					
Record (#Up - #Down)	13-3	11-5	9-7	11-5	11-5
Current streak	D1	D2	D2	D2	D2
Avg % Change	1.6	1.2	1.3	1.1	0.7
Week After Options Expiration 1990-2005					
Record (#Up - #Down)	8-8	9-7	9-7	9-7	9-7
Current streak	U2	U3	U3	U3	U3
Avg % Change	−0.3	−0.2	0.2	−0.2	0.6
2006 Bullish Days based on data from 1984 to 2004					
	3, 6, 11,17, 18, 25	17, 18, 19, 21	5, 10, 11, 17, 19	10, 17, 18, 26	11, 18, 25, 26
		25, 28	26, 27, 28		27, 28
2006 Bearish Days based on data from 1984 to 2004					
	7, 20, 24	24	7	24	3, 7

Dow & S&P 1950-July 2005, NASDAQ 1971-July 2005, Russell 1K & 2K 1979-July 2005. Options data 1990 through August 2005. Bullish/Bearish days based on index rising or falling 60% of the time on a particular trading day 1984-2004 (see pages 66-73).

Good Friday Better in April

When Good Friday falls in April the Thursday before is more positive than when it lands in March. The S&P 500 is up eight of the last ten times. Monday after Easter is still negative though less so than in March. Tuesday is even stronger with a 0.6% average gain.

Indicators and Patterns

Down January + Down April = Bad Sign

Earlier, in the section on January, we discussed a host of indicators that give their readings in January and later we'll touch on the "December Low Indicator." The absence of Santa Claus Rally, a down First Five Days, a down January Barometer or if the Dow Jones Industrials closes below its December closing low suggests bearish implications for the stock market. The more that occur in the same year the more likely the market is ripe for a further decline. We know that January and April are generally strong months. When January is down it is often a negative indication and April has been known to get hammered in bear markets.

The following table shows all years (since 1950 for Dow and S&P, 1971 for NASDAQ) when both January and April were down. You can see that not only were the full years hit hard, all down or flat, but from the end of April to the end of the year was also treacherous. Most of the damage was wrapped up by September with the last three months of these years performing best. June, July, and August of these years have also delivered a smattering of strong gains.

Dow Jones Industrials Monthly % Change

Year	Jan	Feb	Mar	Apr	May	Jun	Jul	Aug	Sep	Oct	Nov	Dec	Year's % Change	April-Dec % Change
1953	-0.7	-1.9	-1.5	-1.8	-0.9	-1.5	2.7	-5.1	1.1	4.5	2.0	-0.2	-3.8	2.2
1960	-8.4	1.2	-2.1	-2.4	4.0	2.4	-3.7	1.5	-7.3	0.04	2.9	3.1	-9.3	2.4
1962	-4.3	1.1	-0.2	-5.9	-7.8	-8.5	6.5	1.9	-5.0	1.9	10.1	0.4	-10.8	-2.0
1970	-7.0	4.5	1.0	-6.3	-4.8	-2.4	7.4	4.1	-0.5	-0.7	5.1	5.6	4.8	14.0
1973	-2.1	-4.4	-0.4	-3.1	-2.2	-1.1	3.9	-4.2	6.7	1.0	-14.0	3.5	-16.6	-7.7
1981	-1.7	2.9	3.0	-0.6	-0.6	-1.5	-2.9	-7.4	-3.6	0.3	4.3	-1.6	-9.2	-12.3
1990	-5.9	1.4	3.0	-1.9	8.3	0.1	0.9	-10.0	-6.2	-0.4	4.8	2.9	-4.3	-0.9
2000	-4.8	-7.4	7.8	-1.7	-2.0	-0.7	0.7	6.6	-5.0	3.0	-5.1	3.6	-6.2	0.5
2002	-1.0	-1.9	2.9	-4.4	-0.2	-6.9	-5.5	-0.8	-12.4	10.6	5.9	-6.2	-16.8	-16.1
2005	-2.7	2.6	-2.4	-3.0										
Average	**-4.0**			**-3.1**	**-0.7**	**-2.2**	**1.2**	**-1.5**	**-3.6**	**2.2**	**1.8**	**1.2**	**-8.0**	**-2.2**

S&P 500 Monthly % Change

Year	Jan	Feb	Mar	Apr	May	Jun	Jul	Aug	Sep	Oct	Nov	Dec	Year's % Change	April-Dec % Change
1953	-0.7	-1.8	-2.4	-2.6	-0.3	-1.6	2.5	-5.8	0.1	5.1	0.9	0.2	-6.6	0.8
1956	-3.6	3.5	6.9	-0.2	-6.6	3.9	5.2	-3.8	-4.5	0.5	-1.1	3.5	2.6	-3.5
1960	-7.1	0.9	-1.4	-1.8	2.7	2.0	-2.5	2.6	-6.0	-0.2	4.0	4.6	-3.0	6.9
1962	-3.8	1.6	-0.6	-6.2	-8.6	-8.2	6.4	1.5	-4.8	0.4	10.2	1.3	-11.8	-3.3
1970	-7.6	5.3	0.1	-9.0	-6.1	-5.0	7.3	4.4	3.3	-1.1	4.7	5.7	0.1	13.0
1973	-1.7	-3.7	-0.1	-4.1	-1.9	-0.7	3.8	-3.7	4.0	-0.1	-11.4	1.7	-17.4	-8.8
1974	-1.0	-0.4	-2.3	-3.9	-3.4	-1.5	-7.8	-9.0	-11.9	16.3	-5.3	-2.0	-29.7	-24.1
1981	-4.6	1.3	3.6	-2.3	-0.2	-1.0	-0.2	-6.2	-5.4	4.9	3.7	-3.0	-9.7	-7.7
1990	-6.9	0.9	2.4	-2.7	9.2	-0.9	-0.5	-9.4	-5.1	-0.7	6.0	2.5	-6.6	-0.2
2000	-5.1	-2.0	9.7	-3.1	-2.2	2.4	-1.6	6.1	-5.3	-0.5	-8.0	0.4	-10.1	-9.1
2002	-1.6	-2.1	3.7	-6.1	-0.9	-7.2	-7.9	0.5	-11.0	8.6	5.7	-6.0	-23.4	-18.3
2005	-2.5	1.9	-1.9	-2.0										
Average	**-4.0**			**-3.8**	**-1.7**	**-1.6**	**-0.4**	**-2.1**	**-4.2**	**3.0**	**0.9**	**0.8**	**-10.5**	**-4.9**

NASDAQ Composite Monthly % Change

Year	Jan	Feb	Mar	Apr	May	Jun	Jul	Aug	Sep	Oct	Nov	Dec	Year's % Change	April-Dec % Change
1973	-4.0	-6.2	-2.4	-8.2	-4.8	-1.6	7.6	-3.5	6.0	0.9	-15.1	-1.4	-17.4	-14.5
1984	-3.7	-5.9	-0.7	-1.3	-5.9	2.9	-4.2	10.9	-1.8	-1.2	-1.8	2.0	1.4	0.04
1990	-8.6	2.4	2.3	-3.6	9.3	0.7	-5.2	-13.0	-9.6	-4.3	8.9	4.1	-6.6	-11.0
2000	-3.2	19.2	-2.6	-15.6	-11.9	16.6	-5.0	11.7	-12.7	-8.3	-22.9	-4.9	-10.1	-36.0
2002	-0.8	-10.5	6.6	-8.5	-4.3	-9.4	-9.2	-1.0	-10.9	13.5	11.2	-9.7	-23.4	-20.9
2005	-5.2	-0.5	2.6	-3.9										
Average	**-4.1**			**-7.4**	**-3.5**	**1.8**	**-3.2**	**1.0**	**-5.8**	**-0.2**	**-3.9**	**-2.1**	**-26.2**	**-16.5**

MAY INDICATORS AND PATTERNS

May Almanac

May has been a tricky month over the years. It used to be part of what we called the "May/June disaster area." From 1965 to 1984 the S&P 500 was down during May fifteen out of twenty times. Then from 1985 through 1997 May was the best month, gaining ground every single year (13 straight gains) on the S&P, up 3.3% on average with the Dow Jones Industrials falling once and two NAS-DAQ losses. In the eight years since 1997, May's performance has been erratic, up only about half the time with marginal advances. NASDAQ has suffered five May losses in a row from 1998 to 2001, down –11.9% in 2000, followed by three straight large gains.

May begins the "Worst Six Months" for the Dow and S&P. Everyone has heard the Wall Street adage, "sell in May and go away." Our "Best Six Months Switching Strategy," that we created in 1986, proves that there is merit to this old trader's tale. A hypothetical $10,000 investment in the Dow Jones Industrials compounded to $499,933 for November-April in 55 years compared to $502 loss for May-October.

Post-Election Years, notoriously the worst year of the four-year election cycle, are May's best performing year. In these years May ranks number one on NAS-DAQ (average gain, 3.4%) and the Russell 2000 (average gain, 4.9%), second on the S&P 500 (average gain, 1.5%) and the Russell 1000 (average gain, 3.1%) and third on the Dow Jones Industrials (average gain, 1.1%).

Midterm election year Mays lose ground about half the time averaging losses except for the Russell 1000 which manages an average 1.3% gain. Pre-election year Mays are especially bullish for small stocks. The Russell 2000 averages a 3.2% advance in these rather bullish years.

Election Year Mays rank at or near the bottom registering net losses on the Dow Jones Industrials and NASDAQ, and fractional gains on and S&P 500, Russell 1000, and Russell 2000.

Monday before May option expiration is much stronger than expiration day itself albeit weaker for small caps. Big caps have only registered two losses in the last fifteen years. Expiration day is a loser across the board. The full week and week after have a bullish bias.

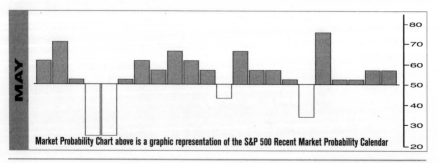

Market Probability Chart above is a graphic representation of the S&P 500 Recent Market Probability Calendar

Typical May

The first two days of May trade higher frequently and the Dow Jones Industrials have been up six of the last seven first trading days. NASDAQ and the Russell 2000 continue to be strong into day three and throughout the month. A bout of weakness often appears the fourth, fifth, and seventeenth trading days for large cap stocks but the middle of the month tends to be rather strong. NASDAQ and the Russell 2000 take the lead again the last three days of May.

May Vital Statistics

	DJIA	S&P 500	NASDAQ	Russell 1K	Russell 2K
Rank	9	8	5	4	4
Up	29	32	21	19	18
Down	27	24	14	8	9
Avg % Change	0.1%	0.3%	1.2%	1.4%	2.0%
4-Year Presidential Election Cycle Performance					
Post-Election Year	1.1%	1.5%	3.4%	3.1%	4.9%
Mid-Term Year	−0.2	−0.4	−0.2	1.3	−0.7
Pre-Election Year	−0.1	0.1	2.0	1.2	3.2
Election Year	−0.3	0.1	−0.6	0.1	0.1
Best & Worst May					
	% Change	% Change	% Change	% Change	% Change
Best	1990 8.3	1990 9.2	1997 11.1	1990 8.9	1997 11
Worst	1962 −7.8	1962 −8.6	2000 −11.9	1984 −5.9	2000 −5.9
Best & Worst May Weeks					
Best	5/29/70 5.8	5/2/97 6.2	5/17/02 8.8	5/2/97 6.4	5/2/97 5.4
Worst	5/25/62 −6.0	5/25/62 −6.8	5/12/00 −7.5	5/2/86 −2.9	5/26/00 −4.7
Best & Worst May Days					
Best	5/27/70 5.1	5/27/70 5.0	5/30/00 7.9	5/8/02 3.7	5/30/00 4.2
Worst	5/28/62 −5.7	5/28/62 −6.7	5/23/00 −5.9	5/19/03 −2.5	5/10/00 −3.4
First Trading Day of Expiration Week 1990-2005					
Record (#Up - #Down)	14-2	14-2	12-4	14-2	10-6
Current streak	U1	U1	U1	U1	U1
Avg % Change	0.7	0.7	0.6	0.7	0.3
Options Expiration Day 1990-2005					
Record (#Up - #Down)	6-10	6-10	7-9	6-10	6-10
Current streak	D1	D1	U2	D1	D1
Avg % Change	−0.3	−0.3	−0.4	−0.3	−0.2
Options Expiration Week 1990-2005					
Record (#Up - #Down)	11-5	10-6	11-5	9-7	12-4
Current streak	U1	U1	U5	U1	U5
Avg % Change	1.1	1.0	1.2	1.0	0.9
Week After Options Expiration 1990-2005					
Record (#Up - #Down)	10-6	10-6	11-5	10-6	12-4
Current streak	U2	U2	U2	U2	U3
Avg % Change	−0.1	0.2	0.2	0.2	0.2
2006 Bullish Days based on data from 1984 to 2004					
	1, 2, 9 ,10, 11	1, 2, 9, 11, 12	1, 2, 3, 8, 11, 15, 17	2, 9, 11, 17	1, 2, 3, 9, 11, 17
	19, 30	17, 24	19, 24, 26, 30, 31	24, 31	24, 26, 30, 31
2006 Bearish Days based on data from 1984 to 2004					
	4, 5, 23	4, 5, 23	None	4, 5, 23	None

Dow & S&P 1950-July 2005, NASDAQ 1971-July 2005, Russell 1K & 2K 1979-July 2005. Options data 1990 through August 2005.
Bullish/Bearish days based on index rising or falling 60% of the time on a particular trading day 1984-2004 (see pages 66-73).

Wall Street Rallies for Moms

On Friday before Mother's Day the Dow Jones Industrials have gained ground nine of the last fifteen years but on the Monday after, the blue-chip average has risen in twelve of those years.

Indicators and Patterns

Memorial Day and the Stock Market

Congress turned Memorial Day into a three-day weekend at the end of May with the National Holiday Act of 1971. It is traditionally the 30th of May but since 1971 has been observed on the last Monday in May.

We have kept track of market action around major holidays since the first edition of the Stock Trader's Almanac in 1968. Memorial Day has had a weak bias ahead of the long weekend and strength after the holiday. Early departures for the first long "summer" weekend have driven the Dow down six of the last twelve years.

The week after Memorial Day has been sporadic, following the short-term trend of the market. The Dow Jones Industrials was up twelve years in a row from 1984 to 1995. The last ten years it has been up six times with some substantial gains: 240.10 Dow points in 1999, 495.52 Dow points in 2000, and 248.88 Dow points in 2003.

	Memorial Day Market Dow Jones Industrial Average Point Changes		
Year	Day Before	Day After	Week After
1971	2.03	5.84	14.34
1972	2.18	−0.07	−9.86
1973	6.40	−5.27	−36.88
1974	11.42	−2.35	−14.48
1975	12.99	−5.79	0.39
1976	9.66	−2.10	−11.33
1977	−9.24	−0.17	13.40
1978	−3.72	2.51	15.85
1979	−1.38	−3.73	−15.07
1980	11.18	3.66	−3.25
1981	−4.87	12.24	20.03
1982	−5.42	−4.57	−14.56
1983	−7.35	−16.16	−3.10
1984	3.67	−5.86	17.25
1985	5.26	−0.45	13.44
1986	16.99	29.74	53.42
1987	17.43	54.74	48.37
1988	−10.31	74.68	114.86
1989	11.18	−18.22	24.06
1990	−34.63	49.57	80.05
1991	13.87	44.95	113.59
1992	8.06	−22.56	10.11
1993	−27.40	24.91	17.71
1994	3.68	1.23	15.08
1995	−43.23	9.68	75.39
1996	0.74	−53.19	−119.68
1997	87.78	37.50	−14.87
1998	−17.93	−150.71	−214.49
1999	92.81	36.52	240.10
2000	−24.68	227.89	495.52
2001	−117.05	33.77	−14.96
2002	−111.82	−122.68	−179.01
2003	7.36	179.97	248.88
2004	−16.75	14.20	54.37
2005	4.95	−75.07	−81.58
Average	−3.03	10.13	27.23
Up	20	18	21
Down	15	17	14

JUNE INDICATORS AND PATTERNS

June Almanac

The first month of summer has shone brighter on NASDAQ stocks over the last 35 years as a rule ranking fourth with a 1.2% average gain, up 22 of 35 years. This contributes to NASDAQ's Best Eight Months which ends in June. June ranks near the bottom on the Dow Jones Industrials along with August and September since 1950.

NASDAQ Best Eight Months MACD buy and sell signals have produced excellent long-term results. $10,000 invested in the NASDAQ composite only during the Best Eight Months implementing MACD timing since 1971 would have yielded a $672,954 gain versus a $7,243 loss during the Worst Four Months, which are July through October.

Post-election year Junes have been much weaker pushing Dow and S&P average returns into negative territory and NASDAQ's down to 0.4%. Midterm election year Junes are the worst S&P 500 month, down 10 of 14 with an average loss of –2.0% and average losses in the other major indexes. The last nine pre-election year Junes have fared well, except 1971 and 1991 (recessions). Election year Junes have been solid and only weak in 1972 (Watergate) and 1992 (third candidate, Perot).

The second Triple-Witching Week of the year brings on some volatile trading. On Monday of Triple-Witching Week the Dow has been up nine of the last fourteen but, down five of the last nine. Triple-Witching Friday is no better and more prone to sizeable drops than gains. Full-week performance is choppy as well, littered with greater than 1% moves in both directions. Weeks After Triple-Witching Day are quite dangerous. This week has experienced Dow losses in twelve of the last fourteen years.

Typical June

June's first trading day is the Dow's best day of the month, up fifteen of the last twenty-one years. Strength picks up day two for the broader market with NASDAQ leading the charge. Gains are sparse throughout the remainder of the month until the last two days when semi-annual Russell index reshuffling pushes

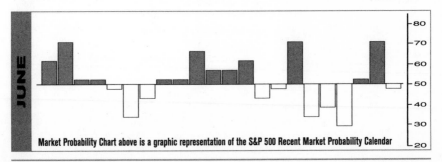

Market Probability Chart above is a graphic representation of the S&P 500 Recent Market Probability Calendar

NASDAQ and Russell 2000 stocks highest. The last day of the second quarter is a bit of a paradox as "portfolio pumping" has driven the Dow down eleven of the last fifteen while buoying the NASDAQ and Russell 2000 higher twelve of the last fifteen years.

June Vital Statistics

	DJIA	S&P 500	NASDAQ	Russell 1K	Russell 2K
Rank	11	9	4	7	7
Up	28	30	22	17	18
Down	28	26	13	10	9
Avg % Change	−0.1%	0.2%	1.2%	0.8%	1.1%
4-Year Presidential Election Cycle Performance					
Post-Election Year	−1.3%	−0.7%	0.4%	0.3%	1.1%
Mid-Term Year	−1.9	−2.0	−1.8	−1.5	−2.1
Pre-Election Year	1.3	1.8	3.0	2.4	2.4
Election Year	1.4	1.9	2.9	1.8	2.5
Best & Worst June					
	% Change	% Change	% Change	% Change	% Change
Best	1955 6.2	1955 8.2	2000 16.6	1999 5.1	2000 8.6
Worst	1962 −8.5	1962 −8.2	2002 −9.4	2002 −7.5	1991 −6.0
Best & Worst June Weeks					
Best	6/7/74 6.4	6/2/00 7.2	6/2/00 19	6/2/00 8	6/2/00 12.2
Worst	6/30/50 −6.8	6/30/50 −7.6	6/15/01 −8.4	6/15/01 −4.2	6/24/94 −4.4
Best & Worst June Days					
Best	6/28/62 3.8	6/28/62 3.4	6/2/00 6.4	6/17/02 2.8	6/2/00 4.2
Worst	6/26/50 −4.7	6/26/50 −5.4	6/14/01 −3.7	6/3/02 −2.4	6/12/00 −2.8
First Trading Day of Expiration Week 1990-2005					
Record (#Up - #Down)	10-6	10-6	7-9	9-7	7-9
Current streak	U1	U1	U1	U1	U1
Avg % Change	0.2	0.1	−0.2	0.1	−0.3
Options Expiration Day 1990-2005					
Record (#Up - #Down)	10-6	10-6	9-7	9-7	9-7
Current streak	U3	U3	U2	U3	U2
Avg % Change	−0.3	−0.1	−0.01	−0.1	−0.01
Options Expiration Week 1990-2005					
Record (#Up - #Down)	9-7	9-7	7-9	8-8	7-9
Current streak	U3	U1	U1	U1	U2
Avg % Change	−0.04	0.1	−0.5	0.02	−0.3
Week After Options Expiration 1990-2005					
Record (#Up - #Down)	2-14	6-10	7-9	7-9	6-10
Current streak	D7	D3	D1	D1	D1
Avg % Change	−1.0	−0.6	−0.03	−0.5	−0.5
2006 Bullish Days based on data from 1984 to 2004					
	1, 6, 14, 22, 29	1,2,14,19,22,29	1, 2, 6, 29, 30	1, 2, 19 22, 29	1, 2, 7, 29, 30
2006 Bearish Days based on data from 1984 to 2004					
	9, 20	8, 23, 26, 27	27	7,8,9,20,23,26,27	8, 19

Dow & S&P 1950-July 2005, NASDAQ 1971-July 2005, Russell 1K & 2K 1979-July 2005. Options data 1990 through August 2005.
Bullish/Bearish days based on index rising or falling 60% of the time on a particular trading day 1984-2004 (see pages 66-73).

ALMANAC INVESTOR

NASDAQ's Powerful 12-Day Mid-Year Rally

Every year when the days get long and the temperature rises on Wall Street, we always hear those infamous buzzwords, the "Summer Rally." As volume begins to shrink he hopes for a Summer Rally catch the ear of investors. On page 75 we illustrate that yes, there is a Summer Rally, but there is a rally for all seasons and the one that occurs in summer is weakest. Sure the market has performed well in a few summers but as a rule it does not. Any outsized summer gains have been predominantly due to extenuating circumstances and after a correction.

NASDAQ however, delivers a short, powerful rally that starts at the end of June. The table on the next page shows NASDAQ averaging a 3.2% gain since 1987 during the 12-day period from June's third to last trading day through July's ninth trading day.

NASDAQ COMPOSITE MID-YEAR RALLY

	June Close	4th Last June Trading Day	3rd Last June Trading Day	8th July Trading Day	9th July Trading Day	July Close	% Change 4th to 8th	% Change 4th to 9th	% Change 3rd to 8th	% Change 3rd to 9th	July Change
1985	296.20	292.30	293.40	300.52	302.39	301.29	2.8%	3.5%	2.4%	3.1%	1.7%
1986	405.51	402.22	402.87	391.55	384.80	371.37	−2.7	−4.3	−2.8	−4.5	−8.4
1987	424.67	427.20	426.68	426.53	431.14	434.93	−0.2	0.9	−0.0	1.0	2.4
1988	394.66	389.00	391.67	393.56	394.67	387.33	1.2	1.5	0.5	0.8	−1.9
1989	435.29	448.55	444.90	447.89	448.90	453.84	−0.1	0.1	0.7	0.9	4.3
1990	462.29	455.38	456.89	467.17	468.44	438.24	2.6	2.9	2.2	2.5	−5.2
1991	475.92	473.30	473.08	488.37	492.71	502.04	3.2	4.1	3.2	4.1	5.5
1992	563.60	548.20	547.84	570.22	575.21	580.83	4.0	4.9	4.1	5.0	3.1
1993	703.95	694.81	702.84	708.47	712.49	704.70	2.0	2.5	0.8	1.4	0.1
1994	705.96	702.68	702.05	719.35	721.56	722.16	2.4	2.7	2.5	2.8	2.3
1995	933.45	919.56	920.52	994.15	999.33	1001.21	8.1	8.7	8.0	8.6	7.3
1996	1185.02	1172.58	1153.29	1106.36	1103.49	1080.59	−5.6	−5.9	−4.1	−4.3	−8.8
1997	1442.07	1446.24	1436.38	1502.62	1523.88	1593.81	3.9	5.4	4.6	6.1	10.5
1998	1894.74	1863.25	1869.53	1965.53	1968.41	1872.39	5.5	5.6	5.1	5.3	−1.2
1999	2686.12	2552.65	2602.44	2778.23	2818.13	2638.49	8.8	10.4	6.8	8.3	−1.8
2000	3966.11	3858.96	3940.34	4174.86	4246.18	3766.99	8.2	10.0	6.0	7.8	−5.0
2001	2160.54	2064.62	2074.74	2075.74	2084.79	2027.13	0.5	1.0	0.0	0.5	−6.2
2002	1463.21	1423.99	1429.33	1374.43	1373.50	1328.26	−3.5	−3.5	−3.8	−3.9	−9.2
2003	1622.80	1602.66	1634.01	1733.93	1754.82	1735.02	8.2	9.5	6.1	7.4	6.9
2004	2047.79	2025.47	2019.82	1931.66	1914.88	1887.36	−4.6	−5.5	−4.4	−5.2	−7.8
2005	2056.96	2045.20	2069.89	2144.11	2152.82	2184.83	4.8	5.3	3.6	4.0	6.2
1985 Average							2.4%	2.8%	2.0%	2.5%	−0.2%
1987 Average							2.6%	3.2%	2.2%	2.8%	0.1%

JULY INDICATORS AND PATTERNS

July Almanac

July may be the best month of the third quarter for the Dow and S&P, but that is not saying much. Performance for the other two months, August and September, is negative for the most part. Only the Dow has consistently racked up gains. Since 1950 the Dow has averaged a 1.1% gain while the S&P posts an average gain of 0.9%.

July begins NASDAQ's worst four months and except for a few select years the over-the-counter index has been hit hard in July with an average loss of –0.3% since 1971. Dynamic trading often accompanies the first full month of summer as the beginning of the second half of the year brings an inflow of new funds—likely from retirement accounts. This creates a bullish beginning, a weak middle and strength towards the end (unless a bear market is in progress). Huge gains in July are often followed by sizeable drops and better buying opportunities later in the year (see Hot July Markets, page 35).

Trading around the Independence Day holiday is nothing to get exited about. The day before barely ekes out a gain and the day after is down more than half of the time, averaging minor losses. Wild market gyrations, both up and down, frequently occur for several days after the 4th. It pays to leave a day or two early with the traders and close out any short-term long positions well before the annual festivities begin. As mentioned in the June section and later with all the Seasonal Rallies, most years it does not pay to get sucked into the "Summer Rally" hype. Lock in any short-term gains and be prepared to capitalize on broad market weakness.

Post-election Julys perform quite well, ranking number one on the S&P 500 and the Dow Jones Industrials. Midterm election Julys are worst for NASDAQ and the Russell 2000 ranking dead last on both. NASDAQ averages a loss of –3.4%, up two, down six. The Russell 2000 has been crushed over the years for a –6.2% drubbing and only one gain. Pre-election Julys, swept up by overall bullish forces, achieve modest gains. Julys have suffered from the heat of the campaign trail in election years with large caps posting fractional gains and losses. Election year Julys are second worst on NASDAQ with an average drop of –1.8%, up 3, down 6.

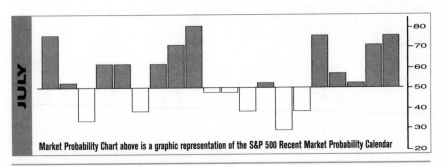

Market Probability Chart above is a graphic representation of the S&P 500 Recent Market Probability Calendar

---

Option expiration in July is generally characterized by flat trading. Monday before expiration has been mixed the last six years, with the Dow down 3 straight then up the last 3. On expiration Friday however, the Dow has been down 4 of the last 6. The week after expiration is one of the worst of the year.

Typical July

The month opens strong with the Dow Jones Industrials, S&P 500 and Russell 1000 up fourteen of the last seventeen first trading days. Day three is weak fol-

July Vital Statistics

	DJIA	S&P 500	NASDAQ	Russell 1K	Russell 2K
Rank	5	7	11	10	12
Up	34	30	17	11	13
Down	22	26	18	16	14
Avg % Change	1.1%	0.9%	-0.3%	0.3%	-0.8%
4-Year Presidential Election Cycle Performance					
Post-Election Year	1.6%	1.6%	2.6%	2.4%	1.6%
Mid-Term Year	0.9	0.4	-3.4	-2.5	-6.2
Pre-Election Year	1.5	1.3	1.2	1.3	2.1
Election Year	0.3	0.2	-1.8	-0.4	-1.5
Best & Worst July					
	% Change	% Change	% Change	% Change	% Change
Best	1989 9	1989 8.8	1997 10.5	1989 8.2	1980 11
Worst	1969 -6.6	2002 -7.9	2002 -9.2	2002 -7.5	2002 -15.2
Best & Worst July Weeks					
Best	7/2/99 5.6	7/2/99 5.8	7/2/99 7.4	7/2/99 5.7	7/18/80 4.2
Worst	7/19/02 -7.7	7/19/02 -8.0	7/28/00 -10.5	7/19/02 -7.4	7/19/02 -6.6
Best & Worst July Days					
Best	7/24/02 6.4	7/24/02 5.7	7/29/02 5.8	7/24/02 5.6	7/29/02 4.9
Worst	7/19/02 -4.6	7/19/02 -3.8	7/28/00 -4.7	7/19/02 -3.6	7/23/02 -4.1
First Trading Day of Expiration Week 1990-2005					
Record (#Up - #Down)	10-6	11-5	11-5	11-5	10-6
Current streak	U3	U3	U1	U3	U1
Avg % Change	-0.1	-0.1	0.1	-0.1	-0.01
Options Expiration Day 1990-2005					
Record (#Up - #Down)	5-11	6-10	6-10	6-10	4-12
Current streak	U1	U1	U1	U1	U1
Avg % Change	-0.6	-0.5	-0.6	-0.5	-0.6
Options Expiration Week 1990-2005					
Record (#Up - #Down)	9-7	6-10	7-9	6-10	8-8
Current streak	U1	U1	U1	U1	U1
Avg % Change	-0.3	-0.6	-0.5	-0.6	-0.6
Week After Options Expiration 1990-2005					
Record (#Up - #Down)	7-9	6-10	5-11	6-10	4-12
Current streak	U1	U1	U1	U1	U1
Avg % Change	-0.5	-0.8	-1.6	-0.8	-1.3
2006 Bullish Days based on data from 1984 to 2004					
	3, 12, 13, 14, 25	3,7,10,12,13,14	3, 10, 12, 13, 14	3,7,12,13,14,25	10, 13, 14, 25
	28, 31	25, 28, 31	25, 26, 31	26, 28, 31	26, 31
2006 Bearish Days based on data from 1984 to 2004					
	6, 19, 21	6, 11, 19, 21,24	6, 19, 21, 24	6, 11, 19, 21, 24	6, 19, 21, 24

Dow & S&P 1950-July 2005, NASDAQ 1971-July 2005, Russell 1K & 2K 1979-July 2005. Options data 1990 through August 2005. Bullish/Bearish days based on index rising or falling 60% of the time on a particular trading day 1984-2004 (see pages 66-73).

lowed by strength until options expiration. The third week of July, frequently the week after options expiration, is July's major trouble spot.

Indicators and Patterns

Hot July Markets Often Precede Fourth Quarter Buying Opportunities

One of the many interesting seasonal patterns we have tracked over the years in the *Stock Trader's Almanac* and our newsletters concerns July gains of 3.5% or more on the Dow that occurred since 1950. The accompanying table illustrates that whenever bulls stampeded in July, investors were likely to be given an opportunity to purchase stocks cheaper sometime later in the fall.

Three times subsequent second half lows were reached rather quickly after hot July markets. The August 1954 low followed the bear market of 1953, when the market bottomed in September 1953 and went straight up until April 1956. August 1958's low followed the 1957 bear market, when the new bull market picked up steam in April 1958. A quick low came in August 1970 as the 1969/1970 bear market ended in May 1970.

All other occasions brought better buying opportunities in the ninety days between mid-September and mid-December.

HOT JULY MARKETS & AUTUMN BUYING OPPORTUNITIES					
July Gains of 3.5% or More			Subsequent 2nd Half Low		
Year	Dow	% Gain	Date	Dow	% Lower
1951	257.86	6.3%	Nov 24	255.95	− 0.7%
1954	347.92	4.3	Aug 31	335.80	− 3.5
1956	517.81	5.1	Nov 28	466.10	− 10.0
1958	502.99	5.2	Aug 18	502.67	− 0.1
1959	674.88	4.9	Sep 22	616.45	− 8.7
1962	597.93	6.5	Oct 23	558.06	− 6.7
1967	904.24	5.1	Nov 8	849.57	− 6.0
1970	734.12	7.4	Aug 13	707.35	− 3.6
1973	926.40	3.9	Dec 5	788.31	− 14.9
1978	862.27	5.3	Nov 14	785.26	− 8.9
1980	935.32	7.8	Dec 11	908.45	− 2.9
1987	2572.07	6.3	Oct 19	1738.74	− 32.4
1989	2660.66	9.0	Oct 13	2569.26	− 3.4
1991	3024.82	4.1	Dec 10	2863.82	− 5.3
1994	3764.50	3.8	Nov 23	3674.63	− 2.4
1997	8222.61	7.2	Oct 27	7161.15	− 12.9
2005	10640.91	3.6			
				Total	− 122.4%
				Average	− 7.7%

AUGUST INDICATORS AND PATTERNS

August Almanac

Money flow from harvesting made August a great stock market month in the first half of the twentieth century. It was the best month from 1901 to 1951. In 1900, 37.5% of the population was farming. Now less than 2% farm and August is one of the worst months of the year. August has become the worst S&P 500 month in the past 15 years.

The shortest bear market in history (45 days) caused by turmoil in Russia, the Asian currency crisis and the Long-Term Capital Management hedge fund debacle ended August 31, 1998. The Dow dropped a record 1344.22 points for the month, off 15.1%—which is the second worst monthly percentage Dow loss since 1950. The Dow lost 512.64 points on the last day alone, –6.4%, the worst one-day drop since October 1987. Saddam Hussein triggered a 10.0% slide in August 1990. The best Dow gains occurred in 1982 (11.5%) and 1984 (9.8%) as bear markets ended.

Trading stocks in August has led to frustration with its propensity for nasty sell-offs. August's woes may be perpetuated by the empty trading floors of the "vacation" month.

August is its typical self in post-election years generating losses and ranking last on the Dow Jones Industrials and S&P 500. It is the penultimate Russell 1000 month and third from the bottom on NASDAQ and the Russell 2000. Midterm Augusts behave on par with the months overall performance. Pre-election Augusts produce decent gains and rank a bit higher on the Dow Industrials and S&P 500. Election year Augusts perform better though; ranked number one on both Russell indices with the small cap Russell 2000 averaging a 3.5% gain, up 4, down 3.

On Monday of expiration week the Dow has been up twelve of the last sixteen times with some big winners while on expiration Friday it has dropped in ten of those sixteen years. Expiration week as a whole is up half the time but some of the losses have been steep. The week after is much stronger up five straight from 2000 to 2004.

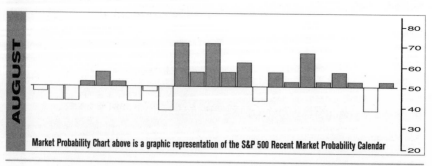

Market Probability Chart above is a graphic representation of the S&P 500 Recent Market Probability Calendar

Typical August

The first nine trading days of the month have exhibited weakness while mid-month is strongest. The end of August tends to get whacked as traders evacuate Wall Street for the summer finale. The last five days have suffered in six of the last nine years with the Dow up only once the next to last day in ten years. In the last nine years, the last five days of August have averaged losses of: Dow Jones Industrials, –2.9%; S&P 500, –2.7%; and NASDAQ, –2.4%.

August Vital Statistics

	DJIA	S&P 500	NASDAQ	Russell 1K	Russell 2K
Rank	10	10	10	9	8
Up	31	30	18	17	15
Down	24	25	16	9	11
Avg % Change	–0.1%	0.02%	0.2%	0.5%	0.6%
4-Year Presidential Election Cycle Performance					
Post-Election Year	–2.0%	–1.8%	–1.9%	–2.2%	–0.7%
Mid-Term Year	–0.9	–0.6	–2.8	–0.4	–2.9
Pre-Election Year	1.8	1.4	2.2	1.9	1.8
Election Year	0.8	0.9	2.8	2.3	3.5
Best & Worst August					
	% Change	% Change	% Change	% Change	% Change
Best	1982 11.5	1982 11.6	2000 11.7	1982 11.3	1984 11.5
Worst	1998 –15.1	1998 –14.6	1998 –19.9	1998 –15.1	1998 –19.5
Best & Worst August Weeks					
Best	8/20/82 10.3	8/20/82 8.8	8/3/84 7.4	8/20/82 8.5	8/3/84 7.0
Worst	8/23/74 –6.1	8/16/74 –6.4	8/28/98 –8.8	8/28/98 –5.4	8/28/98 –9.4
Best & Worst August Days					
Best	8/17/82 4.9	8/17/82 4.8	8/14/02 5.1	8/17/82 4.4	8/6/02 3.7
Worst	8/31/98 –6.4	8/31/98 –6.8	8/31/98 –8.6	8/31/98 –6.7	8/31/98 –5.7
First Trading Day of Expiration Week 1990-2005					
Record (#Up - #Down)	12-4	14-2	14-2	14-2	12-4
Current streak	U3	U3	U8	U3	U6
Avg % Change	0.5	0.5	0.6	0.5	0.4
Options Expiration Day 1990-2005					
Record (#Up - #Down)	6-10	7-9	7-9	7-9	9-7
Current streak	U3	U3	D1	U3	U4
Avg % Change	–0.5	–0.4	–0.4	–0.4	–0.1
Options Expiration Week 1990-2005					
Record (#Up - #Down)	8-8	10-6	10-6	10-6	11-5
Current streak	D1	D1	D1	D1	D1
Avg % Change	–0.2	0.2	0.6	0.2	0.6
Week After Options Expiration 1990-2005					
Record (#Up - #Down)	11-5	12-4	11-5	12-4	11-5
Current streak	D1	D1	D1	D1	D1
Avg % Change	0.2	0.2	0.4	0.2	–0.3
2006 Bullish Days based on data from 1984 to 2004					
	14, 16, 22, 24	14, 16, 18, 24	4, 14, 15, 16, 22	7, 14, 16, 18, 22	9, 14, 15, 16, 22, 24
			23, 29, 31	24	29, 30, 31
2006 Bearish Days based on data from 1984 to 2004					
	30	11, 30	2	2, 11	11

Dow & S&P 1950-July 2005, NASDAQ 1971-July 2005, Russell 1K & 2K 1979-July 2005. Options data 1990 through August 2005. Bullish/Bearish days based on index rising or falling 60% of the time on a particular trading day 1984-2004 (see pages 66-73).

SEPTEMBER INDICATORS AND PATTERNS

September Almanac

September has the dubious honor of being the worst month of the year and was creamed four years straight from 1999-2002 after four banner years from 1996-1998 in the halcyon days of the dot.com bubble madness. (Over the last fifteen years August is the worst on the S&P.) Though the month has opened strong eight of the last ten years, once the summer tans begin to fade and the kids head back to school, fund managers tend to clean house as the end of the third quarter approaches, causing some nasty selloffs near month-end over the years. We steer clear of the long side until the institutions settle up their accounts. The start of the business year, end of vacations, and back-to-school made September a leading barometer month in the first 60 years of the twentieth century.

Post-election Septembers, though not the worst post-election year month, are prone to large declines. Nine of the last thirteen post-election year Septembers took some rather mean hits. The four gains were not without cause. The 1953 bear market ended in September. The 1973 downleg ended in August, but the Yom Kippur War, Watergate, and the OPEC oil embargo forged a wicked bear market through 1973 and 1974. An acceleration of defense spending in September 1965 related to Vietnam created a bullish environment for stocks. President Clinton's signing of the capital gains tax cut into law in July 1997 helped boost stocks in September 1997; August and October were down 7.3% and 6.3% respectively.

POST-ELECTION YEAR SEPTEMBERS	
Year	Dow % Gain
1953	1.1%
1957	− 5.8
1961	− 2.6
1965	4.2
1969	− 2.8
1973	6.7
1977	− 1.7
1981	− 3.6
1985	− 0.4
1989	− 1.6
1993	− 2.6
1997	4.2
2001	− 11.1

Midterm Septembers have punished investors ahead of eight October midterm bottoms since WWII. Along with October, September is the only weak link in

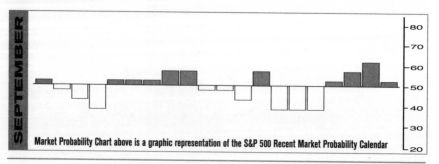

SEPTEMBER

Market Probability Chart above is a graphic representation of the S&P 500 Recent Market Probability Calendar

mighty pre-election years. Only three S&P 500 losses came in the last ten election year Septembers—in 1972 and 1984 when incumbents ran and won; and in 2000, down over 5%, during the incumbentless "fuzzy" campaigns.

Except for the Monday before, September Triple Witching is not to be trifled with. The Dow has risen ten of the last fifteen years on Monday but nine losses were registered on Triple-Witching Friday. Triple-Witching Week can be cruel,

September Vital Statistics

	DJIA	S&P 500	NASDAQ	Russell 1K	Russell 2K
Rank	12	12	12	12	11
Up	19	22	18	11	13
Down	36	32	16	15	13
Avg % Change	−1.1%	−0.7%	−1.0%	−1.1%	−0.8%
4-Year Presidential Election Cycle Performance					
Post-Election Year	−1.2%	−1.3%	−1.8%	−2.4%	−3.1%
Mid-Term Year	−1.9	−1.2	−2.9	−3.3	−2.0
Pre-Election Year	−0.9	−0.6	−0.6	−0.4	−0.1
Election Year	−0.2	0.3	0.8	1.3	1.7
Best & Worst September					
	% Change	% Change	% Change	% Change	% Change
Best	1954 7.3	1954 8.3	1998 13	1998 6.5	1998 7.6
Worst	2002 −12.4	1974 −11.9	2001 −17.0	2002 −10.9	2001 −13.6
Best & Worst September Weeks					
Best	9/28/01 7.4	9/28/01 7.8	9/20/74 5.7	9/28/01 7.6	9/28/01 6.9
Worst	9/21/01 −14.3	9/21/01 −11.6	9/21/01 −16.1	9/21/01 −11.7	9/21/01 −14.0
Best & Worst September Days					
Best	9/8/98 5	9/8/98 5.1	9/8/98 6	9/8/98 5	9/8/98 4.3
Worst	9/17/01 −7.1	9/26/55 −6.6	9/17/01 −6.8	9/17/01 −5.0	9/17/01 −5.2
First Trading Day of Expiration Week 1990-2004					
Record (#Up - #Down)	10-5	9-6	5-10	9-6	6-9
Current streak	U1	U1	U1	U1	U1
Avg % Change	−0.1	−0.1	−0.6	−0.1	−0.3
Options Expiration Day 1990-2004					
Record (#Up - #Down)	6-9	8-7	9-6	8-7	10-5
Current streak	U1	U1	U1	U1	D1
Avg % Change	−0.2	−0.03	−0.1	−0.03	−0.01
Options Expiration Week 1990-2004					
Record (#Up - #Down)	8-7	9-6	8-7	9-6	8-7
Current streak	D1	U2	U2	U2	U2
Avg % Change	−0.9	−0.7	−1.1	−0.7	−1.0
Week After Options Expiration 1990-2004					
Record (#Up - #Down)	3-12	2-13	6-9	3-12	5-10
Current streak	D3	D3	D3	D3	D3
Avg % Change	−1.1	−0.7	−0.8	−0.7	−1.0
2006 Bullish Days based on data from 1984 to 2004					
	13	28	5, 13, 20	13, 27, 28	5, 7, 13, 28, 29
2006 Bearish Days based on data from 1984 to 2004					
	7, 11, 19, 21, 22	7, 21, 22, 25	15, 18, 25	7, 18, 21, 25	15, 18, 26

Dow & S&P 1950-July 2005, NASDAQ 1971-July 2005, Russell 1K & 2K 1979-July 2005. Options data 1990 through August 2005. Bullish/Bearish days based on index rising or falling 60% of the time on a particular trading day 1984-2004 (see pages 66-73).

especially in bear markets, falling in five of the last six years. The week after Triple Witching has been brutal, down twelve of the last fifteen, averaging a Dow loss of −1.1%.

Typical September

Despite its bad reputation, September has a few bullish tendencies. The first two trading days are the month's silver lining with the Dow Jones Industrials posting gains in eight of the last ten years. These two days are often right around Labor Day's bullish influence mentioned below. And above, the Monday before Triple Witching is highlighted. Other than those few days an abundance of hazards shrouds the month, especially the second half. The second to last trading day is the best of the last two weeks with the S&P 500 up eight of the last ten years but the last day was down in seven of those years.

Indicators and Patterns

Trading the Labor Day Market

Over the years the few days before the three-day Labor Day holiday weekend have become prime vacation time. Back in the first half of the twentieth century, approximately one-fourth of the country worked on farms as compared to less than 2% nowadays. Business activity ahead of the long weekend was more energetic in the old days. From 1950 through 1977 the three days before Labor Day pushed the Dow Jones Industrials higher in twenty-five of twenty-eight years. Since then bullishness has shifted to the last day before and the two days after. This frequently coincides with early September strength. The two days after Labor Day are up nine of the last eleven years.

Labor Day Market						
Dow Jones Industrial Average Point Changes						
Year	3-Day Change Before	Day Before	Day After	2-Day Change After	3-Day Change After	Week's Change After
1950	0.13	1.55	1.60	− 0.22	− 0.09	1.61
1951	4.69	0.31	0.38	2.23	2.03	3.64
1952	1.87	0.63	1.36	2.11	1.72	1.46
1953	1.80	0.73	1.08	1.14	− 1.46	− 4.63
1954	7.30	1.95	2.27	2.97	3.63	4.73
1955	7.86	2.90	3.71	2.67	2.53	2.06
1956	− 1.01	6.08	5.62	7.78	7.45	4.72
1957	6.80	8.29	1.78	− 1.75	− 4.84	− 5.72
1958	− 1.00	0.91	3.14	5.08	4.81	4.14
1959	− 3.72	6.28	− 9.49	− 14.51	− 18.80	− 14.82
1960	− 1.18	− 0.88	− 4.37	− 12.95	− 13.80	− 11.10
1961	7.04	1.25	− 2.47	4.82	5.34	− 0.28
1962	3.93	6.86	− 6.73	− 10.04	− 8.37	− 8.32
1963	9.44	2.92	2.70	3.60	8.66	6.05
1964	4.31	2.29	3.60	7.26	11.19	18.82
1965	14.87	7.57	2.14	5.71	9.50	10.98

(table continued on next page)

ALMANAC INVESTOR

Labor Day Market
Dow Jones Industrial Average Point Changes

Year	3-Day Change Before	Day Before	Day After	2-Day Change After	3-Day Change After	Week's Change After
1966	11.97	− 4.40	− 5.35	− 10.30	− 12.81	− 12.14
1967	6.42	− 0.11	2.95	5.78	6.99	6.36
1968	− 0.12	1.68	4.35	10.94	21.51	25.24
1969	13.20	8.31	1.06	− 1.05	− 11.42	− 17.22
1970	13.00	5.88	1.99	− 4.72	− 10.40	− 9.31
1971	14.68	12.12	3.72	8.18	3.14	− 1.75
1972	15.35	6.32	− 0.68	− 6.62	− 7.60	− 8.81
1973	15.50	5.04	7.82	11.51	13.47	11.06
1974	7.04	21.74	− 15.25	− 30.58	− 7.82	− 0.70
1975	32.23	5.87	− 11.65	− 3.05	2.97	0.63
1976	15.37	4.32	7.48	3.83	− 2.24	− 0.75
1977	13.42	7.45	0.96	4.08	− 3.15	− 15.27
1978	− 0.87	2.51	7.28	16.46	14.38	28.41
1979	2.99	3.93	− 15.02	− 21.50	− 20.31	− 13.48
1980	− 20.82	2.21	8.19	20.57	16.22	8.37
1981	− 21.03	− 5.33	− 10.56	− 7.80	0.76	11.13
1982	23.82	15.73	− 10.85	− 9.38	− 12.60	− 18.31
1983	19.41	8.64	23.27	28.66	30.69	24.29
1984	− 7.73	1.10	− 12.03	− 15.35	− 5.52	− 17.00
1985	11.54	− 1.12	− 4.82	− 7.29	− 8.18	1.68
1986	− 5.91	− 1.83	− 27.98	− 17.01	21.37	1.41
1987	− 49.59	− 38.11	− 16.26	− 12.11	14.67	47.36
1988	16.36	52.28	10.67	11.20	8.53	14.22
1989	25.46	14.82	− 7.41	− 32.30	− 45.21	− 42.55
1990	− 0.49	21.04	− 0.99	13.86	− 18.07	5.19
1991	17.44	− 6.04	− 25.93	− 35.10	− 35.10	− 31.97
1992	15.67	− 10.27	− 21.34	− 10.54	23.23	23.77
1993	− 17.32	7.83	− 26.83	− 45.00	− 44.44	− 12.30
1994	− 31.72	− 15.86	13.12	0.67	22.88	− 10.77
1995	39.10	36.98	22.54	36.27	22.18	53.18
1996	− 95.06	− 31.44	32.18	40.69	− 9.25	43.65
1997	− 159.80	− 72.01	257.36	272.22	244.82	199.99
1998	− 187.18	− 41.97	380.53	224.77	− 24.71	155.25
1999	249.17	235.24	− 44.32	− 42.11	0.95	− 50.02
2000	23.68	23.68	21.83	71.86	21.09	− 18.13
2001	− 272.28	30.17	47.74	83.52	− 108.91	− 343.90
2002	− 160.91	− 7.49	− 355.45	− 238.38	− 379.80	− 236.30
2003	75.37	41.61	107.45	152.64	172.08	87.52
2004	86.28	− 30.08	82.59	53.16	28.90	52.87
1950-2004						
Avg	− 3.70	6.55	7.98	9.57	− 1.22	− 0.83
Up	36	40	33	31	30	30
Down	19	15	22	24	25	25
1950-1977						
Avg	7.90	4.42	0.13	− 0.22	0.08	− 0.33
Up	23	25	20	17	15	14
Down	5	3	8	11	13	14
1978-2004						
Avg	− 15.72	8.75	16.11	19.73	− 2.57	− 1.35
Up	13	15	13	14	15	16
Down	14	12	14	13	12	11

OCTOBER INDICATORS AND PATTERNS

October Almanac

October often evokes fear on Wall Street as memories of crashes in 1929, 1987, the 554-point drop on October 27, 1997, back-to-back massacres in 1978 and 1979 and Friday the 13th in 1989 are stirred. The term "Octoberphobia" has been used to describe the phenomenon of major market drops occurring during the month. Market calamities can become a self-fulfilling prophecy, so stay on the lookout and don't get whipsawed if it happens.

But it has become a turnaround month—a "bear killer" if you will. Eleven post-WWII bear markets have ended in October: 1946, 1957, 1960, 1962, 1966, 1974, 1987, 1990, 1998, 2001, and 2002. Eight were midterm bottoms.

Buy! Buy! Buy!

Twice during the four decades of newsletter publishing we have jumped on these major midterm October bottoms and advised subscribers likewise with bold headlines of "BUY! BUY! BUY! BUY! BUY! BUY! BUY! BUY! BUY! BUY!" across the top. In October 1974 Yale Hirsch had the guts to go out on a limb in the face of Watergate, the OPEC Oil Embargo, and the worst bear market since the Great Depression. And most recently in 2002, we repeated the coup de grace on October 16, days after the end of the bear market that brought NASDAQ down 77.9% from its year 2000 top. Even as the worst bear market since the 1970s gnashed its teeth with rampant corporate malfeasance, terrorism, memories of 9/11, Afghanistan, and the looming confrontation with Iraq.

October used to be a horrible month for stocks and from 1950 to 1997 held the record for most cumulative Dow Jones Industrials points lost. Since the beating in 1997 it has been the best month, up significantly six of the last seven years. Only December and November are better for small cap Russell 2000 stocks.

With the exception of the Russell 1000, our "Worst Months" of the year ends with October. With October a rising market star and a frequent bear killer it has become one of the best times of the year to take long positions. We use MACD triggers to better time entries into the market at this time of year.

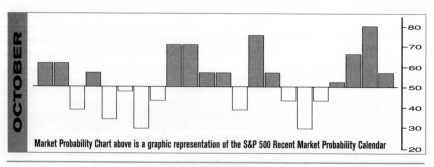

Market Probability Chart above is a graphic representation of the S&P 500 Recent Market Probability Calendar

Much of the churning in October can be related to the October 31 deadline for mutual funds. The Internal Revenue Code requires mutual fund companies to distribute 98 percent of their earnings over every 12-month period ending October 31 and every calendar year ending December 31. Generating the cash for these distributions means selling holdings. October is a great time to buy depressed high-tech stocks. Big October gains five years in a row from 1999 to 2003 came after atrocious Septembers.

October Vital Statistics

	DJIA	S&P 500	NASDAQ	Russell 1K	Russell 2K
Rank	7	6	8	6	10
Up	32	33	18	17	14
Down	23	22	16	9	12
Avg % Change	0.6%	0.9%	0.6%	1.1%	−0.6%
4-Year Presidential Election Cycle Performance					
Post-Election Year	0.7%	1.1%	1.8%	1.1%	1.6%
Mid-Term Year	3.1	3.3	4.1	5.6	3.1
Pre-Election Year	−1.9	−1.3	−2.9	−2.6	−6.0
Election Year	0.3	0.6	−0.1	1.0	−0.1
Best & Worst October					
	% Change	% Change	% Change	% Change	% Change
Best	1982 10.7	1974 16.3	1974 17.2	1982 11.3	1982 14.1
Worst	1987 −23.2	1987 −21.8	1987 −27.2	1987 −21.9	1987 −30.8
Best & Worst October Weeks					
Best	10/11/74 12.6	10/11/74 14.1	10/11/74 9.5	10/16/98 7.6	10/16/98 7.7
Worst	10/23/87 −13.2	10/23/87 −12.2	10/23/87 −19.2	10/23/87 −12.9	10/23/87 −20.4
Best & Worst October Days					
Best	10/21/87 10.2	10/21/87 9.1	10/13/00 7.9	10/21/87 8.9	10/21/87 7.6
Worst	10/19/87 −22.6	10/19/87 −20.5	10/19/87 −11.4	10/19/87 −19.0	10/19/87 −12.5
First Trading Day of Expiration Week 1990-2004					
Record (#Up - #Down)	13-2	11-4	11-4	12-3	15-0
Current streak	U5	U3	U3	U3	U15
Avg % Change	0.5	0.5	0.6	0.5	0.5
Options Expiration Day 1990-2004					
Record (#Up - #Down)	9-6	10-5	10-5	10-5	9-6
Current streak	U1	U1	U1	U1	U15
Avg % Change	0.2	0.10	0.01	0.04	0.2
Options Expiration Week 1990-2004					
Record (#Up - #Down)	10-5	10-5	8-7	10-5	9-6
Current streak	D1	D1	D2	D1	D1
Avg % Change	1.0	1.0	1.4	1.1	1.0
Week After Options Expiration 1990-2004					
Record (#Up - #Down)	8-7	6-9	7-8	6-9	6-9
Current streak	D2	D2	U1	D2	D2
Avg % Change	0.2	0.02	0.2	0.01	0.2
2006 Bullish Days based on data from 1984 to 2004					
	2, 5, 12, 13, 16	2, 3, 12, 13	5, 12, 13, 19	12, 13, 19, 27	5, 12, 13, 16, 19
	19, 27, 30	19, 27, 30	30, 31	30, 31	30, 31
2006 Bearish Days based on data from 1984 to 2004					
	4, 6, 10, 11, 25	4, 6, 10, 18, 24	18, 24, 25, 26	4, 6, 10, 18, 24, 25	4, 6, 9, 24, 26

Dow & S&P 1950-July 2005, NASDAQ 1971-July 2005, Russell 1K & 2K 1979-July 2005. Options data 1990 through August 2005. Bullish/Bearish days based on index rising or falling 60% of the time on a particular trading day 1984-2004 (see pages 66-73).

October does fairly well in post-election years as other months take the brunt of bearish cross-currents. Midterm election year Octobers are downright stellar thanks to the major turnarounds mentioned above; ranking number one on the Dow, S&P 500 and Russell 1000, and second on NASDAQ and the Russell 2000. October has been the weakest link in pre-election years but has produced hefty gains in bull markets, most recently in 1999 and 2003. Octobers average about the same in election years as they do in all years but rise and fall with the incumbent's prospect for reelection.

Options expiration week in October provides plenty of opportunity. On the Monday before expiration the Dow has only been down three times since 1982 and the Russell 2000 is up the last fifteen years straight. Expiration day has a more spotty record as does the week as a whole. After a market bottom in October, the week after is most bullish, otherwise it is susceptible to downdrafts. Any weakness can be used to take new long positions.

Typical October

After mild gains the first couple of days, stocks tend to drift lower. Mid-month trading is more robust around options expiration. Weakness then plagues the third week of the month. Strength the last several days is most dependable the second to last day with the Dow Industrials and S&P 500 up seventeen of the last twenty-one years, averaging one-day gains of about 0.75%.

NOVEMBER INDICATORS AND PATTERNS

November Almanac

Ah November, the holiday season begins and ushers in the start of the best three-month span of the year. November is the number-two S&P 500 month and has been number three on the Dow Jones Industrials since 1950. Since 1971 November ranks third for NASDAQ.

November begins the Best Six Months for the Dow and S&P, and the Best Eight Months for NASDAQ. Small caps come into favor during November but see how they really take off the last two weeks of the year in the December section. Tricky Thanksgiving trading is detailed below.

November maintains its status among the top performing months as fourth-quarter cash inflows from institutions drive November to lead the best consecutive three-month span. The month has taken hits during bear markets and November 2000, down –22.9% (undecided election and the nascent bear), was NASDAQ's second worst month on record since the composite was created February 5, 1971—second only to October 1987.

November's market strength is apparent as it does not suffer from any consistent losses in any of the four years of the Presidential Election Cycle. The Dow Jones Industrials lost ground in only three Novembers in the last fifteen post-election years since 1945 (all during Vietnam); the S&P 500 was down only four.

Midterm Election Novembers team with October for a helluva one-two punch, an 8.5% two-month NASDAQ gain. Pre-election year Novembers are ironically mediocre for such a powerful market year.

Election year Novembers rank number one for the Dow and S&P 500 but have relinquished losses in tumultuous election environments. 2000 was the worst election year November since Truman upset Dewy in 1948 following the first undecided Presidential Election since 1888. The previous seven Republican victories averaged 2.8% in November on the S&P 500 while the last seven Democrats averaged 0.4%.

Options expiration often coincides with the week before Thanksgiving (see page 47). In any event the week is strong. Dow Jones Industrials posted ten straight

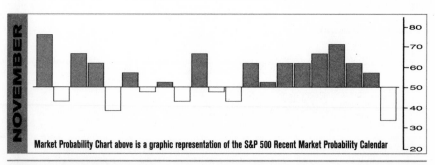

Market Probability Chart above is a graphic representation of the S&P 500 Recent Market Probability Calendar

gains from 1993 to 2002. The Monday before expiration day has been streaky with the Dow up five straight, 1994-1998, during the bulk of the last twentieth century bull market, down five in a row, 1999-2003, and up in 2004. Options expiration day behaves similarly, though moving in the opposite direction of Monday the last three years. The week after expiration has been stronger lately, up the last four.

November Vital Statistics

	DJIA	S&P 500	NASDAQ	Russell 1K	Russell 2K
Rank	3	2	3	1	2
Up	37	37	23	19	17
Down	18	18	11	7	9
Avg % Change	1.7%	1.7%	2.1%	2.2%	2.5%
4-Year Presidential Election Cycle Performance					
Post-Election Year	1.1%	1.2%	1.6%	3.7%	2.2%
Mid-Term Year	2.9	2.9	4.4	3.3	4.2
Pre-Election Year	0.6	0.7	2.1	0.4	2.4
Election Year	2.1	2.0	0.4	1.7	1.5
Best & Worst November					
	% Change	% Change	% Change	% Change	% Change
Best	1962 10.1	1980 10.2	2001 14.2	1980 10.1	2002 8.8
Worst	1973 –14.0	1973 –11.4	2000 –22.9	2000 –9.3	2000 –10.4
Best & Worst November Weeks					
Best	11/2/62 6.3	11/5/82 6.3	11/5/82 6.8	11/5/82 6.4	11/5/82 6.6
Worst	11/2/73 –5.3	11/23/73 –4.3	11/10/00 –12.2	11/10/00 –4.9	11/10/00 –5.3
Best & Worst November Days					
Best	11/26/63 4.5	11/26/63 4.0	11/14/00 5.8	11/3/82 3.7	11/24/00 3.1
Worst	11/30/87 –4.0	11/30/87 –4.2	11/8/00 –5.4	11/30/87 –4.1	11/30/87 –3.4
First Trading Day of Expiration Week 1990-2004					
Record (#Up - #Down)	7-8	6-9	8-7	7-8	9-6
Current streak	U1	D6	U1	U1	U1
Avg % Change	0.1	0.1	0.01	0.04	0.03
Options Expiration Day 1990-2004					
Record (#Up - #Down)	9-6	8-7	5-10	8-7	5-10
Current streak	D1	D1	D1	D1	D1
Avg % Change	–0.1	–0.2	–0.4	–0.2	–0.3
Options Expiration Week 1990-2004					
Record (#Up - #Down)	11-4	10-5	9-6	9-6	9-6
Current streak	D2	D2	D2	D2	D2
Avg % Change	1.0	0.7	0.8	0.7	0.4
Week After Options Expiration 1990-2004					
Record (#Up - #Down)	8-7	8-7	9-6	8-7	8-7
Current streak	U4	U4	U4	U4	U4
Avg % Change	0.3	0.3	0.5	0.3	0.4
2006 Bullish Days based on data from 1984 to 2004					
	1, 3, 6, 8, 14, 17	1, 3, 6, 14, 17	1, 3, 14, 22	1, 3, 6, 14, 17	1,2,3,6,10,14,17
	21, 22, 24, 27	21,22,24,27,28	24, 28, 29	22, 24, 27, 28	24,27,28,29,30
2006 Bearish Days based on data from 1984 to 2004					
	2, 7, 9, 16	7, 30	15, 16	7, 16, 30	13, 16, 21

Dow & S&P 1950-July 2005, NASDAQ 1971-July 2005, Russell 1K & 2K 1979-July 2005. Options data 1990 through August 2005. Bullish/Bearish days based on index rising or falling 60% of the time on a particular trading day 1984-2004 (see pages 66-73).

ALMANAC INVESTOR

Typical November

Being such a bullish month November is not surprisingly chockfull of strong days, though it does have weak points. Day one usually opens strong but on day two stocks often take a breather. The next two days have a bullish bias but the fifth trading day is characterized by market losses. After drifting sideways for several days stock prices tend to move higher the day before mid-month, then fade for several days. Seven days before month-end the market heats up as fourth-quarter rallies frequently take hold until the last day of the month when stocks pause before big December. The bond market closes for Veteran's Day.

Indicators and Patterns

Trading the Thanksgiving Market

The S&P 500 has been up the week before Thanksgiving week eleven of the last thirteen years, 2003 broke the eleven-year run. The day before Thanksgiving Day and the day after have combined for only 9 losses in 53 years on the Dow Jones Industrials. For 35 years the combination of the Wednesday before Thanksgiving and the Friday after had a great track record, except for two occasions.

Attributing this phenomenon to the warm "holiday spirit" was a no-brainer. But publishing it in the *1987 Stock Trader's Almanac* was the "kiss of death." Wednesday, Friday, and Monday were all crushed, down 6.6% over the three days in 1987. Since 1988 Wednesday-Friday lost six of seventeen times with a total Dow point-gain of 442.22 versus a Wednesday-Monday total Dow point-gain of 653.26 with only four losses.

The best strategy seems to be going long into weakness Tuesday or Wednesday and staying in through the following Monday or exiting into strength.

DOW JONES INDUSTRIALS BEFORE AND AFTER THANKSGIVING

	Tuesday Before	Wednesday Before		Friday After	Total Gain Dow Points	Dow Close	Next Monday
1952	− 0.18	1.54		1.22	2.76	283.66	0.04
1953	1.71	0.65		2.45	3.10	280.23	1.14
1954	3.27	1.89		3.16	5.05	387.79	0.72
1955	4.61	0.71		0.26	0.97	482.88	− 1.92
1956	− 4.49	− 2.16		4.65	2.49	472.56	− 2.27
1957	− 9.04	10.69		3.84	14.53	449.87	− 2.96
1958	− 4.37	8.63		8.31	16.94	557.46	2.61
1959	2.94	1.41		1.42	2.83	652.52	6.66
1960	− 3.44	1.37		4.00	5.37	606.47	− 1.04
1961	− 0.77	1.10		2.18	3.28	732.60	− 0.61
1962	6.73	4.31		7.62	11.93	644.87	− 2.81
1963	32.03	− 2.52		9.52	7.00	750.52	1.39
1964	− 1.68	− 5.21	**T**	− 0.28	− 5.49	882.12	6.69
1965	2.56	N/C	**H**	− 0.78	− 0.78	948.16	1.23
1966	− 3.18	1.84	**A**	6.52	8.36	803.34	− 2.18
1967	13.17	3.07	**N**	3.58	6.65	877.60	4.51
1968	8.14	− 3.17	**K**	8.76	5.59	985.08	− 1.74
1969	− 5.61	3.23	**S**	1.78	5.01	812.30	− 7.26
1970	5.21	1.98	**G**	6.64	8.62	781.35	12.74
1971	− 5.18	0.66	**I**	17.96	18.62	816.59	13.14
1972	8.21	7.29	**V**	4.67	11.96	1025.21	− 7.45
1973	− 17.76	10.08	**I**	− 0.98	9.10	854.00	− 29.05
1974	5.32	2.03	**N**	− 0.63	1.40	618.66	− 15.64
1975	9.76	3.15	**G**	2.12	5.27	860.67	− 4.33
1976	− 6.57	1.66		5.66	7.32	956.62	− 6.57
1977	6.41	0.78		1.12	1.90	844.42	− 4.85
1978	− 1.56	2.95		3.12	6.07	810.12	3.72
1979	− 6.05	− 1.80		4.35	2.55	811.77	16.98
1980	3.93	7.00	**D**	3.66	10.66	993.34	− 23.89
1981	18.45	7.90	**A**	7.80	15.70	885.94	3.04
1982	− 9.01	9.01	**Y**	7.36	16.37	1007.36	− 4.51
1983	7.01	− 0.20		1.83	1.63	1277.44	− 7.62
1984	9.83	6.40		18.78	25.18	1220.30	− 7.95
1985	0.12	18.92		− 3.56	15.36	1472.13	− 14.22
1986	6.05	4.64		− 2.53	2.11	1914.23	− 1.55
1987	40.45	− 16.58		− 36.47	− 53.05	1910.48	− 76.93
1988	11.73	14.58		− 17.60	− 3.02	2074.68	6.76
1989	7.25	17.49		18.77	36.26	2675.55	19.42
1990	− 35.15	9.16		− 12.13	− 2.97	2527.23	5.94
1991	14.08	− 16.10		− 5.36	− 21.46	2894.68	40.70
1992	25.66	17.56		15.94	33.50	3282.20	22.96
1993	3.92	13.41		− 3.63	9.78	3683.95	− 6.15
1994	− 91.52	− 3.36		33.64	30.28	3708.27	31.29
1995	40.46	18.06		7.23*	25.29	5048.84	22.04
1996	− 19.38	− 29.07		22.36*	− 6.71	6521.70	N/C
1997	41.03	− 14.17		28.35*	14.18	7823.13	189.98
1998	− 73.12	13.13		18.80*	31.93	9333.08	− 216.53
1999	− 93.89	12.54		− 19.26*	− 6.72	10988.91	− 40.99
2000	31.85	− 95.18		70.91*	− 24.27	10470.23	75.84
2001	− 75.08	− 66.70		125.03*	58.33	9959.71	23.04
2002	− 172.98	255.26		− 35.59*	219.67	8896.09	− 33.52
2003	16.15	15.63		2.89*	18.52	9899.05	116.59
2004	3.18	27.71		1.92*	29.63	10475.90	− 46.33

Shortened trading day

DECEMBER INDICATORS AND PATTERNS

December Almanac

December is the number one month on the Dow Jones Industrials and S&P 500 since 1950, averaging gains of 1.8% and 1.7% respectively. It's also the top Russell 2000 month and ranks second on NASDAQ and the Russell 1000. Rarely does the market fall precipitously in December. When it does it is usually a turning point in the market—near a top or bottom. If the market has experienced fantastic gains leading up to December, stocks are likely ripe for a fall. Conversely if the market has been through the ringer of late and December is down sharply as well, then expect a rally to ensue shortly. In 1998 December was part of best fourth quarter since 1928.

Market trading in December is holiday inspired and fueled by a buying bias throughout the month on the part of NYSE members and brokerage houses. However, the first part of the month tends to be weaker as tax-loss selling and year-end portfolio restructuring crescendos. The month is laden with market seasonality and important events. As small caps tend to start to outperform larger caps near middle of month our "Free Lunch" strategy is served on Wall Street. Our "Santa Claus Rally" is visible in the accompanying bar chart. All three are discussed in detail below. Examination of December trades by NYSE members through the years shows they tend to buy on balance during this month, contrary to other months.

The S&P 500 has been down in only three Decembers the last fifteen post-election years while the Dow was down four. Only four Decembers lost ground in the last fourteen midterm election years. 1966, 1974, and 2002 were major midterm bottoms. 2002 was the worst December since 1931, down over 6% on the Dow Industrials and S&P 500, and off 9.7% on NASDAQ. Since WWII the Dow Industrials have fallen only twice in pre-election year December: 1975 (−1.0%), 1983 (−1.4%). Election year Decembers fare well; the S&P 500 averages 1.5%, up 13.

December Triple-Witching Week is more favorable to the Dow Jones Industrial with Monday up nine of the last fifteen years while Triple-Witching Friday is up eleven of those years. The entire week has logged gains an amazing nineteen times in the last twenty-one years. The week after December Triple Witching is the best of all weeks after and is the only one with a clearly bullish bias.

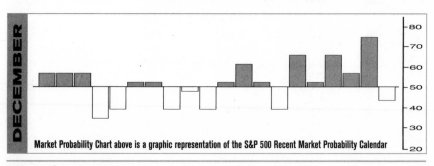

Market Probability Chart above is a graphic representation of the S&P 500 Recent Market Probability Calendar

Typical December

The first three trading days of the month have been strongest for NASDAQ and the Russell 2000. After a few years of first day selling, Dow and S&P 500 have posted solid 1% or better gains the first day of December the last two years. Trading remains guarded through the first half of the month as tax-loss selling wraps up. Once mid-month passes, stocks rise on the majority of days.

December Vital Statistics

	DJIA	S&P 500	NASDAQ	Russell 1K	Russell 2K
Rank	1	1	2	2	1
Up	40	42	21	20	21
Down	15	13	13	6	5
Avg % Change	1.8%	1.7%	2.1%	1.7%	2.8%
4-Year Presidential Election Cycle Performance					
Post-Election Year	1.0%	0.3%	0.4%	1.2%	2.2%
Mid-Term Year	1.3	1.7	0.3	0.4	0.8
Pre-Election Year	3.4	3.6	6.0	4.5	5.1
Election Year	1.5	1.2	1.4	0.6	2.6
Best & Worst December					
	% Change	% Change	% Change	% Change	% Change
Best	1991 9.5	1991 11.2	1999 22	1991 11.2	1999 11.2
Worst	2002 –6.2	2002 –6.0	2002 –9.7	2002 –5.8	2002 –5.7
Best & Worst December Weeks					
Best	12/18/87 5.8	12/18/87 5.9	12/8/00 10.3	12/18/87 6	12/18/87 7.7
Worst	12/4/87 –7.5	12/6/74 –7.1	12/15/00 –9.1	12/4/87 –7.0	12/12/80 –6.5
Best & Worst December Days					
Best	12/14/87 3.5	12/5/00 3.9	12/5/00 10.5	12/5/00 4.4	12/5/00 4.6
Worst	12/3/87 –3.9	12/3/87 –3.5	12/20/00 –7.1	12/20/00 –3.4	12/8/80 –3.6
First Trading Day of Expiration Week 1990-2004					
Record (#Up - #Down)	9-6	8-7	7-8	9-6	8-7
Current streak	U1	U1	U1	U1	U1
Avg % Change	0.3	0.2	0.2	0.2	0.1
Options Expiration Day 1990-2004					
Record (#Up - #Down)	11-4	10-5	9-6	10-5	8-7
Current streak	D1	D2	D2	D2	D2
Avg % Change	0.2	0.2	0.1	0.2	0.3
Options Expiration Week 1990-2004					
Record (#Up - #Down)	13-2	12-3	9-6	11-4	7-8
Current streak	U4	U4	U3	U4	U1
Avg % Change	0.9	0.8	–0.2	0.7	0.1
Week After Options Expiration 1990-2004					
Record (#Up - #Down)	11-4	9-6	10-5	9-6	12-3
Current streak	U2	U2	U2	U2	U2
Avg % Change	0.9	0.7	1.1	0.7	1.2
2006 Bullish Days based on data from 1984 to 2004					
	4, 18, 21, 26	18, 21, 26, 28	1, 4, 5, 21, 22, 26, 28, 29	1, 5, 18, 21, 26, 27, 28	1, 4, 5, 8, 21, 22, 26, 27, 28, 29
2006 Bearish Days based on data from 1984 to 2004					
	7	6, 7, 12, 14, 20	7, 12, 14	6, 7, 12, 14, 20	7, 15

Dow & S&P 1950-July 2005, NASDAQ 1971-July 2005, Russell 1K & 2K 1979-July 2005. Options data 1990 through August 2005. Bullish/Bearish days based on index rising or falling 60% of the time on a particular trading day 1984-2004 (see pages 66-73).

The day before Christmas has been weak the last four years making it a perfect time to get in before the "Santa Claus Rally." On the day after the Christmas holiday the Dow was up nine in a row from 1990 to 1998 but up only three of the last six. NASDAQ had a stellar record of being up the last trading day of the year twenty-nine years in a row, but it has been down the last five in a row. Less bullishness the last trading day of the year is due to last-minute portfolio restructuring.

Indicators and Patterns

Most of the So-Called "January Effect" Starts in Mid-December

The chart below illustrates quite clearly that the "January Effect" of small cap stocks outperforming big cap stocks in the month of January now starts in mid-December. Also noticeable are small stock moves in late October and late November. Any early December weakness in small stocks—such as our Almanac Investor Stock Portfolio—can be used to add to existing positions or make new ones. Note that the bulk of this move is complete by mid-January but runs through early March. Any outsized gains can be taken without prejudice—especially by implementing the standard trading policy we use for small stocks of selling half on a double to take your initial investment off the table.

In the graph below we have taken the twenty-seven years of daily data for the Russell 2000 index of smaller companies and divided it by the Russell 1000 index of largest companies. Then the twenty-seven years are compressed into a single year to show an idealized yearly pattern. When the graph is descending, big blue chips are outperforming smaller companies; when the graph is rising, smaller companies are moving up faster than their larger brethren.

RUSSELL 2000/RUSSELL 1000 ONE-YEAR SEASONAL PATTERN

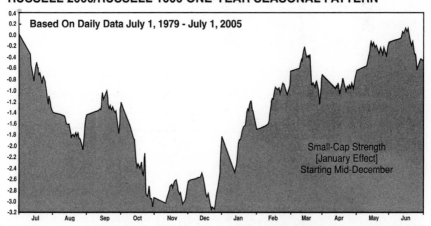

Looking at the graph above comparing the Russell 1000 index of large capitalization stocks to the Russell 2000 smaller capitalization stocks, shows small cap stocks beginning to outperform the blue chips in mid-December. Narrowing the comparison down to half-month segments reveals that most of this gain occurs in the last two weeks of December.

18-YEAR AVERAGE RATES OF RETURN (DEC 1987 – FEB 2005)

	Russell 1000		Russell 2000	
From 12/15	Change	Annualized	Change	Annualized
12/15-12/31	2.1%	69.5%	3.5%	145.1%
12/15-01/15	2.3	30.8	4.3	65.0
12/15-01/31	3.2	28.2	5.0	48.2
12/15-02/15	4.1	27.4	6.7	47.8
12/15-02/28	3.6	19.4	7.0	40.0
From 12/31				
12/31-01/15	0.2	2.4	0.7	8.6
12/31-01/31	1.1	8.9	1.4	12.1
12/31-02/15	2.0	12.8	3.1	19.8
12/31-02/28	1.5	7.8	3.3	17.4

26-YEAR AVERAGE RATES OF RETURN (DEC 1979 – FEB 2005)

	Russell 1000		Russell 2000	
From 12/15	Change	Annualized	Change	Annualized
12/15-12/31	1.7%	56.4%	2.9%	112.8%
12/15-01/15	2.4	32.8	4.6	71.6
12/15-01/31	3.3	29.7	5.4	52.3
12/15-02/15	4.1	27.2	7.0	49.8
12/15-02/28	3.8	20.6	7.2	41.6
From 12/31				
12/31-01/15	0.6	8.1	1.6	21.0
12/31-01/31	1.6	13.2	2.4	20.6
12/31-02/15	2.4	15.0	3.9	25.8
12/31-02/28	2.1	10.8	4.1	22.3

Small-cap strength in the last half of December became even more magnified after the 1987 market crash. Note the dramatic shift in gains in the last half of December during the eighteen-year period starting in 1987, versus the twenty-six years from 1979 to 2005. With all the beaten down small stocks being dumped for tax loss purposes, it generally pays to get a head start on the January Effect in mid-December. The leading small-cap sector was hit hardest in the January 2005 correction.

The Only "Free Lunch" on Wall Street

This bottom-fishing strategy we have implemented over the years feeds off the year-end small-cap strength just discussed. Our "Free Lunch" strategy is only an extremely short-term strategy reserved for the nimblest traders.

Tax-loss selling tends to push losing stocks down to bargain levels near year end. In years past we only selected NYSE stocks selling at their lows on December 15. These stocks usually outperformed the market by February 15 in the following year.

Tax selling in recent years seems to be continuing down to the last few days of the year, so we altered the strategy the last several years to make our selections from stocks making new 52-week lows on the fourth to last trading day of the year—the last settlement day of the year.

The candidates are hand-picked every year from the stocks making new 52-week lows. Preferred stocks, closed-end funds, splits and new issues are eliminated. When there are a huge number of new lows, stocks down the most are selected.

BARGAIN STOCKS VS. THE MARKET**

Short Span** Late Dec - Jan/Feb	New Lows Late Dec	% Change Jan/Feb	% Change NYSE Composite	Bargain Stocks Advantage
1974-75	112	48.9%	22.1%	26.8%
1975-76	21	34.9	14.9	20.0
1976-77	2	1.3	— 3.3	4.6
1977-78	15	2.8	— 4.5	7.3
1978-79	43	11.8	3.9	7.9
1979-80	5	9.3	6.1	3.2
1980-81	14	7.1	— 2.0	9.1
1981-82	21	— 2.6	— 7.4	4.8
1982-83	4	33.0	9.7	23.3
1983-84	13	— 3.2	— 3.8	0.6
1984-85	32	19.0	12.1	6.9
1985-86	4	— 22.5	3.9	— 26.4
1986-87	22	9.3	12.5	— 3.2
1987-88	23	13.2	6.8	6.4
1988-89	14	30.0	6.4	23.6
1989-90	25	— 3.1	— 4.8	1.7
1990-91	18	18.8	12.6	6.2
1991-92	23	51.1	7.7	43.4
1992-93	9	8.7	0.6	8.1
1993-94	10	— 1.4	2.0	— 3.4
1994-95	25	14.6	5.7	8.9
1995-96	5	— 11.3	4.5	—15.8
1996-97	16	13.9	11.2	2.7
1997-98	29	9.9	5.7	4.2
1998-99	40	— 2.8	4.3	— 7.1
1999-00	26*	8.9	— 5.4	14.3
2000-01	51[1]	44.4	0.1	44.3
2001-02	12[2]	31.4	— 2.3	33.7
2002-03	33[3]	28.7	3.9	24.8
2003-04	15[4]	16.7	2.3	14.4
2004-05	36[5]	6.8	— 2.8	9.6
31-Year Totals**		**427.8%**	**122.7%**	**304.9%**
Average**		**13.8%**	**4.0%**	**9.8%**

*** Dec 15 - Feb 15 (1974-1999)* * *Chosen 12/29/99* [1] *Chosen 12/27/00* [2] *12/26/01-1/16/02, incl NAS stocks*
[3] *12/26/02-1/14/03, incl NAS & AMEX stocks* [4] *12/26/03-1/13/04, incl NAS, AMEX & OTCBB stocks*
[5] *12/28/04-1/11/05, incl NAS, AMEX & OTCBB stocks*

The strategy was refined further when few NYSE stocks were left after our screens. Recently we have added selections from NASDAQ, AMEX, and the OTC Bulletin Board. These stocks tend to start giving back their gains in January. We have advised subscribers to sell in mid-January or when quick gains materialize.

The object is to buy bargain stocks near their 52-week lows and sell any quick, generous gains, as the stocks can often be real dogs. It's a quick trade so do not get attached to these stocks. When they pop, sell them. We're just trying to capitalize on any "dead cat bounce." If any of these stocks double, we sell at least half, or use trailing stops so if they continue to rise we stay in, if not, we're out. This Free Lunch strategy has performed better after market corrections and when there are more new lows at year end.

2004 Eat and Run — Free Lunch Gains Gobbled Up Quickly

Gains came fast with our 2004 Free Lunch Year-End Bargain Stocks. Profit taking pushed small stocks and the market down after the powerful post-election rally. Big winners came mostly from the Bulletin Board selections. NASDAQ and Amex bargain stocks firmed up the most in the New Year. The lone NYSE bargain was a dud from the start. Nevertheless, the whole basket outperformed the market by a wide margin. We prefer to have a larger number of stocks from the Big Board.

As gains have come so quickly in recent years we have been revisiting bargain stocks at mid-month and are considering serving two Free Lunches, one a at mid-month and one at year end. Almanac Investor Platform and Newsletter subscribers will receive notice of December Free Lunch Bargain Stocks via email. A free 60-day trial is offered to readers of this book.

2004 Free Lunch Menu of Year-End Bargain Stocks
36 Late-December NYSE, NASDAQ, AMEX, & OTCBB New Lows

NYSE Bargain Stock		52 Week Low	52 Week High	% Down From High	12/28/04 Close	12/29/04 Close	1-Day % Change	1/3/05 Close	4-Day % Change	1/11/05 Close	10-Day % Change
MDZ	MDS Inc	13.80	17.35	−20.5%	14.10	14.06	−0.3%	13.84	−1.8%	12.94	−8.2%
NASDAQ Bargain Stocks											
CNBKA	Century BanCorp	28.15	37.52	−25.0%	28.15	29.00	3.0%	29.77	5.8%	29.60	5.2%
DROOY	DRDGOLD Ltd	1.45	4.10	−64.6%	1.49	1.49	0.0%	1.45	−2.7%	1.45	−2.7%
MWRK	Mothers Work	11.75	28.07	−58.1%	13.10	13.65	4.2%	13.52	3.2%	14.02	7.0%
CVST	Covista Communications	1.52	4.25	−64.2%	1.55	1.73	11.6%	1.78	14.8%	1.91	23.2%
EWST	Energy West	5.41	8.50	−36.4%	5.90	6.48	9.8%	6.67	13.1%	6.84	15.9%
	Average Change NASDAQ Bargain Stocks						5.7%		6.8%		9.7%
AMEX Bargain Stock											
CTE	Cardiotech Int'l	2.40	7.20	−66.7%	2.49	2.66	6.8%	2.88	15.7%	2.48	−0.4%
IHT	Innsuites Hospitality Trust	1.12	2.25	−50.2%	1.12	1.44	28.6%	1.53	36.6%	1.39	24.1%
	Average Change AMEX Bargain Stocks						17.7%		26.1%		11.9%
OTCBB Bargain Stocks											
ADNWE	Auto Data Network	1.54	3.56	−56.7%	1.99	2.08	4.5%	2.12	6.5%	2.04	2.5%
CAAUF	Calais Resources	0.30	2.00	−85.0%	0.31	0.34	9.7%	0.51	64.5%	0.32	3.2%
CIGI	Coach Industries	1.03	2.15	−52.1%	1.07	1.14	6.5%	1.20	12.1%	1.12	4.7%
CROO	Cirond Corp	0.51	1.60	−68.1%	0.51	0.53	3.9%	0.47	−7.8%	0.38	−25.5%
CRWS	Crown Crafts	0.43	0.90	−52.2%	0.43	0.60	39.5%	0.56	30.2%	0.62	44.2%
CSUA	Consumer Direct Amer	0.20	7.80	−97.4%	0.25	0.36	44.0%	0.60	140.0%	0.36	44.0%
DNKY	Donnkenny Inc	0.25	2.75	−90.9%	0.36	0.44	22.2%	0.50	38.9%	0.17	−52.8%
ETIFF	Eiger Tech	0.18	1.05	−82.9%	0.18	0.21	16.7%	0.28	55.6%	0.22	22.8%
EXNT	Enxnet	0.21	0.99	−78.8%	0.22	0.30	36.4%	0.29	31.8%	0.25	13.6%
FDVI	Fortune Diversified	0.65	1.60	−59.4%	0.70	0.74	5.7%	0.72	2.9%	0.50	−28.6%
FNGC	Falcon Natural Gas	0.79	2.02	−60.9%	0.79	0.80	1.3%	1.00	26.6%	0.88	11.4%
FOTO	Photoworks	0.25	0.73	−65.8%	0.29	0.28	−3.4%	0.31	6.9%	0.24	−17.2%
GPXM	Golden Phoenix Minrl	0.16	0.50	−68.0%	0.16	0.18	12.5%	0.20	25.0%	0.19	19.4%
IDIB	IDI Global	0.45	2.25	−80.0%	0.48	0.52	8.3%	0.50	4.2%	0.43	−10.6%
ISSG	Int'l Smart Sourcing	0.45	1.15	−60.9%	0.45	0.65	44.4%	0.75	66.7%	0.67	48.9%
KOLR	Kolorfusion Int'l	0.24	0.80	−70.0%	0.30	0.35	16.7%	0.45	50.0%	0.22	−26.7%
MDTI	MDI Techs	1.70	2.75	−38.2%	1.90	1.98	4.2%	2.00	5.3%	1.92	1.1%
MXUS	Maxus Tech	0.25	1.65	−84.8%	0.32	0.70	118.8%	0.45	40.6%	0.34	6.3%
NJMC	New Jersey Mining	0.49	0.80	−38.8%	0.48	0.50	4.2%	0.57	18.8%	0.54	12.5%
PNAMF	Pan American Gold	0.36	1.13	−68.1%	0.37	0.43	16.2%	0.42	13.5%	0.36	−2.7%
PSED	Poseidis Inc	0.14	2.36	−94.1%	0.16	0.20	25.0%	0.20	25.0%	0.16	0.0%
PSUY	Platinum Superyachts	0.07	1.50	−95.3%	0.09	0.14	64.7%	0.20	135.3%	0.14	64.7%
TELA	Techlabs	0.75	4.20	−82.1%	0.75	1.74	132.0%	1.45	93.3%	1.05	40.0%
TMAS	TIMCO Aviation	0.17	0.90	−81.1%	0.17	0.16	−5.9%	0.29	70.6%	0.22	29.4%
TMEG	Trimedia Entertainment	0.45	2.84	−84.2%	0.53	0.47	−11.3%	0.50	−5.7%	0.38	−28.3%
TUMIF	Tumi Resources	0.66	1.75	−62.3%	0.75	0.74	−1.3%	0.75	0.0%	0.67	−10.5%
UMSY	US Medsys Corp	1.75	7.20	−75.7%	1.69	1.95	15.4%	2.00	18.3%	1.73	2.4%
ZIMCF	Zim Corp	0.25	1.01	−75.2%	0.25	0.33	32.0%	0.33	32.0%	0.28	12.0%
	Average Change OTCBB Bargain Stocks						23.7%		35.8%		6.4%
	Average Change Of Bargain Stocks						20.2%		30.2%		6.8%
	Bargain Stocks Advantage						20.2%		31.1%		9.6%
	NYSE Bargains Advantage Over NYSE Composite						−0.2%		−0.9%		−5.4%
	Bargain Stocks Advantage						20.2%		31.3%		11.3%
	NASDAQ Bargains Advantage Over NASDAQ Composite						5.7%		8.0%		14.2%
	Bargain Stocks Advantage						20.2%		31.3%		9.1%
	AMEX Bargains Advantage Over AMEX Composite						17.7%		27.3%		14.2%

Santa Claus Rally

Beginning just before or right after the market's Christmas closing, we normally experience a brief, yet respectable, rally from the last five trading days of the year through the first two of the New Year. The S&P 500 has averaged a 1.6% gain during this seven-day span since 1969. We refer to this as the "Santa Claus Rally."

It is important to remember, though, that when this reliable seasonality has failed to materialize, it has often been a harbinger of bear markets or sizeable corrections in the coming year. But these were times stocks could have been purchased later in the year at much lower prices. Such occasions provide opportunities. Yale Hirsch discovered this phenomenon in 1972. We have alerted investors to this ominous portent for decades with the mnemonic device, "If Santa Claus should fail to call; bears may come to Broad & Wall."

This rhyme was certainly on the mark in 2000, as the period suffered a horrendous 4.0% loss. On January 14, 2000, the Dow started its 33-month 37.8% slide to the October 2002 midterm election year bottom. NASDAQ cracked eight weeks later falling 37.3% in ten weeks, eventually dropping 77.9% by October 2002. This was reminiscent of the Dow during the Great Depression, when the Dow initially fell 47.9% in just over two months from 381.17 September 3, 1929, only to end down 89.2% at its twentieth century low of 41.22 on July 8, 1932. Perhaps October 9, 2002, will prove to be the low for the twenty-first century.

Saddam Hussein's invasion of Kuwait cancelled 1990s Santa Claus Rally. Three days later, on January 9, 1991, the S&P 500 had dropped 3% one week before the onslaught of Gulf War I. This created a triple bottom at levels that will likely never be seen again.

Energy prices and Middle East terror woes may have grounded Santa in 2004. Corrections and gyrations ensued in early 2005, keeping the averages mixed with single-digit gains at best at press time. Previous absent Santa Claus Rallies in 1979 and 1981 preceded bear market lows in the following years of 1980 and 1982 respectively.

Less bullishness on last day is due to last-minute portfolio restructuring. Pushing gains and losses into the next tax year often affects year's first trading day. This indicator is most effective when confirmed by a down "First Five Days" and a down "January Barometer." Both are discussed in the January section.

DAILY % CHANGE IN S&P 500 AT YEAR END

	Trading Days Before Year End						First Days in January			Rally % Change
	6	5	4	3	2	1	1	2	3	
1969	— 0.4	1.1	0.8	— 0.7	0.4	0.5	1.0	0.5	— 0.7	3.6
1970	0.1	0.6	0.5	1.1	0.2	— 0.1	— 1.1	0.7	0.6	1.9
1971	— 0.4	0.2	1.0	0.3	— 0.4	0.3	— 0.4	0.4	1.0	1.3
1972	— 0.3	— 0.7	0.6	0.4	0.5	1.0	0.9	0.4	— 0.1	3.1
1973	— 1.1	— 0.7	3.1	2.1	— 0.2	0.01	0.1	2.2	— 0.9	6.7
1974	— 1.4	1.4	0.8	— 0.4	0.03	2.1	2.4	0.7	0.5	7.2
1975	0.7	0.8	0.9	— 0.1	— 0.4	0.5	0.8	1.8	1.0	4.3
1976	0.1	1.2	0.7	— 0.4	0.5	0.5	— 0.4	— 1.2	— 0.9	0.8
1977	0.8	0.9	N/C	0.1	0.2	0.2	— 1.3	— 0.3	— 0.8	— 0.3
1978	0.03	1.7	1.3	— 0.9	— 0.4	— 0.2	0.6	1.1	0.8	3.3
1979	— 0.6	0.1	0.1	0.2	— 0.1	0.1	— 2.0	— 0.5	1.2	— 2.2
1980	— 0.4	0.4	0.5	— 1.1	0.2	0.3	0.4	1.2	0.1	2.0
1981	— 0.5	0.2	— 0.2	— 0.5	0.5	0.2	0.2	— 2.2	— 0.7	— 1.8
1982	0.6	1.8	— 1.0	0.3	— 0.7	0.2	— 1.6	2.2	0.4	1.2
1983	— 0.2	— 0.03	0.9	0.3	— 0.2	0.05	— 0.5	1.7	1.2	2.1
1984	— 0.5	0.8	— 0.2	— 0.4	0.3	0.6	— 1.1	— 0.5	— 0.5	— 0.6
1985	— 1.1	— 0.7	0.2	0.9	0.5	0.3	— 0.8	0.6	— 0.1	1.1
1986	— 1.0	0.2	0.1	— 0.9	— 0.5	— 0.5	1.8	2.3	0.2	2.4
1987	1.3	— 0.5	— 2.6	— 0.4	1.3	— 0.3	3.6	1.1	0.1	2.2
1988	— 0.2	0.3	— 0.4	0.1	0.8	— 0.6	— 0.9	1.5	0.2	0.9
1989	0.6	0.8	— 0.2	0.6	0.5	0.8	1.8	— 0.3	— 0.9	4.1
1990	0.5	— 0.6	0.3	— 0.8	0.1	0.5	— 1.1	— 1.4	— 0.3	— 3.0
1991	2.5	0.6	1.4	0.4	2.1	0.5	0.04	0.5	— 0.3	5.7
1992	— 0.3	0.2	— 0.1	— 0.3	0.2	— 0.7	— 0.1	— 0.2	0.04	— 1.1
1993	0.01	0.7	0.1	— 0.1	— 0.4	— 0.5	— 0.2	0.3	0.1	— 0.1
1994	0.01	0.2	0.4	— 0.3	0.1	— 0.4	— 0.03	0.3	— 0.1	0.2
1995	0.8	0.2	0.4	0.04	— 0.1	0.3	0.8	0.1	— 0.6	1.8
1996	— 0.3	0.5	0.6	0.1	— 0.4	— 1.7	— 0.5	1.5	— 0.1	0.1
1997	— 1.5	— 0.7	0.4	1.8	1.8	— 0.04	0.5	0.2	— 1.1	4.0
1998	2.1	— 0.2	— 0.1	1.3	— 0.8	— 0.2	— 0.1	1.4	2.2	1.3
1999	1.6	— 0.1	0.04	0.4	0.1	0.3	— 1.0	— 3.8	0.2	— 4.0
2000	0.8	2.4	0.7	1.0	0.4	— 1.0	— 2.8	5.0	— 1.1	5.7
2001	0.4	— 0.02	0.4	0.7	0.3	— 1.1	0.6	0.9	0.6	1.8
2002	0.2	— 0.5	— 0.3	— 1.6	0.5	0.05	3.3	— 0.05	2.2	1.2
2003	0.3	— 0.2	0.2	1.2	0.01	0.2	— 0.3	1.2	0.1	2.4
2004	0.1	— 0.4	0.7	— 0.01	0.01	— 0.1	— 0.8	— 1.2	— 0.4	—1.8
Avg	0.09	0.33	0.34	0.12	0.19	0.06	0.05	0.50	0.09	1.6

HALF-HOURLY TRADING PATTERNS

Half-hourly data became available for the Dow Jones Industrial Average starting in January 1987. Examination of half-hourly performance from 1987 through July 1, 2005 shows early morning and mid-afternoon weakness with end of day strength.

It is usually the weak hands, or individuals, that try to sell first thing in the morning after having reevaluated their positions overnight or over the weekend. Brokerage houses oblige buying their clients shares on the cheap pushing prices higher before lunch.

Traders eat too and you can see prices flatten out as Wall Street participants take a moment to sustain themselves from noon to 2:00. Around this time the pros get positioned for the big move at the end of the day and stocks tend to fall from two to three. The end of the day is when institutions and professional traders firm up positions driving prices higher the last hour on most days.

MARKET % PERFORMANCE EACH HALF-HOUR OF THE DAY
(JANUARY 1987 – JULY 1, 2005)

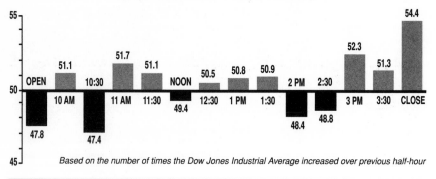

Based on the number of times the Dow Jones Industrial Average increased over previous half-hour

We have separated half-hourly trading since January 1987 by day of the week to illustrate how the typical week behaves. After an opening selloff on Monday the market snaps back in the second half hour and then is quite flat until three o'clock. Monday closes are the strongest followed closely by Friday's close.

Mid-week mornings are generally down with Thursday the worst. Friday tends open strong drift flat to down until the last hour of the day. On all days stocks do tend to firm up near the close with weakness early morning and from 2:00 to 2:30 frequently. Weakness near the close, especially on Friday and Monday can be indicative of a precarious market ripe for a fall.

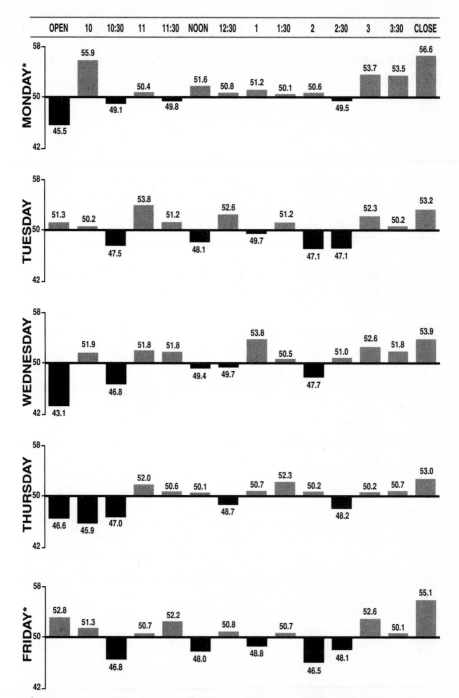

| | OPEN | 10 | 10:30 | 11 | 11:30 | NOON | 12:30 | 1 | 1:30 | 2 | 2:30 | 3 | 3:30 | CLOSE |

MONDAY*
- OPEN: 45.5
- 10: 55.9
- 10:30: 49.1
- 11: 50.4
- 11:30: 49.8
- NOON: 51.6
- 12:30: 50.8
- 1: 51.2
- 1:30: 50.1
- 2: 50.6
- 2:30: 49.5
- 3: 53.7
- 3:30: 53.5
- CLOSE: 56.6

TUESDAY
- OPEN: 51.3
- 10: 50.2
- 10:30: 47.5
- 11: 53.8
- 11:30: 51.2
- NOON: 48.1
- 12:30: 52.6
- 1: 49.7
- 1:30: 51.2
- 2: 47.1
- 2:30: 47.1
- 3: 52.3
- 3:30: 50.2
- CLOSE: 53.2

WEDNESDAY
- OPEN: 43.1
- 10: 51.9
- 10:30: 46.8
- 11: 51.8
- 11:30: 51.8
- NOON: 49.4
- 12:30: 49.7
- 1: 53.8
- 1:30: 50.5
- 2: 47.7
- 2:30: 51.0
- 3: 52.6
- 3:30: 51.8
- CLOSE: 53.9

THURSDAY
- OPEN: 46.6
- 10: 45.9
- 10:30: 47.0
- 11: 52.0
- 11:30: 50.6
- NOON: 50.1
- 12:30: 48.7
- 1: 50.7
- 1:30: 52.3
- 2: 50.2
- 2:30: 48.2
- 3: 50.2
- 3:30: 50.7
- CLOSE: 53.0

FRIDAY*
- OPEN: 52.8
- 10: 51.3
- 10:30: 46.8
- 11: 50.7
- 11:30: 52.2
- NOON: 48.0
- 12:30: 50.8
- 1: 48.8
- 1:30: 50.7
- 2: 46.5
- 2:30: 48.1
- 3: 52.6
- 3:30: 50.1
- CLOSE: 55.1

*Research indicates that where Tuesday is the first trading day of the week, it follows the Monday pattern. Therefore, all such Tuesdays were combined with the Mondays here. Thursdays that are the final trading day of a given week behave like Fridays, and were similarly grouped with Fridays.

WEEKLY TRADING PATTERNS

Dow Gains Most First Two Days of the Week

Since 1989, Monday* and Tuesday have been the most consistently bullish days of the week for the Dow, Thursday and Friday** the most bearish, as traders have become reluctant to stay long going into the weekend. Since 1989 Mondays and Tuesdays gained 8696.37 Dow points, while Thursday and Friday combined for a total loss of 1845.36 points. In past flat and bear market years Friday was the worst day of the week and Monday second worst. In bull years Monday is best and Friday number two.

ANNUAL DOW POINT CHANGES FOR DAYS OF THE WEEK SINCE 1953

Year	Monday*	Tuesday	Wednesday	Thursday	Friday**	Year's DJIA Closing	Year's Point Change
1953	− 36.16	− 7.93	19.63	5.76	7.70	280.90	11.00
1954	15.68	3.27	24.31	33.96	46.27	404.39	123.49
1955	− 48.36	26.38	46.03	− 0.66	60.62	488.40	84.01
1956	− 27.15	− 19.36	− 15.41	8.43	64.56	499.47	11.07
1957	− 109.50	− 7.71	64.12	3.32	− 14.01	435.69	− 63.78
1958	17.50	23.59	29.10	22.67	55.10	583.65	147.96
1959	− 44.48	29.04	4.11	13.60	93.44	679.36	95.71
1960	− 111.04	− 3.75	− 5.62	6.74	50.20	615.89	− 63.47
1961	− 23.65	10.18	87.51	− 5.96	47.17	731.14	115.25
1962	− 101.60	26.19	9.97	− 7.70	− 5.90	652.10	− 79.04
1963	− 8.88	47.12	16.23	22.39	33.99	762.95	110.85
1964	− 0.29	− 17.94	39.84	5.52	84.05	874.13	111.18
1965	− 73.23	39.65	57.03	3.20	68.48	969.26	95.13
1966	− 153.24	− 27.73	56.13	− 46.19	− 12.54	785.69	− 183.57
1967	− 68.65	31.50	25.42	92.25	38.90	905.11	119.42
1968†	− 6.41	34.94	25.16	− 72.06	44.19	943.75	38.64
1969	− 164.17	− 36.70	18.33	23.79	15.36	800.36	− 143.39
1970	− 100.05	− 46.09	116.07	− 3.48	72.11	838.92	38.56
1971	− 2.99	9.56	13.66	8.04	23.01	890.20	51.28
1972	− 87.40	− 1.23	65.24	8.46	144.75	1020.02	129.82
1973	− 174.11	10.52	− 5.94	36.67	− 36.30	850.86	− 169.16
1974	− 149.37	47.51	− 20.31	− 13.70	− 98.75	616.24	− 234.62
1975	39.46	− 109.62	56.93	124.00	125.40	852.41	236.17
1976	70.72	71.76	50.88	− 33.70	− 7.42	1004.65	152.24
1977	− 65.15	− 44.89	− 79.61	− 5.62	21.79	831.17	− 173.48
1978	− 31.29	− 70.84	71.33	64.67	69.31	805.01	− 26.16
1979	− 32.52	9.52	− 18.84	75.18	0.39	838.74	33.73
1980	86.51	135.13	137.67	− 122.00	60.96	963.99	125.25
1981	− 45.68	− 49.51	− 13.95	− 14.67	34.82	875.00	− 88.99
1982	5.71	86.20	28.37	− 1.47	52.73	1046.54	171.54
1983	30.51	30.92	149.68	61.16	1.67	1258.64	212.10
1984	− 73.80	78.02	− 139.24	92.79	− 4.84	1211.57	− 47.07
1985	80.36	52.70	51.26	46.32	104.46	1546.67	335.10
1986	− 39.94	97.63	178.65	29.31	83.63	1895.95	349.28
1987	− 559.15	235.83	392.03	139.73	− 165.56	1938.83	42.88
1988	268.12	166.44	− 60.48	− 230.84	86.50	2168.57	229.74
1989	− 53.31	143.33	233.25	90.25	171.11	2753.20	584.63
SubTotal	− 1937.20	941.79	1708.54	330.82	1417.35		2461.30
1990	219.90	− 25.22	47.96	− 352.55	− 9.63	2633.66	− 119.54
1991	191.13	47.97	174.53	254.79	− 133.25	3168.83	535.17
1992	237.80	− 49.67	3.12	108.74	− 167.71	3301.11	132.28
1993	322.82	− 37.03	243.87	4.97	− 81.65	3754.09	452.98
1994	206.41	− 95.33	29.98	− 168.87	108.16	3834.44	80.35
1995	262.97	210.06	357.02	140.07	312.56	5117.12	1282.68
1996	626.41	155.55	− 34.24	268.52	314.91	6448.27	1331.15
1997	1136.04	1989.17	− 590.17	− 949.80	− 125.26	7908.25	1459.98
1998	649.10	679.95	591.63	− 1579.43	931.93	9181.43	1273.18
1999	980.49	− 1587.23	826.68	735.94	1359.81	11497.12	2315.69
2000	2265.45	306.47	− 1978.34	238.21	− 1542.06	10786.85	− 710.27
2001	− 389.33	336.86	− 396.53	976.41	− 1292.76	10021.50	− 765.35
2002	− 1404.94	− 823.76	1443.69	− 428.12	− 466.74	8341.63	− 1679.87
2003	978.87	482.11	− 425.46	566.22	510.55	10453.92	2112.29
2004 ‡	201.12	523.28	358.76	− 409.72	− 344.35	10783.01	329.09
2005 ‡	77.37	21.58	46.73	− 344.84	− 280.41	10303.44	− 479.57
SubTotal	6561.61	2134.76	699.23	− 939.46	− 905.90		7550.24
Totals	4624.41	3076.55	2407.77	− 608.64	511.45		10011.54

* On Monday holidays, following Tuesday included in Monday figures
** On Friday holidays, preceding Thursday included in Friday figures
† Most Wednesdays closed last 7 months of 1968 ‡ Partial year through July 1, 2005

Monday Now Most Profitable
S&P 500 Day of the Week

Between 1952 and 1989 Monday was the worst trading day of the week. The first trading day of the week (including Tuesday, when Monday is a holiday) rose only 44.3% of the time, while the other trading days closed higher 54.8% of the time. (NYSE Saturday trading discontinued June 1952.)

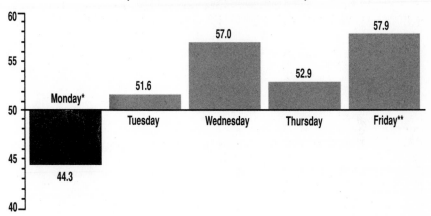

MARKET % PERFORMANCE EACH DAY OF THE WEEK
(JUNE 1952 – DECEMBER 1989)

A dramatic reversal occurred in 1990 — Monday became the most powerful day of the week. However, during the bear market years of 2001 and 2002 combined Monday once again was the worst day of the week and Friday became a day to avoid, as traders were not inclined to stay long over the weekend during uncertain market times.

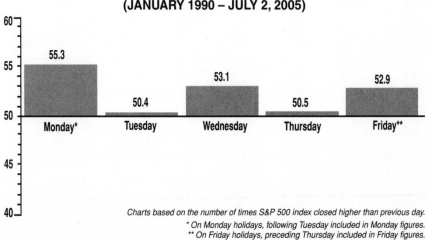

MARKET % PERFORMANCE EACH DAY OF THE WEEK
(JANUARY 1990 – JULY 2, 2005)

Charts based on the number of times S&P 500 index closed higher than previous day.
* On Monday holidays, following Tuesday included in Monday figures.
** On Friday holidays, preceding Thursday included in Friday figures.

Indicators and Patterns

S&P 500 Daily Performance Each Year Since 1952

To determine if market trend alters performance of different days of the week, we separated twenty bear years of 1953, '56, '57, '60, '62, '66, '69, '70, '73, '74, '77, '78, '81, '84, '87, '90, '94, 2000, 2001, and 2002 from 34 bull market years. While Tuesday and Thursday did not vary much between bull and bear years, Mondays and Fridays were sharply affected. There was a swing of 10.3 percentage points in Monday's and 10.9 in Friday's performance. Mondays have been much stronger since 1990.

PERCENTAGE OF TIMES MARKET CLOSED HIGHER THAN PREVIOUS DAY (1953 – JULY 1, 2005)

	Monday*	Tuesday	Wednesday	Thursday	Friday**
1952	48.4%	55.6%	58.1%	51.9%	66.7%
1953	32.7	50.0	54.9	57.5	56.6
1954	50.0	57.5	63.5	59.2	73.1
1955	50.0	45.7	63.5	60.0	78.9
1956	36.5	39.6	46.9	50.0	59.6
1957	25.0	54.0	66.7	48.9	44.2
1958	59.6	52.0	59.6	68.1	72.6
1959	42.3	53.1	55.8	48.9	69.8
1960	34.6	50.0	44.2	54.0	59.6
1961	52.9	54.4	64.7	56.0	67.3
1962	28.3	52.1	54.0	51.0	50.0
1963	46.2	63.3	51.0	57.5	69.2
1964	40.4	48.0	61.5	58.7	77.4
1965	44.2	57.5	55.8	51.0	71.2
1966	36.5	47.8	53.9	42.0	57.7
1967	38.5	50.0	60.8	64.0	69.2
1968†	49.1	57.5	64.3	42.6	54.9
1969	30.8	45.8	50.0	67.4	50.0
1970	38.5	46.0	63.5	48.9	52.8
1971	44.2	64.6	57.7	55.1	51.9
1972	38.5	60.9	57.7	51.0	67.3
1973	32.1	51.1	52.9	44.9	44.2
1974	32.7	57.1	51.0	36.7	30.8
1975	53.9	38.8	61.5	56.3	55.8
1976	55.8	55.3	55.8	40.8	58.5
1977	40.4	40.4	46.2	53.1	53.9
1978	51.9	43.5	59.6	54.0	48.1
1979	54.7	53.2	58.8	66.0	44.2
1980	55.8	54.2	71.7	35.4	59.6
1981	44.2	38.8	55.8	53.2	47.2
1982	46.2	39.6	44.2	44.9	50.0
1983	55.8	46.8	61.5	52.0	55.8
1984	39.6	63.8	31.4	46.0	44.2
1985	44.2	61.2	54.9	56.3	53.9
1986	51.9	44.9	67.3	58.3	55.8
1987	51.9	57.1	63.5	61.7	49.1
1988	51.9	61.7	51.9	48.0	59.6
1989	51.9	47.8	69.2	58.0	69.2
1990	67.9	53.2	52.9	40.0	51.9
1991	44.2	46.9	52.9	49.0	51.9
1992	51.9	49.0	53.9	56.3	45.3
1993	65.4	41.7	55.8	44.9	48.1
1994	55.8	46.8	52.9	48.0	59.6
1995	63.5	56.5	63.5	62.0	63.5
1996	54.7	44.9	51.0	57.1	63.5
1997	67.3	67.4	42.3	41.7	57.7
1998	57.7	62.5	57.7	38.3	60.4
1999	46.2	29.8	67.3	53.1	57.7
2000	51.9	43.5	40.4	56.0	46.2
2001	45.3	51.1	44.0	59.2	43.1
2002	40.4	37.5	56.9	38.8	48.1
2003	59.6	62.5	42.3	58.3	50.0
2004	51.9	61.7	59.6	52.1	52.8
2005 ‡	65.4	52.2	57.7	56.0	38.5
Average	**47.2%**	**51.2%**	**55.8%**	**52.2%**	**56.6%**
34 Bull Years	**51.2%**	**52.9%**	**58.1%**	**53.1%**	**60.7%**
20 Bear Years	**40.9%**	**48.5%**	**52.1%**	**50.6%**	**49.8%**

Based on S&P 500

† Most Wednesdays closed last 7 months of 1968. ‡ Six months only, not included in averages.
* On Monday holidays, following Tuesday included in Monday figures.
** On Friday holidays, preceding Thursday included in Friday figures.

NASDAQ Strongest
Last Three Days of the Week

Despite 20 years less data, daily trading patterns on NASDAQ through 1989 appear to be fairly similar to the S&P 500 except for more bullishness on Thursdays. During the mostly flat markets of the 1970s and early 1980s, it would appear that apprehensive investors decided to throw in the towel over weekends and sell on Mondays and Tuesdays.

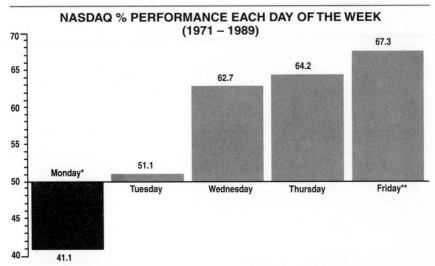

NASDAQ % PERFORMANCE EACH DAY OF THE WEEK (1971 – 1989)

Notice the vast difference in the daily trading pattern between NASDAQ and S&P from January 1, 1990 to recent times. The reason for so much more bullishness is that NASDAQ moved up 1010%, over three times as much during the 1990-2000 period. The gain for the S&P was 332% and for the Dow Jones Industrials, 326%. NASDAQ's weekly patterns are beginning to move in step with the rest of the market. Monday's weakness during the 2000 to 2002 bear market is evident below.

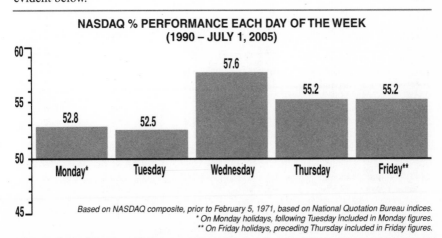

NASDAQ % PERFORMANCE EACH DAY OF THE WEEK (1990 – JULY 1, 2005)

Based on NASDAQ composite, prior to February 5, 1971, based on National Quotation Bureau indices.
* On Monday holidays, following Tuesday included in Monday figures.
** On Friday holidays, preceding Thursday included in Friday figures.

NASDAQ Daily Performance Each Year Since 1971

After dropping a hefty 77.9% from its 2000 high (versus –37.8% on the Dow and –49.1% on the S&P 500), NASDAQ tech stocks still outpace the blue chips and big caps — but not by nearly as much as they did. From January 1, 1971, through June 30, 2005, NASDAQ moved up an impressive 2196%. The Dow (up 1125%) and the S&P (up 1193%) gained just over half as much. Monday's performance on NASDAQ was lackluster during the three-year bear market of 2000 to 2002. As NASDAQ rebounded sharply in 2003, up 50% for the year, strength returned to Monday as well as on Tuesday and Thursday. Wednesday and Friday were weak in 2003 with Friday losing the most ground though Wednesday was down more frequently. Tuesday was best in 2004 with Thursday and Friday net losers. So far in 2005 only Monday has netted a gain.

PERCENTAGE OF TIMES NASDAQ CLOSED HIGHER THAN PREVIOUS DAY
(1971 – JULY 1, 2005)

	Monday*	Tuesday	Wednesday	Thursday	Friday**
1971	51.9%	52.1%	59.6%	65.3%	71.2%
1972	30.8	60.9	63.5	57.1	78.9
1973	34.0	48.9	52.9	53.1	48.1
1974	30.8	44.9	52.9	51.0	42.3
1975	44.2	42.9	63.5	64.6	63.5
1976	50.0	63.8	67.3	59.2	58.5
1977	51.9	40.4	53.9	63.3	73.1
1978	48.1	47.8	73.1	72.0	84.6
1979	45.3	53.2	64.7	86.0	82.7
1980	46.2	64.6	84.9	52.1	73.1
1981	42.3	32.7	67.3	76.6	69.8
1982	34.6	47.9	59.6	51.0	63.5
1983	42.3	44.7	67.3	68.0	73.1
1984	22.6	53.2	35.3	52.0	51.9
1985	36.5	59.2	62.8	68.8	66.0
1986	38.5	55.1	65.4	72.9	75.0
1987	42.3	49.0	65.4	68.1	66.0
1988	50.0	55.3	61.5	66.0	63.5
1989	38.5	54.4	71.2	72.0	75.0
1990	54.7	42.6	60.8	46.0	55.8
1991	51.9	59.2	66.7	65.3	51.9
1992	44.2	53.1	59.6	60.4	45.3
1993	55.8	56.3	69.2	57.1	67.3
1994	51.9	46.8	54.9	52.0	55.8
1995	50.0	52.2	63.5	64.0	63.5
1996	50.9	57.1	64.7	61.2	63.5
1997	65.4	59.2	53.9	52.1	55.8
1998	59.6	58.3	65.4	44.7	58.5
1999	61.5	40.4	63.5	57.1	65.4
2000	40.4	41.3	42.3	60.0	57.7
2001	41.5	57.8	52.0	55.1	47.1
2002	44.2	37.5	56.9	46.9	46.2
2003	57.7	60.4	40.4	60.4	46.2
2004	57.7	59.6	53.9	50.0	50.9
2005†	61.5	60.9	50.0	44.0	50.0
Average	**46.1%**	**51.5%**	**60.6%**	**60.3%**	**62.1%**
24 Bull Years	**48.5%**	**54.1%**	**63.3%**	**62.1%**	**65.4%**
10 Bear Years	**40.5%**	**45.5%**	**54.1%**	**56.1%**	**54.1%**

Based on NASDAQ composite; prior to February 5, 1971 based on National Quotation Bureau indices.
† Six months only, not included in averages.
* On Monday holidays, following Tuesday included in Monday figures.
** On Friday holidays, preceding Thursday included in Friday figures.

MONTHLY TRADING PATTERNS

Typical S&P 500 Month

For many years, the last trading day of the month, plus the first four of the following month, were the best market days of the month. This pattern is quite clear in the first chart showing these five consecutive trading days towering above the other 16 trading days of the average month in the 1953 to 1981 period. The rationale was that individuals and institutions tended to operate similarly, causing a massive flow of cash into stocks near beginnings of months.

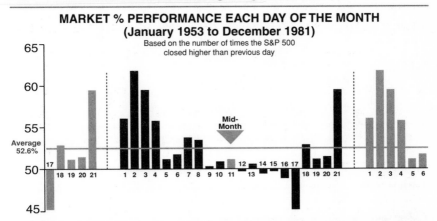

MARKET % PERFORMANCE EACH DAY OF THE MONTH
(January 1953 to December 1981)

Based on the number of times the S&P 500 closed higher than previous day

Clearly "front-running" traders took advantage of this phenomenon, drastically altering the previous pattern. The second chart from 1982 onward shows the trading shift caused by these "anticipators" to the last three trading days of the month plus the first two. Another astonishing development shows the ninth, tenth, and eleventh trading days rising strongly as well. Perhaps the enormous growth of 401(k) retirement plans (participants' salaries are usually paid twice monthly) is responsible for this new mid-month bulge.

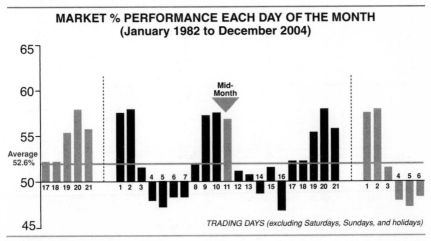

MARKET % PERFORMANCE EACH DAY OF THE MONTH
(January 1982 to December 2004)

TRADING DAYS (excluding Saturdays, Sundays, and holidays)

Typical NASDAQ Month

NASDAQ stocks moved up 58.1% of the time through 1981 compared to 52.6% for the S&P across the page. Ends and beginnings of the month are fairly similar, specifically the last plus the first four trading days. But notice how investors piled into NASDAQ stocks until mid-month. NASDAQ rose 118.6% from January 1, 1971, to December 31, 1981, compared to 33.0% for the S&P.

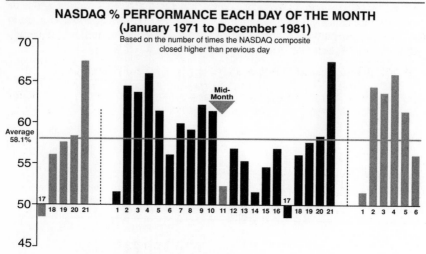

NASDAQ % PERFORMANCE EACH DAY OF THE MONTH
(January 1971 to December 1981)

Based on the number of times the NASDAQ composite closed higher than previous day

After the air was let out of the market 2000-2002, S&P's 889.9% gain over the last 23 years is more evenly matched with NASDAQ's 1010.8% gain. Last three, first four and middle ninth and tenth days rose the most. Where the S&P has six days of the month that go down more often than up, NASDAQ has none. NASDAQ exhibits the most strength on the last trading day of the month.

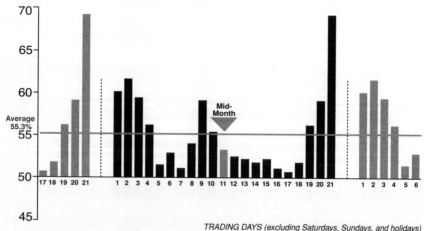
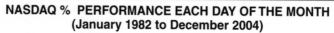

NASDAQ % PERFORMANCE EACH DAY OF THE MONTH
(January 1982 to December 2004)

TRADING DAYS (excluding Saturdays, Sundays, and holidays)

Based on NASDAQ composite, prior to February 5, 1971, based on National Quotation Bureau indices

ALMANAC INVESTOR

Dow Gains More Eight Days a Month
Than on All 13 Remaining Days Combined

The market currently exhibits greater bullish bias from the last three trading days of the previous month through the first two days of the current month, and shows significant bullishness during the middle three trading days nine to eleven, due to 401(k) cash inflows. This pattern was not as pronounced during the boom years of the 1990s, with market strength all month long. But the last five and a half years have experienced monthly bullishness at the ends, beginnings and middles of months versus losses during the rest of the month. Was 1999's "rest of month" heavy bullishness a bearish omen and 2002's "rest of month" large losses a bullish sign?

SUPER EIGHT DAYS* DOW % CHANGES VS. REST OF MONTH

	Super 8 Days	Rest of Month	Super 8 Days	Rest of Month	Super 8 Days	Rest of Month
	1997		**1998**		**1999**	
Jan	0.80%	0.91%	4.18%	− 2.30%	0.98%	0.08%
Feb	4.19	1.46	5.43	1.55	0.76	1.62
Mar	− 3.83	1.58	3.06	2.53	− 0.68	3.74
Apr	− 4.50	2.66	2.29	− 1.47	2.84	7.09
May	5.49	3.81	2.37	− 1.79	− 0.83	− 1.92
Jun	1.63	2.55	− 4.64	4.47	0.20	0.01
Jul	2.85	2.65	3.55	− 3.43	5.87	− 1.74
Aug	− 2.39	− 1.76	− 4.75	0.17	− 0.35	2.41
Sep	4.51	− 3.57	− 4.92	− 0.59	− 5.83	− 2.32
Oct	2.45	− 6.73	0.68	3.59	− 2.86	2.97
Nov	6.56	− 2.84	6.19	4.57	4.25	2.45
Dec	2.53	− 3.57	− 2.75	2.11	0.29	3.92
Totals	**20.29%**	**− 2.85%**	**10.69%**	**9.41%**	**4.64%**	**18.31%**
Average	**1.69%**	**− 0.24%**	**0.89%**	**0.78%**	**0.39%**	**1.53%**
	2000		**2001**		**2002**	
Jan	− 4.09%	0.47%	2.13%	− 2.36%	− 1.92%	− 0.24%
Feb	0.43	− 9.10	1.41	− 3.36	− 1.41	4.27
Mar	2.76	5.62	− 1.50	− 3.30	4.11	− 2.64
Apr	− 2.79	4.77	− 2.61	9.56	− 2.46	0.08
May	0.71	− 7.86	2.02	1.53	3.62	− 4.07
Jun	5.99	− 4.10	− 2.46	− 2.45	− 2.22	− 6.51
Jul	− 0.65	0.83	2.16	− 2.29	− 5.04	− 4.75
Aug	3.08	3.75	0.24	− 2.48	2.08	4.59
Sep	− 3.27	− 2.34	− 3.62	− 12.05	− 6.58	− 5.00
Oct	− 0.85	− 1.47	4.51	5.36	8.48	− 1.50
Nov	5.81	− 4.06	1.01	2.48	4.74	0.99
Dec	− 2.96	4.44	0.19	1.99	− 0.76	− 4.02
Totals	**4.17%**	**− 9.05%**	**3.48%**	**− 7.37%**	**2.64%**	**− 18.80%**
Average	**0.35%**	**− 0.75%**	**0.29%**	**− 0.61%**	**0.22%**	**− 1.57%**
	2003		**2004**		**2005**	
Jan	1.00%	− 4.86%	3.79%	− 1.02%	− 1.96%	− 1.35%
Feb	2.71	− 4.82	− 1.20	0.83	1.76	− 0.07
Mar	5.22	− 0.90	− 1.64	− 1.69	0.31	− 2.05
Apr	2.87	− 1.91	3.20	− 0.60	− 4.62	1.46
May	3.17	2.46	− 2.92	− 0.51	0.57	2.43
Jun	3.09	− 0.38	1.15	1.36	1.43	− 3.00
Jul	1.18	1.64	− 1.91	− 0.88		
Aug	− 0.74	1.55	0.51	0.40		
Sep	3.58	− 3.47	0.47	− 2.26		
Oct	2.87	1.41	0.85	− 1.82		
Nov	− 0.47	0.48	3.08	3.20		
Dec	2.10	3.70	2.03	1.13		
Totals	**26.58%**	**− 5.10%**	**7.41%**	**− 1.86%**	**− 2.51%**	**− 2.57%**
Average	**2.22%**	**− 0.43%**	**0.62%**	**− 0.16%**	**− 0.42%**	**− 0.43%**

	Super 8 Days*		Rest of Month (13 Days)	
102	Net % Changes	**77.39%**	Net % Changes	**− 19.88%**
Month	Average Period	**0.76%**	Average Period	**− 0.195%**
Totals	Average Day	**0.09%**	Average Day	**− 0.015%**

* Super 8 Days = Last 3 + First 2 + Middle 3

S&P 500 MARKET PROBABILITY CALENDAR 2006

THE % CHANCE OF THE MARKET RISING ON ANY TRADING DAY OF THE YEAR*

(Based on the number of times the S&P 500 rose on a particular trading day during **January 1954-December 2004**)

Date	Jan	Feb	Mar	Apr	May	Jun	Jul	Aug	Sep	Oct	Nov	Dec
1	S	56.9	60.8	S	54.9	54.9	S	47.1	62.8	S	64.7	49.0
2	H	56.9	62.8	S	70.6	60.8	S	43.1	S	49.0	54.9	S
3	47.1	51.0	62.8	62.8	58.8	S	66.7	47.1	S	70.6	70.6	S
4	74.5	S	S	56.9	43.1	S	H	52.9	H	52.9	S	51.0
5	52.9	S	S	52.9	41.2	56.9	58.8	S	56.9	62.8	S	60.8
6	49.0	47.1	47.1	54.9	S	56.9	51.0	S	58.8	49.0	52.9	56.9
7	S	49.0	47.1	54.9	S	51.0	60.8	58.8	43.1	S	43.1	41.2
8	S	41.2	58.8	S	49.0	41.2	S	45.1	49.0	S	60.8	49.0
9	45.1	41.2	58.8	S	51.0	41.2	S	54.9	S	49.0	62.8	S
10	49.0	62.8	47.1	60.8	52.9	S	60.8	47.1	S	37.3	56.9	S
11	51.0	S	S	64.7	47.1	S	54.9	47.1	49.0	45.1	S	54.9
12	52.9	S	S	51.0	52.9	62.8	51.0	S	52.9	52.9	S	47.1
13	60.8	47.1	60.8	49.0	S	60.8	47.1	S	62.8	51.0	45.1	47.1
14	S	43.1	45.1	H	S	54.9	72.6	68.6	51.0	S	52.9	43.1
15	S	52.9	62.8	S	54.9	54.9	S	62.8	51.0	S	49.0	47.1
16	H	33.3	62.8	S	49.0	47.1	S	54.9	S	51.0	47.1	S
17	64.7	51.0	54.9	62.8	56.9	S	54.9	51.0	S	54.9	54.9	S
18	54.9	S	S	62.8	41.2	S	41.2	52.9	51.0	37.3	S	56.9
19	52.9	S	S	56.9	45.1	54.9	41.2	S	47.1	68.6	S	47.1
20	47.1	H	51.0	51.0	S	39.2	47.1	S	52.9	49.0	54.9	45.1
21	S	43.1	47.1	54.9	S	51.0	43.1	45.1	52.9	S	58.8	47.1
22	S	41.2	45.1	S	54.9	54.9	S	58.8	37.3	S	64.7	58.8
23	45.1	37.3	43.1	S	43.1	43.1	S	47.1	S	35.3	H	S
24	60.8	56.9	51.0	45.1	54.9	S	43.1	51.0	S	39.2	60.8	S
25	52.9	S	S	58.8	45.1	S	56.9	49.0	49.0	33.3	S	H
26	51.0	S	S	47.1	45.1	39.2	54.9	S	51.0	58.8	S	72.6
27	43.1	51.0	41.2	43.1	S	37.3	51.0	S	54.9	60.8	68.6	54.9
28	S	62.8	49.0	60.8	S	49.0	62.8	45.1	49.0	S	58.8	66.7
29	S		56.9	S	H	60.8	S	52.9	45.1	S	54.9	68.6
30	66.7		35.3	S	52.9	52.9	S	47.1	S	58.8	49.0	S
31	66.7		41.2		60.8		68.6	66.7		54.9		S

RECENT S&P 500 MARKET PROBABILITY CALENDAR 2006

THE % CHANCE OF THE MARKET RISING ON ANY TRADING DAY OF THE YEAR*

(Based on the number of times the S&P 500 rose on a particular trading day during **January 1984-December 2004**)

Date	Jan	Feb	Mar	Apr	May	Jun	Jul	Aug	Sep	Oct	Nov	Dec
1	S	52.4	47.6	S	61.9	61.9	S	47.6	52.4	S	76.2	57.1
2	H	57.1	57.1	S	71.4	71.4	S	42.9	S	61.9	42.9	S
3	38.1	61.9	61.9	57.1	52.4	S	76.2	42.9	S	61.9	66.7	S
4	71.4	S	S	57.1	23.8	S	H	52.4	H	38.1	S	57.1
5	52.4	S	S	47.6	23.8	52.4	52.4	S	47.6	57.1	S	57.1
6	47.6	38.1	47.6	57.1	S	52.4	33.3	S	42.9	33.3	61.9	33.3
7	S	47.6	52.4	42.9	S	47.6	61.9	57.1	38.1	S	38.1	38.1
8	S	47.6	61.9	S	52.4	33.3	S	52.4	52.4	S	57.1	52.4
9	47.6	42.9	42.9	S	61.9	42.9	S	42.9	S	47.6	47.6	S
10	47.6	71.4	42.9	57.1	57.1	S	61.9	47.6	S	28.6	52.4	S
11	47.6	S	S	57.1	66.7	S	38.1	38.1	52.4	42.9	S	52.4
12	52.4	S	S	42.9	61.9	52.4	61.9	S	52.4	71.4	S	38.1
13	57.1	57.1	61.9	47.6	S	52.4	71.4	S	57.1	71.4	42.9	47.6
14	S	42.9	47.6	H	S	66.7	81.0	71.4	57.1	S	66.7	38.1
15	S	71.4	66.7	S	57.1	57.1	S	57.1	47.6	S	47.6	52.4
16	H	28.6	71.4	S	42.9	57.1	S	71.4	S	57.1	42.9	S
17	76.2	33.3	57.1	61.9	66.7	S	47.6	57.1	S	57.1	61.9	S
18	61.9	S	S	66.7	57.1	S	47.6	61.9	47.6	38.1	S	61.9
19	52.4	S	S	61.9	57.1	61.9	38.1	S	42.9	76.2	S	52.4
20	38.1	H	52.4	42.9	S	42.9	52.4	S	57.1	57.1	52.4	38.1
21	S	38.1	38.1	61.9	S	47.6	28.6	42.9	38.1	S	61.9	66.7
22	S	52.4	47.6	S	52.4	71.4	S	57.1	38.1	S	61.9	52.4
23	38.1	38.1	38.1	S	33.3	33.3	S	52.4	S	42.9	H	S
24	52.4	52.4	52.4	33.3	76.2	S	38.1	66.7	S	28.6	66.7	S
25	52.4	S	S	61.9	52.4	S	76.2	52.4	38.1	42.9	S	H
26	47.6	S	S	57.1	52.4	38.1	57.1	S	52.4	52.4	S	66.7
27	52.4	57.1	52.4	52.4	S	28.6	52.4	S	57.1	66.7	71.4	57.1
28	S	66.7	47.6	61.9	S	52.4	71.4	57.1	61.9	S	61.9	76.2
29	S		61.9	S	H	71.4	S	52.4	52.4	S	57.1	42.9
30	66.7		28.6	S	57.1	47.6	S	38.1	S	81.0	33.3	S
31	81.0		47.6		57.1		76.2	52.4		57.1		S

Indicators and Patterns

DOW JONES INDUSTRIALS MARKET PROBABILITY CALENDAR 2006
THE % CHANCE OF THE MARKET RISING ON ANY TRADING DAY OF THE YEAR*

(Based on the number of times the DJIA rose on a particular trading day during **January 1954-December 2004**)

Date	Jan	Feb	Mar	Apr	May	Jun	Jul	Aug	Sep	Oct	Nov	Dec
1	S	54.9	66.7	S	54.9	56.9	S	45.1	60.8	S	64.7	47.1
2	H	54.9	68.6	S	62.8	52.9	S	45.1	S	49.0	49.0	S
3	54.9	39.2	60.8	56.9	52.9	S	60.8	47.1	S	62.8	68.6	S
4	74.5	S	S	56.9	49.0	S	H	52.9	H	51.0	S	54.9
5	49.0	S	S	52.9	43.1	56.9	62.8	S	58.8	60.8	S	62.8
6	54.9	52.9	49.0	60.8	S	58.8	58.8	S	58.8	47.1	56.9	58.8
7	S	45.1	45.1	52.9	S	52.9	56.9	56.9	43.1	S	43.1	45.1
8	S	41.2	54.9	S	47.1	41.2	S	45.1	45.1	S	62.8	43.1
9	49.0	45.1	58.8	S	51.0	35.3	S	49.0	S	51.0	52.9	S
10	47.1	62.8	51.0	58.8	49.0	S	60.8	51.0	S	39.2	58.8	S
11	47.1	S	S	64.7	49.0	S	54.9	45.1	39.2	39.2	S	54.9
12	47.1	S	S	62.8	54.9	60.8	52.9	S	52.9	54.9	S	58.8
13	58.8	41.2	54.9	54.9	S	56.9	37.3	S	58.8	56.9	45.1	41.2
14	S	51.0	49.0	H	S	54.9	64.7	66.7	47.1	S	51.0	51.0
15	S	54.9	58.8	S	52.9	49.0	S	58.8	51.0	S	56.9	47.1
16	H	35.3	62.8	S	45.1	49.0	S	52.9	S	52.9	47.1	S
17	56.9	47.1	56.9	72.6	54.9	S	47.1	43.1	S	51.0	52.9	S
18	60.8	S	S	64.7	45.1	S	43.1	52.9	49.0	41.2	S	58.8
19	41.2	S	S	54.9	49.0	49.0	45.1	S	39.2	62.8	S	52.9
20	37.3	H	51.0	52.9	S	41.2	47.1	S	47.1	49.0	51.0	54.9
21	S	51.0	45.1	51.0	S	52.9	45.1	45.1	47.1	S	60.8	49.0
22	S	35.3	39.2	S	47.1	51.0	S	58.8	41.2	S	68.6	60.8
23	41.2	45.1	49.0	S	33.3	43.1	S	49.0	S	37.3	H	S
24	47.1	60.8	35.3	49.0	54.9	S	47.1	51.0	S	47.1	60.8	S
25	58.8	S	S	58.8	41.2	S	58.8	51.0	51.0	27.5	S	H
26	56.9	S	S	51.0	43.1	41.2	54.9	S	52.9	51.0	S	72.6
27	47.1	47.1	49.0	45.1	S	47.1	47.1	S	47.1	56.9	64.7	51.0
28	S	54.9	47.1	54.9	S	43.1	60.8	45.1	49.0	S	56.9	56.9
29	S		56.9	S	H	56.9	S	52.9	41.2	S	51.0	56.9
30	64.7		41.2	S	52.9	54.9	S	41.2	S	60.8	51.0	S
31	60.8		41.2		62.8		56.9	62.8		54.9		S

RECENT DOW JONES INDUSTRIALS MARKET PROBABILITY CALENDAR 2006

THE % CHANCE OF THE MARKET RISING ON ANY TRADING DAY OF THE YEAR*

(Based on the number of times the DJIA rose on a particular trading day during **January 1984-December 2004****)

Date	Jan	Feb	Mar	Apr	May	Jun	Jul	Aug	Sep	Oct	Nov	Dec
1	S	52.4	57.1	S	61.9	71.4	S	42.9	47.6	S	76.2	52.4
2	H	52.4	66.7	S	66.7	57.1	S	52.4	S	66.7	38.1	S
3	57.1	42.9	61.9	61.9	42.9	S	71.4	42.9	S	47.6	66.7	S
4	71.4	S	S	57.1	38.1	S	H	52.4	H	33.3	S	61.9
5	47.6	S	S	42.9	28.6	57.1	57.1	S	57.1	61.9	S	52.4
6	57.1	38.1	47.6	71.4	S	61.9	33.3	S	47.6	38.1	61.9	42.9
7	S	52.4	52.4	38.1	S	47.6	57.1	52.4	33.3	S	38.1	33.3
8	S	38.1	52.4	S	57.1	42.9	S	47.6	47.6	S	61.9	57.1
9	42.9	47.6	52.4	S	66.7	33.3	S	47.6	S	52.4	38.1	S
10	47.6	61.9	47.6	57.1	61.9	S	57.1	52.4	S	28.6	57.1	S
11	47.6	S	S	61.9	66.7	S	42.9	42.9	38.1	38.1	S	57.1
12	57.1	S	S	57.1	57.1	57.1	71.4	S	57.1	71.4	S	52.4
13	52.4	52.4	47.6	57.1	S	42.9	61.9	S	61.9	71.4	47.6	42.9
14	S	52.4	57.1	H	S	66.7	71.4	66.7	52.4	S	66.7	42.9
15	S	71.4	57.1	S	52.4	47.6	S	52.4	47.6	S	52.4	57.1
16	H	33.3	71.4	S	47.6	57.1	S	66.7	S	61.9	38.1	S
17	61.9	33.3	52.4	76.2	57.1	S	47.6	47.6	S	52.4	61.9	S
18	61.9	S	S	76.2	57.1	S	52.4	57.1	42.9	47.6	S	66.7
19	38.1	S	S	57.1	66.7	52.4	38.1	S	28.6	71.4	S	47.6
20	38.1	H	61.9	38.1	S	38.1	47.6	S	52.4	52.4	52.4	47.6
21	S	47.6	42.9	57.1	S	47.6	38.1	42.9	33.3	S	71.4	61.9
22	S	52.4	33.3	S	47.6	61.9	S	61.9	38.1	S	71.4	57.1
23	33.3	42.9	42.9	S	33.3	42.9	S	47.6	S	42.9	H	S
24	38.1	52.4	28.6	33.3	71.4	S	42.9	61.9	S	42.9	71.4	S
25	71.4	S	S	61.9	42.9	S	71.4	47.6	47.6	38.1	S	H
26	61.9	S	S	57.1	52.4	42.9	57.1	S	57.1	42.9	S	76.2
27	57.1	47.6	57.1	52.4	S	42.9	47.6	S	52.4	71.4	71.4	57.1
28	S	52.4	42.9	52.4	S	47.6	61.9	52.4	57.1	S	57.1	57.1
29	S		66.7	S	H	61.9	S	52.4	47.6	S	47.6	42.9
30	61.9		42.9	S	66.7	42.9	S	28.6	S	81.0	47.6	S
31	66.7		38.1		57.1		66.7	47.6		42.9		S

NASDAQ COMPOSITE MARKET PROBABILITY CALENDAR 2006

THE % CHANCE OF THE MARKET RISING ON ANY TRADING DAY OF THE YEAR*

(Based on the number of times the NASDAQ rose on a particular trading day during **January 1972-December 2004**)

Date	Jan	Feb	Mar	Apr	May	Jun	Jul	Aug	Sep	Oct	Nov	Dec
1	S	63.6	63.6	S	60.6	57.6	S	51.5	54.6	S	72.7	63.6
2	H	69.7	57.6	S	72.7	75.8	S	39.4	S	48.5	51.5	S
3	51.5	60.6	72.7	39.4	66.7	S	51.5	48.5	S	63.6	75.8	S
4	78.8	S	S	60.6	54.6	S	H	63.6	H	54.6	S	60.6
5	60.6	S	S	60.6	54.6	60.6	48.5	S	66.7	63.6	S	63.6
6	66.7	66.7	54.6	51.5	S	60.6	39.4	S	57.6	60.6	54.6	60.6
7	S	54.6	54.6	51.5	S	57.6	51.5	60.6	57.6	S	45.5	42.4
8	S	48.5	57.6	S	57.6	48.5	S	39.4	54.6	S	54.6	51.5
9	51.5	51.5	57.6	S	57.6	45.5	S	54.6	S	60.6	63.6	S
10	57.6	66.7	51.5	63.6	39.4	S	60.6	51.5	S	48.5	63.6	S
11	54.6	S	S	66.7	57.6	S	63.6	54.6	45.5	48.5	S	42.4
12	57.6	S	S	57.6	57.6	60.6	57.6	S	45.5	75.8	S	39.4
13	69.7	51.5	69.7	51.5	S	60.6	72.7	S	60.6	63.6	51.5	45.5
14	S	57.6	48.5	H	S	63.6	75.8	63.6	57.6	S	57.6	39.4
15	S	60.6	54.6	S	60.6	54.6	S	57.6	33.3	S	42.4	45.5
16	H	48.5	66.7	S	57.6	45.5	S	51.5	S	51.5	39.4	S
17	69.7	57.6	54.6	63.6	54.6	S	66.7	57.6	S	51.5	57.6	S
18	69.7	S	S	51.5	42.4	S	45.5	51.5	42.4	36.4	S	54.6
19	66.7	S	S	60.6	45.5	51.5	48.5	S	54.6	75.8	S	51.5
20	45.5	H	60.6	60.6	S	48.5	54.6	S	66.7	63.6	54.6	51.5
21	S	39.4	39.4	54.6	S	60.6	45.5	36.4	54.6	S	54.6	69.7
22	S	48.5	39.4	S	51.5	51.5	S	66.7	48.5	S	69.7	66.7
23	48.5	54.6	60.6	S	48.5	51.5	S	57.6	S	39.4	H	S
24	54.6	57.6	57.6	45.5	60.6	S	51.5	48.5	S	39.4	60.6	S
25	42.4	S	S	48.5	51.5	S	57.6	51.5	48.5	33.3	S	H
26	63.6	S	S	66.7	57.6	48.5	51.5	S	45.5	42.4	S	72.7
27	57.6	54.6	39.4	57.6	S	42.4	48.5	S	45.5	57.6	57.6	51.5
28	S	57.6	48.5	75.8	S	57.6	51.5	54.6	48.5	S	66.7	72.7
29	S		54.6	S	H	69.7	S	54.6	51.5	S	66.7	84.9
30	60.6		48.5	S	51.5	75.8	S	60.6	S	57.6	66.7	S
31	66.7		66.7		72.7		60.6	75.8		66.7		S

RECENT NASDAQ COMPOSITE MARKET PROBABILITY CALENDAR 2006

THE % CHANCE OF THE MARKET RISING ON ANY TRADING DAY OF THE YEAR*

(Based on the number of times the NASDAQ rose on a particular trading day during **January 1984-December 2004****)

Date	Jan	Feb	Mar	Apr	May	Jun	Jul	Aug	Sep	Oct	Nov	Dec
1	S	71.4	66.7	S	66.7	61.9	S	52.4	52.4	S	81.0	71.4
2	H	71.4	47.6	S	71.4	81.0	S	38.1	S	52.4	47.6	S
3	57.1	61.9	76.2	42.9	71.4	S	61.9	42.9	S	57.1	85.7	S
4	85.7	S	S	47.6	42.9	S	H	61.9	H	52.4	S	66.7
5	61.9	S	S	61.9	42.9	57.1	52.4	S	61.9	61.9	S	66.7
6	61.9	61.9	52.4	47.6	S	61.9	38.1	S	47.6	42.9	57.1	57.1
7	S	57.1	57.1	38.1	S	52.4	52.4	52.4	57.1	S	52.4	33.3
8	S	52.4	52.4	S	66.7	42.9	S	47.6	57.1	S	57.1	42.9
9	47.6	47.6	52.4	S	57.1	47.6	S	47.6	S	52.4	57.1	S
10	57.1	57.1	52.4	61.9	42.9	S	66.7	52.4	S	42.9	57.1	S
11	57.1	S	S	61.9	61.9	S	57.1	47.6	52.4	52.4	S	42.9
12	57.1	S	S	52.4	52.4	52.4	61.9	S	47.6	76.2	S	33.3
13	66.7	47.6	61.9	52.4	S	52.4	76.2	S	61.9	66.7	47.6	57.1
14	S	61.9	42.9	H	S	57.1	81.0	76.2	57.1	S	61.9	38.1
15	S	66.7	52.4	S	61.9	57.1	S	61.9	19.1	S	38.1	52.4
16	H	33.3	76.2	S	52.4	47.6	S	61.9	S	57.1	23.8	S
17	61.9	47.6	57.1	66.7	66.7	S	57.1	57.1	S	47.6	57.1	S
18	71.4	S	S	47.6	47.6	S	47.6	47.6	38.1	38.1	S	52.4
19	76.2	S	S	61.9	61.9	47.6	38.1	S	52.4	76.2	S	52.4
20	38.1	H	61.9	47.6	S	47.6	47.6	S	71.4	57.1	57.1	52.4
21	S	42.9	38.1	52.4	S	57.1	33.3	42.9	47.6	S	47.6	76.2
22	S	52.4	33.3	S	47.6	57.1	S	76.2	47.6	S	66.7	61.9
23	47.6	57.1	52.4	S	42.9	42.9	S	61.9	S	42.9	H	S
24	57.1	52.4	52.4	47.6	61.9	S	38.1	52.4	S	38.1	61.9	S
25	42.9	S	S	52.4	47.6	S	66.7	47.6	38.1	28.6	S	H
26	71.4	S	S	61.9	61.9	47.6	61.9	S	47.6	33.3	S	66.7
27	61.9	52.4	38.1	61.9	S	33.3	52.4	S	42.9	52.4	57.1	57.1
28	S	61.9	47.6	76.2	S	57.1	57.1	57.1	47.6	S	61.9	71.4
29	S		52.4	S	H	71.4	S	61.9	57.1	S	71.4	76.2
30	57.1		42.9	S	61.9	81.0	S	57.1	S	71.4	57.1	S
31	71.4		66.7		76.2		71.4	71.4		66.7		S

RUSSELL 1000 MARKET PROBABILITY CALENDAR 2006

THE % CHANCE OF THE MARKET RISING ON ANY TRADING DAY OF THE YEAR

(Based on the number of times the Russell 1K rose on a particular trading day during January 1984-December 2004)

Date	Jan	Feb	Mar	Apr	May	Jun	Jul	Aug	Sep	Oct	Nov	Dec
1	S	66.7	52.4	S	57.1	61.9	S	47.6	52.4	S	76.2	61.9
2	H	57.1	52.4	S	66.7	61.9	S	38.1	S	57.1	42.9	S
3	33.3	66.7	66.7	52.4	57.1	S	71.4	42.9	S	57.1	66.7	S
4	71.4	S	S	57.1	23.8	S	H	52.4	H	38.1	S	57.1
5	57.1	S	S	52.4	23.8	52.4	47.6	S	47.6	57.1	S	61.9
6	47.6	38.1	42.9	57.1	S	52.4	33.3	S	47.6	38.1	61.9	33.3
7	S	52.4	47.6	42.9	S	38.1	61.9	61.9	33.3	S	38.1	38.1
8	S	47.6	61.9	S	57.1	38.1	S	57.1	52.4	S	57.1	52.4
9	47.6	47.6	47.6	S	66.7	38.1	S	42.9	S	47.6	47.6	S
10	52.4	66.7	42.9	61.9	57.1	S	57.1	52.4	S	33.3	52.4	S
11	52.4	S	S	57.1	66.7	S	38.1	33.3	52.4	42.9	S	52.4
12	52.4	S	S	47.6	57.1	52.4	66.7	S	52.4	71.4	S	33.3
13	57.1	57.1	61.9	47.6	S	52.4	71.4	S	61.9	71.4	47.6	47.6
14	S	42.9	47.6	H	S	57.1	85.7	66.7	57.1	S	61.9	38.1
15	S	71.4	61.9	S	57.1	52.4	S	57.1	47.6	S	52.4	57.1
16	H	28.6	66.7	S	52.4	57.1	S	71.4	S	57.1	38.1	S
17	71.4	38.1	52.4	61.9	66.7	S	47.6	57.1	S	57.1	66.7	S
18	66.7	S	S	66.7	57.1	S	47.6	61.9	38.1	38.1	S	61.9
19	52.4	S	S	57.1	57.1	61.9	33.3	S	42.9	76.2	S	52.4
20	33.3	H	52.4	42.9	S	38.1	52.4	S	52.4	52.4	52.4	38.1
21	S	42.9	38.1	57.1	S	47.6	28.6	42.9	38.1	S	57.1	66.7
22	S	52.4	42.9	S	52.4	61.9	S	61.9	42.9	S	61.9	52.4
23	38.1	38.1	38.1	S	33.3	38.1	S	52.4	S	42.9	H	S
24	52.4	57.1	47.6	33.3	71.4	S	33.3	61.9	S	23.8	71.4	S
25	52.4	S	S	52.4	52.4	S	81.0	47.6	38.1	38.1	S	H
26	66.7	S	S	61.9	57.1	38.1	61.9	S	52.4	47.6	S	71.4
27	57.1	57.1	52.4	52.4	S	28.6	47.6	S	66.7	61.9	71.4	66.7
28	S	66.7	42.9	57.1	S	52.4	71.4	57.1	61.9	S	71.4	76.2
29	S		57.1	S	H	71.4	S	52.4	57.1	S	57.1	52.4
30	66.7		33.3	S	57.1	57.1	S	42.9	S	76.2	38.1	S
31	71.4		52.4		61.9		76.2	52.4		66.7		S

RUSSELL 2000 MARKET PROBABILITY CALENDAR 2006

THE % CHANCE OF THE MARKET RISING ON ANY TRADING DAY OF THE YEAR

(Based on the number of times the Russell 2K rose on a particular trading day during January 1984-December 2004)

Date	Jan	Feb	Mar	Apr	May	Jun	Jul	Aug	Sep	Oct	Nov	Dec
1	S	66.7	66.7	S	71.4	71.4	S	42.9	47.6	S	76.2	61.9
2	H	61.9	76.2	S	71.4	71.4	S	52.4	S	47.6	61.9	S
3	38.1	61.9	66.7	38.1	71.4	S	57.1	42.9	S	52.4	76.2	S
4	81.0	S	S	47.6	47.6	S	H	52.4	H	38.1	S	61.9
5	61.9	S	S	42.9	42.9	57.1	57.1	S	61.9	66.7	S	66.7
6	61.9	66.7	61.9	52.4	S	52.4	38.1	S	47.6	38.1	66.7	57.1
7	S	61.9	71.4	38.1	S	61.9	52.4	52.4	66.7	S	57.1	38.1
8	S	66.7	52.4	S	52.4	38.1	S	47.6	52.4	S	52.4	61.9
9	57.1	52.4	52.4	S	66.7	47.6	S	61.9	S	38.1	52.4	S
10	57.1	71.4	38.1	57.1	52.4	S	61.9	52.4	S	42.9	71.4	S
11	52.4	S	S	66.7	66.7	S	57.1	38.1	52.4	57.1	S	42.9
12	71.4	S	S	52.4	52.4	52.4	57.1	S	52.4	71.4	S	52.4
13	71.4	52.4	61.9	52.4	S	52.4	66.7	S	61.9	61.9	38.1	47.6
14	S	66.7	57.1	H	S	57.1	76.2	85.7	52.4	S	61.9	42.9
15	S	66.7	57.1	S	47.6	52.4	S	61.9	23.8	S	42.9	38.1
16	H	38.1	66.7	S	57.1	52.4	S	71.4	S	66.7	14.3	S
17	66.7	42.9	61.9	57.1	61.9	S	57.1	52.4	S	42.9	61.9	S
18	66.7	S	S	61.9	57.1	S	42.9	47.6	38.1	47.6	S	57.1
19	85.7	S	S	57.1	57.1	33.3	33.3	S	42.9	66.7	S	57.1
20	33.3	H	57.1	52.4	S	42.9	42.9	S	42.9	52.4	42.9	52.4
21	S	38.1	52.4	57.1	S	47.6	33.3	47.6	52.4	S	28.6	76.2
22	S	52.4	42.9	S	57.1	47.6	S	66.7	47.6	S	57.1	71.4
23	47.6	61.9	52.4	S	47.6	42.9	S	52.4	S	47.6	H	S
24	57.1	61.9	47.6	47.6	66.7	S	33.3	61.9	S	38.1	66.7	S
25	38.1	S	S	66.7	42.9	S	61.9	57.1	42.9	42.9	S	H
26	61.9	S	S	61.9	66.7	42.9	76.2	S	38.1	38.1	S	81.0
27	52.4	66.7	42.9	66.7	S	42.9	47.6	S	52.4	52.4	61.9	66.7
28	S	71.4	57.1	76.2	S	57.1	52.4	57.1	61.9	S	61.9	71.4
29	S		61.9	S	H	81.0	S	66.7	81.0	S	71.4	81.0
30	61.9		42.9	S	66.7	81.0	S	66.7	S	71.4	61.9	S
31	81.0		81.0		76.2		81.0	81.0		81.0		S

ANNUAL TRADING PATTERNS

Market Behavior Three Days Before and Three Days After Holidays

We have tracked holiday seasonality annually since the first edition of the *Stock Trader's Almanac* in 1968. Stocks used to rise on the day before holidays and sell off the day after, but nowadays each holiday moves to its own rhythm.

HOLIDAYS: 3 DAYS BEFORE, 3 DAYS AFTER (Average % Change 1980 — July 2005)

	−3	−2	−1		+1	+2	+3
S&P 500	0.12	0.26	−0.11	Positive Day After	−0.04	0.46	0.12
DJIA	0.06	0.18	−0.19	New Year's Day	0.17	0.48	0.29
NASDAQ	0.27	0.32	0.29	1/1/06 (Closed 1/2)	−0.10	0.83	0.32
Russell 2K	0.32	0.43	0.62		−0.22	0.41	0.22
S&P 500	0.34	−0.06	−0.27	Negative Before & After	−0.14	−0.07	−0.09
DJIA	0.37	−0.03	−0.19	Presidents' Day	−0.05	−0.12	−0.11
NASDAQ	0.54	0.22	−0.45	2/20/06	−0.55	−0.05	−0.05
Russell 2K	0.39	0.05	−0.16		−0.42	−0.12	−0.04
S&P 500	0.15	−0.03	0.21	Positive Before &	−0.34	0.41	0.15
DJIA	0.13	−0.07	0.14	Negative After	−0.20	0.41	0.14
NASDAQ	0.48	0.30	0.34	Good Friday	−0.55	0.39	0.29
Russell 2K	0.25	0.12	0.28	4/14/06	−0.52	0.28	0.10
S&P 500	0.14	−0.02	0.04	Positive Day After	0.35	0.20	0.18
DJIA	0.12	−0.06	−0.03	Memorial Day	0.43	0.22	0.12
NASDAQ	0.20	0.20	0.02	5/29/06	0.15	−0.03	0.41
Russell 2K	−0.04	0.19	0.16		0.16	0.11	0.33
S&P 500	0.00	0.09	0.07	Negative After	−0.16	−0.05	0.11
DJIA	−0.02	0.07	0.05	Independence Day	−0.10	−0.01	0.09
NASDAQ	0.11	0.11	0.05	7/4/06	−0.16	−0.21	0.32
Russell 2K	0.09	−0.10	0.02		−0.13	−0.21	0.12
S&P 500	−0.07	−0.34	0.22	Positive Day Before	0.01	0.03	−0.08
DJIA	−0.07	−0.40	0.21	Labor Day	0.11	0.10	−0.18
NASDAQ	0.17	−0.04	0.23	9/4/06	−0.16	−0.14	0.13
Russell 2K	0.29	0.02	0.22		−0.07	0.03	0.16
S&P 500	−0.07	0.01	0.25	Positive Before & After	0.24	−0.15	0.15
DJIA	0.03	0.05	0.30	Thanksgiving	0.18	−0.13	0.21
NASDAQ	−0.23	−0.26	0.37	11/23/06	0.62	−0.13	−0.06
Russell 2K	−0.15	−0.17	0.31		0.48	−0.06	0.02
S&P 500	0.20	0.19	0.23	Christmas	0.19	0.09	0.34
DJIA	0.28	0.26	0.30	12/25/06	0.23	0.07	0.27
NASDAQ	−0.16	0.47	0.50		0.13	0.22	0.41
Russell 2K	0.12	0.36	0.40		0.21	0.32	0.54

The eight official New York Stock Exchange holidays are separated into seven groups. Average percent changes for the Dow, S&P 500, NASDAQ and Russell 2000 are shown. The Dow and S&P consist of blue chips and the largest cap stocks, whereas NASDAQ and the Russell 2000 would be more representative of smaller cap stocks. This is evident on the last day of the year with NASDAQ and the Russell 2000 having a field day, while their larger brethren in the Dow and S&P are showing losses on average.

The best six-day span can be seen for the Russell 2000 on the three days before and three days after Christmas, a gain of about 2.0% on average. Thanks to the Santa Claus Rally the six days around New Year's Day are up solidly as well. However, trading around the first day of the year has been mixed. Traders have been selling more the first trading day of the year recently, pushing gains and losses into the New Year.

Bullishness before Labor Day and after Memorial Day is affected by strength the first day of September and June. The worst day after a holiday is the day after Easter. Surprisingly, the following day is one of the best second days after a holiday, right up there with the second day after New Year's Day. Presidents' Day is the least bullish of all the holidays, bearish the day before and three days after. The S&P and NASDAQ have dropped twelve of the last fourteen days before Presidents' Day (Dow, 11 of 14; Russell 2000, 9 of 14).

Seasonal Rallies and Corrections

Most years, especially when the market sells off during the first half, prospects for the perennial summer rally become the buzz on the street. Parameters for this "rally" were defined by the late Ralph Rotnem as the lowest close in the Dow Jones Industrials in May or June to the highest close in July, August, or September.

Such a big deal is made of the "summer rally" that one might get the impression the market puts on its best performance in the summertime. Nothing could be further from the truth! Not only does the market "rally" in every season of the year, but it does so with more gusto in the winter, spring, and fall than in the summer.

Winters in forty-two years averaged a 13.4% gain as measured from the low in November or December to the first quarter closing high. Spring rose 11.1% followed by fall with 10.9%. Last and least was the average 9.3% "summer rally." Even 2003's impressive 14.3% "summer rally" was outmatched by spring and fall. Nevertheless, no matter how thick the gloom or grim the outlook, don't despair! There's always a rally for all seasons, statistically.

While there's a rally for every season, almost always there's a decline or correction, too. Fortunately, corrections tend to be smaller than rallies, and that's what gives the stock market its long-term upward bias. In each season the average bounce outdoes the average setback.

On average the net gain between the rally and the correction is smallest in summer and fall. The summer setback tends to be slightly outdone by the average correction in the fall. Tax selling and portfolio cleaning are the usual explanations —individuals sell to register a tax loss and institutions like to get rid of their losers before preparing year-end statements.

SEASONAL GAINS IN DOW JONES INDUSTRIALS

	WINTER RALLY Nov/Dec Low to Q1 High	SPRING RALLY Feb/Mar Low to Q2 High	SUMMER RALLY May/Jun Low to Q3 High	FALL RALLY Aug/Sep Low to Q4 High
1964	15.3%	6.2%	9.4%	8.3%
1965	5.7	6.6	11.6	10.3
1966	5.9	4.8	3.5	7.0
1967	11.6	8.7	11.2	4.4
1968	7.0	11.5	5.2	13.3
1969	0.9	7.7	1.9	6.7
1970	5.4	6.2	22.5	19.0
1971	21.6	9.4	5.5	7.4
1972	19.1	7.7	5.2	11.4
1973	8.6	4.8	9.7	15.9
1974	13.1	8.2	1.4	11.0
1975	36.2	24.2	8.2	8.7
1976	23.3	6.4	5.9	4.6
1977	8.2	3.1	2.8	2.1
1978	2.1	16.8	11.8	5.2
1979	11.0	8.9	8.9	6.1
1980	13.5	16.8	21.0	8.5
1981	11.8	9.9	0.4	8.3
1982	4.6	9.3	18.5	37.8
1983	15.7	17.8	6.3	10.7
1984	5.9	4.6	14.1	9.7
1985	11.7	7.1	9.5	19.7
1986	31.1	18.8	9.2	11.4
1987	30.6	13.6	22.9	5.9
1988	18.1	13.5	11.2	9.8
1989	15.1	12.9	16.1	5.7
1990	8.8	14.5	12.4	8.6
1991	21.8	11.2	6.6	9.3
1992	14.9	6.4	3.7	3.3
1993	8.9	7.7	6.3	7.3
1994	9.7	5.2	9.1	5.0
1995	13.6	19.3	11.3	13.9
1996	19.2	7.5	8.7	17.3
1997	17.7	18.4	18.4	7.3
1998	20.3	13.6	8.2	24.3
1999	15.1	21.6	8.2	12.6
2000	10.8	15.2	9.8	3.5
2001	6.4	20.8	1.7	23.1
2002	14.8	7.9	2.8	17.6
2003	6.5	23.9	14.3	15.7
2004	11.6	5.2	4.4	10.6
2005	9.0	2.1		
Totals	**562.2%**	**466.0%**	**379.8%**	**448.3%**
Average	**13.4%**	**11.1%**	**9.3%**	**10.9%**

The October jinx also plays a major part. Since 1964, there have been 16 fall declines of over 10%, and in nine of them (1966, 1974, 1978, 1979, 1987, 1990, 1997, 2000, and 2002) much damage was done in October, where so many bear markets end. Important October lows were also seen in 1998 and 1999.

Most often, it has paid to buy after fourth quarter or late third quarter "waterfall declines" for a rally that may continue into January or even beyond. The war in Iraq affected the pattern in 2003. Anticipation of our invasion put the market down in the first quarter. Quick success inspired the bulls which resumed their upward move through the summer.

SEASONAL CORRECTIONS IN DOW JONES INDUSTRIALS

	WINTER SLUMP Nov/Dec High to Q1 Low	SPRING SLUMP Feb/Mar High to Q2 Low	SUMMER SLUMP May/Jun High to Q3 Low	FALL SLUMP Aug/Sep High to Q4 Low
1964	− 0.1%	− 2.4%	− 1.0%	− 2.1%
1965	− 2.5	− 7.3	− 8.3	− 0.9
1966	− 6.0	− 13.2	− 17.7	− 12.7
1967	− 4.2	− 3.9	− 5.5	− 9.9
1968	− 8.8	− 0.3	− 5.5	+ 0.4
1969	− 8.7	− 8.7	− 17.2	− 8.1
1970	− 13.8	− 20.2	− 8.8	− 2.5
1971	− 1.4	− 4.8	− 10.7	− 13.4
1972	− 0.5	− 2.6	− 6.3	− 5.3
1973	− 11.0	− 12.8	− 10.9	− 17.3
1974	− 15.3	− 10.8	− 29.8	− 27.6
1975	− 6.3	− 5.5	− 9.9	− 6.7
1976	− 0.2	− 5.1	− 4.7	− 8.9
1977	− 8.5	− 7.2	− 11.5	− 10.2
1978	− 12.3	− 4.0	− 7.0	− 13.5
1979	− 2.5	− 5.8	− 3.7	− 10.9
1980	− 10.0	− 16.0	− 1.7	− 6.8
1981	− 6.9	− 5.1	− 18.6	− 12.9
1982	− 10.9	− 7.5	− 10.6	− 3.3
1983	− 4.1	− 2.8	− 6.8	− 3.6
1984	− 11.9	− 10.5	− 8.4	− 6.2
1985	− 4.8	− 4.4	− 2.8	− 2.3
1986	− 3.3	− 4.7	− 7.3	− 7.6
1987	− 1.4	− 6.6	− 1.7	− 36.1
1988	− 6.7	− 7.0	− 7.6	− 4.5
1989	− 1.7	− 2.4	− 3.1	− 6.6
1990	− 7.9	− 4.0	− 17.3	− 18.4
1991	− 6.3	− 3.6	− 4.5	− 6.3
1992	+ 0.1	− 3.3	− 5.4	− 7.6
1993	− 2.7	− 3.1	− 3.0	− 2.0
1994	− 4.4	− 9.6	− 4.4	− 7.1
1995	− 0.8	− 0.1	− 0.2	− 2.0
1996	− 3.5	− 4.6	− 7.5	+ 0.2
1997	− 1.8	− 9.8	− 2.2	− 13.3
1998	− 7.0	− 3.1	− 18.2	− 13.1
1999	− 2.7	− 1.7	− 8.0	− 11.5
2000	− 14.8	− 7.4	− 4.1	− 11.8
2001	− 14.5	− 13.6	− 27.4	− 16.2
2002	− 5.1	− 14.2	− 26.7	− 19.5
2003	− 15.8	− 5.3	− 3.1	− 2.1
2004	− 3.9	− 7.7	− 6.3	− 5.7
2005	− 4.5	− 8.5		
Totals	− 259.4%	− 281.2%	− 365.4%	− 375.8%
Average	− 6.2%	− 6.7%	− 8.9%	− 9.2%

Best Months of the Year:
Seasonal Switching Strategies

Top Performing Months Past 55¹/₂ Years
Standard & Poor's 500 & Dow Jones Industrials

January, April, November, and December hold the top four positions in both the Dow and S&P 500 since 1950. This led to our discovery in 1986 of the market's best-kept secret: the "Best Six Months" are November through April.

The most important observation to be made from a chart showing the average

MONTHLY % CHANGES (JANUARY 1950 – JUNE 2005)

	Standard & Poor's 500					Dow Jones Industrials			
Month	Total % Change	Avg. % Change	# Up	# Down	Month	Total % Change	Avg. % Change	# Up	# Down
Jan	77.5%	1.4%	35	21	Jan	74.8%	1.3%	37	19
Feb	— 1.0	— 0.02	30	26	Feb	11.3	0.2	32	24
Mar	55.3	1.0	36	20	Mar	50.3	0.9	35	21
Apr	71.8	1.3	37	19	Apr	99.1	1.8	34	22
May	17.2	0.3	32	24	May	5.6	0.1	29	27
Jun	13.5	0.2	30	26	Jun	— 5.3	— 0.1	28	28
Jul	45.7	0.8	29	26	Jul	55.9	1.0	33	22
Aug	1.1	0.02	30	25	Aug	— 2.7	— 0.1	31	24
Sep*	— 38.3	— 0.7	22	32	Sep	— 58.4	— 1.1	19	36
Oct	50.8	0.9	33	22	Oct	31.5	0.6	32	23
Nov	95.4	1.7	37	18	Nov	91.7	1.7	37	18
Dec	95.7	1.7	42	13	Dec	98.9	1.8	40	15

% Rank					% Rank				
Dec	95.7%	1.7%	42	13	Apr	99.1%	1.8%	34	22
Nov	95.4	1.7	37	18	Dec	98.9	1.8	40	15
Jan	77.5	1.4	35	21	Nov	91.7	1.7	37	18
Apr	71.8	1.3	37	19	Jan	74.8	1.3	37	19
Mar	55.3	1.0	36	20	Jul	55.9	1.0	33	22
Oct	50.8	0.9	33	22	Mar	50.3	0.9	35	21
Jul	45.7	0.8	29	26	Oct	31.5	0.6	32	23
May	17.2	0.3	32	24	Feb	11.3	0.2	32	24
Jun	13.5	0.2	30	26	May	5.6	0.1	29	27
Aug	1.1	0.02	30	25	Aug	— 2.7	— 0.1	31	24
Feb	— 1.0	— 0.02	30	26	Jun	— 5.3	— 0.1	28	28
Sep*	— 38.3	— 0.7	22	32	Sep	— 58.4	— 1.1	19	36
Totals	484.7%	8.6%			Totals	452.7%	8.2%		
Average		0.72%			Average		0.68%		

*No change 1979

monthly percent change in market prices since 1950 is that institutions (mutual funds, pension funds, banks, etc.) determine the trading patterns in today's market. The "investment calendar" reflects the annual, semi-annual and quarterly operations of institutions during January, Apri, and July. August and September tend to combine to make the worst consecutive two-month period. Unusual year-end strength comes from corporate and private pension funds, producing a 4.8% gain on average between November 1 and January 31. September's dismal performance makes it the worst month of the year. In the last twenty-one years it has only been up six times—four in a row, from 1995 to 1998. October is the top month since 1990.

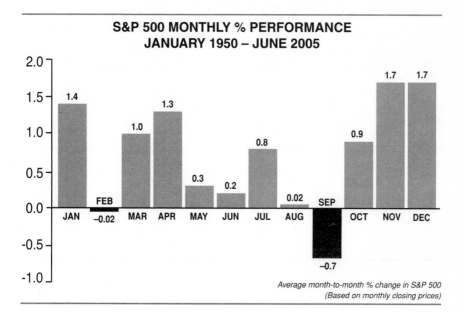

S&P 500 MONTHLY % PERFORMANCE
JANUARY 1950 – JUNE 2005

Average month-to-month % change in S&P 500
(Based on monthly closing prices)

Top Performing NASDAQ Months Past 34¹/₂ Years

NASDAQ stocks run away during three consecutive months, November, December and January, with an average gain of 7.9% despite the slaughter of November 2000, down 22.9%, December 2001, up only 1.0%, January 2002, –0.8%, and December 2002, –9.7% during the three-year bear that shrank the tech-dominated index by 77.9%. Solid gains in November and December 2004 offset January 2005's 5.2% Iraq-turmoil-fueled drop.

January by itself is impressive, up 3.7% on average. April, May, and June also shine, creating our NASDAQ Best Eight Months strategy. A Death Valley abyss occurs during NASDAQ's bleakest four months: July, August, September, and October.

Ample Octobers in six of the last seven years, plus two huge turnarounds in 2001 (+12.8%) and 2002 (+13.5%) has put bear-killing October in the number one spot since 1998. NASDAQ year-end strength is even most impressive, pro-

MONTHLY CHANGES (JANUARY 1971 — JUNE 2005)

	NASDAQ Composite*					Dow Jones Industrials			
Month	Total % Change	Avg. % Change	# Up	# Down	Month	Total % Change	Avg. % Change	# Up	# Down
Jan	128.5%	3.7%	24	11	Jan	64.9%	1.9%	23	12
Feb	21.2	0.6	19	16	Feb	17.0	0.5	20	15
Mar	9.5	0.3	21	14	Mar	29.2	0.8	22	13
Apr	36.9	1.1	22	13	Apr	68.1	1.9	19	16
May	42.3	1.2	21	14	May	19.0	0.5	19	16
Jun	43.4	1.2	22	13	Jun	11.9	0.3	20	15
Jul	— 15.0	— 0.4	16	18	Jul	12.5	0.4	17	17
Aug	7.6	0.2	18	16	Aug	— 5.3	— 0.2	19	15
Sep	— 34.7	— 1.0	18	16	Sep	— 54.5	— 1.6	9	25
Oct	20.0	0.6	18	16	Oct	20.2	0.6	20	14
Nov	70.2	2.1	23	11	Nov	47.6	1.4	23	11
Dec	71.8	2.1	21	13	Dec	62.5	1.8	25	9

% Rank					% Rank				
Jan	128.5%	3.7%	24	11	Apr	68.1%	1.9%	19	16
Dec	71.8	2.1	21	13	Jan	64.9	1.9	23	12
Nov	70.2	2.1	23	11	Dec	62.5	1.8	25	9
Jun	43.4	1.2	22	13	Nov	47.6	1.4	23	11
May	42.3	1.2	21	14	Mar	29.2	0.8	22	13
Apr	36.9	1.1	22	13	Oct	20.2	0.6	20	14
Feb	21.2	0.6	19	16	May	19.0	0.5	19	16
Oct	20.0	0.6	18	16	Feb	17.0	0.5	20	15
Mar	9.5	0.3	21	14	Jun	11.9	0.3	20	15
Aug	7.6	0.2	18	16	Jul	12.5	0.4	17	17
Jul	— 15.0	— 0.4	16	18	Aug	— 5.3	— 0.2	19	15
Sep	— 34.7	— 1.0	18	16	Sep	— 54.5	— 1.6	9	25
Totals	**401.7%**	**11.7%**			**Totals**	**293.1%**	**8.3%**		
Average		**0.98%**			**Average**		**0.69%**		

ducing a 7.9% gain on average between November 1 and January 31—1.6 times greater than that of the S&P 500. September is the worst month of the year for the over-the-counter index as well, posting a deeper average loss of –1.0%. These extremes underscore NASDAQ's higher volatility—and potential for moves of greater magnitude.

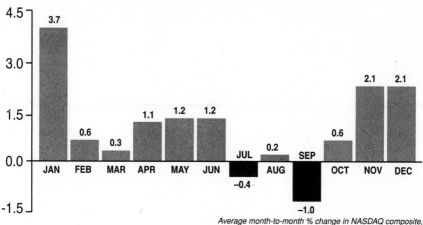

NASDAQ MONTHLY % PERFORMANCE
JANUARY 1971 – JUNE 2005

Average month-to-month % change in NASDAQ composite,
prior to February 5, 1971, based on National Quotation Bureau indices
(Based on monthly closing prices)

Best Six Months Switching Strategy

Our Best Six Months Switching Strategy consistently delivers. Investing between November 1st and April 30th each year and then switching into fixed income for the other six months has produced reliable returns with reduced risk since 1950.

November, December, January, March, and April are the top Dow Jones Industrials and S&P months since 1950. Add February, and an excellent strategy is born! These six consecutive months gained 10764.72 Dow points in 55 years, while the remaining May through October months lost 786.54 points. The S&P gained 1053.79 points in the same best six months versus 84.99 points in the worst six.

A compounding $10,000 investment in the two consecutive six-month periods underscores the low-risk profit power of this investment strategy. The November-April $489,933 Dow gain overshadows the May-October $502 loss. (S&P results were $357,785 to $7,461.) Just two November-April losses were double-digit: April 1970 (Cambodian invasion) and 1973 (OPEC oil embargo). Similarly, Iraq muted the Best six and inflated the Worst six in 2003.

When we discovered this strategy in 1986, the Dow in November-April outperformed May-October by $88,163 to minus $1,522. Results improved substantially these past nineteen years, $401,770 to $1,020. As sensational as these results are, they are nearly tripled with a simple timing indicator (see page 89).

Indicators and Patterns

DJIA SIX-MONTH SWITCHING STRATEGY

	DJIA % Change May 1-Oct 31	Investing $10,000	DJIA % Change Nov 1-Apr 30	Investing $10,000
1950	5.0%	$10,500	15.2%	$11,520
1951	1.2	10,626	− 1.8	11,313
1952	4.5	11,104	2.1	11,551
1953	0.4	11,148	15.8	13,376
1954	10.3	12,296	20.9	16,172
1955	6.9	13,144	13.5	18,355
1956	− 7.0	12,224	3.0	18,906
1957	− 10.8	10,904	3.4	19,549
1958	19.2	12,998	14.8	22,442
1959	3.7	13,479	− 6.9	20,894
1960	− 3.5	13,007	16.9	24,425
1961	3.7	13,488	− 5.5	23,082
1962	− 11.4	11,950	21.7	28,091
1963	5.2	12,571	7.4	30,170
1964	7.7	13,539	5.6	31,860
1965	4.2	14,108	− 2.8	30,968
1966	− 13.6	12,189	11.1	34,405
1967	− 1.9	11,957	3.7	35,678
1968	4.4	12,483	− 0.2	35,607
1969	− 9.9	11,247	− 14.0	30,622
1970	2.7	11,551	24.6	38,155
1971	− 10.9	10,292	13.7	43,382
1972	0.1	10,302	− 3.6	41,820
1973	3.8	10,693	− 12.5	36,593
1974	− 20.5	8,501	23.4	45,156
1975	1.8	8,654	19.2	53,826
1976	− 3.2	8,377	− 3.9	51,727
1977	− 11.7	7,397	2.3	52,917
1978	− 5.4	6,998	7.9	57,097
1979	− 4.6	6,676	0.2	57,211
1980	13.1	7,551	7.9	61,731
1981	− 14.6	6,449	− 0.5	61,422
1982	16.9	7,539	23.6	75,918
1983	− 0.1	7,531	− 4.4	72,578
1984	3.1	7,764	4.2	75,626
1985	9.2	8,478	29.8	98,163
1986	5.3	8,927	21.8	119,563
1987	− 12.8	7,784	1.9	121,835
1988	5.7	8,228	12.6	137,186
1989	9.4	9,001	0.4	137,735
1990	− 8.1	8,272	18.2	162,803
1991	6.3	8,793	9.4	178,106
1992	− 4.0	8,441	6.2	189,149
1993	7.4	9,066	0.0	189,206
1994	6.2	9,628	10.6	209,262
1995	10.0	10,591	17.1	245,046
1996	8.3	11,470	16.2	284,743
1997	6.2	12,181	21.8	346,817
1998	− 5.2	11,548	25.6	435,602
1999	− 0.5	11,490	0.0	435,776
2000	2.2	11,743	− 2.2	426,189
2001	− 15.5	9,923	9.6	467,103
2002	− 15.6	8,375	1.0	471,774
2003	15.6	9,682	4.3	492,060
2004	− 1.9	9,498	1.6	499,933
Average	**0.3%**		**7.9%**	
# Up	**32**		**43**	
# Down	**23**		**12**	
55-Year Gain (Loss)		**($502)**		**$489,933**

S&P 500 SIX-MONTH SWITCHING STRATEGY

	S&P % Change May 1-Oct 31	Investing $10,000	S&P % Change Nov 1-Apr 30	Investing $10,000
1950	8.1%	$10,810	14.8%	$11,480
1951	2.3	11,059	1.7	11,675
1952	5.1	11,623	0.4	11,722
1953	− 0.3	11,588	15.2	13,504
1954	12.1	12,990	19.8	16,178
1955	11.5	14,484	14.3	18,491
1956	− 5.8	13,644	0.4	18,565
1957	− 10.2	12,252	5.8	19,642
1958	18.2	14,482	12.2	22,038
1959	− 0.1	14,468	− 5.5	20,826
1960	− 1.8	14,208	22.3	25,470
1961	5.1	14,933	− 4.9	24,222
1962	− 13.4	12,932	23.5	29,914
1963	6.0	13,708	7.4	32,128
1964	6.8	14,640	5.0	33,734
1965	3.7	15,182	− 1.5	33,228
1966	− 11.9	13,375	17.2	38,943
1967	− 0.1	13,362	3.9	40,462
1968	6.0	14,164	0.3	40,583
1969	− 6.2	13,286	− 16.2	34,009
1970	2.1	13,565	24.9	42,477
1971	− 9.4	12,290	14.3	48,551
1972	3.6	12,732	− 4.1	46,560
1973	1.2	12,885	− 16.6	38,831
1974	− 18.2	10,540	18.1	45,859
1975	2.0	10,751	14.2	52,371
1976	1.2	10,880	− 4.3	50,119
1977	− 6.2	10,205	4.9	52,575
1978	− 3.8	9,817	9.2	57,412
1979	0.1	9,827	4.4	59,938
1980	19.9	11,783	4.2	62,455
1981	− 8.3	10,805	− 4.5	59,645
1982	14.8	12,404	23.0	73,363
1983	− 0.5	12,342	− 2.1	71,822
1984	3.8	12,811	8.3	77,783
1985	5.6	13,528	24.1	96,529
1986	3.6	14,015	18.2	114,097
1987	− 12.7	12,235	3.8	118,433
1988	6.8	13,067	11.0	131,461
1989	9.9	14,361	− 2.8	127,780
1990	− 8.1	13,198	23.5	157,808
1991	4.6	13,805	5.7	166,803
1992	0.9	13,929	5.1	175,310
1993	6.3	14,807	− 3.6	168,999
1994	4.8	15,518	9.0	184,209
1995	13.0	17,535	12.5	207,235
1996	7.8	18,903	13.6	235,419
1997	14.1	21,568	21.6	286,270
1998	− 1.2	21,309	21.5	347,818
1999	2.1	21,756	6.6	370,774
2000	− 1.6	21,408	− 12.6	324,056
2001	− 15.2	18,154	1.6	329,241
2002	− 17.8	14,923	3.5	340,764
2003	14.6	17,102	5.4	359,165
2004	2.1	17,461	2.4	367,785
Average	**1.4%**		**7.3%**	
# Up	**34**		**43**	
# Down	**21**		**12**	
55-Year Gain		**$7,461**		**$357,785**

Best Eight Months Switching Strategy

When we extend our strategy to eight months for NASDAQ and the Russell 2000, both produce consistent gains in May and June.

NASDAQ EIGHT-MONTH SWITCHING STRATEGY

	NASDAQ % Change Jul 1-Oct 31	Investing $10,000	NASDAQ % Change Nov 1-Jun 30	Investing $10,000
1971	− 2.5%	$9,750	23.8%	$12,377
1972	0.1	9,762	− 22.5	9,596
1973	9.1	10,650	− 31.1	6,616
1974	− 14.1	9,146	33.4	8,826
1975	− 11.5	8,092	17.3	10,354
1976	0.0	8,095	10.4	11,429
1977	− 2.2	7,916	23.4	14,099
1978	− 7.6	7,312	24.3	17,526
1979	− 1.9	7,174	16.4	20,403
1980	22.2	8,765	11.9	22,834
1981	− 9.5	7,932	− 12.3	20,034
1982	24.1	9,846	49.9	30,028
1983	− 13.9	8,482	− 12.7	26,211
1984	3.1	8,743	19.9	31,428
1985	− 1.2	8,635	38.6	43,565
1986	− 11.0	7,682	17.7	51,281
1987	− 23.9	5,848	22.1	62,600
1988	− 3.1	5,667	13.8	71,247
1989	4.7	5,932	1.5	72,288
1990	− 28.7	4,232	44.3	104,303
1991	14.1	4,828	3.8	108,264
1992	7.4	5,184	16.3	125,936
1993	10.7	5,739	− 9.4	114,090
1994	10.1	6,320	20.1	136,976
1995	11.0	7,015	14.4	156,670
1996	3.1	7,231	18.1	184,959
1997	10.5	7,991	18.9	219,909
1998	− 6.5	7,471	51.6	333,468
1999	10.4	8,251	33.7	445,846
2000	− 15.0	7,010	− 35.9	285,868
2001	− 21.8	5,484	− 13.4	247,477
2002	− 9.1	4,984	22.0	302,016
2003	19.1	5,934	6.0	320,082
2004	− 3.6	5,723	4.2	333,367
Average	− 0.8%		13.0%	
# Up	16		27	
# Down	18		7	
34-Year Gain (Loss)		($4,277)		$323,367

RUSSELL 2000 EIGHT-MONTH
SWITCHING STRATEGY

	R2K % Change Jul 1-Oct 31	Investing $10,000	R2K % Change Nov 1-Jun 30	Investing $10,000
1979	− 2.2%	$9,776	18.5%	$11,847
1980	26.4	12,357	13.7	13,465
1981	− 11.5	10,935	− 11.5	11,919
1982	25.0	13,673	53.6	18,303
1983	− 12.1	12,021	− 8.1	16,816
1984	2.8	12,353	14.9	19,314
1985	− 1.4	12,181	32.1	25,519
1986	− 9.3	11,053	17.7	30,041
1987	− 28.2	7,934	27.9	38,434
1988	− 2.7	7,722	13.7	43,699
1989	0.0	7,724	0.9	44,109
1990	− 29.7	5,430	41.1	62,216
1991	10.4	5,993	2.0	63,440
1992	5.4	6,319	17.3	74,428
1993	11.1	7,018	− 7.3	69,003
1994	6.1	7,448	11.2	76,744
1995	4.4	7,779	17.0	89,790
1996	− 1.7	7,643	16.4	104,501
1997	9.3	8,354	5.6	110,321
1998	− 17.3	6,907	21.0	133,519
1999	− 6.3	6,469	20.7	161,114
2000	− 3.8	6,224	3.0	165,957
2001	− 16.5	5,198	8.1	179,317
2002	− 19.3	4,196	20.0	215,262
2003	17.8	4,943	12.0	241,058
2004	− 1.3	4,878	9.6	264,128
Average	**− 1.7%**		**14.3%**	
# Up	**11**		**23**	
# Down	**15**		**3**	
26-Year Gain (Loss)		**($5,122)**		**$254,128**

Best Nine Months Switching Strategy

The large cap Russell 1000 index starts its seasonal run one month earlier.

	RUSSELL 1000 NINE-MONTH SWITCHING STRATEGY			
	R1K % Change Jul 1-Sep 30	Investing $10,000	R1K % Change Oct 1-Jun 30	Investing $10,000
1979	6.8%	$10,676	5.4%	$10,536
1980	10.4	11,785	4.5	11,014
1981	− 12.3	10,340	− 6.5	10,302
1982	10.0	11,370	41.4	14,569
1983	− 1.4	11,208	− 10.1	13,103
1984	8.5	12,166	16.7	15,292
1985	− 5.6	11,480	38.5	21,177
1986	− 8.1	10,552	27.2	26,929
1987	5.6	11,145	− 13.9	23,177
1988	− 0.4	11,097	16.5	26,991
1989	9.4	12,145	1.0	27,268
1990	− 15.3	10,290	22.8	33,479
1991	5.3	10,834	5.7	35,379
1992	2.6	11,113	9.3	38,679
1993	2.6	11,397	− 4.4	36,988
1994	4.4	11,896	16.9	43,235
1995	8.3	12,883	14.0	49,282
1996	2.7	13,232	26.2	62,205
1997	8.2	14,313	18.3	73,607
1998	− 10.7	12,780	34.9	99,274
1999	− 7.0	11,888	15.9	115,104
2000	0.4	11,933	− 16.3	96,338
2001	− 15.5	10,084	− 4.2	92,329
2002	− 17.3	8,341	19.8	110,598
2003	2.5	8,553	14.5	126,634
2004	− 2.2	8,361	8.4	137,319
Average	**− 0.3%**		**11.6%**	
# Up	**15**		**20**	
# Down	**11**		**6**	
26-Year Gain (Loss)		**($1,639)**		**$127,319**

MACD-Timing Triples Best Six Months Results
Doubles NASDAQ's Best Eight

Using the simple MACD (Moving Average Convergence Divergence) indicator developed by our friend Gerald Appel to better time entries and exits into and out of the Best Six Months period nearly triples the results.

Sy Harding's *Riding the Bear* dubbed trading our Best Six Months Switching Strategy with MACD triggers the "best mechanical system ever."

Our *Almanac Investor Newsletter* and *Platform* implements this system with quite a degree of success. Starting October 1 we look to catch the market's first hint of an uptrend after the summer doldrums, and beginning April 1 we prepare to exit these seasonal positions as soon as the market falters.

In up-trending markets MACD signals get you in earlier and keep you in longer. But if the market is trending down, entries are delayed until the market turns up and exit points can come a month earlier. Thus, our "Best Six Months" could be lengthened or shortened a month or so.

The results are astounding applying the simple MACD signals. Instead of $10,000 gaining $489,933 over the 55 recent years when invested only during the Best Six Months, the gain nearly tripled to $1,436,723. The $318 loss during the worst six months expanded to a loss of $6,629.

Impressive results for being invested during only 6$^1/_2$ months of the year on average! For the rest of the year you could park in a money market fund, or if a long-term holder, you could write options on your positions (sell call options).

Using the same MACD timing indicators on the NASDAQ as is done for the Dow has enabled us to capture much of October's improved performance, pumping up NASDAQ's results considerably. Over the thirty-four years since NASDAQ began, the gain on the same $10,000 more than doubles to $671,954 and the loss during the four-month void increases to $7,243. Only four sizeable losses occur during the favorable period and the bulk of NASDAQ's bear markets were avoided including the worst of the 2000-2002 bear.

Updated signals are emailed to our monthly *Almanac Investor Newsletter* and *Platform* subscribers as soon as they are triggered. For further information on how the MACD indicator is calculated, dates when signals were given, or for a FREE 2-month trial to our *Almanac Investor Platform*, visit *http://www.hirschorg.com/MACD*.

DJIA BEST SIX MONTHS STRATEGY + TIMING

MACD	Worst 6 Months		MACD	Best 6 Months	
Signal	**May 1-Oct 31***	**Investing**	**Signal**	**Nov 1-Apr 30***	**Investing**
Date	**DJIA**	**% Change**	**$10,000**	**Date**	**DJIA**	**% Change**	**$10,000**
22-Apr-50	213.90	7.3	$10,730	14-Nov-50	229.54	13.3	$11,330
10-May-51	260.07	0.1	10,741	13-Nov-51	260.41	1.9	11,545
5-Apr-52	265.44	1.4	10,891	31-Oct-52	269.23	2.1	11,787
30-Apr-53	274.75	0.2	10,913	23-Oct-53	275.34	17.1	13,803
14-May-54	322.50	13.5	12,386	5-Nov-54	366.00	16.3	16,053
29-Apr-55	425.65	7.7	13,340	21-Oct-55	458.47	13.1	18,156
9-Apr-56	518.52	-6.8	12,433	8-Oct-56	483.38	2.8	18,664
9-May-57	496.76	-12.3	10,904	29-Oct-57	435.76	4.9	19,579
16-May-58	457.10	17.3	12,790	6-Oct-58	536.29	16.7	22,849
5-May-59	625.90	1.6	12,995	6-Oct-59	636.06	-3.1	22,141
22-Apr-60	616.32	-4.9	12,358	7-Oct-60	586.42	16.9	25,883
21-Apr-61	685.26	2.9	12,716	9-Oct-61	705.42	-1.5	25,495
23-Apr-62	694.61	-15.3	10,770	10-Oct-62	588.14	22.4	31,206
1-May-63	719.67	4.3	11,233	18-Oct-63	750.60	9.6	34,202
14-Apr-64	822.95	6.7	11,986	9-Nov-64	878.08	6.2	36,323
19-May-65	932.12	2.6	12,298	26-Oct-65	956.32	-2.5	35,415
2-May-66	931.95	-16.4	10,281	17-Oct-66	778.89	14.3	40,479
12-May-67	890.03	-2.1	10,065	21-Nov-67	870.95	5.5	42,705
8-May-68	918.86	3.4	10,407	14-Oct-68	949.96	0.2	42,790
21-May-69	951.78	-11.9	9,169	16-Oct-69	838.77	-6.7	39,923
15-Apr-70	782.60	-1.4	9,041	6-Nov-70	771.97	20.8	48,227
3-May-71	932.41	-11.0	8,046	29-Nov-71	829.73	15.4	55,654
24-Apr-72	957.48	-0.6	7,998	25-Oct-72	951.38	-1.4	54,875
26-Apr-73	937.76	-11.0	7,118	11-Dec-73	834.18	0.1	54,930
26-Apr-74	834.64	-22.4	5,524	10-Oct-74	648.08	28.2	70,420
1-May-75	830.96	0.1	5,530	17-Oct-75	832.18	18.5	83,448
5-May-76	986.46	-3.4	5,342	28-Oct-76	952.63	-3.0	80,945
27-Apr-77	923.76	-11.4	4,733	31-Oct-77	818.35	0.5	81,350
9-May-78	822.07	-4.5	4,520	14-Nov-78	785.26	9.3	88,916
17-Apr-79	857.93	-5.3	4,280	5-Nov-79	812.63	7.0	95,140
20-Jun-80	869.71	9.3	4,678	10-Oct-80	950.68	4.7	99,612
1-May-81	995.59	-14.6	3,995	14-Oct-81	850.65	0.4	100,010
4-May-82	854.45	15.5	4,614	8-Oct-82	986.85	23.5	123,512
13-May-83	1218.75	2.5	4,729	21-Oct-83	1248.88	-7.3	114,496
11-May-84	1157.14	3.3	4,885	17-Oct-84	1195.89	3.9	118,961
1-May-85	1242.05	7.0	5,227	4-Oct-85	1328.74	38.1	164,285
25-Apr-86	1835.57	-2.8	5,081	6-Oct-86	1784.45	28.2	210,613
13-Apr-87	2287.07	-14.9	4,324	4-Nov-87	1945.29	3.0	216,931
10-May-88	2003.65	6.1	4,588	12-Oct-88	2126.24	11.8	242,529
8-May-89	2376.47	9.8	5,038	14-Nov-89	2610.25	3.3	250,532
20-Apr-90	2695.95	-6.7	4,700	22-Oct-90	2516.09	15.8	290,116
26-Apr-91	2912.38	4.8	4,926	17-Oct-91	3053.00	11.3	322,899
11-May-92	3397.58	-6.2	4,621	21-Oct-92	3187.10	6.6	344,210
26-Apr-93	3398.37	5.5	4,875	7-Oct-93	3583.63	5.6	363,486
13-Jun-94	3783.12	3.7	5,055	17-Oct-94	3923.93	13.1	411,103
23-May-95	4436.44	7.2	5,419	23-Oct-95	4755.48	16.7	479,757
17-Apr-96	5549.93	9.2	5,918	17-Oct-96	6059.20	21.9	584,824
27-May-97	7383.41	3.6	6,131	18-Nov-97	7650.82	18.5	693,016
24-Apr-98	9064.62	-12.4	5,371	13-Oct-98	7938.14	39.9	969,529
13-May-99	11107.19	-6.4	5,027	20-Oct-99	10392.36	5.1	1,018,975
13-Apr-00	10923.55	-6.0	4,725	23-Oct-00	10271.72	5.4	1,074,000
11-May-01	10821.31	-17.3	3,908	2-Oct-01	8950.59	15.8	1,243,692
1-Apr-02	10362.70	-25.2	2,923	2-Oct-02	7755.61	6.0	1,318,314
10-Apr-03	8221.33	16.4	3,402	3-Oct-03	9572.31	7.8	1,421,142
20-Apr-04	10314.50	-0.9	3,371	4-Oct-04	10216.54	1.8	1,446,723
1-Apr-05	10404.30						
	55-Year Loss		**($6,629)**		**55-Year Gain**		**$1,436,723**

*MACD generated entry and exit points (earlier or later) can lengthen or shorten six-month periods

NASDAQ BEST EIGHT MONTHS STRATEGY + TIMING

MACD Signal Date	Worst 4 Months July 1-Oct 31* NASDAQ	% Change	Investing $10,000	MACD Signal Date	Best 8 Months Nov 1-June 30* NASDAQ	% Change	Investing $10,000
22-Jul-71	109.54	− 3.6	$9,640	4-Nov-71	105.56	24.1	$12,410
7-Jun-72	131.00	− 1.8	9,466	23-Oct-72	128.66	−22.7	9,593
25-Jun-73	99.43	− 7.2	8,784	7-Dec-73	92.32	−20.2	7,655
3-Jul-74	73.66	−23.2	6,746	7-Oct-74	56.57	47.8	11,314
11-Jun-75	83.60	− 9.2	6,125	7-Oct-75	75.88	20.8	13,667
22-Jul-76	91.66	− 2.4	5,978	19-Oct-76	89.45	13.2	15,471
27-Jul-77	101.25	− 4.0	5,739	4-Nov-77	97.21	26.6	19,586
7-Jun-78	123.10	− 6.5	5,366	6-Nov-78	115.08	19.1	23,327
3-Jul-79	137.03	− 1.1	5,307	30-Oct-79	135.48	15.5	26,943
20-Jun-80	156.51	26.2	6,697	9-Oct-80	197.53	11.2	29,961
4-Jun-81	219.68	−17.6	5,518	1-Oct-81	181.09	− 4.0	28,763
7-Jun-82	173.84	12.5	6,208	7-Oct-82	195.59	57.4	45,273
1-Jun-83	307.95	−10.7	5,544	3-Nov-83	274.86	−14.2	38,844
1-Jun-84	235.90	5.0	5,821	15-Oct-84	247.67	17.3	45,564
3-Jun-85	290.59	− 3.0	5,646	1-Oct-85	281.77	39.4	63,516
10-Jun-86	392.83	−10.3	5,064	1-Oct-86	352.34	20.5	76,537
30-Jun-87	424.67	−22.7	3,914	2-Nov-87	328.33	20.1	91,921
8-Jul-88	394.33	-6.6	3,656	29-Nov-88	368.15	22.4	112,511
13-Jun-89	450.73	0.7	3,682	9-Nov-89	454.07	1.9	114,649
11-Jun-90	462.79	−23.0	2,835	2-Oct-90	356.39	39.3	159,706
11-Jun-91	496.62	6.4	3,016	1-Oct-91	528.51	7.4	171,524
11-Jun-92	567.68	1.5	3,061	14-Oct-92	576.22	20.5	206,686
7-Jun-93	694.61	9.9	3,364	1-Oct-93	763.23	− 4.4	197,592
17-Jun-94	729.35	5.0	3,532	11-Oct-94	765.57	13.5	224,267
1-Jun-95	868.82	17.2	4,140	13-Oct-95	1018.38	21.6	272,709
3-Jun-96	1238.73	1.0	4,181	7-Oct-96	1250.87	10.3	300,798
4-Jun-97	1379.67	24.4	5,201	3-Oct-97	1715.87	1.8	306,212
1-Jun-98	1746.82	− 7.8	4,795	15-Oct-98	1611.01	49.7	458,399
1-Jun-99	2412.03	18.5	5,682	6-Oct-99	2857.21	35.7	622,047
29-Jun-00	3877.23	−18.2	4,648	18-Oct-00	3171.56	−32.2	421,748
1-Jun-01	2149.44	−31.1	3,202	1-Oct-01	1480.46	5.5	444,944
3-Jun-02	1562.56	−24.0	2,434	2-Oct-02	1187.30	38.5	616,247
20-Jun-03	1644.72	15.1	2,802	6-Oct-03	1893.46	4.3	642,746
21-Jun-04	1974.38	− 1.6	2,757	1-Oct-04	1942.20	6.1	681,954
8-Jun-05	2060.18						
	34-Year Loss		**($7,243)**		**34-Year Gain**		**$671,954**

* MACD generated entry and exit points (earlier or later) can lengthen or shorten eight-month periods

Aura of the Triple Witch:
Fourth Quarter Most Bullish, Down Weeks
Trigger More Weakness Week After

Options expire the third Friday of every month but in March, June, September, and December a powerful coven gathers. Since the S&P index futures began trading on April 21, 1982, stock options, index options as well as index futures all expire at the same time four times each year — known as Triple Witching. Traders have long sought to understand and master the magic of this quarterly phenomenon.

The market is still small for fledgling single-stock futures (160 at this writing) so we do not believe the term "quadruple witching" is applicable just yet.

We have analyzed what the market does prior, during and following Triple Witching expirations in search of consistent trading patterns. This is never easy. For as soon as a pattern becomes obvious, the market almost always starts to anticipate it, and the pattern tends to shift.

To help investors summon an edge and hopefully increased profits while warding off losses we shed some light on the mystical conjurations of Triple Witching patterns and seasonalities.

Increased volatility and trading volume across the equity exchanges is often associated with Triple Witching—the Friday of expiration and the days leading up to it and after. We have analyzed what the market does prior, during and following Triple Witching expirations in search of consistent trading patterns. This is never easy. For as soon as a pattern becomes obvious, the market almost always tends to anticipate them and the pattern tends to shift. These are some of our findings of how the Dow Jones Industrials perform around Triple Witching time.

Triple-Witching Weeks have become more bullish since 1991, except in the second quarter. The weeks following Triple-Witching Weeks have become more bearish. Since Q1 2000 only six of twenty were up and four occurred in December. Triple-Witching Weeks have tended to be down in flat periods and dramatically so during the 2000-2002 bear market.

Down weeks tend to follow down Triple-Witching Weeks. This is a most interesting pattern. Since 1991, of twenty down Triple-Witching Weeks, sixteen following weeks were also down. This is surprising inasmuch as the previous decade had an exactly opposite pattern: There were 13 down Triple-Witching Weeks then, but 12 up weeks followed them.

When we break down Triple Witching Weeks quarter by quarter an even clearer pattern emerges. You can clearly see in the accompanying table that Triple Witching Weeks in the second and third quarter (Worst Six Months May through October) are much weaker and the weeks following, horrendous. But in the first and fourth quarter (Best Six Months period November through April) a solid bullish bias is evident.

It's not coincidental to us that these strong Triple Witches occur during our

Best Six Months period November through April while Triple Witching is rather dismal in the Worst Six months May through October.

Since 1991, second quarter Triple-Witching Weeks have been up eight times and down seven. Following weeks were atrocious, down thirteen and up only twice. One up week followed the Six up Triple-Witching Weeks whereas six down weeks followed seven down Triple-Witching Weeks.

Third quarter Triple-Witching Weeks were slightly better, up eight of the last fourteen times. But weeks following Triple Witching were down eleven of the last fourteen. Two up weeks followed the eight up Triple-Witching Weeks and five down weeks followed the six down Triple-Witching Weeks.

The tables turn dramatically in the first and fourth quarters. First quarter Triple-Witching Weeks perform quite well up ten of the last fifteen but weeks following have been down eleven times. Three up weeks followed the ten up Triple-Witching Weeks and four down weeks followed the five down Triple-Witching Weeks.

Fourth quarter Triple Witching has proved to be the most favorable. Triple-Witching Week was up twelve of the last fourteen times and the following was up eleven of fifteen times. Ten up weeks followed the twelve up Triple-Witching Weeks and one down week followed the two down Triple-Witching Weeks.

TRIPLE-WITCHING WEEK & WEEK AFTER DOW POINT CHANGES

	Expiration Week Q1	Week After	Expiration Week Q2	Week After	Expiration Week Q3	Week After	Expiration Week Q4	Week After
1991	− 6.93	− 89.36	− 34.98	− 58.81	33.54	− 13.19	20.12	167.04
1992	40.48	− 44.95	− 69.01	− 2.94	21.35	− 76.73	9.19	12.97
1993	43.76	− 31.60	− 10.24	− 3.88	− 8.38	− 70.14	10.90	6.15
1994	32.95	−120.92	3.33	−139.84	58.54	−101.60	116.08	26.24
1995	38.04	65.02	86.80	75.05	96.85	− 33.42	19.87	− 78.76
1996	114.52	51.67	55.78	− 50.60	49.94	− 15.54	179.53	76.51
1997	−130.67	− 64.20	14.47	−108.79	174.30	4.91	− 82.01	− 76.98
1998	303.91	−110.35	−122.07	231.67	100.16	133.11	81.87	314.36
1999	27.20	− 81.31	365.05	−303.00	− 224.80	−524.30	32.73	148.33
2000	666.41	517.49	−164.76	− 44.55	− 293.65	− 79.63	−277.95	200.60
2001	−821.21	−318.63	−353.36	− 19.05	−1369.70	611.75	224.19	101.65
2002	34.74	−179.56	−220.42	− 10.53	− 326.67	−284.57	77.61	−207.54
2003	662.26	−376.20	83.63	−211.70	173.27	−331.74	236.06	46.45
2004	− 53.48	26.37	6.31	− 44.57	− 28.61	−237.22	106.70	177.20
2005	−144.69	−186.80	110.44	−325.23				
Up	10	4	8	2	8	3	12	11
Down	5	11	7	13	6	11	2	3

Annual Trading Volume Patterns

With our Best Six Months Strategy and the old saw, "Sell in May and go away" in mind, the inquiring mind is forced to ask "Why?" Changes in average daily trading volume may provide some insight.

We refer to the summer months as the doldrums due to the anemic volume and uninspired trading on Wall Street. The individual investor, if looking to sell a stock, is generally met with disinterest from the street. It becomes very difficult to sell a stock at a good price. That is also why we recommend taking advantage of any summer rally as soon as you recognize it because the rally is often short lived and followed by a sharp correction.

The chart of the NYSE Volume One-Year Seasonal Pattern from 1965 to 2004 is overlaid with 2005's average daily volume pattern at press time. The lines are calculated by taking difference between the volume for each trading day and the average daily volume for the year. If a trading day has been historically heavier than the average for the year, then it is above the zero line, if it has been a light trading day historically, it falls below.

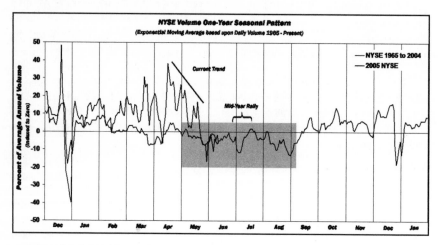

Note the shaded box. These are the summer doldrums. Beginning in May, the historical trend line is predominantly below the zero line illustrating the light trading days.

It is also of note that the mid-year rally we discussed earlier is the only time, historically, that there has been any real interest on The Street during summertime. This is made clear by the brief transient the historical trend line makes above the zero line in the middle of July.

When comparing 2005 volume to the historical trend, there is going to be amplification due the huge increase in average daily volume. In 1965, the average daily volume was about 6.27 **million**. 2005's average has been 1.54 **billion** so the points are not going to line up. The important part of the comparison is the trend, not the level. Notice how from January to March volume was strong while the market was going up. There was a huge volume crescendo in the middle of April corresponding to tax day. From that point on, volume and the market has drifted lower. May started off strong, but there hasn't been a day over the zero line since May 19.

The historical NASDAQ Volume chart has 2003 laid over. Recall that in 2003 there was a major summer rally. Note how the summer volume in 2003 towers over the historical norms.

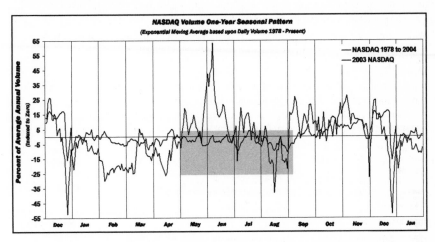

Summer markets tend to drift along until Labor day much like a sailing ship caught in the belt of calms and light winds between the northern and southern trade winds of the Atlantic and Pacific that the sailors of old first dubbed the doldrums. Major deviations from the historical norms can signal a real "summer rally."

The December Low indicator: a Useful Prognosticating Tool

When the Dow closes below its December closing low in the first quarter, it is frequently an excellent warning sign. Jeffrey Saut, managing director of investment strategy at Raymond James, brought this to our attention a few years ago.

The December Low Indicator was originated by Lucien Hooper, a Forbes columnist and Wall Street analyst back in the 1970s. Hooper dismissed the importance of January and January's first week as reliable indicators. He noted that the trend could be random or even manipulated during a holiday-shortened week. Instead, said Hooper, "Pay much more attention to the December low. If that low is violated during the first quarter of the New Year, watch out!"

To make things more clear, we produced two tables. One shows results when the indicator gave a warning—a new first quarter low on a closing basis. The other table shows the history when December's low held.

The results are fairly impressive. To be fair we calculated what happened each year subsequent to a signal as well as the change for the year as a whole. In only one case did the full-year drop and the partial year rise—and negligibly at that.

Since 1950 the December Low Indicator has given twenty-six warning signals. Twelve of the twenty-six occurrences were followed by gains for the rest of the year — and full-year gains — after the low for the year was reached. Fourteen of them were correct, which may not seem good until you consider that the market is rising some 70% of the time.

For perspective we've included the January Barometer readings for the selected years. Hooper's "Watch Out" warning was absolutely correct, though. All but one of the instances since 1952 experienced further declines, as the Dow fell an additional 10.7% on average when December's low was breached in Q1.

Both indicators were wrong only three times and three years ended flat. If the December low is not crossed, turn to our January Barometer for guidance. It has been virtually perfect, right nearly 100% of these times. Used in conjunction with our January Barometer, the December indicator looks even more valuable.

YEARS DOW FELL BELOW DECEMBER LOW IN FIRST QUARTER

Year	Previous Dec Low	Date Crossed	Crossing Price	Subseq. Low	% Change Cross-Low	Rest of Year % Change	Full Year % Change	Jan Bar
1952	262.29	2/19/52	261.37	256.35	— 1.9%	11.7%	8.4%	1.6%[2]
1953	281.63	2/11/53	281.57	255.49	— 9.3	— 0.2	— 3.8	— 0.7
1956	480.72	1/9/56	479.74	462.35	— 3.6	4.1	2.3	— 3.6[2 3]
1957	480.61	1/18/57	477.46	419.79	— 12.1	— 8.7	— 12.8	— 4.2
1960	661.29	1/12/60	660.43	566.05	— 14.3	— 6.7	— 9.3	— 7.1
1962	720.10	1/5/62	714.84	535.76	— 25.1	— 8.8	— 10.8	— 3.8
1966	939.53	3/1/66	938.19	744.32	— 20.7	— 16.3	— 18.9	0.5[1]
1968	879.16	1/22/68	871.71	825.13	— 5.3	8.3	4.3	— 4.4[1 2]
1969	943.75	1/6/69	936.66	769.93	— 17.8	— 14.6	— 15.2	— 0.8
1970	769.93	1/26/70	768.88	631.16	— 17.9	9.1	4.8	— 7.6[2 3]
1973	1000.00	1/29/73	996.46	788.31	— 20.9	— 14.6	— 16.6	— 1.7
1977	946.64	2/7/77	946.31	800.85	— 15.4	— 12.2	— 17.3	— 5.1
1978	806.22	1/5/78	804.92	742.12	— 7.8	0.0	— 3.1	— 6.2
1980	819.62	3/10/80	818.94	759.13	— 7.3	17.7	14.9	5.8[2]
1982	868.25	1/5/82	865.30	776.92	— 10.2	20.9	19.6	— 1.8[1 2]
1984	1236.79	1/25/84	1231.89	1086.57	— 11.8	— 1.6	— 3.7	— 0.9[3]
1990	2687.93	1/15/90	2669.37	2365.10	— 11.4	— 1.3	— 4.3	— 6.9
1991	2565.59	1/7/91	2522.77	2470.30	— 2.1	25.6	20.3	4.2[2]
1993	3255.18	1/8/93	3251.67	3241.95	— 0.3	15.5	13.7	0.7[2]
1994	3697.08	3/30/94	3626.75	3593.35	— 0.9	5.7	2.1	3.3[2 3]
1996	5059.32	1/10/96	5032.94	5032.94	0.0	28.1	26.0	3.3[2]
1998	7660.13	1/9/98	7580.42	7539.07	— 0.5	21.1	16.1	1.0[2]
2000	10998.39	1/4/00	10997.93	9796.03	— 10.9	— 1.9	— 6.2	— 5.1
2001	10318.93	3/12/01	10208.25	8235.81	— 19.3	— 1.8	— 7.1	3.5[1]
2002	9763.96	1/16/02	9712.27	7286.27	— 25.0	— 14.1	— 16.8	— 1.6
2003	8303.78	1/24/03	8131.01	7524.06	— 7.5	28.6	25.3	— 2.7[1 2]
2005	10440.58	1/21/05	10392.99	10071.25	— 3.1	*At Presstime – not in average*		
				Average Drop	**— 10.7%**			

[1] January Barometer wrong   [2] December Low Indicator wrong   [3] Year Flat

Only three significant drops occurred when December's low was not breached in Q1 (1974, 1981, and 1987). The January Barometer was virtually perfect when we did not cross the December low. The only minor discrepancy was in 1992 when the January Barometer was slightly negative and the Dow for the year was virtually flat. Hooper's indicator had two major errors 1974 and 1981, which the January Barometer predicted perfectly.

YEARS DOW DID NOT FALL BELOW ITS DECEMBER LOW IN Q1

Year	Previous Dec Low	Q1 Low	Rest of Year % Change	Full Year % Change	Jan Bar
1950	192.71	196.81	19.6%	17.6%	1.7%
1951	222.33	238.99	12.7	14.4	6.1
1954	278.30	279.87	44.5	44.0	5.1
1955	384.04	388.20	25.8	20.8	1.8
1958	425.65	436.89	33.6	34.0	4.3
1959	556.08	574.46	18.3	16.4	0.4
1961	593.49	610.25	19.8	18.7	6.3
1963	640.14	646.79	18.0	17.0	4.9
1964	751.82	766.08	14.1	14.6	2.7
1965	857.45	869.78	11.4	10.9	3.3
1967	785.69	786.41	15.1	15.2	7.8
1971	794.29	830.57	7.2	6.1	4.0
1972	846.01	889.15	14.7	14.6	1.8
1974	788.31	803.90	— 23.3	— 27.6	— 1.0
1975	577.60	632.04	34.9	38.3	12.3
1976	818.80	858.71	17.0	17.9	11.8
1979	787.51	807.00	3.9	4.2	4.0
1981	908.45	931.57	— 6.1	— 9.2	— 4.6
1983	990.25	1027.04	22.6	20.3	3.3
1985	1163.21	1184.96	30.5	27.7	7.4
1986	1457.91	1502.29	26.2	22.6	0.2
1987	1895.95	1927.31	0.6	2.3	13.2
1988	1766.74	1879.14	15.4	11.8	4.0
1989	2092.28	2144.64	28.4	27.0	7.1
1992	2863.82	3172.41	4.1	4.2	— 2.0
1995	3685.73	3832.08	33.5	33.5	2.4
1997	6268.35	6442.49	22.8	22.6	6.1
1999	8695.60	9120.67	26.1	25.2	4.1
2004	9853.64	10048.23	7.3	3.1	1.7

THE FOUR-YEAR PRESIDENTIAL ELECTION/STOCK MARKET CYCLE

For four decades, the *Stock Trader's Almanac* has discussed—and demonstrated—the importance of the Four-Year Presidential Election/Stock Market Cycle. The *Almanac Investor Platform* website *stocktradersalamanac.com* has a navigation system designed around the Presidential Election Cycle that breaks out the performance of the Dow Jones Industrial for every president since McKinley. Readers of this books are entitled to a Free 60-Day Trial to our *Almanac Investor Platform*.

But first, let's get one thing straight. Yes we are strong proponents of historical and seasonal market patterns but we are fully aware that history never repeats exactly. We use history as a guide for navigating current market conditions and predicting significant future trends with quite a degree of reliability over the years.

The four-year Presidential Election/Stock Market Cycle is the "Old Faithful" of indicators for us. What we try to get Almanac Investors to do is not necessarily follow historical patterns to a tee but to keep them in mind so you know when your radar should perk up.

The 172-Year Saga Continues

This pattern is most compelling. The entire four-year pattern back to Jackson's first administration is detailed at a glance in the following table. It is no mere coincidence that the last two years (pre-election year and election year) of the 43 administrations since 1833 produced a total net market gain of 745.9%, dwarfing the 227.6% gain of the first two years of these administrations.

Presidential elections every four years have a profound impact on the economy and the stock market. Wars, recessions, and bear markets tend to start or occur in the first half of the term; prosperous times and bull markets, in the latter half. Notice the greatest gains in the third years of presidents' terms with weakness in the first two years.

In an effort to gain reelection, presidents tend to take care of most of their more painful initiatives in the first half of their term and "prime the pump" in the second half so the electorate is most prosperous when they enter the voting booths. A good number of these midterm bottoms occur during the worst six months. After nine straight annual Dow gains during the millennial bull, the four-year election cycle appears to be back on track. The years 2001 through 2004 are a textbook example.

STOCK MARKET ACTION SINCE 1833
Annual % Change In Dow Jones Industrial Average[1]

4-Year Cycle Beginning	Elected President	Post-Election Year	Mid-Term Year	Pre-Election Year	Election Year
1833	Jackson (D)	− 0.9	13.0	3.1	− 11.7
1837	Van Buren (D)	− 11.5	1.6	− 12.3	5.5
1841*	W.H. Harrison (W)**	− 13.3	− 18.1	45.0	15.5
1845*	Polk (D)	8.1	− 14.5	1.2	− 3.6
1849*	Taylor (W)	N/C	18.7	− 3.2	19.6
1853*	Pierce (D)	− 12.7	− 30.2	1.5	4.4
1857	Buchanan (D)	− 31.0	14.3	− 10.7	14.0
1861*	Lincoln (R)	− 1.8	55.4	38.0	6.4
1865	Lincoln (R)**	− 8.5	3.6	1.6	10.8
1869	Grant (R)	1.7	5.6	7.3	6.8
1873	Grant (R)	− 12.7	2.8	− 4.1	− 17.9
1877	Hayes (R)	− 9.4	6.1	43.0	18.7
1881	Garfield (R)**	3.0	− 2.9	− 8.5	− 18.8
1885*	Cleveland (D)	20.1	12.4	− 8.4	4.8
1889*	B. Harrison (R)	5.5	− 14.1	17.6	− 6.6
1893*	Cleveland (D)	− 24.6	− 0.6	2.3	− 1.7
1897*	McKinley (R)	21.3	22.5	9.2	7.0
1901	McKinley (R)**	− 8.7	− 0.4	− 23.6	41.7
1905	T. Roosevelt (R)	38.2	− 1.9	− 37.7	46.6
1909	Taft (R)	15.0	− 17.9	0.4	7.6
1913*	Wilson (D)	− 10.3	− 5.4	81.7	− 4.2
1917	Wilson (D)	− 21.7	10.5	30.5	− 32.9
1921*	Harding (R)**	12.7	21.7	− 3.3	26.2
1925	Coolidge (R)	30.0	0.3	28.8	48.2
1929	Hoover (R)	− 17.2	− 33.8	− 52.7	− 23.1
1933*	F. Roosevelt (D)	66.7	4.1	38.5	24.8
1937	F. Roosevelt (D)	− 32.8	28.1	− 2.9	− 12.7
1941	F. Roosevelt (D)	− 15.4	7.6	13.8	12.1
1945	F. Roosevelt (D)**	26.6	− 8.1	2.2	− 2.1
1949	Truman (D)	12.9	17.6	14.4	8.4
1953*	Eisenhower (R)	− 3.8	44.0	20.8	2.3
1957	Eisenhower (R)	− 12.8	34.0	16.4	− 9.3
1961*	Kennedy (D)**	18.7	− 10.8	17.0	14.6
1965	Johnson (D)	10.9	− 18.9	15.2	4.3
1969*	Nixon (R)	− 15.2	4.8	6.1	14.6
1973	Nixon (R)***	− 16.6	− 27.6	38.3	17.9
1977*	Carter (D)	− 17.3	− 3.1	4.2	14.9
1981*	Reagan (R)	− 9.2	19.6	20.3	− 3.7
1985	Reagan (R)	27.7	22.6	2.3	11.8
1989	G. H. W. Bush (R)	27.0	− 4.3	20.3	4.2
1993*	Clinton (D)	13.7	2.1	33.5	26.0
1997	Clinton (D)	22.6	16.1	25.2	− 6.2
2001*	G. W. Bush (R)	− 7.1	− 16.8	25.3	3.1
Total % Gain		67.9 %	159.7%	457.6%	288.3%
Average % Gain		1.6 %	3.7%	10.6%	6.7%
# Up		19	25	32	29
# Down		23	18	11	14

*Party in power ousted   **Death in office   ***Resigned   D—Democrat, W—Whig, R—Republican

[1] Based on annual close; Prior to 1886 based on Cowles and other indices; 12 Mixed Stocks, 10 Rails, 2 Inds 1886-1889; 20 Mixed Stocks, 18 Rails, 2 Inds 1890-1896; Railroad average 1897 (First industrial average published May 26, 1896)

How the Government Manipulates the Economy to Stay in Power

The "making of presidents" is accompanied by an unsubtle manipulation of the economy. Incumbent administrations are duty-bound to retain the reins of power. Subsequently, the "piper must be paid," producing what we have coined the "Post-Presidential Year Syndrome." Most big, bad bear markets began in such years—1929, 1937, 1957, 1969, 1973, 1977, and 1981. Our major wars also began in years following elections—Civil War (1861), WWI (1917), WWII (1941), and Vietnam (1965). Post-election 2001 combined with 2002 for the worst back-to-back years since 1973-1974 (also first and second years). Plus we had 9/11, the war on terror, and the build-up to confrontation with Iraq.

Some cold, hard facts to prove economic manipulation appeared in a book by Edward R. Tufte, *Political Control of the Economy* (Princeton University Press). Stimulative fiscal measures designed to increase per capita disposable income, providing a sense of well-being to the voting public, included: increases in federal budget deficits, government spending and social security benefits; interest rate reductions on government loans; and speed-ups of projected funding.

Federal Spending: During 1962-1973, the average increase was 29% higher in election years than in non-election years.

Social Security: There were nine increases during the 1952-1974 period. Half of the six election-year increases became effective in September eight weeks before Election Day. The average increase was 100% higher in presidential than in midterm election years.

Real Disposable Income: Accelerated in all but one election year between 1947 and 1973 (excluding the Eisenhower years). Only one of the remaining odd-numbered years (1973) showed a marked acceleration.

These moves were obviously not coincidences and explain why we tend to have a political (four-year) stock market cycle.

Under Reagan we paid the piper in 1981 and 1982 followed by eight straight years of expansion. However, we ran up a larger deficit than the total deficit of the previous 200 years of our national existence.

Alan Greenspan took over the Fed from Paul Volker August 11, 1987, and was able to keep the economy rolling until an exogenous event in the Persian Gulf pushed us into a real recession in August 1990 which lasted long enough to choke off the Bush re-election effort in 1992. Three other incumbents in this century failed to retain power: Taft in 1912 when the Republican Party split in two; Hoover in 1932 in the depths of the Great Depression; and Carter in 1980 during the Iran Hostage Crisis.

Bill Clinton, warts and all, presided for two terms over the incredible economic expansion and market gains of the nineties. Mr. Clinton was keen to have former Goldman Sachs chief, Robert Rubin, run the treasury for a stretch, helping his administration create a smooth and beneficial relationship with Wall Street, Main Street, and the Fed.

George W. Bush adeptly navigated the country through recession, the most excruciating bear market since the 1970s, and military action in the first two years of his first administration (2001-2002). Quick initial success in Iraq and major tax cuts, including a bone to Wall Street in a dividend tax cut helped stimulate the economy and the stock market in pre-election year 2003. We would not be surprised if the first two years of President Bush's second term (2005-2006) contained a recession and bear market and perhaps the low for the twenty-first century.

Gridlock on Capitol Hill Is Best for the Markets

There are six possible scenarios on Capitol Hill: Republican President with a Republican Congress, Republican President with a Democratic Congress, Republican President with a split Congress, Democratic President with a Democratic Congress, Democratic President with a Republican Congress, and a Democratic President with a split Congress.

First looking at just the historical performance of the Dow under the Democratic and Republican Presidents, we see a pattern that is contrary to popular belief. Under a Democrat, the Dow has performed much better than under a Republican. The Dow has historically returned 9.1% under the Democrats compared to only a 6.3% return under a Republican executive.

The results are the opposite with a Republican Congress, yielding an average 10.2% gain in the Dow compared to a 7.8% return when the Democrats have control of the Hill.

With total Republican control of Washington, the Dow has been up on average 9.7%. Democrats in power over the two branches have fared a bit worse with 8.4% gains. When power is split, with a Republican President and a Democratic Congress, the Dow has not done very well, averaging only a 6.8% gain. The best scenario for all investors is a Democrat in the White House and Republican control of Congress with average gains of 11.5%. The most of dire circumstance

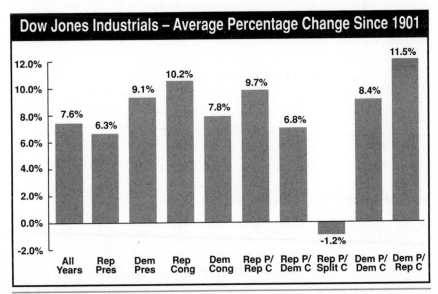

Dow Jones Industrials – Average Percentage Change Since 1901

occurs with a Republican President and a split Congress, averaging a net loss of 1.2%. There has never been a Democratic President and a split Congress. 2003's 25.3% gain boosted market gains for Republican controlled governments.

Post-Election Years: Paying the Piper

Politics being what it is, incumbent administrations during election years try to make the economy look good to impress the electorate and tend to put off unpopular decisions until the votes are counted. This produces an American phenomenon—the Post-Election Year Syndrome. The year begins with an Inaugural Ball, after which the piper must be paid, and we Americans have often paid dearly in the past 91 years.

Victorious candidates rarely succeed in fulfilling campaign promises of "peace and prosperity." In the past 23 Post-Election years, three major wars began: World War I (1917), World War II (1941), and Vietnam (1965); four drastic bear markets started in 1929, 1937, 1969, and 1973; 9/11, a recession and a continuing bear market (2001); and less severe bear markets occurred or were in progress in 1913, 1917, 1921, 1941, 1949, 1953, 1957, 1977, and 1981. Only in 1925, 1989, 1993, and 1997 were Americans blessed with peace and prosperity.

THE RECORD SINCE 1913

1913 Wilson (D)	Minor bear market.
1917 Wilson (D)	World War I and a bear market.
1921 Harding (R)	Post-war depression and bear market.
1925 Coolidge (R)	Peace and prosperity. Hallelujah!
1929 Hoover (R)	Worst market crash in history until 1987.
1933 Roosevelt (D)	Devaluation, bank failures, depression still on but market strong.
1937 Roosevelt (D)	Another crash, 20% unemployment rate.
1941 Roosevelt (D)	World War II and a continuing bear.
1945 Roosevelt (D)	Post-war industrial contraction, strong market precedes 1946 crash.
1949 Truman (D)	Minor bear market.
1953 Eisenhower (R)	Minor post-war (Korea) bear market.
1957 Eisenhower (R)	Major bear market.
1961 Kennedy (D)	Bay of Pigs fiasco, strong market precedes 1962 crash.
1965 Johnson (D)	Vietnam escalation. Bear came in 1966.
1969 Nixon (R)	Start of worst bear market since 1937.
1973 Nixon, Ford (R)	Start of worst bear market since 1929.
1977 Carter (D)	Bear market in blue chip stocks.
1981 Reagan (R)	Bear strikes again.
1985 Reagan (R)	No bear in sight.
1989 Bush (R)	Effect of 1987 Crash wears off.
1993 Clinton (D)	S&P up 7.1%, next year off 1.5%.
1997 Clinton (D)	S&P up 31.0%, next year up 26.7%.
2001 Bush, GW (R)	9/11, recession, worst bear market since 1929 takes hold.

Republicans took back the White House following foreign involvements under the Democrats in 1921 (World War I), 1953 (Korea), 1969 (Vietnam), and 1981 (Iran); and a scandal (2001). Bear markets occurred during all or part of these post-election years.

Democrats recaptured power after domestic problems under the Republicans: in 1913 (GOP split in two), 1933 (Crash and depression), 1961 (recession), 1977 (Watergate), and 1993 (sluggish economy). Democratic post-election years after resuming power were bearish following a Republican Party squabble or scandal and bullish following bad economic times.

Under Democrats $10,000 Grows to $279,705 but Only to $80,466 Under the Republicans

Does the market perform better under Republicans or Democrats? The market surge under Reagan and Bush after Vietnam, OPEC, and Iran inflation almost helped Republicans even up the score in the twentieth century versus the Democrats, who benefited when Roosevelt came in following an 89.2% drop by the Dow. However, under Clinton, the Democrats took the lead again. Both parties were more evenly matched in the last half of the century.

THE STOCK MARKET UNDER REPUBLICANS AND DEMOCRATS

Republican Eras		% Change	Democratic Eras		% Change
1901-1912	12 Years	48.3%	1913-1920	8 Years	29.2%
1921-1932	12 Years	− 24.5%	1933-1952	20 Years	318.4%
1953-1960	8 Years	121.2%	1961-1968	8 Years	58.3%
1969-1976	8 Years	2.1%	1977-1980	4 Years	− 3.0%
1981-1992	12 Years	247.0%	1993-2000	8 Years	236.7%
2001-2004	4 Years	− 8.4%			
Totals	**56 Years**	**383.7%**	**Totals**	**48 Years**	**639.6%**
Average Annual Change 6.9%			**Average Annual Change 13.3%**		

A $10,000 investment compounded during Democratic eras would have grown to $279,705 in 48 years. The same investment during 56 Republican years would have appreciated to $80,466. After lagging for many years, performance under the Republicans improved under Reagan and Bush. But under Clinton, Democratic performance surged way ahead.

Adjusting stock market performance for loss of purchasing power reduced the Democrats' $279,705 to $33,426 and the Republicans' $80,466 to $26,550.

DECLINE OF THE DOLLAR UNDER REPUBLICANS AND DEMOCRATS

Republican Eras		Loss in Purch. Power	Value of Dollar	Democratic Eras		Loss in Purch. Power	Value of Dollar
1901-1912	12 Years	− 23.6%	$0.76	1913-1920	8 Years	− 51.4%	$0.49
1921-1932	12 Years	+ 46.9%	$1.12	1933-1952	20 Years	− 48.6%	$0.25
1953-1960	8 Years	− 10.2%	$1.01	1961-1968	8 Years	− 15.0%	$0.21
1969-1976	8 Years	− 38.9%	$0.62	1977-1980	4 Years	− 30.9%	$0.15
1981-1992	12 Years	− 41.3%	$0.36	1993-2000	8 Years	− 18.5%	$0.12
2001-2004	4 Years	− 8.8%	$0.33				
The Republican Dollar declined to $0.33 in 56 years.				**The Democratic Dollar declined to $0.12 in 48 years.**			

Republicans may point out that all four major wars of the twentieth century began while the Democrats were in power. Democrats can counter that the 46.7 percent increase in purchasing power occurred during the Depression and was not very meaningful to the 25 percent who were unemployed.

For the record, there have been 14 recessions and 14 bear markets under the Republicans and 7 recessions and 10 bear markets under the Democrats

Market Behavior When Incumbent Party Wins and Loses

Looking at the past you can see that when Democrats ousted Republican White House occupants the market fared better in post-election years than when the reverse occurred. In the past Democrats came to power over domestic issues and Republicans won the White House on foreign shores.

POST-ELECTION MARKETS WHEN PARTY IN POWER IS OUSTED

New Democrats		Dow %	New Republicans		Dow %
Wilson	1913	− 10.3%	Harding	1921	12.7%
Roosevelt	1933	66.7	Eisenhower	1953	− 3.8
Kennedy	1961	18.7	Nixon	1969	− 15.2
Carter	1977	− 17.3	Reagan	1981	− 9.2
Clinton	1993	13.7	GW Bush	2001	− 7.1
	Average	14.3		Average	− 4.5

POST-ELECTION MARKETS WHEN PARTY STAYS IN POWER

Democrats		Dow %	Republicans		Dow %
Wilson	1917	− 21.7%	McKinley	1901	− 8.7%
F. Roosevelt	1937	− 32.8	T. Roosevelt	1905	38.2
F. Roosevelt	1941	− 15.4	Taft	1909	15.0
F. Roosevelt	1945	26.6	Coolidge	1925	30.0
Truman	1949	12.9	Hoover	1929	− 17.2
Johnson	1965	10.9	Eisenhower	1957	− 12.8
Clinton	1997	22.6	Nixon	1973	− 16.6
	Average	0.4	Reagan	1985	27.7
			GHW Bush	1989	27.0
				Average	9.2

Wilson won after the Republican Party split in two, and Carter after the Watergate scandal. Roosevelt, Kennedy, and Clinton won elections during bad economies. The Republicans took over after major wars were begun under Democrats, benefiting Harding, Eisenhower, and Nixon.

The Iranians made Jimmy Carter appear helpless, which favored Reagan. With no recession and no embarrassing foreign entanglement, the major advantage for Bush was the Clinton scandal. A disjointed Democratic Party and "wartime President" status helped George W. Bush hold the White House in 2004.

Post-Election High to Midterm Low: −22.2%

Since 1913 the Dow has dropped −22.2% on average from its post-election-year high to its subsequent low in the following midterm year. At press time the Dow's 2005 post-election year high is 10940.55. A 22.2% decline would put the Dow at 8511.75 at the 2006 midterm bottom. Whatever the level, the rally off the 2006 midterm low will likely provide one of the best buying opportunities of the twenty-first century.

% CHANGE IN DOW JONES INDUSTRIALS BETWEEN THE POST-ELECTION HIGH AND THE LOW IN THE FOLLOWING YEAR

	Post-Election Year High		Midterm Year Low		
	Date of High	Dow	Date of Low	Dow	% Loss
1	Jan 9 1913	64.88	Jul 30 1914	52.32	− 19.4%
2	Jan 3 1917	99.18	Jan 15 1918	73.38	− 26.0
3	Dec 15 1921	81.50	Jan 10 1922	78.59	− 3.6
4	Nov 6 1925	159.39	Mar 30 1926	135.20	− 15.2
5	Sep 3 1929	381.17	Dec 16 1930	157.51	− 58.7
6	Jul 18 1933	108.67	Jul 26 1934	85.51	− 21.3
7	Mar 10 1937	194.40	Mar 31 1938	98.95	− 49.1
8	Jan 10 1941	133.59	Apr 28 1942	92.92	− 30.4
9	Dec 11 1945	195.82	Oct 9 1946	163.12	− 16.7
10	Dec 30 1949	200.52	Jan 13 1950	196.81	− 1.9
11	Jan 5 1953	293.79	Jan 11 1954	279.87	− 4.7
12	Jul 12 1957	520.77	Feb 25 1958	436.89	− 16.1
13	Dec 13 1961	734.91	Jun 26 1962	535.76	− 27.1
14	Dec 31 1965	969.26	Oct 7 1966	744.32	− 23.2
15	May 14 1969	968.85	May 26 1970	631.16	− 34.9
16	Jan 11 1973	1051.70	Dec 6 1974	577.60	− 45.1
17	Jan 3 1977	999.75	Feb 28 1978	742.12	− 25.8
18	Apr 27 1981	1024.05	Aug 12 1982	776.92	− 24.1
19	Dec 16 1985	1553.10	Jan 22 1986	1502.29	− 3.3
20	Oct 9 1989	2791.41	Oct 11 1990	2365.10	− 15.3
21	Dec 29 1993	3794.33	Apr 4 1994	3593.35	− 5.3
22	Aug 6 1997	8259.31	Aug 31 1998	7539.07	− 8.7
23	May 21 2001	11337.92	Oct 9 2002	7286.27	− 35.7
				Average	**− 22.2%**

Midterm Election Years:
Where Bottom Pickers Find Paradise

American presidents have danced the Quadrennial Quadrille over the past two centuries. After the midterm congressional election and the invariable seat loss by his party, the president during the next two years jiggles fiscal policies to get federal spending, disposable income, and social security benefits up and interest rates and inflation down. By Election Day, he will have danced his way into the wallets and hearts of the electorate and, hopefully, will have choreographed four more years in the White House for his party.

After the Inaugural Ball is over, however, we pay the piper. Practically all bear markets began and ended in the two years after presidential elections. Bottoms often occurred in an air of crisis: the Cuban Missile Crisis in 1962, tight money in 1966, Cambodia in 1970, Watergate and Nixon's resignation in 1974, and threat of international monetary collapse in 1982. But remember, the word for "crisis" in Chinese is composed of two characters: the first, the symbol for danger; the second, opportunity. Of the 10 quadrennial cycles in the past 44 years, only one bottom was reached in the post-presidential year. All others came in midterm years.

THE RECORD SINCE 1914

1914 Wilson (D)	Bottom in July. War closed markets.
1918 Wilson (D)	**Bottom 12 days prior to start of year.**
1922 Harding (R)	**Bottom 4½ months prior to start of year.**
1926 Coolidge (R)	Only drop (7 wks, –17%) ends Mar. 30.
1930 Hoover (R)	**Crash of 1929 continues through 1930. No bottom.**
1934 Roosevelt (D)	First Roosevelt bear, February to July 26 bottom (–23%).
1938 Roosevelt (D)	Big 1937 break ends in March, DJI off 49%.
1942 Roosevelt (D)	World War II bottom in April.
1946 Truman (D)	Market tops in May, bottoms in October.
1950 Truman (D)	June 1949 bottom, June 1950 Korean War outbreak causes 14% drop.
1954 Eisenhower (R)	**September 1953 bottom, then straight up.**
1958 Eisenhower (R)	**October 1957 bottom, then straight up.**
1962 Kennedy (D)	Bottoms in June and October.
1966 Johnson (D)	Bottom in October.
1970 Nixon (R)	Bottom in May.
1974 Nixon, Ford (R)	December Dow bottom, S&P bottom in October.
1978 Carter (D)	March bottom, despite October massacre later.
1982 Reagan (R)	Bottom in August.
1986 Reagan (R)	**No bottom in 1985 or 1986.**
1990 Bush (R)	Bottom October 11 (Kuwaiti Invasion).
1994 Clinton (D)	Bottom April 4 after 10% drop.
1998 Clinton (D)	October 8 bottom (Asian currency crisis, hedge fund debacle).
2002 Bush, GW (R)	October 9 bottom (Corp malfeasance, terrorism, Iraq).

Bold = No bottom in midterm election year

50% Gain From Midterm Low to Pre-election High

Normally, major corrections occur sometime in the first or second years following presidential elections. In the last eleven midterm election years, bear markets began or were in progress nine times — we experienced a bull year in 1986 and a flat year in 1994.

The puniest midterm advance, 14.5% from the 1946 low, was during the industrial contraction after World War II. The next four smallest advances were: 1978 (OPEC–Iran) 20.9%, 1930 (economic collapse) 23.4%, 1966 (Vietnam) 26.7%, and 1990 (Persian Gulf War) 34.0%.

Since 1914 the Dow has gained 50% on average from its midterm election year low to its subsequent high in the following pre-election year. A swing of such magnitude is equivalent to a move from 7,300 to 10,950 or from 10,000 to 15,000.

% CHANGE IN DOW JONES INDUSTRIALS BETWEEN THE MIDTERM YEAR LOW AND THE HIGH IN THE FOLLOWING YEAR

	Midterm Year Low			Pre-Election Year High		
	Date of Low		Dow	Date of High	Dow	% Gain
1	Jul 30 1914 *		52.32	Dec 27 1915	99.21	89.6%
2	Jan 15 1918 **		73.38	Nov 3 1919	119.62	63.0
3	Jan 10 1922 **		78.59	Mar 20 1923	105.38	34.1
4	Mar 30 1926 *		135.20	Dec 31 1927	202.40	49.7
5	Dec 16 1930 *		157.51	Feb 24 1931	194.36	23.4
6	Jul 26 1934 *		85.51	Nov 19 1935	148.44	73.6
7	Mar 31 1938 *		98.95	Sep 12 1939	155.92	57.6
8	Apr 28 1942 *		92.92	Jul 14 1943	145.82	56.9
9	Oct 9 1946		163.12	Jul 24 1947	186.85	14.5
10	Jan 13 1950 **		196.81	Sep 13 1951	276.37	40.4
11	Jan 11 1954 **		279.87	Dec 30 1955	488.40	74.5
12	Feb 25 1958 **		436.89	Dec 31 1959	679.36	55.5
13	Jun 26 1962 *		535.74	Dec 18 1963	767.21	43.2
14	Oct 7 1966 *		744.32	Sep 25 1967	943.08	26.7
15	May 26 1970 *		631.16	Apr 28 1971	950.82	50.6
16	Dec 6 1974 *		577.60	Jul 16 1975	881.81	52.7
17	Feb 28 1978 *		742.12	Oct 5 1979	897.61	21.0
18	Aug 12 1982 *		776.92	Nov 29 1983	1287.20	65.7
19	Jan 22 1986		1502.29	Aug 25 1987	2722.42	81.2
20	Oct 11 1990 *		2365.10	Dec 31 1991	3168.84	34.0
21	Apr 4 1994		3593.35	Dec 13 1995	5216.47	45.2
22	Aug 31 1998 *		7539.07	Dec 31 1999	11497.12	52.5
23	Oct 9 2002 *		7286.27	Dec 31 2003	10453.92	43.5
*Bear Market ended **Bear previous year				**Average**	**50.0%**

Prosperity More Than Peace Determines
Outcome of Midterm Congressional Races

Though the stock market in presidential election years very often is able to predict if the party in power will retain or lose the White House, the outcome of congressional races in midterm years is another matter entirely. Typically, the president's party will lose a number of House seats in these elections (1934, 1998, and 2002 were exceptions). It is considered a victory for the president when his party loses a small number of seats, and a repudiation of sorts when a large percentage of seats is lost.

The table below would seem to indicate that there is no relationship between the stock market's behavior in the ten months prior to the midterm election and the magnitude of seats lost in the House. Roaring bull markets preceded the elections of 1954 and 1958, yet Republicans lost few seats during one, and a huge number in the other.

If the market does not offer a clue to the outcome of House races, does anything besides the popularity and performance of the administration? Yes! In the two years prior to the elections in the first ten midterm years listed, no war or major recession began. As a result, the percentage of House seats lost was minimal. A further observation is that the market gained ground in the last seven weeks of the year, except 2002.

Our four major wars last century began under the four Democrats in the shaded area. The percentage of seats lost was greater during these midterm elections. But the seven worst repudiations of the president are at the bottom of the list. These were preceded by: the sick economy in 1930, the botched health proposals in 1994, the severe recession in 1937, the post-war contraction in 1946, the recession in 1957, Watergate in 1974, and rumors of corruption (Teapot Dome) in 1922. Obviously, prosperity is of greater importance to the electorate than peace!

LAST 21 MIDTERM ELECTIONS RANKED BY
% LOSS OF SEATS BY PRESIDENT'S PARTY

	% Seats Gained or Lost	Year	President	Dow Jones Industrials Jan 1 to Elec Day	Elec Day to Dec 31	Year's CPI % Change
1.	3.6%	2002	R: G.W. Bush	− 14.5%	− 2.7%	1.6%
2.	2.9	1934	D: Roosevelt	− 3.8	8.3	1.5
3.	1.9	1998	D: Clinton	10.1	5.5	1.6
4.	− 1.5	1962	D: Kennedy	− 16.5	6.8	1.3
5.	− 2.7	1986	R: Reagan	22.5	0.1	1.1
6.	− 4.0	1926	R: Coolidge	− 3.9	4.4	− 1.1
7.	− 4.6	1990	R: G.H.W. Bush	− 9.1	5.3	6.1
8.	− 5.1	1978	D: Carter	− 3.7	0.6	9.0
9.	− 6.3	1970	R: Nixon	− 5.3	10.7	5.6
10.	− 8.1	1954	R: Eisenhower	26.0	14.2	− 0.7
11.	− 9.0	1918	D: Wilson (WW1)	15.2	− 4.1	20.4
12.	− 11.0	1950	D: Truman (Korea)	11.2	− 5.8	5.9
13.	− 13.5	1982	R: Reagan	14.9	4.1	3.8
14.	− 15.9	1966	D: Johnson (Vietnam)	− 17.2	− 2.1	3.5
15.	− 16.9	1942	D: Roosevelt (WW2)	3.4	4.1	9.0
16.	− 18.4	1930	R: Hoover	− 25.4	− 11.2	− 6.4
17.	− 20.9	1994	D: Clinton	1.5	0.7	2.7
18.	− 21.3	1938	D: Roosevelt	28.2	− 0.1	− 2.8
19.	− 22.6	1946	D: Truman	− 9.6	1.6	18.1
20.	− 23.9	1958	R: Eisenhower	25.1	7.1	1.8
21.	− 25.0	1974	R: Ford	− 22.8	− 6.2	12.3
22.	− 25.0	1922	R: Harding	21.4	0.3	− 2.3

Midterm Election Time Unusually Bullish

Presidential election years tend to produce high drama and frenetic campaigns. Midterm years with only local or state candidates running are less stressful. Could this be the reason for the bullishness that seems to occur in the five days before and three days after midterm congressional elections? We don't think so. So many bear markets seem to occur in midterm years, very often bottoming in October. Also, major military involvements began or were in their early stages in midterm years, such as: World War II, Korea, Vietnam, Kuwait, and Iraq. Solidly bullish midterm years such as 1954, 1958, and 1986 were exceptions. With so many negative occurrences in midterm years, perhaps the opportunity for investors to make a change for the better by casting their votes translates into an inner bullish feeling before and after midterm elections.

An impressive 2.9% has been the average gain during the eight trading days surrounding midterm election days since 1934. This is equivalent to roughly 40 Dow points per day at present levels. There was only one losing period in 1994 when the Republicans took control of both the House and the Senate for the first time in 40 years. Two other midterm switches occurred in 1946 when control of Congress passed to the Republicans for just two years, and in 1954, when Democrats took back control after two years.

There were nine occasions when the percentage of House seats lost by the president's party was in double digits. The average market gain during the eight-day trading period was 2.3%. In contrast, the average gain in the eight occasions when there were no losses, or losses were in single digits, gains averaged 3.4%.

BULLS WIN BATTLE BETWEEN ELEPHANTS AND DONKEYS

Midterm Year	Dow Jones Industrials 5 Trading Days Before E. Day	Dow Jones Industrials 3 Trading Days After E. Day	% Change	President's Party % Seats Lost	President in Power
1934	93.05	99.02	**6.4%**	2.9%	Dem
1938	152.21	158.41	**4.1**	− 21.3	Dem
1942	113.11	116.12	**2.7**	− 16.9	Dem
1946	164.20	170.79	**4.0**	− 22.6	**Dem***
1950	225.69	229.29	**1.6**	− 11.0	Dem
1954	356.32	366.00	**2.7**	− 8.1	**Rep***
1958	536.88	554.26	**3.2**	− 23.9	Rep
1962	588.98	616.13	**4.6**	− 1.5	Dem
1966	809.63	819.09	**1.2**	− 15.9	Dem
1970	754.45	771.97	**2.3**	− 6.3	Rep
1974	659.34	667.16	**1.2**	− 25.0	Rep
1978	792.45	807.09	**1.8**	− 5.1	Dem
1982	1006.07	1051.78	**4.5**	− 13.5	Rep
1986	1845.47	1886.53	**2.2**	− 2.7	Rep
1990	2448.02	2488.61	**1.7**	− 4.6	Rep
1994	3863.37	3801.47	**− 1.6**	− 20.9	**Dem***
1998	8366.04	8975.46	**7.3**	1.9	Dem
2002	8368.94	8537.13	**2.0**	3.6	Rep
		Total	**51.9%**		
		Average	**2.9%**		

Control switches to other Party

Pre-Election Years: No Losers Since 1939

There hasn't been a down year in the third year of a presidential term since war-torn 1939, when the Dow was off 2.9%. The only severe loss in a pre-presidential election year going back 84 years occurred in 1931 during the Depression.

Electing a president every four years has set in motion a political stock market cycle. Most bear markets take place in the first or second years after elections. Then, the market improves. What happens is that each administration usually does everything in its power to juice up the economy so that voters are in a positive mood at election time.

THE RECORD SINCE 1915

1915 Wilson (D)	World War I in Europe, but U.S. stocks up 81.7%.
1919 Wilson (D)	Post-Armistice 45.5% gain through November 3rd top. Dow up 30.5% for the year.
1923 Harding/Coolidge (R)	Teapot Dome scandal a depressant. Dow loses 3.3%.
1927 Coolidge (R)	Bull market rolls on, up 28.8%.
1931 Hoover (R)	Depression, stocks slashed in half. Dow −52.7%, S&P −47.1%.
1935 Roosevelt (D)	Almost a straight up year, S&P 500 up 41.2%, Dow 38.5%.
1939 Roosevelt (D)	War clouds, Dow off 2.9% but 23.7% April/December gain. S&P −5.5%.
1943 Roosevelt (D)	U.S. at war, prospects brighter, S&P +19.4%, Dow +13.8%.
1947 Truman (D)	S&P unchanged, Dow up 2.2%.
1951 Truman (D)	Dow +14.4%, S&P +16.5%.
1955 Eisenhower (R)	Dow +20.8%, S&P +26.4%.
1959 Eisenhower (R)	Dow +16.4%, S&P +8.5%.
1963 Kennedy/Johnson (D)	Dow +17.0%, S&P +18.9%.
1967 Johnson (D)	Dow +15.2%, S&P +20.1%.
1971 Nixon (R)	Dow +6.1%, S&P +10.8%, NASDAQ +27.4%.
1975 Ford (R)	Dow +38.3%, S&P +31.5%, NASDAQ +29.8%.
1979 Carter (D)	Dow +4.2%, S&P +12.3%, NASDAQ +28.1%.
1983 Reagan (R)	Dow +20.3%, S&P +17.3%, NASDAQ +19.9%.
1987 Reagan (R)	Dow +2.3%, S&P +2.0% despite the meltdown in October. NASDAQ −5.4%.
1991 Bush (R)	Dow +20.3%, S&P +26.3%, NASDAQ +56.8%.
1995 Clinton (D)	Dow +33.5%, S&P +34.1%, NASDAQ +39.9%.
1999 Clinton (D)	Millennial fever crescendo: Dow +25.2%, S&P +19.5%, NASDAQ +85.6%.
2003 Bush, GW (R) +26.4%,	First bull market of the twenty-first century: +25.3%, S&P NASDAQ +50.0%.

Only One Loss Last 7 Months of Election Years

Election years are traditionally up years. Incumbent administrations attempt to massage the economy so voters will keep them in power. But, sometimes over-powering events occur and the market crumbles, usually resulting in a change of political control.

The Republicans won in 1920 as the post-war economy contracted and President Wilson ailed. The Democrats came back during the 1932 Depression when the Dow hit its lowest level of the twentieth century. A world at war and the fall of France jolted the market in 1940 but Roosevelt won an unprecedented third term. Cold War confrontations and Truman's historic upset of Dewey held markets down through the end of 1948.

Since 1948, investors have barely been bruised during election years, except for a brief span early in the year—until 2000. An undecided election plagued the country with uncertainty, hammering stock prices in November and keeping them down until mid-December.

The table below presents a very positive picture for the last seven or eight months of election years.

- Since 1952, January through April losses occurred in seven of fourteen election years. Incumbent parties were ousted on five of these seven losses. Ironically, bear markets began the year following four of seven gainers in 1957, 1969, 1973, and 1977.

- Of the thirteen election-year Julys since 1952, seven were losers (1960, 1968, 1976, 1984, 1988, 1996, and 2000). Four were years when, at convention time, no strong incumbent was running for re-election. Note that April through July periods had only five losers: 1972 by a small margin,

S&P 500 DURING ELECTION YEARS

Election Year	% Change First 4 Months	April	May	June	July	Dec	% Change Last 8 Months	% Change Last 7 Months
1952*	− 1.9%	**23.32**	23.86	24.96	25.40	26.57	13.9%	11.4%
1956	6.4	**48.38**	**45.20**	46.97	49.39	46.67	− 3.5	3.3
1960*	− 9.2	**54.37**	55.83	56.92	**55.51**	58.11	6.9	4.1
1964	5.9	79.46	80.37	81.69	83.18	84.75	6.7	5.4
1968*	1.2	97.59	98.68	99.58	**97.74**	**103.86**	6.4	5.2
1972	5.5	107.67	109.53	**107.14**	107.39	118.05	9.6	7.8
1976*	12.7	**101.64**	**100.18**	104.28	**103.44**	107.46	5.7	7.3
1980*	− 1.5	106.29	111.24	114.24	121.67	**135.76**	27.7	22.0
1984	− 3.0	160.05	**150.55**	153.18	**150.66**	167.24	4.5	11.1
1988	5.8	261.33	262.16	273.50	**272.02**	277.72	6.3	5.9
1992*	− 0.5	414.95	415.35	**408.14**	424.21	435.71	5.0	4.9
1996	6.2	654.17	669.12	670.63	**639.95**	**740.74**	13.2	10.7
2000**	− 1.1	**1452.43**	**1420.60**	1454.60	**1430.83**	1320.28	− 9.1	− 7.1
2004	−0.4	**1107.30**	1120.68	1140.68	**1101.72**	1211.92	9.4	8.1
Totals	**26.1%**						**102.7%**	**100.1%**
Average	**1.9%**						**7.3%**	**7.2%**

*Incumbents ousted ** Incumbent ousted & undecided election*
Down months are bold

1984 as the market was turning around, 1996, 2000 as the bubble began to work off its excesses, and 2004 negligibly.

■ For a longer perspective, we extended the table to December. Just two losing eight-month periods in an election year are revealed and only one loss in the last seven months of all these years—in undecided 2000.

Incumbent Victories versus Incumbent Defeats

Since 1944 stocks have tended to move up earlier when White House occupants are popular but do even better in November and December when unpopular administrations are ousted.

Actual percent changes reveal that March, June, October, and December are best when incumbents stay in power and February, July, and September are the worst when they are removed. Ironically, November is best when incumbents are ousted and second worst when they win.

Other interesting tidbits: there were no major losses in October (1984 off fractionally) and only one in March, June and December when incumbent parties retained the White House; Republican wins in November resulted in total gains of 23.6% (excluding no-decision 2000); Democratic victories produced total gains of 2.6%; however, Democrats "gained" 15.6% in December, the Republicans 7.9%.

Trend of S&P 500 Index in Election Years 1944-2004

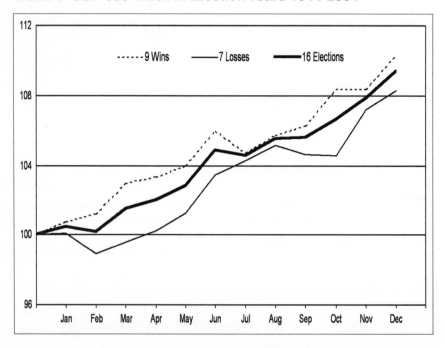

S&P 500 MONTHLY % CHANGES DURING ELECTION YEARS

Incumbents Win

Year	Jan	Feb	Mar	Apr	May	Jun	Jul	Aug	Sep	Oct	Nov	Dec
1944	1.5	—0.3	1.7	—1.3	4.0	5.1	—2.1	0.9	—0.3	N/C	0.4	3.5
1948	—4.0	—4.7	7.7	2.7	7.8	0.3	—5.3	0.8	—3.0	6.8	—10.8	3.1
1956	—3.6	3.5	6.9	—0.2	—6.6	3.9	5.2	—3.8	—4.5	0.5	—1.1	3.5
1964	2.7	1.0	1.5	0.6	1.1	1.6	1.8	—1.6	2.9	0.8	—0.5	0.4
1972	1.8	2.5	0.6	0.4	1.7	—2.2	0.2	3.4	—0.5	0.9	4.6	1.2
1984	—0.9	—3.9	1.3	0.5	—5.9	1.7	—1.6	10.6	—0.3	—0.01	—1.5	2.2
1988	4.0	4.2	—3.3	0.9	0.3	4.3	—0.5	—3.9	4.0	2.6	—1.9	1.5
1996	3.3	0.7	0.8	1.3	2.3	0.2	—4.6	1.9	5.4	2.6	7.3	—2.2
2004	1.7	1.2	—1.6	—1.7	1.2	1.8	—3.4	0.2	0.9	1.4	3.9	3.2
Totals	**6.5**	**4.2**	**15.6**	**3.2**	**5.9**	**16.7**	**—10.3**	**8.5**	**4.6**	**15.6**	**0.4**	**16.4**
Average	**0.7**	**0.5**	**1.7**	**0.4**	**0.7**	**1.9**	**—1.1**	**0.9**	**0.5**	**1.9**	**0.04**	**1.8**

Incumbents Lose

Year	Jan	Feb	Mar	Apr	May	Jun	Jul	Aug	Sep	Oct	Nov	Dec
1952	1.6	—3.6	4.8	—4.3	2.3	4.6	1.8	—1.5	—2.0	—0.1	4.6	3.5
1960	—7.1	0.9	—1.4	—1.8	2.7	2.0	—2.5	2.6	—6.0	—0.2	4.0	4.6
1968	—4.4	—3.1	0.9	8.2	1.1	0.9	—1.8	1.1	3.9	0.7	4.8	—4.2
1976	11.8	—1.1	3.1	—1.1	—1.4	4.1	—0.8	—0.5	2.3	—2.2	—0.8	5.2
1980	5.8	—0.4	—10.2	4.1	4.7	2.7	6.5	0.6	2.5	1.6	10.2	—3.4
1992	—2.0	1.0	—2.2	2.8	0.1	—1.7	3.9	—2.4	0.9	0.2	3.0	1.0
2000	—5.1	—2.0	9.7	—3.1	—2.2	2.4	—1.6	6.1	—5.3	—0.5	—8.0	0.4
Totals	**0.6**	**—8.3**	**4.7**	**4.8**	**7.3**	**15.0**	**5.5**	**6.0**	**—3.7**	**—0.5**	**17.8**	**7.1**
Average	**0.1**	**—1.2**	**0.7**	**0.7**	**1.0**	**2.1**	**0.8**	**0.9**	**—0.5**	**—0.1**	**2.5**	**1.0**
16 Elections	**7.1**	**—4.1**	**20.3**	**8.0**	**13.2**	**31.7**	**—4.8**	**14.5**	**0.9**	**15.1**	**18.2**	**23.5**
Average	**0.4**	**—0.3**	**1.3**	**0.5**	**0.8**	**2.0**	**—0.3**	**0.9**	**0.1**	**1.0**	**1.1**	**1.5**

Undecided election

Market Acts as a Barometer Between the Last Convention and Election Day

Another election-year phenomenon, one with an outstanding track record, is the Post-Convention-to-Election-Day Forecaster. Here the direction of the Dow between the close of the last presidential convention and Election Day reflects voter sentiment.

Of the sixteen presidential elections since 1900 where the incumbent parties were victorious, fourteen were foretold by rising stock prices. The two exceptions were minor (–2.3% in 1956 and –0.6% in 1984). Gains for the period averaged 8.6%. Conversely, dissatisfaction with an incumbent party is most times reflected by a decline between the last convention and Election Day. Here, seven out of ten election years produced declines.

Though the average change when incumbent parties lost is +3.4%, this reflects the Dow hitting bottom in 1932 (losing 89.2% since 1929), then moving up over 100% intraday in 60 days before giving back half by Election Day. Excluding 1932 changes the average to –1.6%. Even 1968's post-convention gain is suspect because riots and two assassinations disrupted the market and depressed it prior to the last convention.

In 2004 President Bush had one major factor on his side (aside from the shortcomings of the Democratic challenger): two wars in progress, Iraq and the War on Terror.

POST-CONVENTION-TO-ELECTION MARKETS

Year Incumbent Party Won	% Change	Year Incumbent Party Lost	% Change
1900	7.7%	1912	— 1.4%
1904	30.7	1920	— 9.1
1908	10.0	1932	48.6
1916	16.7	1952	— 2.8
1924	7.5	1960	— 3.1
1928	22.4	1968	5.6
1936	11.8	1976	— 0.8
1940	10.7	1980	— 3.1
1944	1.6	1992	1.1
1948	1.1*	2000	— 0.6
1956	— 2.5**	**Average**	**3.4%**
1964	4.3	**Excluding 1932**	**— 1.6%**
1972	2.8		
1984	— 0.6		
1988	5.4		
1996	7.6		
2004	— 2.0†		
Average	**8.0%**		

% change based on Dow Jones Industrials
*Truman upsets Dewey
** Russian tanks in Hungary in October
† Two wars in progress, Iraq & War on Terror

Election Year Perspectives and Observations

If we could predict the outcome of the fourth-year presidential election twelve to eighteen months ahead of time, it sure would provide insight as to what the market might do during election years. As we can't, we added up the seventeen times since 1900 that parties retained the White House and find the Dow gained 15.1 percent in the average election year. The ten other times "ins" were ousted the Dow lost 1.4 percent on average.

ELECTION YEAR MARKETS SINCE 1900

	17 Wins	10 Losses
DJIA Changes	256.3%	-14.2%
Average	**15.1%**	**-1.4%**

George W. Bush is the first president who failed to win the popular vote to win a second term. John Quincy Adams, a son of a former president, and Benjamin Harrison both failed in their bids for reelection. Rutherford B. Hayes chose not to run in 1880.

PRESIDENTS WHO LOST THE POPULAR VOTE

Election Year	Elected President	Next Election	What Happened
1824	John Quincy Adams	1828	Not Reelected
1876	Rutherford B. Hayes	1880	Chose not to run
1888	Benjamin Harrison	1892	Not Reelected
2000	**George W. Bush**	**2004**	**Reelected**

Presidential popularity during wartime often fades by the time the war ends, or seems to be ending, and the next presidential election rolls around.

The Democrats lost power after WWI (1920), Korea (1952), and Vietnam (1968); the Republicans gave up the White House in 1992, despite their very high ratings during and after Desert Storm. (Even the greatest leader of the century, England's Sir Winston Churchill, lost power in July 1945 shortly after the Allies' overwhelming defeat of the enemy.)

In the modern era only Truman, in 1948, managed to retain power for the Democrats when he ran against a candidate (Dewey), who was heavily favored to win. With Iraq and the War on Terror still in progress during 2004 Bush's popularity was still strong. Stocks did not run away during these six election years.

HOW WARS AFFECT POLITICAL PARTIES

Election Year	War	Party Ousted	Retains Power	Dow % Elec Day	Dow % Full Year
1920	WWI	Dem		−20.3%	−32.9%
1948	WWII		Dem	4.7%	−2.1%
1952	Korea	Dem		0.4%	8.4%
1968	Vietnam	Dem		4.5%	4.3%
1992	Gulf War	Rep		2.9%	4.2%
2004	Iraq/Terror		Rep	−4.0%	3.1%

Presidents Are Reelected During Wars or Threats of War

Voters usually "rally round the flag" when wars are in progress or threatening. During the twentieth century, elected presidents successfully running for second terms included Wilson (1916) prior to World War I and Roosevelt (1940) for a third term prior to America being involved in the Second World War. Roosevelt was elected again (1944) for a fourth term and Nixon (1972) won his second term, as wars were in progress. The Dow declined in the first two instances and climbed in the latter two. In the previous century Madison was reelected during the War of 1812 and Lincoln (1864) in the midst of the Civil War.

ELECTED PRESIDENTS RUNNING FOR SECOND TERM

Year	President	Reelected Dow %	Ousted Dow %	Reason for Loss
1912	Taft (R)		7.6%	Party Split
1916	**Wilson (D)**	**–4.2%**		
1932	Hoover (R)		–23.1	Depression
1936	Roosevelt (D)	24.8		
1940	**Roosevelt (D)**	**–12.7**		
1944	**Roosevelt (D)**	**12.1**		
1956	Eisenhower (R)	2.3		
1972	**Nixon (R)**	**14.6**		
1980	Carter (D)		14.9	Iran Hostage Crisis
1984	Reagan (R)	–3.7		
1992	Bush (R)		4.2	Post-Kuwait Recession
1996	Clinton (D)	26.0		
2004	**Bush GW (R)**	**3.1**		
	Totals	62.3%	3.6%	
	Average	6.9%	0.9%	

Bold: War in progress

The Stock Market as a Popularity Poll

Excepting exogenous events, markets tend to do better when incumbent presidents are reelected, rather than ousted. If you tally up the thirteen occasions in the last 100 years when elected presidents ran for reelection, you get an average gain of 6.9% on the Dow when incumbents are reelected, compared to 0.9% on average when they lose. Of the nine winners, the five running during wars (or when there was a threat of war) saw average gains on the Dow of 2.6%. Gains for the four others, Roosevelt, Eisenhower, Reagan, and Clinton, averaged 12.4%.

Democrats Lose Overseas, Republicans Here, Till 1992

Power in Washington changed hands ten times since 1900. For most of the century Democrats gave up the White House after foreign entanglements were over or turned sour, while Republicans had to move out after things went awry on our own shores. Democrats lost power in 1920 (WW1), 1952 (Korea), 1968 (Vietnam), and 1980 (Iran Hostage Crisis). Republicans lost it domestically in 1912 (Party Split), 1932 (Depression), 1960 (Recession), and 1976 (Watergate).

Did the two parties trade places in the last two switches? Obviously, the Democrats lost in 2000 because of the domestic scandal, in spite of the biggest bull market on record. But, did the Republicans lose it in 1992 because of, "It's the economy, stupid," fading popularity after the Persian Gulf War, or Ross Perot siphoning off almost 20 million votes as a third party candidate? For that matter, would someone else be occupying the White House now if Ralph Nader hadn't entered the race in 2000 and grabbed several million Democratic votes?

Beating the Election Odds

In his reelection victory President Bush defied the historical odds. He is the first president ever to win reelection after losing the popular vote the first time. His reelection is the second time since 1952 the incumbent party has held the White House after the S&P 500 was down during the first four months of the year. Five of the six previous first four-month losses preceded an incumbent party ouster.

Our Post-Convention-to-Election Day Forecaster was flouted as Mr. Bush won despite a 2% drop in the Dow after the Republican Convention through Election Day. President Bush's stature was boosted by two wars in progress, Iraq and the War on Terror. As mentioned earlier, "voters usually 'rally around the flag' when wars are in progress or threatening." We reminded subscribers in our *Almanac Investor 2004 Forecast* that, "the situation in Iraq looks likely to continue so that a 'wartime' president is up for reelection."

DECENNIAL CYCLE: A MARKET PHENOMENON

By arranging each year's market gain or loss so the first and succeeding years of each decade fall into the same column, certain interesting patterns emerge — strong fifth and eighth years; weak first, seventh and zero years.

This fascinating phenomenon was first presented by Edgar Lawrence Smith in *Common Stocks and Business Cycles* (William-Frederick Press, 1959). Anthony Gaubis co-pioneered the decennial pattern with Smith.

When Smith first cut graphs of market prices into ten-year segments and placed them above one another, he observed that each decade tended to have three bull market cycles and that the longest and strongest bull markets seem to favor the middle years of a decade.

Don't place too much emphasis on the decennial cycle nowadays, other than the extraordinary fifth and zero years, as the stock market is more influenced by the quadrennial presidential election cycle. Also, the last half-century, which has been the most prosperous in U.S. history, has distributed the returns among most years of the decade. Interestingly, NASDAQ suffered its worst bear market ever in a zero year, giving us the rare experience of witnessing a bubble burst.

2005 looks likely to keep fifth years' twelve-and-zero winning streak, but with the gyrations experienced to date, we don't expect 2005 to be a huge gainer year-over-year. After another test of the 2004 lows in 2005, recovery highs are likely to be revisited in late 2005/early 2006. Midterm 2006 promises another correction and perhaps the next bear market. Midterm election years have historically been host to a plethora of major bottoms.

THE TEN-YEAR STOCK MARKET CYCLE
Annual % Change in Dow Jones Industrial Average
Year of Decade

DECADES	1st	2nd	3rd	4th	5th	6th	7th	8th	9th	10th
1881-1890	3.0%	- 2.9%	- 8.5%	-18.8%	20.1%	12.4%	- 8.4%	4.8%	5.5%	-14.1%
1891-1900	17.6	- 6.6	-24.6	- 0.6	2.3	- 1.7	21.3	22.5	9.2	7.0
1901-1910	- 8.7	- 0.4	-23.6	41.7	38.2	- 1.9	-37.7	46.6	15.0	-17.9
1911-1920	0.4	7.6	-10.3	- 5.4	81.7	- 4.2	-21.7	10.5	30.5	-32.9
1921-1930	12.7	21.7	- 3.3	26.2	30.0	0.3	28.8	48.2	-17.2	-33.8
1931-1940	-52.7	-23.1	66.7	4.1	38.5	24.8	-32.8	28.1	- 2.9	-12.7
1941-1950	-15.4	7.6	13.8	12.1	26.6	- 8.1	2.2	- 2.1	12.9	17.6
1951-1960	14.4	8.4	- 3.8	44.0	20.8	2.3	-12.8	34.0	16.4	- 9.3
1961-1970	18.7	-10.8	17.0	14.6	10.9	-18.9	15.2	4.3	-15.2	4.8
1971-1980	6.1	14.6	-16.6	-27.6	38.3	17.9	-17.3	- 3.1	4.2	14.9
1981-1990	- 9.2	19.6	20.3	- 3.7	27.7	22.6	2.3	11.8	27.0	- 4.3
1991-2000	20.3	4.2	13.7	2.1	33.5	26.0	22.6	16.1	25.2	- 6.2
2001-2010	- 7.1	-16.8	25.3	3.1						
Total % Change	0.1%	23.1%	66.1%	91.8%	368.6%	71.5%	-38.3%	221.7%	110.6%	-86.9%
Avg % Change	0.01%	1.8%	5.1%	7.1%	30.7%	6.0%	- 3.2%	18.5%	9.2%	-7.2%
Up Years	8	7	6	8	12	7	6	10	9	4
Down Years	5	6	7	5	0	5	6	2	3	8

Based on annual close; Cowles indices 1881-1885; 12 Mixed Stocks, 10 Rails, 2 Inds 1886-1889;
20 Mixed Stocks, 18 Rails, 2 Inds 1890-1896; Railroad average 1897 (First industrial average published May 26, 1896)

ALMANAC INVESTOR

BULL AND BEAR MARKETS SINCE 1900

— Beginning —		— Ending —		— Bull —		— Bear —	
Date	DJIA	Date	DJIA	% Gain	Days	%Change	Days
9/24/00	38.80	6/17/01	57.33	47.8%	266	− 46.1%	875
11/9/03	30.88	1/19/06	75.45	144.3	802	− 48.5	665
11/15/07	38.83	11/19/09	73.64	89.6	735	− 27.4	675
9/25/11	53.43	9/30/12	68.97	29.1	371	− 24.1	668
7/30/14	52.32	11/21/16	110.15	110.5	845	− 40.1	393
12/19/17	65.95	11/3/19	119.62	81.4	684	− 46.6	660
8/24/21	63.90	3/20/23	105.38	64.9	573	− 18.6	221
10/27/23	85.76	9/3/29	381.17	344.5	2138	− 47.9	71
11/13/29	198.69	4/17/30	294.07	48.0	155	− 86.0	813
7/8/32	41.22	9/7/32	79.93	93.9	61	− 37.2	173
2/27/33	50.16	2/5/34	110.74	120.8	343	− 22.8	171
7/26/34	85.51	3/10/37	194.40	127.3	958	− 49.1	386
3/31/38	98.95	11/12/38	158.41	60.1	226	− 23.3	147
4/8/39	121.44	9/12/39	155.92	28.4*	157	− 40.4	959
4/28/42	92.92	5/29/46	212.50	128.7	1492	− 23.2	353
5/17/47	163.21	6/15/48	193.16	18.4	395	− 16.3	363
6/13/49	161.60	1/5/53	293.79	81.8	1302	− 13.0	252
9/14/53	255.49	4/6/56	521.05	103.9	935	− 19.4	564
10/22/57	419.79	1/5/60	685.47	63.3	805	− 17.4	294
10/25/60	566.05	12/13/61	734.91	29.8	414	− 27.1	195
6/26/62	535.76	2/9/66	995.15	85.7	1324	− 25.2	240
10/7/66	744.32	12/3/68	985.21	32.4	788	− 35.9	539
5/26/70	631.16	4/28/71	950.82	50.6	337	− 16.1	209
11/23/71	797.97	1/11/73	1051.70	31.8	415	− 45.1	694
12/6/74	577.60	9/21/76	1014.79	75.7	655	− 26.9	525
2/28/78	742.12	9/8/78	907.74	22.3	192	− 16.4	591
4/21/80	759.13	4/27/81	1024.05	34.9	371	− 24.1	472
8/12/82	776.92	11/29/83	1287.20	65.7	474	− 15.6	238
7/24/84	1086.57	8/25/87	2722.42	150.6	1127	− 36.1	55
10/19/87	1738.74	7/17/90	2999.75	72.5	1002	− 21.2	86
10/11/90	2365.10	7/17/98	9337.97	294.8	2836	− 19.3	45
8/31/98	7539.07	1/14/00	11722.98	55.5	501	− 29.7	616
9/21/01	8235.81	3/19/02	10635.25	29.1	179	− 31.5	204
10/9/02	7286.27	3/4/05	10940.55	50.2*	877*	*At Press Time	
			Average	**84.4%**	**728**	**− 30.8%**	**406**

Based on Dow Jones industrial average   1900-2000 Data: Ned Davis Research
The NYSE was closed from 7/31/1914 to 12/11/1914 due to World War I.
DJIA figures were then adjusted back to reflect the composition change from 12 to 20 stocks in September 1916.

Bear markets begin at the end of one bull market and end at the start of the next bull market (7/17/90 to 10/11/90 as an example). The high at Dow 3978.36 on 1/31/94, was followed by a 9.7% correction. A 10.3% correction occurred between the 5/22/96, closing high of 5778 and the intraday low on 7/16/96. The longest bull market on record ended on 7/17/98, and the shortest bear market on record ended on 8/31/98, when the new bull market began. The greatest bull super cycle in history that began 8/12/82 ended in 2000 after the Dow gained 1,409% and NASDAQ climbed 3,072%. The Dow gained only 497% in the eight-year super bull from 1921 to the top in 1929. NASDAQ suffered its worst loss ever, down 77.9%, nearly as much as the 89.2% drop in the Dow from 1929 to the bottom in 1932. The Dow has rallied 50.2% since the 10/9/02 bear market low; S&P 500, 60.3% and NASDAQ 99.1%! From their late 2004/early 2005 highs the Dow corrected 8.5%; S&P, 7.2% and NASDAQ 12.6%. The Dow has not been able to surpass its March 2005 high but the S&P and NASDAQ have cleared those levels, albeit by less than 2% at press time.

HOW WAR AND PEACE IMPACT THE MARKETS

The cycle of war and peace has developed into a predictable pattern. It was recognition of the post-war bullishness that led Yale Hirsch to make his now famous call of Dow 3,420 by 1990 in April 1976, based on 500% moves following wartime inflations. Dow 3,420 was a 500% move from the 1,974 intraday low of 570. In the summer of 1990 the S&P 500 realized this 500% gain, the Dow come up short, reaching only 3,024 (not a typo). Two years later the Dow reached 3,420 intraday in May 1992. That is tantamount to predicting Dow 43,068 by 2018 using the 2002 intraday low of 7,178. And, with patterns and cycles compressing, could we see Dow 43K even sooner?

Parameters

For World War I, the markets were closed from July 31, 1914 until December 12, 1914. Much of the escalation of the war occurred during this time, so we opted to use the close from July 30, 1914. The armistice that ended WWI was signed Sunday, November 11, 1918; so, the close from November 9, 1918 was used.

German tanks rolled into Poland on September 1, 1939, signifying the start of World War II. The end of WWII for this study is September 2, 1945, when the Japanese surrendered to the United States.

Korea was fairly simple. North Korea invaded South Korea on June 25, 1950 and the armistice that ended the Korean War was signed on July 27, 1953.

Vietnam is a little trickier. No declaration of War was ever asked of, or granted, by Congress for the Vietnam "conflict." Technically, the United States was involved in conflict there starting in 1950. There were various levels of escalation throughout the Eisenhower, Kennedy, and Johnson administrations. In lieu of an actual declaration of war and not wanting to skew the study by using the original presence of troops; August 7, 1964 was used; the approval of the Gulf of Tonkin Resolution. The War officially came to an end on January 27, 1973 with the signing of the Paris Peace Accords.

The first Gulf War started on August 2, 1990 when Iraq invaded Kuwait and ended on February 27, 1991 when President Bush (41) declared a ceasefire.

The current situation is not cut and dried. There were three possible dates to use for the onset of the war on terror (we prefer to call this Gulf War II seeing as terror is a tactic not an enemy). September 11, 2001 could be used for obvious reasons but, we chose not to. March 20, 2003; the date that the air bombardment of Iraq started is equally justifiable, but we did not use this date either. Instead, we opted to use a date in-between these; October 7, 2001—the date when we invaded Afghanistan.

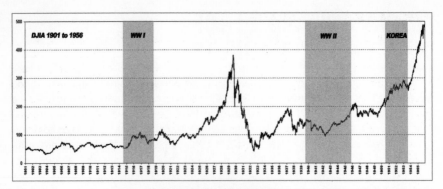

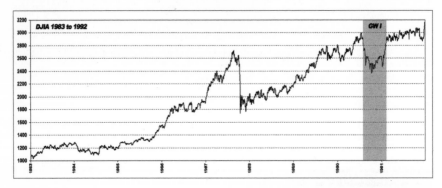

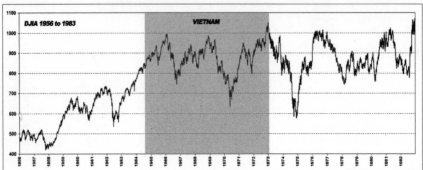

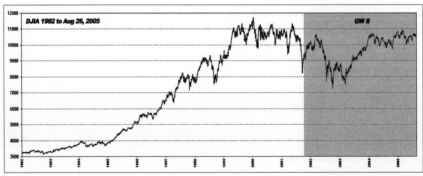

Fearless Projections

We have broken the periods out into wartime and peacetime. Average annual return is calculated by dividing the total return from the start of the period to the end of the period by the length of the period. For wartime the % change peace high to war low and % change peace low to war high is from the peace period before the war. For example, for Korea, the peace low and high is taken from the period after WWII. The same is true for the % change war low to peace high and % change war high to peace low. For example, for peacetime after WWII, the % change is from low made during WWII to the ensuing high during the peace after the war.

DOW PERFORMANCE DURING WARTIME

	WW I	WW II	Korea	Vietnam	Gulf War I	War Time Stats		Projected Gulf War II	
Dow at the Start	52.32	135.25	224.35	829.16	2864.60	Average % Chg during War	27.7%	Dow at the Start GW II	9,119.77
Dow at the End	88.06	174.29	268.46	1003.54	2889.11	Average Length of War	4y178d	Projected Dow at End	11650.02
% Chg at End of War	68.3%	28.9%	19.7%	21.0%	0.9%	Average Annual % Change	6.2%	High to Date	10940.55
Duration	4y104d	6y3d	3y33d	8y175d	209 Days	Average % Chg High	39.9%	Projected High	12760.98
Average Annual % Change	16.0%	4.8%	6.4%	2.5%	1.5%	Average % Chg at Low	-16.9%	Low to Date	7286.27
High	110.15	174.29	293.79	1051.70	2934.65	Average % Chg Low to High	67.5%	Projected Low	7576.71
% Chg at High	110.5%	28.9%	31.0%	26.8%	2.4%	Avg % Chg Peace Hi - War Lo	-34.0%		
Low	52.32	92.92	197.46	631.16	2365.10	Avg % Chg Peace Lo - War Hi	281.1%		
% Chg at Low	0.0%	-31.3%	-12.0%	-23.9%	-17.4%				
% Chg Low to High	110.5%	87.6%	48.8%	66.6%	24.1%				
% Chg Peace Hi - War Lo	NA	-75.6%	-13.5%	-25.9%	-21.2%				
% Chg Peace Lo -War Hi	NA	322.8%	81.8%	311.6%	408.1%				

DOW PERFORMANCE DURING PEACETIME AFTER

	WWI	WWII	Korea	Vietnam	Gulf War I	Peace Time Stats		Projected Gulf War II	
Dow at the Start	88.06	174.29	268.46	1003.54	2889.11	Average % Chg during Peace	139.3%	Projected Dow at Start	11650.02
Dow at the End	135.25	224.35	829.16	2864.60	9119.77	Average Length of Peace	12y351d	Projected Dow at End	27883.32
% Chg at End of Peace	53.6%	28.7%	213.3%	185.4%	215.7%	Average Annual % Change	11.8%	Projected High	36946.68
Duration Years/Days	20y338d	4y297d	10y379d	17y191d	10y225d	Average % Chg at High	217.1%	Projected Low	9112.36
Average Annual % Change	2.6%	6.0%	19.3%	10.6%	20.3%	Average % Chg at Low	-21.8%		
High	381.17	228.38	851.35	2999.75	11722.98	Average % Chg Low to High	365.8%		
% Chg at High	332.9%	31.0%	217.1%	198.9%	305.8%	Avg % Chg War Hi - Peace Lo	-26.1%		
Low	41.22	161.60	255.49	577.60	2855.45	Avg % Chg War Lo - Peace Hi	375.3%		
% Chg at Low	-53.2%	-7.3%	-4.8%	-42.4%	-1.2%				
% Chg Low to High	824.7%	41.3%	233.2%	419.3%	310.5%				
% Chg War Hi - Peace Lo	-62.6%	-7.3%	-13.0%	-45.1%	-2.7%				
% Chg War Lo -Peace Hi	628.5%	145.8%	331.2%	375.3%	395.7%				

These are not our prognostications! The numbers for the Projected Gulf War II and after Projected Gulf War II are simple extrapolations utilizing the wartime stats and peacetime stats from current levels in the Dow.

War and the Markets

A close examination of the major events throughout history during war time and the correlating reaction of the markets are revealing. Looking at the charts above, several key conclusions can be made.

1) **No new all-time highs**—The Dow has never made a significant high during wartime. The lack of a big breakout can be attributed to muted investor enthusiasm. Every time the market tried to rally to new all-time high, inevitably a negative exogenous event pertaining to the war dampened spirits.

2) **The war machine props up the market**—After the initial shock of once again being in a war, the markets do not fall significantly lower. The combination of government spending, investor bargain hunting, and good old American pride insulate the market from making serious lows.

3) **The Market (as always) is a barometer**—Markets rally on sustained good news and fall on sustained bad news. The markets also tend to be more reactive early in wartime. By the end of a prolonged engagement, investors tend to be more callous to news. The markets will also anticipate the end of the war by moving to a high-water mark. This contributes to the inevitable letdown when peace breaks out.

4) **Wartime presidents do not lose**—Presidents tend to shape their political decisions pertaining to a foreign war around the presidential election cycle making unpopular decisions only after they are reelected while creating as much good news as possible leading up to the election.

500%+ Moves Follow Wartime Inflation

What makes the market range bound during wartime and soar during peacetime? The simple answer is inflation. The government empties the treasury during a war. It also focuses on foreign issues rather than domestic concerns and the economy. The result is a sustained rise in inflation. Only after the economy settles down and Washington refocuses on domestic issues will the stock market soar to new heights.

It is important to note that the scope and focus of this study is long-, to very-long-term. It will be impossible to predict the start of the next secular bull market until the major worldwide conflicts that the United States is involved in are over or perceived to be ending. Moreover, the inevitable inflationary cycle associated has just started to rear its ugly head. Historically, war-related inflation has lasted one year for World War I, a year and a half for World War II and almost two decades for Vietnam! The secular bull will not start until that inflation levels off.

There have been three highly inflationary eras since the Civil War's 74% rate of inflation. These periods of high inflation were also war-related—World War I, World War II, and Vietnam.

World War I

Prices slightly more than doubled in five years between 1915 and 1920. The Consumer Price Index (1967 = 100) climbed from approximately 30 to a dizzying 60. While the nation was suffering from two years of severe deflation and depression with stock market prices being slashed in half, the Dow began to rise out of the ashes. From 63.90 on August 24, 1921, it climbed to an intraday high of 386.10

on September 3, 1929, a spectacular rise of 504 percent for the 8-year period. Who could have dreamed it? This era likely gave birth to the adage, "Buy and Hold."

Bear in mind that the Dow accomplished its feat despite many unfavorable conditions: the growth of communism and the beginning of fascism in Germany and Italy; monetary horrors such as the German "nightmare" inflation and the inability of our Allies to repay their war debts; the Teapot Dome scandal; prohibition and gangsterism; et al. Through it all the Dow rolled on!

After World War I, deflation brought the CPI down to the 50 level where it remained almost stationary throughout most of the twenties. The early thirties' deflation knocked the CPI down further to the 40 level, and there it stayed for the rest of the decade. Interestingly, the rise in stock prices between the 1932 bottom and the 1937 top was quite respectable too—up 284%.

World War II

The onset of the war brought rising prices as usual. This resulted in a 74% rise in the cost of living between 1941 and 1948. The CPI rose from approximately 42 to 73.

After spending three years in the doldrums, the market began a long 16-year rise on June 14, 1949 at Dow 160.63 (intraday). By January 19, 1966, when the Dow hit 1000.55 (intraday), investors once again had experienced a giant 500-percent climb following a super-inflationary period. To be precise, the rise measured 523 percent. It should be noted that a small inflationary rate (averaging under 2% a year) accompanied the market rise, bringing the CPI up to the 95 level in January 1966.

Once again, we must add that the Dow moved up despite many unsettling events along the way: (the Korean War; the French defeat and withdrawal from Vietnam; McCarthyism; revolts in Poland, Hungary, Argentina; the Egyptian seizure of the Suez Canal and war with Israel, France, and Britain; the civil rights movement; the Cuban missile crisis; the Kennedy assassination; etc.).

Vietnam War

The 1970s brought back crunching inflation, unseen for a generation. War, as usual, was primarily responsible although the OPEC fiascos played a substantial role. Vietnam helped drive the CPI up from 95 to OVER 300 by the time it leveled off in the early eighties, an increase of over 200%. This helps explain the ensuing super bull that powered the markets for the next two decades.

In the April 1976 issue of *Smart Money Newsletter* (a predecessor of the *Almanac Investor Newsletter*) Yale Hirsch wrote an article entitled: "Stocks Catch Up With Inflation Eventually—500% Moves After Both WW1 & WW 2—Can It Happen Again? Dow 3,420?"

A truly bold and amazing prediction made when many pundits were making a case for the Dow to NEVER cross 1,000 again! The market crested in 1990 on July 17 at Dow 3,024.26 (good for a 430% move—not quite 500%, but respectfully close) and crossed Dow 3,420 on May 20 1992. The S&P, however, did do it in July 1990 by gaining 506.6% from its October 4, 1974 intraday low of 60.96 to its July 16, 1990 intraday high of 369.78!

Little did Yale (or anyone else for that matter) realize at the time that the market would wind up making a 1,957% move from the Vietnam low to the bubble high! With the benefit of hindsight we now know that the end of the launching pad—when inflation leveled off was in August 1982. From its intraday low on August 11, 1982 at 770 the Dow climbed 1,447% to its intraday high of 11,908.50 on January 14, 2000.

Gulf War I, Gulf War II, War in Afghanistan, War on Terror, et al.

Correlating today's market to a historical point, we see a strikingly similar situation to the Markets circa late 1965. The market had already hit "rock bottom" in 1962 and was well on its way to the February 1966 top. This is just before the numbing inflation of the late 1960s to early 1980s. Vietnam was in full swing, but it was well before the major anti-war protests and the stark reality of war hit home after the Tet Offensive. The market managed to move along nicely for another year or so topping in February 1966. Then things started to get ugly. Inflation rose and rose and rose. Three significant bottoms were reached as the market failed to breakthrough Dow 1,000—first in late 1966, then again in the summer of 1970 and finally the post-war bottom in the winter of 1974, each time making lower lows.

There are a few differences in looking at the pattern this time around. This is not your daddy's CPI. The U.S. Department of Labor has tweaked and manipulated the CPI many times over the past twenty years or so in an attempt to mask inflation. This is important to note, because this time around we may only see a 40-50% increase in the CPI—or it could be another 200%. The point is that no one is really sure how this new and improved version of the CPI will react in a hyperinflationary environment. Inflation may be best illustrated by another index, or the dollar, or the increase in a gallon of milk or a can of Campbell's chicken noodle soup. The dollar may actually be the best way to judge inflation moving forward. The important concept is that prices are going to rise sharply in the near future and that is what will be the catalyst for the next secular bull.

As it stands right now, the war low is Dow 7,178 intraday. Will the market make another 500% move to Dow 43,000? How about another 1,447% move to Dow 111,044? The answer depends on how much inflation we get. The last move took twenty-six years to play out from the 1974 bottom to the 2000 top. At this juncture, the projected level and timeframe are less important than the understanding of how the markets have historically performed and the looming cycle of inflation that lies just around the corner.

In the future, we can expect revolts, revolutions, environmental problems, monetary crises, scandals, droughts, more inflation, a few recessions and bear markets, not to mention a "plague" or two along the way. However, during the three previous "500%" moves—or for that matter, the last 5,000 or more years—

people were always afraid of something or other in the future. Somehow, we do seem to survive and overcome adversity.

The Big Picture Explained

From the chart showing the Dow and the CPI plotted together, we first point out the correlation between war, inflation, and the subsequent "catch-up" of the market. We have also highlighted the rectangular consolidation areas surrounding wartimes that possess roughly the same percentage range. These give the appearance of "launching pads" for the giant moves.

The inflation/catch-up correlation is clear. World War I inflation (up 100%) followed by the 504% rise in the stock prices during the twenties. Then we see the inflation of World War II (up 74%) and the subsequent long rise of the Dow of 523%. Finally, the Vietnam inflation of over 300% and the subsequent super-bull to end all super-bulls is a hopeful reminder as well as a warning.

During prolonged military conflicts, the market basically stayed within a defined trading range. Once peace had set in for several years the stock market took off to new heights. When the current battle against terror and our involvement in Iraq has passed then we can expect the Dow to leave 10,000 behind for good and put 20,000 and beyond in our sights.

Dow 43,000 is where we will set our sights. The verdict on how long it will take to get there is out until the dust begins to settle.

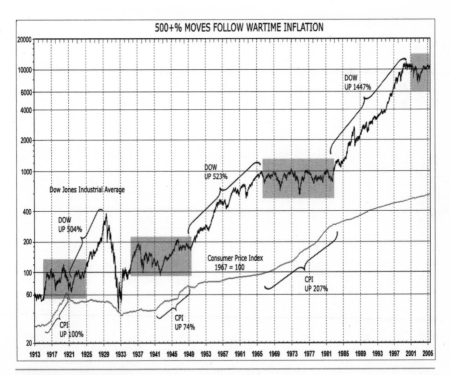

THE THREE PEAKS AND DOMED HOUSE RECURRING MARKET PATTERN

This modern treatise stands on shoulders of George Lindsay, the late, great technician, and his unrivaled research and revelations. Here we recap all that has been covered, further explain the nature of this phenomenon and bring us fully up-to-date as to where the market stands right now with respect to this Three Peaks and Domed House Pattern.

"Three Peaks and a Domed House" is an easy way to remember and recognize this amazing recurring market pattern. Occurring at nearly every major U. S. equity market top, the pattern illustrates consistent market behavior.

The pattern describes how markets tend to come off a low and move up until a resistance point is reached (point 3). Then after two attempts to move higher (points 5 and 7) there is a sell-off to point 10. This is the "Separating Decline" that separates the Three Peaks from the Domed House. Point 10 is always lower than either point 4 or 6, often both. If is not lower it does not qualify and the pattern is nullified. The Domed House starts with a base between points 10 and 14. A rally usually ensues and forms another higher base (points 15 to 20, Roof of the First Story). Then from there the final surge to the high creates the Dome from points 21 to 25. The drop-off returns to the vicinity of point 10.

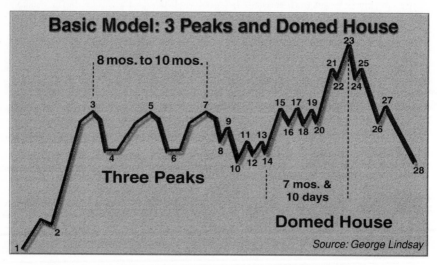

Lindsay based these formations after studying 150 years of market charts back in 1968. When looking at the point 23 dates in Lindsay's original work we noticed that they all matched up with a bull market high on page 119. Additionally, Lindsay stated that the pattern "may occur on either a major or minor scale. When it is of major scope, a typical formation begins at a bear market low." This inspired us to reconcile our study of this phenomenal pattern to the bull and bear markets defined on page 119. In the end, that's what we are after, where and when the next major top and bottom will be.

Lindsay noted that minor and major formations of Three Peaks and a Domed House often overlapped with a Peak of one being a Dome of another. Sometimes Three Peaks followed a Domed House. Some tops could not be fit into the pattern and do not qualify. But Lindsay did find that, "...the market has followed [the formations] at least 60% of the time..." and that, "The majority of all major advances ended in a pattern which resembled the Three Peaks and a Domed House."

The formations at major tops that Lindsay defined went through 1968. We picked up from there and plotted the points of all the formations at major tops that match the bull markets. Lindsay did not identify starting points so we applied the nearest or most logical bear market low. Our current analysis is based on a more recent time frame, starting with the top in 1916. This is the first major top after the four-plus month market closure from August to December 1914 during WWI. It is also a more modern era, more relevant to present time.

The table on the next page details moves and durations of the instances of Three Peaks and Domed House patterns that have topped out at major bull market tops since 1916. Projections for the current pattern are based on the average moves and durations from different points.

Three Peaks and Domed House Moves & Durations

Pt 1 - Peaks High % Gain	Pt 1 - Pt 3 Days	Peak 1 - Peak 3 Days	Peaks High - Sep Dec Low % Loss	Domed House Top Date	Domed House Top Point 23 DJIA	Point 10 - Point 23 Days	Point 14 - Point 23 Days	Sep Low - Dome Top % Gain	Peaks High - Dome top % Gain	Point 1 - Point 23 Days	Point 1 - Point 23 % Gain	Top - Point 28 % Loss	Top - Point 28 Days	Sep Low (10) - House Low (28) % Loss	Days (10)
83.0%	240	146	-14.4%	11/21/16	110.15	213	81	29.6%	11.0%	636	103.2%	-21.0%	73	2.4%	286
41.8%	117	68	-12.3%	11/3/19	119.62	75	68	21.5%	6.6%	268	51.1%	-24.8%	114	-8.6%	189
61.9%	383	58	-11.0%	3/20/23	105.38	113	82	14.5%	1.9%	573	64.9%	-12.0%	62	0.8%	175
27.1%	59	88	-10.3%	9/3/29	381.17	99	76	29.9%	16.5%	269	48.1%	-39.6%	56	-21.6%	155
116.6%	141	63	-23.0%	2/5/34	110.74	107	82	32.4%	1.9%	343	120.8%	-22.8%	171	2.2%	278
28.6%	114	77	-10.1%	5/29/46	212.50	92	62	14.2%	2.7%	307	32.1%	-21.3%	104	-10.1%	196
40.0%	427	200	-7.2%	1/5/53	293.79	249	216	14.6%	6.3%	907	48.8%	-13.0%	252	-0.3%	501
103.9%	935	269	-12.7%	7/12/57	520.77	150	123	14.5%	-0.1%	1397	103.8%	-19.4%	102	-7.7%	252
63.3%	650	311	-17.4%	12/13/61	734.61	414	303	29.8%	7.2%	1513	75.0%	-27.1%	195	-5.4%	609
75.4%	876	177	-10.5%	2/9/66	995.15	226	170	18.4%	5.9%	1324	85.7%	-22.9%	201	-8.8%	427
26.7%	213	245	-12.5%	12/3/68	985.21	294	257	19.4%	4.5%	788	32.4%	-18.6%	238	-2.8%	532
50.6%	337	133	-16.1%	1/11/73	1051.70	415	304	31.8%	10.6%	961	66.6%	-25.0%	328	-1.2%	743
52.7%	159	117	-11.1%	9/21/76	1014.79	356	291	29.4%	15.1%	655	75.7%	-26.9%	525	-5.4%	881
16.8%	62	36	-7.0%	9/8/78	907.74	65	46	12.7%	4.8%	192	22.3%	-13.5%	67	-2.5%	132
31.8%	116	97	-9.2%	4/27/81	1024.05	137	73	12.7%	2.4%	371	34.9%	-19.5%	151	-9.3%	288
60.7%	271	77	-6.8%	11/29/83	1287.20	113	97	10.7%	3.1%	474	65.7%	-15.6%	238	-6.6%	351
76.7%	636	136	-8.6%	8/25/87	2722.42	330	237	55.1%	41.8%	1127	150.6%	-36.1%	55	-0.9%	385
61.6%	683	123	-9.5%	7/17/90	2999.75	168	144	17.9%	6.7%	1002	72.5%	-21.2%	86	-7.0%	254
249.2%	2491	121	-8.2%	7/17/98	9337.97	189	175	23.2%	13.1%	2836	294.8%	-19.3%	45	-0.5%	234
50.2%	255	104	-11.5%	1/14/00	11722.98	91	73	17.0%	3.5%	501	55.5%	-16.4%	53	-2.2%	144
65.9%	**458**	**132**	**-11.5%**	avg		**195**	**148**	**22.5%**	**8.3%**	**822**	**80.2%**	**-21.8%**	**156**	**-4.8%**	**351**
16.8%	**59**	**36**	**-23.0%**	min		**65**	**46**	**10.7%**	**-0.1%**	**192**	**22.3%**	**-12.0%**	**45**	**2.4%**	**132**
249.2%	**2491**	**311**	**-6.8%**	max		**415**	**304**	**55.1%**	**41.8%**	**2836**	**294.8%**	**-39.6%**	**525**	**-21.6%**	**881**
47.4%	490	133	-9.2%	3/4/05	10940.55	204	130	12.2%	1.9%	877	50.2%*	8555.59*		9284.56*	

CURRENT PATTERN, *PROJECTIONS BASED ON AVERAGES

130   ALMANAC INVESTOR

The Points Defined

Points 1 through 7 form the Three Peaks section. The base is formed at points 1 and 2 with points 3, 5 and 7 constituting the peaks. The first two peaks have a corresponding retrenching level at points 4 and 6. The tops and the bottoms of the peaks are all in the same basic price range.

After the third peak comes the Separating Decline. Points 7 through 10 separate the Three Peaks from the Domed House section. This phase of the cycle has at least two selling waves and point 10 is always lower than either 4 or 6 and often both. Unless one of the two prior lows is broken, it doesn't qualify as a Separating Decline and the pattern is nullified.

During the Separating Decline the general direction of the market is noticeably downward. As the market stabilizes, the foundation of the Domed House is formed from points 10 through 14. The Domed House is a two-story house with a flat roof on the first floor and a domed top on the second. To form a satisfactory foundation the market rebounds off point 10 to point 11 and then retreats twice to 12 and 14. Lindsay is emphatic that the model states that the low must be tested twice; one test is not sufficient to form the foundation.

The first story of the house occurs from point 14 through 20. Points 14 through 15 form the Wall of the First Story of the Domed House. This is a rapid rise in the market that is according to Lindsay, "a short lived advance." After this rise a base is formed, known as the Roof of the First Story. The roof is a series of market reversals occurring in the same general price range. Five Reversals generally form the roof.

After the fifth reversal, the Wall of the Second Story of the Domed House is formed between points 20 and 21. The Roof of the Second Story of the Domed House begins at point 21. The market hesitates between points 21 and 22 before pushing higher to the apex of the Domed House at point 23. Point 23 is the market top.

Once the top is made there is a quick retreat to point 24 which is at the same general level as point 22. On a chart this, "suggests a cupola or small dome on a building," hence, Domed House. The market holds on for a while between points 24 and 25 before a rapid retreat to point 26. This drop is back to the level of points 15-20 thus giving back all the gain made during the formation of the Second Story of the Domed House.

Following point 26 the market tries to rally to a new high, but the rally is futile and the market has always returned to the level seen at point 10! Lindsay states that there has never been an exception to this rule and that all of the gains made during the formation of the Domed House have always eventually been given back. And our research of the nine major bull market tops from 1973 to 2000 confirms this.

Historical Examples

The counts for the 1968-1969 formation are courtesy of the late George Lindsay from his September 8, 1969 newsletter. Counts up to point 26 in the 1999-2000 were plotted by us in our February 11, 2000 newsletter. In that issue we wrote, "It appears to us that the Domed House section may have been completed in record time. This fast-paced, quick reacting market seems to have built the Domed House section in three months instead of seven..."

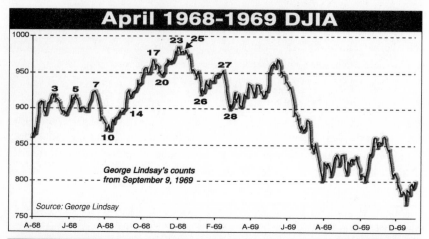

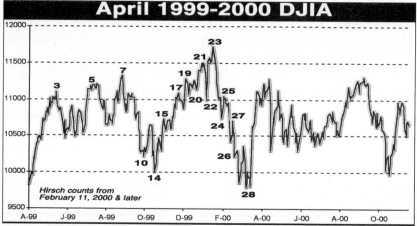

These two formations in conjunction with the current pattern illustrate both the similarities and the differences. Remember, no two patterns are the same and none follow the model to a tee. Note the shortness of Three Peaks (less than Lindsay's basic model time span of 8-10 months) and the swiftness of the rise and fall of the Domed House. Our current research of the twenty formations since WWI, shows an average of 4-5 months for both the Three Peaks and Domed House formations with the shortest being about one month and the longest about 10 months. Notice in December 1968 how point 25 is asymmetrical and quite close to point 23.

     ALMANAC INVESTOR

In both instances strong rallies followed the point 28 low. In 1969 a further drop ensued rather quickly and in 2000 sideways action preceded a deeper fall in 2001. Continued declines followed in both cases with bottoms about a year and a half latter, May 1970 and September 2001 respectively. It was not until January 1973 that the Dow exceeded that December 1968 top—another Domed House top. The Dow has yet to surpass its 2000 high-water mark.

Current Situation

Before applying this model to the current situation in the Dow, it is important to note that the Three Peaks and the Domed House pattern is not a magic eight ball. We are not omnipotent oracles who can divine the markets exactly. Following this pattern will not make you a fortune overnight. As most seasoned investors know and all green investors will find out, one does not trade by indicators and patterns alone. The purpose of indicators and patterns is to gain a grasp on how markets have acted in the past. No pattern repeats itself exactly and moreover, no pattern or indicator has 100% accuracy. That being said, this pattern will show you an approximation of level, general market direction, and an advanced warning to be on the lookout for sentiment and conditions on The Street to change. George Santayana once stated that, "Those who cannot remember the past are condemned to repeat it." We are in the business of remembering and explaining the past in order to make money in the future.

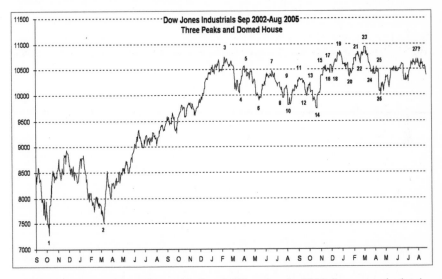

We are using the base formed in late 2002 and early 2003 for our as the beginning of the current pattern. Point 1 was put in at the low made October 9, 2002 with point 2 occurring March 12, 2003. It is not important to get hung up on where the starting point is, for Lindsay makes it a point to discount its significance.

What is important is the Three Peaks formation. We have the Three Peaks being made in spring 2004 with Peak 1 (Point 3) being reached February 11, 2004, Peak 2 (Point 5) on April 6, 2004, and the last Peak (Point 7) logged on June 23, 2004.

The Separating Decline was put in during the difficult market conditions summer 2004. After hitting Dow 10480, the market plummeted over 500 points to Point 8 on July 26. After a short rally Point 9 was set on August 2 before Point 10 was made on August 12 completing this leg of the pattern.

The foundation of the house was made during fall 2004's tight trading range with Point 11 made on September 7, Point 12 on September 27, and Point 13 on October 6. Point 14, the last point of the foundation of the house, was reached on October 25.

The Dow rallied over 820 points off of the foundation of the Domed House's last reversal thus creating the Wall of the First Story of the Domed House on November 18 corresponding to Point 15. The Dow went through a series of reversals from December 2004 through January 2005 forming Points 16-20. The Five Reversals that constitute the Roof of the First Story were made mid-November through the end of January with Point 16 logged on November 30, Point 17 on December 3, Point 18 December 7, Point 19 December 28 and finally Point 20 on January 24.

The Dow then rallied almost 500 points to Dow 10,837 until the middle of February creating the Wall of the Second Story on February 15. From that level, the left side of the cupola was made with a slight retreat to Dow 10,611 setting Point 22 on February 22. Another rally to the high of Dow 10,940.55 on March 4, 2005 created what we feel at this writing is the Point 23 Domed House Top. An 8.5% correction ended April 20, 2005 at Point 26.

At this juncture the Dow has failed to reach a new high and Point 27 may have been logged on July 28, 2005 at Dow 10,705.55. Currently the Dow is in retreat. Already giving back the gains made by the Second Story of the Domed House (Point 20, Dow 10368). We anticipate a further drop to the neighborhood of Point 14 (Dow 9750).

Why the Dow?

Why use the antiquated and unrepresentative Dow? Some pattern followers have plotted the Three Peaks out on other indices such as the S&P 500—and they do fit the formation. But the Dow is "the right average to use" as Lindsay stated in 1969. Lindsay went on to write, "If you want to know the true level of the market, look at the broader averages. If you want to predict the future, go by the Dow...some technicians get the most reliable results by using an index of only ten or twelve sensitive and influential stocks." The Dow still possesses thirty of the most sensitive and influential stocks in the world.

We will continue to monitor and explain this pattern until its completion which we expect sometime during the summer and fall.

Sources:

Recurrent Stock Market Patterns: the Three Peaks and the Domed House
by George Lindsay, George Lindsay's Opinion September 4, 1968

One Year Later: A Follow-Up of the Three Peaks and Domed House
by George Lindsay, George Lindsay's Opinion September 8, 1969

PART 2: SEASONAL SECTOR INVESTING

SECTOR INDICIES

Sector seasonality was featured in the first *1968 Stock Trader's Almanac*. A Merrill Lynch study showed that buying seven sectors around September or October and selling in the first few months of 1954-1964 tripled the gains of holding them for ten years. Over the past few years we have honed this strategy significantly and now devote a large portion of our time and resources to investing during seasonably favorable periods for different sectors with Exchange Traded Funds (ETFs).

As the ETF universe expands at breakneck speed, more seasonal investment options become available to Almanac Investors. We are constantly reviewing and revamping existing seasonalities as well as delving for new ones. Twenty years ago who would have thought that the Internet would be a major sector on The Street?

The seasonalities in this section of the book help drive selections for our Exchange Traded Fund (ETF) Portfolio. We hand select ETFs that correlate to sectors that are coming into favor.

Illustrated within first section of Part 2 are the major facets of the sector indices we used to create our seasonal sector investment strategies. Section two is a detailed look at Exchange Traded Funds available at the time of publication.

It is important to note that many elements of these indices and ETFs are constantly in flux. We advocate using a recent set of data prior to the commencement of new research. The research available on our website is periodically refreshed and all of the recommendations made in our newsletter or via email alerts are based on the most recent data possible.

AI Seasonality

The seasonality is derived by analyzing the dataset of an index in a year over year fashion. It is important to use a dataset that is long enough to be statistically significant. This is the primary reason we use the indices and not ETFs to determine seasonalities. Most ETFs have not been around long enough.

We have specified beginning third, middle third, or last third of the month which corresponds to the first seven, middle seven, or last seven trading days of the month.

Recommended ETF

This is the ETF that corresponds best to the sector index and seasonality. In some instances there is only one ETF available that accurately tracks the index or seasonal pattern. Often times there are many and we analyze and recommend several.

Volatility

Volitility is based on an index's tendency to have severe daily or weekly moves.

Risk

Risk is based on the probability of the seasonality either failing or underperforming.

Key Consideration

What to take into account when deciding whether to trade the AI Seasonality and for setting buy limits above or below the market.

Components

Chosen by the issuer of the index based on their set of rules, they are subject to change. It is important to note that while components change, most indices are composed of industry stalwarts that by and large set the trend and direction of movement.

Performance

Split into seasonal and buy and hold. Brokerage fees and tax implications have not been factored in.

Monthly Performance

Listed by best performance as well as chronologically.

SECTOR INDEX SEASONALITY TABLE

Ticker	Sector Index	Seasonality Start		Finish		Average % Return † 10-Year	5-Year
XNG	Natural Gas	February	E	June	B	19.6	10.4
RXH	Healthcare Prov	March	E	June	M	15.1	14.4
XCI	Computer Tech	April	M	July	M	16.2	6.8
RXP	Healthcare Prod	April	M	July	B	10.4	4.2
MSH	High-Tech	April	M	July	M	16.5	7.8
IIX	Internet	April	M	July	B	17.4	10.3
BTK	Biotech	July	E	March	B	44.9	8.0
XAU	Gold & Silver	July	E	September	E	18.6	18.6
UTY	Utilities	July	E	January	B	12.9	16.8
CMR	Consumer	September	E	June	B	16.4	12.5
RXP	Healthcare Prod ‡	September	B	February	M	14.9	11.0
RXH	Healthcare Prov ‡	September	E	January	B	12.6	12.9
DRG	Pharmaceutical	September	B	February	M	16.0	6.1
XTC	Telecom	September	E	January	M	22.5	21.2
BKX	Banking	October	B	June	B	21.2	16.0
XBD	Broker/Dealer	October	B	April	M	44.5	16.1
XCI	Computer Tech	October	B	February	B	24.3	13.2
CYC	Cyclical	October	B	May	M	21.0	21.8
MSH	High-Tech	October	B	January	M	28.5	22.8
IIX	Internet	October	B	January	B	39.5	25.6
S5MATR *	Materials	October	M	May	M	17.2	20.0
RMS**	Real Estate	October	E	July	B	18.8	23.3
SOX	Semiconductor	October	E	December	B	22.1	20.7
DJT	Transports	October	B	May	B	20.4	16.8
XOI	Oil	December	M	June	M	16.2	19.0

† Average % Return based on full seasonality completion through July 2005 ‡ Only nine years of data
* S5MATR Available @ bloomberg.com ** RMS changed to RMZ June 2005

Sector Index Seasonality Strategy Calendar

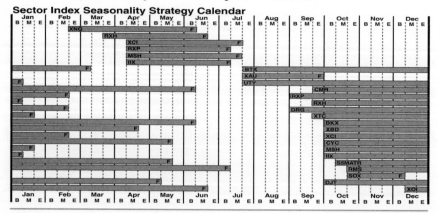

ALMANAC INVESTOR

BANKING
Ticker **BKX**   Index **PLHX BANKING**

AI SEASONALITY

Start	Finish	Data Since
October (Beginning)	June (Beginning)	2/22/93

HISTORICAL PERFORMANCE

Buy & Hold	5-Year Avg	10-Year Avg	Avg Since Inception	Best Year	% Change	Worst Year	% Change
12 Months	7.3%	17.0%	12.3%	1995	54.6%	2002	−13.0%

AI Seasonality	5-Year Avg	10-Year Avg	Avg Since Inception	Best Year	% Change	Worst Year	% Change
9 Months	19.8%	23.5%	21.6%	1999	44.0%	1994	2.3%

Recommended ETF:	Merrill Lynch Regional Bank HOLDRS (RKH)	Volatility: Low
Key Consideration:	Recent industry consolidation and mergers	Risk: Low

COMPONENTS

Ticker	Name	Ticker	Name
BAC	Bank of America	NCC	National City
BK	Bank of New York	NFB	North Fork Bank
BBT	BB&T	TRS	Northern Trust
COF	Capital One Financial	PNC	PNC Financial Services
C	Citigroup	RF	Regions Financial
CMA	Comerica	STT	State Street
FITB	Fifth Third Bancorp	STI	SunTrust Banks
GDW	Golden West Financial	USB	US Bancorp
JPM	JPMorgan Chase	WB	Wachovia
KEY	Keycorp	WM	Washington Mutual
MTB	M&T Bank	WFC	Wells Fargo
MEL	Mellon Financial	ZION	Zion Bancorporation

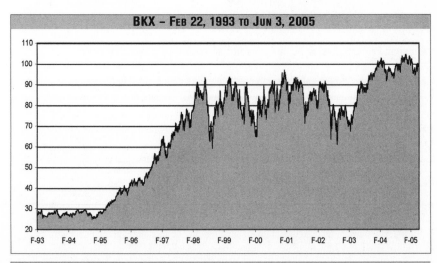

BKX – Feb 22, 1993 to Jun 3, 2005

Ticker BKX   **Index PLHX Banking**

DETAILED PERFORMANCE AI SEASONALITY

Start		Finish		Percent	Investing
Date	Close	Date	Close	Change	$1,000
Oct 6 1994	26.60	Jun 5 1995	32.98	23.98%	$1239.80
Oct 2 1995	37.80	Jun 5 1996	44.94	18.89	1474.00
Oct 1 1996	48.12	Jun 10 1997	63.10	31.13	1932.85
Oct 1 1997	72.72	Jun 8 1998	85.72	17.88	2278.45
Oct 8 1998	59.20	Jun 7 1999	85.26	44.02	3281.42
Oct 1 1999	74.58	Jun 2 2000	89.26	19.68	3927.20
Oct 10 2000	82.86	Jun 5 2001	93.24	12.53	4419.28
Oct 8 2001	75.14	Jun 3 2002	86.44	15.04	5083.94
Oct 9 2002	61.11	Jun 5 2003	87.25	42.78	7258.85
Oct 2 2003	90.08	Jun 7 2004	98.35	9.18	7925.22
			Average:	**23.51**	**$6925.22 Gain**

DETAILED PERFORMANCE BUY & HOLD

Start		Finish		Percent	Investing
Date	Close	Date	Close	Change	$1,000
Dec 30 1994	25.48	Dec 29 1995	39.38	54.55	1545.50
Dec 29 1995	39.38	Dec 31 1996	53.77	36.54	2110.23
Dec 31 1996	53.77	Dec 31 1997	75.54	40.49	2964.66
Dec 31 1997	75.54	Dec 31 1998	80.52	6.59	3160.03
Dec 31 1998	80.52	Dec 31 1999	77.00	−4.37	3021.93
Dec 31 1999	77.00	Dec 29 2000	90.14	17.06	3537.48
Dec 29 2000	90.14	Dec 31 2001	86.01	−4.58	3375.46
Dec 31 2001	86.01	Dec 31 2002	74.80	−13.03	2935.64
Dec 31 2002	74.80	Dec 31 2003	97.48	30.32	3825.72
Dec 31 2003	97.48	Dec 31 2004	104.11	6.80	4085.87
			Average:	**17.04**	**$3085.87 Gain**

Almanac Investor Sector Seasonality out-performance factor 124.42%

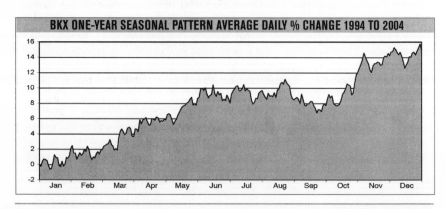

BKX ONE-YEAR SEASONAL PATTERN AVERAGE DAILY % CHANGE 1994 TO 2004

MONTHLY PERFORMANCE BY RANK
MARCH 1993 TO MAY 2005

Month	Total Change	Average Change	# Up	# Down
October	44.1%	3.7%	7	5
May	31.0	2.4	10	3
March	21.0	1.6	6	7
January	19.5	1.6	7	5
April	19.3	1.5	8	5
November	17.8	1.5	8	4
July	16.2	1.3	8	4
December	10.4	0.9	7	5
February	−1.4	−0.1	6	6
June	−2.7	−0.2	6	6
August	−9.4	−0.8	7	5
September	−9.4	−0.8	6	6

MONTHLY PERFORMANCE
MARCH 1993 TO MAY 2005

Month	Total Change	Average Change	# Up	# Down
January	19.5%	1.6%	7	5
February	−1.4	−0.1	6	6
March	21.0	1.6	6	7
April	19.3	1.5	8	5
May	31.0	2.4	10	3
June	−2.7	−0.2	6	6
July	16.2	1.3	8	4
August	−9.4	−0.8	7	5
September	−9.4	−0.8	6	6
October	44.1	3.7	7	5
November	17.8	1.5	8	4
December	10.4	0.9	7	5

BEST & WORST MONTHS BY PERCENT MARCH 1993 TO MAY 2005

Month	Best Close	Change	Month	Worst Close	Change
Mar-2000	79.54	17.7%	Aug-1998	64.16	−25.6%
Oct-1999	88.42	17.5	Jun-2000	73.26	−11.7
Oct-1998	74.32	13.8	Feb-2000	67.59	−11.7
Jul-1997	71.39	12.7	Sep-2002	69.71	−11.4
Apr-2003	79.24	12.0	Jul-2002	75.65	−8.8
Aug-2000	89.56	11.9	May-1999	84.44	−8.3
May-1995	32.31	9.9	Feb-2001	88.24	−7.9
Nov-1996	56.57	9.9	Sep-1994	27.29	−7.8
Feb-1998	79.26	9.8	Nov-1994	25.77	−7.5
Oct-2002	76.34	9.5	Mar-1997	56.09	−7.5
Dec-2000	90.14	9.4	Jul-1999	82.89	−7.5
Jul-2000	80.06	9.3	Sep-2001	79.28	−7.4
May-2000	82.98	9.1	Oct-1993	26.78	−7.2
Mar-2002	89.77	9.0	Dec-1999	77.00	−7.0
Apr-1999	92.09	8.9	Nov-1999	82.80	−6.4
Jan-1997	57.98	7.8	Aug-1997	67.03	−6.1
Oct-1996	51.49	7.7	Jun-2002	82.96	−5.9
Nov-2001	83.29	7.4	Aug-2001	85.58	−5.8
Oct-2003	94.19	7.3	Apr-1993	26.41	−5.6
Nov-1995	39.51	7.2	Nov-2000	82.38	−5.4

BEST YEARS BY PERCENT

Year	Close	Point Change	Percent Change
1995	39.38	13.90	54.6%
1997	75.54	21.77	40.5
1996	53.77	14.39	36.5
2003	97.48	22.68	30.3
2000	90.14	13.14	17.1

WORST YEARS BY PERCENT

Year	Close	Point Change	Percent Change
2002	74.80	−11.21	−13.0%
1994	25.48	−1.79	−6.6
2001	86.01	−4.13	−4.6
1999	77.00	−3.52	−4.4
1998	80.52	4.98	6.6

BEST & WORST WEEKS BY % CHANGE FEB 22, 1993 TO JUN 3, 2005

Week	Best Close	Change	Week	Worst Close	Change
3/17/00	76.11	17.93%	9/21/01	71.26	−11.66%
10/22/99	80.87	13.92	10/15/99	70.99	−10.33
9/28/01	79.28	11.25	8/28/98	68.10	−9.28
6/2/00	89.26	10.63	4/23/93	26.60	−8.78
10/18/02	74.74	10.59	1/9/98	69.46	−8.34
10/16/98	70.51	10.34	10/4/02	63.82	−8.20
8/4/00	86.51	9.71	6/16/00	75.51	−8.13
5/2/97	60.55	9.36	6/9/00	82.19	−7.92
10/29/99	88.42	9.34	9/4/98	62.74	−7.87
7/7/00	79.66	8.74	7/19/02	71.48	−7.85
8/9/02	77.43	8.02	10/13/00	80.76	−7.15
1/8/99	86.89	7.91	2/8/02	81.08	−6.91
3/21/03	75.30	7.51	9/20/02	68.65	−6.74
4/9/99	90.65	7.46	2/23/01	86.94	−6.71
12/22/00	89.57	7.28	1/21/00	72.54	−6.41
12/5/97	77.63	6.81	2/18/00	66.68	−6.39
7/2/99	90.91	6.68	8/7/98	80.78	−6.37
11/21/97	73.40	6.59	7/12/02	77.57	−6.28
11/3/00	87.84	6.56	11/17/00	80.98	−6.20
3/30/01	85.83	6.30	1/15/99	81.51	−6.19

BEST & WORST DAYS BY % CHANGE FEB 22, 1993 TO JUN 3, 2005

Day	Best Close	Change	Day	Worst Close	Change
3/16/00	76.37	9.18%	10/27/97	68.08	−7.53%
10/9/98	63.90	7.94	4/14/00	75.22	−7.09
10/15/02	73.26	7.55	7/23/02	63.61	−7.00
3/15/00	69.95	7.50	8/27/98	69.90	−5.85
9/8/98	67.10	6.95	8/31/98	64.16	−5.79
7/29/02	74.23	6.84	6/16/00	75.51	−5.60
10/15/98	68.31	6.60	8/4/98	80.11	−5.58
7/24/02	67.75	6.51	9/3/02	74.37	−5.43
10/28/99	88.84	6.33	3/14/01	82.26	−5.39
1/3/01	94.43	6.27	10/3/02	65.58	−5.34
9/11/98	66.26	6.22	10/12/00	76.68	−5.19
9/23/98	72.02	5.93	2/4/02	80.28	−5.16
4/3/00	84.11	5.75	9/24/98	68.39	−5.04
9/24/01	75.18	5.50	1/29/02	82.36	−5.02
3/23/01	80.74	5.46	3/12/01	84.37	−4.94
10/10/02	64.42	5.42	6/15/00	79.99	−4.75
8/8/02	76.90	5.40	9/17/01	76.87	−4.71
6/17/02	86.76	5.39	1/3/00	73.46	−4.60
10/13/00	80.76	5.32	10/2/02	69.28	−4.43
12/5/00	84.68	5.13	10/5/98	62.66	−4.41

BIOTECH

Ticker **BTK**   Index **AMEX BIOTECH**

AI SEASONALITY

Start	Finish	Data Since
July (End)	March (Beginning)	12/5/94

HISTORICAL PERFORMANCE

Buy & Hold	5-Year Avg	10-Year Avg	Avg Since Inception	Best Year	% Change	Worst Year	% Change
12 Months	13.6%	27.7%	27.7%	1999	111.4%	2002	−41.7%

AI Seasonality	5-Year Avg	10-Year Avg	Avg Since Inception	Best Year	% Change	Worst Year	% Change
7.67 Months	8.0%	44.9%	44.9%	2000	244.0%	2001	−1.5%

Recommended ETF: iShares NASDAQ Biotechnology (IBB)	Volatility: High
Key Consideration: Recent FDA and legal actions & scientific breakthroughs	Risk: High

COMPONENTS

Ticker	Name	Ticker	Name
AFFX	Affymetrix	GENZ	Genzyme
AMGN	Amgen	GILD	Gilead Sciences
CRA	Applera Corp-Celera Genomics	HGSI	Human Genome Sciences
BIIB	Biogen Idec	IVGN	Invitrogen
CELG	Celgene	MEDI	Medimmune
CEPH	Cephalon	MLNM	Millennium Pharmaceuticals
CHIR	Chiron	PDLI	Protein Design Labs
ENZN	Enzon Pharmaceuticals	VRTX	Vertex Pharmaceuticals
DNA	Genentech		

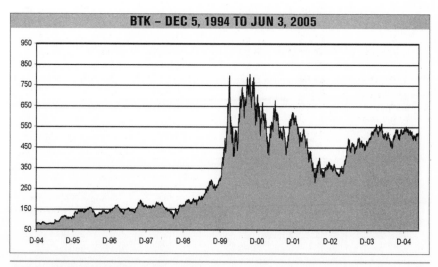

BTK – DEC 5, 1994 TO JUN 3, 2005

DETAILED PERFORMANCE AI SEASONALITY

| Start | | Finish | | Percent | Investing |
Date	Close	Date	Close	Change	$1,000
Jul 21 1995	90.47	Mar 7 1996	147.74	63.30%	$1633.00
Jul 24 1996	111.77	Mar 7 1997	158.80	42.08	2320.17
Jul 31 1997	138.03	Mar 10 1998	168.59	22.14	2833.85
Jul 31 1998	137.98	Mar 8 1999	189.06	37.02	3882.94
Jul 26 1999	230.96	Mar 6 2000	794.53	244.01	13357.71
Jul 31 2000	591.44	Mar 2 2001	582.74	−1.47	13161.35
Jul 24 2001	495.76	Mar 6 2002	513.69	3.62	13637.79
Jul 23 2002	304.88	Mar 7 2003	318.69	4.53	14255.59
Jul 24 2003	456.62	Mar 5 2004	560.97	22.85	17512.99
Jul 26 2004	455.73	Mar 2 2005	503.71	10.53	19357.11
			Average:	**44.86**	**$18357.11 Gain**

DETAILED PERFORMANCE BUY & HOLD

| Start | | Finish | | Percent | Investing |
Date	Close	Date	Close	Change	$1,000
Dec 30 1994	82.06	Dec 29 1995	133.77	63.01	1630.10
Dec 29 1995	133.77	Dec 31 1996	144.30	7.87	1758.39
Dec 31 1996	144.30	Dec 31 1997	162.42	12.56	1979.24
Dec 31 1997	162.42	Dec 31 1998	185.13	13.98	2255.94
Dec 31 1998	185.13	Dec 31 1999	391.44	111.44	4769.96
Dec 31 1999	391.44	Dec 29 2000	634.32	62.05	7729.72
Dec 29 2000	634.32	Dec 31 2001	580.58	−8.47	7075.01
Dec 31 2001	580.58	Dec 31 2002	338.22	−41.74	4121.90
Dec 31 2002	338.22	Dec 31 2003	490.10	44.91	5973.05
Dec 31 2003	490.10	Dec 31 2004	544.25	11.05	6633.07
			Average:	**27.67**	**$5633.07 Gain**

Almanac Investor Sector Seasonality out-performance factor 225.88%

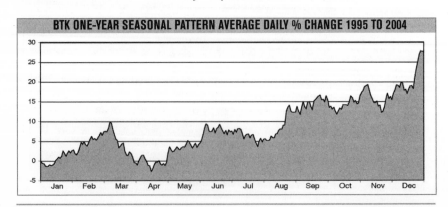

BTK ONE-YEAR SEASONAL PATTERN AVERAGE DAILY % CHANGE 1995 TO 2004

BIOTECH

MONTHLY PERFORMANCE BY RANK
JANUARY 1995 TO MAY 2005

Month	Total Change	Average Change	# Up	# Down
December	85.2%	8.5%	7	3
August	44.6	4.5	7	3
September	37.4	3.7	5	5
February	37.1	3.4	4	7
May	33.4	3.0	6	5
April	31.2	2.8	7	4
October	30.5	3.1	5	5
June	22.3	2.2	5	5
January	21.7	2.0	6	5
November	8.2	0.8	6	4
July	−18.4	−1.8	4	6
March	−55.1	−5.0	4	7

MONTHLY PERFORMANCE
JANUARY 1995 TO MAY 2005

Month	Total Change	Average Change	# Up	# Down
January	21.7%	2.0%	6	5
February	37.1	3.4	4	7
March	−55.1	−5.0	4	7
April	31.2	2.8	7	4
May	33.4	3.0	6	5
June	22.3	2.2	5	5
July	−18.4	−1.8	4	6
August	44.6	4.5	7	3
September	37.4	3.7	5	5
October	30.5	3.1	5	5
November	8.2	0.8	6	4
December	85.2	8.5	7	3

BEST & WORST MONTHS BY PERCENT JANUARY 1995 TO MAY 2005

Month	Best Close	Change	Month	Worst Close	Change
Feb-2000	701.46	61.9%	Mar-2000	499.90	−28.7%
Jun-2000	644.23	37.4	Aug-1998	104.51	−24.3
Dec-1999	391.44	35.9	Nov-2000	580.40	−20.9
Sep-1998	139.39	33.4	Mar-2001	470.24	−20.6
Aug-2000	773.30	30.8	Jul-1996	116.18	−17.4
Dec-1995	133.77	22.8	Sep-2001	450.43	−15.6
Oct-2001	548.68	21.8	Mar-1997	139.54	−14.8
Apr-2001	568.04	20.8	Jan-2002	500.02	−13.9
May-2003	449.36	20.4	Jun-2002	348.90	−13.9
Oct-1998	164.10	17.7	Jul-2001	529.72	−13.4
Jul-1999	250.49	16.9	Apr-2002	436.49	−12.8
Sep-1997	176.53	15.9	Feb-1999	176.81	−10.0
Jun-1995	89.94	15.7	Jun-1996	140.68	−9.6
Jan-1997	166.13	15.1	Jun-1998	146.84	−9.0
May-1997	148.82	13.4	Dec-2002	338.22	−8.4
Aug-1995	110.56	13.3	Oct-1995	104.82	−8.2
Dec-1998	185.13	13.1	Jul-2000	591.44	−8.2
Apr-2003	373.22	12.0	May-1998	161.27	−7.9
Apr-1996	149.63	11.0	Sep-2002	320.01	−7.6
Jan-2000	433.40	10.7	Jul-2004	482.32	−7.6

BEST YEARS BY PERCENT

Year	Close	Point Change	Percent Change
1999	391.44	206.31	111.4%
1995	133.77	51.71	63.0
2000	634.32	242.88	62.1
2003	490.10	151.88	44.9
1998	185.13	22.71	14.0

WORST YEARS BY PERCENT

Year	Close	Point Change	Percent Change
2002	338.22	−242.36	−41.7%
2001	580.58	−53.74	−8.5
1996	144.30	10.53	7.9
2004	544.25	54.15	11.1
1997	162.42	18.12	12.6

BEST & WORST WEEKS BY % CHANGE DEC 5, 1994 TO JUN 3, 2005

Week	Best Close	Change	Week	Worst Close	Change
6/2/00	535.77	23.15%	4/14/00	408.36	−24.87%
2/18/00	630.72	22.98	9/21/01	417.64	−16.57
12/23/99	368.15	19.49	1/5/01	533.57	−15.88
10/26/01	577.05	15.15	1/28/00	424.66	−13.66
1/21/00	491.83	15.06	7/28/00	605.60	−13.51
4/12/01	514.09	14.76	3/17/00	597.05	−13.33
3/3/00	759.15	14.26	10/6/00	669.00	−13.09
12/8/00	685.67	14.03	8/28/98	113.35	−12.37
4/28/00	487.31	13.78	11/17/00	623.23	−12.13
6/9/00	609.31	13.73	3/16/01	468.05	−11.84
8/25/00	750.68	13.34	4/26/02	428.94	−11.37
12/22/95	125.86	12.67	5/26/00	435.06	−10.88
7/7/00	724.32	12.43	6/7/02	361.90	−10.65
2/4/00	476.11	12.12	8/30/02	346.38	−9.32
8/24/01	550.20	11.65	9/26/03	450.18	−9.27
6/16/95	90.28	11.17	3/10/00	688.88	−9.26
1/26/01	639.44	10.65	6/21/96	135.20	−9.07
5/18/01	600.96	10.63	3/9/01	530.90	−8.90
5/2/97	139.41	10.63	10/15/99	243.15	−8.74
9/11/98	126.09	10.17	3/31/00	499.90	−8.69

BEST & WORST DAYS BY % CHANGE DEC 5, 1994 TO JUN 3, 2005

Day	Best Close	Change	Day	Worst Close	Change
4/28/00	487.31	14.14%	3/14/00	550.24	−13.23%
6/12/95	91.37	12.51	4/14/00	408.36	−11.81
2/16/00	605.67	12.32	3/20/00	526.83	−11.76
6/17/02	375.34	10.25	8/11/98	125.92	−11.22
4/18/00	446.86	10.22	11/13/00	630.77	−11.06
12/8/00	685.67	10.22	11/20/00	557.82	−10.50
3/22/00	566.06	9.99	10/27/97	165.33	−9.86
6/19/00	680.66	9.43	3/12/01	479.74	−9.64
9/8/98	124.98	9.20	1/4/00	361.41	−8.66
4/5/01	451.18	9.05	1/5/01	533.57	−8.51
5/8/02	414.80	8.88	12/20/00	598.74	−8.42
12/5/00	626.79	8.83	3/21/01	423.47	−8.38
1/10/00	440.64	8.70	6/11/02	336.93	−8.13
1/7/00	405.38	8.66	3/13/00	634.16	−7.94
2/17/00	658.09	8.65	9/17/01	461.12	−7.88
6/2/00	535.77	8.35	8/31/98	104.51	−7.80
5/30/00	471.25	8.32	3/29/00	507.26	−7.71
8/12/98	136.15	8.12	6/22/00	642.61	−7.69
12/21/95	123.63	7.76	10/2/00	711.80	−7.52
4/6/00	537.42	7.43	3/20/01	462.20	−7.46

BROKER DEALER — Ticker **XBD**   Index **AMEX BROKER/DEALER**

AI SEASONALITY

Start	Finish	Data Since
October (Beginning)	April (Middle)	4/15/94

HISTORICAL PERFORMANCE

Buy & Hold	5-Year Avg	10-Year Avg	Avg Since Inception	Best Year	% Change	Worst Year	% Change
12 Months	14.5%	33.1%	33.1%	1997	91.5%	2002	−18.8%

AI Seasonality	5-Year Avg	10-Year Avg	Avg Since Inception	Best Year	% Change	Worst Year	% Change
6.67 Months	16.1%	44.5%	43.4%	1999	254.6%	2001	−11.0%

Recommended ETF: iShares Dow Jones U.S. Financials (IYF)	Volatility: Moderate
Key Consideration: Trading volume & phase of bull/bear market	Risk: Low

COMPONENTS

Ticker	Name	Ticker	Name
AGE	A.G. Edwards	JEF	Jefferies Group
AMTD	Ameritrade	LM	Legg Mason
BSC	Bear Stearns	LEH	Lehman Brothers
SCH	Charles Schwab	MER	Merrill Lynch
ET	E*Trade Financial	MWD	Morgan Stanley
GS	Goldman Sachs	RJF	Raymond James

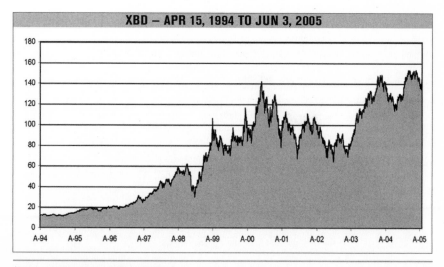

XBD – APR 15, 1994 TO JUN 3, 2005

BROKER DEALER — Ticker **XBD**   Index **AMEX BROKER/DEALER**

DETAILED PERFORMANCE AI SEASONALITY

Start Date	Close	Finish Date	Close	Percent Change	Investing $1,000
Oct 10 1995	18.38	Apr 19 1996	19.50	6.09%	$1060.90
Oct 1 1996	20.75	Apr 10 1997	27.18	30.99	1389.67
Oct 1 1997	42.70	Apr 14 1998	59.70	39.81	1942.90
Oct 7 1998	29.90	Apr 13 1999	106.01	254.55	6888.56
Oct 1 1999	73.72	Apr 12 2000	98.50	33.61	9203.80
Oct 10 2000	116.88	Apr 18 2001	104.06	−10.97	8194.15
Oct 1 2001	76.00	Apr 10 2002	100.04	31.63	10785.95
Oct 7 2002	64.18	Apr 17 2003	84.22	31.22	14153.33
Oct 1 2003	121.34	Apr 16 2004	137.45	13.28	16032.89
Oct 8 2004	125.71	Apr 12 2005	144.69	15.10	18453.86
			Average:	**44.53**	**$17453.86 Gain**

DETAILED PERFORMANCE BUY & HOLD

Start Date	Close	Finish Date	Close	Percent Change	Investing $1,000
Dec 30 1994	11.91	Dec 29 1995	16.67	39.97%	$1399.70
Dec 29 1995	16.67	Dec 31 1996	24.57	47.39	2063.02
Dec 31 1996	24.57	Dec 31 1997	47.06	91.53	3951.30
Dec 31 1997	47.06	Dec 31 1998	55.14	17.17	4629.74
Dec 31 1998	55.14	Dec 31 1999	89.26	61.88	7494.62
Dec 31 1999	89.26	Dec 29 2000	112.30	25.81	9428.98
Dec 29 2000	112.30	Dec 31 2001	102.52	−8.71	8607.71
Dec 31 2001	102.52	Dec 31 2002	83.30	−18.75	6993.77
Dec 31 2002	83.30	Dec 31 2003	132.36	58.90	11113.10
Dec 31 2003	132.36	Dec 31 2004	152.60	15.29	12812.29
			Average:	**33.05**	**$11812.29 Gain**

Almanac Investor Sector Seasonality out-performance factor 47.76%

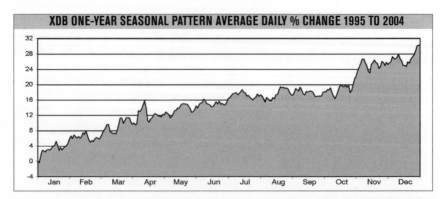

XDB ONE-YEAR SEASONAL PATTERN AVERAGE DAILY % CHANGE 1995 TO 2004

MONTHLY PERFORMANCE BY RANK
MAY 1994 TO MAY 2005

Month	Total Change	Average Change	# Up	# Down
October	60.2%	5.5%	8	3
January	55.5	5.1	6	5
December	43.3	3.9	9	2
November	41.3	3.8	8	3
May	30.2	2.5	7	5
March	27.4	2.5	6	5
April	27.3	2.5	6	5
June	16.3	1.5	7	4
February	7.5	0.7	6	5
July	5.8	0.5	6	5
August	0.2	0.01	7	4
September	−7.0	−0.6	5	6

MONTHLY PERFORMANCE
MAY 1994 TO MAY 2005

Month	Total Change	Average Change	# Up	# Down
January	55.5%	5.1%	6	5
February	7.5	0.7	6	5
March	27.4	2.5	6	5
April	27.3	2.5	6	5
May	30.2	2.5	7	5
June	16.3	1.5	7	4
July	5.8	0.5	6	5
August	0.2	0.01	7	4
September	−7.0	−0.6	5	6
October	60.2	5.5	8	3
November	41.3	3.8	8	3
December	43.3	3.9	9	2

BEST & WORST MONTHS BY PERCENT MAY 1994 TO MAY 2005

Month	Best Close	Change	Month	Worst Close	Change
Jan-1999	70.84	28.5%	Aug-1998	38.19	−31.6%
Nov-1998	51.21	20.0	Nov-2000	97.90	−22.0
Mar-2000	107.39	19.2	Feb-2001	103.34	−18.3
Sep-1997	42.79	19.2	Mar-2001	88.69	−14.2
Oct-1998	42.67	19.1	Mar-1997	24.52	−13.2
Aug-2000	135.43	18.2	Jul-1999	77.94	−12.6
May-2003	100.91	17.5	Sep-2001	77.35	−12.6
Mar-1999	80.87	16.0	Apr-2000	94.48	−12.0
Jul-2000	114.62	15.7	Jul-2002	75.95	−11.0
Apr-1997	28.21	15.1	Apr-2002	92.24	−11.0
Dec-2000	112.30	14.7	Sep-1994	11.65	−10.0
Feb-1998	49.58	14.5	Dec-1995	16.67	−9.8
Apr-2001	101.57	14.5	Oct-1995	17.98	−9.7
Jul-1997	36.97	14.3	Sep-2002	72.74	−9.7
Oct-1999	84.68	13.3	Jun-1994	11.47	−9.0
Jun-2000	99.05	13.2	Apr-2004	128.45	−8.5
Jan-1996	18.85	13.1	Dec-2002	83.30	−8.1
Nov-2002	90.65	13.0	Jan-1998	43.29	−8.0
Oct-2001	87.20	12.7	Aug-2001	88.46	−7.8
Jan-2001	126.48	12.6	May-2000	87.47	−7.4

BEST YEARS BY PERCENT

Year	Close	Point Change	Percent Change
1997	47.06	22.49	91.5%
1999	89.26	34.12	61.9
2003	132.36	49.06	58.9
1996	24.57	7.90	47.4
1995	16.67	4.76	40.0

WORST YEARS BY PERCENT

Year	Close	Point Change	Percent Change
2002	83.30	−19.22	−18.8%
2001	102.52	−9.78	−8.7
2004	152.60	20.24	15.3
1998	55.14	8.08	17.2
2000	112.30	23.04	25.8

BROKER DEALER   Ticker **XBD**   Index **AMEX BROKER/DEALER**

BEST & WORST WEEKS BY % CHANGE APR 15, 1994 TO JUN 3, 2005

Week	Best Close	Change	Week	Worst Close	Change
6/2/00	99.00	20.22%	9/21/01	68.84	−16.53%
1/8/99	65.62	19.01	8/28/98	42.44	−15.98
4/9/99	94.42	17.15	4/14/00	84.22	−15.42
3/3/00	97.54	16.51	9/4/98	36.44	−14.14
4/12/01	97.87	16.39	2/23/01	105.15	−9.85
7/14/00	117.59	15.80	5/26/00	82.35	−9.70
10/16/98	38.09	15.49	11/10/00	114.61	−9.64
12/24/98	56.03	14.98	12/4/98	49.09	−9.56
12/8/00	112.53	13.33	10/2/98	34.83	−9.56
10/18/02	80.01	13.01	4/26/02	90.85	−9.10
3/21/03	81.47	12.98	10/20/95	18.26	−8.43
9/28/01	77.35	12.36	6/4/99	79.82	−8.27
3/8/02	105.98	11.73	1/24/03	78.70	−8.25
9/1/00	136.94	11.62	10/4/02	67.25	−8.22
5/2/97	29.16	11.09	10/15/99	70.78	−8.19
7/2/99	87.75	11.06	1/7/00	81.96	−8.18
11/27/98	54.28	10.62	1/9/98	42.61	−8.07
11/20/98	49.07	10.44	9/7/01	81.52	−7.85
3/24/00	116.34	10.27	8/6/99	71.89	−7.76
10/22/99	77.69	9.76	3/31/00	107.39	−7.69

BEST & WORST DAYS BY % CHANGE APR 15, 1994 TO JUN 3, 2005

Day	Best Close	Change	Day	Worst Close	Change
1/3/01	122.25	13.46%	4/14/00	84.22	−12.73%
4/5/01	87.07	11.50	8/31/98	38.19	−10.01
4/18/00	93.18	9.95	10/27/97	38.59	−9.56
8/30/00	134.20	9.39	9/17/01	74.74	−9.37
12/5/00	108.09	9.17	4/4/00	97.16	−9.30
9/8/98	39.69	8.92	8/27/98	44.49	−9.19
11/23/98	53.44	8.91	10/7/98	29.90	−7.49
6/2/00	99.00	8.73	4/19/99	84.71	−6.64
11/12/99	91.87	8.62	10/1/98	33.48	−6.58
10/28/99	85.69	8.32	3/12/01	90.42	−6.41
10/15/98	36.15	8.27	10/5/98	32.61	−6.37
12/8/00	112.53	7.97	9/9/98	37.19	−6.30
4/13/99	106.01	7.87	9/24/98	38.17	−6.26
10/22/99	77.69	7.74	9/3/98	37.28	−6.19
12/21/98	52.42	7.57	4/15/99	94.10	−6.01
4/10/01	91.21	7.47	9/20/01	67.23	−5.81
7/12/00	114.76	7.38	11/30/98	51.21	−5.66
4/18/01	104.06	7.38	4/3/01	80.88	−5.65
9/23/98	40.72	7.30	9/19/02	73.75	−5.58
10/11/01	88.22	7.27	4/14/99	100.12	−5.56

COMPUTER TECHNOLOGY Ticker **XCI**   Index **AMEX Computer Technology**

AI SEASONALITY

Start	Finish	Data Since
April (Middle)	July (Middle)	8/26/83
October (Beginning)	February (Beginning)	

HISTORICAL PERFORMANCE

Buy & Hold	5-Year Avg	10-Year Avg	Avg Since Inception	Best Year	% Change	Worst Year	% Change
12 Months	−8.2%	23.5%	13.8%	1998	81.5%	2000	−35.1%

AI Seasonality	5-Year Avg	10-Year Avg	Avg Since Inception	Best Year	% Change	Worst Year	% Change
3.33 Months	7.3%	18.6%	11.0%	1997	48.7%	2002	−14.9%
4.67 Months	13.2%	24.3%	17.7%	1999	89.9%	1988	−27.4%

Recommended ETF: iShares Goldman Sachs Technology (IGM)	**Volatility: High**
Key Consideration: NASDAQ level with respect to 50 and 200-day MA	**Risk: Low**

COMPONENTS

Ticker	Name	Ticker	Name
COMS	3Com	IBM	International Business Machines
ADBE	Adobe Systems	MU	Micron Technology
AMD	Advanced Micro Devices	MSFT	Microsoft
AAPL	Apple Computer	MOT	Motorola
AMAT	Applied Materials	NSM	National Semiconductor
ADP	Automatic Data Processing	NOVL	Novell
CSCO	Cisco Systems	ORCL	Oracle
CA	Computer Associates	PALM	Palm
CSC	Computer Sciences	SEBL	Siebel Systems
DELL	Dell	SGI	Silicon Graphics
EMC	EMC	STK	Storage Technology
EDS	Electronic Data Systems	SUNW	Sun Microsystems
GTW	Gateway	SYMC	Symantec
HPQ	Hewlett-Packard	TXN	Texas Instruments
INTC	Intel	YHOO	Yahoo

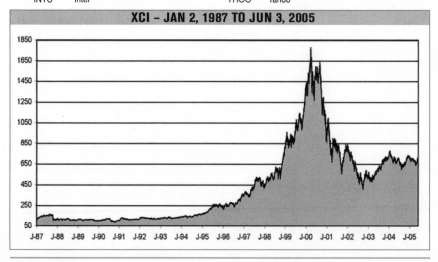

XCI – JAN 2, 1987 TO JUN 3, 2005

Seasonal Sector Investing: Indices

DETAILED PERFORMANCE AI SEASONALITY

| Start | | Finish | | Percent | Investing |
Date	Close	Date	Close	Change	$1,000
Apr 12 1995	185.49	Jul 17 1995	259.70	40.01%	$1400.10
Oct 10 1995	226.42	Feb 6 1996	253.75	12.07	1569.09
Apr 12 1996	241.52	Jul 18 1996	250.59	3.76	1628.09
Oct 1 1996	293.59	Feb 3 1997	381.09	29.80	2113.26
Apr 11 1997	333.13	Jul 16 1997	495.50	48.74	3143.26
Oct 1 1997	501.27	Feb 10 1998	508.40	1.42	3187.90
Apr 13 1998	500.72	Jul 20 1998	617.27	23.28	3930.04
Oct 8 1998	504.15	Feb 1 1999	957.30	89.88	7462.36
Apr 19 1999	809.10	Jul 16 1999	1080.71	33.57	9967.48
Oct 1 1999	1051.08	Feb 8 2000	1506.64	43.34	14287.38
Apr 14 2000	1336.93	Jul 17 2000	1589.30	18.88	16984.84
Oct 10 2000	1173.37	Feb 1 2001	1075.33	−8.36	15564.91
Apr 16 2001	763.07	Jul 13 2001	826.89	8.36	16866.13
Oct 2 2001	573.09	Feb 4 2002	754.93	31.73	22217.76
Apr 11 2002	650.01	Jul 17 2002	553.43	−14.86	18916.20
Oct 9 2002	405.34	Feb 3 2003	497.94	22.85	23238.55
Apr 11 2003	503.63	Jul 16 2003	631.44	25.38	29136.49
Oct 2 2003	663.38	Feb 3 2004	742.25	11.89	32600.82
Apr 20 2004	673.53	Jul 13 2004	666.37	−1.06	32255.25
		Average:		**22.14**	**$31255.25 Gain**

DETAILED PERFORMANCE BUY & HOLD

| Start | | Finish | | Percent | Investing |
Date	Close	Date	Close	Change	$1,000
Dec 30 1994	161.50	Dec 29 1995	228.62	41.56%	$1415.60
Dec 29 1995	228.62	Dec 31 1996	339.92	48.68	2104.71
Dec 31 1996	339.92	Dec 31 1997	438.99	29.15	2718.24
Dec 31 1997	438.99	Dec 31 1998	796.58	81.46	4932.52
Dec 31 1998	796.58	Dec 31 1999	1394.19	75.02	8632.89
Dec 31 1999	1394.19	Dec 29 2000	904.61	−35.12	5601.02
Dec 29 2000	904.61	Dec 31 2001	768.08	−15.09	4755.82
Dec 31 2001	768.08	Dec 31 2002	504.49	−34.32	3123.63
Dec 31 2002	504.49	Dec 31 2003	720.79	42.87	4462.72
Dec 31 2003	720.79	Dec 31 2004	724.12	0.46	4483.25
		Average:		**23.47**	**$3483.25 Gain**

Almanac Investor Sector Seasonality out-performance factor 797.30%

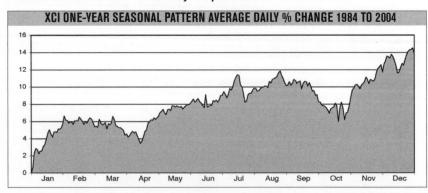

XCI ONE-YEAR SEASONAL PATTERN AVERAGE DAILY % CHANGE 1984 TO 2004

ALMANAC INVESTOR

MONTHLY PERFORMANCE BY RANK
SEPTEMBER 1983 TO MAY 2005

Month	Total Change	Average Change	# Up	# Down
January	113.9%	5.2%	17	5
November	61.3	2.8	13	9
April	40.7	1.9	12	10
May	35.9	1.6	13	9
December	27.9	1.3	13	9
October	26.8	1.2	13	9
June	16.7	0.8	10	11
July	8.2	0.4	12	9
August	5.9	0.3	12	9
February	−1.3	−0.1	13	9
March	−19.1	−0.9	8	14
September	−43.1	−2.0	9	13

MONTHLY PERFORMANCE
SEPTEMBER 1983 TO MAY 2005

Month	Total Change	Average Change	# Up	# Down
January	113.9%	5.2%	17	5
February	−1.3	−0.1	13	9
March	−19.1	−0.9	8	14
April	40.7	1.9	12	10
May	35.9	1.6	13	9
June	16.7	0.8	10	11
July	8.2	0.4	12	9
August	5.9	0.3	12	9
September	−43.1	−2.0	9	13
October	26.8	1.2	13	9
November	61.3	2.8	13	9
December	27.9	1.3	13	9

BEST & WORST MONTHS BY PERCENT SEPTEMBER 1983 TO MAY 2005

Month	Best Close	Change	Month	Worst Close	Change
Oct-2002	511.74	22.1%	Oct-1987	114.01	−23.9%
Jul-1997	500.24	20.2	Feb-2001	817.30	−22.9
Jan-1999	956.43	20.1	Sep-2000	1296.79	−20.8
Dec-1999	1394.19	20.0	Nov-2000	1041.58	−17.9
Jan-2001	1060.25	17.2	Sep-2002	418.99	−17.8
Sep-1998	591.49	17.2	Sep-2001	577.86	−17.3
Oct-2001	674.97	16.8	Aug-1998	504.86	−14.3
Nov-1996	348.09	16.7	Dec-2002	504.49	−14.0
Nov-2001	783.45	16.1	Feb-1999	828.75	−13.4
Jan-1991	114.98	15.9	Dec-2000	904.61	−13.2
Apr-2001	843.48	15.3	Feb-2002	682.70	−12.9
Jan-1987	120.13	15.0	Aug-2001	698.49	−12.6
Nov-2002	586.73	14.7	Aug-1990	94.64	−12.2
Dec-1998	796.58	14.0	Apr-2002	634.34	−11.5
Aug-1984	98.30	13.0	May-2000	1353.26	−10.9
Jun-1999	988.85	13.0	Mar-2001	731.30	−10.5
Jan-1997	382.95	12.7	Aug-1988	100.97	−10.4
Jun-2000	1524.46	12.7	Nov-1987	102.29	−10.3
May-1990	117.23	12.6	Jun-2002	554.19	−10.2
Feb-2000	1514.98	12.5	Jun-1991	104.38	−10.0

BEST YEARS BY PERCENT

Year	Close	Point Change	Percent Change
1998	796.58	357.59	81.5%
1999	1394.19	597.61	75.0
1996	339.92	111.30	48.7
2003	720.79	216.30	42.9
1995	228.62	67.12	41.6

WORST YEARS BY PERCENT

Year	Close	Point Change	Percent Change
2002	504.49	−263.59	−34.3%
2001	768.08	−136.53	−15.1
1989	95.49	−10.91	−10.3
1986	104.43	−10.74	−9.3
1984	94.73	−5.68	−5.7

BEST & WORST WEEKS BY % CHANGE AUGUST 26, 1983 TO JUN 3, 2005

Week	Best Close	Change	Week	Worst Close	Change
6/2/00	1483.57	14.24%	4/14/00	1336.93	−20.58%
4/20/01	895.02	14.19	10/23/87	108.46	−18.65
4/12/01	783.81	12.58	9/21/01	553.64	−15.77
5/17/02	676.78	11.86	11/10/00	1122.58	−13.22
8/3/84	96.28	11.65	12/1/00	1035.61	−11.50
2/4/00	1456.31	11.19	12/12/97	432.02	−10.43
10/5/01	640.85	10.90	4/16/99	848.39	−9.68
5/2/97	391.75	10.31	12/15/00	986.19	−9.08
10/11/02	454.03	10.21	3/1/96	243.13	−9.05
1/29/99	956.43	9.83	2/9/01	932.07	−9.02
1/18/91	106.20	9.54	10/2/98	558.75	−9.02
1/19/01	1077.55	9.35	10/16/87	133.33	−9.00
4/20/00	1460.49	9.24	6/15/01	786.55	−8.85
3/24/00	1770.47	8.96	7/26/02	477.80	−8.73
12/18/87	113.71	8.83	12/15/95	226.38	−8.59
1/8/99	864.37	8.51	1/28/00	1309.80	−8.52
7/2/99	1014.23	8.32	6/21/02	540.41	−8.41
9/25/98	614.15	7.71	8/31/01	698.49	−8.30
6/26/98	557.59	7.52	1/17/03	518.42	−8.28
12/27/91	113.60	7.51	4/26/02	626.22	−8.24

BEST & WORST DAYS BY % CHANGE AUGUST 26, 1983 TO JUN 3, 2005

Day	Best Close	Change	Day	Worst Close	Change
1/3/01	996.34	16.16%	10/19/87	103.31	−22.52%
5/8/02	648.81	11.39	10/26/87	98.03	−9.62
4/17/00	1476.21	10.42	8/31/98	504.86	−9.27
10/19/00	1266.67	10.15	1/8/88	109.60	−8.29
4/18/01	843.62	9.93	10/27/97	434.96	−7.77
4/5/01	729.10	9.75	3/9/01	790.98	−7.47
12/5/00	1136.33	9.73	12/20/00	876.02	−7.27
10/13/00	1227.09	8.85	4/14/00	1336.93	−7.17
10/28/97	471.79	8.47	10/16/02	452.38	−7.16
10/3/01	616.66	7.60	3/28/01	743.95	−7.15
12/22/00	957.23	7.53	11/10/00	1122.58	−6.80
10/15/02	487.28	7.17	4/12/00	1465.64	−6.69
7/29/02	511.59	7.07	7/25/02	471.13	−6.43
5/30/00	1388.20	6.89	9/17/01	615.46	−6.37
7/12/01	820.56	6.82	10/13/89	98.81	−6.15
8/14/02	525.08	6.61	1/5/01	934.98	−6.10
9/24/01	589.66	6.51	7/19/95	236.15	−6.10
11/14/00	1191.82	6.50	5/10/00	1314.23	−6.04
10/11/02	454.03	6.50	3/12/01	743.65	−5.98
4/19/01	897.25	6.36	11/8/00	1210.81	−5.83

CONSUMER
Ticker **CMR**   Index **MS CONSUMER**

AI SEASONALITY

Start	Finish	Data Since
September (End)	June (Beginning)	3/14/94

HISTORICAL PERFORMANCE

Buy & Hold	5-Year Avg	10-Year Avg	Avg Since Inception	Best Year	% Change	Worst Year	% Change
12 Months	2.6%	12.1%	12.1%	1997	32.7%	2002	−12.7%

AI Seasonality	5-Year Avg	10-Year Avg	Avg Since Inception	Best Year	% Change	Worst Year	% Change
8.67 Months	12.4%	17.6%	17.6%	1998	27.7%	2000	8.4%

Recommended ETF:	Merrill Lynch Retail HOLDRS (RTH)	Volatility: Low
Key Consideration:	Recent inflation, income & employment stats	Risk: Low

COMPONENTS

Ticker	Name	Ticker	Name
ABT	Abbott Laboratories	KMB	Kimberly-Clark
ABS	Albertson's	MCD	McDonald's
MO	Altria Group	MDT	Medtronic
AIG	American International Group	MRK	Merck
BUD	Anheuser-Busch	NWL	Newell Rubbermaid
ADP	Automatic Data Processing	PEP	Pepsico
KO	Coca-Cola	PG	Procter & Gamble
CL	Colgate-Palmolive	SWY	Safeway Stores
CAG	Conagra Foods	SGP	Schering-Plough
EMR	Emerson Electric	SEE	Sealed Air
GIS	General Mills	SYY	Sysco
G	Gillette	WAG	Walgreen
GWW	Grainger WW	WMT	Wal-Mart Stores
IFF	International Flavors & Fragrances	DIS	Walt Disney
JNJ	Johnson & Johnson	WYE	Wyeth

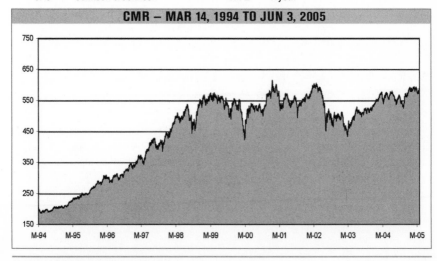

CMR – MAR 14, 1994 TO JUN 3, 2005

DETAILED PERFORMANCE AI SEASONALITY

| Start | | Finish | | Percent | Investing |
Date	Close	Date	Close	Change	$1,000
Sep 23 1994	201.62	Jun 6 1995	243.61	20.83%	$1208.30
Sep 21 1995	260.48	Jun 5 1996	308.92	18.60	1433.04
Sep 20 1996	320.40	Jun 10 1997	399.55	24.70	1787.01
Sep 25 1997	401.82	Jun 9 1998	513.04	27.68	2281.65
Sep 30 1998	464.40	Jun 4 1999	565.72	21.82	2779.50
Sep 29 1999	495.59	Jun 1 2000	537.39	8.43	3013.82
Sep 21 2000	507.38	Jun 5 2001	570.31	12.40	3387.53
Sep 21 2001	494.21	Jun 5 2002	578.65	17.09	3966.46
Sep 30 2002	469.92	Jun 6 2003	518.46	10.33	4376.19
Sep 30 2003	507.26	Jun 8 2004	576.60	13.67	4974.42
			Average:	**17.56**	**$3974.42 Gain**

DETAILED PERFORMANCE BUY & HOLD

| Start | | Finish | | Percent | Investing |
Date	Close	Date	Close	Change	$1,000
Dec 30 1994	208.53	Dec 29 1995	284.75	36.55%	$1365.50
Dec 29 1995	284.75	Dec 31 1996	335.95	17.98	1611.02
Dec 31 1996	335.95	Dec 31 1997	445.64	32.65	2137.01
Dec 31 1997	445.64	Dec 31 1998	558.10	25.24	2676.40
Dec 31 1998	558.10	Dec 31 1999	534.77	−4.18	2564.52
Dec 31 1999	534.77	Dec 29 2000	613.91	14.80	2944.07
Dec 29 2000	613.91	Dec 31 2001	564.87	−7.99	2708.84
Dec 31 2001	564.87	Dec 31 2002	493.41	−12.65	2366.17
Dec 31 2002	493.41	Dec 31 2003	548.25	11.11	2629.05
Dec 31 2003	548.25	Dec 31 2004	590.79	7.76	2833.07
			Average:	**12.13**	**$1833.07 Gain**

Almanac Investor Sector Seasonality out-performance factor 116.82%

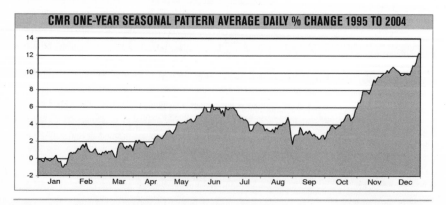

CMR ONE-YEAR SEASONAL PATTERN AVERAGE DAILY % CHANGE 1995 TO 2004

Ticker **CMR**   Index **MS CONSUMER**

MONTHLY PERFORMANCE BY RANK
APRIL 1994 TO MAY 2005

Month	Total Change	Average Change	# Up	# Down
October	38.7%	3.5%	10	1
November	36.0	3.3	10	1
May	23.4	2.0	10	2
April	22.0	1.8	8	4
December	21.0	1.9	8	3
March	4.1	0.4	6	5
January	3.9	0.4	6	5
June	3.1	0.3	7	4
September	1.5	0.1	5	6
February	−1.8	−0.2	7	4
August	−13.2	−1.2	6	5
July	−15.1	−1.4	4	7

MONTHLY PERFORMANCE
APRIL 1994 TO MAY 2005

Month	Total Change	Average Change	# Up	# Down
January	3.9%	0.4%	6	5
February	−1.8	−0.2	7	4
March	4.1	0.4	6	5
April	22.0	1.8	8	4
May	23.4	2.0	10	2
June	3.1	0.3	7	4
July	−15.1	−1.4	4	7
August	−13.2	−1.2	6	5
September	1.5	0.1	5	6
October	38.7	3.5	10	1
November	36.0	3.3	10	1
December	21.0	1.9	8	3

BEST & WORST MONTHS BY PERCENT APRIL 1994 TO MAY 2005

Month	Best Close	Change	Month	Worst Close	Change
Oct-1998	517.25	11.4%	Aug-1998	443.66	−12.1%
Oct-2000	568.34	8.6	Feb-2000	453.24	−12.0
Mar-2000	492.14	8.6	Aug-1997	392.31	−8.1
Oct-1999	540.31	8.5	Jul-2002	501.90	−7.5
Nov-1997	431.80	8.3	Jun-2002	542.32	−7.0
Apr-1997	373.71	7.5	Sep-1999	497.84	−6.9
Sep-1996	324.01	6.9	Sep-2002	469.92	−6.8
Dec-2000	613.91	6.4	Jun-2001	536.92	−5.1
Sep-1995	263.52	6.1	Mar-2001	541.18	−5.1
Apr-2003	486.79	6.0	Jul-2004	549.62	−4.5
Nov-1996	344.76	5.9	Jul-1996	298.99	−4.2
Feb-1998	480.44	5.8	Jan-2003	473.50	−4.0
Aug-1994	206.48	5.7	Jan-2001	589.50	−4.0
Jan-1997	353.79	5.3	Sep-2001	527.67	−4.0
Dec-2004	590.79	5.2	Feb-2003	455.30	−3.8
Nov-1995	281.79	5.2	Jan-2000	514.74	−3.8
Jun-1998	518.05	5.2	Mar-1997	347.81	−3.7
May-1997	392.13	4.9	Feb-2001	570.25	−3.3
Jul-1997	426.91	4.9	Jul-2000	515.42	−3.1
Oct-2002	492.91	4.9	Jul-1999	542.57	−3.1

BEST YEARS BY PERCENT

Year	Close	Point Change	Percent Change
1995	284.75	76.22	36.6%
1997	445.64	109.69	32.7
1998	558.10	112.46	25.2
1996	335.95	51.20	18.0
2000	613.91	79.14	14.8

WORST YEARS BY PERCENT

Year	Close	Point Change	Percent Change
2002	493.41	−71.46	−12.7%
2001	564.87	−49.04	−8.0
1999	534.77	−23.33	−4.2
2004	590.79	42.54	7.8
2003	548.25	54.84	11.1

Seasonal Sector Investing: Indices

CONSUMER

Ticker **CMR**   Index **MS CONSUMER**

BEST & WORST WEEKS BY % CHANGE MAR 14, 1994 TO JUN 3, 2005

Week	Best Close	Change	Week	Worst Close	Change
3/17/00	478.65	10.70%	7/19/02	454.27	−10.00%
3/21/03	483.01	8.33	9/21/01	494.21	−9.56
10/16/98	501.63	7.63	3/16/01	532.14	−7.76
7/26/02	488.80	7.60	7/12/02	504.77	−6.58
10/22/99	523.64	6.82	10/15/99	490.20	−6.39
9/28/01	527.67	6.77	1/5/01	579.69	−5.57
12/29/00	613.91	5.37	3/10/00	432.40	−5.14
5/2/97	377.27	5.23	9/24/99	505.28	−5.01
4/18/97	360.61	4.93	2/25/00	447.05	−4.92
10/8/99	523.66	4.84	1/24/03	476.79	−4.73
9/13/96	319.66	4.69	1/28/00	512.66	−4.62
11/8/96	339.37	4.27	8/15/97	396.31	−4.37
4/20/00	515.48	4.26	4/12/96	288.62	−4.18
6/13/97	412.39	4.23	9/4/98	457.69	−3.92
11/21/97	434.07	4.19	6/21/02	546.84	−3.88
3/30/01	541.18	4.12	2/18/00	470.20	−3.87
1/3/03	506.20	3.95	9/20/02	479.77	−3.85
1/16/98	447.52	3.85	3/28/03	464.44	−3.84
7/2/99	562.47	3.84	2/11/00	489.11	−3.76
2/9/96	305.84	3.84	2/7/03	457.64	−3.35

BEST & WORST DAYS BY % CHANGE MAR 14, 1994 TO JUN 3, 2005

Day	Best Close	Change	Day	Worst Close	Change
3/15/00	458.21	6.73%	8/31/98	443.66	−6.86%
3/16/00	485.27	5.91	10/27/97	384.84	−5.81
7/24/02	475.59	5.00	3/7/00	422.65	−5.31
9/8/98	479.94	4.86	4/14/00	494.41	−4.68
9/1/98	464.02	4.59	7/19/02	454.27	−4.42
10/28/97	402.32	4.54	3/12/01	555.67	−3.68
10/15/98	494.96	4.07	3/24/03	466.67	−3.38
4/3/00	511.93	4.02	7/18/02	475.26	−3.35
1/7/00	549.79	3.76	9/27/02	476.07	−3.31
7/29/02	506.94	3.71	8/27/98	482.93	−3.30
10/30/00	568.85	3.32	9/3/02	488.01	−3.23
3/17/03	460.36	3.25	9/21/01	494.21	−3.12
4/21/99	571.69	3.14	8/4/98	485.87	−3.07
3/21/03	483.01	3.01	8/15/97	396.31	−2.95
10/1/02	483.91	2.98	1/4/01	578.90	−2.93
8/14/02	511.79	2.97	9/10/98	457.79	−2.83
10/28/99	534.45	2.94	9/30/98	464.40	−2.76
9/2/97	403.48	2.85	8/5/02	478.91	−2.74
5/16/01	569.67	2.70	3/8/96	299.20	−2.68
12/30/97	447.05	2.69	9/17/02	490.85	−2.64

CYCLICAL

Ticker **CYC**   Index **MS CYCLICAL**

AI SEASONALITY

Start	Finish	Data Since
October (Beginning)	May (Middle)	2/22/94

HISTORICAL PERFORMANCE

Buy & Hold	5-Year Avg	10-Year Avg	Avg Since Inception	Best Year	% Change	Worst Year	% Change
12 Months	8.5%	11.9%	11.9%	2003	51.2%	2002	−15.5%

AI Seasonality	5-Year Avg	10-Year Avg	Avg Since Inception	Best Year	% Change	Worst Year	% Change
7.67 Months	21.8%	21.0%	20.2%	1999	55.5%	2000	0.9%

Recommended ETF:	Select Sector SPDR Materials (XLB)	Volatility: Low
Key Consideration:	Phase of bull/bear market & G	Risk: Low

COMPONENTS

Ticker	Name	Ticker	Name
MMM	3M	HON	Honeywell
AA	Alcoa	IR	Ingersoll-Rand
CAT	Caterpillar	IP	International Paper
C	Citigroup	JCI	Johnson Controls
CSX	CSX	KRI	Knight Ridder
DCN	Dana	MAS	Masco
DE	Deere	MOT	Motorola
DOW	Dow Chemical	PTV	Pactiv
DD	DuPont	PD	Phelps Dodge
ETN	Eaton	PPG	PPG Industries
FDX	Fedex	R	Ryder Systems
F	Ford Motor	SHLD	Sears Holdings
GP	Georgia-Pacific	X	U.S. Steel
GT	Goodyear Tire & Rubber	UTX	United Technologies
HPQ	Hewlett-Packard	WHR	Whirlpool

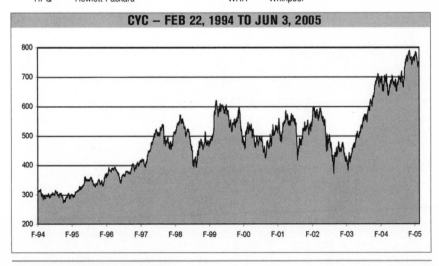

CYC – FEB 22, 1994 TO JUN 3, 2005

DETAILED PERFORMANCE AI SEASONALITY

| Start | | Finish | | Percent | Investing |
Date	Close	Date	Close	Change	$1,000
Oct 10 1995	331.39	May 20 1996	392.35	18.40	1184.00
Oct 9 1996	372.75	May 15 1997	447.10	19.95	1420.21
Oct 1 1997	525.46	May 13 1998	556.95	5.99	1505.28
Oct 8 1998	392.20	May 12 1999	609.71	55.46	2340.11
Oct 1 1999	534.29	May 16 2000	539.15	0.91	2361.40
Oct 2 2000	447.60	May 18 2001	578.27	29.19	3050.69
Oct 1 2001	446.00	May 17 2002	592.41	32.83	4052.24
Oct 9 2002	371.05	May 15 2003	474.29	27.82	5179.57
Oct 1 2003	559.48	May 13 2004	650.72	16.31	6024.36
Oct 11 2004	699.88	May 18 2005	720.30	2.92	6200.27
			Average:	**20.98**	**$5200.27 Gain**

DETAILED PERFORMANCE BUY & HOLD

| Start | | Finish | | Percent | Investing |
Date	Close	Date	Close	Change	$1,000
Dec 30 1994	291.08	Dec 29 1995	340.22	16.88%	$1168.80
Dec 29 1995	340.22	Dec 31 1996	388.56	14.21	1334.89
Dec 31 1996	388.56	Dec 31 1997	475.01	22.25	1631.90
Dec 31 1997	475.01	Dec 31 1998	476.84	0.39	1638.26
Dec 31 1998	476.84	Dec 31 1999	585.78	22.85	2012.61
Dec 31 1999	585.78	Dec 29 2000	511.18	−12.74	1756.20
Dec 29 2000	511.18	Dec 31 2001	531.87	4.05	1827.33
Dec 31 2001	531.87	Dec 31 2002	449.63	−15.46	1544.82
Dec 31 2002	449.63	Dec 31 2003	679.71	51.17	2335.31
Dec 31 2003	679.71	Dec 31 2004	784.10	15.36	2694.01
			Average:	**11.90**	**$1694.01 Gain**

Almanac Investor Sector Seasonality out-performance factor 206.98%

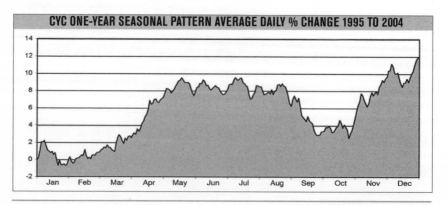

CYC ONE-YEAR SEASONAL PATTERN AVERAGE DAILY % CHANGE 1995 TO 2004

CYCLICAL

Ticker **CYC**   Index **MS CYCLICAL**

MONTHLY PERFORMANCE BY RANK
MARCH 1994 TO MAY 2005

Month	Total Change	Average Change	# Up	# Down
November	42.1%	3.8%	7	4
April	39.8	3.3	8	4
December	23.9	2.2	6	5
October	21.3	1.9	7	4
February	10.8	1.0	8	3
May	10.4	0.9	8	4
March	10.0	0.8	6	6
July	6.6	0.6	6	5
June	−1.7	−0.2	5	6
January	−5.2	−0.5	5	6
August	−17.0	−1.6	4	7
September	−34.1	−3.1	4	7

MONTHLY PERFORMANCE
MARCH 1994 TO MAY 2005

Month	Total Change	Average Change	# Up	# Down
January	−5.2%	−0.5%	5	6
February	10.8	1.0	8	3
March	10.0	0.8	6	6
April	39.8	3.3	8	4
May	10.4	0.9	8	4
June	−1.7	−0.2	5	6
July	6.6	0.6	6	5
August	−17.0	−1.6	4	7
September	−34.1	−3.1	4	7
October	21.3	1.9	7	4
November	42.1	3.8	7	4
December	23.9	2.2	6	5

BEST & WORST MONTHS BY PERCENT MARCH 1994 TO MAY 2005

Month	Best Close	Change	Month	Worst Close	Change
Apr-1999	596.74	20.6%	Aug-1998	397.74	−18.2%
Oct-2003	613.45	12.3	Sep-2001	451.73	−16.2
Nov-2001	523.70	12.1	Sep-2002	412.93	−14.3
Apr-2003	458.02	11.9	Jan-2000	521.32	−11.0
Nov-2002	477.68	11.0	Jul-2002	496.03	−10.0
Nov-2004	760.55	10.2	Feb-2000	478.15	−8.3
Dec-2000	511.18	10.1	Jun-2000	458.93	−8.2
Oct-1998	453.14	9.8	Oct-1997	481.76	−7.7
Dec-1999	585.78	9.7	Nov-1994	281.29	−7.7
Apr-2001	541.68	9.3	Sep-2000	450.91	−6.7
Dec-2003	679.71	9.0	Apr-2005	697.44	−6.6
Nov-1996	403.92	8.8	Jul-1998	486.05	−6.1
Mar-2000	517.73	8.3	Dec-2002	449.63	−5.9
Jul-1997	517.32	8.2	May-2000	499.78	−5.5
Jul-2003	535.99	8.2	Oct-1995	328.80	−5.3
May-1997	448.96	7.3	May-1999	565.43	−5.3
Feb-1998	515.96	7.0	Aug-2001	539.24	−5.2
Jun-1997	477.92	6.5	Sep-1999	540.67	−5.2
Oct-2000	479.47	6.3	Jul-1996	350.11	−5.0
Nov-1998	479.82	5.9	Mar-2001	495.42	−4.9

BEST YEARS BY PERCENT

Year	Close	Point Change	Percent Change
2003	679.71	230.08	51.2%
1999	585.78	108.94	22.9
1997	475.01	86.45	22.3
1995	340.22	49.14	16.9
2004	784.10	104.39	15.4

WORST YEARS BY PERCENT

Year	Close	Point Change	Percent Change
2002	449.63	−82.24	−15.5%
2000	511.18	−74.60	−12.7
1998	476.84	1.83	0.4
2001	531.87	20.69	4.1
1996	388.56	48.34	14.2

Seasonal Sector Investing: Indices

BEST & WORST WEEKS BY % CHANGE FEB 22, 1994 TO JUN 3, 2005

Week	Best Close	Change	Week	Worst Close	Change
4/16/99	573.71	11.81%	9/21/01	416.25	−17.37%
3/21/03	441.15	10.84	3/16/01	500.63	−9.03
9/28/01	451.73	8.52	7/19/02	468.84	−8.30
1/8/99	513.06	7.60	7/12/02	511.29	−7.99
12/22/00	497.64	7.58	2/11/00	474.91	−7.20
10/16/98	435.96	7.45	4/15/05	692.85	−6.72
11/3/00	477.92	7.11	9/24/99	528.35	−6.71
3/17/00	499.00	6.82	8/28/98	417.40	−6.68
7/7/95	356.57	6.25	1/21/00	547.44	−6.30
11/6/98	480.55	6.05	10/31/97	481.76	−6.09
5/18/01	578.27	5.87	5/26/00	493.84	−6.08
11/5/04	730.16	5.79	1/28/00	516.25	−5.70
3/1/02	577.09	5.59	3/28/03	416.31	−5.63
6/2/00	520.95	5.49	12/15/00	462.57	−5.45
4/2/04	700.32	5.16	4/30/04	666.58	−5.28
7/13/01	563.74	5.04	1/9/98	453.80	−5.18
7/14/00	497.79	5.03	9/20/02	433.36	−5.18
11/16/01	518.64	5.02	10/15/99	522.93	−5.10
10/31/03	613.45	4.93	9/7/01	511.82	−5.08
5/20/05	719.99	4.87	1/15/99	487.11	−5.06

BEST & WORST DAYS BY % CHANGE FEB 22, 1994 TO JUN 3, 2005

Day	Best Close	Change	Day	Worst Close	Change
10/15/02	431.73	6.43%	9/17/01	455.67	−9.54%
7/29/02	505.05	6.19	10/27/97	473.23	−7.75
10/30/00	472.58	5.92	4/14/00	507.45	−5.67
9/24/01	440.50	5.83	9/20/01	419.97	−5.49
4/18/01	542.71	5.76	8/31/98	397.74	−4.71
3/16/00	510.08	5.62	10/9/02	371.05	−4.67
7/24/02	470.92	5.47	3/24/03	421.10	−4.54
10/11/02	408.78	5.42	8/2/02	466.41	−4.44
3/15/00	482.95	5.09	7/19/02	468.84	−4.08
9/8/98	416.96	4.66	8/27/98	421.20	−4.06
3/21/03	441.15	4.54	9/10/98	394.22	−3.94
10/10/02	387.75	4.50	10/1/98	396.54	−3.93
12/22/00	497.64	4.38	9/7/01	511.82	−3.80
4/14/99	553.77	4.36	3/7/00	454.96	−3.79
3/17/03	415.20	4.32	1/9/98	453.80	−3.77
5/16/01	572.99	4.28	10/2/02	413.87	−3.76
11/21/02	461.12	4.25	10/16/02	415.78	−3.69
10/15/98	423.54	4.15	9/3/02	463.87	−3.68
10/1/02	430.04	4.14	7/22/02	452.06	−3.58
1/3/01	521.22	4.10	8/5/02	450.40	−3.43

GOLD & SILVER   Ticker **XAU**   Index **PHLX GOLD & SILVER**

AI SEASONALITY

Start	Finish	Data Since
July (End)	September (End)	12/19/83

HISTORICAL PERFORMANCE

Buy & Hold	5-Year Avg	10-Year Avg	Avg Since Inception	Best Year	% Change	Worst Year	% Change
12 Months	11.1%	1.8%	3.3%	1993	85.0%	1997	−36.5%

AI Seasonality	5-Year Avg	10-Year Avg	Avg Since Inception	Best Year	% Change	Worst Year	% Change
2.33 Months	18.6%	18.6%	14.2%	1986	46.0%	1991	−9.4%

Recommended ETF:	streetTRACKS Gold Shares (GLD)	Volatility: Moderate
Key Consideration:	Strength of dollar & global economy	Risk: Moderate

COMPONENTS

Ticker	Name	Ticker	Name
AEM	Agnico-Eagle Mines	G.TO	Goldcorp
AU	AngloGold Ashanti	HMY	Harmony Gold Mining
ABX	Barrick Gold	MDG	Meridian Gold
FCX	Freeport McMoran Copper & Gold	NEM	Newmont Mining
GLG.T	Glamis Gold	PAAS	Pan American Silver
GFI	Gold Fields	PDG.T	Placer Dome

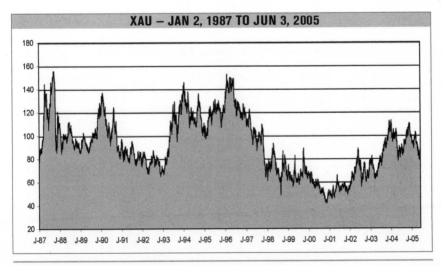

XAU – JAN 2, 1987 TO JUN 3, 2005

GOLD & SILVER   Ticker **XAU**   Index **PHLX GOLD & SILVER**

DETAILED PERFORMANCE AI SEASONALITY

Start Date	Close	Finish Date	Close	Percent Change	Investing $1,000
Jul 31 1995	118.70	Sep 21 1995	125.88	6.05	1060.50
Jul 24 1996	116.81	Sep 24 1996	121.57	4.07	1103.66
Jul 23 1997	93.71	Sep 30 1997	109.50	16.85	1289.63
Jul 31 1998	62.92	Sep 28 1998	78.46	24.70	1608.17
Jul 26 1999	61.14	Sep 27 1999	86.52	41.51	2275.72
Jul 25 2000	50.20	Sep 27 2000	50.90	1.39	2307.35
Jul 31 2001	53.06	Sep 20 2001	59.31	11.78	2579.16
Jul 26 2002	55.73	Sep 24 2002	75.47	35.42	3492.69
Jul 30 2003	80.64	Sep 24 2003	97.50	20.91	4223.02
Jul 26 2004	82.64	Sep 30 2004	101.95	23.37	5209.94
			Average:	**18.61**	**$4209.94 Gain**

DETAILED PERFORMANCE BUY & HOLD

Start Date	Close	Finish Date	Close	Percent Change	Investing $1,000
Dec 30 1994	109.33	Dec 29 1995	120.42	10.14	1101.40
Dec 29 1995	120.42	Dec 31 1996	116.75	−3.05	1067.81
Dec 31 1996	116.75	Dec 31 1997	74.19	−36.45	678.59
Dec 31 1997	74.19	Dec 31 1998	64.97	−12.43	594.24
Dec 31 1998	64.97	Dec 31 1999	67.97	4.62	621.70
Dec 31 1999	67.97	Dec 29 2000	51.41	−24.36	470.25
Dec 29 2000	51.41	Dec 31 2001	54.43	5.87	497.86
Dec 31 2001	54.43	Dec 31 2002	76.76	41.03	702.13
Dec 31 2002	76.76	Dec 31 2003	108.84	41.79	995.54
Dec 31 2003	108.84	Dec 31 2004	99.35	−8.72	908.73
			Average:	**1.84**	**$-91.27 Loss**

Almanac Investor Sector Seasonality out-performance factor 473.32%

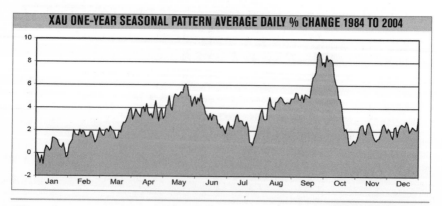

XAU ONE-YEAR SEASONAL PATTERN AVERAGE DAILY % CHANGE 1984 TO 2004

GOLD & SILVER

Ticker **XAU**   Index **PHLX GOLD & SILVER**

MONTHLY PERFORMANCE BY RANK
JANUARY 1984 TO MAY 2005

Month	Total Change	Average Change	# Up	# Down
September	94.4%	4.5%	16	5
February	63.1	2.9	14	8
May	54.6	2.5	16	6
August	43.5	2.1	14	7
December	26.9	1.3	10	11
March	24.4	1.1	10	12
November	6.5	0.3	11	10
July	−4.1	−0.2	12	9
January	−12.5	−0.6	12	10
April	−38.7	−1.8	7	15
June	−42.2	−2.0	9	12
October	−117.9	−5.6	8	13

MONTHLY PERFORMANCE
JANUARY 1984 TO MAY 2005

Month	Total Change	Average Change	# Up	# Down
January	−12.5%	−0.6%	12	10
February	63.1	2.9	14	8
March	24.4	1.1	10	12
April	−38.7	−1.8	7	15
May	54.6	2.5	16	6
June	−42.2	−2.0	9	12
July	−4.1	−0.2	12	9
August	43.5	2.1	14	7
September	94.4	4.5	16	5
October	−117.9	−5.6	8	13
November	6.5	0.3	11	10
December	26.9	1.3	10	11

BEST & WORST MONTHS BY PERCENT JANUARY 1984 TO MAY 2005

Month	Best Close	Change	Month	Worst Close	Change
Sep-1998	74.99	53.4%	Oct-1987	96.78	−36.9%
Apr-1999	73.42	22.9	Aug-1998	48.89	−22.3
Mar-1987	114.07	22.0	Apr-2004	81.94	−21.9
Dec-2002	76.76	21.1	Jul-1984	81.84	−19.8
Jul-1987	137.95	20.7	Oct-1997	87.91	−19.7
Mar-1985	93.39	19.4	Nov-1997	70.82	−19.4
Sep-1999	80.26	19.2	Jan-1988	89.01	−18.9
Oct-1993	123.45	18.6	Jan-1991	80.31	−17.2
Mar-1995	121.97	17.5	Oct-1990	89.78	−17.1
Jan-1996	141.05	17.1	May-1999	60.87	−17.1
Nov-1987	113.12	16.9	Jun-1996	123.76	−16.9
Apr-2001	55.13	15.9	Jul-2002	60.54	−15.3
Aug-2002	69.46	14.7	Jun-2002	71.46	−15.2
Mar-1993	86.82	14.3	May-1998	74.71	−15.0
Aug-1984	93.51	14.3	Mar-1997	104.12	−15.0
Feb-1984	127.70	14.1	Apr-1994	114.43	−14.4
May-2002	84.24	13.9	Oct-1995	107.18	−13.7
Dec-1990	97.04	13.8	Aug-1991	75.91	−13.7
Apr-1993	98.81	13.8	Oct-1999	69.55	−13.3
Apr-1987	129.68	13.7	Nov-1992	65.81	−13.0

BEST YEARS BY PERCENT

Year	Close	Point Change	Percent Change
1993	131.91	60.61	85.0%
1987	109.72	33.46	43.9
2003	108.84	32.08	41.8
2002	76.76	22.33	41.0
1989	119.93	32.92	37.8

WORST YEARS BY PERCENT

Year	Close	Point Change	Percent Change
1984	76.06	−35.76	−32.0%
2000	51.41	−16.56	−24.4
1988	87.01	−22.71	−20.7
1990	97.04	−22.89	−19.1
1994	109.33	−22.58	−17.1

Seasonal Sector Investing: Indices

GOLD & SILVER   Ticker XAU   Index PHLX GOLD & SILVER

BEST & WORST WEEKS BY % CHANGE DEC 19, 1983 TO JUN 3, 2005

Week	Best Close	Change	Week	Worst Close	Change
11/27/87	120.74	30.56%	7/26/02	55.73	−21.83%
9/4/98	64.69	25.83	10/23/87	105.65	−19.64
3/27/87	115.77	18.10	8/28/98	51.41	−16.62
3/27/98	83.22	16.87	1/9/98	63.65	−15.52
10/1/99	82.91	16.02	12/4/87	102.34	−15.24
2/4/00	68.25	15.58	7/6/84	88.77	−13.04
8/3/84	96.07	15.54	3/16/01	48.37	−12.07
4/16/99	67.72	14.33	8/6/93	114.21	−11.40
7/30/93	128.90	14.17	2/25/00	60.59	−10.95
12/11/87	116.78	14.11	1/16/04	98.52	−10.87
9/5/86	82.68	13.81	6/7/96	133.34	−10.44
8/2/02	63.23	13.46	12/3/99	64.79	−10.14
1/16/98	71.82	12.84	10/16/87	131.47	−10.04
7/25/03	84.27	12.54	12/4/98	67.16	−9.99
12/6/02	71.29	12.48	11/13/92	68.66	−9.80
1/8/99	72.95	12.28	1/6/95	98.77	−9.66
6/3/88	111.06	12.16	5/22/87	123.26	−9.65
9/24/99	71.46	12.02	1/29/88	89.01	−9.37
4/10/87	133.95	11.99	8/14/92	74.64	−9.00
8/30/02	69.46	11.98	9/27/02	68.61	−8.98

BEST & WORST DAYS BY % CHANGE DEC 19, 1983 TO JUN 3, 2005

Day	Best Close	Change	Day	Worst Close	Change
9/27/99	86.52	21.07%	10/20/87	96.07	−18.15%
9/3/98	58.28	12.68	5/7/99	72.05	−12.80
10/21/87	108.14	12.56	10/26/87	92.29	−12.65
2/4/00	68.25	12.20	10/27/97	85.64	−11.26
9/10/98	67.90	11.60	7/23/02	59.24	−11.05
9/4/98	64.69	11.00	10/19/87	117.37	−10.72
1/23/98	76.13	10.56	9/7/93	99.57	−9.46
5/2/00	61.02	9.85	10/24/97	96.51	−8.65
3/19/85	92.62	9.60	4/27/87	125.27	−8.63
11/27/87	120.74	9.27	7/7/97	87.01	−8.12
12/17/97	74.81	9.15	1/17/91	85.00	−8.11
11/4/98	79.18	8.32	10/9/98	76.68	−8.09
1/3/94	142.85	8.29	7/5/84	89.19	−7.98
10/27/98	74.63	8.27	5/19/93	104.10	−7.57
3/27/87	115.77	8.21	8/27/90	108.04	−7.54
1/13/98	66.51	8.16	4/15/87	133.79	−7.28
4/9/87	130.48	8.15	4/28/04	81.20	−7.15
1/9/92	82.08	8.14	2/9/99	63.63	−7.14
11/23/87	99.86	7.98	12/15/87	108.88	−7.08
3/26/98	80.94	7.95	10/16/87	131.47	−6.90

HEALTHCARE PRODUCTS Ticker **RXP** Index **MS HEALTHCARE PRODUCTS**

AI SEASONALITY

Start	Finish	Data Since
April (Middle)	July (Beginning)	1/19/96
September (Beginning)	February (Middle)	

HISTORICAL PERFORMANCE

Buy & Hold	5-Year Avg	10-Year Avg	Avg Since Inception	Best Year	% Change	Worst Year	% Change
12 Months	11.5%	NA	18.0%	1998	53.4%	2002	−15.8%

AI Seasonality	5-Year Avg	10-Year Avg	Avg Since Inception	Best Year	% Change	Worst Year	% Change
3 Months	7.7%	NA	11.1%	1997	31.4%	2002	−16.5%
5.67 Months	11.0%	NA	14.9%	1999	29.2%	2000	1.1%

Recommended ETF:	PowerShares Dynamic Biotechnology & Genome (PBE)	Volatility: Low
Key Consideration:	Driven by Biotech & Pharmaceuticals	Risk: Moderate

COMPONENTS

Ticker	Name	Ticker	Name
ABT	Abbott Laboratories	DNA	Genentech
AGN	Allergan	GENZ	Genzyme
AMGN	Amgen	GSK	GlaxoSmithKline
AZN	AstraZeneca	GDT	Guidant
BAX	Baxter International	JNJ	Johnson & Johnson
BDX	Becton, Dickinson	MDT	Medtronic
BIIB	Biogen Idec	MRK	Merck
BSX	Boston Scientific	MYL	Mylan Laboratories
BMY	Bristol-Myers Squibb	PFE	Pfizer
BCR	C.R. Bard	SGP	Schering-Plough
CHIR	Chiron	STJ	St. Jude Medical
EW	Edwards Lifesciences	SYK	Stryker
LLY	Eli Lilly	WYE	Wyeth
FRX	Forest Laboratories		

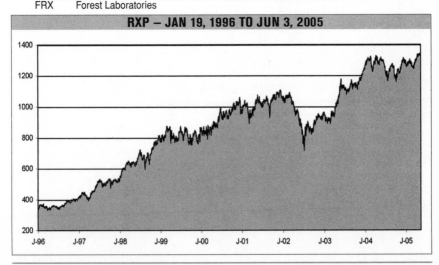

RXP – JAN 19, 1996 TO JUN 3, 2005

HEALTHCARE PRODUCTS — Ticker **RXP** — Index **MS HEALTHCARE PRODUCTS**

DETAILED PERFORMANCE AI SEASONALITY

Start Date	Close	Finish Date	Close	Percent Change	Investing $1,000
Apr 11 1996	332.36	Jul 1 1996	358.12	7.75%	$1077.50
Sep 5 1996	354.63	Feb 18 1997	447.66	26.23	1360.13
Apr 11 1997	393.16	Jul 8 1997	516.76	31.44	1787.75
Sep 10 1997	492.54	Feb 18 1998	601.98	22.22	2184.99
Apr 16 1998	620.01	Jul 10 1998	696.93	12.41	2456.15
Sep 1 1998	624.48	Feb 16 1999	806.64	29.17	3172.61
Apr 19 1999	764.43	Jul 12 1999	840.18	9.91	3487.01
Sep 2 1999	836.39	Feb 17 2000	845.36	1.07	3524.32
Apr 14 2000	815.49	Jul 10 2000	994.45	21.95	4297.91
Sep 6 2000	920.99	Feb 12 2001	1039.62	12.88	4851.48
Apr 11 2001	932.33	Jul 2 2001	1025.23	9.96	5334.69
Sep 18 2001	982.87	Feb 15 2002	1072.47	9.12	5821.22
Apr 17 2002	1018.07	Jul 5 2002	849.86	−16.52	4859.55
Sep 3 2002	832.74	Feb 18 2003	926.49	11.26	5406.74
Apr 16 2003	933.57	Jul 8 2003	1137.82	21.88	6589.73
Sep 3 2003	1114.56	Feb 11 2004	1315.72	18.05	7779.18
Apr 13 2004	1271.80	Jul 1 2004	1284.67	1.01	7857.75
Sep 1 2004	1243.21	Feb 18 2005	1291.73	3.90	8164.20
			Average:	**12.98**	**$7164.20 Gain**

DETAILED PERFORMANCE BUY & HOLD

Start Date	Close	Finish Date	Close	Percent Change	Investing $1,000
Dec 31 1996	397.13	Dec 31 1997	529.71	33.38	1333.80
Dec 31 1997	529.71	Dec 31 1998	812.71	53.43	2046.45
Dec 31 1998	812.71	Dec 31 1999	812.36	−0.04	2045.63
Dec 31 1999	812.36	Dec 29 2000	1052.86	29.61	2651.34
Dec 29 2000	1052.86	Dec 31 2001	1092.97	3.81	2752.36
Dec 31 2001	1092.97	Dec 31 2002	920.74	−15.76	2318.59
Dec 31 2002	920.74	Dec 31 2003	1226.00	33.15	3087.20
Dec 31 2003	1226.00	Dec 31 2004	1308.37	6.72	3294.66
			Average:	**18.04**	**$2294.66 Gain**

Almanac Investor Sector Seasonality out-performance factor 212.21%

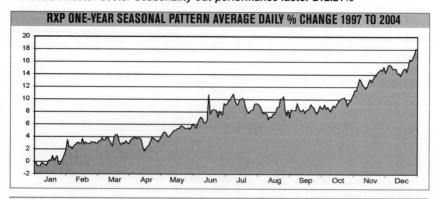

RXP ONE-YEAR SEASONAL PATTERN AVERAGE DAILY % CHANGE 1997 TO 2004

HEALTHCARE PRODUCTS — Ticker **RXP**   Index **MS HEALTHCARE PRODUCTS**

MONTHLY PERFORMANCE BY RANK
FEBRUARY 1996 TO MAY 2005

Month	Total Change	Average Change	# Up	# Down
November	30.9%	3.4%	9	0
December	22.3	2.5	6	3
May	20.0	2.0	6	4
June	18.5	2.1	5	4
September	17.3	1.9	6	3
October	16.4	1.8	6	3
April	12.8	1.3	7	3
January	10.1	1.1	6	3
February	7.9	0.8	6	4
July	−2.4	−0.3	4	5
March	−4.4	−0.4	5	5
August	−9.2	−1.0	4	5

MONTHLY PERFORMANCE
FEBRUARY 1996 TO MAY 2005

Month	Total Change	Average Change	# Up	# Down
January	10.1%	1.1%	6	3
February	7.9	0.8	6	4
March	−4.4	−0.4	5	5
April	12.8	1.3	7	3
May	20.0	2.0	6	4
June	18.5	2.1	5	4
July	−2.4	−0.3	4	5
August	−9.2	−1.0	4	5
September	17.3	1.9	6	3
October	16.4	1.8	6	3
November	30.9	3.4	9	0
December	22.3	2.5	6	3

BEST & WORST MONTHS BY PERCENT FEBRUARY 1996 TO MAY 2005

Month	Best Close	Change	Month	Worst Close	Change
Sep-1998	680.61	14.4%	Aug-1998	594.97	−13.1%
Sep-1996	389.12	9.1	Jun-2002	878.16	−8.7
Dec-1998	812.71	8.8	Sep-1999	762.69	−8.7
Jun-1997	493.11	7.9	Apr-2002	976.42	−7.9
Dec-2004	1308.37	7.6	Mar-1997	403.93	−6.8
Jun-2000	955.21	7.6	Apr-1999	792.29	−6.6
Jan-1997	426.87	7.5	Aug-1997	490.75	−5.5
Oct-2002	894.77	7.4	Jul-2004	1226.43	−5.5
May-2003	1072.96	7.1	Jan-2001	998.40	−5.2
Jan-1998	566.55	7.0	Mar-2001	978.38	−4.1
Apr-2003	1001.68	6.9	Jul-2000	916.30	−4.1
May-1997	456.89	6.8	Jan-2005	1259.61	−3.7
Oct-1998	724.36	6.4	Mar-2004	1250.88	−3.7
Aug-2000	973.84	6.3	Jan-2002	1053.41	−3.6
Jun-1998	662.99	6.2	Sep-2002	833.19	−3.5
Feb-1998	600.33	6.0	Oct-2004	1206.19	−3.3
Apr-1997	427.81	5.9	Jul-1996	344.41	−3.2
Mar-1999	847.87	5.7	Oct-1997	501.19	−2.4
Nov-1996	403.68	5.5	Feb-1996	356.67	−2.3
Jul-1997	519.37	5.3	Jun-2001	1014.36	−2.2

BEST YEARS BY PERCENT

Year	Close	Point Change	Percent Change
1998	812.71	283.00	53.4%
1997	529.71	132.58	33.4
2003	1226.00	305.26	33.2
2000	1052.86	240.50	29.6

WORST YEARS BY PERCENT

Year	Close	Point Change	Percent Change
2002	920.74	−172.23	−15.8%
1999	812.36	−0.35	−0.04
2001	1092.97	40.11	3.8
2004	1308.37	82.37	6.7

HEALTHCARE PRODUCTS   Ticker **RXP**   Index **MS HEALTHCARE PRODUCTS**

BEST & WORST WEEKS BY % CHANGE JAN 19, 1996 TO JUN 3, 2005

Week	Best Close	Change	Week	Worst Close	Change
9/28/01	1017.25	9.39%	1/5/01	953.68	−9.42%
7/26/02	807.58	8.50	9/21/01	929.89	−8.91
3/21/03	968.56	7.83	10/15/99	751.99	−7.74
12/23/99	817.64	7.35	7/12/02	784.11	−7.74
10/16/98	688.66	7.18	4/16/99	801.06	−7.28
7/2/99	838.16	7.12	9/24/99	766.36	−6.41
3/30/01	978.38	6.93	3/16/01	929.64	−6.27
5/2/97	436.47	6.58	4/30/99	792.29	−5.71
1/7/00	864.50	6.42	6/7/02	909.01	−5.52
1/29/99	814.76	5.92	8/15/97	479.57	−5.49
6/30/00	955.21	5.74	10/8/04	1194.64	−5.09
3/3/00	871.07	5.52	7/19/02	744.28	−5.08
1/26/01	1006.86	5.42	4/14/00	815.49	−5.08
10/8/99	815.11	5.16	12/10/99	779.08	−4.80
6/16/00	915.04	5.13	7/23/99	831.29	−4.79
4/20/00	855.40	4.89	8/6/04	1169.65	−4.63
4/23/99	840.26	4.89	4/12/96	340.27	−4.60
6/13/97	484.46	4.81	4/11/97	393.16	−4.48
10/18/02	907.95	4.79	9/26/03	1112.66	−4.37
8/2/02	845.97	4.75	4/5/02	1015.05	−4.26

BEST & WORST DAYS BY % CHANGE JAN 19, 1996 TO JUN 3, 2005

Day	Best Close	Change	Day	Worst Close	Change
7/24/02	764.08	6.55%	8/31/98	594.97	−8.09%
1/7/00	864.50	6.28	10/27/97	474.58	−7.88
3/16/00	878.39	5.92	7/10/02	759.91	−5.24
10/28/97	500.52	5.47	4/14/00	815.49	−5.02
9/8/98	662.84	5.25	7/18/02	768.66	−4.99
9/1/98	624.48	4.96	1/24/00	815.83	−4.62
3/15/00	829.29	4.92	4/19/99	764.43	−4.57
4/21/99	828.47	4.71	4/11/97	393.16	−4.33
7/29/02	843.55	4.45	8/5/02	809.65	−4.29
4/18/00	855.15	4.32	3/8/96	357.11	−4.29
6/17/02	917.47	4.27	3/7/00	813.04	−4.28
10/19/99	782.88	3.88	1/4/00	773.84	−4.22
2/2/98	588.10	3.80	7/9/02	801.95	−4.17
9/27/01	1015.05	3.68	1/4/01	973.72	−4.11
1/20/98	552.82	3.67	6/11/02	887.08	−3.93
7/25/02	791.99	3.65	10/1/98	653.88	−3.93
7/5/02	849.86	3.54	2/17/99	774.99	−3.92
4/20/99	791.24	3.51	8/27/98	658.33	−3.91
12/22/99	792.02	3.50	3/13/00	813.88	−3.75
3/17/03	928.50	3.37	7/1/02	846.23	−3.64

AI SEASONALITY

Start	Finish	Data Since
March (End)	June (Middle)	1/19/96
September (End)	January (Beginning)	

HISTORICAL PERFORMANCE

Buy & Hold	5-Year Avg	10-Year Avg	Avg Since Inception	Best Year	% Change	Worst Year	% Change
12 Months	22.7%	NA	8.9%	2000	88.1%	1999	−37.5%

AI Seasonality	5-Year Avg	10-Year Avg	Avg Since Inception	Best Year	% Change	Worst Year	% Change
3 Months	22.2%	NA	16.2%	1999	36.4%	1998	−6.8%
3.67 Months	12.9%	NA	12.6%	2001	33.2%	2003	−5.2%

Recommended ETF: Vanguard Health Care VIPERs (VHT) **Volatility: Low**

Key Consideration: State of government reform especially in pre-election years **Risk: Moderate**

COMPONENTS

Ticker	Name	Ticker	Name
AHG	Apria Healthcare	HCR	Manor Care
CYH	Community Health Systems	OCR	Omnicare
DVA	DaVita	RCI	Renal Care Group
HCA	HCA	SRZ	Sunrise Senior Living
HMA	Health Management Assoc	THC	Tenet Healthcare
LPNT	LifePoint Hospitals	TRI	Triad Hospitals
LNCR	Lincare Holdings	UHS	Universal Health Services

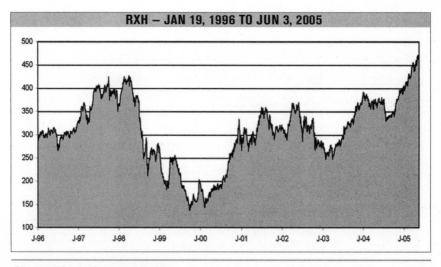

RXH – JAN 19, 1996 TO JUN 3, 2005

DETAILED PERFORMANCE AI SEASONALITY

| Start | | Finish | | Percent | Investing |
Date	Close	Date	Close	Change	$1,000
Mar 21 1996	294.12	Jun 14 1996	313.67	6.65%	$1066.50
Sep 25 1996	299.64	Jan 10 1997	323.92	8.10	1152.89
Mar 31 1997	335.15	Jun 17 1997	399.06	19.07	1372.74
Sep 24 1997	391.18	Jan 5 1998	393.46	0.58	1380.70
Mar 30 1998	407.33	Jun 10 1998	379.67	−6.79	1286.95
Sep 30 1998	249.88	Jan 6 1999	281.10	12.49	1447.69
Mar 23 1999	181.76	Jun 16 1999	247.90	36.39	1974.51
Sep 24 1999	158.16	Jan 7 2000	202.64	28.12	2529.74
Mar 23 2000	157.29	Jun 20 2000	194.54	23.68	3128.79
Sep 21 2000	231.49	Jan 3 2001	308.25	33.16	4166.29
Mar 22 2001	263.89	Jun 20 2001	329.37	24.81	5199.95
Sep 21 2001	311.52	Jan 2 2002	316.96	1.75	5290.95
Mar 25 2002	318.54	Jun 19 2002	368.91	15.81	6127.45
Sep 24 2002	302.31	Jan 6 2003	286.64	−5.18	5810.05
Mar 24 2003	262.31	Jun 17 2003	288.65	10.04	6393.37
Sep 26 2003	316.02	Jan 12 2004	374.26	18.43	7571.67
Mar 24 2004	355.22	Jun 10 2004	371.00	4.44	7907.85
Sep 27 2004	337.94	Jan 3 2005	393.09	16.32	9198.42
			Average:	**13.77**	**$8198.42 Gain**

DETAILED PERFORMANCE BUY & HOLD

| Start | | Finish | | Percent | Investing |
Date	Close	Date	Close	Change	$1,000
Dec 31 1996	315.95	Dec 31 1997	395.16	25.07	1250.70
Dec 31 1997	395.16	Dec 31 1998	277.83	−29.69	879.37
Dec 31 1998	277.83	Dec 31 1999	173.75	−37.46	549.96
Dec 31 1999	173.75	Dec 29 2000	326.80	88.09	1034.41
Dec 29 2000	326.80	Dec 31 2001	320.52	−1.92	1014.55
Dec 31 2001	320.52	Dec 31 2002	278.59	−13.08	881.85
Dec 31 2002	278.59	Dec 31 2003	366.89	31.70	1161.39
Dec 31 2003	366.89	Dec 31 2004	398.43	8.60	1261.27
			Average:	**8.91**	**$261.27 Gain**

Almanac Investor Sector Seasonality out-performance factor 3037.86%

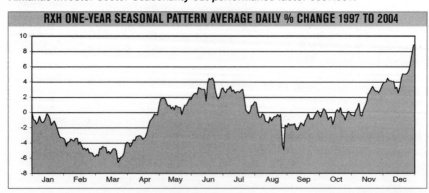

RXH ONE-YEAR SEASONAL PATTERN AVERAGE DAILY % CHANGE 1997 TO 2004

HEALTHCARE PROVIDERS

Ticker **RXH**   Index **MS HEALTHCARE PROVIDER**

MONTHLY PERFORMANCE BY RANK
FEBRUARY 1996 TO MAY 2005

Month	Total Change	Average Change	# Up	# Down
April	47.5%	4.8%	9	1
December	38.5	4.3	8	1
November	34.4	3.8	8	1
March	24.1	2.4	6	4
June	13.0	1.4	5	4
September	12.2	1.4	6	3
May	10.2	1.0	4	6
October	−8.8	−1.0	4	5
February	−11.9	−1.2	5	5
January	−26.4	−2.9	4	5
August	−26.4	−2.9	3	6
July	−28.0	−3.1	4	5

MONTHLY PERFORMANCE
FEBRUARY 1996 TO MAY 2005

Month	Total Change	Average Change	# Up	# Down
January	−26.4%	−2.9%	4	5
February	−11.9	−1.2	5	5
March	24.1	2.4	6	4
April	47.5	4.8	9	1
May	10.2	1.0	4	6
June	13.0	1.4	5	4
July	−28.0	−3.1	4	5
August	−26.4	−2.9	3	6
September	12.2	1.4	6	3
October	−8.8	−1.0	4	5
November	34.4	3.8	8	1
December	38.5	4.3	8	1

BEST & WORST MONTHS BY PERCENT FEBRUARY 1996 TO MAY 2005

Month	Best Close	Change	Month	Worst Close	Change
Apr-1999	241.71	20.7%	Aug-1998	247.69	−25.3%
Mar-2000	168.88	16.7	Feb-2000	144.66	−18.6
Jun-2001	340.79	15.3	Feb-1999	199.50	−16.9
Dec-2000	326.80	13.7	Jul-1999	196.23	−15.8
Mar-2002	328.86	13.0	Jan-1999	240.04	−13.6
Sep-2000	240.11	12.6	Jan-2001	283.91	−13.1
Feb-1998	410.22	12.2	Jul-1998	331.53	−12.4
Jul-2003	312.37	12.0	Oct-2001	304.12	−10.8
Oct-2000	265.80	10.7	Jul-1996	273.06	−10.3
Apr-2002	363.18	10.4	Aug-1999	179.92	−8.3
Feb-2001	312.60	10.1	Mar-2001	286.71	−8.3
Aug-2000	213.28	9.8	Jul-2004	348.37	−8.3
Nov-2004	379.90	8.8	May-1998	385.85	−8.0
Apr-2000	183.23	8.5	Sep-1999	165.69	−7.9
May-2003	281.69	8.4	Oct-1999	153.03	−7.6
Nov-2000	287.43	8.1	Jan-1998	365.47	−7.5
May-1997	368.59	8.0	Oct-2002	296.49	−6.6
Dec-1999	173.75	7.8	Jun-1999	233.08	−6.4
Jun-1997	395.37	7.3	Feb-2002	291.05	−5.9
Aug-1996	292.75	7.2	Apr-2003	259.94	−5.6

BEST YEARS BY PERCENT

Year	Close	Point Change	Percent Change
2000	326.80	153.05	88.1%
2003	366.89	88.30	31.7
1997	395.16	79.21	25.1
2004	398.43	31.54	8.6

WORST YEARS BY PERCENT

Year	Close	Point Change	Percent Change
1999	173.75	−104.08	−37.5%
1998	277.83	−117.33	−29.7
2002	278.59	−41.93	−13.1
2001	320.52	−6.28	−1.9

HEALTHCARE PROVIDERS   Ticker **RXH**   Index **MS HEALTHCARE PROVIDER**

BEST & WORST WEEKS BY % CHANGE JAN 19, 1996 TO JUN 3, 2005

Week	Best Close	Change	Week	Worst Close	Change
4/23/99	247.43	16.86%	10/2/98	236.93	−17.31%
1/7/00	202.64	16.63	1/5/01	281.67	−13.81
3/3/00	163.26	12.97	7/24/98	334.28	−10.52
9/28/01	340.82	9.41	11/1/02	301.91	−9.90
1/26/01	290.54	9.36	11/8/02	274.14	−9.20
4/16/99	211.73	9.19	1/9/98	356.27	−9.12
12/31/98	277.83	8.31	1/19/01	265.67	−9.09
9/18/98	279.41	8.00	8/28/98	262.86	−9.06
12/31/99	173.75	7.36	2/5/99	220.04	−8.33
8/4/00	203.63	7.30	10/15/99	137.24	−8.07
4/27/01	301.85	7.26	7/30/99	196.23	−8.02
10/6/00	257.54	7.26	2/18/00	155.92	−8.01
10/16/98	236.82	7.22	1/29/99	240.04	−7.84
11/19/99	170.00	7.18	2/25/00	144.52	−7.31
9/15/00	224.42	7.12	9/21/01	311.52	−7.17
12/22/99	312.97	7.05	10/8/99	149.29	−7.03
8/2/02	323.86	6.93	2/11/00	169.50	−7.01
2/9/01	301.17	6.82	7/12/96	275.29	−6.87
3/31/00	168.88	6.62	10/9/98	220.87	−6.78
9/22/00	238.86	6.43	3/9/01	291.57	−6.65

BEST & WORST DAYS BY % CHANGE JAN 19, 1996 TO JUN 3, 2005

Day	Best Close	Change	Day	Worst Close	Change
1/7/00	202.64	8.05%	11/8/02	274.14	−9.76%
3/3/00	163.26	6.96	7/23/98	335.50	−9.36
7/24/02	303.55	6.09	1/4/01	279.44	−9.35
4/14/99	207.76	5.59	10/27/97	374.05	−8.24
4/21/99	232.90	5.59	9/29/98	263.57	−6.98
1/6/00	187.55	5.52	10/1/98	233.86	−6.41
12/18/00	308.13	5.39	1/2/01	306.62	−6.18
10/28/97	394.13	5.37	10/31/02	296.49	−6.11
3/16/00	162.72	5.02	8/31/98	247.69	−5.77
11/15/99	166.50	4.97	4/15/03	256.85	−5.60
4/25/01	299.53	4.96	11/1/00	250.99	−5.57
10/19/98	248.45	4.91	7/11/96	275.75	−5.38
1/22/01	278.67	4.89	4/14/00	165.06	−5.38
1/15/99	274.00	4.76	12/14/98	245.71	−5.30
2/12/01	315.27	4.68	8/27/02	318.97	−5.25
12/4/02	288.91	4.63	9/30/98	249.88	−5.19
4/23/99	247.43	4.46	7/22/02	285.52	−5.01
10/9/98	220.87	4.44	1/19/01	265.67	−4.79
11/12/99	158.61	4.26	8/27/98	264.37	−4.73
11/20/01	315.96	4.22	2/2/99	222.71	−4.73

HIGH TECH

Ticker **MSH** Index **MS TECHNOLOGY**

AI SEASONALITY

Start	Finish	Data Since
April (Middle)	July (Middle)	6/30/95
October (Beginning)	January (Middle)	

HISTORICAL PERFORMANCE

Buy & Hold	5-Year Avg	10-Year Avg	Avg Since Inception	Best Year	% Change	Worst Year	% Change
12 Months	−4.5%	NA	24.6%	1999	110.6%	2002	−43.3%

AI Seasonality	5-Year Avg	10-Year Avg	Avg Since Inception	Best Year	% Change	Worst Year	% Change
3.33 Months	10.5%	NA	16.3%	2000	43.0%	2002	−17.2%
3.67 Months	22.9%	NA	28.5%	1999	106.0%	1998	−11.2%

Recommended ETF: Select Sector SPDR Technology (XLK) **Volatility: High**

Key Consideration: Availability of venture capital in the market **Risk: High**

COMPONENTS

Ticker	Name	Ticker	Name
ACN	Accenture	IBM	International Business Machines
AMZN	Amazon.com	INTU	Intuit
AMAT	Applied Materials	JNPR	Juniper Networks
ADP	Automatic Data Processing	MXIM	Maxim Integrated Products
AV	Avaya	MSFT	Microsoft
BRCM	Broadcom	MOT	Motorola
CSCO	Cisco Systems	NTAP	Network Appliance
CA	Computer Associates	NOK	Nokia
DELL	Dell	NT	Nortel Networks
EBAY	eBay	NVDA	NVIDIA
ERTS	Electronic Arts	ORCL	Oracle
EDS	Electronic Data Systems	QCOM	Qualcomm
EMC	EMC	SAP	SAP
FDC	First Data	TX	Seagate Technology
FLEX	Flextronics	SYMC	Symantec
GOOG	Google	TXN	Texas Instruments
HPQ	Hewlett-Packard	YHOO	Yahoo
INTC	Intel		

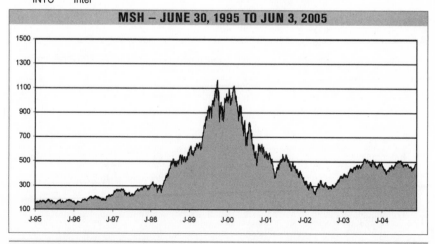

MSH – JUNE 30, 1995 TO JUN 3, 2005

DETAILED PERFORMANCE AI SEASONALITY

Start Date	Close	Finish Date	Close	Percent Change	Investing $1,000
Oct 9 1995	149.27	Jan 19 1996	153.10	2.57%	$1025.70
Apr 12 1996	156.65	Jul 18 1996	151.03	−3.59	988.88
Oct 1 1996	174.55	Jan 20 1997	210.99	20.88	1195.35
Apr 18 1997	176.15	Jul 16 1997	251.87	42.99	1709.24
Oct 1 1997	256.80	Jan 20 1998	228.13	−11.16	1518.49
Apr 13 1998	264.60	Jul 20 1998	327.46	23.76	1879.28
Oct 8 1998	240.52	Jan 19 1999	495.45	105.99	3871.13
Apr 19 1999	475.71	Jul 16 1999	621.90	30.73	5060.73
Oct 1 1999	618.74	Jan 20 2000	945.77	52.85	7735.32
Apr 14 2000	822.11	Jul 17 2000	1091.61	32.78	10270.96
Oct 10 2000	870.25	Jan 19 2001	807.50	−7.21	9530.42
Apr 11 2001	538.22	Jul 13 2001	561.06	4.24	9934.51
Oct 1 2001	368.80	Jan 11 2002	535.04	45.08	14412.99
Apr 11 2002	406.82	Jul 15 2002	336.81	−17.21	11932.51
Oct 7 2002	227.32	Jan 14 2003	327.87	44.23	17210.26
Apr 11 2003	289.78	Jul 14 2003	396.90	36.97	23572.90
Oct 1 2003	419.45	Jan 20 2004	521.82	24.41	29327.04
Apr 20 2004	475.07	Jul 13 2004	455.17	−4.19	28098.24
Oct 8 2004	453.13	Jan 18 2005	488.13	7.72	30267.42
		Average:		**22.73**	**$29267.42 Gain**

DETAILED PERFORMANCE BUY & HOLD

Start Date	Close	Finish Date	Close	Percent Change	Investing $1,000
Dec 29 1995	157.88	Dec 31 1996	191.52	21.31	1213.10
Dec 31 1996	191.52	Dec 31 1997	223.76	16.83	1417.26
Dec 31 1997	223.76	Dec 31 1998	437.23	95.40	2769.34
Dec 31 1998	437.23	Dec 31 1999	920.78	110.59	5831.94
Dec 31 1999	920.78	Dec 29 2000	668.22	−27.43	4232.24
Dec 29 2000	668.22	Dec 31 2001	507.03	−24.12	3211.42
Dec 31 2001	507.03	Dec 31 2002	287.69	−43.26	1822.16
Dec 31 2002	287.69	Dec 31 2003	475.82	65.39	3013.67
Dec 31 2003	475.82	Dec 31 2004	507.67	6.69	3215.29
		Average:		**24.60**	**$2215.29 Gain**

Almanac Investor Sector Seasonality out-performance factor 1221.16%

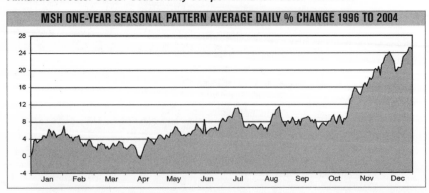

MSH ONE-YEAR SEASONAL PATTERN AVERAGE DAILY % CHANGE 1996 TO 2004

HIGH TECH

MONTHLY PERFORMANCE BY RANK
JULY 1995 TO MAY 2005

Month	Total Change	Average Change	# Up	# Down
November	65.7%	6.6%	8	2
October	59.1	5.9	7	3
January	43.6	4.4	7	3
May	21.1	2.1	5	5
June	19.5	2.2	5	4
April	17.9	1.8	6	4
December	10.1	1.0	4	6
July	−4.7	−0.5	4	6
August	−6.2	−0.6	5	5
March	−6.7	−0.7	4	6
September	−13.1	−1.3	6	4
February	−25.3	−2.5	3	7

MONTHLY PERFORMANCE
JULY 1995 TO MAY 2005

Month	Total Change	Average Change	# Up	# Down
January	43.6%	4.4%	7	3
February	−25.3	−2.5	3	7
March	−6.7	−0.7	4	6
April	17.9	1.8	6	4
May	21.1	2.1	5	5
June	19.5	2.2	5	4
July	−4.7	−0.5	4	6
August	−6.2	−0.6	5	5
September	−13.1	−1.3	6	4
October	59.1	5.9	7	3
November	65.7	6.6	8	2
December	10.1	1.0	4	6

BEST & WORST MONTHS BY PERCENT JULY 1995 TO MAY 2005

Month	Best Close	Change	Month	Worst Close	Change
Oct-2002	291.05	22.0%	Feb-2001	593.79	−24.6%
Dec-1998	437.23	20.5	Nov-2000	708.83	−23.6
Dec-1999	920.78	19.9	Sep-2001	373.77	−22.0
Sep-1998	286.89	19.5	Aug-1998	240.07	−19.6
Jul-1997	252.76	18.6	Sep-2002	238.60	−18.6
Jan-1999	517.13	18.3	Feb-2002	423.22	−15.9
Oct-2001	441.58	18.1	Dec-2002	287.69	−15.9
Feb-2000	1037.32	17.9	Sep-2000	951.21	−14.8
Jan-2001	787.27	17.8	Jun-2002	332.22	−14.0
Nov-2002	341.93	17.5	Oct-1997	227.93	−12.4
Nov-1999	767.72	17.2	Apr-2002	399.20	−12.2
Nov-2001	513.61	16.3	Aug-2001	479.18	−12.1
Apr-2001	607.53	15.9	Mar-2001	524.28	−11.7
May-2003	366.82	15.6	Jul-2004	438.01	−11.1
Nov-1998	362.88	15.4	Jul-2002	299.94	−9.7
Nov-1996	200.45	14.7	Feb-1999	466.95	−9.7
May-1997	214.74	14.5	Feb-1997	186.66	−8.6
Jun-1999	579.62	13.8	Dec-1995	157.88	−8.6
Feb-1998	266.33	13.6	Apr-2000	978.49	−7.9
Aug-2000	1116.79	13.4	May-2000	907.17	−7.3

BEST YEARS BY PERCENT

Year	Close	Point Change	Percent Change
1999	920.78	483.55	110.6%
1998	437.23	213.47	95.4
2003	475.82	188.13	65.4
1996	191.52	33.64	21.3
1997	223.76	32.24	16.8

WORST YEARS BY PERCENT

Year	Close	Point Change	Percent Change
2002	287.69	−219.34	−43.3%
2000	668.22	−252.56	−27.4
2001	507.03	−161.19	−24.1
2004	507.67	31.85	6.7

BEST & WORST WEEKS BY % CHANGE JUN 30, 1995 TO JUN 3, 2005

Week	Best Close	Change	Week	Worst Close	Change
6/2/00	1011.59	18.58%	4/14/00	822.11	−23.70%
5/2/97	200.04	15.60	9/21/01	361.47	−17.70
4/12/01	560.85	14.46	11/10/00	819.04	−14.18
2/4/00	964.56	13.07	12/12/97	209.61	−11.51
4/20/01	631.15	12.53	9/20/02	253.54	−10.77
4/20/00	921.13	12.04	3/1/96	158.29	−10.25
5/17/02	420.49	11.27	8/28/98	268.99	−10.17
12/8/00	811.56	11.25	12/15/00	733.56	−9.61
10/5/01	411.08	9.98	10/2/98	270.31	−9.59
10/16/98	280.35	9.95	1/28/00	853.09	−9.36
3/8/02	492.14	9.78	9/7/01	434.48	−9.33
10/11/02	254.31	9.33	6/15/01	543.59	−9.15
1/12/01	740.64	9.29	7/26/02	283.16	−9.02
1/8/99	476.93	9.08	6/21/02	330.61	−9.02
1/29/99	517.13	9.03	2/9/01	685.68	−8.86
1/19/01	807.50	9.03	3/16/01	527.19	−8.83
9/25/98	298.99	8.59	12/15/95	154.54	−8.72
7/2/99	590.91	8.59	7/6/01	528.79	−8.65
10/12/01	445.86	8.46	12/1/00	729.47	−8.51
3/23/01	570.66	8.25	1/17/03	299.73	−8.31

BEST & WORST DAYS BY % CHANGE JUN 30, 1995 TO JUN 3, 2005

Day	Best Close	Change	Day	Worst Close	Change
1/3/01	731.78	16.52%	8/31/98	240.07	−10.75%
4/5/01	515.30	10.79	10/27/97	216.37	−9.04
5/8/02	405.38	10.53	4/14/00	822.11	−8.42
4/17/00	902.26	9.75	9/17/01	404.25	−7.96
4/18/01	608.17	9.37	12/20/00	642.34	−7.34
12/5/00	810.75	9.17	7/25/02	281.94	−7.27
10/13/00	905.11	8.69	4/12/00	916.84	−7.12
9/8/98	276.14	8.57	3/28/01	539.39	−7.04
5/30/00	921.73	8.04	2/16/01	677.95	−7.00
12/22/00	675.82	7.57	4/19/99	475.71	−6.69
10/28/97	232.18	7.31	3/9/01	578.24	−6.56
10/3/01	396.38	7.30	1/5/01	677.66	−6.48
10/19/00	935.73	7.30	10/1/98	268.52	−6.40
9/1/98	257.52	7.27	1/9/96	142.66	−6.40
4/25/00	951.81	6.70	10/25/00	873.22	−6.29
7/12/01	557.68	6.68	1/2/01	628.03	−6.01
4/10/01	525.27	6.65	4/3/01	473.84	−5.90
12/8/00	811.56	6.51	5/10/00	837.88	−5.87
7/5/02	338.65	6.38	11/10/00	819.04	−5.87
7/29/02	301.21	6.37	1/4/00	894.78	−5.83

INTERNET

AI SEASONALITY

Start	Finish	Data Since
April (Middle)	July (Beginning	10/4/95
October (Beginning)	January (Beginning)	

HISTORICAL PERFORMANCE

Buy & Hold	5-Year Avg	10-Year Avg	Avg Since Inception	Best Year	% Change	Worst Year	% Change
12 Months	−9.6%	NA	30.9%	1999	168.3%	2000	−51.2%

AI Seasonality	5-Year Avg	10-Year Avg	Avg Since Inception	Best Year	% Change	Worst Year	% Change
3 Months	10.3%	NA	17.6%	2003	43.1%	2002	−22.3%
3.33 Months	25.6%	NA	41.6%	1999	164.0%	2001	−34.6%

Recommended ETF: Merrill Lynch Internet HOLDRS (HHH)	Volatility: High
Key Consideration: Ecommerce & Ad numbers	Risk: High

COMPONENTS

Ticker	Name	Ticker	Name
AMZN	Amazon.com	MNST	Monster Worldwide
AQNT	aQuantive	NTBK	NetBank
BEAS	BEA Systems	NFLX	Netflix
BRCM	Broadcom	PALM	Palm
CHKP	Check Point Software	QCOM	Qualcomm
CKFR	Checkfree	Q	Qwest Communications
CIEN	Ciena	RNWK	RealNetworks
CSCO	Cisco Systems	RHAT	Red Hat
CNET	CNET Networks	RIMM	Research In Motion
DGIN	Digital Insight	SONE	S1 Corporation
DRIV	Digital River	SEBL	Siebel Systems
ET	E*Trade Financial	SUNW	Sun Microsystems
ELNK	Earthlink	SYMC	Symantec
EBAY	eBay	TIBX	TIBCO Software
FFIV	F5 Networks	TWX	Time Warner
FDRY	Foundry Networks	UNTD	United Online
GOOG	Google	VRSN	Verisign
IACI	IAC/InterActiveCorp	VRTY	Verity
ISSX	Internet Security	WEBX	WebEx Communication
INTU	Intuit	HLTH	WebMD
JNPR	Juniper Networks	WEBM	webMethods
MACR	Macromedia	WBSN	Websense
MFE	McAfee	YHOO	Yahoo

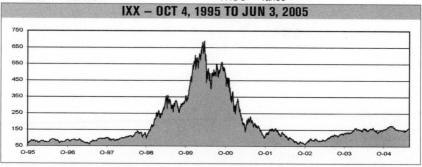

IXX – OCT 4, 1995 TO JUN 3, 2005

INTERNET
Ticker **IIX** Index **INTER@ACTIVE WEEK INTERNET**

DETAILED PERFORMANCE AI SEASONALITY

Start		Finish		Percent	Investing
Date	Close	Date	Close	Change	$1,000
Apr 12 1996	73.09	Jul 1 1996	86.39	18.20%	$1182.00
Oct 1 1996	84.17	Jan 10 1997	85.80	1.94	1204.93
Apr 18 1997	63.02	Jul 9 1997	88.75	40.83	1696.90
Oct 1 1997	95.29	Jan 5 1998	89.69	−5.88	1597.13
Apr 13 1998	101.99	Jul 6 1998	132.14	29.56	2069.24
Oct 8 1998	96.59	Jan 11 1999	255.01	164.01	5462.99
Apr 19 1999	277.74	Jul 9 1999	327.96	18.08	6450.70
Oct 1 1999	322.68	Jan 3 2000	601.53	86.42	12025.40
Apr 14 2000	435.52	Jul 12 2000	504.89	15.93	13941.04
Oct 10 2000	455.27	Jan 3 2001	297.75	−34.60	9117.44
Apr 11 2001	174.27	Jul 2 2001	189.51	8.75	9915.22
Oct 1 2001	100.35	Jan 4 2002	158.11	57.56	15622.42
Apr 11 2002	104.03	Jul 5 2002	80.84	−22.29	12140.18
Oct 8 2002	58.59	Jan 10 2003	95.25	62.57	19736.29
Apr 10 2003	85.28	Jul 9 2003	122.00	43.06	28234.74
Oct 1 2003	121.94	Jan 12 2004	155.66	27.65	36041.64
Apr 20 2004	149.69	Jul 1 2004	158.82	· 6.10	38240.18
Oct 8 2004	149.51	Jan 3 2005	171.64	14.80	43899.73
		Average:		**29.59**	**$42899.73 Gain**

DETAILED PERFORMANCE BUY & HOLD

Start		Finish		Percent	Investing
Date	Close	Date	Close	Change	$1,000
Dec 29 1995	77.73	Dec 31 1996	81.36	4.67	1046.70
Dec 31 1996	81.36	Dec 31 1997	86.75	6.62	1115.99
Dec 31 1997	86.75	Dec 31 1998	213.71	146.35	2749.25
Dec 31 1998	213.71	Dec 31 1999	573.37	168.29	7375.95
Dec 31 1999	573.37	Dec 29 2000	279.60	−51.24	3596.51
Dec 29 2000	279.60	Dec 31 2001	145.94	−47.80	1877.38
Dec 31 2001	145.94	Dec 31 2002	82.99	−43.13	1067.67
Dec 31 2002	82.99	Dec 31 2003	143.67	73.12	1848.34
Dec 31 2003	143.67	Dec 31 2004	173.74	20.93	2235.20
		Average:		**30.87**	**$1235.20 Gain**

Almanac Investor Sector Seasonality out-performance factor 3373.10%

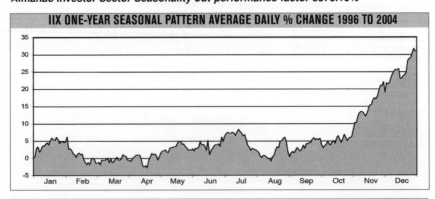

IIX ONE-YEAR SEASONAL PATTERN AVERAGE DAILY % CHANGE 1996 TO 2004

MONTHLY PERFORMANCE BY RANK
NOVEMBER 1995 TO MAY 2005

Month	Total Change	Average Change	# Up	# Down
November	93.5%	9.4%	8	2
October	50.8	5.6	6	3
January	30.1	3.0	6	4
May	29.0	2.9	5	5
December	27.0	2.7	4	6
June	25.2	2.8	5	4
April	17.4	1.7	6	4
September	7.4	0.8	5	4
March	−1.0	−0.1	4	6
August	−13.8	−1.5	5	4
July	−41.9	−4.7	2	7
February	−52.1	−5.2	3	7

MONTHLY PERFORMANCE
NOVEMBER 1995 TO MAY 2005

Month	Total Change	Average Change	# Up	# Down
January	30.1%	3.0%	6	4
February	−52.1	−5.2	3	7
March	−1.0	−0.1	4	6
April	17.4	1.7	6	4
May	29.0	2.9	5	5
June	25.2	2.8	5	4
July	−41.9	−4.7	2	7
August	−13.8	−1.5	5	4
September	7.4	0.8	5	4
October	50.8	5.6	6	3
November	93.5	9.4	8	2
December	27.0	2.7	4	6

BEST & WORST MONTHS BY PERCENT NOVEMBER 1995 TO MAY 2005

Month	Best Close	Change	Month	Worst Close	Change
Dec-1999	573.37	31.0%	Feb-2001	215.15	−30.8%
Dec-1998	213.71	28.7	Nov-2000	315.41	−28.1
Mar-1999	305.59	25.5	Sep-2001	102.32	−23.4
May-1997	82.34	25.2	Mar-2001	167.47	−22.2
Nov-1998	166.03	24.6	Aug-1998	101.32	−20.7
Jan-1999	265.09	24.0	Aug-2001	133.65	−20.6
Nov-2002	96.34	24.0	Feb-2002	110.41	−19.8
Oct-2002	77.67	23.8	May-2000	421.32	−17.8
Sep-1998	124.65	23.0	Apr-2000	512.27	−17.6
Nov-2001	147.46	23.0	Feb-1997	71.42	−17.6
Nov-1999	437.70	22.9	Apr-2002	100.05	−17.2
Jun-1998	127.73	20.7	Jul-1996	70.75	−15.9
Apr-2001	199.63	19.2	Jun-2002	82.04	−14.6
Jul-1997	94.21	18.6	Dec-2002	82.99	−13.9
Feb-2000	628.34	17.7	Jul-2002	70.76	−13.8
Jun-2000	495.32	17.6	Sep-2002	62.74	−13.1
Oct-2001	119.92	17.2	Oct-2000	438.94	−12.7
May-2003	108.42	15.8	Dec-2000	279.60	−11.4
Aug-2000	560.18	15.2	Jul-2004	144.18	−11.3
Apr-1996	84.72	15.2	Jul-1999	278.33	−11.0

BEST YEARS BY PERCENT

Year	Close	Point Change	Percent Change
1999	573.37	359.66	168.3%
1998	213.71	126.96	146.4
2003	143.67	60.68	73.1
2004	173.74	30.07	20.9
1997	86.75	5.39	6.6

WORST YEARS BY PERCENT

Year	Close	Point Change	Percent Change
2000	279.60	−293.77	−51.2%
2001	145.94	−133.66	−47.8
2002	82.99	−62.95	−43.1
1996	81.36	3.63	4.7

Ticker **IIX**   Index **INTER@ACTIVE WEEK INTERNET**

BEST & WORST WEEKS BY % CHANGE OCT 4, 1995 TO JUN 3, 2005

Week	Best Close	Change	Week	Worst Close	Change
6/2/00	490.27	23.12%	4/14/00	435.52	−28.10%
4/12/01	181.97	22.59	9/21/01	101.58	−16.96
5/2/97	71.12	18.08	11/10/00	391.19	−15.48
12/8/00	373.46	15.60	2/8/02	124.70	−12.82
5/17/02	105.04	14.07	12/22/00	292.92	−12.28
4/20/01	207.53	14.05	10/2/98	115.04	−11.80
11/20/98	161.54	13.70	6/15/01	174.19	−11.51
3/8/02	133.78	13.65	4/26/02	98.62	−11.39
1/12/01	299.91	13.29	4/6/01	148.44	−11.36
1/29/99	265.09	13.27	1/28/00	520.99	−11.28
11/9/01	139.02	13.18	7/28/00	472.23	−11.10
10/12/01	126.78	12.40	8/28/98	116.71	−11.06
12/10/99	532.75	12.37	9/7/01	118.99	−10.97
1/8/99	240.04	12.32	12/12/97	81.65	−10.95
10/16/98	115.29	11.90	12/15/00	333.91	−10.59
4/9/99	347.75	11.83	2/9/01	259.28	−10.51
4/20/00	486.60	11.73	10/9/98	103.03	−10.44
7/2/99	321.57	11.03	6/21/02	82.82	−10.29
5/4/01	213.40	10.72	8/31/01	133.65	−10.13
11/27/98	178.57	10.54	2/23/01	229.98	−10.06

BEST & WORST DAYS BY % CHANGE OCT 4, 1995 TO JUN 3, 2005

Day	Best Close	Change	Day	Worst Close	Change
1/3/01	297.75	21.07%	8/31/98	101.32	−13.19%
5/8/02	99.30	13.93	4/19/99	277.74	−12.82
4/5/01	155.40	13.62	1/2/01	245.93	−12.04
12/5/00	368.49	13.50	4/3/01	139.09	−11.82
12/22/00	292.92	12.33	3/28/01	167.37	−10.92
4/18/01	195.17	9.76	12/20/00	265.31	−9.78
5/30/00	436.62	9.65	10/27/97	84.24	−9.70
4/10/01	167.52	9.60	1/5/01	264.73	−9.40
6/2/00	490.27	9.34	4/14/00	435.52	−9.05
10/13/00	452.38	9.09	7/25/02	65.69	−8.79
12/19/95	78.21	8.93	10/5/98	105.26	−8.50
2/23/00	621.03	8.91	9/17/01	112.14	−8.33
2/11/99	245.16	8.50	4/3/00	569.87	−8.30
6/16/99	284.33	8.47	10/1/98	114.68	−8.00
10/3/01	109.94	8.43	6/14/99	256.70	−7.98
5/21/01	228.75	8.12	4/12/00	497.80	−7.89
7/12/01	178.01	7.99	5/23/00	400.96	−7.89
10/11/01	125.64	7.86	10/17/01	119.09	−7.80
4/18/00	505.33	7.86	2/4/02	127.15	−7.61
9/8/98	117.19	7.82	4/23/01	192.11	−7.43

MATERIALS Ticker **S5MATR** Index **S&P 500 MATERIALS***

AI SEASONALITY

Start	Finish	Data Since
October (Middle)	May (Middle)	9/11/89

HISTORICAL PERFORMANCE

Buy & Hold	5-Year Avg	10-Year Avg	Avg Since Inception	Best Year	% Change	Worst Year	% Change
12 Months	4.2%	7.3%	6.8%	2003	34.8%	2000	−17.7%

AI Seasonality	5-Year Avg	10-Year Avg	Avg Since Inception	Best Year	% Change	Worst Year	% Change
7.33 Months	20.0%	17.2%	16.0%	2001	46.3%	1990	0.3%

Recommended ETF: Vanguard Materials VIPERs (VAW)	**Volatility: Moderate**
Key Consideration: China & state of commodity bull/bear market	**Risk: Moderate**

COMPONENTS

Ticker	Name	Ticker	Name
APD	Air Products & Chemicals	LPX	Louisiana-Pacific
AA	Alcoa	MWV	Meadwestvaco
ATI	Allegheny Technologies	MON	Monsanto
ASH	Ashland	NEM	Newmont Mining
BLL	Ball	NUE	Nucor
BMS	Bemis Co	PTV	Pactiv
DOW	Dow Chemical	PD	Phelps Dodge
DD	DuPont	PPG	PPG Industries
EMN	Eastman Chemical	PX	Praxair
ECL	Ecolab	ROH	Rohm & Haas
EC	Engelhard	SEE	Sealed Air
FCX	Freeport McMoran Copper & Gold	SIAL	Sigma-Aldrich
GP	Georgia-Pacific	TIN	Temple-Inland
HPC	Hercules	X	U.S. Steel
IFF	International Flavors & Fragrances	VMC	Vulcan Materials
IP	International Paper	WY	Weyerhaeuser

* S5MATR Available @ bloomberg.com

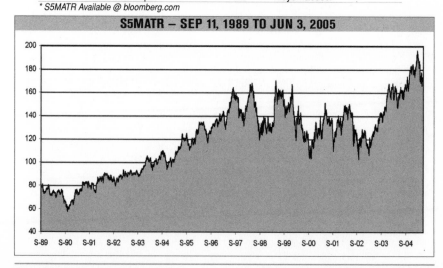

S5MATR – SEP 11, 1989 TO JUN 3, 2005

DETAILED PERFORMANCE AI SEASONALITY

| Start | | Finish | | Percent | Investing |
Date	Close	Date	Close	Change	$1,000
Oct 19 1995	114.28	May 14 1996	133.96	17.22%	$1172.20
Oct 16 1996	131.54	May 15 1997	144.37	9.75	1286.49
Oct 20 1997	151.26	May 14 1998	167.85	10.97	1427.62
Oct 14 1998	123.59	May 12 1999	164.29	32.93	1897.73
Oct 15 1999	141.24	May 15 2000	142.50	0.89	1914.62
Oct 17 2000	103.14	May 17 2001	150.86	46.27	2800.52
Oct 10 2001	122.13	May 15 2002	148.36	21.48	3402.07
Oct 10 2002	107.15	May 12 2003	126.48	18.04	4015.80
Oct 10 2003	140.80	May 13 2004	149.79	6.38	4272.01
Oct 19 2004	161.65	May 11 2005	173.93	7.60	4596.68
			Average:	**17.15**	**$3596.68 Gain**

DETAILED PERFORMANCE BUY & HOLD

| Start | | Finish | | Percent | Investing |
Date	Close	Date	Close	Change	$1,000
Dec 30 1994	100.00	Dec 29 1995	117.29	17.29%	$1172.90
Dec 29 1995	117.29	Dec 31 1996	132.99	13.39	1329.95
Dec 31 1996	132.99	Dec 31 1997	141.37	6.30	1413.74
Dec 31 1997	141.37	Dec 31 1998	130.09	−7.98	1300.92
Dec 31 1998	130.09	Dec 31 1999	159.96	22.96	1599.61
Dec 31 1999	159.96	Dec 29 2000	131.61	−17.72	1316.16
Dec 29 2000	131.61	Dec 31 2001	132.93	1.00	1329.32
Dec 31 2001	132.93	Dec 31 2002	122.69	−7.70	1226.97
Dec 31 2002	122.69	Dec 31 2003	165.34	34.76	1653.46
Dec 31 2003	165.34	Dec 31 2004	183.15	10.77	1831.54
			Average:	**7.31**	**$831.54 Gain**

Almanac Investor Sector Seasonality out-performance factor 332.53%

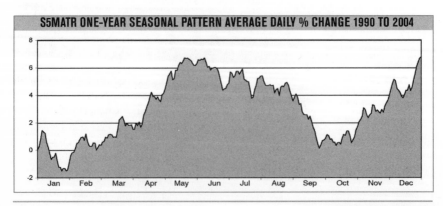

S5MATR ONE-YEAR SEASONAL PATTERN AVERAGE DAILY % CHANGE 1990 TO 2004

MATERIALS

Ticker **S5MATR**   Index **S&P 500 MATERIALS***

MONTHLY PERFORMANCE BY RANK
OCTOBER 1989 TO MAY 2005

Month	Total Change	Average Change	# Up	# Down
December	45.7%	2.9%	10	6
November	40.5	2.5	12	4
April	37.0	2.3	10	6
May	27.7	1.7	10	6
February	25.5	1.6	12	4
March	15.9	1.0	9	7
October	12.5	0.8	10	6
July	7.1	0.5	10	5
January	−16.4	−1.0	7	9
June	−21.6	−1.4	5	10
August	−25.9	−1.7	6	9
September	−42.3	−2.8	6	9

MONTHLY PERFORMANCE
OCTOBER 1989 TO MAY 2005

Month	Total Change	Average Change	# Up	# Down
January	−16.4%	−1.0%	7	9
February	25.5	1.6	12	4
March	15.9	1.0	9	7
April	37.0	2.3	10	6
May	27.7	1.7	10	6
June	−21.6	−1.4	5	10
July	7.1	0.5	10	5
August	−25.9	−1.7	6	9
September	−42.3	−2.8	6	9
October	12.5	0.8	10	6
November	40.5	2.5	12	4
December	45.7	2.9	10	6

BEST & WORST MONTHS BY PERCENT OCTOBER 1989 TO MAY 2005

Month	Best Close	Change	Month	Worst Close	Change
Apr-1999	162.59	24.1%	Aug-1998	119.40	−13.3%
Dec-2000	131.61	14.5	Sep-2002	109.47	−13.1
Nov-2002	128.39	11.7	Jan-2000	141.06	−11.8
Nov-2001	136.35	11.6	Sep-2001	119.34	−11.3
Apr-2001	137.19	11.2	Aug-1990	66.51	−11.3
Dec-1999	159.96	10.7	Jul-2002	126.82	−11.3
Dec-2003	165.34	10.0	Sep-2000	108.23	−10.0
Mar-2000	139.59	9.8	Feb-2000	127.19	−9.8
Oct-2000	118.63	9.6	Jun-2000	118.08	−9.1
May-1991	82.25	9.3	Oct-1997	141.89	−8.8
Dec-1991	81.67	9.2	Jul-1998	137.71	−8.4
Apr-2003	123.44	9.2	Nov-1991	74.80	−8.3
Oct-2003	147.31	9.1	Nov-1994	96.62	−7.9
Jul-1997	162.32	8.4	May-1999	149.87	−7.8
Jan-1994	104.47	7.9	Jan-1990	72.01	−7.8
Jul-2003	137.78	7.8	Sep-1990	61.51	−7.5
Feb-2005	190.91	7.6	Apr-2005	172.50	−7.0
Nov-2004	180.96	7.5	Oct-1995	111.55	−6.4
May-1990	75.15	7.5	Aug-1992	83.69	−5.5
Nov-1990	63.80	7.2	Oct-1989	74.48	−5.5

BEST YEARS BY PERCENT

Year	Close	Point Change	Percent Change
2003	165.34	42.65	34.8%
1999	159.96	29.87	23.0
1991	81.67	14.47	21.5
1995	117.29	17.29	17.3
1996	132.99	15.70	13.4

WORST YEARS BY PERCENT

Year	Close	Point Change	Percent Change
2000	131.61	−28.35	−17.7%
1990	67.20	−10.88	−13.9
1998	130.09	−11.28	−8.0
2002	122.69	−10.24	−7.7
2001	132.93	1.32	1.0

Seasonal Sector Investing: Indices

MATERIALS
Ticker **S5MATR** Index **S&P 500 MATERIALS***

BEST & WORST WEEKS BY % CHANGE SEP 11, 1989 TO JUN 3, 2005

Week	Best Close	Change	Week	Worst Close	Change
4/16/99	153.05	14.28%	9/21/01	109.44	−13.98%
12/22/00	131.50	10.96	3/16/01	124.50	−9.32
9/28/01	119.34	9.05	7/19/02	120.98	−9.22
3/21/03	121.31	8.79	4/15/05	169.67	−8.06
3/17/00	132.90	8.43	1/9/98	131.24	−7.90
5/31/91	82.25	7.45	5/26/00	128.88	−7.55
5/18/01	150.16	7.21	10/13/89	74.28	−7.16
1/8/99	139.43	7.18	1/21/00	149.00	−7.07
1/25/02	133.10	7.17	2/11/00	132.21	−6.86
3/2/01	132.06	6.99	8/14/98	127.14	−6.79
11/3/00	117.11	6.86	10/12/90	58.56	−6.57
8/9/02	128.37	6.35	1/12/01	122.14	−6.50
2/5/93	93.20	6.31	9/24/99	138.78	−6.32
7/7/95	123.52	6.17	7/12/02	133.27	−6.19
7/14/00	124.51	6.16	10/13/00	104.49	−6.17
11/6/98	138.94	6.09	5/13/05	165.85	−6.14
12/27/91	79.27	6.05	9/15/00	110.49	−5.93
10/27/00	109.59	5.86	5/28/99	149.87	−5.78
11/29/02	128.39	5.77	12/4/98	130.13	−5.55
6/4/99	158.37	5.67	1/18/02	124.20	−5.31

BEST & WORST DAYS BY % CHANGE SEP 11, 1989 TO JUN 3, 2005

Day	Best Close	Change	Day	Worst Close	Change
10/30/00	117.51	7.23%	9/17/01	116.13	−8.72%
7/24/02	121.96	6.78	10/27/97	138.18	−7.73
3/15/00	130.04	6.77	10/13/89	74.28	−6.06
3/16/00	137.75	5.93	10/2/02	110.07	−5.05
10/1/02	115.93	5.90	4/14/00	137.58	−4.93
7/29/02	132.02	5.62	9/7/00	118.51	−4.71
4/14/99	146.72	5.55	8/2/02	120.71	−4.53
7/11/00	126.55	5.50	7/19/02	120.98	−4.45
12/4/00	125.13	5.16	7/22/02	115.78	−4.30
10/15/02	117.26	5.15	9/30/98	126.67	−4.17
10/3/00	112.24	5.13	10/9/02	102.55	−4.07
10/24/00	108.57	5.06	8/31/98	119.40	−4.05
5/16/01	149.47	4.96	7/30/02	126.79	−3.96
4/28/99	163.41	4.88	9/24/02	110.18	−3.92
9/24/01	114.75	4.85	3/24/03	116.60	−3.88
10/11/02	112.09	4.61	10/13/98	125.70	−3.88
12/22/00	131.50	4.52	9/20/01	111.37	−3.81
10/10/02	107.15	4.49	3/7/00	119.02	−3.78
2/26/01	128.91	4.44	12/20/99	150.58	−3.70
10/15/98	129.06	4.43	1/9/98	131.24	−3.68

NATURAL GAS — Ticker **XNG**   Index **AMEX NATURAL GAS**

AI SEASONALITY

Start	Finish	Data Since
February (End)	June (Beginning)	3/18/94

HISTORICAL PERFORMANCE

Buy & Hold	5-Year Avg	10-Year Avg	Avg Since Inception	Best Year	% Change	Worst Year	% Change
12 Months	27.4%	16.8%	16.8%	2000	105.5%	1998	−36.2%

AI Seasonality	5-Year Avg	10-Year Avg	Avg Since Inception	Best Year	% Change	Worst Year	% Change
3 .33 Months	29.9%	19.5%	19.5%	2000	65.9%	1998	−0.02%

Recommended ETF: iShares Dow Jones U.S. Oil and Gas (IYE)   Volatility: Moderate

Key Consideration: Stablity of energy prices and geopolitics   Risk: Moderate

COMPONENTS

Ticker	Name	Ticker	Name
APC	Anadarko Petroleum	GAS	Nicor
APA	Apache	NI	NiSource
BR	Burlington Resources	NBL	Noble Energy
DVN	Devon Energy	PPP	Pogo Producing
EP	El Paso	STR	Questar
EOG	EOG Resources	WMB	Williams
KMI	Kinder Morgan	XTO	XTO Energy
NFG	National Fuel Gas		

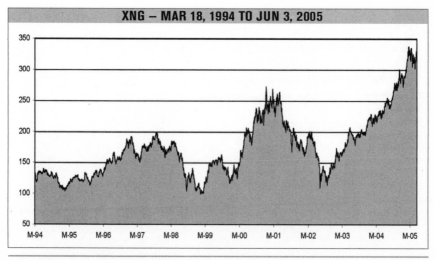

XNG – MAR 18, 1994 TO JUN 3, 2005

DETAILED PERFORMANCE AI SEASONALITY

Start Date	Close	Finish Date	Close	Percent Change	Investing $1,000
Feb 21 1995	109.12	Jun 1 1995	128.34	17.61%	$1176.10
Feb 29 1996	132.58	Jun 4 1996	151.52	14.29	1344.16
Feb 28 1997	158.71	Jun 3 1997	179.40	13.04	1519.44
Feb 24 1998	166.43	Jun 5 1998	166.40	−0.02	1519.14
Feb 24 1999	101.29	Jun 7 1999	152.63	50.69	2289.19
Feb 25 2000	123.79	Jun 1 2000	205.32	65.86	3796.85
Feb 28 2001	238.23	Jun 4 2001	247.71	3.98	3947.97
Feb 20 2002	164.84	Jun 4 2002	167.99	1.91	4023.37
Feb 20 2003	160.88	Jun 4 2003	204.76	27.27	5120.55
Feb 24 2004	213.25	Jun 1 2004	232.81	9.17	5590.10
			Average:	**20.38**	**$4590.10 Gain**

DETAILED PERFORMANCE BUY & HOLD

Start Date	Close	Finish Date	Close	Percent Change	Investing $1,000
Dec 30 1994	111.56	Dec 29 1995	136.54	22.39%	$1223.90
Dec 29 1995	136.54	Dec 31 1996	182.06	33.34	1631.95
Dec 31 1996	182.06	Dec 31 1997	175.41	−3.65	1572.38
Dec 31 1997	175.41	Dec 31 1998	111.95	−36.18	1003.49
Dec 31 1998	111.95	Dec 31 1999	128.94	15.18	1155.82
Dec 31 1999	128.94	Dec 29 2000	264.93	105.47	2374.87
Dec 29 2000	264.93	Dec 31 2001	185.84	−29.85	1665.97
Dec 31 2001	185.84	Dec 31 2002	146.12	−21.37	1309.95
Dec 31 2002	146.12	Dec 31 2003	219.36	50.12	1966.50
Dec 31 2003	219.36	Dec 31 2004	290.46	32.41	2603.85
			Average:	**16.79**	**$1603.85 Gain**

Almanac Investor Sector Seasonality out-performance factor 186.19%

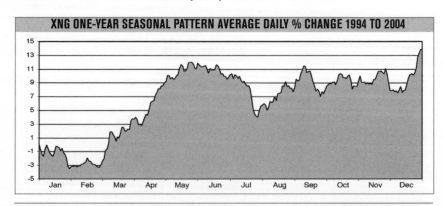

XNG ONE-YEAR SEASONAL PATTERN AVERAGE DAILY % CHANGE 1994 TO 2004

NATURAL GAS

MONTHLY PERFORMANCE BY RANK
APRIL 1993 TO MAY 2005

Month	Total Change	Average Change	# Up	# Down
March	75.6%	6.9%	9	2
April	54.5	4.5	9	3
December	47.2	4.3	7	4
May	26.8	2.2	7	5
February	22.2	2.0	9	2
October	14.1	1.3	7	4
August	11.4	1.0	6	5
September	5.8	0.5	5	6
November	−16.9	−1.5	5	6
June	−18.4	−1.7	4	7
January	−31.8	−2.9	3	8
July	−44.7	−4.1	5	6

MONTHLY PERFORMANCE
APRIL 1993 TO MAY 2005

Month	Total Change	Average Change	# Up	# Down
January	−31.8%	−2.9%	3	8
February	22.2	2.0	9	2
March	75.6	6.9	9	2
April	54.5	4.5	9	3
May	26.8	2.2	7	5
June	−18.4	−1.7	4	7
July	−44.7	−4.1	5	6
August	11.4	1.0	6	5
September	5.8	0.5	5	6
October	14.1	1.3	7	4
November	−16.9	−1.5	5	6
December	47.2	4.3	7	4

BEST & WORST MONTHS BY PERCENT APRIL 1993 TO MAY 2005

Month	Best Close	Change	Month	Worst Close	Change
Mar-2000	167.84	25.9%	Aug-1998	104.00	−24.6%
Dec-2000	264.93	25.7	Jul-2002	132.44	−17.4
Sep-1998	126.45	21.6	Jul-1998	137.89	−15.5
Aug-2000	221.31	21.0	Jun-2001	212.62	−13.9
May-2000	206.07	20.0	Nov-1998	113.88	−13.8
Apr-1999	144.26	19.9	Feb-1997	158.71	−12.3
Mar-1999	120.30	17.3	Nov-1994	116.82	−11.5
Mar-2002	194.09	12.2	Jan-2001	234.85	−11.4
Jan-2003	163.98	12.2	Jan-1999	99.91	−10.8
Feb-2005	327.63	11.7	Sep-2001	180.06	−10.5
Apr-1994	133.91	11.7	Nov-2001	173.06	−10.4
May-2003	196.92	11.4	Nov-1999	125.78	−9.9
Nov-2002	144.19	11.3	Jan-2002	168.35	−9.4
Apr-1996	152.85	11.1	Sep-2002	127.00	−8.6
Dec-2003	219.36	9.7	Jul-1996	147.71	−8.5
Oct-1996	171.82	9.6	May-2002	174.13	−8.1
Nov-2004	296.96	9.3	Jun-2002	160.31	−7.9
Nov-1995	125.18	9.1	May-1998	165.87	−7.4
Dec-1995	136.54	9.1	Oct-1995	114.75	−7.3
Sep-2004	268.19	9.0	Jul-2000	182.84	−6.8

BEST YEARS BY PERCENT

Year	Close	Point Change	Percent Change
2000	264.93	135.99	105.5%
2003	219.36	73.24	50.1
1996	182.06	45.52	33.3
2004	290.46	71.10	32.4
1995	136.54	24.98	22.4

WORST YEARS BY PERCENT

Year	Close	Point Change	Percent Change
1998	111.95	−63.46	−36.2%
2001	185.84	−79.09	−29.9
2002	146.12	−39.72	−21.4
1997	175.41	−6.65	−3.7
1999	128.94	16.99	15.2

BEST & WORST WEEKS BY % CHANGE MAR 18, 1994 TO JUN 3, 2005

Week	Best Close	Change	Week	Worst Close	Change
3/3/00	138.78	12.11%	7/26/02	114.64	−12.74%
8/2/02	128.30	11.92	9/21/01	181.32	−10.48
3/31/00	167.84	11.86	7/19/02	131.38	−9.64
1/21/00	146.23	9.87	1/5/01	240.79	−9.11
12/29/00	264.93	9.15	9/22/00	216.04	−8.80
3/9/01	266.62	8.78	1/28/00	133.65	−8.60
11/22/02	147.62	8.29	10/27/00	214.88	−8.12
10/13/00	235.40	7.89	3/16/01	245.01	−8.11
3/8/02	189.68	7.75	7/12/02	145.39	−7.77
10/5/01	193.67	7.56	2/25/00	123.79	−7.11
5/5/00	184.24	7.28	12/1/00	218.14	−6.88
1/3/03	151.61	7.03	11/16/01	179.03	−6.76
1/17/03	171.19	6.77	11/2/01	186.40	−6.72
4/27/01	259.51	6.56	9/20/02	126.61	−6.61
2/9/01	252.96	6.29	4/15/05	304.08	−6.47
3/10/00	147.27	6.12	4/26/02	186.94	−5.97
5/12/00	195.31	6.01	1/30/04	214.19	−5.92
4/19/02	198.80	5.88	6/7/02	163.93	−5.86
2/21/03	163.55	5.88	11/30/01	173.06	−5.42
11/26/04	299.94	5.77	1/7/05	275.06	−5.30

BEST & WORST DAYS BY % CHANGE MAR 18, 1994 TO JUN 3, 2005

Day	Best Close	Change	Day	Worst Close	Change
12/26/00	264.44	8.94%	7/23/02	109.15	−9.15%
7/29/02	122.83	7.14	7/22/02	120.14	−8.56
3/7/00	149.44	6.82	7/19/02	131.38	−6.70
3/7/01	265.06	6.37	7/5/00	184.68	−6.63
3/29/00	160.97	6.34	11/15/01	176.03	−6.19
1/6/00	129.19	5.29	8/5/02	120.40	−6.16
1/18/00	139.93	5.14	3/12/01	253.29	−5.00
7/25/01	209.44	5.05	11/29/00	221.18	−4.98
7/30/02	128.97	5.00	9/18/01	188.70	−4.97
9/28/01	180.06	4.96	11/30/00	210.72	−4.73
2/29/00	133.32	4.73	1/3/00	122.90	−4.68
10/10/01	203.73	4.61	6/3/02	166.25	−4.53
11/14/02	137.84	4.49	11/28/01	173.86	−4.51
7/11/00	195.03	4.33	10/25/00	213.86	−4.51
10/21/02	129.71	4.33	1/3/01	244.76	−4.36
11/15/00	226.27	4.16	1/3/05	277.90	−4.32
11/19/02	144.30	4.02	5/2/01	244.73	−4.25
5/4/00	180.97	4.02	9/19/01	180.80	−4.19
2/15/00	140.57	3.97	3/22/01	232.21	−4.14
10/10/00	230.89	3.86	1/4/01	234.67	−4.12

OIL

AI SEASONALITY

Start	Finish	Data Since
December (Middle)	June (Middle)	8/26/83

HISTORICAL PERFORMANCE

Buy & Hold	5-Year Avg	10-Year Avg	Avg Since Inception	Best Year	% Change	Worst Year	% Change
12 Months	8.7%	11.6%	10.5%	1989	37.0%	2002	−14.1%

AI Seasonality	5-Year Avg	10-Year Avg	Avg Since Inception	Best Year	% Change	Worst Year	% Change
6.33 Months	15.0%	14.8%	14.4%	1987	39.4%	1990	1.7%

Recommended ETF:	Select Sector SPDR Energy Select Sector (XLE)	Volatility: Moderate
Key Consideration:	Stablity of energy prices and geopolitcs	Risk: Moderate

COMPONENTS

Ticker	Name	Ticker	Name
AHC	Amerada Hess	OXY	Occidental Petroleum
BP	BP	REP	Repsol
CVX	Chevron	RDS-A	Royal Dutch Shell
COP	ConocoPhillips	SUN	Sunoco
XOM	ExxonMobil	TOT	Total
KMG	Kerr-Mcgee	VLO	Valero Energy
MRO	Marathon Oil		

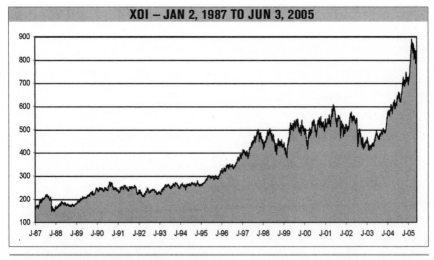

XOI – JAN 2, 1987 TO JUN 3, 2005

OIL

DETAILED PERFORMANCE AI SEASONALITY

Start Date	Close	Finish Date	Close	Percent Change	Investing $1,000
Dec 14 1994	259.83	Jun 19 1995	298.73	14.97%	$1149.70
Dec 18 1995	310.94	Jun 12 1996	340.69	9.57	1259.73
Dec 13 1996	374.07	Jun 16 1997	443.21	18.48	1492.52
Dec 18 1997	445.93	Jun 17 1998	472.89	6.05	1582.82
Dec 15 1998	425.29	Jun 15 1999	526.05	23.69	1957.79
Dec 20 1999	495.20	Jun 16 2000	542.26	9.50	2143.78
Dec 14 2000	490.20	Jun 12 2001	588.69	20.09	2574.47
Dec 13 2001	482.36	Jun 17 2002	539.23	11.79	2878.00
Dec 13 2002	443.44	Jun 11 2003	495.11	11.65	3213.28
Dec 10 2003	519.80	Jun 18 2004	634.58	22.08	3922.78
			Average:	**14.79**	**$2922.78 Gain**

DETAILED PERFORMANCE BUY & HOLD

Start Date	Close	Finish Date	Close	Percent Change	Investing $1,000
Dec 30 1994	261.75	Dec 29 1995	320.80	22.56%	$1225.60
Dec 29 1995	320.80	Dec 31 1996	390.17	21.62	1490.57
Dec 31 1996	390.17	Dec 31 1997	454.36	16.45	1735.77
Dec 31 1997	454.36	Dec 31 1998	433.19	−4.66	1654.89
Dec 31 1998	433.19	Dec 31 1999	503.00	16.12	1921.65
Dec 31 1999	503.00	Dec 29 2000	536.25	6.61	2048.68
Dec 29 2000	536.25	Dec 31 2001	519.99	−3.03	1986.60
Dec 31 2001	519.99	Dec 31 2002	446.84	−14.07	1707.09
Dec 31 2002	446.84	Dec 31 2003	562.61	25.91	2149.39
Dec 31 2003	562.61	Dec 31 2004	721.12	28.17	2754.88
			Average:	**11.57**	**$1754.88 Gain**

Almanac Investor Sector Seasonality out-performance factor 66.55%

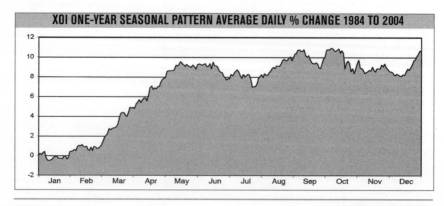

XOI ONE-YEAR SEASONAL PATTERN AVERAGE DAILY % CHANGE 1984 TO 2004

OIL

MONTHLY PERFORMANCE BY RANK
SEPTEMBER 1983 TO MAY 2005

Month	Total Change	Average Change	# Up	# Down
March	80.3%	3.7%	16	6
April	57.3	2.6	17	5
December	42.8	2.0	14	8
August	37.1	1.8	13	8
May	31.4	1.4	15	7
February	30.6	1.4	12	10
January	11.1	0.5	12	10
July	7.7	0.4	12	9
September	−1.9	−0.1	10	12
October	−10.8	−0.5	9	13
November	−17.3	−0.8	11	11
June	−29.0	−1.4	7	14

MONTHLY PERFORMANCE
SEPTEMBER 1983 TO MAY 2005

Month	Total Change	Average Change	# Up	# Down
January	11.1%	0.5%	12	10
February	30.6	1.4	12	10
March	80.3	3.7	16	6
April	57.3	2.6	17	5
May	31.4	1.4	15	7
June	−29.0	−1.4	7	14
July	7.7	0.4	12	9
August	37.1	1.8	13	8
September	−1.9	−0.1	10	12
October	−10.8	−0.5	9	13
November	−17.3	−0.8	11	11
December	42.8	2.0	14	8

BEST & WORST MONTHS BY PERCENT SEPTEMBER 1983 TO MAY 2005

Month	Best Close	Change	Month	Worst Close	Change
Aug-1986	145.28	18.7%	Oct-1987	164.61	−19.7%
Mar-1999	450.59	17.1	Jul-2002	483.07	−11.9
Mar-2000	501.99	16.7	Nov-1991	226.38	−10.3
Feb-2005	861.39	15.5	Nov-1987	148.30	−9.9
Mar-1987	190.18	15.5	Aug-1998	390.71	−9.6
Apr-1999	515.08	14.3	Sep-2002	444.58	−9.4
Dec-2003	562.61	13.7	Sep-2001	498.16	−9.2
Aug-1984	117.71	12.9	Jan-1999	394.97	−8.8
Sep-1998	440.84	12.8	Feb-2000	430.30	−8.0
Jan-1987	168.94	12.0	Jul-1998	432.34	−7.6
Jan-1984	111.99	11.3	Jan-1986	124.06	−7.2
Apr-2001	584.80	10.5	Jan-2000	467.79	−7.0
Apr-1992	234.82	10.4	Jul-1984	104.22	−6.8
May-2000	537.97	10.0	Nov-1993	250.88	−6.4
Jul-1990	262.88	9.7	Jul-1986	122.43	−6.4
May-2003	471.29	9.4	Jun-2001	548.85	−6.4
Sep-2004	698.74	9.3	Jun-2000	505.35	−6.1
Dec-1987	161.88	9.2	Nov-1994	263.34	−5.9
Aug-2000	520.25	8.3	May-1984	114.05	−5.7
Feb-1991	251.89	8.2	Jun-1992	227.45	−5.6

BEST YEARS BY PERCENT

Year	Close	Point Change	Percent Change
1989	245.94	66.39	37.0%
2004	721.12	158.51	28.2
2003	562.61	115.77	25.9
1995	320.80	59.05	22.6
1996	390.17	69.37	21.6

WORST YEARS BY PERCENT

Year	Close	Point Change	Percent Change
2002	446.84	−73.15	−14.1%
1998	433.19	−21.17	−4.7
2001	519.99	−16.26	−3.0
1992	229.11	−7.00	−3.0
1990	240.57	−5.37	−2.2

BEST & WORST WEEKS BY % CHANGE AUG 26, 1983 TO JUN 3, 2005

Week	Best Close	Change	Week	Worst Close	Change
11/12/99	520.67	10.14%	9/21/01	482.33	−12.06%
10/26/84	121.73	8.51	10/23/87	166.44	−9.48
4/16/99	497.16	7.27	7/19/02	457.97	−8.73
3/12/99	434.09	7.14	9/12/86	138.64	−8.69
8/9/02	486.56	7.11	1/9/98	414.63	−8.57
8/8/86	130.89	7.01	7/12/02	501.79	−8.33
3/20/87	187.10	6.74	11/16/01	477.17	−8.06
4/30/99	515.08	6.72	1/28/00	462.30	−7.74
3/10/00	468.64	6.55	8/28/98	400.74	−7.60
2/8/91	246.25	6.55	10/16/87	183.87	−6.85
1/16/98	441.42	6.46	10/13/89	218.00	−6.65
7/13/90	253.47	6.43	11/5/99	472.75	−6.10
8/15/86	139.20	6.35	12/4/98	428.15	−6.09
3/31/00	501.99	6.24	4/15/05	802.53	−6.06
12/24/87	165.14	6.14	10/19/84	112.18	−6.04
3/3/00	439.83	5.96	9/22/00	516.21	−6.02
9/11/98	432.70	5.85	10/25/02	433.89	−5.98
1/29/93	233.85	5.84	3/16/01	527.53	−5.91
12/11/87	155.37	5.78	1/10/92	224.69	−5.78
3/14/86	126.29	5.77	3/31/94	244.09	−5.71

BEST & WORST DAYS BY % CHANGE AUG 26, 1983 TO JUN 3, 2005

Day	Best Close	Change	Day	Worst Close	Change
10/21/87	167.42	9.15%	10/19/87	146.71	−20.21%
3/7/00	466.78	7.11	10/26/87	152.94	−8.11
10/22/84	118.30	5.46	8/1/02	454.40	−5.93
5/26/92	248.19	5.29	10/27/97	447.43	−5.93
9/23/98	457.05	5.22	10/13/89	218.00	−5.91
7/29/02	472.17	5.09	1/8/88	161.68	−5.81
7/24/02	447.63	5.07	7/22/02	432.24	−5.62
3/29/00	489.41	4.85	7/19/02	457.97	−5.55
3/10/99	425.25	4.75	11/14/01	491.07	−5.35
3/11/86	124.40	4.70	9/11/86	140.22	−4.70
10/20/87	153.39	4.55	7/5/00	490.68	−4.60
9/27/01	484.99	4.48	11/15/01	469.26	−4.44
11/8/99	493.81	4.45	11/30/87	148.30	−4.43
10/10/83	104.31	4.21	9/3/02	469.64	−4.27
8/5/86	132.25	4.11	9/19/01	498.94	−4.16
2/6/91	243.37	4.07	5/2/01	560.16	−4.10
1/25/93	229.93	4.06	10/29/02	414.61	−4.09
11/27/98	455.90	4.06	9/30/98	440.84	−3.99
4/15/99	479.98	4.04	4/14/88	183.76	−3.77
10/28/97	465.51	4.04	5/12/05	800.12	−3.68

PHARMACEUTICAL · Ticker **DRG** · Index **AMEX PHARMACEUTICAL**

AI SEASONALITY

Start	Finish	Data Since
September (Beginning)	February (Middle)	2/28/94

HISTORICAL PERFORMANCE

Buy & Hold	5-Year Avg	10-Year Avg	Avg Since Inception	Best Year	% Change	Worst Year	% Change
12 Months	−1.0%	15.4%	15.4%	1995	51.1%	2002	−22.5%

AI Seasonality	5-Year Avg	10-Year Avg	Avg Since Inception	Best Year	% Change	Worst Year	% Change
5.67 Months	6.1%	16.0%	15.8%	1998	34.9%	2005	−1.8%

Recommended ETF: PowerShares Dynamic Pharmaceuticals (PJP)	Volatility: Moderate
Key Consideration: FDA, Medicare & HMO issues	Risk: Moderate

COMPONENTS

Ticker	Name	Ticker	Name
ABT	Abbott Laboratories	JNJ	Johnson & Johnson
AMGN	Amgen	KG	King Pharmaceuticals
AZN	AstraZeneca	MRK	Merck
BMY	Bristol-Myers Squibb	PFE	Pfizer
LLY	Eli Lilly	SNY	Sanofi-Aventis
FRX	Forest Laboratories	SGP	Schering-Plough
GSK	GlaxoSmithKline	WYE	Wyeth
IVX	IVAX		

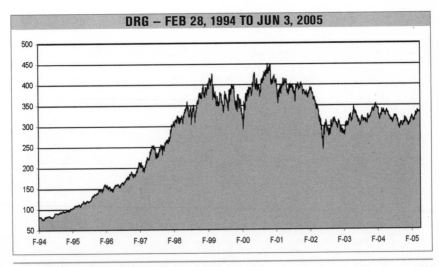

DRG – FEB 28, 1994 TO JUN 3, 2005

Seasonal Sector Investing: Indices

DETAILED PERFORMANCE AI SEASONALITY

| Start | | Finish | | Percent | Investing |
Date	Close	Date	Close	Change	$1,000
Sep 1 1995	118.68	Feb 20 1996	159.49	34.39%	$1343.90
Sep 6 1996	159.24	Feb 20 1997	210.96	32.48	1780.40
Sep 2 1997	223.55	Feb 17 1998	301.65	34.94	2402.47
Sep 4 1998	304.32	Feb 10 1999	389.74	28.07	3076.84
Sep 7 1999	364.20	Feb 14 2000	362.67	−0.42	3063.92
Sep 7 2000	370.59	Feb 13 2001	421.95	13.86	3488.58
Sep 10 2001	376.82	Feb 21 2002	382.70	1.56	3543.00
Sep 3 2002	284.47	Feb 18 2003	291.19	2.36	3626.62
Sep 3 2003	308.34	Feb 11 2004	353.08	14.51	4152.84
Sep 10 2004	320.73	Feb 18 2005	314.83	−1.84	4076.43
			Average:	**15.99**	**$3076.43 Gain**

DETAILED PERFORMANCE BUY & HOLD

| Start | | Finish | | Percent | Investing |
Date	Close	Date	Close	Change	$1,000
Dec 30 1994	97.07	Dec 29 1995	146.71	51.14%	$1511.40
Dec 29 1995	146.71	Dec 31 1996	184.26	25.59	1898.17
Dec 31 1996	184.26	Dec 31 1997	257.10	39.53	2648.51
Dec 31 1997	257.10	Dec 31 1998	378.45	47.20	3898.61
Dec 31 1998	378.45	Dec 31 1999	358.99	−5.14	3698.22
Dec 31 1999	358.99	Dec 29 2000	449.18	25.12	4627.22
Dec 29 2000	449.18	Dec 31 2001	385.25	−14.23	3968.76
Dec 31 2001	385.25	Dec 31 2002	298.53	−22.51	3075.39
Dec 31 2002	298.53	Dec 31 2003	335.59	12.41	3457.05
Dec 31 2003	335.59	Dec 31 2004	316.62	−5.65	3261.73
			Average:	**15.35**	**$2261.73 Gain**

Almanac Investor Sector Seasonality out-performance factor 36.02%

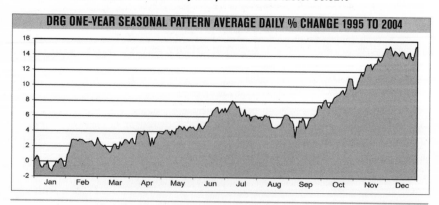

DRG ONE-YEAR SEASONAL PATTERN AVERAGE DAILY % CHANGE 1995 TO 2004

MONTHLY PERFORMANCE BY RANK
MARCH 1994 TO MAY 2005

Month	Total Change	Average Change	# Up	# Down
November	45.3%	4.1%	9	2
February	41.6	3.8	9	2
October	30.4	2.8	8	3
April	21.6	1.8	8	4
June	17.4	1.6	6	5
August	12.0	1.1	7	4
May	10.7	0.9	8	4
December	5.9	0.5	4	7
September	5.2	0.5	7	4
July	−10.1	−0.9	5	6
January	−11.7	−1.1	4	7
March	−12.9	−1.1	5	7

MONTHLY PERFORMANCE
MARCH 1994 TO MAY 2005

Month	Total Change	Average Change	# Up	# Down
January	−11.7%	−1.1%	4	7
February	41.6	3.8	9	2
March	−12.9	−1.1	5	7
April	21.6	1.8	8	4
May	10.7	0.9	8	4
June	17.4	1.6	6	5
July	−10.1	−0.9	5	6
August	12.0	1.1	7	4
September	5.2	0.5	7	4
October	30.4	2.8	8	3
November	45.3	4.1	9	2
December	5.9	0.5	4	7

BEST & WORST MONTHS BY PERCENT MARCH 1994 TO MAY 2005

Month	Best Close	Change	Month	Worst Close	Change
Apr-2000	383.15	13.5%	Sep-1999	345.15	−9.7%
Nov-1997	259.64	12.8	Jan-2001	406.79	−9.4
Feb-1997	210.66	12.1	May-1999	354.61	−9.2
Oct-1999	384.13	11.3	Jun-2002	307.03	−8.4
Nov-1998	378.68	10.5	Dec-1999	358.99	−8.3
Jan-1998	283.35	10.2	Aug-1997	228.32	−8.1
Jun-1997	243.35	10.2	Mar-2001	380.53	−7.0
Aug-1994	89.25	9.7	Apr-2002	351.45	−6.6
Feb-1998	309.67	9.3	Sep-2002	278.99	−6.2
May-1997	220.90	9.0	Mar-2004	320.58	−6.0
Sep-1995	128.95	8.4	Mar-1994	77.75	−5.5
Feb-1999	399.08	8.2	Jan-2005	299.78	−5.3
Oct-2002	301.74	8.2	Oct-1997	230.12	−4.6
Aug-1999	382.34	7.5	May-2002	335.26	−4.6
Mar-1995	108.75	7.4	Dec-2002	298.53	−4.5
Jun-1995	117.49	7.4	Jan-2000	343.52	−4.3
Nov-1996	186.24	7.3	Sep-2004	308.77	−4.3
Dec-1995	146.71	6.8	Aug-2003	303.53	−4.2
Oct-1995	137.51	6.6	Feb-2000	329.70	−4.0
Dec-2003	335.59	6.3	Jul-2000	387.47	−3.9

BEST YEARS BY PERCENT

Year	Close	Point Change	Percent Change
1995	146.71	49.64	51.1%
1998	378.45	121.35	47.2
1997	257.10	72.84	39.5
1996	184.26	37.55	25.6
2000	449.18	90.19	25.1

WORST YEARS BY PERCENT

Year	Close	Point Change	Percent Change
2002	298.53	−86.72	−22.5%
2001	385.25	−63.93	−14.2
2004	316.62	−18.97	−5.7
1999	358.99	−19.46	−5.1
2003	335.59	37.06	12.4

BEST & WORST WEEKS BY % CHANGE FEB 28,1994 TO JUN 3, 2005

Week	Best Close	Change	Week	Worst Close	Change
7/26/02	277.28	11.04%	4/23/99	363.81	−14.39%
11/7/97	249.96	8.62	9/4/98	304.32	−10.46
3/21/03	306.71	8.54	1/5/01	405.28	−9.77
4/7/00	363.98	7.85	7/19/02	249.71	−9.26
7/9/99	379.88	7.64	1/28/00	342.04	−8.75
10/15/99	385.63	7.56	7/12/02	275.19	−8.21
8/27/99	373.61	7.51	7/21/00	398.26	−6.88
3/30/01	380.53	7.31	10/31/97	230.12	−6.82
4/30/99	390.31	7.28	12/10/99	370.97	−6.75
10/18/02	311.79	7.01	3/23/01	354.60	−6.34
2/6/98	302.94	6.91	6/7/02	314.82	−6.10
6/23/00	403.51	6.85	6/29/01	389.02	−5.53
4/28/00	383.15	6.76	12/17/99	350.94	−5.40
3/24/00	342.69	6.28	10/9/98	323.55	−5.38
2/4/00	363.51	6.28	10/22/99	365.40	−5.25
2/5/99	392.03	6.27	12/14/01	375.16	−5.08
5/9/97	216.29	6.15	10/1/99	344.96	−5.07
11/14/03	326.44	5.99	4/4/97	191.61	−5.00
1/3/03	310.37	5.88	5/23/03	311.92	−4.93
2/7/97	198.41	5.62	2/18/00	338.79	−4.89

BEST & WORST DAYS BY % CHANGE FEB 28, 1994 TO JUN 3, 2005

Day	Best Close	Change	Day	Worst Close	Change
1/13/00	374.51	7.57%	9/4/98	304.32	−8.39%
3/21/00	340.34	7.40	10/31/97	230.12	−7.54
7/24/02	258.64	6.15	4/23/99	363.81	−5.69
3/14/00	309.47	5.86	8/14/00	383.72	−5.63
11/3/97	243.43	5.78	7/10/02	269.13	−5.29
3/15/00	326.35	5.45	7/19/02	249.71	−4.90
3/22/00	357.87	5.15	3/13/00	292.33	−4.65
1/26/98	290.42	5.10	1/28/00	342.04	−4.61
9/8/98	319.42	4.96	8/5/02	277.40	−4.39
4/7/00	363.98	4.78	7/9/02	284.15	−4.38
7/29/02	289.80	4.52	5/19/03	313.79	−4.36
10/25/99	381.86	4.50	4/20/99	403.79	−4.35
9/14/98	333.90	4.35	6/12/02	308.83	−4.33
10/1/02	290.36	4.08	9/3/02	284.47	−4.30
5/6/94	82.03	4.07	1/5/01	405.28	−4.28
6/30/97	243.35	4.06	7/18/00	402.72	−4.17
10/14/99	382.12	3.99	4/4/97	191.61	−4.07
8/8/02	304.36	3.87	4/21/99	387.38	−4.06
8/4/00	407.77	3.77	9/27/02	280.23	−4.04
7/5/02	299.79	3.77	1/4/01	423.40	−4.01

REAL ESTATE Ticker **RMS**   Index **MS REIT***

AI SEASONALITY

Start	Finish	Data Since
October (End)	July (Beginning)	6/13/95

HISTORICAL PERFORMANCE

Buy & Hold	5-Year Avg	10-Year Avg	Avg Since Inception	Best Year	% Change	Worst Year	% Change
12 Months	22.3%	NA	16.1%	2003	36.7%	1998	−16.9%

AI Seasonality	5-Year Avg	10-Year Avg	Avg Since Inception	Best Year	% Change	Worst Year	% Change
8.67 Months	23.2%	NA	18.3%	2003	27.1%	1998	2.8%

Recommended ETF: iShares Cohen & Steers Realty Majors (ICF)	Volatility: Moderate
Key Consideration: Housing bubble & interest rate	Risk: Moderate

COMPONENTS

Ticker	Name	Ticker	Name
AFR	American Financial Reallty	MHX	Meristar Hospitality
NNN	Commercial Net Lease	MAA	Mid-Amer Apart Communities
OFC	Corporate Office Prop	MLS	Mills Corp
EPR	Entertainment Propertie	NHP	Nationwide Health Prop
ENN	Equity Inns	NXL	New Plan Excel Realty
ELS	Equity Lifestyle Properties	OHI	Omega Healthcare Inv
EOP	Equity Office Properties	PNP	Pan Pacific Retail Prop
EQY	Equity One	PKY	Parkway Properties
EQR	Equity Residential	PEI	Pennsylvania REIT
ESS	Essex Property Trust	PPS	Post Properties
EXR	Extra Space Storage	PP	Prentiss Properties Trust
FRT	Federal Realty Investment	PLD	Prologis
FCH	Felcor Lodging Trust	PSB	PS Business Parks
FR	First Industrial Realty	PSA	Public Storage
GBP	Gables Residential Trust	RPT	Ramco-Gershenson Prop
GGP	Genl Growth Properties	O	Realty Income
GTY	Getty Realty	RA	Reckson Associates Realty
GLB	Glenborough Realty Trust	REG	Regency Centers
GRT	Glimcher Realty Trust	SNH	Senior Housing Properties
GCT	GMH Communities Trust	SHU	Shurgard Storage Centers
HCP	Health Care Prop Inv	SPG	Simon Property Group
HCN	Health Care REIT	SLG	SL Green Realty
HR	Healthcare Realty	SSS	Sovran Self Storage
HTG	Heritage Property Inv	SUI	Sun Communities
HIH	Highland Hospitality	SHO	Sunstone Hotel Investors
HIW	Highwoods Properties	SMA	Symmetry Medical
HME	Home Properties	SKT	Tanger Factory Outlet Ctrs
HPT	Hospitality Properties	TCO	Taubman Centers
HMT	Host Marriott	TCT	Town & Country Trust
HRP	HRPT Properties	TRZ	Trizec Properties
IRC	Inland Real Estate	TSY	Trustreet Properties
KPA	Innkeepers Usa Trust	UDR	United Dominion Realty
IRETS	Investors Real Estate	UHT	Universal Health Realty
KRC	Kilroy Realty	UBA	Urstadt Biddle Properties
KIM	Kimco Realty	YSI	U-Store-It Trust
LHO	Lasalle Hotel Properties	VTR	Ventas Inc
LXP	Lexington Corporate Prop	VNO	Vornado Realty Trust
LRY	Liberty Property Trust	WRE	Washington REIT
MAC	Macerich	WRI	Weingarten Realty Inv
MPG	Maguire Properties		

* RMS Changed to RMZ June 2005

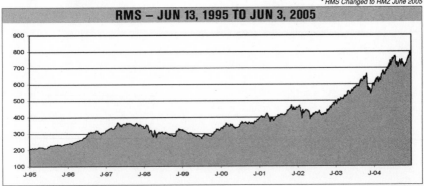

RMS – JUN 13, 1995 TO JUN 3, 2005

DETAILED PERFORMANCE AI SEASONALITY

Start Date	Close	Finish Date	Close	Percent Change	Investing $1,000
Oct 31 1995	209.51	Jul 3 1996	241.25	15.15%	$1151.50
Oct 23 1996	260.30	Jul 8 1997	324.28	24.58	1434.54
Oct 27 1997	343.31	Jul 9 1998	352.86	2.78	1474.42
Oct 28 1998	298.44	Jul 2 1999	316.16	5.94	1562.00
Oct 26 1999	278.18	Jul 10 2000	343.62	23.52	1929.38
Oct 25 2000	328.03	Jul 3 2001	404.34	23.26	2378.16
Oct 24 2001	374.94	Jul 1 2002	464.32	23.84	2945.11
Oct 23 2002	398.22	Jul 8 2003	505.98	27.06	3742.05
Oct 24 2003	535.84	Jul 7 2004	633.48	18.22	4423.86
			Average:	**18.26**	**$3423.86 Gain**

DETAILED PERFORMANCE BUY & HOLD

Start Date	Close	Finish Date	Close	Percent Change	Investing $1,000
Dec 29 1995	225.81	Dec 31 1996	306.86	35.89%	$1358.90
Dec 31 1996	306.86	Dec 31 1997	363.87	18.58	1611.38
Dec 31 1997	363.87	Dec 31 1998	302.36	−16.90	1339.06
Dec 31 1998	302.36	Dec 31 1999	288.60	−4.55	1278.13
Dec 31 1999	288.60	Dec 29 2000	365.98	26.81	1620.80
Dec 29 2000	365.98	Dec 31 2001	412.94	12.83	1828.75
Dec 31 2001	412.94	Dec 31 2002	427.99	3.64	1895.31
Dec 31 2002	427.99	Dec 31 2003	585.25	36.74	2591.65
Dec 31 2003	585.25	Dec 31 2004	769.52	31.49	3407.77
			Average:	**16.06**	**$2407.77 Gain**

Almanac Investor Sector Seasonality out-performance factor 42.20%

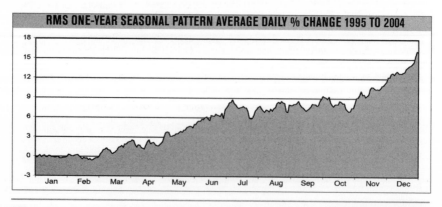

RMS ONE-YEAR SEASONAL PATTERN AVERAGE DAILY % CHANGE 1995 TO 2004

Ticker **RMS**   Index **MS REIT***

MONTHLY PERFORMANCE BY RANK
JULY 1995 TO MAY 2005

Month	Total Change	Average Change	# Up	# Down
December	40.1%	4.0%	9	1
November	28.4	2.8	9	1
May	27.2	2.7	9	1
June	21.8	2.4	7	2
March	19.2	1.9	7	3
September	14.7	1.5	6	4
April	7.9	0.8	6	4
February	2.7	0.3	5	5
August	2.2	0.2	6	4
July	0.9	0.1	6	4
January	−9.2	−0.9	5	5
October	−13.3	−1.3	3	7

MONTHLY PERFORMANCE
JULY 1995 TO MAY 2005

Month	Total Change	Average Change	# Up	# Down
January	−9.2%	−0.9%	5	5
February	2.7	0.3	5	5
March	19.2	1.9	7	3
April	7.9	0.8	6	4
May	27.2	2.7	9	1
June	21.8	2.4	7	2
July	0.9	0.1	6	4
August	2.2	0.2	6	4
September	14.7	1.5	6	4
October	−13.3	−1.3	3	7
November	28.4	2.8	9	1
December	40.1	4.0	9	1

BEST & WORST MONTHS BY PERCENT JULY 1995 TO MAY 2005

Month	Best Close	Change	Month	Worst Close	Change
Dec-1996	306.86	11.6%	Apr-2004	558.58	−14.8%
Apr-1999	315.65	9.7	Aug-1998	290.80	−9.3
Sep-1997	360.33	9.5	Jan-2005	703.30	−8.6
Jul-2000	356.65	9.1	Jul-1998	320.69	−7.2
Aug-2004	668.61	8.0	Jul-2002	442.57	−5.6
May-2004	598.68	7.2	Oct-2002	405.75	−5.0
Dec-2000	365.98	7.1	Oct-2000	335.81	−4.8
Apr-2000	316.17	6.7	Sep-1999	290.75	−4.2
Mar-2002	447.21	6.4	Aug-2000	342.02	−4.1
Dec-1995	225.81	6.4	Sep-2001	393.51	−4.0
Sep-1998	308.83	6.2	Sep-2002	427.20	−3.6
Jun-2001	403.99	6.0	Apr-1998	348.46	−3.5
Apr-2005	754.62	5.9	Oct-2001	380.32	−3.4
Nov-2001	402.49	5.8	Apr-1997	297.55	−3.3
May-2003	476.29	5.7	Jul-1999	306.39	−3.2
Mar-2004	655.77	5.6	Oct-1995	209.51	−3.1
Oct-2004	703.78	5.5	Jan-2003	416.21	−2.8
Jul-2003	513.07	5.3	Oct-1997	350.59	−2.7
Jun-1997	322.69	5.3	Jan-1999	294.24	−2.7
Dec-2004	769.52	4.9	Oct-1999	284.11	−2.3

BEST YEARS BY PERCENT

Year	Close	Point Change	Percent Change
2003	585.25	157.26	36.7%
1996	306.86	81.05	35.9
2004	769.52	184.27	31.5
2000	365.98	77.38	26.8
1997	363.87	57.01	18.6

WORST YEARS BY PERCENT

Year	Close	Point Change	Percent Change
1998	302.36	−61.51	−16.9%
1999	288.60	−13.76	−4.6
2002	427.99	15.05	3.6
2001	412.94	46.96	12.8

Seasonal Sector Investing: Indices

BEST & WORST WEEKS BY % CHANGE JUN 13, 1995 TO JUN 3, 2005

Week	Best Close	Change	Week	Worst Close	Change
4/16/99	307.42	8.15%	4/8/04	601.55	−8.21%
9/28/01	393.51	6.56	9/21/01	369.27	−7.44
9/25/98	312.54	6.30	10/9/98	279.93	−6.89
5/28/04	598.68	6.26	9/4/98	287.30	−6.00
9/18/98	294.03	5.97	1/7/05	726.95	−5.53
3/21/03	442.39	5.93	7/12/02	432.23	−5.47
8/20/04	652.28	5.13	7/19/02	410.96	−4.92
7/7/00	343.24	4.97	7/31/98	320.69	−4.51
11/12/04	737.18	4.86	4/19/02	452.69	−3.95
5/20/05	792.18	4.57	10/2/98	300.64	−3.81
10/16/98	291.86	4.26	4/4/97	301.77	−3.78
10/3/03	549.16	4.21	4/16/04	579.19	−3.72
4/12/02	471.30	3.95	5/10/02	441.49	−3.58
10/3/97	364.81	3.57	10/4/02	413.37	−3.53
3/7/97	316.96	3.56	3/11/05	720.65	−3.44
3/5/04	642.35	3.42	11/19/04	711.88	−3.43
10/1/04	679.41	3.40	9/11/98	277.46	−3.42
12/13/96	288.33	3.37	7/24/98	335.84	−3.31
2/4/05	728.60	3.35	1/28/05	705.00	−3.30
12/8/95	219.33	3.33	6/12/98	332.30	−3.25

BEST & WORST DAYS BY % CHANGE JUN 13, 1995 TO JUN 3, 2005

Day	Best Close	Change	Day	Worst Close	Change
7/29/02	435.66	4.77%	4/12/04	570.91	−5.09%
12/17/99	276.89	3.98	8/31/98	290.80	−4.85
9/22/98	314.50	3.89	4/6/04	603.07	−4.20
4/16/99	307.42	3.60	4/5/04	629.54	−3.94
7/26/02	415.82	3.54	1/5/05	722.01	−3.76
8/20/04	652.28	3.01	4/20/04	561.24	−3.63
9/21/98	302.72	2.96	9/17/01	384.85	−3.54
7/3/00	335.54	2.61	10/8/98	273.03	−3.50
10/9/98	279.93	2.53	5/7/04	544.80	−3.48
10/10/02	394.80	2.51	10/27/97	343.31	−3.22
7/25/02	401.59	2.49	7/23/02	390.00	−3.14
8/7/98	316.18	2.49	10/9/02	385.13	−3.11
9/18/98	294.03	2.46	10/5/98	291.59	−3.01
11/12/04	737.18	2.38	3/9/05	722.89	−2.99
10/15/02	405.61	2.34	9/10/98	277.69	−2.99
1/7/00	295.93	2.24	6/30/00	327.00	−2.88
4/15/04	573.11	2.23	8/4/98	307.98	−2.79
9/16/98	286.42	2.23	11/5/04	703.03	−2.76
4/1/03	441.70	2.11	10/7/02	402.12	−2.72
10/16/98	291.86	2.09	2/22/05	719.86	−2.64

SEMICONDUCTOR   Ticker **SOX**   Index **PHLX SEMICONDUCTOR**

AI SEASONALITY

Start	Finish	Data Since
October (End)	December (Beginning)	5/4/94

HISTORICAL PERFORMANCE

Buy & Hold	5-Year Avg	10-Year Avg	Avg Since Inception	Best Year	% Change	Worst Year	% Change
12 Months	−2.3%	19.5%	19.5%	1999	101.0%	2002	−44.6%

AI Seasonality	5-Year Avg	10-Year Avg	Avg Since Inception	Best Year	% Change	Worst Year	% Change
1.67 Months	20.7%	22.1%	20.7%	1998	42.7%	1995	−8.2%

Recommended ETF: iShares Goldman Sachs Semiconductor (IGW)	**Volatility:** High
Key Consideration: Capitol investment and book to bill numbers	**Risk:** High

COMPONENTS

Ticker	Name	Ticker	Name
ALTR	Altera	MXIM	Maxim Integrated Products
AMD	Advanced Micro Devices	MU	Micron Technology
AMAT	Applied Materials	NSM	National Semiconductor
BRCM	Broadcom	NVLS	Novellus Systems
FSL-B	Freescale Semiconductor	STM	STMicroelectronics
IFX	Infineon Technologies	TSM	Taiwan Semiconductor
INTC	Intel	TER	Teradyne
KLAC	KLA-Tencor	TXN	Texas Instruments
LLTC	Linear Technology	XLNX	Xilinx
MRVL	Marvell Technology		

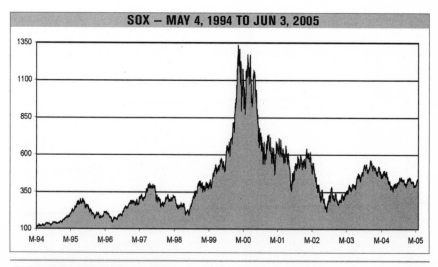

SOX – MAY 4, 1994 TO JUN 3, 2005

SEMICONDUCTOR Ticker **SOX** Index **PHLX SEMICONDUCTOR**

DETAILED PERFORMANCE AI SEASONALITY

Start Date	Close	Finish Date	Close	Percent Change	Investing $1,000
Oct 25 1995	247.42	Dec 4 1995	227.11	−8.21%	$917.90
Oct 29 1996	183.46	Dec 9 1996	252.28	37.51	1262.20
Oct 27 1997	284.66	Dec 1 1997	305.17	7.21	1353.21
Oct 22 1998	247.30	Dec 8 1998	352.81	42.66	1930.49
Oct 27 1999	493.58	Dec 6 1999	681.82	38.14	2666.78
Oct 25 2000	665.09	Dec 11 2000	682.77	2.66	2737.71
Oct 30 2001	429.68	Dec 5 2001	585.80	36.33	3732.32
Oct 24 2002	278.50	Dec 2 2002	375.24	34.74	5028.93
Oct 23 2003	456.80	Dec 1 2003	532.53	16.58	5862.73
Oct 22 2004	395.16	Dec 6 2004	446.88	13.09	6630.16
			Average:	**22.07**	**$5630.16 Gain**

DETAILED PERFORMANCE BUY & HOLD

Start Date	Close	Finish Date	Close	Percent Change	Investing $1,000
Dec 30 1994	140.09	Dec 29 1995	200.66	43.24%	$1432.40
Dec 29 1995	200.66	Dec 31 1996	240.30	19.75	1715.30
Dec 31 1996	240.30	Dec 31 1997	263.63	9.71	1881.85
Dec 31 1997	263.63	Dec 31 1998	350.56	32.97	2502.30
Dec 31 1998	350.56	Dec 31 1999	704.56	100.98	5029.13
Dec 31 1999	704.56	Dec 29 2000	576.61	−18.16	4115.84
Dec 29 2000	576.61	Dec 31 2001	522.16	−9.44	3727.30
Dec 31 2001	522.16	Dec 31 2002	289.24	−44.61	2064.55
Dec 31 2002	289.24	Dec 31 2003	508.12	75.67	3626.80
Dec 31 2003	508.12	Dec 31 2004	433.31	−14.72	3092.93
			Average:	**19.54**	**$2092.93 Gain**

Almanac Investor Sector Seasonality out-performance factor 169.01%

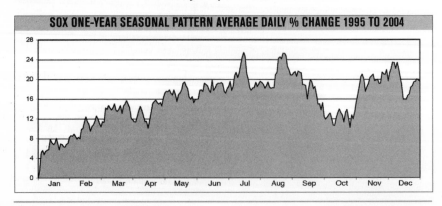

SOX ONE-YEAR SEASONAL PATTERN AVERAGE DAILY % CHANGE 1995 TO 2004

MONTHLY PERFORMANCE BY RANK
JUNE 1995 TO MAY 2005

Month	Total Change	Average Change	# Up	# Down
January	75.3%	6.8%	7	4
October	72.9	6.6	7	4
November	60.8	5.5	7	4
April	46.0	4.2	6	5
February	35.8	3.3	5	6
March	9.2	0.8	5	6
June	8.0	0.7	4	7
May	7.8	0.7	6	5
August	5.7	0.5	6	5
July	–3.3	–0.3	6	5
December	–5.1	–0.5	7	4
September	–71.1	–6.5	4	7

MONTHLY PERFORMANCE
JUNE 1995 TO MAY 2005

Month	Total Change	Average Change	# Up	# Down
January	75.3%	6.8%	7	4
February	35.8	3.3	5	6
March	9.2	0.8	5	6
April	46.0	4.2	6	5
May	7.8	0.7	6	5
June	8.0	0.7	4	7
July	–3.3	–0.3	6	5
August	5.7	0.5	6	5
September	–71.1	–6.5	4	7
October	72.9	6.6	7	4
November	60.8	5.5	7	4
December	–5.1	–0.5	7	4

BEST & WORST MONTHS BY PERCENT JUNE 1995 TO MAY 2005

Month	Best Close	Change	Month	Worst Close	Change
Feb-2000	1170.46	50.4%	Sep-2001	373.70	–33.6%
Nov-1996	237.94	27.2	Nov-2000	536.99	–27.6
Jan-2001	732.19	27.0	Sep-2000	851.57	–26.1
Nov-2002	373.53	26.6	Feb-2001	541.23	–26.1
Jun-1999	484.45	24.8	Aug-1998	193.47	–24.2
Oct-2002	295.15	23.9	Dec-2002	289.24	–22.6
Oct-1998	262.62	23.4	Oct-1997	301.90	–20.9
Apr-2001	662.66	21.6	Sep-2002	238.24	–20.6
Jan-1997	288.73	20.2	Jun-2002	387.58	–18.6
Jan-1999	420.45	19.9	May-1998	259.31	–17.9
Oct-2001	448.02	19.9	Feb-1999	356.26	–15.3
Jul-1997	366.24	19.8	Jun-1996	174.71	–15.2
Oct-2003	496.52	18.3	May-2000	998.43	–14.8
Apr-1996	206.09	17.1	Jul-2002	330.94	–14.6
Aug-2003	456.06	17.1	Jul-2004	416.43	–14.2
Nov-1998	306.15	16.6	Oct-2000	741.83	–12.9
Mar-2002	595.24	16.5	Jul-2000	993.85	–12.9
Feb-1995	162.16	16.2	Dec-1995	200.66	–11.8
Aug-2000	1152.98	16.0	Apr-2002	525.74	–11.7
Nov-2001	518.95	15.8	Aug-2004	371.02	–10.9

BEST YEARS BY PERCENT

Year	Close	Point Change	Percent Change
1999	704.56	354.00	101.0%
2003	508.12	218.88	75.7
1995	200.66	60.57	43.2
1998	350.56	86.93	33.0
1996	240.30	39.64	19.8

WORST YEARS BY PERCENT

Year	Close	Point Change	Percent Change
2002	289.24	–232.92	–44.6%
2000	576.61	–127.95	–18.2
2004	433.31	–74.81	–14.7
2001	522.16	–54.45	–9.4
1997	263.63	23.33	9.7

SEMICONDUCTOR   Ticker **SOX**   Index **PHLX SEMICONDUCTOR**

BEST & WORST WEEKS BY % CHANGE MAY 4, 1994 TO JUN 3, 2005

Week	Best Close	Change	Week	Worst Close	Change
6/2/00	1157.75	27.27%	4/14/00	892.16	−27.07%
4/12/01	597.92	22.64	9/21/01	381.01	−25.17
8/18/00	1134.82	18.99	12/1/00	538.35	−20.21
3/23/01	642.09	18.63	11/10/00	624.20	−15.72
12/8/00	638.34	18.57	3/30/01	545.04	−15.11
3/3/00	1211.34	17.38	12/12/97	248.18	−14.74
1/14/00	809.87	17.25	6/21/02	380.01	−13.83
10/12/01	473.78	16.67	7/26/02	315.01	−13.48
2/4/00	868.02	15.89	3/1/96	178.76	−12.81
5/2/97	302.90	15.14	7/21/00	1082.51	−12.64
10/16/98	230.98	15.03	8/28/98	210.97	−12.54
4/20/00	1024.28	14.81	1/17/03	297.53	−12.25
4/28/00	1171.64	14.39	4/26/02	514.73	−11.67
11/22/02	362.64	13.44	7/28/00	957.28	−11.57
10/26/01	480.74	13.43	12/6/02	331.35	−11.29
5/17/02	541.97	12.69	9/20/02	248.87	−11.28
3/8/02	637.94	12.46	5/12/00	982.15	−11.13
4/20/01	669.50	11.97	10/17/97	347.01	−10.98
11/5/99	621.21	11.76	8/30/02	300.19	−10.73
4/17/03	332.96	11.66	4/6/01	487.53	−10.55

BEST & WORST DAYS BY % CHANGE MAY 4, 1994 TO JUN 3, 2005

Day	Best Close	Change	Day	Worst Close	Change
1/3/01	670.23	17.51%	4/14/00	892.16	−11.64%
10/19/00	758.74	17.22	10/10/00	706.51	−10.11
4/17/00	1009.88	13.19	7/25/02	318.05	−10.08
4/5/01	522.69	12.77	10/27/97	284.66	−9.75
3/22/01	626.39	12.25	7/5/00	1070.81	−9.32
12/8/00	638.34	12.09	10/17/00	648.09	−9.29
4/18/01	640.94	11.70	10/16/02	245.37	−8.82
5/8/02	522.35	11.11	9/17/01	464.49	−8.77
5/30/00	1010.30	11.06	7/6/01	566.51	−8.58
3/1/02	567.27	11.05	5/10/00	908.94	−8.56
10/11/01	474.60	10.74	2/26/99	356.26	−8.32
10/28/97	313.59	10.16	4/12/00	1037.70	−8.32
12/5/00	607.41	10.14	8/31/98	193.47	−8.30
10/13/00	758.32	10.04	11/7/02	302.61	−8.26
2/29/00	1170.46	9.75	7/27/00	949.90	−8.15
12/22/00	587.14	9.66	11/28/00	577.12	−8.11
10/3/01	388.81	9.64	9/26/01	370.63	−7.90
4/10/01	520.12	9.45	10/24/00	716.37	−7.83
10/15/02	269.10	9.44	1/15/96	165.77	−7.79
3/22/00	1304.59	9.22	5/23/00	869.74	−7.74

TELECOM
Ticker **XTC** Index **AMEX N. AMER TELECOM**

AI SEASONALITY

Start	Finish	Data Since
September (End)	January (Middle)	11/4/93

HISTORICAL PERFORMANCE

Buy & Hold	5-Year Avg	10-Year Avg	Avg Since Inception	Best Year	% Change	Worst Year	% Change
12 Months	−9.4%	15.9%	13.7%	1999	73.9%	2002	−45.5%

AI Seasonality	5-Year Avg	10-Year Avg	Avg Since Inception	Best Year	% Change	Worst Year	% Change
4 Months	21.2%	22.5%	19.7%	2003	62.4%	1995	−7.8%

Recommended ETF:	iShares S&P Global Telecommunications (IXP)	Volatility: High
Key Consideration:	Advances in VoiP and wireless networks	Risk: High

COMPONENTS

Ticker	Name	Ticker	Name
AT	Alltel	MOT	Motorola
AMX	America Movil	Q	Qwest
T	AT&T	SBC	SBC COMMUNICATIONS
BCE	BCE	S	Sprint Nextel
BLS	BellSouth	TMX	Telefonos de Mexico
CTL	CenturyTel	TDS	TELETelephone & Data Systems
CZN	Citizens Communications	VZ	Verizon
LU	Lucent Technologies		

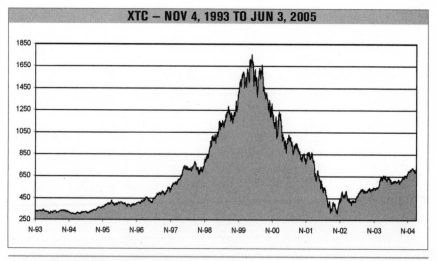

XTC – NOV 4, 1993 TO JUN 3, 2005

TELECOM Ticker **XTC** Index **AMEX N. AMER TELECOM**

DETAILED PERFORMANCE AI SEASONALITY

Start Date	Close	Finish Date	Close	Percent Change	Investing $1,000
Sep 25 1995	358.53	Jan 16 1996	397.95	10.99%	$1109.90
Sep 27 1996	378.59	Jan 21 1997	430.12	13.61	1260.96
Sep 25 1997	507.63	Jan 22 1998	610.68	20.30	1516.93
Sep 22 1998	696.95	Jan 20 1999	1005.44	44.26	2188.33
Sep 24 1999	1191.73	Jan 21 2000	1546.52	29.77	2839.79
Sep 27 2000	1232.91	Jan 19 2001	1231.31	−0.13	2836.10
Sep 21 2001	780.38	Jan 11 2002	819.39	5.00	2977.90
Sep 30 2002	317.47	Jan 14 2003	515.54	62.39	4835.82
Sep 30 2003	510.64	Jan 20 2004	642.74	25.87	6086.84
Sep 27 2004	626.25	Jan 18 2005	707.15	12.92	6873.26
			Average:	**22.50**	**$5873.26 Gain**

DETAILED PERFORMANCE BUY & HOLD

Start Date	Close	Finish Date	Close	Percent Change	Investing $1,000
Dec 30 1994	300.81	Dec 29 1995	392.17	30.37%	$1303.70
Dec 29 1995	392.17	Dec 31 1996	412.48	5.18	1371.23
Dec 31 1996	412.48	Dec 31 1997	590.98	43.27	1964.56
Dec 31 1997	590.98	Dec 31 1998	908.08	53.66	3018.75
Dec 31 1998	908.08	Dec 31 1999	1578.94	73.88	5249.00
Dec 31 1999	1578.94	Dec 29 2000	1026.48	−34.99	3412.37
Dec 29 2000	1026.48	Dec 31 2001	827.02	−19.43	2749.35
Dec 31 2001	827.02	Dec 31 2002	450.44	−45.53	1497.57
Dec 31 2002	450.44	Dec 31 2003	572.89	27.18	1904.61
Dec 31 2003	572.89	Dec 31 2004	720.69	25.80	2396.00
			Average:	**15.94**	**$1396.00 Gain**

Almanac Investor Sector Seasonality out-performance factor 320.72%

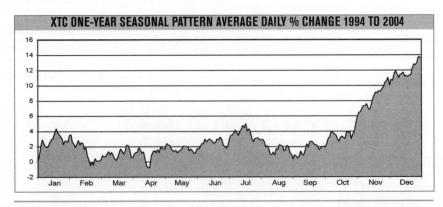

XTC ONE-YEAR SEASONAL PATTERN AVERAGE DAILY % CHANGE 1994 TO 2004

ALMANAC INVESTOR

MONTHLY PERFORMANCE BY RANK
DECEMBER 1993 TO MAY 2005

Month	Total Change	Average Change	# Up	# Down
October	53.6%	4.9%	9	2
November	46.8	4.3	9	2
January	33.6	2.8	8	4
December	22.9	1.9	8	4
April	8.6	0.7	7	5
May	4.5	0.4	5	7
September	1.4	0.1	6	5
June	−1.2	−0.1	7	4
March	−3.0	−0.3	4	8
July	−5.0	−0.5	6	5
August	−17.1	−1.6	4	7
February	−32.7	−2.7	5	7

MONTHLY PERFORMANCE
DECEMBER 1993 TO MAY 2005

Month	Total Change	Average Change	# Up	# Down
January	33.6%	2.8%	8	4
February	−32.7	−2.7	5	7
March	−3.0	−0.3	4	8
April	8.6	0.7	7	5
May	4.5	0.4	5	7
June	−1.2	−0.1	7	4
July	−5.0	−0.5	6	5
August	−17.1	−1.6	4	7
September	1.4	0.1	6	5
October	53.6	4.9	9	2
November	46.8	4.3	9	2
December	22.9	1.9	8	4

BEST & WORST MONTHS BY PERCENT DECEMBER 1993 TO MAY 2005

Month	Best Close	Change	Month	Worst Close	Change
Oct-2002	415.24	30.8%	Jun-2002	386.89	−26.8%
Nov-2002	502.15	20.9	Sep-2002	317.47	−19.1
Jan-2001	1191.79	16.1	Nov-2000	1097.54	−16.0
Dec-1998	908.08	12.8	Feb-2002	638.50	−15.7
Oct-1999	1380.84	12.4	Feb-2001	1009.17	−15.3
Jan-1999	1014.76	11.8	Apr-2002	545.14	−12.3
Mar-1998	727.58	11.4	Aug-1998	663.63	−11.6
May-2003	493.16	10.9	Dec-2002	450.44	−10.3
Nov-1997	571.03	10.6	Oct-2001	759.28	−8.9
Aug-2002	392.45	10.4	Mar-2001	922.19	−8.6
Jun-1999	1228.07	10.1	Jan-2002	757.70	−8.4
Mar-2000	1688.47	10.0	Jul-2002	355.36	−8.2
Nov-2001	833.43	9.8	May-2000	1453.19	−7.8
Oct-1998	764.20	9.2	Aug-2001	850.49	−7.8
Apr-2003	444.78	8.2	Mar-1997	416.25	−7.3
Dec-1999	1578.94	8.2	Jul-2000	1435.69	−7.3
Sep-1999	1228.75	8.1	Apr-2000	1576.51	−6.6
Sep-1997	513.40	7.8	Sep-2000	1304.73	−6.5
Jan-2004	613.66	7.1	Aug-1999	1136.27	−6.5
Jun-2000	1548.55	6.6	Dec-2000	1026.48	−6.5

BEST YEARS BY PERCENT

Year	Close	Point Change	Percent Change
1999	1578.94	670.86	73.9%
1998	908.08	317.10	53.7
1997	590.98	178.50	43.3
1995	392.17	91.36	30.4
2003	572.89	122.45	27.2

WORST YEARS BY PERCENT

Year	Close	Point Change	Percent Change
2002	450.44	−376.58	−45.5%
2000	1026.48	−552.46	−35.0
2001	827.02	−199.46	−19.4
1994	300.81	−30.81	−9.3
1996	412.48	20.31	5.2

BEST & WORST WEEKS BY % CHANGE NOV 4, 1993 TO JUN 3, 2005

Week	Best Close	Change	Week	Worst Close	Change
3/3/00	1701.60	13.40%	7/26/02	316.34	−19.44%
10/18/02	369.11	9.94	4/14/00	1468.98	−12.85
6/2/00	1524.27	9.01	12/22/00	1006.69	−12.66
11/22/02	476.89	8.93	2/8/02	672.07	−9.45
2/4/00	1584.25	8.80	7/28/00	1420.36	−9.43
1/5/01	1115.38	8.66	6/28/02	386.89	−9.03
10/25/02	400.17	8.41	4/12/02	550.06	−8.96
1/12/01	1206.64	8.18	9/27/02	320.16	−8.88
8/2/02	341.86	8.07	9/20/02	351.36	−8.76
8/23/02	399.94	8.01	6/7/02	482.51	−8.74
10/29/99	1380.84	7.98	2/16/01	1010.53	−7.60
4/9/99	1142.89	7.75	1/7/00	1463.87	−7.29
10/8/99	1322.13	7.47	1/24/03	445.60	−6.90
3/8/02	699.70	7.34	2/15/02	625.96	−6.86
11/1/02	428.91	7.18	6/14/02	449.72	−6.80
8/16/02	370.27	7.14	10/15/99	1233.93	−6.67
5/17/02	537.69	7.00	10/13/00	1229.92	−6.11
9/28/01	833.76	6.84	1/26/01	1156.94	−6.04
4/12/01	947.42	6.73	11/10/00	1160.04	−5.91
11/16/01	850.66	6.25	10/19/01	801.65	−5.86

BEST & WORST DAYS BY % CHANGE NOV 4, 1993 TO JUN 3, 2005

Day	Best Close	Change	Day	Worst Close	Change
4/16/02	602.96	10.24%	7/23/02	340.40	−7.87%
1/3/01	1120.76	8.94	2/4/02	703.95	−7.09
7/29/02	339.40	7.29	6/26/02	378.45	−6.86
3/1/00	1643.01	6.99	10/27/97	500.07	−6.56
4/23/03	439.76	6.46	12/9/02	450.68	−6.50
5/8/02	546.29	6.37	12/20/00	1013.63	−6.09
1/2/03	477.34	5.97	7/22/02	369.46	−5.91
10/10/02	326.26	5.90	5/10/02	502.53	−5.66
10/15/02	361.29	5.84	8/31/98	663.63	−5.40
4/5/01	910.26	5.80	2/5/02	666.44	−5.33
1/6/03	502.21	5.59	3/28/01	918.99	−5.17
7/5/02	393.77	5.53	4/11/02	536.76	−5.06
9/28/00	1300.13	5.45	6/2/02	478.45	−4.85
3/6/02	696.47	5.36	10/11/00	1224.81	−4.85
10/1/02	334.27	5.29	4/14/00	1468.98	−4.85
8/14/02	358.68	5.27	1/4/00	1489.76	−4.83
4/25/00	1595.57	5.16	12/19/00	1079.36	−4.82
1/31/00	1530.80	5.13	5/19/00	1424.82	−4.82
10/28/99	1372.44	5.04	2/16/01	1010.53	−4.82
11/21/02	472.70	5.01	4/22/02	552.81	−4.75

TRANSPORTS

Ticker **DJT**   Index **DJ TRANSPORTS**

AI SEASONALITY

Start	Finish	Data Since
October (Beginning)	May (Beginning)	1/2/30

HISTORICAL PERFORMANCE

Buy & Hold	5-Year Avg	10-Year Avg	Avg Since 1984	Best Year	% Change	Worst Year	% Change
12 Months	6.5%	11.8%	11.1%	1980	57.7%	1974	−26.9%

AI Seasonality	5-Year Avg	10-Year Avg	Avg Since 1984	Best Year	% Change	Worst Year	% Change
7.33 Months	16.8%	20.4%	17.4%	1998	60.8%	1932	−52.5%

Recommended ETF: iShares Dow Jones Transportation Average (IYT)	Volatility:Low
Key Consideration: Fuel prices & inflation	Risk: Moderate

COMPONENTS

Ticker	Name	Ticker	Name
ALEX	Alexander & Baldwin	GMT	GATX
AMR	AMR	JBHT	JB Hunt Transport Services
BNI	Burlington Northern Santa Fe	LSTR	Landstar System
CHRW	C.H. Robinson Worldwide	NSC	Norfolk Southern
CNF	CNF	NWAC	Northwest Airlines
CAL	Continental Airlines	R	Ryder System
CSX	CSX	LUV	Southwest Airlines
DAL	Delta Air Lines	UNP	Union Pacific
EXPD	Expeditors International	UPS	United Parcel Service
FDX	FedEx	YELL	Yellow Roadway

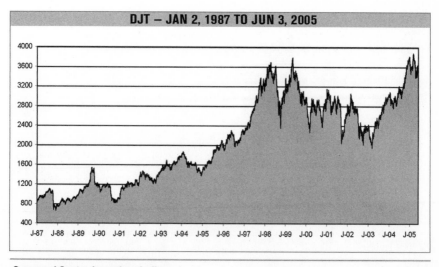

DJT – JAN 2, 1987 TO JUN 3, 2005

DETAILED PERFORMANCE AI SEASONALITY

| Start | | Finish | | Percent | Investing |
Date	Close	Date	Close	Change	$1,000
Oct 10 1995	1892.30	May 1 1996	2209.40	16.76%	$1167.60
Oct 9 1996	2049.60	May 5 1997	2624.01	28.03	1494.88
Oct 1 1997	3203.59	May 1 1998	3588.04	12.00	1674.26
Oct 8 1998	2345.00	May 11 1999	3770.91	60.81	2692.38
Oct 1 1999	2868.34	May 8 2000	2935.87	2.35	2755.65
Oct 2 2000	2464.42	May 4 2001	2869.19	16.42	3208.13
Oct 9 2001	2128.67	May 8 2002	2753.01	29.33	4149.08
Oct 9 2002	2013.02	May 6 2003	2486.35	23.51	5124.53
Oct 1 2003	2736.34	May 3 2004	2923.10	6.83	5474.53
Oct 1 2004	3298.80	May 9 2005	3559.06	7.89	5906.47
			Average:	**20.39**	**$4906.47 Gain**

DETAILED PERFORMANCE BUY & HOLD

| Start | | Finish | | Percent | Investing |
Date	Close	Date	Close	Change	$1,000
Dec 30 1994	1455.00	Dec 29 1995	1981.00	36.15%	$1361.50
Dec 29 1995	1981.00	Dec 31 1996	2255.70	13.87	1550.34
Dec 31 1996	2255.70	Dec 31 1997	3256.50	44.37	2238.23
Dec 31 1997	3256.50	Dec 31 1998	3149.31	−3.29	2164.59
Dec 31 1998	3149.31	Dec 31 1999	2977.20	−5.47	2046.19
Dec 31 1999	2977.20	Dec 29 2000	2946.60	−1.03	2025.11
Dec 29 2000	2946.60	Dec 31 2001	2639.99	−10.41	1814.30
Dec 31 2001	2639.99	Dec 31 2002	2309.96	−12.50	1587.51
Dec 31 2002	2309.96	Dec 31 2003	3007.05	30.18	2066.62
Dec 31 2003	3007.05	Dec 31 2004	3798.05	26.30	2610.14
		Average:	**11.82**		**$1610.14 Gain**

Almanac Investor Sector Seasonality out-performance factor 204.72%

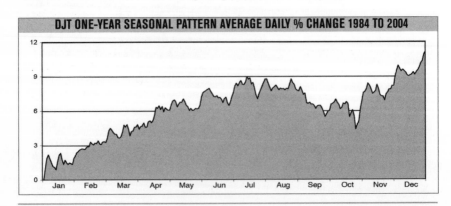

DJT ONE-YEAR SEASONAL PATTERN AVERAGE DAILY % CHANGE 1984 TO 2004

MONTHLY PERFORMANCE BY RANK
JANUARY 1984 TO MAY 2005

Month	Total Change	Average Change	# Up	# Down
December	61.7%	2.9%	17	4
March	34.8	1.6	13	9
January	33.8	1.5	14	8
October	32.1	1.5	16	5
November	31.3	1.5	15	6
February	30.3	1.4	15	7
May	26.2	1.2	13	9
April	19.4	0.9	11	11
July	19.3	0.9	11	10
June	6.6	0.3	8	13
August	−23.7	−1.1	8	13
September	−41.8	−2.0	7	14

MONTHLY PERFORMANCE
JANUARY 1984 TO MAY 2005

Month	Total Change	Average Change	# Up	# Down
January	33.8%	1.5%	14	8
February	30.3	1.4	15	7
March	34.8	1.6	13	9
April	19.4	0.9	11	11
May	26.2	1.2	13	9
June	6.6	0.3	8	13
July	19.3	0.9	11	10
August	−23.7	−1.1	8	13
September	−41.8	−2.0	7	14
October	32.1	1.5	16	5
November	31.3	1.5	15	6
December	61.7	2.9	17	4

BEST & WORST MONTHS BY PERCENT JANUARY 1984 TO MAY 2005

Month	Best Close	Change	Month	Worst Close	Change
Aug-1989	1509.40	18.1%	Oct-1987	757.20	−27.7%
Jan-1991	1069.10	17.5	Sep-2001	2194.68	−22.0
Dec-1991	1358.00	15.8	Aug-1990	901.40	−17.6
Mar-2000	2763.24	15.7	Oct-1989	1205.00	−16.9
Nov-2001	2511.78	14.4	Aug-1998	2752.51	−14.8
Apr-2003	2408.87	13.0	Jan-2000	2571.65	−13.6
May-1985	645.20	12.5	Jul-2002	2370.05	−13.2
Jul-1989	1277.70	11.2	Jan-1990	1045.90	−11.2
Sep-1997	3179.74	10.8	Sep-1994	1491.60	−9.2
Apr-1999	3647.29	10.6	Nov-1991	1172.30	−8.6
Jan-1989	1071.50	10.5	Jul-1986	716.10	−8.5
Jul-1997	2992.11	10.3	Nov-1987	695.10	−8.2
Jun-1988	908.20	9.9	Jul-1996	2008.00	−8.0
Aug-1984	520.51	9.9	Feb-1984	511.11	−7.9
Oct-1998	2891.92	9.4	Apr-2005	3426.44	−7.8
Feb-1988	835.00	9.3	Aug-1999	3076.10	−7.7
Jan-1985	609.50	9.2	Sep-2000	2521.64	−7.4
Apr-1997	2572.54	9.1	Jan-1984	554.69	−7.3
Oct-2003	2913.11	9.0	Aug-1992	1221.30	−7.3
Oct-2000	2744.62	8.8	Apr-2002	2704.72	−7.3

BEST YEARS BY PERCENT

Year	Close	Point Change	Percent Change
1991	1358.00	447.80	49.2%
1997	3256.50	1000.80	44.4
1995	1981.00	526.00	36.2
2003	3007.05	697.09	30.2
1988	969.80	220.90	29.5

WORST YEARS BY PERCENT

Year	Close	Point Change	Percent Change
1990	910.20	−267.60	−22.7%
1994	1455.00	−307.30	−17.4
2002	2309.96	−330.03	−12.5
2001	2639.99	−306.61	−10.4
1987	748.90	−58.30	−7.2

TRANSPORTS

Ticker **DJT**   Index **DJ TRANSPORTS**

BEST & WORST WEEKS BY % CHANGE JAN 3, 1984 TO JUN 3, 2005

Week	Best Close	Change	Week	Worst Close	Change
10/16/98	2780.87	14.46%	9/21/01	2054.84	−23.23%
8/11/89	1413.20	13.06	10/23/87	749.60	−20.40
3/21/03	2263.49	11.66	10/20/89	1230.80	−12.48
3/17/00	2623.83	10.93	3/16/01	2631.37	−10.56
8/3/84	516.78	10.75	12/4/87	661.00	−9.25
1/18/91	1001.10	10.56	10/16/87	941.70	−9.18
12/18/87	767.30	9.77	8/3/90	1039.10	−8.43
11/3/00	2761.75	9.20	1/24/03	2163.33	−7.73
12/27/91	1314.80	8.93	9/4/98	2616.75	−7.46
11/16/01	2497.37	7.61	10/15/99	2855.58	−7.34
10/8/99	3081.71	7.44	10/2/98	2602.23	−6.92
1/4/02	2830.20	7.08	10/9/98	2429.52	−6.64
7/13/01	2940.35	6.96	2/11/00	2436.13	−6.62
10/29/99	3058.98	6.84	6/15/01	2693.62	−6.54
9/28/01	2194.68	6.81	10/13/89	1406.30	−6.53
8/9/02	2351.65	6.79	7/12/02	2480.14	−6.50
1/8/99	3360.28	6.70	1/15/99	3148.53	−6.30
12/7/90	909.70	6.65	12/15/00	2698.68	−6.29
5/20/05	3620.99	6.43	8/10/90	974.80	−6.19
5/31/91	1229.00	6.38	1/28/00	2581.75	−6.17

BEST & WORST DAYS BY % CHANGE JAN 3, 1984 TO JUN 3, 2005

Day	Best Close	Change	Day	Worst Close	Change
8/7/89	1344.10	7.53%	10/19/87	776.90	−17.50%
10/15/98	2664.28	6.92	9/17/01	2271.68	−15.12
10/15/02	2286.46	6.91	10/26/87	674.90	−9.97
1/17/91	979.60	6.75	10/16/89	1304.20	−7.26
10/21/87	787.00	6.31	10/27/97	3004.58	−7.24
10/30/00	2686.61	6.23	9/20/01	2033.86	−6.09
3/16/00	2678.88	6.23	4/14/00	2727.04	−6.08
9/28/01	2194.68	6.07	8/6/90	980.30	−5.66
3/15/00	2521.71	5.88	1/8/88	745.00	−5.62
10/29/87	725.50	5.82	10/13/89	1406.30	−5.26
7/29/02	2380.95	5.60	10/9/02	2013.02	−4.84
8/2/84	511.49	5.35	9/5/02	2204.26	−4.79
3/4/02	3049.96	5.28	3/7/00	2263.59	−4.73
9/8/98	2749.30	5.07	10/20/87	740.30	−4.71
1/3/01	3015.07	4.90	8/2/02	2202.03	−4.60
8/6/02	2235.50	4.84	11/30/87	695.10	−4.57
9/26/02	2269.42	4.72	10/22/87	751.70	−4.49
9/14/98	2805.14	4.70	11/15/91	1225.50	−4.44
10/10/01	2228.61	4.69	9/11/86	749.00	−4.29
12/16/87	764.70	4.61	10/8/98	2345.00	−4.20

AI SEASONALITY

Start	Finish	Data Since
July (End)	January (Beginning)	9/22/87

HISTORICAL PERFORMANCE

Buy & Hold	5-Year Avg	10-Year Avg	Avg Since Inception	Best Year	% Change	Worst Year	% Change
12 Months	9.3%	7.3%	6.1%	2000	43.6%	2002	−21.9%

AI Seasonality	5-Year Avg	10-Year Avg	Avg Since Inception	Best Year	% Change	Worst Year	% Change
5.67 Months	16.8%	12.9%	9.9%	2001	28.3%	2000	−9.5%

Recommended ETF: Select Sector SPDR Utilities (XLU)   **Volatility: Low**

Key Consideration: EPA reform, energy prices, weather & alt. energy   **Risk: Low**

COMPONENTS

Ticker	Name	Ticker	Name
AES	AES	EXC	Exelon
AEE	Ameren	FE	FirstEnergy
AEP	American Electric Power	FPL	FPL Group
CNP	CenterPoint Energy	NU	Northeast Utilities
ED	Consolidated Edison	PCG	PG&E
D	Dominion Resources	PGN	Progress Energy
DTE	DTE Energy	PEG	Public Service Enterprise
DUK	Duke Energy	SO	Southern Company
EIX	Edison International	TXU	TXU
ETR	Entergy	XEL	Xcel Energy

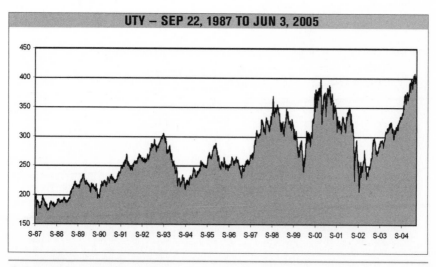

UTY – SEP 22, 1987 TO JUN 3, 2005

DETAILED PERFORMANCE AI SEASONALITY

Start Date	Close	Finish Date	Close	Percent Change	Investing $1,000
Jul 21 1995	248.73	Jan 9 1996	282.29	13.49%	$1134.90
Jul 29 1996	244.04	Jan 9 1997	259.65	6.40	1207.53
Jul 23 1997	253.30	Jan 2 1998	309.01	21.99	1473.07
Jul 31 1998	310.16	Jan 6 1999	348.18	12.26	1653.67
Jul 29 1999	315.15	Jan 7 2000	285.31	−9.47	1497.07
Jul 31 2000	297.53	Jan 2 2001	381.67	28.28	1920.44
Jul 24 2001	330.03	Jan 2 2002	334.00	1.20	1943.48
Jul 23 2002	224.57	Jan 6 2003	276.59	23.16	2393.59
Jul 30 2003	273.01	Jan 7 2004	308.77	13.10	2707.15
Jul 26 2004	312.04	Jan 3 2005	369.13	18.30	3202.56
			Average:	**12.87**	**$2202.56 Gain**

DETAILED PERFORMANCE BUY & HOLD

Start Date	Close	Finish Date	Close	Percent Change	Investing $1,000
Dec 30 1994	227.26	Dec 29 1995	277.60	22.15%	$1221.50
Dec 29 1995	277.60	Dec 31 1996	256.56	−7.58	1128.91
Dec 31 1996	256.56	Dec 31 1997	310.03	20.84	1364.18
Dec 31 1997	310.03	Dec 31 1998	348.69	12.47	1534.29
Dec 31 1998	348.69	Dec 31 1999	273.82	−21.47	1204.88
Dec 31 1999	273.82	Dec 29 2000	393.26	43.62	1730.44
Dec 29 2000	393.26	Dec 31 2001	330.01	−16.08	1452.19
Dec 31 2001	330.01	Dec 31 2002	257.67	−21.92	1133.87
Dec 31 2002	257.67	Dec 31 2003	308.03	19.54	1355.43
Dec 31 2003	308.03	Dec 31 2004	373.61	21.29	1644.00
			Average:	**7.29**	**$644.00 Gain**

Almanac Investor Sector Seasonality out-performance factor 242.01%

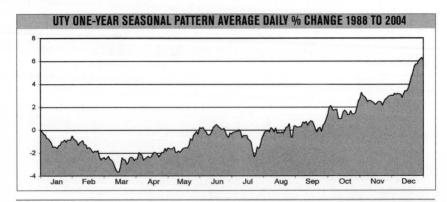

UTY ONE-YEAR SEASONAL PATTERN AVERAGE DAILY % CHANGE 1988 TO 2004

MONTHLY PERFORMANCE BY RANK
OCTOBER 1987 TO MAY 2005

Month	Total Change	Average Change	# Up	# Down
March	80.3%	3.7%	16	6
April	57.3	2.6	17	5
December	42.8	2.0	14	8
August	37.1	1.8	13	8
May	31.4	1.4	15	7
February	30.6	1.4	12	10
January	11.1	0.5	12	10
July	7.7	0.4	12	9
September	−1.9	−0.1	10	12
October	−10.8	−0.5	9	13
November	−17.3	−0.8	11	11
June	−29.0	−1.4	7	14

MONTHLY PERFORMANCE
OCTOBER 1987 TO MAY 2005

Month	Total Change	Average Change	# Up	# Down
January	11.1%	0.5%	12	10
February	30.6	1.4	12	10
March	80.3	3.7	16	6
April	57.3	2.6	17	5
May	31.4	1.4	15	7
June	−29.0	−1.4	7	14
July	7.7	0.4	12	9
August	37.1	1.8	13	8
September	−1.9	−0.1	10	12
October	−10.8	−0.5	9	13
November	−17.3	−0.8	11	11
December	42.8	2.0	14	8

BEST & WORST MONTHS BY PERCENT OCTOBER 1987 TO MAY 2005

Month	Best Close	Change	Month	Worst Close	Change
Apr-2000	295.53	14.2%	Jul-2002	273.26	−12.9%
Aug-2000	334.24	12.3	Feb-2000	255.68	−11.7
Sep-2000	374.70	12.1	Jan-2001	348.19	−11.5
Jan-1988	198.73	10.7	Sep-2002	252.23	−10.3
Oct-1990	217.72	10.7	Nov-1999	280.18	−9.1
May-2003	289.34	9.9	Sep-2001	315.10	−9.1
Mar-2002	341.63	8.3	Aug-1990	198.71	−8.0
Mar-1998	326.71	7.8	Jul-1996	244.98	−7.2
Nov-1997	289.42	7.6	Jun-2000	283.37	−7.1
Jan-1995	243.91	7.3	Jun-1999	321.36	−6.4
Apr-2003	263.30	7.3	Jun-2001	360.18	−6.3
Dec-1997	310.03	7.1	Jul-2003	273.67	−6.3
May-1999	343.22	7.0	Feb-1999	310.40	−6.2
Aug-1998	331.63	6.9	May-1994	226.61	−6.2
May-1995	255.49	6.7	May-2002	326.35	−6.1
Sep-1995	262.67	6.2	Feb-1994	253.30	−6.1
Dec-2003	308.03	6.2	Nov-1993	273.94	−5.8
Jul-1989	222.29	5.9	Jan-1992	253.76	−5.7
Jul-1992	269.30	5.9	Sep-1999	302.34	−5.6
Dec-1995	277.60	5.9	Apr-1990	204.11	−5.5

BEST YEARS BY PERCENT

Year	Close	Point Change	Percent Change
2000	393.26	119.44	43.6%
1989	233.12	43.78	23.1
1995	277.60	50.34	22.2
2004	373.61	65.58	21.3
1991	268.99	47.12	21.2

WORST YEARS BY PERCENT

Year	Close	Point Change	Percent Change
2002	257.67	−72.34	−21.9%
1999	273.82	−74.87	−21.5
1994	227.26	−50.72	−18.3
2001	330.01	−63.25	−16.1
1996	256.56	−21.04	−7.6

UTILITIES

BEST & WORST WEEKS BY % CHANGE SEP 22, 1987 TO JUN 3, 2005

Week	Best Close	Change	Week	Worst Close	Change
3/30/01	368.58	10.03%	1/5/01	337.89	−14.08%
9/8/00	363.76	8.41	7/12/02	272.57	−9.82
10/25/02	238.54	7.87	7/19/02	245.95	−9.77
4/14/00	279.86	6.57	2/25/00	251.15	−6.36
9/29/00	374.70	6.40	11/5/93	273.91	−5.81
3/17/00	257.11	6.28	10/11/02	225.59	−5.59
10/5/01	334.07	6.02	3/10/00	241.91	−5.42
2/9/01	369.55	5.91	9/22/00	352.16	−5.40
8/4/00	320.54	5.79	6/7/02	308.81	−5.37
8/9/02	275.84	5.71	9/24/99	299.62	−5.27
1/26/01	352.32	5.50	8/24/90	193.84	−5.27
10/2/98	355.96	5.36	5/6/94	228.78	−5.27
3/20/98	327.45	5.36	10/6/00	355.09	−5.23
10/5/90	207.03	5.27	3/16/01	351.91	−5.18
5/24/02	337.90	5.26	5/17/02	321.00	−5.13
5/2/97	241.66	5.12	5/13/94	217.74	−4.83
3/21/03	249.38	4.86	3/23/01	334.97	−4.81
11/25/94	228.05	4.86	9/28/01	315.10	−4.75
4/12/01	369.86	4.83	6/30/00	283.37	−4.67
10/29/99	308.28	4.71	9/20/02	249.53	−4.40

BEST & WORST DAYS BY % CHANGE SEP 22, 1987 TO JUN 3, 2005

Day	Best Close	Change	Day	Worst Close	Change
7/24/02	245.43	9.29%	10/19/87	164.17	−14.49%
10/10/02	224.11	8.61	10/9/02	206.34	−9.14
10/20/87	175.95	7.18	7/23/02	224.57	−7.65
7/30/02	270.09	7.04	1/4/01	338.73	−6.07
10/21/87	187.96	6.83	7/10/02	273.71	−5.91
10/21/02	233.68	5.68	1/3/01	360.63	−5.51
3/16/00	263.50	5.06	3/6/00	242.52	−5.18
3/26/01	351.02	4.79	1/11/01	321.34	−5.08
3/15/00	250.81	4.66	7/19/02	245.95	−4.70
1/6/03	276.59	4.49	10/8/02	227.10	−4.70
1/5/00	279.97	4.30	9/26/01	311.63	−4.57
7/25/02	255.54	4.12	9/19/00	354.52	−4.34
9/26/02	253.91	3.82	11/7/02	246.18	−4.05
5/23/03	287.53	3.74	10/16/02	213.93	−3.99
7/11/02	283.60	3.61	10/4/02	238.94	−3.99
8/6/02	269.29	3.55	10/9/98	353.68	−3.96
6/1/98	325.58	3.40	10/12/98	339.89	−3.90
10/13/87	200.48	3.36	7/12/02	272.57	−3.89
10/1/90	203.23	3.34	3/22/01	336.18	−3.64
9/18/02	257.81	3.20	5/9/94	220.73	−3.52

EXCHANGE TRADED FUNDS (ETFs)

The ETF universe continues to expand at an accelerated clip. When ETFs were first introduced in 1993 with the issuing of the S&P Depositary Receipt (SPY, AKA the "Spyder") it barely made a ripple in the world of equities. The volume was often under 100,000 whereas now the SPY trades tens of millions of shares daily. In the *2002 Stock Trader's Almanac* we featured the top 50 ETFs as determined by market cap. In 2003 the list grew to 69. 2004 saw the list grow to expand to 96. 2005's edition has a whopping 140. For the 2006 Almanac, we were unable to fit them all on one page. Understanding ETFs is becoming vital for all individual investors.

When we were creating this book it became evident that there is no one-stop website where you can get all of the information you need on ETFs.

This section of the book illustrates all of the Exchange Traded Funds that were traded for at least one month at the time we complied our database. As you read this, more ETFs are likely available. For a complete list of funds available, as well as up to date information, please visit our website.

There are two ways to look up ETFs in this section. The ETFs are listed alphanumerically by fund name. There is an alphanumeric index of all the ETFs as well as an index that lists the ETFs by category.

Every family of funds operates differently. By and large they track specific indices, but there is a growing trend amongst issuers to offer specialized or customized products.

Generally the top holdings comprise a large percentage of the overall holdings of the fund. The top ten holdings can change daily, but rarely do they change drastically in the long run. So before you buy an ETF verify what you are buying. We include the top ten holdings to give you an understanding of what the fund managers invest in. Many ETFs contain dozens if not hundreds of stocks. Before you buy an ETF verify that the top holdings are stocks that you would want to own individually. Weak or undesirable stocks in an ETF's top holdings are a warning sign.

The top three sectors are listed in order of size provided that they represent at least 10% of the fund's overall makeup. Some ETFs have only one or two sectors of at least 10%.

ETF ALPHANUMERIC LISTING

ETF CATEGORY LISTING

ADRA | BLDRS Asia 50

CATEGORY   Pacific Markets

DESCRIPTION

Tracks the Bank of New York Asia 50 ADR Index comprised of a basket of 50 publicly traded Depositary Receipts from Asian based markets

TOP TEN HOLDINGS

Toyota
Mitsubishi Tokyo Financial Group
BHP Billiton
Honda
Canon

National Australia Bank
Sony Corp
Matsushita Electric
Taiwan Semiconductor
Australia & New Zealand Banking Group

TOP SECTORS

Automobile & Parts
Technology Equipment
Banking

Inception Date:	11/15/2002
Exchange:	NASDAQ
Shares Outstanding:	850,000
Minimum Lot:	1
Options Traded:	No
Recent Dividends:	Yes

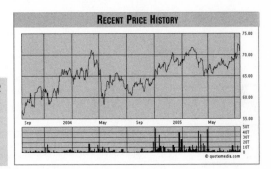

RECENT PRICE HISTORY

ADRD | BLDRS Developed Markets 100

CATEGORY   Global Developed Markets

DESCRIPTION

Tracks the Bank of New York Developed Markets 100 ADR Index comprised of a 100 publicly traded Depositary Receipts from international developed markets

TOP TEN HOLDINGS

BP
HSBC Holdings
Vodafone
GlaxoSmithKline
Total

Royal Dutch Petroleum
Novartis
Toyota
Shell Transport and Trading
Sanofi-Aventis

TOP SECTORS

Banking
Oil & Gas Producers
Pharmaceutical & Biotechnology

Inception Date:	11/15/2002
Exchange:	NASDAQ
Shares Outstanding:	600,000
Minimum Lot:	1
Options Traded:	No
Recent Dividends:	Yes

RECENT PRICE HISTORY

ADRE — BLDRS Emerging Markets 50

CATEGORY   Global Emerging Markets

DESCRIPTION

Tracks the Bank of New York Emerging Markets 50 ADR index comprised of a basket of 50 Depositary Receipts from international emerging markets

TOP TEN HOLDINGS

Taiwan Semiconductor
Teva Pharmaceutical
Infosys Technologies
America Movil
Petroleo Brasileiro (Preferred)

China Mobile
POSCO
Petroleo Brasileiro
Kookmin Bank
Sasol

TOP SECTORS

Oil & Gas Producers
Technology Equipment
Banking

Inception Date:	11/15/2002
Exchange:	NASDAQ
Shares Outstanding:	850,000
Minimum Lot:	1
Options Traded:	No
Recent Dividends:	Yes

RECENT PRICE HISTORY

ADRU — BLDRS Europe 100

CATEGORY   European Markets

DESCRIPTION

Tracks the Bank of New York Europe 100 ADR Index comprised of a basket of 100 Depositary Receipts from European markets

TOP TEN HOLDINGS

BP
HSBC Holdings
Vodafone
GlaxoSmithKline
Total

Royal Dutch Petroleum
Novartis
Shell Transport and Trading
Sanofi-Aventis
UBS

TOP SECTORS

Oil & Gas Producers
Banking
Pharmaceutical & Biotechnology

Inception Date:	11/15/2002
Exchange:	NASDAQ
Shares Outstanding:	200,000
Minimum Lot:	1
Options Traded:	No
Recent Dividends:	Yes

RECENT PRICE HISTORY

DIA | DIAMONDS

CATEGORY Broad Index

DESCRIPTION

Tracks the Dow Jones Industrial Average

TOP TEN HOLDINGS

United Technologies
IBM
Caterpillar
3M
American International Group

Johnson & Johnson
Altria
American Express
Proctor & Gamble
Wal-Mart

TOP SECTORS

Industrials
Information Technology
Financials

Inception Date:	6/20/1998
Exchange:	AMEX
Shares Outstanding:	65,982,000
Minimum Lot:	1
Options Traded:	Yes
Recent Dividends:	Yes

ONEQ | Fidelity NASDAQ Composite

CATEGORY Broad Index

DESCRIPTION

Tracks the NASDAQ composite index

TOP TEN HOLDINGS

Microsoft
Intel
Cisco Systems
Dell
Amgen

Oracle
Qualcomm
Google
Yahoo
eBay

TOP SECTORS

Information Technology
Health Care
Consumer Discretionary

Inception Date:	9/25/2003
Exchange:	NASDAQ
Shares Outstanding:	1,100,000
Minimum Lot:	1
Options Traded:	Yes
Recent Dividends:	Yes

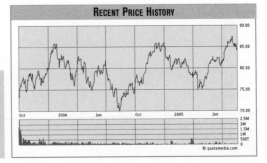

Seasonal Sector Investing: ETFs

ICF — iShares Cohen & Steers Realty Majors

CATEGORY Real Estate

DESCRIPTION
Tracks the Cohen & Steers Realty Majors Index of large, actively traded U.S. real estate investment trusts

TOP TEN HOLDINGS

Simon Property Group Inc REIT
Equity Office Properties Trust REIT
Vornado Realty Trust REIT
Equity Residential REIT
General Growth Properties Inc REIT

Boston Properties Inc REIT
Public Storage Inc REIT
ProLogis REIT
Kimco Realty Corp REIT
Archstone-Smith Trust REIT

TOP SECTORS
Real Estate

Inception Date:	1/29/2001
Exchange:	AMEX
Shares Outstanding:	22,300,000
Minimum Lot:	1
Options Traded:	Yes
Recent Dividends:	Yes

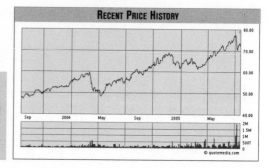

IAU — iShares COMEX Gold

CATEGORY Gold

DESCRIPTION
The price of the ETF corresponds to 1/10 of the price of gold

TOP TEN HOLDINGS
Gold Bullion

TOP SECTORS
Gold

Inception Date:	1/21/2005
Exchange:	AMEX
Shares Outstanding:	4,450,000
Minimum Lot:	1
Options Traded:	No
Recent Dividends:	No

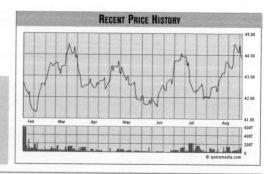

DVY | iShares Dow Jones Select Dividend

CATEGORY Dividend

DESCRIPTION

Tracks the Dow Jones Select Dividend Index of the top 100 highest dividend-yielding securities (excluding REITs) in the Dow Jones U.S. Total Market Index

TOP TEN HOLDINGS

Altria
FPL
DTE Energy
Bank of America
Unitrin

Pinnacle West Capital
PNC Financial Services
Comerica
FirstEnergy
People's Bank

TOP SECTORS

Banking
Electricity

Inception Date:	11/3/2003
Exchange:	NYSE
Shares Outstanding:	115,250,000
Minimum Lot:	1
Options Traded:	No
Recent Dividends:	Yes

IYT | iShares Dow Jones Transportation Average

CATEGORY Transports

DESCRIPTION

Tracks the Dow Jones Transportation Average Index

TOP TEN HOLDINGS

FedEx
United Parcel Service
Union Pacific
CH Robinson Worldwide
Expeditors International of Washington

Yellow Roadway
Burlington Northern Santa Fe
CNF
GATX
CSX

TOP SECTORS

Industrial Transportation
Travel & Leisure

Inception Date:	10/6/2003
Exchange:	AMEX
Shares Outstanding:	2,300,000
Minimum Lot:	1
Options Traded:	No
Recent Dividends:	Yes

IYM   iShares Dow Jones U.S. Basic Materials

CATEGORY   Materials

DESCRIPTION
Tracks the Dow Jones U.S. Basic Materials Index

TOP TEN HOLDINGS

Dow Chemical
du Pont
Alcoa
Monsanto
Praxair

Newmont Mining
Weyerhaeuser
International Paper
Air Products & Chemicals
PPG Industries

TOP SECTORS

Chemicals
Mining
Industrial Metals

Inception Date:	6/12/2000
Exchange:	AMEX
Shares Outstanding:	7,850,000
Minimum Lot:	1
Options Traded:	No
Recent Dividends:	Yes

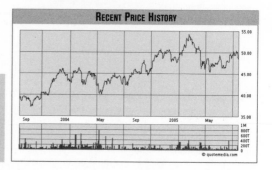

IYK   iShares Dow Jones U.S. Consumer Goods

CATEGORY   Consumer Goods

DESCRIPTION
Tracks the Dow Jones U.S. Goods Index

TOP TEN HOLDINGS

Procter & Gamble
Altria Group
Coca-Cola
PepsiCo
Gillette

Anheuser-Busch
Kimberly-Clark
Colgate-Palmolive
Ford Motor
Electronic Arts

TOP SECTORS

Household Goods
Beverages
Personal Goods

Inception Date:	6/12/2000
Exchange:	AMEX
Shares Outstanding:	8,350,000
Minimum Lot:	1
Options Traded:	No
Recent Dividends:	Yes

IYC — iShares Dow Jones U.S. Consumer

CATEGORY   Consumer Goods

DESCRIPTION
Tracks the Dow Jones U.S. Consumer Services Index

TOP TEN HOLDINGS

Wal-Mart	Viacom
Home Depot	Target
Time Warner	Lowe's
Disney	eBay
Walgreen	McDonald's

TOP SECTORS

General Retailers
Media
Travel & Leisure

Inception Date:	6/12/2000
Exchange:	AMEX
Shares Outstanding:	3,550,000
Minimum Lot:	1
Options Traded:	No
Recent Dividends:	Yes

RECENT PRICE HISTORY

IYG — iShares Dow Jones U.S. Financial Services

CATEGORY   Financial

DESCRIPTION
Tracks the Dow Jones U.S. Financial Services Index

TOP TEN HOLDINGS

Citigroup	American Express
Bank of America	US Bancorp
JPMorgan Chase	Federal National Mortgage Association
Wells Fargo	Morgan Stanley
Wachovia	Merrill Lynch

TOP SECTORS

Banking
General Financial

Inception Date:	6/12/2000
Exchange:	AMEX
Shares Outstanding:	2,500,000
Minimum Lot:	1
Options Traded:	No
Recent Dividends:	Yes

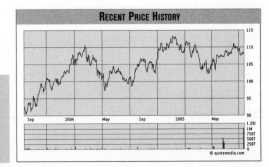

RECENT PRICE HISTORY

IYF   iShares Dow Jones U.S. Financials

CATEGORY   Financial

DESCRIPTION

Tracks the Dow Jones U.S. Financials Index

TOP TEN HOLDINGS

Citigroup
Bank of America
American International Group
JPMorgan Chase
Wells Fargo

Wachovia
American Express
US Bancorp
Federal National Mortgage Association
Morgan Stanley

TOP SECTORS

Banking
General Financial
Non-life Insurance

Inception Date:	5/22/2000
Exchange:	AMEX
Shares Outstanding:	3,600,000
Minimum Lot:	1
Options Traded:	Yes
Recent Dividends:	Yes

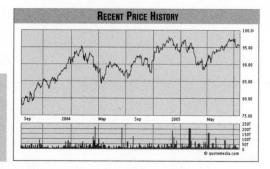

IYH   iShares Dow Jones U.S. Healthcare

CATEGORY   Healthcare

DESCRIPTION

Tracks the Dow Jones U.S. Health Care Index

TOP TEN HOLDINGS

Pfizer
Johnson & Johnson
Amgen
Abbott Laboratories
Merck

UnitedHealth Group
Medtronic
Wyeth
Eli Lilly
Bristol-Myers Squibb

TOP SECTORS

Pharmaceutical & Biotechnology
Health Care Equip & Services

Inception Date:	6/12/2000
Exchange:	AMEX
Shares Outstanding:	20,800,000
Minimum Lot:	1
Options Traded:	Yes
Recent Dividends:	Yes

IYJ   iShares Dow Jones U.S. Industrials

CATEGORY   Industrials

DESCRIPTION

Tracks the Dow Jones U.S. Industrials Index which includes companies in the industrials sector

TOP TEN HOLDINGS

General Electric
Tyco International
3M
Boeing
United Technologies

United Parcel Service
Caterpillar
First Data Corp
Honeywell International
Emerson Electric

TOP SECTORS

General Industrials
Aerospace & Defense
Support Services

Inception Date:	6/12/2000
Exchange:	AMEX
Shares Outstanding:	4,250,000
Minimum Lot:	1
Options Traded:	No
Recent Dividends:	Yes

RECENT PRICE HISTORY

IYE   iShares Dow Jones U.S. Oil and Gas

CATEGORY   Oil & Gas

DESCRIPTION

Tracks the Dow Jones U.S. Oil and Gas Index

TOP TEN HOLDINGS

Exxon Mobil
ChevronTexaco
ConocoPhillips
Schlumberger
Occidental Petroleum

Burlington Resources
Devon Energy
Baker Hughes
Halliburton
Apache

TOP SECTORS

Oil & Gas Producers
Oil Equipment Svces & Distrib

Inception Date:	6/12/2000
Exchange:	AMEX
Shares Outstanding:	9,300,000
Minimum Lot:	1
Options Traded:	Yes
Recent Dividends:	Yes

RECENT PRICE HISTORY

IYR — iShares Dow Jones U.S. Real Estate

CATEGORY   Real Estate

DESCRIPTION
Tracks the Dow Jones U.S. Real Estate Index

TOP TEN HOLDINGS

Simon Property Group Inc REIT
Equity Office Properties Trust REIT
Equity Residential REIT
General Growth Properties REIT
Vornado Realty Trust REIT

Archstone-Smith Trust REIT
ProLogis REIT
Boston Properties REIT
Plum Creek Timber REIT
Host Marriott Corp REIT

TOP SECTORS

Real Estate

Inception Date:	6/12/2000
Exchange:	AMEX
Shares Outstanding:	19,750,000
Minimum Lot:	1
Options Traded:	Yes
Recent Dividends:	Yes

RECENT PRICE HISTORY

IYW — iShares Dow Jones U.S. Technology

CATEGORY   Technology

DESCRIPTION
Tracks the Dow Jones U.S. Technology Index

TOP TEN HOLDINGS

Microsoft
Intel
IBM
Cisco Systems
Dell

Hewlett-Packard
QUALCOMM
Texas Instruments
Motorola
Oracle

TOP SECTORS

Tech Hardware & Equipment
Software & Computer Services

Inception Date:	5/15/2000
Exchange:	AMEX
Shares Outstanding:	8,650,000
Minimum Lot:	1
Options Traded:	Yes
Recent Dividends:	Yes

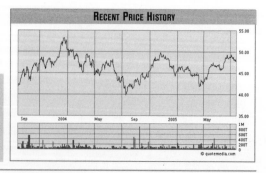

RECENT PRICE HISTORY

IYZ   iShares Dow Jones U.S. Telecommunications

CATEGORY   Telecom

DESCRIPTION

Tracks the Dow Jones U.S. Telecommunications Index

TOP TEN HOLDINGS

Verizon	Nextel
SBC	AT&T
ALLTEL	BCE
BellSouth	CenturyTel
Sprint	Vodafone

TOP SECTORS

Fixed Line Telecommunications
Mobile Telecommunications

Inception Date:	5/22/2000
Exchange:	AMEX
Shares Outstanding:	20,750,000
Minimum Lot:	1
Options Traded:	Yes
Recent Dividends:	Yes

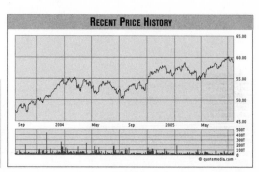

IYY   iShares Dow Jones U.S. Total Market

CATEGORY   Broad Index - Total Market

DESCRIPTION

Tracks the Dow Jones U.S. Total Market Index

TOP TEN HOLDINGS

Exxon Mobil	Johnson & Johnson
General Electric	Bank of America
Microsoft	Intel
Citigroup	American International Group
Pfizer	Altria Group

TOP SECTORS

Financials
Technology
Consumer Services

Inception Date:	6/12/2000
Exchange:	AMEX
Shares Outstanding:	7,500,000
Minimum Lot:	1
Options Traded:	No
Recent Dividends:	Yes

IDU — iShares Dow Jones U.S. Utilities

CATEGORY   Utilities

DESCRIPTION
Tracks the Dow Jones U.S. Utilities Index

TOP TEN HOLDINGS

Exelon Corp
Dominion Resources
Duke Energy
Southern
TXU

Entergy
FirstEnergy
FPL Group
Public Service Enterprise Group
American Electric Power

TOP SECTORS

Electricity
Gas, Water & Multi-utilities

Inception Date:	6/12/2000
Exchange:	AMEX
Shares Outstanding:	10,050,000
Minimum Lot:	1
Options Traded:	Yes
Recent Dividends:	Yes

RECENT PRICE HISTORY

IGE — iShares Goldman Sachs Natural Resources

CATEGORY   Natural Resources

DESCRIPTION
Tracks the Goldman Sachs Natural Resources Index

TOP TEN HOLDINGS

BP
ChevronTexaco
Exxon Mobil
ConocoPhillips
Schlumberger

EnCana
Occidental Petroleum
Halliburton
Devon Energy
Burlington Resources

TOP SECTORS

Oil
Oil Services
Metals & Mining

Inception Date:	10/22/2001
Exchange:	AMEX
Shares Outstanding:	10,150,000
Minimum Lot:	1
Options Traded:	No
Recent Dividends:	Yes

RECENT PRICE HISTORY

IGN iShares Goldman Sachs Networking

CATEGORY   Networking

DESCRIPTION

Tracks the Goldman Sachs Networking Index

TOP TEN HOLDINGS

Motorola
Corning
QUALCOMM
Research In Motion
Cisco Systems

Nortel Networks
Juniper Networks
Lucent Technologies
Broadcom
Marvell Technology Group

TOP SECTORS

Networking
Semiconductors

Inception Date:	7/10/2001
Exchange:	AMEX
Shares Outstanding:	4,950,000
Minimum Lot:	1
Options Traded:	Yes
Recent Dividends:	No

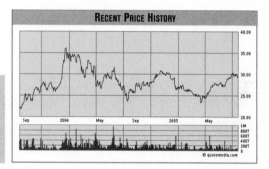

IGW iShares Goldman Sachs Semiconductor

CATEGORY   Semiconductors

DESCRIPTION

Tracks the Goldman Sachs Semiconductor Index

TOP TEN HOLDINGS

Motorola
Texas Instruments
Applied Materials
Intel
STMicroelectronics

Maxim Integrated Products
Analog Devices
Marvell Technology Group
Linear Technology
Broadcom

TOP SECTORS

Semiconductors
Multimedia Networking

Inception Date:	7/10/2001
Exchange:	AMEX
Shares Outstanding:	9,750,000
Minimum Lot:	1
Options Traded:	Yes
Recent Dividends:	No

IGV iShares Goldman Sachs Software

CATEGORY   Software

DESCRIPTION

Tracks the Goldman Sachs Software Index

TOP TEN HOLDINGS

Symantec	Adobe Systems
Microsoft	Intuit
Oracle	Autodesk
Electronic Arts	VeriSign
Computer Associates	Amdocs

TOP SECTORS

Software

Inception Date:	7/10/2001
Exchange:	AMEX
Shares Outstanding:	4,900,000
Minimum Lot:	1
Options Traded:	Yes
Recent Dividends:	Yes

IGM iShares Goldman Sachs Technology

CATEGORY   Technology

DESCRIPTION

Tracks the Goldman Sachs Technology Index

TOP TEN HOLDINGS

Microsoft	Hewlett-Packard
Intel	Oracle
IBM	QUALCOMM
Cisco Systems	eBay
Dell	Motorola

TOP SECTORS

Semiconductors
Computer Hardware
Software

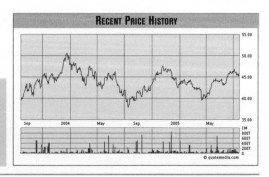

Inception Date:	3/13/2001
Exchange:	AMEX
Shares Outstanding:	6,400,000
Minimum Lot:	1
Options Traded:	Yes
Recent Dividends:	Yes

LQD iShares Goldman Sachs InvesTop Corporate Bond

CATEGORY Bonds

DESCRIPTION

Tracks the performance of the corporate bond market as defined by the Goldman Sachs InvesTop Index

TOP TEN HOLDINGS

Sprint 8.75% 3/15/2032 Baa3/BBB-
Verizon 7.75% 12/1/2030 A2/A+
Time Warner 7.70% 5/1/2032 Baa1/BBB+
Sprint 8.38% 3/15/2012 Baa3/BBB-
General Elec 6.75% 3/15/2032 Aaa/AAA

Weyerhaeuser 7.38% 3/15/2032 Baa2/BBB
TXU Energy 7.00% 3/15/2013 Baa2/BBB-
AT&T Wireless 7.88% 3/1/2011 Baa2/A
Time Warner 6.88% 5/1/2012 Baa1/BBB+
Bellsouth 6.55% 6/15/2034 A2/A

TOP SECTORS

Financials
Consumer
Industrials

Inception Date:	7/22/2002
Exchange:	AMEX
Shares Outstanding:	22,300,000
Minimum Lot:	1
Options Traded:	Yes
Recent Dividends:	Yes

KLD iShares KLD Select Social

CATEGORY Specialty

DESCRIPTION

Tracks the KLD Select Social Index comprised of companies with positive social and environmental characteristics

TOP TEN HOLDINGS

Wells Fargo
Bristol-Myers Squibb
Microsoft
Johnson & Johnson
General Mills

Intel
Bank of America
St Paul Travelers
Exxon Mobil
General Electric

TOP SECTORS

Financials
Technology
Health Care

Inception Date:	1/24/2005
Exchange:	NYSE
Shares Outstanding:	1,450,000
Minimum Lot:	1
Options Traded:	No
Recent Dividends:	Yes

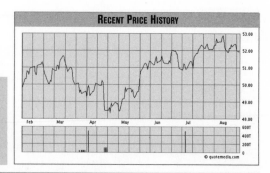

Seasonal Sector Investing: ETFs

SHY   iShares Lehman 1-3 Year Treasury Bond

CATEGORY   Bonds

DESCRIPTION

Tracks the Lehman Brothers 1-3 Year US Treasury Index

TOP TEN HOLDINGS

US Treasury Notes

TOP SECTORS

US Treasury Notes

Inception Date:	7/22/2002
Exchange:	AMEX
Shares Outstanding:	51,000,000
Minimum Lot:	1
Options Traded:	Yes
Recent Dividends:	Yes

IEF   iShares Lehman 7-10 Year Treasury Bond

CATEGORY   Bonds

DESCRIPTION

Tracks the Lehman Brothers 7-10 Year Treasury Index

TOP TEN HOLDINGS

US Treasury Notes

TOP SECTORS

US Treasury Notes

Inception Date:	7/22/2002
Exchange:	AMEX
Shares Outstanding:	12,000,000
Minimum Lot:	1
Options Traded:	Yes
Recent Dividends:	Yes

TLT   iShares Lehman 20 Year Treasury Bond

CATEGORY   Bonds

DESCRIPTION

Tracks the Lehman Brothers 20+ Year Treasury Index

TOP TEN HOLDINGS

US Treasury Notes

TOP SECTORS

US Treasury Notes

Inception Date:	7/22/2002
Exchange:	AMEX
Shares Outstanding:	9,200,000
Minimum Lot:	1
Options Traded:	Yes
Recent Dividends:	Yes

RECENT PRICE HISTORY

© quotemedia.com

AGG   iShares Lehman Aggregate Bond

CATEGORY   Bonds

DESCRIPTION

Tracks the Lehman Brothers U.S. Aggregate Bond Index

TOP TEN HOLDINGS

US Treasury Notes
Corporate Bonds

TOP SECTORS

US Treasury Notes

Inception Date:	9/22/2003
Exchange:	AMEX
Shares Outstanding:	21,700,000
Minimum Lot:	1
Options Traded:	Yes
Recent Dividends:	Yes

RECENT PRICE HISTORY

© quotemedia.com

TIP   iShares Lehman TIPS Bond

CATEGORY   Bonds

DESCRIPTION

Tracks the Lehman Brothers U.S. Treasury Inflation Notes Index

TOP TEN HOLDINGS

US Treasury Notes

TOP SECTORS

US Treasury Notes

Inception Date:	12/4/2003
Exchange:	NYSE
Shares Outstanding:	25,500,000
Minimum Lot:	1
Options Traded:	Yes
Recent Dividends:	Yes

JKD   iShares Morningstar Large Cap Core

CATEGORY   Large Cap

DESCRIPTION

Tracks the Morningstar Large Core Index

TOP TEN HOLDINGS

General Electric
Pfizer
American International Group
IBM
Procter & Gamble

Wells Fargo
Coca-Cola
PepsiCo
Home Depot
Time Warner

TOP SECTORS

Industrial Materials
Financial Services
Health Care

Inception Date:	6/28/2004
Exchange:	NYSE
Shares Outstanding:	1,150,000
Minimum Lot:	1
Options Traded:	No
Recent Dividends:	Yes

JKE   iShares Morningstar Large Growth

CATEGORY   Large Cap

DESCRIPTION

Tracks the Morningstar Large Growth Index

TOP TEN HOLDINGS

Microsoft	Amgen
Johnson & Johnson	Dell
Intel	UnitedHealth Group
Wal-Mart	QUALCOMM
Cisco Systems	Medtronic

TOP SECTORS

Health Care
Computer Hardware
Consumer Services

Inception Date:	6/28/2004
Exchange:	NYSE
Shares Outstanding:	1,300,000
Minimum Lot:	1
Options Traded:	No
Recent Dividends:	Yes

RECENT PRICE HISTORY

© quotemedia.com

JKF   iShares Morningstar Large Cap Value

CATEGORY   Large Cap - Value

DESCRIPTION

US large-cap value stocks, as represented by the Morningstar Large Value Index

TOP TEN HOLDINGS

Exxon Mobil	ChevronTexaco
Citigroup	Verizon
Bank of America	SBC Communications
Altria	ConocoPhillips
JPMorgan Chase	Wachovia

TOP SECTORS

Financial Services
Energy

Inception Date:	6/28/2004
Exchange:	NYSE
Shares Outstanding:	1,050,000
Minimum Lot:	1
Options Traded:	No
Recent Dividends:	Yes

RECENT PRICE HISTORY

© quotemedia.com

JKG · iShares Morningstar Mid Cap Core

CATEGORY   Mid Cap

DESCRIPTION

Tracks the Morningstar Mid-cap Core Index

TOP TEN HOLDINGS

Harrah's Entertainment
Williams
DR Horton
Phelps Dodge
ITT Industries

Pulte Homes
Murphy Oil
Kinder Morgan
Centex
Chesapeake Energy

TOP SECTORS

Financial Services
Consumer Services
Industrial Materials

Inception Date:	6/28/2004
Exchange:	NYSE
Shares Outstanding:	1,100,000
Minimum Lot:	1
Options Traded:	No
Recent Dividends:	Yes

JKH · iShares Morningstar Mid Cap Growth

CATEGORY   Mid Cap - Growth

DESCRIPTION

Tracks the Morningstar Mid Cap Growth Index

TOP TEN HOLDINGS

Legg Mason
Nabors Industries
SunGard Data Systems
Liberty Global
General Growth Properties REIT

GlobalSantaFe
BJ Services
KLA-Tencor
National-Oil well Varco
Network Appliance

TOP SECTORS

Health Care
Computer Hardware
Business Services

Inception Date:	6/28/2004
Exchange:	NYSE
Shares Outstanding:	550,000
Minimum Lot:	1
Options Traded:	No
Recent Dividends:	Yes

JKI iShares Morningstar Mid Cap Value

CATEGORY   Mid Cap - Value

DESCRIPTION
Tracks the Morningstar Mid Cap Value Index.

TOP TEN HOLDINGS

Federated Department Stores
Safeway
Constellation Energy Group
Vornado Realty Trust REIT
Amerada Hess

AmSouth Bancorp
CSX
CIT Group
Sovereign Bancorp
Sunoco

TOP SECTORS

Financial Services
Utilities
Consumer Goods

Inception Date:	6/28/2004
Exchange:	NYSE
Shares Outstanding:	750,000
Minimum Lot:	1
Options Traded:	No
Recent Dividends:	Yes

JKJ iShares Morningstar Small Cap Core

CATEGORY   Small Cap

DESCRIPTION
Tracks the Morningstar Small-cap Core Index

TOP TEN HOLDINGS

Cimarex Energy
New Century Financial REIT
Meritage Homes
Flowserve
Meridian Gold

STERIS
MoneyGram International
Mentor
St Mary Land & Exploration
Capital Automotive REIT

TOP SECTORS

Financial Services
Industrial Materials
Business Services

Inception Date:	6/28/2004
Exchange:	NYSE
Shares Outstanding:	700,000
Minimum Lot:	1
Options Traded:	No
Recent Dividends:	Yes

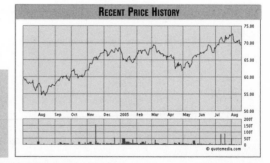

JKK   iShares Morningstar Small Cap Growth

CATEGORY   Small Cap - Growth

DESCRIPTION

Tracks the Morningstar Small-cap Growth Index

TOP TEN HOLDINGS

Advanced Medical Optics
Intuitive Surgical
LifePoint Hospitals
Cal Dive International
Todco

Unit Corp
SCP Pool
Medicis Pharmaceutical
Quiksilver
Tractor Supply

TOP SECTORS

Health Care
Hardware
Business Services

Inception Date:	6/28/2004
Exchange:	NYSE
Shares Outstanding:	450,000
Minimum Lot:	1
Options Traded:	No
Recent Dividends:	No

JKL   iShares Morningstar Small Cap Value

CATEGORY   Small Cap - Value

DESCRIPTION

Tracks the Morningstar Small Value Index

TOP TEN HOLDINGS

Chemtura
Cabot Oil & Gas
AMR Corp
Crescent Real Estate Equities REIT
Hudson United Bancorp

Sybase
Briggs & Stratton
Nicor
American Financial Realty Trust REIT
AGCO Corp

TOP SECTORS

Financial Services
Industrial Materials

Inception Date:	·6/28/2004
Exchange:	NYSE
Shares Outstanding:	700,000
Minimum Lot:	1
Options Traded:	No
Recent Dividends:	Yes

EWA | iShares MSCI Australia

CATEGORY   Foreign Market

DESCRIPTION
Tracks publicly traded securities in the Australian stock market

TOP TEN HOLDINGS

BHP Billiton
Commonwealth Bank of Australia
National Australia Bank
Australia and New Zealand Banking Group
Westpac Banking

Westfield Group
Woolworths
Wesfarmers
Woodside Petroleum
Macquarie Bank

TOP SECTORS

Banking
Materials
Real Estate

Inception Date:	3/12/1996
Exchange:	AMEX
Shares Outstanding:	19,600,000
Minimum Lot:	1
Options Traded:	No
Recent Dividends:	Yes

EWO | iShares MSCI Austria

CATEGORY   Foreign Market

DESCRIPTION
Tracks publicly traded securities in the Austrian stock market

TOP TEN HOLDINGS

OMV
Erste Bank der oesterreichischen
Telekom Austria
Bank Austria Creditanstalt
Oesterreichische Elek

Immofinanz Immobilien Anlagen
Wienerberger
Voestalpine
Meinl European Land
Boehler-Uddeholm

TOP SECTORS

Banking
Energy
Telecommunication Services

Inception Date:	3/12/1996
Exchange:	AMEX
Shares Outstanding:	7,800,000
Minimum Lot:	1
Options Traded:	No
Recent Dividends:	Yes

Seasonal Sector Investing: ETFs

EWK iShares MSCI Belgium

CATEGORY   Foreign Market

DESCRIPTION

Tracks publicly traded securities in the Belgium Stock Market

TOP TEN HOLDINGS

Fortis
Dexia Group
KBC Bankverzekerings Holding
Belgacom
Groupe Bruxelles Lambert

Electrabel
InBev
Solvay
UCB
Delhaize Group

TOP SECTORS

Diversified Financials
Banking

Inception Date:	3/12/1996
Exchange:	AMEX
Shares Outstanding:	2,480,000
Minimum Lot:	1
Options Traded:	No
Recent Dividends:	Yes

EWZ iShares MSCI Brazil

CATEGORY   Foreign Market

DESCRIPTION

Tracks publicly traded securities in the Brazilian stock market

TOP TEN HOLDINGS

Petroleo Brasileiro
Petroleo Brasileiro
Companhia Vale do Rio Doce
Companhia Vale do Rio Doce (ADR)
Banco Itau Holding Financeira

Banco Bradesco
Companhia de Bedidas das Americas
Tele Norte Leste Participacoes
Unibanco - Uniao de Bancos Brasileiros
Companhia Energetica de Minas Gerais

TOP SECTORS

Materials
Energy
Banking

Inception Date:	7/10/2000
Exchange:	AMEX
Shares Outstanding:	22,000,000
Minimum Lot:	1
Options Traded:	No
Recent Dividends:	Yes

EWC iShares MSCI Canada

CATEGORY   Foreign Market

DESCRIPTION

Tracks publicly traded securities in the Canadian stock market

TOP TEN HOLDINGS

Royal Bank of Canada   Canadian Imperial Bank of Commerce
Manulife Financial   Suncor Energy
EnCana   Sun Life Financial
Bank of Nova Scotia   Canadian Natural Resources
Bank of Montreal   Canadian National Railway

TOP SECTORS

Energy
Banking
Materials

Inception Date:	3/12/1996
Exchange:	AMEX
Shares Outstanding:	18,900,000
Minimum Lot:	1
Options Traded:	No
Recent Dividends:	Yes

EFA iShares MSCI EAFE

CATEGORY   Global Developed Markets

DESCRIPTION

Tracks the EAFE index an index of stocks that trade in Europe Australia Asia and the Far East

TOP TEN HOLDINGS

BP   Royal Dutch Petroleum
HSBC Holdings   Novartis
Vodafone Group   Nestle
GlaxoSmithKline   Toyota
Total   Royal Bank of Scotland Group

TOP SECTORS

Financials
Consumer Discretionary
Industrials

Inception Date:	8/14/2001
Exchange:	AMEX
Shares Outstanding:	330,000,000
Minimum Lot:	1
Options Traded:	Yes
Recent Dividends:	Yes

EEM | iShares MSCI Emerging Markets

CATEGORY   Global Emerging Markets

DESCRIPTION

Tracks the MSCI Emerging Markets Index

TOP TEN HOLDINGS

Samsung Electronics
Taiwan Semiconductor
Kookmin Bank
Posco
United Microelectronics

AU Optronics
Korea Electric Power
Chunghwa Telecom
Siliconware Precision Industries
LUKOIL

TOP SECTORS

Telecommunication Services
Banking
Semiconductors

Inception Date:	4/7/2003
Exchange:	AMEX
Shares Outstanding:	91,350,000
Minimum Lot:	1
Options Traded:	No
Recent Dividends:	Yes

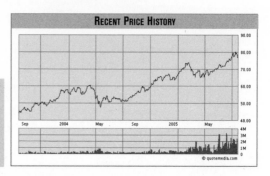

EZU | iShares MSCI EMU Markets

CATEGORY   European Markets

DESCRIPTION

Tracks the MSCI European Monetary Union Index

TOP TEN HOLDINGS

Royal Dutch Petroleum
Total
Sanofi-Aventis
Nokia
Telefonica

Banco Santander Central Hispano
Eni SpA
Siemens
E.ON
BNP Paribas

TOP SECTORS

Banking
Energy

Inception Date:	7/25/2000
Exchange:	AMEX
Shares Outstanding:	7,300,000
Minimum Lot:	1
Options Traded:	No
Recent Dividends:	Yes

EWQ   iShares MSCI France

CATEGORY   Foreign Market

DESCRIPTION

Tracks publicly traded securities in the French stock market

TOP TEN HOLDINGS

Total	Societe Generale
Sanofi-Aventis	Vivendi Universal
BNP Paribas	Carrefour
France Telecom	Suez
AXA	L'Oreal

TOP SECTORS

Energy
Banking
Pharmaceutical & Biotechnology

Inception Date:	3/12/1996
Exchange:	AMEX
Shares Outstanding:	3,000,000
Minimum Lot:	1
Options Traded:	No
Recent Dividends:	Yes

EWG   iShares MSCI Germany

CATEGORY   Foreign Market

DESCRIPTION

Tracks publicly traded securities in the German stock market

TOP TEN HOLDINGS

Siemens	DaimlerChrysler
E.ON	BASF
Deutsche Telekom	SAP
Allianz	RWE
Deutsche Bank	Bayer

TOP SECTORS

Utilities
Automobiles & Components
Capital Goods

Inception Date:	3/12/1996
Exchange:	AMEX
Shares Outstanding:	16,500,000
Minimum Lot:	1
Options Traded:	No
Recent Dividends:	Yes

EWH   iShares MSCI Hong Kong

CATEGORY   Foreign Market

DESCRIPTION
Tracks publicly traded securities in the Hong Kong stock market

TOP TEN HOLDINGS
Hutchison Whampoa
Cheung Kong Holdings
Sun Hung Kai Properties
Hang Seng Bank
CLP Holdings

Swire Pacific Ltd
Hong Kong & China Gas
Esprit Holdings
BOC Hong Kong Holdings
Hongkong Electric Holdings

TOP SECTORS
Real Estate
Utilities
Banking

Inception Date:	3/12/1996
Exchange:	AMEX
Shares Outstanding:	48,300,000
Minimum Lot:	1
Options Traded:	Yes
Recent Dividends:	Yes

EWI   iShares MSCI Italy

CATEGORY   Foreign Market

DESCRIPTION
Tracks publicly traded securities in the Italian stock market

TOP TEN HOLDINGS
Eni
Telecom Italia
Assicurazioni Generali
Enel
UniCredito Italiano

Telecom Italia
San Paolo IMI
Banca Intesa
Mediaset
Mediobanca

TOP SECTORS
Banking
Energy
Telecommunication Services

Inception Date:	3/12/1996
Exchange:	AMEX
Shares Outstanding:	1,650,000
Minimum Lot:	1
Options Traded:	No
Recent Dividends:	Yes

EWJ | iShares MSCI Japan

CATEGORY   Foreign Market

DESCRIPTION

Tracks publicly traded securities in the Japanese stock market

TOP TEN HOLDINGS

Toyota	Mizuho Financial Group
Takeda Pharmaceutical	Sony
Mitsubishi Tokyo Financial Group	Matsushita Electric Industrial
Honda	Sumitomo Mitsui Financial Group
Canon	Tokyo Electric Power

TOP SECTORS

Automobiles & Components
Technology Hardware & Equip

Inception Date:	3/12/1996
Exchange:	AMEX
Shares Outstanding:	615,600,000
Minimum Lot:	1
Options Traded:	No
Recent Dividends:	Yes

RECENT PRICE HISTORY

EWM | iShares MSCI Malaysia

CATEGORY   Foreign Market

DESCRIPTION

Tracks publicly traded securities in the Malaysian stock market

TOP TEN HOLDINGS

Toyota	Mizuho Financial Group
Takeda Pharmaceutical	Sony
Mitsubishi Tokyo Financial Group	Matsushita Electric Industrial
Honda	Sumitomo Mitsui Financial Group
Canon	Tokyo Electric Power

TOP SECTORS

Automobiles & Components
Technology Hardware & Equip

Inception Date:	3/12/1996
Exchange:	AMEX
Shares Outstanding:	615,600,000
Minimum Lot:	1
Options Traded:	No
Recent Dividends:	Yes

RECENT PRICE HISTORY

EWW   iShares MSCI Mexico

CATEGORY   Foreign Market

DESCRIPTION
Tracks publicly traded securities in the Mexican stock market

TOP TEN HOLDINGS
America Movil
Telefonos de Mexico
Cemex
Fomento Economico Mexicano
Wal-Mart de Mexico

Grupo Televisa
Grupo Financiero Banorte
Grupo Carso
Kimberly-Clark de Mexico
Grupo Modelo

TOP SECTORS
Telecommunication Services
Materials
Food Beverage & Tobacco

Inception Date:	3/12/1996
Exchange:	AMEX
Shares Outstanding:	9,100,000
Minimum Lot:	1
Options Traded:	No
Recent Dividends:	Yes

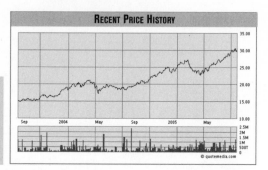

EWN   iShares MSCI Netherlands

CATEGORY   Foreign Market

DESCRIPTION
Tracks publicly traded securities in the Dutch stock market

TOP TEN HOLDINGS
Royal Dutch Petroleum
ING Groep
Unilever
ABN AMRO Holding
Koninklijke (Royal) Philips Elec

Aegon
Koninklijke (Royal) KPN
TPG
Akzo Nobel
Reed Elsevier

TOP SECTORS
Energy
Food Beverage & Tobacco
Diversified Financials

Inception Date:	3/12/1996
Exchange:	AMEX
Shares Outstanding:	3,350,000
Minimum Lot:	1
Options Traded:	No
Recent Dividends:	Yes

EPP   iShares MSCI Pacific Ex-Japan

CATEGORY   Pacific Markets

DESCRIPTION

Tracks the MSCI Pacific Ex-Japan Index including securities traded in the Australia, Hong Kong, New Zealand, and Singapore markets

TOP TEN HOLDINGS

BHP Billiton
Commonwealth Bank of Australia
National Australia Bank
Australia and New Zealand Banking Group
Westpac Banking

Westfield Group
Hutchison Whampoa
Cheung Kong Holdings
Sun Hung Kai Properties
Woolworths

TOP SECTORS

Banking
Real Estate
Materials

Inception Date:	10/25/2001
Exchange:	AMEX
Shares Outstanding:	15,400,000
Minimum Lot:	1
Options Traded:	No
Recent Dividends:	Yes

EWS   iShares MSCI Singapore

CATEGORY   Foreign Market

DESCRIPTION

Tracks publicly traded securities in the Singapore stock market

TOP TEN HOLDINGS

Singapore Telecommunications
United Overseas Bank
DBS Group Holdings
Oversea-Chinese Banking
Keppel

Singapore Press Holdings
Singapore Airlines
City Developments
Singapore Technologies Engineering
Venture

TOP SECTORS

Banking
Capital Goods
Telecommunication Services

Inception Date:	3/12/1996
Exchange:	AMEX
Shares Outstanding:	43,700,000
Minimum Lot:	1
Options Traded:	No
Recent Dividends:	Yes

EZA — iShares MSCI South Africa

CATEGORY   Foreign Market

DESCRIPTION
Tracks publicly traded securities in the South African stock market

TOP TEN HOLDINGS

Sasol
Standard Bank Group
MTN Group
Old Mutual
FirstRand

Impala Platinum Holdings
AngloGold Ashanti
Sanlam
Telkom
Gold Fields

TOP SECTORS

Materials
Banking
Energy

Inception Date:	2/3/2003
Exchange:	AMEX
Shares Outstanding:	1,850,000
Minimum Lot:	1
Options Traded:	No
Recent Dividends:	Yes

RECENT PRICE HISTORY

EWY — iShares MSCI South Korea

CATEGORY   Foreign Market

DESCRIPTION
Tracks publicly traded securities in the South Korean stock market

TOP TEN HOLDINGS

Samsung Electronics
Kookmin
Posco
Hyundai
Korea Electric Power

LG Electronics
Shinhan Financial Group
SK Telecom
SK Corp
Shinsegae

TOP SECTORS

Semiconductors
Banking

Inception Date:	5/9/2000
Exchange:	AMEX
Shares Outstanding:	19,750,000
Minimum Lot:	1
Options Traded:	No
Recent Dividends:	Yes

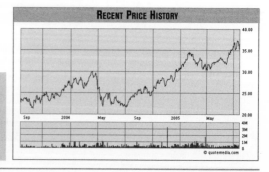

RECENT PRICE HISTORY

EWP iShares MSCI Spain

CATEGORY   Foreign Market

DESCRIPTION

Tracks publicly traded securities in the Spanish stock market

TOP TEN HOLDINGS

Telefonica
Banco Santander Central Hispano
Banco Bilbao Vizcaya Argentaria
Endesa
Repsol YPF

Iberdrola
Banco Popular Espanol
Altadis
ACS Actividades de Construccion y Servs
Union Fenosa

TOP SECTORS

Banking
Telecommunication Services
Utilities

Inception Date:	3/12/1996
Exchange:	AMEX
Shares Outstanding:	1,875,000
Minimum Lot:	1
Options Traded:	No
Recent Dividends:	Yes

RECENT PRICE HISTORY

EWD iShares MSCI Sweden

CATEGORY   Foreign Market

DESCRIPTION

Tracks publicly traded securities in the Swedish stock market

TOP TEN HOLDINGS

Telefonaktiebolaget LM Ericsson
Nordea
Hennes & Mauritz
Svenska Handelsbanken
Volvo

TeliaSonera
Skandinaviska Enskilda Banken
Sandvik
Svenska Cellulosa
Electrolux

TOP SECTORS

Technology Hardware & Equip
Capital Goods
Banking

Inception Date:	3/12/1996
Exchange:	AMEX
Shares Outstanding:	2,850,000
Minimum Lot:	1
Options Traded:	No
Recent Dividends:	Yes

RECENT PRICE HISTORY

EWL — iShares MSCI Switzerland

CATEGORY   Foreign Market

DESCRIPTION
Tracks publicly traded securities in the Swiss stock market

TOP TEN HOLDINGS

Novartis
Nestle
Roche Holding
UBS
Credit Suisse Group

Zurich Financial Services
Swiss Reinsurance Registered
Holcim
Compagnie Financiere Richemont
Syngenta

TOP SECTORS

Pharmaceutical & Biotechnology
Diversified Financials
Food Beverage & Tobacco

Inception Date:	3/12/1996
Exchange:	AMEX
Shares Outstanding:	4,000,000
Minimum Lot:	1
Options Traded:	No
Recent Dividends:	Yes

RECENT PRICE HISTORY

EWT — iShares MSCI Taiwan

CATEGORY   Foreign Market

DESCRIPTION
Tracks publicly traded securities in the Taiwanese stock market

TOP TEN HOLDINGS

Taiwan Semiconductor
Hon Hai Precision Industry
United Microelectronics
Cathay Financial
China Steel

AU Optronics
Formosa Plastic
Nan Ya Plastic
MediaTek
Chunghwa Telecom

TOP SECTORS

Technology Hardware & Equip
Semiconductors
Banking

Inception Date:	6/20/2000
Exchange:	AMEX
Shares Outstanding:	65,450,000
Minimum Lot:	1
Options Traded:	No
Recent Dividends:	Yes

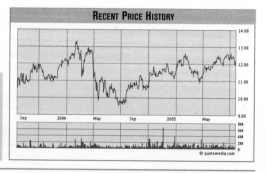

RECENT PRICE HISTORY

EWU   iShares MSCI United Kingdom

CATEGORY   Foreign Market

DESCRIPTION

Tracks publicly traded securities in the British stock market

TOP TEN HOLDINGS

BP
HSBC
Vodafone
GlaxoSmithKline
Royal Bank of Scotland Group

Shell Transport & Trading
AstraZeneca
Barclays
HBOS
Lloyds TSB Group

TOP SECTORS

Banking
Energy

Inception Date:	3/12/1996
Exchange:	AMEX
Shares Outstanding:	26,000,000
Minimum Lot:	1
Options Traded:	No
Recent Dividends:	Yes

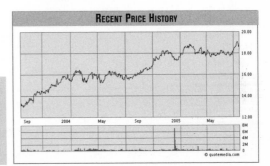

RECENT PRICE HISTORY

IBB   iShares NASDAQ Biotechnology

CATEGORY   Biotechnology

DESCRIPTION

Tracks the NASDAQ Biotechnology Index

TOP TEN HOLDINGS

Amgen
Gilead Sciences
Genzyme
Biogen Idec
Teva Pharmaceutical

Celgene
Sepracor
Kos Pharmaceuticals
MedImmune
Chiron

TOP SECTORS

Biotechnology

Inception Date:	2/5/2001
Exchange:	AMEX
Shares Outstanding:	21,350,000
Minimum Lot:	1
Options Traded:	Yes
Recent Dividends:	No

RECENT PRICE HISTORY

Seasonal Sector Investing: ETFs

NY   iShares NYSE 100

CATEGORY   Broad Index

DESCRIPTION

Tracks the performance of the largest 100 US Companies by market cap listed on the NYSE

TOP TEN HOLDINGS

Exxon Mobil
General Electric
Citigroup
Pfizer
Johnson & Johnson

Bank of America
American International Group
Altria
IBM
Procter & Gamble

TOP SECTORS

Financials
Health Care
Industrials

Inception Date:	3/29/2004
Exchange:	NYSE
Shares Outstanding:	500,000
Minimum Lot:	1
Options Traded:	Yes
Recent Dividends:	Yes

NYC   iShares NYSE Composite

CATEGORY   Broad Index

DESCRIPTION

Tracks the performance of all common stocks, ADRs, real estate investment trusts and tracking stocks listed on the NYSE

TOP TEN HOLDINGS

Exxon Mobil
General Electric
BP
Citigroup
Pfizer

Johnson & Johnson
HSBC Holdings
Bank of America
Vodafone
Total

TOP SECTORS

Financials
Oil & Gas
Health Care

Inception Date:	3/30/2004
Exchange:	NYSE
Shares Outstanding:	200,000
Minimum Lot:	1
Options Traded:	Yes
Recent Dividends:	Yes

IWF   iShares Russell 1000 Growth

CATEGORY   Broad Index - Growth

DESCRIPTION

Tracks the performance of stocks with the highest price-to-book ratios and forecasted growth within the Russell 1000

TOP TEN HOLDINGS

General Electric
Microsoft
Johnson & Johnson
Intel
Procter & Gamble

Cisco Systems
Wal-Mart
IBM
Amgen
Dell

TOP SECTORS

Technology
Health Care
Consumer Discretionary

Inception Date:	5/22/2000
Exchange:	AMEX
Shares Outstanding:	79,650,000
Minimum Lot:	1
Options Traded:	Yes
Recent Dividends:	Yes

IWB   iShares Russell 1000

CATEGORY   Broad Index

DESCRIPTION

Tracks the Russell 1000 Index

TOP TEN HOLDINGS

Exxon Mobil
General Electric
Microsoft Corp
Citigroup
Pfizer

Johnson & Johnson
Bank of America
Intel
American International Group
Altria

TOP SECTORS

Financial Services
Consumer Discretionary
Technology

Inception Date:	5/15/2000
Exchange:	AMEX
Shares Outstanding:	35,250,000
Minimum Lot:	1
Options Traded:	Yes
Recent Dividends:	Yes

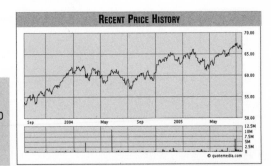

Seasonal Sector Investing: ETFs

IWD iShares Russell 1000 Value

CATEGORY   Broad Index - Value

DESCRIPTION
Tracks the performance of stocks with forecasted growth and the lowest price-to-book ratios within the Russell 1000

TOP TEN HOLDINGS

Exxon Mobil
Citigroup
Pfizer
Bank of America
ChevronTexaco

JPMorgan Chase
American International Group
Verizon Communications
Wells Fargo
ConocoPhillips

TOP SECTORS

Financial Services
Utilities
Integrated Oils

Inception Date:	5/22/2000
Exchange:	AMEX
Shares Outstanding:	77,250,000
Minimum Lot:	1
Options Traded:	Yes
Recent Dividends:	Yes

IWO iShares Russell 2000 Growth

CATEGORY   Broad Index - Growth

DESCRIPTION
Tracks the performance of small-cap growth stocks with the highest price-to-book ratios within the Russell 2000 Index

TOP TEN HOLDINGS

Intuitive Surgical
Cal Dive International
Amylin Pharmaceuticals
Eagle Materials
MGI Pharma

Cypress Semiconductor
Medicis Pharmaceutical
Headwaters
Pediatrix Medical Group
SVB Financial Group

TOP SECTORS

Consumer Discretionary
Health Care
Technology

Inception Date:	7/24/2000
Exchange:	AMEX
Shares Outstanding:	31,700,000
Minimum Lot:	1
Options Traded:	Yes
Recent Dividends:	Yes

IWM   iShares Russell 2000

CATEGORY   Broad Index

DESCRIPTION

Tracks the Russell 2000 Index

TOP TEN HOLDINGS

Cimarex Energy	Fairchild Semiconductor International
Intuitive Surgical	Valassis Communications
Cal Dive International	Eagle Materials
Cabot Oil & Gas	MGI Pharma
Amylin Pharmaceuticals	Hudson United Bancorp

TOP SECTORS

Financial Services
Consumer Discretionary
Technology

Inception Date:	5/22/2000
Exchange:	AMEX
Shares Outstanding:	127,450,000
Minimum Lot:	1
Options Traded:	Yes
Recent Dividends:	Yes

IWN   iShares Russell 2000 Value

CATEGORY   Broad Index - Value

DESCRIPTION

Tracks the performance of small-cap value stocks with forecasted growth and the lowest price-to-book ratios and within the Russell 2000

TOP TEN HOLDINGS

Cimarex Energy	AGCO
Bowater	Nicor
Flowserve	Corn Products International
Briggs & Stratton	Kennametal
Calpine	BancorpSouth

TOP SECTORS

Financial Services
Consumer Discretionary
Materials & Processing

Inception Date:	7/24/2000
Exchange:	AMEX
Shares Outstanding:	45,400,000
Minimum Lot:	1
Options Traded:	Yes
Recent Dividends:	Yes

IWZ iShares Russell 3000 Growth

CATEGORY   Broad Index - Growth

DESCRIPTION

Tracks the Russell 3000 Growth Index which measures the performance of stocks with forecasted growth and the highest price-to-book ratios and within the Russell 1000 and Russell 2000

TOP TEN HOLDINGS

General Electric
Microsoft
Johnson & Johnson
Intel
Procter & Gamble

Cisco Systems
Wal-Mart
IBM
Amgen
Dell

TOP SECTORS

Technology
Consumer Discretionary
Health Care

Inception Date:	7/24/2000
Exchange:	AMEX
Shares Outstanding:	4,250,000
Minimum Lot:	1
Options Traded:	Yes
Recent Dividends:	Yes

RECENT PRICE HISTORY

IWV iShares Russell 3000

CATEGORY   Broad Index

DESCRIPTION

Tracks the performance of the Russell 3000 Index

TOP TEN HOLDINGS

Exxon Mobil
General Electric
Microsoft
Citigroup
Pfizer

Johnson & Johnson
Bank of America
Intel
American International Group
Altria

TOP SECTORS

Financial Services
Consumer Discretionary
Technology

Inception Date:	5/22/2000
Exchange:	AMEX
Shares Outstanding:	28,450,000
Minimum Lot:	1
Options Traded:	Yes
Recent Dividends:	Yes

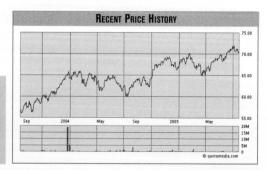

RECENT PRICE HISTORY

IWW iShares Russell 3000 Value

CATEGORY   Broad Index - Value

DESCRIPTION

Tracks the Russell 3000 Value Index which measures the performance of stocks with forecasted growth and the lowest price-to-book ratios and within the Russell 1000 and Russell 2000

TOP TEN HOLDINGS

Exxon Mobil   JPMorgan Chase
Citigroup   American International Group
Pfizer   Verizon
Bank of America   Wells Fargo
ChevronTexaco   ConocoPhillips

TOP SECTORS

Financial Services
Utilities

Inception Date:	7/24/2000
Exchange:	AMEX
Shares Outstanding:	4,800,000
Minimum Lot:	1
Options Traded:	Yes
Recent Dividends:	Yes

IWP iShares Russell Mid Cap Growth

CATEGORY   Mid Cap - Growth

DESCRIPTION

Tracks the mid cap growth sector of the U.S. equity market as represented by the Russell Mid Cap Growth Index a subset of the Russell Mid Cap Index which includes stocks with higher price-to-book ratios and higher forecasted growth

TOP TEN HOLDINGS

EOG Resources   XTO Energy
Maxim Integrated Products   Bed Bath & Beyond
Forest Laboratories   Coach
Analog Devices   Linear Technology
Fortune Brands   Moody's

TOP SECTORS

Consumer Discretionary
Health Care
Technology

Inception Date:	7/17/2001
Exchange:	AMEX
Shares Outstanding:	11,050,000
Minimum Lot:	1
Options Traded:	Yes
Recent Dividends:	Yes

IWR   iShares Russell Mid Cap

CATEGORY   Mid Cap

DESCRIPTION

Tracks the performance of the 800 smallest U.S. companies within the Russell 1000 Index as represented by the Russell Mid Cap Index

TOP TEN HOLDINGS

Norfolk Southern	CIGNA
Public Service Enterprise Group	Forest Laboratories
EOG Resources	Kroger
Maxim Integrated Products	McKesson
American Electric Power	KeyCorp

TOP SECTORS

Financial Services
Consumer Discretionary
Technology

Inception Date:	7/17/2001
Exchange:	AMEX
Shares Outstanding:	17,350,000
Minimum Lot:	1
Options Traded:	Yes
Recent Dividends:	Yes

RECENT PRICE HISTORY

© quotemedia.com

IWS   iShares Russell Mid Cap Value

CATEGORY   Mid Cap - Value

DESCRIPTION

Tracks Russell Mid Cap Value Index, a subset of the Russell Mid Cap Index which consists of companies with lower price-to-book ratios and lower forecasted growth

TOP TEN HOLDINGS

Public Service Enterprise Group	PG&E
American Electric Power	Archer-Daniels-Midland
CIGNA	Equity Office Properties Trust REIT
Kroger	Edison International
KeyCorp	Principal Financial Group

TOP SECTORS

Financial Services
Utilities
Consumer Discretionary

Inception Date:	7/17/2001
Exchange:	AMEX
Shares Outstanding:	12,700,000
Minimum Lot:	1
Options Traded:	Yes
Recent Dividends:	Yes

RECENT PRICE HISTORY

© quotemedia.com

OEF iShares S&P 100

CATEGORY Broad Index

DESCRIPTION

Tracks the performance of U.S. large-cap stocks as represented by the S&P 100 Index

TOP TEN HOLDINGS

Exxon Mobil
General Electric
Microsoft
Citigroup
Pfizer

Johnson & Johnson
Bank of America
Intel
Wal-Mart
American International Group

TOP SECTORS

Financials
Information Technology
Consumer Staples

Inception Date:	10/23/2000
Exchange:	AMEX
Shares Outstanding:	11,350,000
Minimum Lot:	1
Options Traded:	Yes
Recent Dividends:	Yes

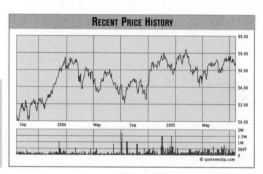

RECENT PRICE HISTORY

IVV iShares S&P 500

CATEGORY Broad Index

DESCRIPTION

Tracks U.S. large-cap stocks, as represented by the S&P 500 Index

TOP TEN HOLDINGS

Exxon Mobil
General Electric
Microsoft
Citigroup
Pfizer

Johnson & Johnson
Bank of America
Intel
Wal-Mart
American International Group

TOP SECTORS

Financials
Information Technology
Health Care

Inception Date:	5/15/2000
Exchange:	AMEX
Shares Outstanding:	111,300,000
Minimum Lot:	1
Options Traded:	No
Recent Dividends:	Yes

RECENT PRICE HISTORY

IVW | iShares S&P 500/BARRA Growth

CATEGORY Large Cap - Growth

DESCRIPTION

Tracks U.S. large-cap growth stocks, as represented by the S&P 500/Barra Growth Index consisting of companies with the highest price-to-book ratios within the S&P 500 Index

TOP TEN HOLDINGS

Exxon Mobil
General Electric
Microsoft
Johnson & Johnson
Intel

Wal-Mart
Altria
IBM
Procter & Gamble
Cisco Systems

TOP SECTORS

Information Technology
Health Care
Consumer Staples

Inception Date:	5/22/2000
Exchange:	AMEX
Shares Outstanding:	49,100,000
Minimum Lot:	1
Options Traded:	No
Recent Dividends:	Yes

RECENT PRICE HISTORY

IVE | iShares S&P 500/BARRA Value

CATEGORY Large Cap - Value

DESCRIPTION

Tracks U.S. large-cap value stocks, as represented by the S&P 500/Barra Value Index consisting of companies with the lowest price-to-book ratios within the S&P 500 Index

TOP TEN HOLDINGS

Citigroup
Pfizer
Bank of America
American International Group
ChevronTexaco

JPMorgan Chase
Wells Fargo
Verizon
ConocoPhillips
Time Warner

TOP SECTORS

Financials
Consumer Discretionary

Inception Date:	5/22/2000
Exchange:	AMEX
Shares Outstanding:	47,750,000
Minimum Lot:	1
Options Traded:	No
Recent Dividends:	Yes

RECENT PRICE HISTORY

ALMANAC INVESTOR

ISI — iShares S&P 1500 Index Fund

CATEGORY Broad Index

DESCRIPTION
Tracks the Standard & Poor's Composite 1500 Index

TOP TEN HOLDINGS
Exxon Mobil
General Electric
Microsoft
Citigroup
Pfizer

Johnson & Johnson
Bank of America
Intel
Wal-Mart
American International Group

TOP SECTORS
Financials
Information Technology
Health Care

Inception Date:	1/20/2004
Exchange:	AMEX
Shares Outstanding:	1,200,000
Minimum Lot:	1
Options Traded:	No
Recent Dividends:	Yes

IEV — iShares S&P Europe 350

CATEGORY European Markets

DESCRIPTION
Tracks the S&P Europe 350 Index a broad range a broad range stocks across diverse industries in continental Europe

TOP TEN HOLDINGS
BP
HSBC Holdings
Vodafone
Total
GlaxoSmithKline

Royal Dutch Shell
Novartis
Nestle
Roche
Royal Bank of Scotland

TOP SECTORS
Financials
Energy

Inception Date:	7/25/2000
Exchange:	AMEX
Shares Outstanding:	15,250,000
Minimum Lot:	1
Options Traded:	Yes
Recent Dividends:	Yes

100   iShares S&P Global 100

CATEGORY   Global Developed Markets

DESCRIPTION

Tracks the performance of large-cap stocks in leading transnational companies, as represented by the S&P Global 100 Index

TOP TEN HOLDINGS

Exxon Mobil	Pfizer
General Electric	Johnson & Johnson
Microsoft	HSBC Holdings
BP	Intel
Citigroup	Vodafone

TOP SECTORS

Financials
Energy
Information Technology

Inception Date:	12/5/2000
Exchange:	NYSE
Shares Outstanding:	5,550,000
Minimum Lot:	1
Options Traded:	No
Recent Dividends:	Yes

IXC   iShares S&P Global Energy

CATEGORY   Energy

DESCRIPTION

Tracks the S&P Global 1200 Index which includes domestic, foreign and multinational securities in the oil equipment and services, oil exploration and production, and oil refineries sectors

TOP TEN HOLDINGS

Exxon Mobil	ConocoPhillips
BP	Royal Dutch Shell
Total	Eni
Royal Dutch Shell	Schlumberger
ChevronTexaco	EnCana

TOP SECTORS

Energy
Oil & Gas

Inception Date:	11/12/2001
Exchange:	AMEX
Shares Outstanding:	4,350,000
Minimum Lot:	1
Options Traded:	No
Recent Dividends:	Yes

IXG — iShares S&P Global Financial

CATEGORY   Financial

DESCRIPTION

Tracks the S&P Global Financials Sector Index which includes foreign and multinational financial securities

TOP TEN HOLDINGS

Citigroup
HSBC Holdings
Bank of America
American International Group
JPMorgan Chase

Wells Fargo
Royal Bank of Scotland
UBS
Wachovia
Banco Santander Central Hispano

TOP SECTORS

Banking
Diversified Financials
Insurance

Inception Date:	11/12/2001
Exchange:	AMEX
Shares Outstanding:	1,200,000
Minimum Lot:	1
Options Traded:	Yes
Recent Dividends:	Yes

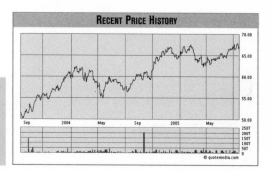

RECENT PRICE HISTORY

© quotemedia.com

IXJ — iShares S&P Global Healthcare

CATEGORY   Healthcare

DESCRIPTION

Tracks the S&P Global Healthcare Sector Index foreign and multinational healthcare securities

TOP TEN HOLDINGS

Pfizer
Johnson & Johnson
GlaxoSmithKline
Novartis
Amgen

Roche
Sanofi-Aventis
AstraZeneca
Abbott Laboratories
Merck

TOP SECTORS

Pharmaceutical & Biotechnology
Health Care Equip & Services

Inception Date:	11/12/2001
Exchange:	AMEX
Shares Outstanding:	7,700,000
Minimum Lot:	1
Options Traded:	No
Recent Dividends:	Yes

RECENT PRICE HISTORY

© quotemedia.com

IXN | iShares S&P Global Technology

CATEGORY Technology

DESCRIPTION

Tracks the S&P Global Technology Sector Index which includes foreign and multinational companies involved in various segments of the technology sector

TOP TEN HOLDINGS

Microsoft	Samsung
Intel	Nokia
IBM	Hewlett-Packard
Cisco Systems	QUALCOMM
Dell	Oracle

TOP SECTORS

Technology Hardware & Equip
Software & Services
Semiconductors

Inception Date:	11/12/2001
Exchange:	AMEX
Shares Outstanding:	1,100,000
Minimum Lot:	1
Options Traded:	No
Recent Dividends:	Yes

RECENT PRICE HISTORY

IXP | iShares S&P Global Telecommunications

CATEGORY Telecom

DESCRIPTION

Tracks the S&P Global Telecommunications Sector Index which includes domestic, foreign and multinational companies involved in the telecom sector

TOP TEN HOLDINGS

Vodafone	France Telecom
Verizon	Deutsche Telekom
Telefonica	Nippon Telegraph & Telephone
SBC Communications	Sprint
BellSouth	Nextel

TOP SECTORS

Telecommunication Services

Inception Date:	11/12/2001
Exchange:	AMEX
Shares Outstanding:	900,000
Minimum Lot:	1
Options Traded:	No
Recent Dividends:	Yes

RECENT PRICE HISTORY

ALMANAC INVESTOR

ILF   iShares S&P Latin America 40

CATEGORY   Latin American Markets

DESCRIPTION

Tracks companies in the Mexican and South American equity markets as represented by the S&P Latin America 40 Index

TOP TEN HOLDINGS

Petroleo Brasileiro

America Movil

Cemex

Companhia Vale do Rio Doce

Telefonos de Mexico

Companhia Vale do Rio Doce

Banco Itau Holding Financiera

Banco Bradesco

Wal-Mart de Mexico

Companhia de Bebidas das Americas

TOP SECTORS

Materials

Telecommunication Services

Financials

Inception Date:	10/25/2001
Exchange:	AMEX
Shares Outstanding:	5,400,000
Minimum Lot:	1
Options Traded:	No
Recent Dividends:	Yes

RECENT PRICE HISTORY

© quotemedia.com

IJH   iShares S&P Mid Cap 400

CATEGORY   Mid Cap

DESCRIPTION

Tracks mid cap stocks as represented by the S&P Mid Cap 400 Index

TOP TEN HOLDINGS

Legg Mason

Murphy Oil

Lennar

Whole Foods Market

Coventry Health

Peabody Energy

Noble Energy

Smith International

Chico's FAS

PacifiCare Health Systems

TOP SECTORS

Consumer Discretionary

Financials

Information Technology

Inception Date:	5/22/2000
Exchange:	AMEX
Shares Outstanding:	40,700,000
Minimum Lot:	1
Options Traded:	Yes

RECENT PRICE HISTORY

© quotemedia.com

IJK   iShares S&P Mid Cap 400/BARRA Growth

CATEGORY   Mid Cap - Growth

DESCRIPTION

Tracks companies with the highest price-to-book ratios within the S&P 400 Index as represented by the S&P Mid Cap 400/Barra Growth Index

TOP TEN HOLDINGS

Legg Mason	Smith International
Murphy Oil	Chico's FAS
Whole Foods Market	Cognizant Technology Solutions
Coventry Health Care	Microchip Technology
Peabody Energy	Toll Brothers

TOP SECTORS

Consumer Discretionary
Health Care
Information Technology

Inception Date:	7/24/2000
Exchange:	AMEX
Shares Outstanding:	18,650,000
Minimum Lot:	1
Options Traded:	Yes
Recent Dividends:	Yes

IJJ   iShares S&P Mid Cap 400/Barra Value

CATEGORY   Mid Cap - Value

DESCRIPTION

Tracks companies with the lowest price-to-book ratios within the S&P Mid Cap 400 Index, as represented by the S&P Mid Cap 400/Barra Value Index

TOP TEN HOLDINGS

Lennar	Lyondell Chemical
Noble Energy	ENSCO International
PacifiCare Health Systems	Pioneer Natural Resources
Fidelity National Financial	Newfield Exploration
SanDisk	Tyson Foods

TOP SECTORS

Financials
Information Technology
Utilities

Inception Date:	7/24/2000
Exchange:	AMEX
Shares Outstanding:	33,450,000
Minimum Lot:	1
Options Traded:	Yes
Recent Dividends:	Yes

IJR   iShares S&P Small Cap 600

CATEGORY   Small Cap

DESCRIPTION
Tracks the S&P Small Cap 600 Index

TOP TEN HOLDINGS

NVR
Southwestern Energy
Cimarex Energy
Massey Energy
Roper Industries

Oshkosh Truck
Standard-Pacific
MDC Holdings
Cooper
Florida Rock Industries

TOP SECTORS

Industrials
Consumer Discretionary
Financials

Inception Date:	5/22/2000
Exchange:	AMEX
Shares Outstanding:	68,250,000
Minimum Lot:	1
Options Traded:	Yes
Recent Dividends:	Yes

ITF   iShares S&P/TOPIX 150

CATEGORY   Foreign Market

DESCRIPTION
Tracks the Japanese equity market as represented by the S&P/Tokyo Stock Price 150 Index

TOP TEN HOLDINGS

Toyota
Nippon Telegraph & Telephone
Takeda Pharmaceutical
Honda
Canon

Matsushita Electric
Sony
Mitsubishi Tokyo Financial Group
Mizuho Financial Group
NTT DoCoMo

TOP SECTORS

Consumer Discretionary
Financials
Industrials

Inception Date:	10/23/2001
Exchange:	AMEX
Shares Outstanding:	1,050,000
Minimum Lot:	1
Options Traded:	No
Recent Dividends:	Yes

Seasonal Sector Investing: ETFs

IJT iShares Small Cap 600/BARRA Growth

CATEGORY   Small Cap - Growth

DESCRIPTION

Tracks publicly traded U.S. small-cap stocks with the highest price-to-book ratios within the S&P Small Cap 600 Index represented by the S&P Small Cap 600/Barra Growth Index

TOP TEN HOLDINGS

NVR	Florida Rock Industries
Southwestern Energy	Pharmaceutical Product Development
Massey Energy	UGI
Roper Industries	Respironics
Oshkosh Truck	Energen

TOP SECTORS

Consumer Discretionary
Health Care
Industrials

Inception Date:	7/24/2000
Exchange:	AMEX
Shares Outstanding:	10,100,000
Minimum Lot:	1
Options Traded:	Yes
Recent Dividends:	Yes

RECENT PRICE HISTORY

IJS iShares Small Cap 600/BARRA Value

CATEGORY   Small Cap - Value

DESCRIPTION

Tracks publicly traded U.S. small-cap stocks with the lowest price-to-book ratios within the S&P Small Cap 600 Index represented by the S&P Small Cap 600/Barra Value Index

TOP TEN HOLDINGS

Cimarex Energy	Southern Union
Standard-Pacific	New Century Financial REIT
MDC Holdings	Atmos Energy
Cooper	South Financial Group
Timken	Whitney Holding

TOP SECTORS

Financials
Industrials
Information Technology

Inception Date:	7/24/2000
Exchange:	AMEX
Shares Outstanding:	26,350,000
Minimum Lot:	1
Options Traded:	Yes
Recent Dividends:	Yes

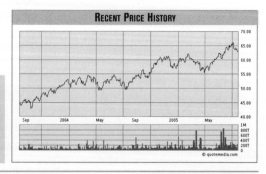

RECENT PRICE HISTORY

FXI — IShares Trust FTSE-Xinhua China 25

CATEGORY   Foreign Market

DESCRIPTION
Tracks publicly traded companies in the FTSE/Xinhua China 25 Index

TOP TEN HOLDINGS
China Mobile
PetroChina
BOC Hong Kong Holdings
CNOOC
China Petroleum and Chemical

China Life Insurance
Denway Motors
China Merchants Holdings
China Telecom
Huaneng Power International

TOP SECTORS
Resources
Non-Cyclical Services
Financials

Inception Date:	10/5/2004
Exchange:	NYSE
Shares Outstanding:	17,050,000
Minimum Lot:	1
Options Traded:	Yes
Recent Dividends:	No

BHH — Merrill Lynch B2B Internet HOLDRS

CATEGORY   Internet

DESCRIPTION
Represents ownership in a fixed basket of securities that participate in business to business (B2B), Internet companies whose products and services are developed for and marketed to companies who conduct business on the Internet

TOP TEN HOLDINGS
Checkfree
Agile Software
Pegasus Solutions
Ariba
Internet Cap Group

Verticalnet

TOP SECTORS
Internet

Inception Date:	2/24/2000
Exchange:	AMEX
Shares Outstanding:	3,500,000
Minimum Lot:	100
Options Traded:	No
Recent Dividends:	Yes

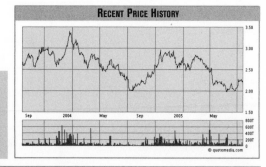

BBH — Merrill Lynch Biotech HOLDRS

CATEGORY Biotechnology

DESCRIPTION

Represents ownership in a fixed basket of securities that are involved in various segments of the Biotechnology Industry

TOP TEN HOLDINGS

Genentech	Chiron
Amgen	MedImmune
Gilead	Applied Biosystems
Biogen	Sepracore
Genzyme	Shire Pharmaceutical

TOP SECTORS

Biotechnology

Inception Date:	11/23/1999
Exchange:	AMEX
Shares Outstanding:	4,500,000
Minimum Lot:	100
Options Traded:	Yes
Recent Dividends:	No

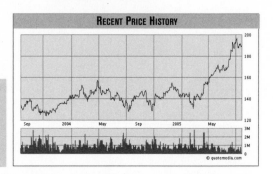

RECENT PRICE HISTORY

BDH — Merrill Lynch Broadband HOLDRS

CATEGORY Broadband

DESCRIPTION

Represents ownership in a fixed basket of securities involved in the broadband industry

TOP TEN HOLDINGS

Qualcomm	Broadcom
Motorola	Scientific-Atlanta
Corning	Comverse Technology
Nortel	Tellabs
Lucent	JDS Uniphase

TOP SECTORS

Telecom
Information Technology

Inception Date:	11/23/1999
Exchange:	AMEX
Shares Outstanding:	5,900,000
Minimum Lot:	100
Options Traded:	Yes
Recent Dividends:	No

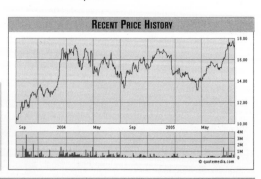

RECENT PRICE HISTORY

EKH Merrill Lynch Europe 2001 HOLDRS

CATEGORY   European Markets

DESCRIPTION

Represents ownership in a fixed basket of securities that are among the largest in Europe who are listed for trading on the NYSE, AMEX or quoted on the NASDAQ National Market

TOP TEN HOLDINGS

Total	BP
Ryanair Holdings	Scottish Power
Respol	USB
GlaxoSmithKline	Novartis
Diageo	Daimler Chrysler

TOP SECTORS

Oil & Gas
Banking
Pharmaceutical & Biotechnology

Inception Date:	1/18/2001
Exchange:	AMEX
Shares Outstanding:	1,000,000
Minimum Lot:	100
Options Traded:	Yes
Recent Dividends:	Yes

IAH Merrill Lynch Internet Architecture HOLDRS

CATEGORY   Internet

DESCRIPTION

Represents ownership in a fixed basket of securities that develop and market hardware and software designed to enhance the Internet, connections within a company's internal networks and end user access to the internet and networks

TOP TEN HOLDINGS

IBM	Apple
Dell	Sun Microsystems
Hewlett Packard	Juniper Networks
Cisco Systems	Network Appliances
EMC	Symantec

TOP SECTORS

Information Technology
Internet

Inception Date:	2/25/2000
Exchange:	AMEX
Shares Outstanding:	2,700,000
Minimum Lot:	100
Options Traded:	Yes
Recent Dividends:	Yes

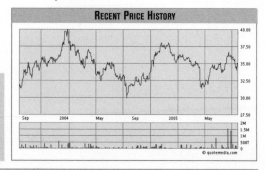

Seasonal Sector Investing: ETFs

HHH   Merrill Lynch Internet HOLDRS

CATEGORY   Internet

DESCRIPTION

Represents ownership in ownership in a fixed basket of securities that are involved in various segments of the Internet Industry

TOP TEN HOLDINGS

eBay	E Trade Financial
Yahoo!	EarthLink
Amazon.com	CNET Networks
Time Warner	Realnetworks
McAfee	Priceline.com

TOP SECTORS

Internet

Inception Date:	2/25/2000
Exchange:	AMEX
Shares Outstanding:	6,500,000
Minimum Lot:	100
Options Traded:	Yes
Recent Dividends:	Yes

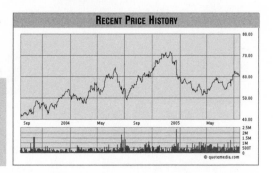

RECENT PRICE HISTORY

IIH   Merrill Lynch Internet Infrastructure HOLDRS

CATEGORY   Internet

DESCRIPTION

Represents ownership in a fixed basket of securities that provide software and technology services, which enhance Internet content and functionality, network performance and web site service and analysis to Internet companies

TOP TEN HOLDINGS

Verisign	4.00%
BEA Systems	Vignette
Akami Technologies	E Piphany
Realnetworks	Vitria Technology
Infospace	Broadvision

TOP SECTORS

Internet
Information Technology

Inception Date:	2/25/2000
Exchange:	AMEX
Shares Outstanding:	4,900,000
Minimum Lot:	100
Options Traded:	No
Recent Dividends:	No

RECENT PRICE HISTORY

MKH — Merrill Lynch Market 2000+ HOLDRS

CATEGORY   Specialty

DESCRIPTION

Represents ownership in a fixed basket of securities that were among the largest companies listed for trading on the NYSE or the AMEX or quoted on the NASDAQ National Market as of the fund inception date

TOP TEN HOLDINGS

Johnson & Johnson	Royal Dutch Petroleum
Total	Wal-Mart
Novartis	Astrazeneca
Exxon Mobil	Dell
BP	IBM

TOP SECTORS

Oil & Gas
Technology

Inception Date:	2/25/2000
Exchange:	AMEX
Shares Outstanding:	1,000,000
Minimum Lot:	100
Options Traded:	No

OIH — Merrill Lynch Market Oil Service HOLDRS

CATEGORY   Oil & Gas Services

DESCRIPTION

Represents ownership in a fixed basket of securities that among other things, provide drilling, well site management and related products and services for the oil service industry

TOP TEN HOLDINGS

Halliburton	BJ Services
Baker Hughes	Nabors Industries
Transocean	Noble
Schlumberger	Diamond Offshore Drilling
Globalsantafe	Weatherford International

TOP SECTORS

Oil Services

Inception Date:	2/26/2001
Exchange:	AMEX
Shares Outstanding:	1,200,000
Minimum Lot:	100
Options Traded:	Yes
Recent Dividends:	Yes

Seasonal Sector Investing: ETFs

PPH Merrill Lynch Pharmaceutical HOLDRS

CATEGORY   Pharmaceuticals

DESCRIPTION

Represents ownership in a fixed basket of securities that are involved in various segments of the Pharmaceutical Industry

TOP TEN HOLDINGS

Johnson & Johnson
Pfizer
Merck
Abbott Laboratories
Wyeth

Eli Lilly
Bristol-Myers Squibb
Schering-Plough
Forest Laboratories
Zimmer Holdings

TOP SECTORS

Pharmaceuticals

Inception Date:	2/1/2000
Exchange:	AMEX
Shares Outstanding:	6,812,000
Minimum Lot:	100
Options Traded:	Yes
Recent Dividends:	Yes

RKH Merrill Lynch Regional Bank HOLDRS

CATEGORY   Banking

DESCRIPTION

Represents ownership in a fixed basket of securities that are involved in various segments of the regional banking industry

TOP TEN HOLDINGS

Wachovia
US Bancorp
JPMorgan Chase
Wells Fargo
Bank of America

National City
SunTrust
Fifth Third Bancorp
PNC Financial
State Street

TOP SECTORS

Banking

Inception Date:	6/23/2000
Exchange:	AMEX
Shares Outstanding:	1,440,000
Minimum Lot:	100
Options Traded:	Yes
Recent Dividends:	Yes

ALMANAC INVESTOR

RTH — Merrill Lynch Retail HOLDRS

CATEGORY Consumer Discretionary

DESCRIPTION

Represents ownership in a fixed basket of securities that are involved in the retailing industry

TOP TEN HOLDINGS

Wal-Mart

Home Depot

Walgreen

Lowes

Target

Best Buy

CVS

The Gap

Costco

Kohls

TOP SECTORS

Consumer Discretionary

RECENT PRICE HISTORY

Inception Date:	5/17/2001
Exchange:	AMEX
Shares Outstanding:	1,000,000
Minimum Lot:	100
Options Traded:	Yes
Recent Dividends:	Yes

SMH — Merrill Lynch Semiconductor HOLDRS

CATEGORY Semiconductors

DESCRIPTION

Represents ownership in a fixed basket of securities that, develop, manufacture and market integrated circuitry and other products made from semiconductors

TOP TEN HOLDINGS

Intel

Texas Instruments

Applied Materials

Analog Devices

Maxim Integrated Products

Linear Technologies

KLA Tencor

National Semiconductor

Xilinx

Altera

TOP SECTORS

Semiconductors

RECENT PRICE HISTORY

Inception Date:	6/5/2000
Exchange:	AMEX
Shares Outstanding:	12,631,000
Minimum Lot:	100
Options Traded:	Yes
Recent Dividends:	Yes

Seasonal Sector Investing: ETFs

SWH Merrill Lynch Software HOLDRS

CATEGORY   Software

DESCRIPTION

Represents ownership in a fixed basket of securities that are involved in various segments of the software industry

TOP TEN HOLDINGS

Microsoft
SAP Aktiengesellschaft
Computer Associates International
Adobe Systems
Oracle

Intuit
Symantec
BMC Software
Check Point Software
Mercury Interactive

TOP SECTORS

Software

RECENT PRICE HISTORY

Inception Date:	9/27/2000
Exchange:	AMEX
Shares Outstanding:	1,150,000
Minimum Lot:	100
Options Traded:	Yes
Recent Dividends:	Yes

TTH Merrill Lynch Telecom HOLDRS

CATEGORY   Telecom

DESCRIPTION

Represents ownership in a fixed basket of securities that are involved in various segments of the telecommunications Industry

TOP TEN HOLDINGS

Verizon
SBC Communications
BellSouth
Sprint
Nextel

BCE
Alltel
AT&T
Qwest
Telephone and Data Systems

TOP SECTORS

Telecom

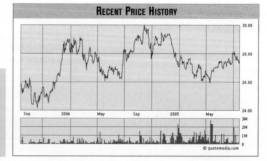

RECENT PRICE HISTORY

Inception Date:	2/1/2000
Exchange:	AMEX
Shares Outstanding:	9,900,000
Minimum Lot:	100
Options Traded:	Yes
Recent Dividends:	Yes

UTH   Merrill Lynch Utilities HOLDRS

CATEGORY   Utilities

DESCRIPTION

Represents ownership in a fixed basket of securities that are involved in various segments of the utilities industry

TOP TEN HOLDINGS

Exelon	Entergy
TXU	FPL
The Southern Company	PG&E
Duke Energy	Edison International
Dominion Resources	Public Service Enterprise Group

TOP SECTORS

Utilities

Inception Date:	6/23/2000
Exchange:	AMEX
Shares Outstanding:	1,000,000
Minimum Lot:	100
Options Traded:	Yes
Recent Dividends:	Yes

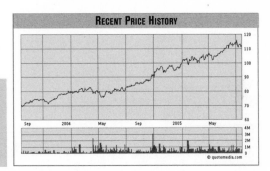

WMH   Merrill Lynch Wireless HOLDRS

CATEGORY   Telecom - Wireless

DESCRIPTION

Represents ownership in a fixed basket of securities that are involved in various segments of the Wireless industry

TOP TEN HOLDINGS

Qualcomm	Nokia
Motorola	Deutsche Telekom
Verizon	Korea Mobile Telecommunications
Vodafone	Sprint
Nextel	Research in Motion

TOP SECTORS

Telecom

Inception Date:	11/1/2000
Exchange:	AMEX
Shares Outstanding:	1,700,000
Minimum Lot:	100
Options Traded:	Yes
Recent Dividends:	Yes

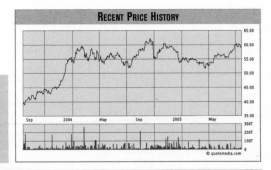

Seasonal Sector Investing: ETFs

MDY — Mid Cap SPDR

CATEGORY Mid Cap

DESCRIPTION
Tracks the Standard & Poor's Mid Cap 400 Index

TOP TEN HOLDINGS

Washington Post
DR Horton
Lennar
Harman International
Fidelity

Murphy Oil
Legg Mason
Lyondell Chemical
Weatherford International
Tyson Foods

TOP SECTORS

Consumer Discretionary
Financials
Information Technology

Inception Date:	8/18/1995
Exchange:	AMEX
Shares Outstanding:	63,523,000
Minimum Lot:	1
Options Traded:	Yes
Recent Dividends:	Yes

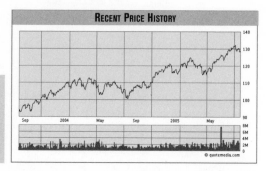

RECENT PRICE HISTORY

© quotemedia.com

QQQQ — NASDAQ 100

CATEGORY Broad Index

DESCRIPTION
Tracks the NASDAQ 100 Index

TOP TEN HOLDINGS

Microsoft
QUALCOMM
Intel
Nextel Communications
Apple Computer

Amgen
Cisco Systems
eBay
Dell
Comcast

TOP SECTORS

Information Technology
Computer Software/Services
Health Care

Inception Date:	3/10/1999
Exchange:	NASDAQ
Shares Outstanding:	492,800,000
Minimum Lot:	1
Options Traded:	Yes
Recent Dividends:	Yes

RECENT PRICE HISTORY

© quotemedia.com

PBE | PowerShares Dynamic Biotechnology & Genome

CATEGORY   Biotechnology

DESCRIPTION

Tracks the Dynamic Biotechnology & Genome Index comprised of biotech & Genome companies selected through the proprietary Intellidex methodology

TOP TEN HOLDINGS

Amgen
Applera
Biogen
Genentech
Gilead Sciences

Medimmune
Sigma-Aldrich
Waters
Affymetrix
Alexion

TOP SECTORS

Biotechnology

Inception Date:	6/23/2005
Exchange:	AMEX
Shares Outstanding:	2,801,000
Minimum Lot:	1
Options Traded:	Yes
Recent Dividends:	No

PBJ | PowerShares Dynamic Food & Beverage

CATEGORY   Specialty

DESCRIPTION

Tracks the Dynamic Food & Beverage Index comprised of food and beverage companies selected through the proprietary Intellidex methodology

TOP TEN HOLDINGS

McDonald's
Kellogg
Sara Lee
General Mills
Hershey

Kraft Foods
Sysco
ConAgra Foods
Seaboard
Domino's Pizza

TOP SECTORS

Consumer Staples
Consumer Discretionary

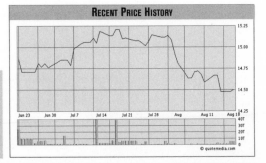

Inception Date:	6/23/2005
Exchange:	AMEX
Shares Outstanding:	1,600,000
Minimum Lot:	1
Options Traded:	Yes
Recent Dividends:	No

Seasonal Sector Investing: ETFs

PWB PowerShares Dynamic Large Cap Growth

CATEGORY Large Cap - Growth

DESCRIPTION

Tracks the Dynamic Large Cap Growth Index comprised of large-cap growth companies selected through the proprietary Intellidex methodology

TOP TEN HOLDINGS

Medtronic
Comcast
Unitedhealth Group
Disney
Intel

Lowes
Dell
Time Warner
Target
American Express

TOP SECTORS

Information Technology
Health Care
Consumer Discretionary

Inception Date:	3/3/2005
Exchange:	AMEX
Shares Outstanding:	2,000,000
Minimum Lot:	1
Options Traded:	Yes
Recent Dividends:	No

PWV PowerShares Dynamic Large Cap Value

CATEGORY Large Cap - Value

DESCRIPTION

Tracks the Dynamic Large Cap Value Index comprised of large-cap value companies selected through the proprietary Intellidex methodology

TOP TEN HOLDINGS

ConocoPhillips
Merck
Exxon Mobil
Altria
ChevronTexaco

Pfizer
Wachovia
US Bancorp
Bank of America
IBM

TOP SECTORS

Financials
Energy
Consumer Staples

Inception Date:	3/3/2005
Exchange:	AMEX
Shares Outstanding:	1,200,000
Minimum Lot:	1
Options Traded:	Yes
Recent Dividends:	Yes

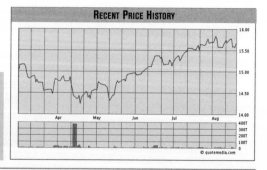

PEJ PowerShares Dynamic Leisure & Entertainment

CATEGORY   Specialty

DESCRIPTION

Tracks the Dynamic Leisure & Entertainment Index comprised of leisure & entertainment companies selected through the proprietary Intellidex methodology

TOP TEN HOLDINGS

Caesars Entertainment
Fox Entertainment
Hilton Hotels
International Gaming Technology
Marriott

McDonald's
Starwood Hotels
Yum Brands
Ameristar Casinos
Aramark

TOP TEN HOLDINGS

Consumer Discretionary

Inception Date:	6/23/2005
Exchange:	AMEX
Shares Outstanding:	1,600,000
Minimum Lot:	1
Options Traded:	Yes
Recent Dividends:	No

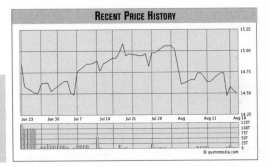

RECENT PRICE HISTORY

PWC PowerShares Dynamic Market

CATEGORY   Hybrid - Broad Markets

DESCRIPTION

Tracks the Dynamic Market Intellidex Index comprised of 100 US stocks from the NYSE, AMEX and NASDAQ having the greatest capital appreciation selected through the proprietary Intellidex methodology

TOP TEN HOLDINGS

Valero Energy
Kellogg
Altria
ConocoPhillips
Coach

Nordstrom
Federated
Cigna
CSX
Unitedhealth

TOP SECTORS

Financials
Consumer Discretionary
Information Technology

Inception Date:	5/1/2003
Exchange:	AMEX
Shares Outstanding:	10,052,000
Minimum Lot:	1
Options Traded:	Yes
Recent Dividends:	Yes

RECENT PRICE HISTORY

Seasonal Sector Investing: ETFs

PBS | PowerShares Dynamic Media

CATEGORY   Specialty

DESCRIPTION

Tracks the Dynamic Media Index comprised of media companies selected through the proprietary intellidex methodology

TOP TEN HOLDINGS

Comcast

Disney

Fox Entertainment

Liberty Media

McGraw-Hill

Omnicom

Time Warner

Washington Post

Advo

Arbitron

TOP SECTORS

Consumer Discretionary

Inception Date:	6/23/2005
Exchange:	AMEX
Shares Outstanding:	1,700,000
Minimum Lot:	1
Options Traded:	Yes
Recent Dividends:	No

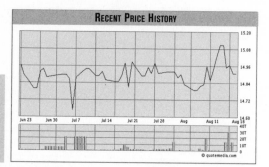

PWJ | PowerShares Dynamic Mid Cap Growth

CATEGORY   Mid Cap - Growth

DESCRIPTION

Tracks the Dynamic Mid Cap Growth Index comprised of mid-cap growth companies selected through the proprietary Intellidex methodology

TOP TEN HOLDINGS

Rockwell Automat

AES

Legg Mason

Bard

Starwood Hotels

Coach

Chicago Mercantile Exchange

T. Rowe Price

Hilton Hotels

Expeditors International

TOP SECTORS

Information Technology

Consumer Discretionary

Healthcare

Inception Date:	3/3/2005
Exchange:	AMEX
Shares Outstanding:	1,100,000
Minimum Lot:	1
Options Traded:	Yes
Recent Dividends:	No

PWP | PowerShares Dynamic Mid Cap Value

CATEGORY   Mid Cap - Value

DESCRIPTION

Tracks the Dynamic Mid Cap value Index comprised of mid-cap value companies selected through the proprietary Intellidex methodology

TOP TEN HOLDINGS

Cigna
UST
Aon
Constellation Energy
JC Penny

Fidelity Financial
Sempra Energy
Lincoln National
Eaton
Genuine Parts

TOP SECTORS

Financials
Consumer Discretionary
Materials

Inception Date:	3/3/2005
Exchange:	AMEX
Shares Outstanding:	800,000
Minimum Lot:	1
Options Traded:	Yes
Recent Dividends:	Yes

PXQ | PowerShares Dynamic Networking

CATEGORY   Networking

DESCRIPTION

Tracks the Dynamic Networking Index comprised of networking companies selected through the proprietary Intellidex methodology

TOP TEN HOLDINGS

Avaya
Cisco Systems
Juniper Networks
Lucent
Motorola

Qualcomm
Scientific-Atlanta
Symantec
ADC Telecom
Altiris

TOP SECTORS

Information Technology

Inception Date:	6/23/2005
Exchange:	AMEX
Shares Outstanding:	1,600,000
Minimum Lot:	1
Options Traded:	Yes
Recent Dividends:	No

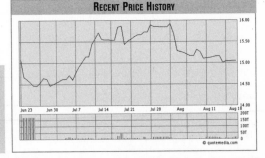

Seasonal Sector Investing: ETFs

PWO PowerShares Dynamic OTC

CATEGORY   Broad Index

DESCRIPTION
Tracks the Dynamic OTC Intellidex index which is comprised of 100 US stocks from the NASDAQ having the greatest capital appreciation selected through the proprietary Intellidex methodology

TOP TEN HOLDINGS

Intuit
American
BEA Systems
Fiserv
NVIDIA

Linear Technology
Microsoft
Intel
Qlogic
Autodesk

TOP SECTORS

Information Technology
Consumer Discretionary
Health Care

Inception Date:	5/1/2003
Exchange:	AMEX
Shares Outstanding:	2,801,000
Minimum Lot:	1
Options Traded:	No
Recent Dividends:	No

RECENT PRICE HISTORY

PJP PowerShares Dynamic Pharmaceuticals

CATEGORY   Pharmaceuticals

DESCRIPTION
Tracks the Dynamic Pharmaceutical Index comprised of pharmaceutical companies selected through the proprietary Intellidex methodology

TOP TEN HOLDINGS

Abbott Laboratories
Amgen
Bristol-Myers Squibb
Genetech
Johnson & Johnson

Merck
Pfizer
Wyeth
Allergan
American Pharmaceutical

TOP SECTORS

Pharmaceuticals

Inception Date:	6/23/2005
Exchange:	AMEX
Shares Outstanding:	1,700,000
Minimum Lot:	1
Options Traded:	Yes
Recent Dividends:	No

RECENT PRICE HISTORY

PSI — PowerShares Dynamic Semiconductors

CATEGORY   Semiconductors

DESCRIPTION

Tracks the Dynamic Semiconductor Index comprised of semiconductor companies selected through the proprietary Intellidex methodology

TOP TEN HOLDINGS

Altera
Applied Materials
Intel
KLA Tencor
Linear Technology

National Semiconductor
Qualcomm
Texas Instruments
Cymer
DSP Group

TOP SECTORS

Semiconductors

Inception Date:	6/23/2005
Exchange:	AMEX
Shares Outstanding:	3,700,000
Minimum Lot:	1
Options Traded:	Yes
Recent Dividends:	No

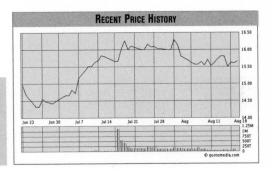

RECENT PRICE HISTORY

© quotemedia.com

PWT — PowerShares Dynamic Small Cap Growth

CATEGORY   Small Cap - Growth

DESCRIPTION

Tracks the Dynamic Small Cap Growth Index comprised of small-cap growth companies selected through the proprietary Intellidex methodology

TOP TEN HOLDINGS

Guitar Center
Cal Dive International
Trimble Navigation
Hyperion Solutions
bebe stores

Navigant Consulting
Kronos
SCP Pool
Simpson Manufacturing
Parametric Tech

TOP SECTORS

Information Technology
Health Care
Industrials

Inception Date:	3/3/2005
Exchange:	AMEX
Shares Outstanding:	3,700,000
Minimum Lot:	1
Options Traded:	Yes
Recent Dividends:	No

RECENT PRICE HISTORY

© quotemedia.com

PWY PowerShares Dynamic Small Cap Value

CATEGORY   Small Cap - Value

DESCRIPTION
Tracks the Dynamic Small Cap Value Index comprised of small-cap value companies selected through the proprietary Intellidex methodology

TOP TEN HOLDINGS

Beazer Homes
Denbury Resources
Toro
Pediatrix Medical Group
Ohio Casualty

Sybase
Apria Healthcare
Alexander & Baldwin
Eagle Materials
Sybron Dental

TOP SECTORS

Financials
Consumer Discretionary
Industrials

Inception Date:	3/3/2005
Exchange:	AMEX
Shares Outstanding:	1,300,000
Minimum Lot:	1
Options Traded:	Yes
Recent Dividends:	Yes

PSJ PowerShares Dynamic Software

CATEGORY   Software

DESCRIPTION
Tracks the Dynamic Software Index comprised of software companies selected through the proprietary Intellidex methodology

TOP TEN HOLDINGS

Adobe Systems
Autodesk
Intuit
MacAfee
Microsoft

Oracle
SEI Investments
Symantec
Activision
Ansys

TOP SECTORS

Software

Inception Date:	6/23/2005
Exchange:	AMEX
Shares Outstanding:	1,900,000
Minimum Lot:	1
Options Traded:	Yes
Recent Dividends:	No

PGJ PowerShares Golden Dragon Halter USX China

CATEGORY   Foreign Market

DESCRIPTION
Tracks the Halter USX China Index comprised of U.S. listed companies which derive most of their revenue from China

TOP TEN HOLDINGS
PetroChina
China Mobile
CNOOC
Sinopec Shanghai
Yanzhou

Shanda International
Aluminum Corp
Huaneng Power
China Petro
China Life Insurance

TOP SECTORS
Information Technology
Telecom
Energy

Inception Date:	12/9/2004
Exchange:	AMEX
Shares Outstanding:	4,600,000
Minimum Lot:	1
Options Traded:	Yes
Recent Dividends:	Yes

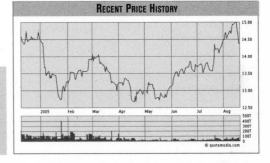

RECENT PRICE HISTORY

PEY PowerShares High Yield Equity Dividend Achievers

CATEGORY   Dividend

DESCRIPTION
Tracks the Mergent Dividend Achievers 50 Index comprised of the 50 highest yielding companies with at least 10 years of consecutive dividend increases

TOP TEN HOLDINGS
Progress Energy
Consolidated Edison
Nicor
Peoples Energy
SBC Communications

First Commonwealth
FNB
Otter Tail
Atmos Energy
Vectren

TOP SECTORS
Financials
Utilities

Inception Date:	12/9/2004
Exchange:	AMEX
Shares Outstanding:	29,200,000
Minimum Lot:	1
Options Traded:	Yes
Recent Dividends:	Yes

RECENT PRICE HISTORY

PBW | PowerShares WilderHill Clean Energy

CATEGORY   Specialty

DESCRIPTION

Tracks the WilderHill Clean Energy Index comprised of companies that focus on alternative energy, renewable sources of energy and cleaner energy

TOP TEN HOLDINGS

Magnetek
Maxwell Tech
Ormat Tech
Ultralife Batteries
Intermagnetics

UGM Technologies
Impco Technologies
Evergreen Solar
Cypress Semiconductor
Kyocera

TOP SECTORS

xIndustrials
Information Technology

Inception Date:	3/4/2005
Exchange:	AMEX
Shares Outstanding:	3,600,000
Minimum Lot:	1
Options Traded:	Yes
Recent Dividends:	No

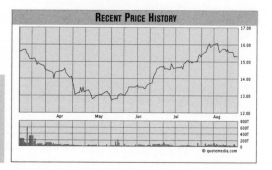

XLG | Rydex Russell Top 50

CATEGORY   Large Cap

DESCRIPTION

Tracks the Russell Top 50 Index made up of the 50 largest stocks in the Russell 3000

TOP TEN HOLDINGS

Exxon Mobil
General Electric
Microsoft
Citigroup
Pfizer

Johnson & Johnson
Bank of America
Intel
Procter & Gamble
Altria

TOP SECTORS

Financials
Information Technology
Health Care

Inception Date:	5/10/2005
Exchange:	AMEX
Shares Outstanding:	1,200,000
Minimum Lot:	1
Options Traded:	Yes
Recent Dividends:	Yes

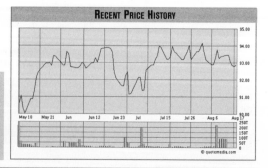

RSP — Rydex S&P Equal Weight ETF

CATEGORY Broad Index

DESCRIPTION

Tracks the S&P Equal Weight Index Rydex which equally balances all stocks in the S&P 500

TOP TEN HOLDINGS

N/A

TOP SECTORS

Consumer Discretionary
Financials
Information Technology

Inception Date:	4/28/2003
Exchange:	AMEX
Shares Outstanding:	6,401,000
Minimum Lot:	1
Options Traded:	No
Recent Dividends:	Yes

RECENT PRICE HISTORY
© quotemedia.com

XLY — Select Sector SPDR Consumer Discretionary

CATEGORY Consumer Discretionary

DESCRIPTION

Consists of all of the consumer discretionary stocks that trade on the S&P 500

TOP TEN HOLDINGS

Home Depot
Time Warner
Comcast
Viacom
Walt Disney

eBay
Lowe's
Target
The News Corporation
McDonald's

TOP SECTORS

Media
Retail
Hotels, Restaurant & Leisure

Inception Date:	12/22/1998
Exchange:	AMEX
Shares Outstanding:	12,001,000
Minimum Lot:	1
Options Traded:	Yes
Recent Dividends:	Yes

RECENT PRICE HISTORY
© quotemedia.com

XLP Select Sector SPDR Consumer Staples

CATEGORY   Consumer Staples

DESCRIPTION

Consists of all the consumer staples stocks that trade on the S&P 500

TOP TEN HOLDINGS

Wal-Mart
Altria
Procter & Gamble
Coca-Cola
Gillette

PepsiCo
Walgreen
Anheuser-Busch
Kimberly-Clark
Colgate-Palmolive

TOP SECTORS

Retail
Beverages
Household Products

Inception Date:	12/22/1998
Exchange:	AMEX
Shares Outstanding:	32,102,000
Minimum Lot:	1
Options Traded:	Yes
Recent Dividends:	Yes

XLE Select Sector SPDR Energy Select Sector

CATEGORY   Energy

DESCRIPTION

Consists of all the energy stocks that trade on the S&P 500

TOP TEN HOLDINGS

Exxon Mobil
Chevron
ConocoPhillips
Occidental Petroleum
Halliburton

Devon Energy
Burlington Resources
Schlumberger
Marathon Oil
EOG Resources

TOP SECTORS

Oil & Gas
Energy

Inception Date:	12/22/1998
Exchange:	AMEX
Shares Outstanding:	59,955,000
Minimum Lot:	1
Options Traded:	Yes
Recent Dividends:	Yes

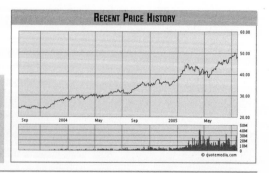

ALMANAC INVESTOR

XLF Select Sector SPDR Financial

CATEGORY   Financial

DESCRIPTION

Consists of all the financial stocks that trade on the S&P 500

TOP TEN HOLDINGS

Citigroup	Wachovia
Bank of America	American Express
American International Group	Morgan Stanley
JPMorgan Chase	Merrill Lynch
Wells Fargo	U.S. Bancorp

TOP SECTORS

Financials
Banking
Insurance

Inception Date:	12/22/1998
Exchange:	AMEX
Shares Outstanding:	41,160,000
Minimum Lot:	1
Options Traded:	Yes
Recent Dividends:	Yes

XLV Select Sector SPDR Healthcare

CATEGORY   Healthcare

DESCRIPTION

Consists of all of the health care stocks that trade on the S&P 500

TOP TEN HOLDINGS

Pfizer	Medtronic
Johnson & Johnson	Abbott Laboratories
Amgen	Eli Lilly
Merck	Wyeth
UnitedHealth Group	Bristol-Myers Squibb

TOP SECTORS

Pharmaceuticals
Healthcare Products
Healthcare Providers

Inception Date:	12/22/1998
Exchange:	AMEX
Shares Outstanding:	55,752,000
Minimum Lot:	1
Options Traded:	Yes
Recent Dividends:	Yes

XLI   Select Sector SPDR Industrial

CATEGORY   Industrials

DESCRIPTION
Consists of all of the industrial stocks that trade in the S&P 500

TOP TEN HOLDINGS

General Electric
United Parcel Service
Tyco International
Boeing
3M

United Technologies
Caterpillar
Honeywell International
Emerson Electric
FedEx

TOP SECTORS

Industrials
Aerospace
Machinery

Inception Date:	12/22/1998
Exchange:	AMEX
Shares Outstanding:	26,752,000
Minimum Lot:	1
Options Traded:	Yes
Recent Dividends:	Yes

RECENT PRICE HISTORY

XLB   Select Sector SPDR Materials

CATEGORY   Materials

DESCRIPTION
Consists of all of the basic material stocks that trade on the S&P 500

TOP TEN HOLDINGS

Dow Chemical
du Pont
Alcoa
Monsanto
Praxair

Weyerhaeuser
International Paper
Newmont Mining
Air Products & Chemicals
PPG Industries

TOP SECTORS

Chemicals
Metals & Mining
Paper & Forest

Inception Date:	12/22/1998
Exchange:	AMEX
Shares Outstanding:	26,858,000
Minimum Lot:	1
Options Traded:	Yes
Recent Dividends:	Yes

RECENT PRICE HISTORY

XLK Select Sector SPDR Technology

CATEGORY Technology

DESCRIPTION

Consists of all of the technology stocks that trade in the S&P 500

TOP TEN HOLDINGS

Microsoft	Verizon
Intel	Hewlett-Packard
IBM	Qualcomm
Cisco Systems	SBC Communications
Dell	Oracle

TOP SECTORS

Computers & Peripherals
Software
Semiconductors

Inception Date:	12/22/1998
Exchange:	AMEX
Shares Outstanding:	62,253,000
Minimum Lot:	1
Options Traded:	Yes
Recent Dividends:	Yes

RECENT PRICE HISTORY

XLU Select Sector SPDR Utilities

CATEGORY Utilities

DESCRIPTION

Consists of all of the utility stocks that trade in the S&P 500

TOP TEN HOLDINGS

Exelon	FirstEnergy
Duke Energy	FPL Group
Dominion Resources	Entergy
Southern	Public Service Enterprise Group
TXU	American Electric Power Co. Inc.

TOP SECTORS

Utilities

Inception Date:	12/22/1998
Exchange:	AMEX
Shares Outstanding:	57,875,000
Minimum Lot:	1
Options Traded:	Yes
Recent Dividends:	Yes

RECENT PRICE HISTORY

OOO | SPDR O-Strip

CATEGORY Hybrid - Broad Market

DESCRIPTION

Tracks the S&P 500 O-Strip Index which includes all of the S&P 500 stocks that are also listed on NASDAQ

TOP TEN HOLDINGS

Microsoft
Intel
Cisco Systems
Amgen
Dell

Comcast
Qualcomm
Oracle
EBay
Yahoo

TOP SECTORS

Information Technology
Consumer Discretionary
Health Care

Inception Date:	9/9/2004
Exchange:	AMEX
Shares Outstanding:	1,000,000
Minimum Lot:	1
Options Traded:	Yes
Recent Dividends:	Yes

RECENT PRICE HISTORY

SPY | SPDR S&P 500

CATEGORY Broad Index

DESCRIPTION

Tracks the S&P 500

TOP TEN HOLDINGS

General Electric
Exxon Mobil
Microsoft
Citigroup
Wal-Mart

Pfizer
Bank of America
Johnson & Johnson
American International Group
IBM

TOP SECTORS

Financials
Information Technology
Health Care

Inception Date:	1/29/1993
Exchange:	AMEX
Shares Outstanding:	402,054,000
Minimum Lot:	1
Options Traded:	Yes
Recent Dividends:	Yes

RECENT PRICE HISTORY

FEZ · streetTRACKS DJ EURO STOXX 50

CATEGORY European Markets

DESCRIPTION

Tracks the Dow Jones EURO STOXX 50 Index of the market sector leaders in the represented countries of the Eurozone which are countries that have adopted the Euro as its currency

TOP TEN HOLDINGS

Total	Nokia
Sanofi-Aventis	E.On
Banco Sant Cent Hisp	Siemens
Eni	Bnp Paribas
Telefonica	Ing Groep

TOP SECTORS

Financials
Energy
Telecom

Inception Date:	10/15/2002
Exchange:	NYSE
Shares Outstanding:	4,350,032
Minimum Lot:	1
Options Traded:	No
Recent Dividends:	Yes

RECENT PRICE HISTORY

© quotemedia.com

FEU · streetTRACKS DJ STOXX 50

CATEGORY European Markets

DESCRIPTION

Tracks the Dow Jones STOXX 50 Index of the market sector leaders in Europe

TOP TEN HOLDINGS

BP	GlaxoSmithKline
HSBC Holdings	Novartis
Vodafone	Nestle
Total	Roche Holdings
Royal Dutch Shell	Royal Bank of Scotland

TOP SECTORS

Financials
Energy
Healthcare

Inception Date:	10/15/2002
Exchange:	NYSE
Shares Outstanding:	800,019
Minimum Lot:	1
Options Traded:	No
Recent Dividends:	Yes

RECENT PRICE HISTORY

© quotemedia.com

DGT   streetTRACKS Dow Jones Global Titans

CATEGORY   Global Developed Markets

DESCRIPTION

Tracks the Dow Jones Global Titans Index of multinational corporations

TOP TEN HOLDINGS

Exxon Mobil
General Electric
Microsoft
BP
Citigroup

Pfizer
Johnson & Johnson
HSBD Holdings
Bank Of America
Intel

TOP SECTORS

Financials
Health Care
Energy

Inception Date:	9/25/2000
Exchange:	AMEX
Shares Outstanding:	1,650,144
Minimum Lot:	1
Options Traded:	Yes
Recent Dividends:	Yes

ELG   streetTRACKS Dow Jones U.S. Large Cap Growth

CATEGORY   Large Cap - Growth

DESCRIPTION

Tracks the Dow Jones US Large Cap Growth Index

TOP TEN HOLDINGS

Microsoft
Johnson & Johnson
Intel
American International Group
IBM

Procter & Gamble
Wal Mart
Cisco Systems
Amgen
Coca Cola

TOP SECTORS

Information Technology
Consumer Discretionary
Health Care

Inception Date:	9/25/2000
Exchange:	AMEX
Shares Outstanding:	2,400,110
Minimum Lot:	1
Options Traded:	No
Recent Dividends:	Yes

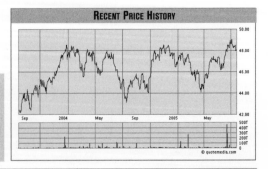

ELV streetTRACKS Dow Jones U.S. Large Cap Value

CATEGORY Large Cap - Value

DESCRIPTION

Tracks the Dow Jones Large Cap Value Index

TOP TEN HOLDINGS

Exxon Mobil
General Electric
Citigroup
Pfizer
Bank Of America

Altria
JPMorgan Chase
Chevron
Wells Fargo
Verizon

TOP SECTORS

Financials
Energy
Industrials

Inception Date:	9/25/2000
Exchange:	AMEX
Shares Outstanding:	750,102
Minimum Lot:	1
Options Traded:	No
Recent Dividends:	Yes

RECENT PRICE HISTORY

DSG streetTRACKS Dow Jones U.S. Small Cap Growth

CATEGORY Small Cap - Growth

DESCRIPTION

Tracks the Dow Jones US Small Cap Growth Index

TOP TEN HOLDINGS

Southwestern Energy
Arch Coal
Ryland Group
Jacobs Energy Group
O Reilly Automotive

Corporate Executive Brand
Roper Industrials
Renal Care Group
Dade Behring Holdings
Federal Realty

TOP SECTORS

Consumer Discretionary
Health Care
Industrials

Inception Date:	9/25/2000
Exchange:	AMEX
Shares Outstanding:	700,100
Minimum Lot:	1
Options Traded:	No
Recent Dividends:	Yes

RECENT PRICE HISTORY

Seasonal Sector Investing: ETFs

DSV   streetTRACKS Dow Jones U.S. Small Cap Value

CATEGORY   Small Cap - Value

DESCRIPTION

Tracks the Dow Jones US Small Cap Value Index

TOP TEN HOLDINGS

Chemtura	Aqua America
Tesoro	Western Digital
Massey Energy	Ventas
CMS Energy	Catellus
Goodyear Tire & Rubber	UGI

TOP SECTORS

Financials
Information Technology
Consumer Discretionary

Inception Date:	9/25/2000
Exchange:	AMEX
Shares Outstanding:	500,197
Minimum Lot:	1
Options Traded:	No
Recent Dividends:	Yes

GLD   streetTRACKS Gold Shares

CATEGORY   Gold

DESCRIPTION

The price of the ETF corresponds to 1/10 of the price of gold

TOP TEN HOLDINGS

Gold Bullion

TOP SECTORS

Gold

Inception Date:	11/18/2004
Exchange:	NYSE
Shares Outstanding:	61,700,000
Minimum Lot:	1
Options Traded:	No
Recent Dividends:	No

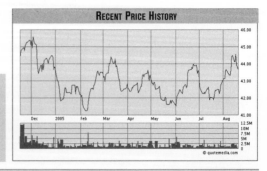

MTK   streetTRACKS Morgan Stanley Technology

CATEGORY   Technology

DESCRIPTION
Tracks the Morgan Stanley Technology Index

TOP TEN HOLDINGS

Google
Broadcom
Texas Instruments
Motorola
Intel

Hewlett Packard
Amazon
Seagate Technology
NVIDIA
Intuit

TOP SECTORS

Information Technology

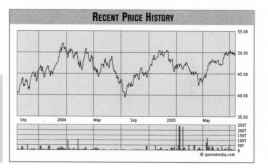

Inception Date:	9/25/2000
Exchange:	AMEX
Shares Outstanding:	850,102
Minimum Lot:	1
Options Traded:	No
Recent Dividends:	Yes

TMW   streetTRACKS Total Market

CATEGORY   Broad Index - Total Market

DESCRIPTION
Tracks the Dow Jones Wilshire 5000 Index

TOP TEN HOLDINGS

Exxon Mobil
General Electric
Microsoft
Citigroup
Pfizer

Johnson & Johnson
Intel
Bank Of America
American International Group
IBM

TOP SECTORS

Financials
Information Technology
Consumer Discretionary

Inception Date:	10/4/2000
Exchange:	AMEX
Shares Outstanding:	1,250,111
Minimum Lot:	1
Options Traded:	Yes
Recent Dividends:	Yes

Seasonal Sector Investing: ETFs

RWR | streetTRACKS Wilshire REIT

CATEGORY   Real Estate

DESCRIPTION

Tracks the Dow Jones Wilshire REIT Index

TOP TEN HOLDINGS

Simon Property Group
Equity Office Properties
Equity Residential
Vornado Reality
General Growth Properties

Boston Properties
Archstone Smith
Prologis
Kimco Realty
Host Marriott

TOP SECTORS

Real Estate

Inception Date:	4/23/2001
Exchange:	AMEX
Shares Outstanding:	3,901,586
Minimum Lot:	1
Options Traded:	No
Recent Dividends:	Yes

RECENT PRICE HISTORY

VCR | Vanguard Consumer Discretionary VIPERs

CATEGORY   Consumer Discretionary

DESCRIPTION

Tracks the MSCI U.S. Investable Market Consumer Discretionary Index

TOP TEN HOLDINGS

Home Depot
Time Warner
Comcast
Disney
Viacom

Target
Lowe's
McDonald's
eBay
The News Corporation

TOP SECTORS

Consumer Discretionary

Inception Date:	1/26/2004
Exchange:	AMEX
Shares Outstanding:	500,000
Minimum Lot:	1
Options Traded:	No
Recent Dividends:	Yes

RECENT PRICE HISTORY

VDC | Vanguard Consumer Staples VIPERs

CATEGORY   Consumer Staples

DESCRIPTION

Tracks the MSCI U.S. Investable Market Consumer Staples Index

TOP TEN HOLDINGS

xxxxxAltria	Gillette
Procter & Gamble	Walgreen
Wal-Mart	Anheuser-Busch
Coca-Cola	Kimberly-Clark
PepsiCo	Colgate-Palmolive

TOP SECTORS

Consumer Staples
Consumer Discretionary

Inception Date:	1/26/2004
Exchange:	AMEX
Shares Outstanding:	1,300,000
Minimum Lot:	1
Options Traded:	No
Recent Dividends:	Yes

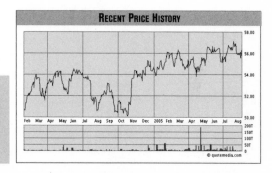

RECENT PRICE HISTORY

VWO | Vanguard Emerging Markets VIPERs

CATEGORY   Global Emerging Markets

DESCRIPTION

Tracks the Vanguard Emerging Markets Stock Index Fund which is made up of approximately 600 common stocks of companies located in emerging markets around the world

TOP TEN HOLDINGS

Samsung	Sasol
Taiwan Semiconductor	America Movil
Teva Pharmaceutical	Petroleo Brasileiro
China Mobile	Hon Hai Precision
Petroleo Brasileiro	Kookmin Bank

TOP SECTORS

Financials
Information Technology
Materials

Inception Date:	3/4/2005
Exchange:	AMEX
Shares Outstanding:	4,090,000
Minimum Lot:	1
Options Traded:	No

RECENT PRICE HISTORY

VDE   Vanguard Energy VIPERs

CATEGORY   Energy

DESCRIPTION

Tracks the MSCI U.S. Investable Market Energy Index

TOP TEN HOLDINGS

Exxon Mobil	Halliburton
Chevron	Devon Energy
ConocoPhillips	Burlington Resources
Schlumberger	Apache
Occidental Petroleum	Anadarko Petroleum

TOP SECTORS

Oil Production
Energy

Inception Date:	9/23/2004
Exchange:	AMEX
Shares Outstanding:	2,300,000
Minimum Lot:	1
Options Traded:	No
Recent Dividends:	Yes

VGK   Vanguard European VIPERs

CATEGORY   European Markets

DESCRIPTION

Tracks the MSCI Europe Index which is made up of approximately 560 stocks in 16 European countries

TOP TEN HOLDINGS

BP	Total
HSBC Holdings	Novartis
Vodafone	Nestle
GlaxoSmithKline	Royal Bank of Scotland
Royal Dutch Petroleum	Shell

TOP SECTORS

Financials

Inception Date:	3/4/2005
Exchange:	AMEX
Shares Outstanding:	2,745,000
Minimum Lot:	1
Options Traded:	No
Recent Dividends:	No

VXF | Vanguard Extended Market VIPERs

CATEGORY   Hybrid - Mid & Small Cap

DESCRIPTION

Tracks the Wilshire 4500 Equity Index made up primarily of mid and small cap U.S. stocks.

TOP TEN HOLDINGS

Berkshire Hathaway	Accenture
Google	Liberty Global
Genentech	Juniper Networks
Liberty Media	Legg Mason
Genworth Financial	MGM Mirage

TOP SECTORS

Financial Services
Consumer Discretionary
Health Care

Inception Date:	12/27/2001
Exchange:	AMEX
Shares Outstanding:	3,372,000
Minimum Lot:	1
Options Traded:	Yes
Recent Dividends:	Yes

VFH | Vanguard Financials VIPERs

CATEGORY   Financial

DESCRIPTION

Tracks the performance of the MSCI US Investable Market Financials Index

TOP TEN HOLDINGS

Citigroup	Wachovia
Bank of America	American Express
American International Group	Fannie Mae
JPMorgan Chase	U.S. Bancorp
Wells Fargo	Morgan Stanley

TOP SECTORS

Financial Services

Inception Date:	1/26/2001
Exchange:	AMEX
Shares Outstanding:	800,000
Minimum Lot:	1
Options Traded:	No
Recent Dividends:	Yes

Seasonal Sector Investing: ETFs

VUG Vanguard Growth VIPERs

CATEGORY   Large Cap - Growth

DESCRIPTION

Tracks the MSCI US Prime Market Growth Index, made up of large-cap US traded growth stocks

TOP TEN HOLDINGS

Microsoft
Johnson & Johnson
General Electric Co
Intel
Procter & Gamble

Cisco Systems
Wal-Mart
IBM
PepsiCo
Dell

TOP SECTORS

Technology
Consumer Discretionary
Health Care

Inception Date:	1/26/2004
Exchange:	AMEX
Shares Outstanding:	3,433,000
Minimum Lot:	1
Options Traded:	Yes
Recent Dividends:	Yes

VHT Vanguard Health Care VIPERs

CATEGORY   Healthcare

DESCRIPTION

Tracks MSCI US Investable Market Health Care Index

TOP TEN HOLDINGS

Pfizer
Johnson & Johnson
Amgen
Abbott Laboratories
Merck

UnitedHealth Group
Medtronic
Wyeth
Eli Lilly
Bristol-Myers Squibb

TOP SECTORS

Health Care

Inception Date:	1/26/2004
Exchange:	AMEX
Shares Outstanding:	3,700,000
Minimum Lot:	1
Options Traded:	No
Recent Dividends:	Yes

VIS   Vanguard Industrials VIPERs

CATEGORY   Industrials

DESCRIPTION

Tracks the MSCI US Investable Market Industrials Index made up of U.S. companies in the industrials sector

TOP TEN HOLDINGS

General Electric
Tyco International
3M
United Technologies
Boeing

United Parcel Service
Caterpillar
Honeywell International
Emerson Electric
Lockheed Martin

TOP SECTORS

Industrials

Inception Date:	9/23/2004
Exchange:	AMEX
Shares Outstanding:	300,000
Minimum Lot:	1
Options Traded:	No
Recent Dividends:	Yes

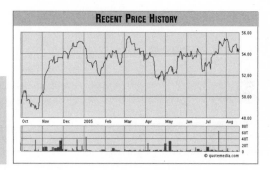

VGT   Vanguard Information Technology VIPERs

CATEGORY   Technology

DESCRIPTION

Tracks MSCI US Investable Market Information Technology Index

TOP TEN HOLDINGS

Microsoft
Intel
Cisco Systems
IBM
Dell

Hewlett-Packard
QUALCOMM
Oracle
Texas Instruments
Google

TOP SECTORS

Technology

Inception Date:	1/26/2004
Exchange:	AMEX
Shares Outstanding:	900,000
Minimum Lot:	1
Options Traded:	No
Recent Dividends:	Yes

Seasonal Sector Investing: ETFs

VV   Vanguard Large Cap VIPERs

CATEGORY   Large Cap

DESCRIPTION

Tracks the MSCI US Prime Market 750 Index U.S. an index of broadly diversified predominantly large-cap companies

TOP TEN HOLDINGS

Exxon Mobil
General Electric
Microsoft
Citigroup
Pfizer

Johnson & Johnson
Bank of America
Intel
Altria
American International Group

TOP SECTORS

Financial Services
Consumer Discretionary
Health Care

Inception Date:	1/27/2004
Exchange:	AMEX
Shares Outstanding:	2,803,000
Minimum Lot:	1
Options Traded:	No
Recent Dividends:	Yes

VAW   Vanguard Materials VIPERs

CATEGORY   Materials

DESCRIPTION

Tracks the MSCI US Investable Market Materials Index

TOP TEN HOLDINGS

du Pont
Dow Chemical
Alcoa
Newmont Mining
Monsanto

Weyerhaeuser
Praxair
International Paper
Air Products & Chemicals
PPG Industries

TOP SECTORS

Materials and Processing

Inception Date:	1/26/2004
Exchange:	AMEX
Shares Outstanding:	1,000,000
Minimum Lot:	1
Options Traded:	No
Recent Dividends:	Yes

VO Vanguard Mid Cap VIPERs

CATEGORY   Mid Cap

DESCRIPTION

Tracks the MSCI US Mid Cap 450 Index, an index of broadly diversified medium-sized U.S. stocks

TOP TEN HOLDINGS

EOG Resources
Coach
Starwood Hotels & Resorts Worldwide
PPL
XTO Energy

Liberty Global
D. R. Horton
Williams
Legg Mason
Constellation Energy Group

TOP SECTORS

Financial Services
Consumer Discretionary
Technology

Inception Date:	1/26/2004
Exchange:	AMEX
Shares Outstanding:	11,822,000
Minimum Lot:	1
Options Traded:	No
Recent Dividends:	Yes

VPL Vanguard Pacific VIPERs

CATEGORY   Pacific Markets

DESCRIPTION

Tracks the MSCI Pacific Index which consists of approximately 500 common stocks of companies located in Japan, Australia, Hong Kong, Singapore, and New Zealand

TOP TEN HOLDINGS

Toyota
BHP Billiton
Takeda Chemical Industries
Mitsubishi Tokyo Financial Group
Canon

Honda
Mizuho Financial Group
Commonwealth Bank of Australia
National Australia Bank
Sony

TOP SECTORS

Financials
Consumer Discretionary
Indusrtials

Inception Date:	3/4/2005
Exchange:	AMEX
Shares Outstanding:	1,880,000
Minimum Lot:	1
Options Traded:	No
Recent Dividends:	No

VNQ — Vanguard REIT VIPERs

CATEGORY   Real Estate

DESCRIPTION

Tracks the MSCI US REIT Index comprised of real estate investment trusts

TOP TEN HOLDINGS

Simon Property Group REIT
Equity Office Properties Trust REIT
Equity Residential REIT
Vornado Realty Trust REIT
General Growth Properties REIT

Archstone-Smith Trust REIT
Boston Properties REIT
ProLogis REIT
Avalonbay Communities REIT
Host Marriott REIT

TOP SECTORS

Real Estate

Inception Date:	9/23/2004
Exchange:	AMEX
Shares Outstanding:	5,737,000
Minimum Lot:	1
Options Traded:	No
Recent Dividends:	Yes

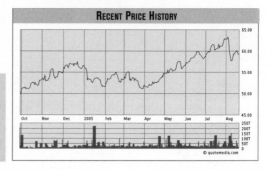

RECENT PRICE HISTORY

VB — Vanguard Small Cap VIPERs

CATEGORY   Small Cap

DESCRIPTION

Tracks the MSCI US Small Cap 1750 Index of diversified small-cap stocks

TOP TEN HOLDINGS

NII Holdings
AmeriCredit
Western Wireless
Reliant Energy
SpectraSite

Ryland Group
American Capital Strategies
Allegheny Energy
Southwestern Energy
Arch Coal

TOP SECTORS

Financial Services
Consumer Discretionary
Health Care

Inception Date:	1/26/2004
Exchange:	AMEX
Shares Outstanding:	3,324,000
Minimum Lot:	1
Options Traded:	No
Recent Dividends:	Yes

RECENT PRICE HISTORY

VBK | Vanguard Small Cap Growth VIPERs

CATEGORY Small Cap - Growth

DESCRIPTION
Tracks the MSCI US Small Cap Growth Index of diversified small-cap US growth stocks

TOP TEN HOLDINGS

NII Holdings
Western Wireless
SpectraSite
Southwestern Energy
Catellus Development

Affymetrix
Grant Prideco
O'Reilly Automotive
Renal Care Group
Activision

TOP SECTORS

Consumer Discretionary
Health Care
Technology

Inception Date:	1/26/2004
Exchange:	AMEX
Shares Outstanding:	1,818,000
Minimum Lot:	1
Options Traded:	No
Recent Dividends:	Yes

VBR | Vanguard Small Cap Value VIPERs

CATEGORY Small Cap - Value

DESCRIPTION
Tracks the MSCI US Small Cap Value Index of diversified small-cap value stocks

TOP TEN HOLDINGS

AmeriCredit
Reliant Energy
American Capital Strategies
Arch Coal
Mills REIT

Conseco
United Dominion Realty Trust REIT
Martin Marietta Materials
CMS Energy
ONEOK

TOP SECTORS

Financial Services
Consumer Discretionary
Materials & Processing

Inception Date:	1/26/2004
Exchange:	AMEX
Shares Outstanding:	1,823,000
Minimum Lot:	1
Options Traded:	No
Recent Dividends:	Yes

Seasonal Sector Investing: ETFs

VOX | Vanguard Telecommunication Services VIPERs

CATEGORY Telecom

DESCRIPTION

Tracks the MSCI US Investable Market Telecommunication Services Index

TOP TEN HOLDINGS

Verizon
SBC Communications
BellSouth
ALLTEL
Sprint

Nextel
AT&T
MCI
Qwest Communications
American Tower

TOP SECTORS

Telecom

RECENT PRICE HISTORY

Inception Date:	9/23/2004
Exchange:	AMEX
Shares Outstanding:	300,000
Minimum Lot:	1
Options Traded:	No
Recent Dividends:	Yes

VTI | Vanguard Total Stock Market VIPERs

CATEGORY Broad Index - Total Market

DESCRIPTION

Tracks the MSCI US Broad Market Index made up of all regularly traded U.S. common stocks

TOP TEN HOLDINGS

Exxon Mobil
General Electric
Microsoft
Citigroup
Pfizer

Johnson & Johnson
Bank of America
Intel
Altria
American International Group

TOP SECTORS

Financial Services
Consumer Discretionary
Health Care

RECENT PRICE HISTORY

Inception Date:	5/24/2001
Exchange:	AMEX
Shares Outstanding:	40,257,000
Minimum Lot:	1
Options Traded:	Yes
Recent Dividends:	Yes

318

VPU   Vanguard Utilities VIPERs

CATEGORY   Utilities

DESCRIPTION

Tracks the MSCI US Investable Market Utilities Index

TOP TEN HOLDINGS

Exelon
Duke Energy
Southern
Dominion Resources
TXU

Entergy
FirstEnergy
FPL
American Electric Power
Public Service Enterprise Group

TOP SECTORS

Utilities

Inception Date:	1/26/2004
Exchange:	AMEX
Shares Outstanding:	1,300,000
Minimum Lot:	1
Options Traded:	No
Recent Dividends:	Yes

VTV   Vanguard Value VIPERs

CATEGORY   Large Cap - Value

DESCRIPTION

Tracks the MSCI US Prime Market Value Index of diversified index of large-cap value stocks

TOP TEN HOLDINGS

Exxon Mobil
Citigroup
Pfizer
Bank of America
General Electric

Altria.
JPMorgan Chase
Chevron
Wells Fargo
Verizon

TOP SECTORS

Financial Services
Oil & Gas
Utilities

Inception Date:	1/26/2004
Exchange:	AMEX
Shares Outstanding:	9,630,000
Minimum Lot:	1
Options Traded:	No
Recent Dividends:	Yes

PART 3:
DATABANK

1950 — DOW JONES INDUSTRIAL AVERAGE

Previous Month Close	Jan	Feb	Mar	Apr	May	Jun	Jul	Aug	Sep	Oct	Nov	Dec
	200.13	201.79	203.44	206.05	214.33	223.42	209.11	209.40	216.87	226.36	225.01	227.60
1	C	201.89	203.62	206.37	215.81	223.23	C	211.87	218.42	C	225.69	228.89
2	C	204.11	203.54	C	214.87	223.71	C	211.26	C	228.94	227.25	227.55
3	198.89	204.53	204.48	208.44	216.26	C	208.35	211.26	C	228.89	228.10	C
4	200.20	205.03	204.71	209.05	214.87	C	C	212.66	C	231.15	227.42	222.33
5	200.57	C	C	210.34	215.72	221.76	210.03	C	220.02	229.85	C	225.44
6	200.96	204.59	204.88	212.10	217.03	223.46	210.85	C	218.20	231.74	222.52	226.16
7	201.94	203.53	203.69	C	C	223.68	208.59	215.82	218.33	231.81	C	225.94
8	C	202.71	203.71	212.55	216.71	225.52	C	215.44	220.03	C	224.25	226.74
9	201.98	203.80	202.33	C	217.40	226.86	C	216.97	C	230.02	227.17	227.30
10	201.17	203.49	202.44	212.29	218.64	C	208.09	216.64	C	227.60	229.29	C
11	201.61	203.36	202.96	211.47	218.72	C	204.60	215.03	218.10	228.97	C	229.19
12	197.93	C	C	213.94	217.61	228.38	199.09	C	220.81	C	C	229.27
13	196.81	C	203.09	214.13	217.78	226.44	197.46	C	223.42	228.54	229.44	228.82
14	196.92	202.02	204.70	215.31	C	223.32	199.83	215.31	224.48	227.63	229.54	225.89
15	C	201.93	207.46	214.48	218.04	222.46	C	215.31	225.85	C	229.52	224.70
16	197.17	201.69	207.89	C	219.70	222.71	C	215.78	C	227.50	228.94	228.34
17	198.78	203.17	207.57	214.41	220.60	C	197.63	217.76	C	229.22	230.27	C
18	199.50	203.97	208.09	215.05	220.63	C	201.88	219.23	226.78	230.60	231.64	231.01
19	199.80	C	C	215.21	222.11	222.09	205.13	C	225.78	230.83	C	231.54
20	200.13	203.47	207.78	213.72	222.41	220.72	207.73	C	224.33	230.33	231.53	231.20
21	200.97	203.35	208.27	214.14	C	222.53	207.65	220.21	226.01	230.88	231.16	230.43
22	C	C	209.31	213.90	221.55	224.51	C	219.79	226.64	C	233.81	231.54
23	200.42	203.32	209.62	C	222.47	224.35	C	221.51	C	230.62	C	C
24	199.62	204.15	209.78	212.58	222.57	C	206.95	221.13	C	231.39	235.47	C
25	198.39	204.15	210.62	212.55	222.44	C	203.83	218.10	226.06	231.49	235.06	C
26	198.53	C	C	211.72	221.93	213.91	204.39	C	222.84	226.65	C	229.65
27	199.08	204.33	209.10	212.44	221.71	212.22	206.37	C	225.74	228.28	234.96	234.21
28	200.08	203.44	209.50	213.56	C	214.68	208.21	218.55	225.93	228.56	228.61	235.34
29	C		208.40	214.33	222.47	206.72	C	218.29	226.36	C	226.42	235.42
30	201.39		206.43	C	C	209.11	C	217.05	C	226.42	227.60	235.41
31	201.79		206.05		223.42		209.40	216.87		225.01		C
Close	201.79	203.44	206.05	214.33	223.42	209.11	209.40	216.87	226.36	225.01	227.60	235.41
Month Pt Change	1.66	1.65	2.61	8.28	9.09	−14.31	0.29	7.47	9.49	−1.35	2.59	7.81
Month % Change	0.8	0.8	1.3	4.0	4.2	−6.4	0.1	3.6	4.4	−0.6	1.2	3.4
QTR % Change			3.0			1.5			8.2			4.0
Year % Change												17.6

HIGHLIGHTS

Mid-Term Election Year	Bull Market	Best Six Months 15.2%	High	Nov-24	235.47
Truman	Expansion	Worst Six Months 5.0%	Low	Jan-13	196.81

DOW JONES INDUSTRIAL AVERAGE   1951

Previous Month Close	Jan	Feb	Mar	Apr	May	Jun	Jul	Aug	Sep	Oct	Nov	Dec
	235.41	248.83	252.05	247.94	259.13	249.65	242.64	257.86	270.25	271.16	262.35	261.27
1	C	250.76	252.80	C	260.71	249.33	C	259.89	C	272.56	264.06	262.29
2	239.92	252.78	253.61	246.63	261.27	C	243.98	262.89	C	274.34	261.94	C
3	238.99	253.92	253.43	246.02	263.13	C	245.92	262.98	C	275.87	259.57	263.24
4	240.86	C	C	247.31	262.77	246.79	C	C	270.63	275.35	C	264.29
5	240.96	255.17	251.82	250.32	261.76	247.59	250.27	C	272.48	275.63	259.76	263.72
6	240.68	254.62	251.55	250.83	C	249.64	250.01	265.21	272.28	275.53	C	266.23
7	C	252.70	252.45	250.28	261.23	250.81	C	264.94	273.89	C	257.14	266.99
8	242.29	253.34	252.81	C	261.10	250.39	C	263.73	C	275.14	257.14	266.90
9	243.50	254.24	252.75	250.57	261.49	C	250.65	262.69	C	273.38	259.91	C
10	240.40	254.80	252.02	250.42	260.07	C	250.00	261.92	275.25	272.76	261.29	267.38
11	244.72	C	C	249.76	258.56	251.56	250.97	C	273.88	274.10	C	265.77
12	243.81	C	249.89	251.66	257.26	250.57	252.59	C	275.31	C	C	266.09
13	243.61	255.71	245.88	254.75	C	250.03	254.32	263.06	276.37	275.13	260.41	265.81
14	C	255.10	243.95	256.18	256.08	252.46	C	262.88	276.06	C	261.27	265.71
15	245.02	253.61	244.85	C	252.08	254.03	C	264.27	C	275.74	260.91	265.48
16	246.65	254.90	248.62	254.85	252.14	C	252.31	265.48	C	274.40	260.39	C
17	248.01	254.70	249.03	255.34	254.57	C	253.89	266.17	275.09	273.53	260.82	265.79
18	247.39	C	C	256.01	250.10	253.80	253.67	C	274.38	273.51	C	266.61
19	246.76	251.67	248.08	254.92	250.63	253.53	253.75	C	274.27	269.68	259.70	267.61
20	246.91	251.12	247.87	254.82	C	251.86	253.73	266.19	274.10	267.42	259.30	267.45
21	C	252.28	249.37	255.02	249.98	250.43	C	265.30	272.11	C	258.72	266.34
22	244.33	C	250.52	C	249.30	247.86	C	264.07	C	262.29	C	265.94
23	245.30	252.18	C	255.12	247.03	C	255.68	265.65	C	263.50	256.95	C
24	244.36	252.93	248.14	254.19	245.78	C	258.94	266.30	270.77	264.95	255.95	265.79
25	242.22	C	C	254.75	245.27	245.30	258.11	C	272.24	264.17	C	C
26	244.51	253.18	249.13	257.13	245.83	246.28	259.09	C	272.24	262.27	257.44	264.06
27	247.36	251.34	248.74	258.96	C	246.84	259.23	265.59	271.31	258.53	259.46	266.74
28	C	252.05	246.19	259.08	247.03	244.00	C	265.56	271.16	C	258.64	268.18
29	248.64		246.90	C	248.44	242.64	C	268.18	C	260.43	258.96	268.52
30	249.58		248.53	259.13	C	C	260.70	269.94	C	260.52	261.27	C
31	248.83		247.94		249.65		257.86	270.25		262.35		269.23
Close	248.83	252.05	247.94	259.13	249.65	242.64	257.86	270.25	271.16	262.35	261.27	269.23
Month Pt Change	13.42	3.22	-4.11	11.19	-9.48	-7.01	15.22	12.39	0.91	-8.81	-1.08	7.96
Month % Change	5.7	1.3	-1.6	4.5	-3.7	-2.8	6.3	4.8	0.3	-3.2	-0.4	3.0
QTR % Change			5.3			-2.1			11.8			-0.7
Year % Change												14.4

HIGHLIGHTS

Pre-Election Year	Bull Market	Best Six Months -1.8%	High Sep-13	276.37
Truman	Expansion	Worst Six Months 1.2%	Low Jan-01	235.41

1952 DOW JONES INDUSTRIAL AVERAGE

Previous Month Close	Jan 269.23	Feb 270.69	Mar 260.08	Apr 269.46	May 257.63	Jun 262.94	Jul 274.26	Aug 279.56	Sep 275.04	Oct 270.61	Nov 269.23	Dec 283.66
1	C	271.68	260.27	267.22	256.35	C	275.46	279.80	C	270.17	C	283.70
2	269.86	272.51	C	267.03	260.00	262.31	274.87	C	276.40	270.75	C	283.78
3	270.38	C	260.08	266.80	260.55	262.09	274.95	C	277.15	270.55	270.23	282.89
4	271.03	269.79	263.95	265.62	C	263.67	C	279.87	276.76	C	C	281.63
5	271.26	269.04	264.66	265.44	261.54	266.29	C	279.50	276.50	C	271.30	282.06
6	C	268.77	264.03	C	261.01	268.03	C	279.07	C	270.00	272.58	C
7	270.34	268.35	263.87	263.38	261.99	C	274.20	279.38	C	269.88	273.47	C
8	268.66	269.85	264.14	265.29	262.39	C	274.43	279.84	275.87	271.40	C	283.62
9	268.08	269.83	C	265.04	262.74	269.15	273.25	C	273.53	270.98	C	285.12
10	269.46	C	262.76	265.75	262.50	267.67	272.58	C	271.65	270.61	273.47	284.55
11	270.31	268.45	262.76	C	C	267.93	274.22	280.29	272.11	C	C	284.57
12	270.73	C	263.78	266.29	261.72	267.91	C	278.14	271.02	C	271.97	285.20
13	C	266.21	264.24	C	261.99	268.56	C	277.88	C	C	272.54	C
14	271.59	265.88	264.05	264.10	260.99	C	275.08	277.75	C	270.43	273.27	C
15	270.46	266.27	264.43	261.29	260.10	C	276.76	277.37	268.38	267.12	C	285.99
16	271.13	266.30	C	261.48	259.82	267.83	276.76	C	269.03	264.87	C	286.16
17	271.91	C	264.08	259.85	259.88	268.03	275.62	C	270.43	267.30	274.45	285.67
18	272.10	265.35	264.10	260.52	C	267.09	273.90	274.31	269.72	C	278.04	285.36
19	272.93	261.37	264.37	260.14	260.06	269.54	C	274.14	270.55	C	280.05	286.52
20	C	258.49	265.33	C	261.26	270.19	C	274.35	C	266.63	279.50	C
21	274.10	259.60	265.62	261.63	261.78	C	274.91	274.45	C	265.84	279.32	C
22	275.40	C	265.69	261.10	263.33	C	275.95	274.43	270.77	263.06	C	288.02
23	274.27	261.40	C	259.97	263.27	269.50	277.63	C	271.65	263.87	C	286.99
24	273.90	C	265.60	258.86	263.23	269.92	279.26	C	272.26	265.46	281.08	287.37
25	273.41	260.58	264.28	259.80	C	270.45	277.71	273.57	272.42	C	280.90	C
26	273.69	259.30	263.87	260.27	264.22	271.24	C	273.17	271.95	C	282.44	288.23
27	C	259.68	265.21	C	263.92	272.44	C	273.84	C	265.90	C	C
28	274.17	260.49	266.96	259.95	262.78	C	277.94	274.41	C	265.72	283.66	C
29	274.00	260.08	269.00	259.34	262.94	C	278.57	275.04	271.73	265.46	C	289.65
30	270.71		C	257.63	C	274.26	279.24	C	270.61	265.72	C	292.00
31	270.69		269.46		C		279.56	C		269.23		291.90
Close	270.69	260.08	269.46	257.63	262.94	274.26	279.56	275.04	270.61	269.23	283.66	291.90
Month Pt Change	1.46	–10.61	9.38	–11.83	5.31	11.32	5.30	–4.52	–4.43	–1.38	14.43	8.24
Month % Change	0.5	–3.9	3.6	–4.4	2.1	4.3	1.9	–1.6	–1.6	–0.5	5.4	2.9
QTR % Change			0.1			1.8			–1.3			7.9
Year % Change												8.4

HIGHLIGHTS

Election Year	Bull Market	Best Six Months	2.1%	High	Dec-30	292.00
Truman	Expansion	Worst Six Months	4.5%	Low	May-01	256.35

DOW JONES INDUSTRIAL AVERAGE — 1953

Previous Month Close	Jan	Feb	Mar	Apr	May	Jun	Jul	Aug	Sep	Oct	Nov	Dec
Close	291.90	289.77	284.27	279.87	274.75	272.28	268.26	275.38	261.22	264.04	275.81	281.37
1	C	C	C	280.09	275.66	268.40	269.39	C	262.54	265.68	C	281.10
2	292.14	290.03	284.71	280.03	C	269.84	270.23	C	263.96	266.70	276.72	282.81
3	C	290.19	285.99	C	C	269.60	270.53	276.13	263.61	C	C	283.25
4	C	289.08	283.70	C	278.34	267.63	C	275.68	264.34	C	276.82	282.71
5	293.79	286.20	283.86	C	278.22	268.32	C	275.08	C	265.48	279.09	C
6	292.18	282.85	284.82	274.10	278.14	C	270.88	275.77	C	264.26	278.83	C
7	290.76	C	C	275.16	277.43	C	272.13	275.54	C	266.53	C	282.00
8	290.36	C	C	276.84	278.22	267.91	272.19	C	265.42	266.72	C	281.45
9	287.52	281.96	284.90	276.23	C	263.39	271.32	C	265.48	267.04	278.26	281.12
10	C	281.67	285.22	275.50	C	263.35	271.06	275.32	262.88	C	275.89	279.89
11	C	281.57	288.02	C	278.79	264.99	C	275.30	259.71	C	C	279.91
12	285.24	C	288.00	C	277.09	265.78	C	276.42	C	C	276.23	C
13	286.85	283.11	289.04	274.73	276.80	C	268.52	276.74	C	266.09	277.53	C
14	287.37	C	C	275.85	277.96	C	268.06	275.71	255.49	267.51	C	279.26
15	288.18	C	C	277.35	277.90	263.87	268.75	C	257.67	271.22	C	279.52
16	287.17	282.18	289.52	276.74	C	262.88	269.41	C	259.07	272.80	275.93	282.87
17	C	281.51	290.64	274.41	C	265.74	270.96	275.04	259.88	C	273.88	282.67
18	C	281.14	290.32	C	276.92	265.86	C	273.29	258.78	C	274.51	283.54
19	286.97	281.55	289.97	C	275.91	265.80	C	271.50	C	273.31	276.09	C
20	288.00	281.89	289.69	275.99	278.04	C	269.74	271.73	C	273.90	276.05	C
21	287.60	C	C	275.48	278.51	C	268.99	271.93	258.01	273.74	C	282.99
22	287.84	C	C	273.55	278.16	267.26	269.39	C	261.28	274.89	C	279.99
23	286.89	C	287.39	270.73	C	268.48	269.94	C	262.35	275.34	275.42	279.84
24	C	282.99	288.83	271.26	C	267.79	269.76	268.70	262.45	C	277.13	280.92
25	C	284.45	287.98	C	277.47	268.93	C	267.45	263.31	C	277.78	C
26	286.54	284.35	286.60	C	276.37	269.05	C	266.51	C	274.43	C	C
27	286.81	284.27	287.33	272.70	273.96	C	268.46	265.68	C	273.35	280.23	C
28	287.39	C	C	273.96	271.48	C	269.13	265.74	264.79	274.14	C	279.91
29	287.96		C	275.38	272.28	268.20	270.43	C	264.77	276.31	C	278.30
30	289.77		283.07	274.75	C	268.26	272.82	C	264.04	275.81	281.37	280.43
31	C		279.87		C		275.38	261.22		C		280.90
Close	289.77	284.27	279.87	274.75	272.28	268.26	275.38	261.22	264.04	275.81	281.37	280.90
Month Pt Change	-2.13	-5.50	-4.40	-5.12	-2.47	-4.02	7.12	-14.16	2.82	11.77	5.56	-0.47
Month % Change	-0.7	-1.9	-1.5	-1.8	-0.9	-1.5	2.7	-5.1	1.1	4.5	2.0	-0.2
QTR % Change			-4.1			-4.1			-1.6			6.4
Year % Change												-3.8

HIGHLIGHTS

Post-Election Year	Bull Market	Best Six Months 15.8%	High Jan-05 293.79
Eisenhower (1st term)	Recession Begins Q3	Worst Six Months 0.4%	Low Sep-14 255.49

Data Bank

1954 — DOW JONES INDUSTRIAL AVERAGE

Previous Month Close	Jan	Feb	Mar	Apr	May	Jun	Jul	Aug	Sep	Oct	Nov	Dec
	280.90	292.39	294.54	303.51	319.33	327.49	333.53	347.92	335.80	360.46	352.14	386.77
1	C	291.84	296.55	306.27	C	328.67	334.12	C	338.13	359.88	353.96	384.04
2	C	291.17	297.48	306.67	C	328.36	337.66	349.57	341.15	C	C	385.63
3	C	292.32	297.03	C	319.35	328.63	C	349.61	343.10	C	361.50	389.60
4	282.89	294.03	297.48	C	319.82	327.63	C	349.74	C	362.73	366.95	C
5	284.19	293.97	299.45	307.04	317.93	C	C	347.79	C	363.37	366.00	C
6	283.96	C	C	304.26	320.41	C	341.12	343.06	C	364.43	C	392.48
7	282.60	C	C	305.41	321.30	327.96	340.34	C	345.37	363.79	C	393.88
8	281.51	293.58	298.64	307.79	C	321.00	339.81	C	346.07	363.77	369.46	393.08
9	C	293.79	299.45	309.39	C	319.27	341.25	340.87	346.73	C	371.07	391.53
10	C	292.95	299.59	C	321.32	320.12	C	343.56	347.83	C	371.88	390.08
11	279.87	292.45	300.83	C	319.74	322.09	C	346.41	C	361.43	374.91	C
12	281.51	293.99	299.71	309.19	321.61	C	340.91	345.84	C	359.57	377.10	C
13	283.03	C	C	308.98	320.39	C	340.04	346.64	351.10	358.91	C	389.79
14	284.49	C	C	311.76	322.50	322.65	340.44	C	351.78	354.69	C	387.03
15	286.72	292.55	298.88	313.77	C	325.21	341.06	C	350.63	353.20	376.74	388.92
16	C	289.61	298.09	C	C	327.28	339.96	349.61	352.37	C	379.39	393.14
17	C	290.11	298.31	C	323.33	327.21	C	348.38	355.32	C	379.69	394.94
18	286.03	291.51	300.10	C	324.14	327.91	C	348.51	C	354.35	377.44	C
19	288.27	291.07	301.44	311.78	323.21	C	338.64	349.89	C	354.75	378.01	C
20	289.14	C	C	311.89	323.88	C	337.62	350.38	353.48	357.42	C	397.32
21	289.48	C	C	310.91	326.09	328.56	339.98	C	356.40	358.08	C	398.11
22	289.65	C	301.60	311.48	C	329.51	342.97	C	358.36	358.61	379.47	397.07
23	C	290.03	299.02	313.37	C	330.72	343.48	347.64	359.63	C	382.74	397.15
24	C	289.54	296.89	C	326.09	332.20	C	346.32	361.67	C	384.63	C
25	290.40	291.41	296.40	C	325.02	332.53	C	344.60	C	356.34	C	C
26	292.85	294.54	299.08	314.54	327.11	C	343.39	343.35	C	356.32	387.79	C
27	292.22	C	C	313.49	326.37	C	344.69	344.48	362.26	355.73	C	393.88
28	291.51	C	C	313.75	327.49	336.12	345.11	C	363.32	354.56	C	398.51
29	292.39		300.06	318.22	C	336.90	346.15	C	361.73	352.14	388.51	401.97
30	C		300.89	319.33	C	333.53	347.92	341.25	360.46	C	386.77	401.97
31	C		303.51		C		C	335.80		C		404.39
Close	292.39	294.54	303.51	319.33	327.49	333.53	347.92	335.80	360.46	352.14	386.77	404.39
Month Pt Change	11.49	2.15	8.97	15.82	8.16	6.04	14.39	−12.12	24.66	−8.32	34.63	17.62
Month % Change	4.1	0.7	3.0	5.2	2.6	1.8	4.3	−3.5	7.3	−2.3	9.8	4.6
QTR % Change			8.0			9.9			8.1			12.2
Year % Change												44.0

HIGHLIGHTS

Mid-Term Year	Bull Market	Best Six Months 20.9%	High Dec-31	404.39
Eisenhower (1st term)	Expansion Begins Q3	Worst Six Months 10.3%	Low Jan-11	279.87

DOW JONES INDUSTRIAL AVERAGE 1955

Previous Month Close	Jan 404.39	Feb 408.83	Mar 411.87	Apr 409.70	May 425.65	Jun 424.86	Jul 451.38	Aug 465.85	Sep 468.18	Oct 466.62	Nov 454.87	Dec 483.26
1	C	409.70	413.71	413.84	C	424.88	453.82	460.25	469.63	C	454.89	481.39
2	C	407.11	417.18	C	426.30	425.80	C	460.82	472.53	C	454.92	482.72
3	408.89	405.85	418.33	C	422.78	428.53	C	460.98	C	455.70	461.97	C
4	406.17	409.76	419.68	412.97	422.54	C	C	454.18	C	458.85	467.35	C
5	397.24	C	C	415.90	423.39	C	459.42	456.40	C	461.14	C	487.16
6	391.89	C	C	416.42	423.84	431.49	467.41	C	476.24	458.19	C	486.73
7	395.60	409.59	416.84	418.20	C	434.55	460.23	C	475.20	454.41	470.58	486.35
8	C	405.70	409.13	C	C	436.95	461.18	454.05	475.06	C	C	487.80
9	C	410.32	404.90	C	424.32	435.07	C	448.84	474.59	C	473.90	487.64
10	400.89	412.89	406.83	C	423.80	437.72	C	450.29	C	441.14	472.52	C
11	400.25	413.99	401.08	418.77	420.29	C	464.24	455.18	C	438.59	476.54	C
12	399.78	C	C	420.94	418.20	C	462.97	457.01	476.51	445.58	C	483.72
13	398.34	C	C	421.57	419.57	440.17	457.40	C	480.93	444.91	C	484.29
14	396.54	411.39	391.36	422.46	C	438.20	458.49	C	482.90	444.68	484.88	480.84
15	C	411.95	399.28	425.45	C	441.93	460.23	456.09	481.56	C	487.07	480.72
16	C	409.98	403.14	C	415.01	442.48	C	453.26	483.67	C	487.38	482.08
17	388.20	410.41	405.23	C	414.12	444.08	C	452.85	C	446.13	485.26	C
18	390.98	411.63	404.75	428.42	417.83	C	460.07	452.53	C	448.58	482.91	C
19	392.31	C	C	427.88	419.72	C	456.72	453.57	483.80	453.09	C	481.80
20	393.03	C	C	428.62	422.89	444.38	458.10	C	483.67	457.66	C	481.84
21	395.90	411.28	402.40	428.45	C	446.80	461.07	C	485.98	458.47	477.30	485.49
22	C	C	404.47	425.52	C	447.37	464.69	452.55	485.96	C	481.91	486.08
23	C	411.48	410.87	C	420.32	448.82	C	457.35	487.45	C	482.62	486.59
24	396.00	410.30	414.49	C	420.39	448.93	C	459.39	C	460.82	C	C
25	397.00	409.50	414.77	426.86	421.77	C	468.02	461.27	C	458.40	482.88	C
26	401.97	C	C	430.64	424.95	C	468.41	463.70	455.56	455.72	C	C
27	402.60	C	C	428.10	425.66	449.86	468.45	C	465.93	453.77	C	485.81
28	404.68	411.87	412.91	423.19	C	449.02	466.46	C	472.61	454.85	480.96	484.22
29	C		413.73	425.65	C	449.70	465.85	464.37	468.68	C	482.60	484.56
30	C		410.13	C	C	451.38	C	464.67	466.62	C	483.26	488.40
31	408.83		409.70		424.86		C	468.18		454.87		C
Close	408.83	411.87	409.70	425.65	424.86	451.38	465.85	468.18	466.62	454.87	483.26	488.40
Month Pt Change	4.44	3.04	−2.17	15.95	−0.79	26.52	14.47	2.33	−1.56	−11.75	28.39	5.14
Month % Change	1.1	0.7	−0.5	3.9	−0.2	6.2	3.2	0.5	−0.3	−2.5	6.2	1.1
QTR % Change			1.3			10.2			3.4			4.7
Year % Change												20.8

HIGHLIGHTS

Pre-Election Year	Bull Market	Best Six Months 13.5%	High Dec-30	488.40
Eisenhower (1st term)	Expansion	Worst Six Months 6.9%	Low Jan-17	388.20

1956　DOW JONES INDUSTRIAL AVERAGE

Previous Month Close	Jan	Feb	Mar	Apr	May	Jun	Jul	Aug	Sep	Oct	Nov	Dec
	488.40	470.74	483.65	511.79	516.12	478.05	492.78	517.81	502.04	475.25	479.85	472.78
1	C	473.28	486.69	C	513.96	480.63	C	518.69	C	468.70	487.62	C
2	C	473.43	488.84	515.10	512.78	C	491.92	520.95	C	475.41	490.47	C
3	485.78	477.44	C	515.91	514.03	C	495.74	520.27	C	482.04	C	480.61
4	484.00	C	C	518.65	516.44	483.22	C	C	507.66	481.24	C	481.38
5	484.02	C	491.68	516.57	C	483.19	500.54	C	509.82	482.39	495.37	488.55
6	485.68	478.57	491.41	521.05	C	480.54	504.14	513.88	509.49	C	C	492.74
7	C	476.56	491.26	C	512.89	482.99	C	515.88	506.76	C	491.15	494.79
8	C	471.23	492.36	C	509.13	475.29	C	518.74	C	483.38	488.72	C
9	479.74	467.22	497.84	518.52	508.16	C	506.52	519.04	C	481.32	485.35	C
10	476.12	467.66	C	510.04	501.56	C	508.34	517.38	505.56	487.32	C	493.18
11	478.42	C	C	512.70	501.25	479.41	509.65	C	502.16	488.06	C	490.36
12	481.80	C	500.24	509.15	C	485.49	507.44	C	499.97	490.19	487.05	487.51
13	481.80	467.17	499.33	509.99	C	487.08	511.10	514.40	499.69	C	486.69	490.47
14	C	465.72	503.88	C	497.28	485.52	C	517.27	500.32	C	482.36	492.08
15	C	470.64	507.50	C	494.83	485.91	C	517.70	C	489.40	480.20	C
16	476.24	469.61	507.60	509.15	492.69	C	512.98	517.19	C	487.57	480.67	C
17	477.73	477.05	C	507.95	496.63	C	514.43	515.79	498.76	484.66	C	493.75
18	472.89	C	C	506.55	496.39	483.91	513.39	C	493.45	486.31	C	495.09
19	468.49	C	509.76	504.33	C	484.52	513.86	C	488.72	486.12	474.56	493.81
20	464.40	476.46	512.62	507.20	C	485.00	514.57	511.24	487.13	C	470.07	490.44
21	C	476.93	507.92	C	491.62	488.26	C	505.43	490.33	C	467.91	494.38
22	C	C	510.94	C	484.13	487.95	C	502.34	C	485.27	C	C
23	462.35	481.50	513.03	507.28	480.16	C	513.61	507.06	C	485.05	472.56	C
24	467.88	485.66	C	503.36	473.51	C	513.17	507.91	487.70	482.67	C	C
25	470.71	C	C	503.02	472.49	486.43	514.13	C	481.08	481.08	C	C
26	466.82	C	512.42	507.12	C	489.37	515.85	C	481.60	486.06	470.29	496.74
27	466.56	485.00	508.68	512.03	C	492.04	512.30	505.70	479.76	C	470.18	496.38
28	C	485.71	510.25	C	468.81	492.50	C	503.05	475.25	C	466.10	496.41
29	C	483.65	511.79	C	477.68	492.78	C	500.90	C	486.94	466.62	C
30	467.56		C	516.12	C	C	513.42	495.96	C	486.47	472.78	C
31	470.74		C		478.05		517.81	502.04		479.85		499.47
Close	470.74	483.65	511.79	516.12	478.05	492.78	517.81	502.04	475.25	479.85	472.78	499.47
Month Pt Change	−17.66	12.91	28.14	4.33	−38.07	14.73	25.03	−15.77	−26.79	4.60	−7.07	26.69
Month % Change	−3.6	2.7	5.8	0.8	−7.4	3.1	5.1	−3.0	−5.3	1.0	−1.5	5.6
QTR % Change			4.8			−3.7			−3.6			5.1
Year % Change												2.3

HIGHLIGHTS

Election Year	Bear Market Begins 4/6/56	Best Six Months	3.0%	High	Apr-06	521.05
Eisenhower (1st term)	Expansion	Worst Six Months	-7.0%	Low	Jan-23	462.35

DOW JONES INDUSTRIAL AVERAGE — 1957

Previous Month Close	Jan	Feb	Mar	Apr	May	Jun	Jul	Aug	Sep	Oct	Nov	Dec
	499.47	479.16	464.62	474.81	494.36	504.93	503.29	508.52	484.35	456.30	441.04	449.87
1	C	477.22	468.91	474.98	495.76	C	503.29	506.21	C	460.80	434.71	C
2	496.03	C	C	477.55	498.56	C	507.55	505.10	C	465.03	C	446.91
3	499.20	C	C	478.31	497.54	503.76	513.25	C	486.13	465.82	C	446.55
4	498.22	477.19	471.48	477.43	C	502.97	C	C	482.60	461.70	434.04	448.87
5	C	469.96	472.88	477.61	C	502.07	516.89	500.78	479.51	C	C	449.55
6	C	470.81	474.87	C	496.32	504.55	C	494.13	478.63	C	435.82	447.20
7	495.20	468.71	474.17	C	494.68	505.63	C	498.48	C	452.42	438.91	C
8	493.86	466.29	471.63	479.04	496.73	C	518.41	496.87	C	450.56	434.12	C
9	493.21	C	C	482.66	496.76	C	516.37	496.78	474.28	451.40	C	443.76
10	495.51	C	C	485.17	498.30	503.76	519.81	C	470.23	441.71	C	439.24
11	493.81	457.44	469.50	484.70	C	509.48	517.97	C	474.40	441.16	434.94	439.36
12	C	454.82	470.31	486.72	C	509.66	520.77	492.32	480.56	C	429.75	438.48
13	C	462.14	472.53	C	502.21	511.58	C	492.14	481.02	C	430.07	440.48
14	489.29	461.56	473.93	C	500.46	511.79	C	485.93	C	443.78	427.94	C
15	484.75	468.07	474.28	485.84	501.98	C	520.16	487.30	C	447.90	439.35	C
16	485.05	C	C	484.32	504.84	C	517.42	488.20	478.08	443.93	C	433.40
17	484.01	C	C	485.02	505.60	513.19	515.11	C	478.28	436.87	C	425.65
18	477.46	467.40	472.30	488.03	C	511.32	515.64	C	478.60	433.83	434.96	426.18
19	C	466.84	473.93	C	C	505.92	515.73	478.95	476.12	C	431.73	431.26
20	C	469.00	473.93	C	505.98	503.56	C	483.86	468.42	C	433.37	427.20
21	475.90	466.93	474.02	C	506.04	500.00	C	485.14	C	423.06	439.80	C
22	477.49	C	472.94	488.79	504.43	C	515.32	481.46	C	419.79	442.68	C
23	479.93	C	C	491.88	504.02	C	515.61	475.74	458.96	437.13	C	428.08
24	481.30	C	C	493.66	504.02	497.08	515.78	C	462.87	436.40	C	429.11
25	478.34	466.90	471.51	492.29	C	501.98	516.69	C	456.95	435.15	444.38	C
26	C	467.72	472.24	491.50	C	500.78	514.59	470.14	457.01	C	435.34	434.16
27	C	466.26	473.12	C	499.21	503.03	C	477.55	456.89	C	446.03	432.90
28	474.59	464.62	475.01	C	497.72	503.29	C	477.79	C	432.14	C	C
29	476.92		474.81	493.95	502.18	C	508.25	476.06	C	435.76	449.87	C
30	480.53		C	494.36	C	C	508.93	484.35	456.30	440.28	C	431.78
31	479.16		C		504.93		508.52	C		441.04		435.69
Close	479.16	464.62	474.81	494.36	504.93	503.29	508.52	484.35	456.30	441.04	449.87	435.69
Month Pt Change	−20.31	−14.54	10.19	19.55	10.57	−1.64	5.23	−24.17	−28.05	−15.26	8.83	−14.18
Month % Change	−4.1	−3.0	2.2	4.1	2.1	−0.3	1.0	−4.8	−5.8	−3.3	2.0	−3.2
QTR % Change			−4.9			6.0			−9.3			−4.5
Year % Change												−12.8

HIGHLIGHTS

Post-Election Year	Bull Market Begins 10/22/57	Best Six Months	3.4%	High Jul-12	520.77
Eisenhower (2nd term)	Recession Begins Q2	Worst Six Months	-10.8%	Low Oct-22	419.79

1958   DOW JONES INDUSTRIAL AVERAGE

Previous Month Close	Jan 435.69	Feb 450.02	Mar 439.92	Apr 446.76	May 455.86	Jun 462.70	Jul 478.18	Aug 502.99	Sep 508.63	Oct 532.09	Nov 543.22	Dec 557.46
1	C	C	C	445.47	457.01	C	478.82	505.43	C	530.94	C	560.07
2	439.27	C	C	441.21	459.56	466.11	480.15	C	511.77	532.09	C	558.57
3	444.56	453.98	443.38	440.50	C	468.14	480.17	C	513.71	533.73	545.16	558.81
4	C	458.65	445.06	C	C	468.58	C	510.33	513.44	C	C	559.10
5	C	454.89	446.58	C	461.12	468.55	C	506.95	512.77	C	550.68	556.75
6	442.56	453.13	450.96	C	463.67	469.60	C	503.11	C	536.29	554.85	C
7	447.79	448.76	451.49	440.09	462.88	C	481.85	506.10	C	539.40	554.26	C
8	446.61	C	C	442.59	462.50	C	480.00	510.13	515.23	539.31	C	556.08
9	443.24	C	C	441.88	462.56	469.46	477.59	C	518.64	539.61	C	558.13
10	438.68	445.94	451.90	441.06	C	468.19	478.97	C	516.20	543.36	557.72	564.98
11	C	442.35	455.92	441.24	C	467.93	482.85	512.42	520.43	C	561.13	563.07
12	C	441.21	454.60	C	460.74	471.42	C	508.19	519.43	C	562.39	562.27
13	439.71	440.24	454.10	C	459.86	474.77	C	509.22	C	545.95	560.75	C
14	441.80	444.44	453.04	443.76	455.45	C	476.89	510.30	C	541.72	564.68	C
15	445.20	C	C	447.58	457.86	C	478.82	506.13	523.40	536.14	C	563.98
16	445.23	C	C	444.35	457.10	476.56	481.00	C	526.57	540.11	C	565.18
17	444.12	442.27	448.23	445.09	C	478.97	485.70	C	525.89	546.36	567.44	569.38
18	C	442.71	447.38	449.31	C	476.65	486.55	502.67	522.34	C	564.89	572.38
19	C	443.06	449.96	C	455.98	471.57	C	503.64	526.48	C	565.97	573.17
20	447.29	439.74	449.46	C	459.83	473.60	C	503.96	C	544.19	566.24	C
21	446.64	439.62	452.49	450.72	458.50	C	493.36	507.10	C	543.72	559.57	C
22	445.70	C	C	449.55	460.24	C	494.89	508.28	524.01	542.31	C	571.23
23	447.93	C	C	450.11	461.03	471.66	494.06	C	525.89	540.72	C	566.39
24	450.66	437.19	453.75	453.42	C	470.43	497.12	C	528.15	539.52	544.89	572.73
25	C	436.89	450.96	454.92	C	471.54	501.76	508.28	525.83	C	540.52	C
26	C	440.42	449.70	C	461.06	474.01	C	509.63	526.83	C	549.15	C
27	448.46	437.80	448.64	C	460.68	475.42	C	510.39	C	535.00	C	C
28	448.67	439.92	448.61	454.51	460.44	C	502.81	507.72	C	536.88	557.46	C
29	451.16		C	451.78	462.70	C	501.38	508.63	529.04	542.72	C	577.31
30	449.72		C	455.86	C	478.18	504.37	C	532.09	543.31	C	581.80
31	450.02		446.76		C		502.99	C		543.22		583.65
Close	450.02	439.92	446.76	455.86	462.70	478.18	502.99	508.63	532.09	543.22	557.46	583.65
Month Pt Change	14.33	−10.10	6.84	9.10	6.84	15.48	24.81	5.64	23.46	11.13	14.24	26.19
Month % Change	3.3	−2.2	1.6	2.0	1.5	3.3	5.2	1.1	4.6	2.1	2.6	4.7
QTR % Change			2.5			7.0			11.3			9.7
Year % Change												34.0

HIGHLIGHTS

Mid-Term Year	Bull Market	Best Six Months 14.8%	High Dec-31 583.65
Eisenhower (2nd term)	Expansion Begins Q3	Worst Six Months 19.2%	Low Jan-01 435.69

DOW JONES INDUSTRIAL AVERAGE — 1959

Previous Month	Jan	Feb	Mar	Apr	May	Jun	Jul	Aug	Sep	Oct	Nov	Dec
Close	583.65	593.96	603.50	601.71	623.75	643.79	643.60	674.88	664.41	631.68	646.60	659.18
1	C	C	C	602.94	625.06	643.51	650.88	C	655.90	633.60	C	664.38
2	587.59	592.23	605.03	607.52	C	637.45	654.76	C	655.80	636.57	645.46	661.29
3	C	592.34	610.78	611.93	C	637.39	C	678.10	645.90	C	C	662.96
4	C	589.38	611.84	C	625.06	630.54	C	676.30	652.18	C	645.74	664.00
5	590.17	586.12	611.87	C	625.90	629.98	C	672.33	C	637.01	647.57	C
6	591.37	582.33	609.52	611.16	624.39	C	660.09	671.98	C	636.06	650.92	C
7	583.15	C	C	610.34	615.64	C	663.21	668.57	C	635.37	C	665.67
8	588.14	C	C	606.44	621.36	621.62	663.81	C	642.69	633.04	C	675.39
9	592.72	574.46	609.96	605.50	C	617.62	663.09	C	637.67	636.98	650.92	671.26
10	C	582.65	611.14	605.97	C	627.17	663.56	653.79	633.38	C	648.14	672.74
11	C	584.03	611.49	C	625.03	627.49	C	658.07	637.36	C	647.32	670.50
12	592.64	581.89	613.75	C	627.66	627.42	C	655.14	C	638.55	644.26	C
13	590.70	587.97	614.69	607.76	633.05	C	657.35	655.43	C	637.83	641.71	C
14	591.64	C	C	609.53	637.04	C	657.70	658.74	633.79	634.27	C	675.07
15	594.81	C	C	612.50	634.53	624.59	660.57	C	630.80	637.48	C	673.78
16	595.75	587.91	607.88	617.58	C	621.40	658.29	C	632.41	643.22	634.46	675.20
17	C	586.71	612.69	624.06	C	628.05	657.13	658.42	629.00	C	635.62	673.90
18	C	588.82	610.87	C	633.53	629.41	C	650.79	625.78	C	641.99	676.65
19	594.40	595.04	610.02	C	635.44	629.76	C	646.53	C	639.66	643.32	C
20	595.69	602.21	610.37	627.08	631.87	C	654.54	655.02	C	635.37	645.46	C
21	597.66	C	C	629.23	631.65	C	661.48	655.39	618.15	632.69	C	675.92
22	595.69	C	C	625.15	634.74	631.71	664.38	C	616.45	625.59	C	671.82
23	596.07	C	605.56	623.27	C	630.73	664.63	C	624.02	633.07	646.75	670.18
24	C	602.91	606.73	627.39	C	634.27	663.72	653.22	632.85	C	649.69	670.69
25	C	601.18	606.47	C	632.35	637.23	C	655.96	632.59	C	651.10	C
26	592.37	602.00	606.58	C	632.38	639.25	C	657.57	C	637.61	C	C
27	594.66	603.50	C	629.87	636.68	C	669.08	663.34	C	642.18	652.52	C
28	588.53	C	C	628.87	639.58	C	672.04	663.06	636.47	643.60	C	669.77
29	590.40		C	625.87	643.79	643.06	673.18	C	640.10	645.11	C	672.23
30	593.96		602.65	623.75	C	643.60	673.37	C	631.68	646.60	659.18	676.97
31	C		601.71		C		674.88	664.41		C		679.36
Close	593.96	603.50	601.71	623.75	643.79	643.60	674.88	664.41	631.68	646.60	659.18	679.36
Month Pt Change	10.31	9.54	−1.79	22.04	20.04	−0.19	31.28	−10.47	−32.73	14.92	12.58	20.18
Month % Change	1.8	1.6	−0.3	3.7	3.2	−0.03	4.9	−1.6	−4.9	2.4	1.9	3.1
QTR % Change			3.1			7.0			−1.9			7.5
Year % Change												16.4

HIGHLIGHTS				
Pre-Election Year	Bull Market	Best Six Months -6.9%	High Dec-31	679.36
Eisnehower (2nd Term)	Expansion	Worst Six Months 3.7%	Low Feb-09	574.46

1960   DOW JONES INDUSTRIAL AVERAGE

Previous Month Close	Jan	Feb	Mar	Apr	May	Jun	Jul	Aug	Sep	Oct	Nov	Dec
	679.36	622.62	630.12	616.59	601.70	625.50	640.62	616.73	625.99	580.14	580.36	597.22
1	C	626.20	626.87	615.98	C	624.89	641.30	617.85	626.10	C	585.24	594.56
2	C	636.92	621.37	C	599.61	627.87	C	613.68	625.22	C	588.23	596.00
3	C	630.97	612.05	C	607.73	628.98	C	608.69	C	577.81	590.82	C
4	679.06	631.14	609.79	618.54	610.99	C	C	609.23	C	573.15	596.07	C
5	685.47	626.77	C	622.19	608.32	C	640.91	614.29	C	578.88	C	593.49
6	682.62	C	C	628.31	607.62	636.92	640.37	C	620.85	583.69	C	597.11
7	677.66	C	604.02	629.03	C	645.58	644.89	C	612.27	586.42	597.63	604.62
8	675.73	619.43	599.10	628.10	C	650.35	646.91	614.79	611.42	C	C	605.17
9	C	628.45	607.16	C	607.48	656.42	C	615.69	614.12	C	602.25	610.90
10	C	623.36	602.31	C	604.82	654.88	C	617.52	C	587.31	612.01	C
11	667.16	618.57	605.83	624.89	606.54	C	640.44	622.88	C	588.75	608.61	C
12	660.43	622.23	C	626.50	607.87	C	634.12	626.18	609.35	585.83	C	611.94
13	656.44	C	C	626.50	616.03	655.85	632.11	C	611.79	591.49	C	611.72
14	660.53	C	606.79	630.12	C	654.88	631.32	C	605.69	596.48	604.80	612.68
15	659.68	617.58	612.18	C	C	649.42	630.24	624.17	602.69	C	606.87	610.76
16	C	611.33	616.73	C	617.39	648.27	C	625.43	602.18	C	604.77	617.78
17	C	613.55	615.09	C	621.63	650.89	C	626.54	C	593.34	602.18	C
18	653.86	622.19	616.42	630.77	623.00	C	626.00	625.82	C	588.75	603.62	C
19	645.07	628.45	C	626.40	624.68	C	624.78	629.27	586.76	587.01	C	615.56
20	643.69	C	C	618.71	625.24	647.52	624.13	C	588.20	582.69	C	614.82
21	645.43	C	617.00	619.15	C	644.93	616.63	C	594.26	577.55	604.54	615.42
22	645.85	C	618.09	616.32	C	645.36	609.87	630.71	592.15	C	601.10	613.31
23	C	626.19	622.06	C	623.66	647.41	C	638.29	585.20	C	602.47	613.23
24	C	623.73	624.00	C	621.39	647.01	C	641.56	C	571.93	C	C
25	639.07	628.51	622.47	611.13	621.28	C	601.68	637.16	C	566.05	606.47	C
26	639.84	632.00	C	610.92	622.79	C	606.75	636.13	577.14	575.18	C	C
27	637.67	C	C	609.96	624.78	642.49	601.76	C	574.81	580.95	C	613.38
28	629.84	C	621.78	604.33	C	637.46	605.67	C	569.08	577.92	605.43	615.75
29	622.62	630.12	620.35	601.70	C	638.39	616.73	634.46	570.59	C	602.40	616.19
30	C		619.94	C	C	640.62	C	626.40	580.14	C	597.22	615.89
31	C		616.59		625.50		C	625.99		580.36		C
Close	622.62	630.12	616.59	601.70	625.50	640.62	616.73	625.99	580.14	580.36	597.22	615.89
Month Pt Change	−56.74	7.50	−13.53	−14.89	23.80	15.12	−23.89	9.26	−45.85	0.22	16.86	18.67
Month % Change	−8.4	1.2	−2.1	−2.4	4.0	2.4	−3.7	1.5	−7.3	0.04	2.9	3.1
QTR % Change			−9.2			3.9			−9.4			6.2
Year % Change												−9.3

Previous Month Close	Jan 615.89	Feb 648.20	Mar 662.08	Apr 676.63	May 678.71	Jun 696.72	Jul 683.96	Aug 705.37	Sep 719.94	Oct 701.21	Nov 703.92	Dec 721.60
1	C	649.39	663.03	C	677.05	695.37	C	713.94	721.19	C	703.84	728.80
2	C	653.62	669.39	C	682.34	697.70	C	710.46	C	699.83	706.83	C
3	610.25	652.97	671.57	677.59	688.90	C	689.81	715.71	C	698.66	709.26	C
4	621.49	C	C	678.73	692.25	C	C	720.69	C	703.31	C	731.22
5	622.67	C	C	677.32	690.67	703.43	692.77	C	718.72	708.49	C	731.31
6	621.64	645.65	674.46	679.34	C	703.79	694.27	C	726.01	708.25	714.60	730.09
7	C	643.94	667.14	683.68	C	700.86	692.73	719.58	726.53	C	C	726.45
8	C	648.85	666.15	C	689.06	701.69	C	720.22	720.91	C	723.74	728.23
9	624.42	645.12	663.33	C	686.92	700.90	C	717.57	C	705.42	722.28	C
10	625.72	639.67	663.56	692.06	686.61	C	693.16	720.49	C	706.67	724.83	C
11	627.21	C	C	694.11	686.49	C	694.47	722.61	714.36	705.62	C	732.56
12	628.50	C	C	690.16	687.91	696.76	690.79	C	722.61	705.50	C	734.02
13	633.65	637.04	664.44	692.02	C	694.15	685.90	C	722.20	703.31	728.43	734.91
14	C	642.91	661.08	693.72	C	695.81	690.95	718.93	715.00	C	732.56	730.94
15	C	648.89	662.88	C	692.37	691.27	C	716.18	716.30	C	734.34	729.40
16	633.19	651.86	670.38	C	697.74	685.50	C	718.20	C	703.15	733.33	C
17	628.96	651.67	676.48	696.72	705.52	C	684.59	721.84	C	701.98	729.53	C
18	634.10	C	C	690.60	701.14	C	679.30	723.54	711.24	704.20	C	727.71
19	632.39	C	C	686.21	705.96	680.68	682.74	C	702.54	704.85	C	722.41
20	634.37	653.65	678.84	684.24	C	687.87	682.97	C	707.32	705.62	730.09	722.57
21	C	652.40	678.73	685.26	C	686.09	682.81	724.75	706.31	C	729.32	720.10
22	C	C	679.38	C	702.44	685.62	C	725.76	701.57	C	730.42	720.87
23	639.82	654.42	675.45	C	700.59	688.66	C	720.46	C	698.98	C	C
24	638.79	655.60	672.48	672.66	696.52	C	682.14	714.03	C	697.24	732.60	C
25	637.72	C	C	683.09	690.16	C	686.37	716.70	691.86	700.72	C	C
26	638.87	C	C	682.18	696.28	681.16	694.19	C	693.20	700.68	C	723.09
27	643.59	660.44	671.03	679.54	C	683.88	702.80	C	701.13	698.74	731.99	731.43
28	C	662.08	669.58	678.71	C	684.59	705.13	716.01	700.28	C	728.07	731.51
29	C		676.41	C	C	681.95	C	714.15	701.21	C	727.18	731.14
30	650.64		676.63	C	C	683.96	C	716.90	C	701.09	721.60	C
31	648.20		C		696.72		705.37	719.94		703.92		C
Close	648.20	662.08	676.63	678.71	696.72	683.96	705.37	719.94	701.21	703.92	721.60	731.14
Month Pt Change	32.31	13.88	14.55	2.08	18.01	-12.76	21.41	14.57	-18.73	2.71	17.68	9.54
Month % Change	5.2	2.1	2.2	0.3	2.7	-1.8	3.1	2.1	-2.6	0.4	2.5	1.3
QTR % Change			9.9			1.1			2.5			4.3
Year % Change												18.7

Bear Market Begins 12/13/61	Bear Market Begins 12/13	Best Six Months −5.5%	High Dec-13 734.91
Kennedy	Expansion Begins Q2	Worst Six Months 3.7%	Low Jan-03 610.25

1962   DOW JONES INDUSTRIAL AVERAGE

Previous Month Close	Jan	Feb	Mar	Apr	May	Jun	Jul	Aug	Sep	Oct	Nov	Dec
	731.14	700.00	708.05	706.95	665.33	613.36	561.28	597.93	609.18	578.98	589.77	649.30
1	C	702.54	711.81	C	671.24	611.05	C	591.36	C	571.95	597.13	C
2	724.71	706.55	711.00	705.42	669.96	C	573.75	593.83	C	578.73	604.58	C
3	726.01	C	C	700.60	675.49	C	579.48	596.38	C	578.52	C	646.41
4	722.53	C	C	696.88	671.20	593.68	C	C	602.45	582.41	C	651.48
5	714.84	706.14	709.99	700.88	C	594.96	583.87	C	599.14	586.59	610.48	653.99
6	C	710.39	708.17	699.63	C	603.91	576.17	593.24	600.81	C	C	651.73
7	C	715.73	706.63	C	670.99	602.20	C	588.35	600.86	C	615.75	652.10
8	708.98	716.82	713.75	C	663.90	601.61	C	590.94	C	586.09	609.14	C
9	707.64	714.27	714.44	692.96	654.70	C	580.82	591.19	C	587.18	616.13	C
10	706.02	C	C	695.46	647.23	C	586.01	592.32	602.03	588.14	C	645.08
11	710.67	C	C	694.90	640.63	595.17	589.06	C	603.99	586.47	C	645.16
12	711.73	714.92	714.68	685.67	C	580.94	590.27	C	606.34	586.47	624.41	647.33
13	C	714.32	716.58	687.90	C	574.04	590.19	595.29	603.99	C	623.11	645.20
14	C	713.67	720.95	C	646.20	563.00	C	601.90	605.84	C	630.48	648.09
15	709.50	717.27	723.54	C	655.36	578.18	C	606.76	C	589.69	629.14	C
16	705.29	716.46	722.27	684.06	654.04	C	588.10	606.71	C	589.35	630.98	C
17	697.41	C	C	688.43	649.79	C	577.85	610.02	607.63	587.68	C	645.49
18	696.03	C	C	691.01	650.70	574.21	571.24	C	607.09	581.15	C	640.14
19	700.72	714.36	720.38	694.25	C	571.61	573.16	C	607.09	573.29	626.21	647.00
20	C	717.55	719.66	C	C	563.08	577.18	612.86	601.65	C	632.94	648.55
21	C	713.02	716.62	C	648.59	550.49	C	608.64	591.78	C	637.25	646.41
22	701.98	C	716.70	C	636.34	539.19	C	615.54	C	568.60	C	C
23	698.54	709.54	716.46	694.61	626.52	C	577.47	616.00	C	558.06	644.87	C
24	698.17	C	C	693.00	622.56	C	574.12	613.74	582.91	576.68	C	647.71
25	696.52	C	C	683.69	611.88	536.77	574.67	C	588.22	570.86	C	651.64
26	692.19	706.22	710.67	678.68	C	535.76	579.61	C	578.48	569.02	642.06	651.64
27	C	709.22	707.28	672.20	C	536.98	585.00	612.57	574.12	C	648.05	650.56
28	C	708.05	712.25	C	576.93	557.35	C	605.25	578.98	C	651.85	651.43
29	689.92		711.28	C	603.96	561.28	C	603.24	C	579.35	652.61	C
30	694.09		706.95	665.33	C	C	591.44	602.32	C	588.98	649.30	C
31	700.00		C		613.36		597.93	609.18		589.77		652.10
Close	700.00	708.05	706.95	665.33	613.36	561.28	597.93	609.18	578.98	589.77	649.30	652.10
Month Pt Change	−31.14	8.05	−1.10	−41.62	−51.97	−52.08	36.65	11.25	−30.20	10.79	59.53	2.80
Month % Change	−4.3	1.1	−0.2	−5.9	−7.8	−8.5	6.5	1.9	−5.0	1.9	10.1	0.4
QTR % Change			−3.3			−20.6			3.2			12.6
Year % Change												−10.8

HIGHLIGHTS

Mid-Term Election Year	Recession Q1 - Q2	Best Six Months	21.7%	High Jan-03	726.01
Kennedy	Expansion	Worst Six Months	−11.4%	Low Jun-26	535.76

Previous Month	Jan	Feb	Mar	Apr	May	Jun	Jul	Aug	Sep	Oct	Nov	Dec
Close	652.10	682.85	662.94	682.52	717.70	726.96	706.88	695.43	729.32	732.79	755.23	750.52
1	C	683.19	659.72	685.86	719.67	C	701.35	694.87	C	738.33	753.73	C
2	646.79	C	C	684.27	721.09	C	708.94	697.83	C	737.94	C	751.91
3	657.42	C	C	690.51	718.08	726.27	713.36	C	732.02	744.25	C	751.82
4	662.23	682.01	667.04	697.12	C	726.49	C	C	732.92	745.06	749.22	755.51
5	C	681.30	667.16	702.43	C	725.93	716.45	702.55	737.98	C	C	763.86
6	C	682.52	668.08	C	713.77	726.87	C	707.06	735.37	C	744.03	760.25
7	662.14	679.09	671.43	C	712.55	722.41	C	703.92	C	743.86	745.66	C
8	669.88	679.92	672.43	706.03	718.54	C	710.66	704.18	C	743.90	750.81	C
9	668.00	C	C	706.03	721.97	C	714.09	708.39	732.92	739.83	C	759.08
10	669.51	C	C	704.35	723.30	716.49	712.12	C	737.43	740.56	C	759.25
11	671.60	674.74	674.02	708.45	C	718.38	709.76	C	740.34	741.76	753.77	757.21
12	C	676.62	675.20	C	C	723.36	707.70	710.27	740.26	C	750.21	757.43
13	C	681.72	677.66	C	723.01	721.43	C	711.13	740.13	C	751.11	760.17
14	675.74	684.86	673.73	C	719.84	722.03	C	714.95	C	741.84	747.04	C
15	675.36	686.07	676.33	711.38	724.34	C	703.28	718.55	C	742.19	740.00	C
16	669.00	C	C	710.92	722.84	C	702.12	719.32	738.46	748.45	C	761.64
17	672.98	C	C	710.25	724.81	718.21	699.72	C	740.13	750.77	C	766.38
18	672.52	688.96	673.56	708.16	C	718.90	695.90	C	737.86	750.60	734.85	767.21
19	C	686.83	672.06	711.68	C	719.84	693.89	718.81	743.22	C	736.65	763.86
20	C	682.06	677.12	C	720.18	718.85	C	717.27	743.60	C	742.06	762.08
21	675.24	681.64	675.57	C	724.04	720.78	C	715.72	C	752.31	732.65	C
22	675.53	C	677.83	711.01	722.84	C	688.74	718.47	C	747.21	711.49	C
23	677.58	C	C	714.98	721.38	C	687.84	723.14	740.43	746.48	C	758.30
24	676.99	C	C	717.74	720.53	718.42	690.88	C	745.96	751.80	C	756.86
25	679.71	674.61	678.17	718.33	C	716.32	687.71	C	743.69	755.61	C	C
26	C	675.28	680.38	717.16	C	708.99	689.38	724.17	736.95	C	743.52	760.21
27	C	670.80	684.73	C	718.25	706.03	C	719.88	737.98	C	741.00	762.95
28	682.89	662.94	682.47	C	717.95	706.88	C	725.07	C	759.39	C	C
29	683.73		682.52	715.11	722.50	C	690.71	726.40	C	760.50	750.52	C
30	678.58		C	717.70	C	C	696.42	729.32	732.79	755.19	C	759.90
31	682.85		C		726.96		695.43	C		755.23		762.95
Close	682.85	662.94	682.52	717.70	726.96	706.88	695.43	729.32	732.79	755.23	750.52	762.95
Month Pt Change	30.75	−19.91	19.58	35.18	9.26	−20.08	−11.45	33.89	3.47	22.44	−4.71	12.43
Month % Change	4.7	−2.9	3.0	5.2	1.3	−2.8	−1.6	4.9	0.5	3.1	−0.6	1.7
QTR % Change			4.7			3.6			3.7			4.1
Year % Change												17.0

HIGHLIGHTS

Pre-Election Year	Bull Market	Best Six Months	7.4%	High Dec-18	767.21
Kennedy (Johnson 11/22/63)	Expansion	Worst Six Months	5.2%	Low Jan-02	646.79

	Jan	Feb	Mar	Apr	May	Jun	Jul	Aug	Sep	Oct	Nov	Dec
Previous Month Close	762.95	785.34	800.14	813.29	810.77	820.56	831.50	841.10	838.48	875.37	873.08	875.43
1	C	C	C	816.08	817.10	818.56	838.06	C	844.00	872.00	C	864.43
2	766.08	C	802.75	820.87	C	813.78	841.47	C	845.08	872.65	875.51	867.16
3	767.68	784.72	805.72	822.99	C	811.79	C	840.35	846.02	C	C	870.79
4	C	783.30	804.70	C	823.83	802.48	C	832.77	848.31	C	873.82	870.93
5	C	783.04	803.77	C	826.63	806.03	C	833.05	C	877.15	873.54	C
6	769.51	786.41	806.03	824.76	828.18	C	844.24	823.40	C	875.14	876.87	C
7	771.73	791.59	C	822.77	830.17	C	844.94	829.16	C	873.78	C	873.99
8	774.46	C	C	824.19	828.57	800.31	845.45	C	851.91	874.90	C	870.69
9	776.55	C	807.18	821.35	C	805.54	845.13	C	855.57	878.08	874.57	863.81
10	774.33	788.71	809.39	821.75	C	807.53	847.51	829.35	859.50	C	870.64	863.14
11	C	792.16	813.87	C	827.07	811.25	C	828.08	867.13	C	873.59	864.34
12	C	794.82	814.22	C	827.38	809.39	C	834.08	C	877.57	874.62	C
13	773.12	794.42	816.22	821.31	825.78	C	845.55	838.52	C	876.21	874.11	C
14	774.49	794.56	C	822.95	824.45	C	843.63	838.81	866.24	875.18	C	860.65
15	774.71	C	C	825.43	826.23	813.56	844.80	C	862.54	868.44	C	857.45
16	776.13	C	816.48	825.65	C	818.16	847.47	C	864.18	873.54	880.10	860.08
17	775.69	796.19	818.16	827.33	C	823.35	851.35	840.21	868.67	C	885.39	863.57
18	C	795.40	820.25	C	821.31	823.98	C	842.83	865.12	C	891.71	868.73
19	C	794.91	819.36	C	817.28	825.25	C	841.76	C	876.21	888.71	C
20	773.03	796.99	814.93	824.54	820.11	C	849.39	838.71	C	881.50	890.72	C
21	776.44	C	C	826.45	819.80	C	846.95	838.62	871.58	879.72	C	869.74
22	781.31	C	C	823.57	820.87	826.38	847.65	C	872.47	877.01	C	870.36
23	782.86	C	813.60	821.66	C	822.70	846.48	C	871.95	877.62	889.29	868.02
24	783.04	797.12	811.43	814.89	C	827.01	845.64	837.31	872.98	C	887.61	868.16
25	C	796.59	813.16	C	820.25	827.48	C	832.20	874.71	C	882.40	C
26	C	799.38	815.91	C	818.92	830.99	C	829.21	C	877.01	C	C
27	785.34	797.04	C	811.87	817.94	C	841.05	835.25	C	875.98	882.12	C
28	787.78	800.14	C	816.70	820.56	C	837.35	839.09	875.46	871.16	C	867.01
29	782.60	C	C	812.81	C	830.94	838.67	C	875.74	871.86	C	862.18
30	783.44		815.29	810.77	C	831.50	839.37	C	875.37	873.08	875.43	868.69
31	785.34		813.29		C		841.10	838.48		C		874.13
Close	785.34	800.14	813.29	810.77	820.56	831.50	841.10	838.48	875.37	873.08	875.43	874.13
Month Pt Change	22.39	14.80	13.15	−2.52	9.79	10.94	9.60	−2.62	36.89	−2.29	2.35	−1.30
Month % Change	2.9	1.9	1.6	−0.3	1.2	1.3	1.2	−0.3	4.4	−0.3	0.3	−0.1
QTR % Change			6.6			2.2			5.3			−0.1
Year % Change												14.6

HIGHLIGHTS

Election Year	Bull Market	Best Six Months	5.6%	High Nov-18	891.71
Johnson	Expansion	Worst Six Months	7.7%	Low Jan-02	766.08

DOW JONES INDUSTRIAL AVERAGE 1965

Previous Month Close	Jan	Feb	Mar	Apr	May	Jun	Jul	Aug	Sep	Oct	Nov	Dec
	874.13	902.86	903.48	889.05	922.31	918.04	868.03	881.74	893.10	930.58	960.82	946.71
1	C	903.68	899.76	890.33	C	908.53	871.59	C	893.60	929.65	958.96	947.60
2	C	903.77	901.91	893.38	C	904.06	875.16	881.85	900.40	C	C	944.59
3	C	906.30	900.76	C	922.11	899.22	C	881.20	907.97	C	961.13	946.10
4	869.78	904.06	897.75	C	928.22	900.87	C	883.88	C	930.86	961.85	C
5	875.86	901.57	895.98	893.23	932.22	C	C	881.63	C	938.70	959.46	C
6	879.68	C	C	891.90	933.52	C	873.18	882.51	C	936.84	C	939.53
7	884.36	C	C	892.94	932.52	902.15	870.77	C	910.11	934.42	C	951.33
8	882.60	897.89	896.84	897.90	C	889.05	877.85	C	913.68	938.32	953.95	946.60
9	C	901.24	894.07	901.29	C	879.84	879.49	879.77	917.47	C	951.72	949.55
10	C	892.92	892.39	C	931.47	876.49	C	878.89	918.95	C	951.22	952.72
11	883.22	881.88	896.51	C	930.92	881.70	C	881.47	C	942.65	953.28	C
12	885.89	888.47	900.33	906.36	934.17	C	877.96	881.96	C	941.12	956.29	C
13	886.85	C	C	908.01	938.87	C	876.97	888.82	920.92	941.01	C	951.55
14	887.18	C	C	912.86	939.62	868.71	883.23	C	916.59	937.50	C	954.06
15	891.15	885.32	899.85	911.91	C	874.57	880.98	C	922.95	940.68	955.90	958.74
16	C	881.35	898.90	C	C	878.07	880.43	891.13	931.18	C	956.51	959.13
17	C	882.93	899.37	C	930.67	883.06	C	894.26	928.99	C	956.57	957.85
18	895.21	883.69	896.55	C	930.62	879.17	C	894.37	C	945.84	950.50	C
19	896.27	885.61	895.79	912.76	932.12	C	880.26	891.79	C	947.76	952.72	C
20	895.31	C	C	911.96	927.27	C	868.79	889.92	931.18	948.47	C	952.22
21	893.26	C	C	910.71	922.01	874.12	865.01	C	926.52	950.28	C	959.46
22	893.59	C	896.12	915.06	C	875.43	861.77	C	931.62	952.42	946.38	965.86
23	C	891.96	898.69	916.41	C	870.22	863.97	887.07	927.45	C	948.94	966.36
24	C	897.84	900.56	C	914.21	857.76	C	887.12	929.54	C	948.94	C
25	896.46	899.90	898.34	C	921.00	854.36	C	890.85	C	948.14	C	C
26	897.84	903.48	891.66	916.86	917.16	C	867.26	896.18	C	956.32	948.16	C
27	899.52	C	C	918.16	913.22	C	863.53	895.96	937.88	959.50	C	959.79
28	900.95	C	C	918.86	918.04	840.59	867.92	C	935.85	959.11	C	957.96
29	902.86		887.82	918.71	C	851.40	874.23	C	932.39	960.82	946.93	960.30
30	C		889.05	922.31	C	868.03	881.74	895.63	930.58	C	946.71	963.69
31	C		889.05		C		C	893.10		C		969.26
Close	902.86	903.48	889.05	922.31	918.04	868.03	881.74	893.10	930.58	960.82	946.71	969.26
Month Pt Change	28.73	0.62	−14.43	33.26	−4.27	−50.01	13.71	11.36	37.48	30.24	−14.11	22.55
Month % Change	3.3	0.1	−1.6	3.7	−0.5	−5.4	1.6	1.3	4.2	3.2	−1.5	2.4
QTR % Change			1.7			−2.4			7.2			4.2
Year % Change												10.9

HIGHLIGHTS

Post Election Year	Bull Market	Best Six Months	-2.8%	High Dec-31	969.26
Johnson	Expansion	Worst Six Months	4.2%	Low Jun-28	840.59

1966   DOW JONES INDUSTRIAL AVERAGE

Previous Month	Jan	Feb	Mar	Apr	May	Jun	Jul	Aug	Sep	Oct	Nov	Dec
Close	969.26	983.51	951.89	924.77	933.68	884.07	870.10	847.38	788.41	774.22	807.07	791.59
1	C	975.89	938.19	931.29	C	883.63	877.06	835.18	792.09	C	809.63	789.75
2	C	982.29	932.01	C	931.95	882.73	C	832.57	787.69	C	807.29	789.47
3	968.54	981.23	936.35	C	921.77	887.86	C	841.70	C	757.96	804.34	C
4	969.26	986.35	932.34	937.86	914.86	C	C	851.50	C	763.19	805.06	C
5	981.62	C	C	944.71	899.77	C	875.27	852.39	C	755.45	C	791.59
6	985.46	C	C	945.26	902.83	881.68	888.86	C	782.34	749.61	C	797.43
7	986.13	989.69	917.76	945.76	C	877.33	891.64	C	777.39	744.32	802.22	808.01
8	C	991.03	919.98	C	C	879.34	894.04	849.05	774.88	C	C	812.80
9	C	995.15	929.84	C	886.80	882.62	C	844.82	775.55	C	809.91	813.02
10	985.41	990.81	929.23	C	895.48	891.75	C	838.53	C	754.51	816.87	C
11	986.85	989.03	927.95	942.42	895.43	C	893.09	837.91	C	758.63	819.09	C
12	983.96	C	C	937.24	885.57	C	886.19	840.53	790.59	778.17	C	820.54
13	985.69	C	C	938.36	876.11	897.60	881.40	C	795.48	772.93	C	816.70
14	987.30	987.69	917.09	945.48	C	903.17	887.80	C	806.23	771.71	813.75	817.98
15	C	981.57	911.08	947.77	C	901.11	889.36	834.85	814.30	C	815.31	809.18
16	C	982.40	916.03	C	867.53	897.16	C	823.83	814.30	C	820.87	807.18
17	989.75	975.27	919.32	C	864.14	894.26	C	819.59	C	778.89	816.03	C
18	994.20	975.22	922.88	941.98	878.50	C	888.41	810.74	C	791.87	809.40	C
19	991.14	C	C	941.64	872.99	C	884.07	804.62	810.85	785.35	C	798.99
20	987.80	C	C	951.28	876.89	892.76	874.49	C	806.01	783.68	C	794.59
21	988.14	966.48	929.17	954.73	C	894.98	873.99	C	793.59	787.30	798.16	797.43
22	C	C	934.52	949.83	C	901.00	869.15	792.03	797.77	C	794.98	801.67
23	C	960.13	929.00	C	882.46	896.43	C	790.14	790.97	C	796.82	799.10
24	991.42	950.66	928.61	C	888.41	897.16	C	799.55	C	787.75	C	C
25	991.64	953.00	929.95	950.55	890.42	C	852.83	792.37	C	793.09	803.34	C
26	990.92	C	C	947.21	891.75	C	852.17	780.56	792.70	801.11	C	C
27	990.36	C	C	944.54	897.04	888.97	856.23	C	794.09	809.57	C	792.20
28	985.35	951.89	932.62	937.41	C	880.90	854.06	C	780.95	807.96	801.16	788.58
29	C		929.39	933.68	C	871.60	847.38	767.03	772.66	C	795.26	786.35
30	C		919.76	C	C	870.10	C	775.72	774.22	C	791.59	785.69
31	983.51		924.77		884.07		C	788.41		807.07		C
Close	983.51	951.89	924.77	933.68	884.07	870.10	847.38	788.41	774.22	807.07	791.59	785.69
Month Pt Change	14.25	–31.62	–27.12	8.91	–49.61	–13.97	–22.72	–58.97	–14.19	32.85	–15.48	–5.90
Month % Change	1.5	–3.2	–2.8	1.0	–5.3	–1.6	–2.6	–7.0	–1.8	4.2	–1.9	–0.7
QTR % Change			–4.6			–5.9			–11.0			1.5
Year % Change												–18.9

HIGHLIGHTS

Mid-Term Election Year	Bear Market 2/9 - 10/7	Best Six Months	11.1%	High	Feb-09	995.15
Johnson	Expansion	Worst Six Months	–13.6%	Low	Oct-07	744.32

DOW JONES INDUSTRIAL AVERAGE   1967

	Jan	Feb	Mar	Apr	May	Jun	Jul	Aug	Sep	Oct	Nov	Dec
Previous Month Close	785.69	849.89	839.37	865.98	897.05	852.56	860.26	904.24	901.29	926.66	879.74	875.81
1	C	848.39	843.49	C	892.93	864.98	C	912.97	901.18	C	867.08	879.16
2	C	853.12	846.71	C	891.65	863.31	C	922.27	C	921.00	864.83	C
3	786.41	857.46	846.60	859.97	896.77	C	859.69	921.98	C	924.47	856.62	C
4	791.14	C	C	859.19	901.95	C	C	923.77	C	921.29	C	883.50
5	805.51	C	C	861.19	905.96	847.77	864.94	C	904.13	927.13	C	888.12
6	808.74	855.12	842.20	861.25	C	862.71	864.02	C	906.96	928.74	855.29	892.28
7	C	852.51	841.76	853.34	C	869.19	869.05	920.37	908.17	C	C	892.22
8	C	860.97	843.32	C	909.63	873.20	C	922.45	907.54	C	849.57	887.25
9	813.47	857.52	844.15	C	899.89	874.89	C	926.72	C	933.31	856.97	C
10	814.14	855.73	848.50	842.43	894.10	C	875.52	925.22	C	926.61	862.81	C
11	822.49	C	C	847.66	896.21	C	879.45	920.65	909.62	920.25	C	882.05
12	829.95	C	C	844.65	890.03	878.93	878.70	C	911.75	913.20	C	881.30
13	835.13	853.34	844.82	848.83	C	886.15	878.53	C	923.77	918.17	859.74	882.34
14	C	856.90	844.27	859.74	C	880.61	882.05	916.32	929.44	C	852.40	883.44
15	C	855.79	854.06	C	882.41	883.26	C	919.15	933.48	C	855.18	880.61
16	833.24	851.56	868.49	C	885.80	885.00	C	915.68	C	908.52	859.74	C
17	843.65	850.84	869.77	866.59	882.24	C	882.74	918.23	C	904.36	862.11	C
18	847.49	C	C	873.00	877.34	C	896.09	919.04	938.74	903.49	C	881.65
19	846.44	C	C	873.94	874.55	884.54	903.32	C	930.07	903.72	C	881.36
20	847.16	847.88	870.43	878.62	C	880.61	908.69	C	929.79	896.73	857.78	886.90
21	C	844.10	866.59	883.18	C	877.66	909.56	912.27	930.48	C	870.95	888.35
22	C	C	870.55	C	871.05	875.69	C	907.48	934.35	C	874.02	887.37
23	847.72	846.77	876.67	C	868.71	877.37	C	905.11	C	894.65	C	C
24	847.72	847.33	C	887.53	862.42	C	904.53	898.46	C	888.18	877.60	C
25	840.59	C	C	891.20	870.71	C	901.29	894.07	943.08	886.73	C	C
26	838.70	C	C	889.03	870.32	872.11	903.14	C	937.18	890.89	C	888.12
27	844.04	836.64	873.72	894.82	C	869.39	903.14	C	933.14	888.18	882.11	894.94
28	C	839.37	875.28	897.05	C	868.87	901.53	894.71	929.38	C	884.88	897.83
29	C		871.10	C	864.98	861.94	C	894.76	926.66	C	883.15	905.11
30	848.11		869.99	C	C	860.26	C	893.72	C	886.62	875.81	C
31	849.89		865.98		852.56		904.24	901.29		879.74		C
Close	849.89	839.37	865.98	897.05	852.56	860.26	904.24	901.29	926.66	879.74	875.81	905.11
Month Pt Change	64.20	−10.52	26.61	31.07	−44.49	7.70	43.98	−2.95	25.37	−46.92	−3.93	29.30
Month % Change	8.2	−1.2	3.2	3.6	−5.0	0.9	5.1	−0.3	2.8	−5.1	−0.4	3.3
QTR % Change			10.2			−0.7			7.7			−2.3
Year % Change												15.2

HIGHLIGHTS

Pre-Election Year	Bull Market	Best Six Months	3.7%	High Sep-25 943.08
Johnson	Expansion	Worst Six Months	-1.9%	Low Jan-03 786.41

1968   DOW JONES INDUSTRIAL AVERAGE

Previous Month Close	Jan	Feb	Mar	Apr	May	Jun	Jul	Aug	Sep	Oct	Nov	Dec
	905.11	855.47	840.50	840.67	912.22	899.00	897.80	883.00	896.01	935.79	952.39	985.08
1	C	861.36	840.44	861.25	913.20	C	896.35	878.07	C	942.32	948.41	C
2	906.84	863.56	C	863.96	918.05	C	896.84	871.27	C	C	C	983.34
3	904.13	C	C	869.11	919.21	905.38	903.51	C	900.36	949.47	C	985.21
4	899.39	C	830.56	872.52	C	916.63	C	C	906.95	952.95	946.23	C
5	901.24	861.13	827.03	865.81	C	907.42	C	872.53	917.52	C	C	977.69
6	C	861.25	837.21	C	914.53	910.13	C	876.92	921.25	C	949.47	978.24
7	C	859.92	836.22	C	919.90	914.88	C	C	C	956.68	950.65	C
8	908.92	850.32	835.24	884.42	918.86	C	912.60	870.37	C	956.24	958.98	C
9	908.29	840.04	C	C	911.35	C	920.42	869.65	924.98	C	C	979.36
10	903.95	C	C	892.63	912.91	913.38	C	C	919.38	949.78	C	977.69
11	899.79	C	843.04	905.69	C	917.95	922.82	C	C	949.59	C	C
12	898.98	C	843.22	C	C	C	922.46	881.02	915.65	C	964.20	977.13
13	C	831.77	842.23	C	909.96	913.86	C	884.68	917.21	C	967.43	981.29
14	C	837.38	830.91	C	908.06	913.62	C	C	C	949.96	963.89	C
15	892.74	839.23	837.55	910.19	907.82	C	923.72	879.51	C	955.31	965.88	C
16	887.14	836.34	C	906.78	903.72	C	921.20	885.89	921.37	C	C	976.32
17	883.78	C	C	908.17	898.98	903.45	C	C	923.05	958.91	C	970.91
18	882.80	C	840.09	909.21	C	900.20	917.95	C	C	967.49	963.70	C
19	880.32	838.65	832.99	897.65	C	C	913.92	887.68	923.98	C	C	975.14
20	C	843.10	830.85	C	894.19	898.28	C	888.67	924.42	C	C	966.99
21	C	849.23	825.13	C	896.32	900.93	C	C	C	967.49	965.13	C
22	871.71	C	826.05	891.99	896.79	C	900.32	888.30	C	963.14	967.06	C
23	864.77	849.80	C	897.48	893.15	C	898.10	892.34	930.45	C	C	953.75
24	862.23	C	C	898.46	895.28	901.83	C	C	938.28	956.68	C	952.32
25	864.25	C	827.27	905.57	C	901.41	885.47	C	C	961.28	971.35	C
26	865.06	841.77	831.54	906.03	C	C	888.47	896.13	933.24	C	979.49	954.25
27	C	846.68	836.57	C	891.60	898.76	C	893.65	933.80	C	976.32	952.51
28	C	844.72	835.12	C	896.78	897.80	C	C	C	957.73	C	C
29	863.67	840.50	840.67	908.34	895.21	C	883.36	894.33	C	951.08	985.08	C
30	859.57		C	912.22	C	C	883.00	896.01	935.79	C	C	945.11
31	855.47		C		899.00		C	C		952.39		943.75
Close	855.47	840.50	840.67	912.22	899.00	897.80	883.00	896.01	935.79	952.39	985.08	943.75
Month Pt Change	−49.64	−14.97	0.17	71.55	−13.22	−1.20	−14.80	13.01	39.78	16.60	32.69	−41.33
Month % Change	−5.5	−1.7	0.02	8.5	−1.4	−0.1	−1.6	1.5	4.4	1.8	3.4	−4.2
QTR % Change			−7.1			6.8			4.2			0.9
Year % Change												4.3

HIGHLIGHTS

Election Year	Bear Market Begins 12/3	Best Six Months	−0.2%	High	Dec-03	985.21
Johnson	Expansion	Worst Six Months	4.4%	Low	Mar-21	825.13

DOW JONES INDUSTRIAL AVERAGE — 1969

Previous Month Close	Jan	Feb	Mar	Apr	May	Jun	Jul	Aug	Sep	Oct	Nov	Dec
	943.75	946.05	905.21	935.48	950.18	937.56	873.19	815.47	836.72	813.09	855.99	812.30
1	C	C	C	933.08	949.22	C	875.90	826.59	C	806.89	C	805.04
2	947.73	C	C	930.92	957.17	933.17	880.69	C	837.78	811.84	C	801.35
3	951.89	946.85	908.63	927.30	C	930.78	886.12	C	835.67	808.41	854.54	793.36
4	C	945.11	919.51	C	C	928.84	C	822.58	825.30	C	853.48	796.53
5	C	945.98	923.11	C	958.95	930.71	C	821.23	819.50	C	854.08	793.03
6	936.66	946.67	913.54	C	962.06	924.77	C	825.88	C	809.40	855.20	C
7	925.72	947.85	911.18	918.78	959.60	C	883.21	826.27	C	806.23	860.48	C
8	921.25	C	C	923.17	963.68	C	870.35	824.46	811.84	802.20	C	785.04
9	927.46	C	C	929.97	961.61	918.05	861.62	C	815.67	803.79	C	783.79
10	925.53	C	917.14	932.89	C	912.49	847.79	C	828.01	806.96	863.05	783.99
11	C	948.97	920.93	933.46	C	904.60	852.25	819.83	825.77	C	859.75	783.53
12	C	949.09	917.52	C	957.86	892.58	C	812.96	824.25	C	855.99	786.69
13	923.11	952.70	907.14	C	962.97	894.84	C	809.13	C	819.30	849.85	C
14	928.33	951.95	904.28	932.64	968.85	C	843.14	813.23	C	832.43	849.26	C
15	931.75	C	C	931.94	965.16	C	841.13	820.88	830.45	830.06	C	784.05
16	938.59	C	C	923.49	967.30	891.16	849.34	C	831.64	838.77	C	773.83
17	935.54	937.72	904.03	924.12	C	885.73	853.09	C	826.56	836.06	842.53	769.93
18	C	930.82	907.38	924.82	C	887.09	845.92	827.68	831.57	C	845.17	783.79
19	C	925.10	912.11	C	959.02	882.37	C	833.69	830.39	C	839.96	789.86
20	931.25	916.65	920.13	C	949.26	876.16	C	833.22	C	839.23	831.18	C
21	929.82	C	920.00	917.51	951.78	C	C	834.87	C	846.88	823.13	C
22	934.17	C	C	918.59	950.04	C	834.02	837.25	831.77	860.35	C	785.97
23	940.20	C	C	917.64	947.45	870.86	827.95	C	834.81	855.73	C	783.79
24	938.59	903.97	917.08	921.20	C	877.20	826.53	C	834.68	862.26	812.90	794.15
25	C	899.80	917.08	924.00	C	874.10	818.06	831.44	829.92	C	807.29	C
26	C	905.77	923.30	C	946.94	870.28	C	823.52	824.18	C	810.52	797.65
27	937.47	903.03	930.88	C	938.66	869.76	C	824.78	C	860.28	C	C
28	938.40	905.21	935.48	925.08	936.92	C	806.23	828.41	C	855.86	812.30	C
29	938.09		C	934.10	937.56	C	801.96	836.72	818.04	848.34	C	792.37
30	942.13		C	950.18	C	873.19	803.58	C	813.09	850.51	C	794.68
31	946.05		C		C		815.47	C		855.99		800.36
Close	946.05	905.21	935.48	950.18	937.56	873.19	815.47	836.72	813.09	855.99	812.30	800.36
Month Pt Change	2.30	−40.84	30.27	14.70	−12.62	−64.37	−57.72	21.25	−23.63	42.90	−43.69	−11.94
Month % Change	0.2	−4.3	3.3	1.6	−1.3	−6.9	−6.6	2.6	−2.8	5.3	−5.1	−1.5
QTR % Change			−0.9			−6.7			−6.9			−1.6
Year % Change												−15.2

HIGHLIGHTS

Post Election Year	Bear Market	Best Six Months -14.0%	High	May-14	968.85
Nixon (1st Term)	Expansion	Worst Six Months -9.9%	Low	Dec-17	769.93

Data Bank

1970   DOW JONES INDUSTRIAL AVERAGE

Previous Month	Jan	Feb	Mar	Apr	May	Jun	Jul	Aug	Sep	Oct	Nov	Dec
Close	800.36	744.06	777.59	785.57	736.07	700.44	683.53	734.12	764.58	760.68	755.61	794.09
1	C	C	C	792.04	733.63	710.36	687.64	C	758.15	760.68	C	794.29
2	809.20	746.44	780.23	792.37	C	709.61	689.14	C	756.64	766.16	758.01	802.64
3	C	757.46	787.42	791.84	C	713.86	C	722.96	765.27	C	768.07	808.53
4	C	754.49	788.15	C	714.56	706.53	C	725.90	771.15	C	770.81	816.06
5	811.31	750.26	787.55	C	709.74	695.03	C	724.81	C	776.70	771.56	C
6	803.66	752.77	784.12	791.18	718.39	C	675.66	722.82	C	782.45	771.97	C
7	801.81	C	C	791.64	723.07	C	669.36	725.70	C	783.68	C	818.66
8	802.07	C	C	791.64	717.73	700.23	682.09	C	773.14	777.04	C	815.10
9	798.11	755.68	778.31	792.50	C	700.16	692.77	C	766.43	768.69	777.66	815.24
10	C	746.63	779.70	790.46	C	694.35	700.10	713.92	760.75	C	777.38	821.06
11	C	757.33	778.12	C	710.07	684.42	C	712.55	761.84	C	779.50	825.92
12	790.52	755.61	776.47	C	704.59	684.21	C	710.64	C	764.24	768.00	C
13	788.01	753.30	772.11	785.90	693.84	C	702.22	707.35	C	760.06	759.79	C
14	787.16	C	C	780.56	684.79	C	703.04	710.84	757.12	762.73	C	823.18
15	785.04	C	C	782.60	702.22	687.36	711.66	C	750.55	767.87	C	819.62
16	782.60	753.70	765.05	775.87	C	706.26	723.44	C	754.31	763.35	760.13	819.07
17	C	747.43	767.42	775.94	C	704.68	735.08	709.06	757.67	C	760.47	822.15
18	C	756.80	767.95	C	702.81	712.69	C	716.66	758.49	C	754.24	822.77
19	776.07	757.92	764.98	C	691.40	720.43	C	723.99	C	756.50	755.82	C
20	777.85	757.46	763.66	775.87	676.55	C	733.91	729.60	C	758.83	761.57	C
21	782.27	C	C	772.51	665.25	C	722.07	745.41	751.92	759.65	C	821.54
22	786.10	C	C	762.61	662.17	716.11	724.67	C	747.47	757.87	C	822.77
23	775.54	C	763.60	750.59	C	698.11	732.68	C	754.38	759.38	767.52	823.11
24	C	754.42	773.76	747.29	C	692.29	730.22	759.58	759.31	C	772.73	828.38
25	C	768.28	790.13	C	641.36	693.59	C	758.97	761.77	C	774.71	C
26	768.88	764.45	791.05	C	631.16	687.84	C	760.47	C	756.43	C	C
27	763.99	777.59	C	735.15	663.20	C	730.08	759.79	C	754.45	781.35	C
28	758.84	C	C	724.33	684.15	C	731.45	765.81	758.97	755.96	C	830.91
29	748.35		C	737.39	700.44	682.91	735.56	C	760.88	753.56	C	842.00
30	744.06		784.65	736.07	C	683.53	734.73	C	760.68	755.61	794.09	841.32
31	C		785.57		C		734.12	764.58		C		838.92
Close	744.06	777.59	785.57	736.07	700.44	683.53	734.12	764.58	760.68	755.61	794.09	838.92
Month Pt Change	−56.30	33.53	7.98	−49.50	−35.63	−16.91	50.59	30.46	−3.90	−5.07	38.48	44.83
Month % Change	−7.0	4.5	1.0	−6.3	−4.8	−2.4	7.4	4.1	−0.5	−0.7	5.1	5.6
QTR % Change			−1.8			−13.0			11.3			10.3
Year % Change												4.8

HIGHLIGHTS

Mid-Term Election Year	Bull Market Begins 5/26	Best Six Months	24.6%	High Dec-29 842.00
Nixon (1st Term)	Recession	Worst Six Months	2.7%	Low May-26 631.16

DOW JONES INDUSTRIAL AVERAGE 1971

Previous Month Close	Jan 838.92	Feb 868.50	Mar 878.83	Apr 904.37	May 941.75	Jun 907.81	Jul 891.14	Aug 858.43	Sep 898.07	Oct 887.19	Nov 839.00	Dec 831.34
1	C	877.81	882.53	903.88	C	913.65	893.03	C	899.02	893.98	825.86	846.01
2	C	874.59	883.01	903.04	C	919.62	890.19	864.92	900.63	C	827.98	848.79
3	C	876.23	882.39	C	932.41	921.30	C	850.03	912.75	C	842.58	859.59
4	830.57	874.79	891.36	C	938.45	922.15	C	844.92	C	895.66	843.17	C
5	835.77	876.57	898.00	905.07	939.92	C	C	849.45	C	891.14	840.39	C
6	837.97	C	C	912.73	937.39	C	892.30	850.61	C	900.55	C	855.72
7	837.83	C	C	918.49	936.97	923.06	895.88	C	916.47	901.80	C	857.40
8	837.01	882.12	898.62	920.39	C	915.01	900.99	C	920.93	893.91	837.54	854.85
9	C	879.79	899.10	C	C	912.46	901.80	842.65	915.89	C	837.91	852.15
10	C	881.09	895.88	C	932.55	915.96	C	839.59	911.00	C	826.15	856.75
11	837.21	885.34	899.44	C	937.25	916.47	C	846.38	C	891.94	814.91	C
12	844.19	888.83	898.34	926.64	937.46	C	903.40	859.01	C	893.55	812.94	C
13	841.11	C	C	927.28	936.34	C	892.38	856.02	909.39	888.80	C	858.79
14	843.31	C	C	932.55	936.06	907.71	891.21	C	901.65	878.36	C	855.14
15	845.70	C	908.20	938.17	C	907.20	888.87	C	904.86	874.58	810.53	863.76
16	C	890.06	914.64	940.21	C	908.59	888.51	888.95	903.11	C	818.71	871.39
17	C	887.87	914.02	C	921.30	906.25	C	899.90	908.22	C	822.14	873.80
18	847.82	885.06	916.83	C	918.56	889.16	C	886.17	C	872.44	815.35	C
19	849.47	878.56	912.92	948.85	920.04	C	886.39	880.77	C	868.43	810.67	C
20	849.95	C	C	944.42	923.41	C	892.30	880.91	905.15	855.65	C	885.01
21	854.74	C	C	941.33	921.87	876.53	890.84	C	903.40	854.85	C	888.32
22	861.31	868.98	910.60	940.63	C	874.42	886.68	C	893.55	852.37	803.15	884.86
23	C	870.00	908.89	947.79	C	879.45	887.78	892.38	891.28	C	797.97	881.17
24	C	875.62	899.37	C	913.15	877.26	C	904.13	889.31	C	798.63	C
25	865.62	881.98	900.81	C	906.69	876.68	C	908.37	C	848.50	C	C
26	866.79	878.83	903.48	944.00	906.41	C	888.87	906.10	C	845.36	816.59	C
27	860.83	C	C	947.09	905.78	C	880.70	908.15	883.47	836.38	C	881.47
28	865.14	C	C	950.82	907.81	873.10	872.01	C	884.42	837.62	C	889.98
29	868.50		903.48	948.15	C	882.30	861.42	C	883.83	839.00	829.73	893.66
30	C		903.39	941.75	C	891.14	858.43	901.43	887.19	C	831.34	889.07
31	C		904.37		C		C	898.07		C		890.20
Close	868.50	878.83	904.37	941.75	907.81	891.14	858.43	898.07	887.19	839.00	831.34	890.20
Month Pt Change	29.58	10.33	25.54	37.38	−33.94	−16.67	−32.71	39.64	−10.88	−48.19	−7.66	58.86
Month % Change	3.5	1.2	2.9	4.1	−3.6	−1.8	−3.7	4.6	−1.2	−5.4	−0.9	7.1
QTR % Change			7.8			−1.5			−0.4			0.3
Year % Change												6.1

HIGHLIGHTS

Pre-Election Year	Bear Market 4/26 - 11/23	Best Six Months 13.7%	High Apr-28	950.82
Nixon (1st Term)	Expansion	Worst Six Months−10.9%	Low Nov-23	797.97

1972 — DOW JONES INDUSTRIAL AVERAGE

Previous Month	Jan	Feb	Mar	Apr	May	Jun	Jul	Aug	Sep	Oct	Nov	Dec
Close	890.20	902.17	928.13	940.70	954.17	960.72	929.03	924.74	963.73	953.27	955.52	1018.21
1	C	901.79	935.43	C	942.28	960.72	C	930.46	970.05	C	968.54	1023.93
2	C	905.85	933.77	C	935.20	961.39	C	941.15	C	953.27	973.06	C
3	889.30	903.15	942.43	940.92	933.47	C	928.66	947.70	C	954.47	984.12	C
4	892.23	906.68	C	943.41	937.31	C	C	951.76	C	951.31	C	1027.02
5	904.43	C	C	954.55	941.23	954.39	933.47	C	969.37	941.30	C	1022.95
6	908.49	C	950.18	959.44	C	951.46	942.13	C	963.43	945.36	984.80	1027.54
7	910.37	903.97	946.87	962.60	C	944.08	938.06	953.12	962.45	C	C	1033.26
8	C	907.13	945.59	C	937.84	941.30	C	952.44	961.24	C	983.74	1033.19
9	C	918.72	942.81	C	925.12	934.45	C	951.16	C	948.75	988.26	C
10	907.96	921.28	939.87	958.08	931.07	C	932.27	952.89	C	951.84	995.26	C
11	912.10	917.59	C	962.60	934.83	C	925.87	964.18	955.00	946.42	C	1036.27
12	910.82	C	C	966.96	941.83	936.71	923.69	C	946.04	937.46	C	1033.19
13	905.18	C	928.66	965.53	C	938.29	916.99	C	949.88	930.46	997.07	1030.48
14	906.68	910.90	934.00	967.72	C	946.79	922.26	973.51	947.55	C	1003.16	1025.06
15	C	914.51	937.31	C	942.20	945.97	C	969.97	947.32	C	998.42	1027.24
16	C	922.94	936.71	C	939.27	945.06	C	964.25	C	921.66	1003.69	C
17	911.12	922.03	942.88	966.59	941.15	C	914.96	961.39	C	926.48	1005.57	C
18	917.22	917.52	C	968.92	951.23	C	911.72	965.83	945.36	932.34	C	1013.25
19	914.96	C	C	964.78	961.54	941.83	916.69	C	943.18	932.12	C	1009.18
20	910.30	C	941.15	966.29	C	948.22	910.45	C	940.25	942.81	1005.04	1004.82
21	907.44	C	934.00	963.80	C	951.61	920.45	967.19	939.49	C	1013.25	1000.00
22	C	913.46	933.93	C	965.31	950.71	C	973.51	943.03	C	1020.54	1004.21
23	C	911.88	944.69	C	962.30	944.69	C	970.35	C	951.31	C	C
24	896.82	912.70	942.28	957.48	965.46	C	935.36	958.38	C	952.51	1025.21	C
25	894.72	922.79	C	946.49	969.07	C	934.45	959.36	935.73	951.38	C	C
26	889.15	C	C	946.94	971.25	936.41	932.57	C	936.56	950.56	C	1006.70
27	899.83	C	939.72	945.97	C	935.28	926.85	C	947.25	946.42	1017.76	1007.68
28	906.38	924.29	937.01	954.17	C	930.84	926.70	956.95	955.15	C	1019.34	C
29	C	928.13	933.02	C	C	926.25	C	954.70	953.27	C	1018.81	1020.02
30	C		940.70	C	971.18	929.03	C	957.86	C	946.42	1018.21	C
31	902.17		C		960.72		924.74	963.73		955.52		C
Close	902.17	928.13	940.70	954.17	960.72	929.03	924.74	963.73	953.27	955.52	1018.21	1020.02
Month Pt Change	11.97	25.96	12.57	13.47	6.55	−31.69	−4.29	38.99	−10.46	2.25	62.69	1.81
Month % Change	1.3	2.9	1.4	1.4	0.7	−3.3	−0.5	4.2	−1.1	0.2	6.6	0.2
QTR % Change			5.7			−1.2			2.6			7.0
Year % Change												14.6

HIGHLIGHTS

Election Year	Bull Market	Best Six Months −3.6%	High Dec-11	1036.27
Nixon (1st Term)	Expansion	Worst Six Months 0.1%	Low Jan-26	889.15

DOW JONES INDUSTRIAL AVERAGE · 1973

Previous Month Close	Jan	Feb	Mar	Apr	May	Jun	Jul	Aug	Sep	Oct	Nov	Dec
	1020.02	999.02	955.07	951.01	921.43	901.41	891.71	926.40	887.57	947.10	956.58	822.25
1	C	985.78	949.65	C	921.21	893.96	C	912.18	C	948.83	948.83	C
2	1031.68	980.81	961.32	936.18	932.34	C	880.57	910.14	C	956.80	935.28	C
3	1043.80	C	C	927.75	945.67	C	874.17	908.87	C	964.55	C	806.52
4	1039.81	C	C	925.05	953.87	885.91	C	C	895.39	955.90	C	803.21
5	1047.49	978.40	966.89	923.46	C	900.81	874.32	C	899.08	971.25	919.40	788.31
6	C	979.91	979.00	931.07	C	898.18	870.11	912.78	901.04	C	913.08	814.12
7	C	968.32	979.98	C	950.71	909.62	C	911.95	898.63	C	920.08	838.05
8	1047.86	967.19	976.44	C	956.58	920.00	C	902.02	C	977.65	932.65	C
9	1047.11	979.46	972.23	947.55	949.05	C	877.26	901.49	C	974.19	908.41	C
10	1046.06	C	C	960.49	939.34	C	888.32	892.38	891.33	960.57	C	851.14
11	1051.70	C	C	967.41	927.98	915.11	908.19	C	885.76	976.07	C	834.18
12	1039.36	991.57	969.75	964.03	C	927.00	901.94	C	881.32	978.63	897.65	810.73
13	C	996.76	976.07	959.36	C	915.49	885.99	883.20	880.57	C	891.03	800.43
14	C	979.91	978.85	C	909.69	902.92	C	870.71	886.36	C	869.88	815.65
15	1025.59	973.13	969.82	C	917.44	888.55	C	874.17	C	967.04	874.55	C
16	1024.31	979.23	963.05	956.73	917.14	C	897.58	872.74	C	967.41	891.33	C
17	1029.12	C	C	953.42	911.72	C	898.03	871.84	892.99	962.52	C	811.12
18	1029.12	C	C	958.31	895.17	875.08	905.40	C	891.26	959.74	C	829.49
19	1026.19	C	952.06	963.20	C	881.55	906.68	C	910.37	963.73	862.66	829.57
20	C	983.59	949.43	C	C	884.71	910.90	867.40	920.53	C	844.90	828.11
21	C	974.34	938.37	C	886.51	873.65	C	857.84	927.90	C	854.98	818.73
22	1018.81	971.78	925.20	C	892.46	879.82	C	851.90	C	960.57	C	C
23	1018.66	959.89	922.71	955.37	895.02	C	913.15	864.46	C	966.51	854.00	C
24	1004.59	C	C	940.77	924.44	C	918.72	863.49	936.71	971.85	C	814.81
25	C	C	C	930.54	930.84	869.13	933.02	C	940.55	974.49	C	C
26	1003.54	953.79	927.90	937.76	C	879.44	934.53	C	949.50	987.06	824.95	837.56
27	C	947.92	944.91	922.19	C	884.63	936.71	870.71	953.27	C	817.73	851.01
28	C	955.07	948.00	C	C	894.64	C	872.07	947.10	C	839.78	848.02
29	996.46		959.14	C	925.57	891.71	C	883.43	C	984.80	835.11	C
30	992.93		951.01	921.43	908.87	C	933.77	882.53	C	968.54	822.25	C
31	999.02		C		901.41		926.40	887.57		956.58		850.86
Close	999.02	955.07	951.01	921.43	901.41	891.71	926.40	887.57	947.10	956.58	822.25	850.86
Month Pt Change	–21.00	–43.95	–4.06	–29.58	–20.02	–9.70	34.69	–38.83	59.53	9.48	–134.33	28.61
Month % Change	–2.1	–4.4	–0.4	–3.1	–2.2	–1.1	3.9	–4.2	6.7	1.0	–14.0	3.5
QTR % Change			–6.8			–6.2			6.2			–10.2
Year % Change												–16.6

HIGHLIGHTS

Post Election Year	Bear Market Begins 1/11	Best Six Months –12.5%	High Jan-11	1051.70
Nixon (2nd Term)	Expansion	Worst Six Months 3.8%	Low Dec-05	788.31

1974   DOW JONES INDUSTRIAL AVERAGE

Previous Month	Jan	Feb	Mar	Apr	May	Jun	Jul	Aug	Sep	Oct	Nov	Dec
Close	850.86	855.55	860.53	846.68	836.75	802.17	802.41	757.43	678.58	607.87	665.52	618.66
1	C	843.94	851.92	843.48	853.88	C	806.24	751.10	C	604.82	665.28	C
2	855.32	C	C	846.61	851.06	C	790.68	752.58	C	601.53	C	603.02
3	880.69	C	C	858.03	845.90	821.26	792.87	C	663.33	587.61	C	596.61
4	880.23	821.50	853.18	858.89	C	828.69	C	C	648.00	584.56	657.23	598.64
5	C	820.64	872.42	847.54	C	830.18	791.77	760.40	670.76	C	674.75	587.06
6	C	824.62	879.85	C	844.88	845.35	C	773.78	677.88	C	669.12	577.60
7	876.85	828.46	869.06	C	847.15	853.72	C	797.56	C	607.56	671.93	C
8	861.78	820.40	878.05	839.96	850.99	C	770.57	784.89	C	602.63	667.16	C
9	834.79	C	C	846.84	865.77	C	772.29	777.30	662.94	631.02	C	579.94
10	823.11	C	C	843.71	850.44	859.67	762.12	C	658.17	648.08	C	593.87
11	841.48	803.90	888.45	844.81	C	852.08	759.62	C	654.72	658.17	672.64	595.35
12	C	806.63	887.12	C	C	848.56	787.23	767.29	641.74	C	659.18	596.37
13	C	806.87	891.66	C	845.59	852.08	C	756.44	627.19	C	659.18	592.77
14	840.18	809.92	889.78	C	847.86	843.09	C	740.54	C	673.50	658.40	C
15	846.40	820.32	887.83	843.79	846.06	C	786.61	737.88	C	658.40	647.61	C
16	856.09	C	C	861.23	835.34	C	775.97	731.54	639.79	642.29	C	586.83
17	872.16	C	C	867.41	818.84	833.23	784.97	C	648.78	651.44	C	597.54
18	855.47	C	874.22	869.92	C	830.26	789.19	C	651.91	654.88	624.92	603.49
19	C	819.54	867.57	859.90	C	826.11	787.94	721.84	674.05	C	614.05	604.43
20	C	831.04	872.34	C	812.42	820.79	C	726.85	670.76	C	609.59	598.48
21	854.63	846.84	875.47	C	809.53	815.39	C	711.59	C	669.82	608.57	C
22	863.47	855.99	878.13	858.57	802.57	C	790.36	704.63	C	662.86	615.30	C
23	871.00	C	C	845.98	805.23	C	797.72	686.80	663.72	645.03	C	589.64
24	863.08	C	C	832.37	816.65	816.33	805.77	C	654.10	636.26	C	598.40
25	859.39	851.38	881.02	827.68	C	828.85	795.68	C	649.95	636.19	611.94	C
26	C	859.51	883.68	834.64	C	816.96	784.57	688.13	637.98	C	617.26	604.74
27	C	863.42	871.17	C	C	803.66	C	671.54	621.95	C	619.29	602.16
28	853.01	860.53	854.35	C	814.30	802.41	C	666.61	C	633.84	C	C
29	852.32		846.68	835.42	795.37	C	770.89	656.84	C	659.34	618.66	C
30	862.32		C	836.75	803.58	C	765.57	678.58	607.87	673.03	C	603.25
31	855.55		C		802.17		757.43	C		665.52		616.24
Close	855.55	860.53	846.68	836.75	802.17	802.41	757.43	678.58	607.87	665.52	618.66	616.24
Month Pt Change	4.69	4.98	−13.85	−9.93	−34.58	0.24	−44.98	−78.85	−70.71	57.65	−46.86	−2.42
Month % Change	0.6	0.6	−1.6	−1.2	−4.1	0.03	−5.6	−10.4	−10.4	9.5	−7.0	−0.4
QTR % Change			−0.5			−5.2			−24.2			1.4
Year % Change												−27.6

HIGHLIGHTS

Mid-Term Election Year	Bull Market Begins 12/6	Best Six Months	23.4%	High	Mar-13	891.66
Nixon (2nd Term) Ford 8/9/74 Recession		Worst Six Months	-20.5%	Low	Dec-06	577.60

DOW JONES INDUSTRIAL AVERAGE — 1975

Previous Month Close	Jan	Feb	Mar	Apr	May	Jun	Jul	Aug	Sep	Oct	Nov	Dec
Closee	616.24	703.69	739.05	768.15	821.34	832.29	878.99	831.51	835.34	793.88	836.04	860.67
1	C	C	C	761.58	830.96	C	877.42	826.50	C	784.16	C	856.34
2	632.04	C	C	760.56	848.48	846.61	870.38	C	823.69	794.55	C	843.20
3	634.54	711.44	753.13	752.19	C	846.14	871.79	C	832.29	813.21	825.72	825.49
4	C	708.07	757.74	747.26	C	839.96	C	818.05	838.31	C	830.13	829.11
5	C	717.85	752.82	C	855.60	842.15	C	810.15	835.97	C	836.27	818.80
6	637.20	714.17	761.81	C	834.72	839.64	C	813.67	C	819.66	840.92	C
7	641.19	711.91	770.10	742.88	836.44	C	861.08	815.79	C	816.51	835.80	C
8	635.40	C	C	749.22	840.50	C	857.79	817.74	840.11	823.91	C	821.63
9	645.26	C	C	767.99	850.13	830.10	871.87	C	827.75	824.54	C	824.15
10	658.79	708.39	776.13	781.29	C	822.12	871.87	C	817.66	823.91	835.48	833.99
11	C	707.60	770.89	789.50	C	824.55	871.09	823.76	812.66	C	838.55	832.73
12	C	715.03	763.69	C	847.47	819.31	C	828.54	809.23	C	852.25	832.81
13	654.18	726.92	762.98	C	850.13	824.47	C	820.56	C	837.77	851.23	C
14	648.70	734.20	773.47	806.95	858.73	C	875.86	817.04	C	835.25	853.67	C
15	653.39	C	C	815.08	848.80	C	881.81	825.64	803.19	837.22	C	836.59
16	655.74	C	C	815.71	837.61	834.56	872.11	C	795.13	837.85	C	844.30
17	644.63	C	786.53	819.46	C	828.61	864.28	C	799.05	832.18	856.66	846.27
18	C	731.30	779.41	808.43	C	827.83	862.41	822.75	814.61	C	855.24	852.09
19	C	736.39	769.48	C	837.69	845.35	C	808.51	829.79	C	848.24	844.38
20	647.45	745.38	764.00	C	830.49	855.44	C	793.26	C	842.25	843.51	C
21	641.90	749.77	763.06	815.86	818.68	C	854.74	791.69	C	846.82	840.76	C
22	652.61	C	C	814.14	818.91	C	846.76	804.76	820.40	849.57	C	838.63
23	656.76	C	C	802.49	831.90	864.83	836.67	C	819.85	855.16	C	843.75
24	666.61	736.94	743.43	803.66	C	869.06	840.27	C	826.19	840.52	845.64	851.94
25	C	719.18	747.89	811.80	C	872.73	834.09	812.34	820.24	C	855.40	C
26	C	728.10	766.19	C	C	874.14	C	803.11	818.60	C	858.55	859.81
27	692.66	731.15	770.26	C	826.11	873.12	C	807.20	C	838.48	C	C
28	694.77	739.05	C	810.00	817.04	C	827.83	829.47	C	851.46	860.67	C
29	705.96		C	803.04	815.00	C	824.86	835.34	805.23	838.63	C	856.66
30	696.42		C	821.34	832.29	878.99	831.66	C	793.88	839.42	C	852.41
31	703.69		768.15		C		831.51	C		836.04		852.41
Close	703.69	739.05	768.15	821.34	832.29	878.99	831.51	835.34	793.88	836.04	860.67	852.41
Month Pt Change	87.45	35.36	29.10	53.19	10.95	46.70	-47.48	3.83	-41.46	42.16	24.63	-8.26
Month % Change	14.2	5.0	3.9	6.9	1.3	5.6	-5.4	0.5	-5.0	5.3	2.9	-1.0
QTR % Change			24.7			14.4			-9.7			7.4
Year % Change												38.3

HIGHLIGHTS

Pre-Election Year	Bull Market	Best Six Months	19.2%	High	Jul-15	881.81
Ford	Expansion Begins Q2	Worst Six Months	1.8%	Low	Jan-02	632.04

1976 DOW JONES INDUSTRIAL AVERAGE

Previous Month	Jan	Feb	Mar	Apr	May	Jun	Jul	Aug	Sep	Oct	Nov	Dec
Close	852.41	975.28	972.61	999.45	996.85	975.23	1002.78	984.64	973.74	990.19	964.93	947.22
1	C	C	975.36	994.10	C	973.13	994.84	C	985.95	979.89	966.09	949.38
2	858.71	971.35	985.12	991.58	C	975.93	999.84	982.26	984.79	C	C	946.64
3	C	972.61	978.83	C	990.32	973.80	C	990.33	989.11	C	956.53	950.55
4	C	976.62	970.64	C	993.70	963.90	C	992.28	C	977.98	960.44	C
5	877.83	964.81	972.92	1004.09	986.46	C	C	986.68	C	966.76	943.07	C
6	890.82	954.90	C	1001.65	989.53	C	991.81	986.00	C	959.69	C	961.77
7	898.69	C	C	986.22	996.22	958.09	991.16	C	996.59	965.09	C	960.69
8	907.98	C	988.74	977.09	C	959.97	991.98	C	992.94	952.38	933.68	963.26
9	911.13	957.18	993.70	968.28	C	958.09	1003.11	983.46	986.87	C	930.77	970.74
10	C	968.75	995.28	C	1007.48	964.39	C	993.43	988.36	C	924.04	973.15
11	C	971.90	1003.31	C	1006.61	978.80	C	986.79	C	940.82	931.43	C
12	922.39	966.78	987.64	971.27	1005.67	C	1011.21	987.12	C	932.35	927.69	C
13	912.94	958.36	C	984.26	1001.10	C	1006.06	990.19	983.29	948.30	C	974.24
14	929.63	C	C	974.65	992.60	991.24	1005.16	C	978.64	935.92	C	980.63
15	924.51	C	974.50	980.48	C	985.92	997.46	C	979.31	937.00	935.42	983.79
16	929.63	C	983.47	C	C	988.62	993.21	992.77	987.95	C	935.34	981.30
17	C	950.57	985.99	C	987.64	1003.19	C	999.34	995.10	C	938.08	979.06
18	C	960.09	979.85	C	989.45	1001.88	C	995.01	C	946.56	950.13	C
19	943.72	975.76	979.85	988.11	988.90	C	990.83	983.88	C	949.97	948.80	C
20	949.86	987.80	C	1003.46	997.27	C	988.29	974.07	994.51	954.87	C	972.41
21	946.24	C	C	1011.02	990.75	1007.45	989.44	C	1014.79	944.90	C	978.39
22	943.48	C	982.29	1007.71	C	997.63	991.08	C	1014.05	938.75	955.87	984.54
23	953.95	985.28	995.43	1000.71	C	996.56	990.91	971.49	1010.80	C	949.30	985.62
24	C	993.55	1009.21	C	971.53	1003.77	C	962.93	1009.31	C	950.96	C
25	C	994.57	1002.13	C	971.69	999.84	C	970.83	C	938.00	C	C
26	961.51	978.83	1003.46	1002.76	968.63	C	991.51	960.44	C	948.14	956.62	C
27	957.81	972.61	C	995.51	965.57	C	984.13	963.93	1013.13	956.12	C	996.09
28	951.35	C	C	1000.70	975.23	997.38	981.33	C	994.93	952.63	C	1000.08
29	968.75	C	997.40	1002.13	C	1000.65	979.29	C	991.19	964.93	950.05	994.93
30	975.28		992.13	996.85	C	1002.78	984.64	968.92	990.19	C	947.22	999.09
31	C		999.45		C		C	973.74		C		1004.65
Close	975.28	972.61	999.45	996.85	975.23	1002.78	984.64	973.74	990.19	964.93	947.22	1004.65
Month Pt Change	122.87	-2.67	26.84	-2.60	-21.62	27.55	-18.14	-10.90	16.45	-25.26	-17.71	57.43
Month % Change	14.4	-0.3	2.8	-0.3	-2.2	2.8	-1.8	-1.1	1.7	-2.6	-1.8	6.1
QTR % Change			17.2			0.3			-1.3			1.5
Year % Change												17.9

HIGHLIGHTS

Election Year	Bear Market Begins 9/21	Best Six Months −3.9%	High Sep-21	1014.79
Ford	Expansion	Worst Six Months −3.2%	Low Jan-02	858.71

DOW JONES INDUSTRIAL AVERAGE 1977

Previous Month	Jan	Feb	Mar	Apr	May	Jun	Jul	Aug	Sep	Oct	Nov	Dec
Close	1004.65	954.37	936.42	919.13	926.90	898.66	916.30	890.07	861.49	847.11	818.35	829.70
1	C	958.36	944.73	927.36	C	906.55	912.65	891.81	864.86	C	806.91	825.71
2	C	952.79	942.07	C	931.22	903.15	C	887.39	872.31	C	800.85	823.98
3	999.75	947.14	948.64	C	934.19	912.23	C	886.00	C	851.96	802.67	C
4	987.87	947.89	953.46	915.56	940.72	C	C	888.17	C	842.00	809.94	C
5	978.06	C	C	916.14	943.44	C	913.59	888.69	C	837.32	C	821.03
6	979.89	C	C	914.73	936.74	903.04	907.73	C	873.27	842.08	C	806.91
7	983.13	946.31	955.12	918.88	C	908.67	909.51	C	876.39	840.35	816.44	807.43
8	C	942.24	952.04	C	C	912.99	907.99	879.42	869.16	C	816.27	806.91
9	C	933.84	942.90	C	933.09	909.85	C	879.42	857.04	C	818.43	815.23
10	986.87	937.92	946.73	C	936.14	910.79	C	887.04	C	840.26	832.55	C
11	976.65	931.52	947.72	924.10	926.90	C	905.53	877.43	C	832.29	845.89	C
12	968.25	C	C	937.16	925.54	C	903.41	871.10	854.38	823.98	C	815.75
13	976.15	C	C	938.18	928.34	912.40	902.99	C	854.56	818.17	C	815.23
14	972.16	938.33	958.36	947.00	C	922.57	C	C	858.71	821.64	838.36	822.68
15	C	944.32	965.01	947.76	C	917.57	905.95	874.13	860.79	C	842.78	817.91
16	C	948.30	968.00	C	932.50	920.45	C	869.28	856.81	C	837.06	815.32
17	967.25	943.73	964.84	C	936.48	920.45	C	864.69	C	820.34	831.86	C
18	962.43	940.24	961.02	942.76	941.91	C	910.60	864.26	C	820.51	835.76	C
19	968.67	C	C	938.77	936.48	C	919.27	863.48	851.52	812.20	C	807.95
20	959.03	C	C	942.59	930.46	924.27	920.48	C	851.78	814.80	C	806.22
21	962.43	C	953.54	935.80	C	928.60	921.78	C	840.96	808.30	836.11	813.93
22	C	939.91	950.96	927.07	C	926.31	923.42	867.29	839.41	C	842.52	821.81
23	C	938.25	942.32	C	917.06	925.37	C	865.56	839.14	C	843.30	829.87
24	963.60	932.60	935.67	C	912.40	929.70	C	862.87	C	802.32	C	C
25	965.92	933.43	928.86	914.60	903.24	C	914.24	854.12	C	801.54	844.42	C
26	958.53	C	C	915.62	908.07	C	908.18	855.42	841.65	813.41	C	C
27	954.54	C	C	923.76	898.83	924.10	888.43	C	835.85	818.61	C	829.70
28	957.53	936.42	926.11	927.32	C	915.62	889.99	C	834.72	822.68	839.57	829.70
29	C		932.01	926.90	C	913.33	890.07	864.09	840.09	C	827.27	830.39
30	C		921.21	C	C	916.30	C	858.89	847.11	C	829.70	831.17
31	954.37		919.13		898.66		C	861.49		818.35		C
Close	954.37	936.42	919.13	926.90	898.66	916.30	890.07	861.49	847.11	818.35	829.70	831.17
Month Pt Change	−50.28	−17.95	−17.29	7.77	−28.24	17.64	−26.23	−28.58	−14.38	−28.76	11.35	1.47
Month % Change	−5.0	−1.9	−1.8	0.8	−3.0	2.0	−2.9	−3.2	−1.7	−3.4	1.4	0.2
QTR % Change			−8.5			−0.3			−7.6			−1.9
Year % Change												−17.3

HIGHLIGHTS

Post Election Year	Bear Market	Best Six Months	2.3%	High Jan-03 999.75
Carter	Expansion	Worst Six Months	-11.7%	Low Nov-02 800.85

Data Bank

1978 — DOW JONES INDUSTRIAL AVERAGE

Previous Month Close	Jan	Feb	Mar	Apr	May	Jun	Jul	Aug	Sep	Oct	Nov	Dec
	831.17	769.92	742.12	757.36	837.32	840.61	818.95	862.27	876.82	865.82	792.45	799.03
1	C	774.34	743.33	C	844.33	840.70	C	860.71	879.33	C	827.79	811.50
2	C	775.38	746.45	C	840.18	847.54	C	883.49	C	871.36	816.96	C
3	817.74	770.96	747.31	751.04	828.83	C	812.89	886.87	C	867.90	823.11	C
4	813.58	C	C	755.37	824.41	C	C	888.43	C	873.96	C	806.83
5	804.92	C	C	763.08	829.09	863.83	805.79	C	886.61	876.47	C	820.51
6	793.49	768.62	742.72	763.95	C	866.51	807.17	C	895.79	880.02	814.88	821.90
7	C	778.85	746.79	769.58	C	861.92	812.46	885.05	893.71	C	800.07	816.09
8	C	782.66	750.87	C	824.58	862.09	C	889.21	907.74	C	807.61	811.85
9	784.56	777.81	750.00	C	822.07	859.23	C	891.63	C	893.19	803.97	C
10	781.53	775.99	758.58	773.65	822.16	C	816.79	885.48	C	891.63	807.09	C
11	775.90	C	C	770.18	834.20	C	821.29	890.85	907.74	901.42	C	817.65
12	778.15	C	C	766.29	840.70	856.72	824.93	C	906.44	896.74	C	814.97
13	775.73	774.43	759.96	775.21	C	856.98	824.76	C	899.60	897.09	792.01	809.86
14	C	765.16	762.56	795.13	C	854.56	839.83	888.17	887.04	C	785.26	812.54
15	C	761.69	758.58	C	846.76	844.25	C	887.13	878.55	C	785.60	805.35
16	771.74	753.29	762.82	C	854.30	836.97	C	894.58	C	875.17	794.18	C
17	779.02	752.69	768.71	810.12	858.37	C	839.05	900.12	C	866.34	797.73	C
18	786.30	C	C	803.27	850.92	C	829.00	896.83	870.15	859.67	C	787.51
19	778.67	C	C	808.04	846.85	838.62	840.70	C	861.57	846.41	C	789.85
20	776.94	C	773.82	814.54	C	830.04	838.62	C	857.16	838.01	805.61	793.66
21	C	749.31	762.82	812.80	C	824.93	833.42	888.95	861.14	C	804.05	794.79
22	C	749.05	757.54	C	855.42	827.70	C	892.41	862.44	C	807.00	808.47
23	770.70	750.95	756.50	C	845.29	823.02	C	897.00	C	839.66	C	C
24	771.57	756.24	C	826.06	837.92	C	831.60	897.35	C	832.55	810.12	C
25	772.44	C	C	833.59	835.41	C	839.57	895.53	862.35	830.21	C	C
26	763.34	C	C	836.97	831.69	812.28	847.19	C	868.16	821.12	C	816.01
27	764.12	748.35	753.21	826.92	C	817.31	850.57	C	860.19	806.05	813.84	808.56
28	C	742.12	758.84	837.32	C	819.91	856.29	884.88	861.31	C	804.14	805.96
29	C		761.78	C	C	821.64	C	880.20	865.82	C	790.11	805.01
30	772.44		759.62	C	834.20	818.95	C	880.72	C	811.85	799.03	C
31	769.92		757.36		840.61		862.27	876.82		792.45		C
Close	769.92	742.12	757.36	837.32	840.61	818.95	862.27	876.82	865.82	792.45	799.03	805.01
Month Pt Change	−61.25	−27.80	15.24	79.96	3.29	−21.66	43.32	14.55	−11.00	−73.37	6.58	5.98
Month % Change	−7.4	−3.6	2.1	10.6	0.4	−2.6	5.3	1.7	−1.3	−8.5	0.8	0.7
QTR % Change			−8.9			8.1			5.7			−7.0
Year % Change												−3.1

HIGHLIGHTS

Mid-Term Election Year	Bull Market 2/28 - 9/8	Best Six Months 7.9%	High Sep-08 907.74
Carter	Expansion	Worst Six Months −5.4%	Low Feb-28 742.12

Previous Month	Jan	Feb	Mar	Apr	May	Jun	Jul	Aug	Sep	Oct	Nov	Dec
Close	805.01	839.22	808.82	862.18	854.90	822.33	841.98	846.42	887.63	878.58	815.70	822.35
1	C	840.87	815.84	C	855.51	821.21	C	850.34	C	872.95	820.14	C
2	811.42	834.63	815.75	855.25	855.51	C	834.04	847.95	C	885.32	818.94	C
3	817.39	C	C	868.33	857.59	C	835.58	846.16	C	885.15	C	819.62
4	826.14	C	C	869.80	847.54	821.90	C	C	872.61	890.10	C	824.91
5	830.73	823.98	827.36	877.60	C	831.34	835.75	C	866.13	897.61	812.63	828.41
6	C	822.85	826.58	875.69	C	835.50	846.16	848.55	867.32	C	806.48	835.07
7	C	816.01	834.29	C	833.42	836.97	C	859.81	874.15	C	796.67	833.19
8	828.14	818.87	844.85	C	834.89	835.15	C	863.14	C	884.04	797.61	C
9	831.43	822.23	842.86	873.70	838.62	C	852.99	858.28	C	857.59	806.48	C
10	824.93	C	C	878.72	828.92	C	850.34	867.06	876.88	849.32	C	833.87
11	828.05	C	C	871.71	830.56	837.58	843.86	C	869.71	844.62	C	833.70
12	836.28	824.84	844.68	870.50	C	845.29	836.86	C	870.90	838.99	821.93	835.67
13	C	830.21	846.93	C	C	842.17	833.53	875.26	870.73	C	814.08	836.09
14	C	829.78	845.37	C	825.02	842.34	C	876.71	879.10	C	816.55	842.75
15	848.67	829.09	847.02	C	825.88	843.30	C	885.84	C	831.06	821.33	C
16	835.59	827.01	852.82	860.45	828.48	C	834.90	884.04	C	829.52	815.70	C
17	834.20	C	C	857.93	842.95	C	828.50	883.36	881.31	830.72	C	844.62
18	839.14	C	C	860.27	841.91	839.40	828.58	C	874.15	830.12	C	838.65
19	837.49	C	857.59	855.25	C	839.40	827.30	C	876.45	814.68	815.27	838.91
20	C	834.55	850.31	856.98	C	839.83	828.07	886.52	893.69	C	809.22	843.34
21	C	834.55	857.76	C	842.43	843.64	C	886.01	893.94	C	807.42	838.91
22	838.53	828.57	861.31	C	845.37	849.10	C	885.84	C	809.13	C	C
23	846.85	823.28	859.75	860.10	837.40	C	825.51	880.38	C	806.83	811.77	C
24	846.41	C	C	866.86	837.66	C	829.78	880.20	885.84	808.36	C	839.16
25	854.64	C	C	867.46	836.28	844.25	839.51	C	886.18	805.46	C	C
26	859.75	821.12	854.82	860.97	C	837.66	839.76	C	886.35	809.30	828.75	838.14
27	C	807.00	871.36	856.64	C	840.52	839.76	885.41	887.46	C	825.85	840.10
28	C	808.82	866.25	C	C	843.04	C	884.64	878.58	C	830.46	838.91
29	855.77		866.77	C	832.55	841.98	C	884.90	C	808.62	831.74	C
30	851.78		862.18	854.90	822.16	C	838.74	883.70	C	823.81	822.35	C
31	839.22		C		822.33		846.42	887.63		815.70		838.74
Close	839.22	808.82	862.18	854.90	822.33	841.98	846.42	887.63	878.58	815.70	822.35	838.74
Month Pt Change	34.21	−30.40	53.36	−7.28	−32.57	19.65	4.44	41.21	−9.05	−62.88	6.65	16.39
Month % Change	4.2	−3.6	6.6	−0.8	−3.8	2.4	0.5	4.9	−1.0	−7.2	0.8	2.0
QTR % Change			7.1			−2.3			4.3			−4.5
Year % Change												4.2

Pre-Election Year	Bear Market	Best Six Months	0.2%	High	Oct-05	897.61
Carter	Expansion	Worst Six Months	-4.6%	Low	Nov-07	796.67

1980   DOW JONES INDUSTRIAL AVERAGE

Previous Month Close	Jan	Feb	Mar	Apr	May	Jun	Jul	Aug	Sep	Oct	Nov	Dec
	838.74	875.85	863.14	785.75	817.06	850.85	867.92	935.32	932.59	932.42	924.49	993.34
1	C	881.48	C	784.47	808.79	C	872.27	931.48	C	939.42	C	969.45
2	824.57	C	C	787.80	810.92	847.35	876.02	C	940.78	942.24	C	974.40
3	820.31	C	854.35	784.13	C	843.77	888.91	C	953.16	950.68	937.20	972.27
4	828.84	875.09	856.48	C	C	858.02	C	931.06	948.81	C	C	970.48
5	C	876.62	844.88	C	816.30	858.70	C	929.78	940.96	C	953.16	956.23
6	C	881.83	828.07	C	816.04	861.52	C	938.23	C	965.70	935.41	C
7	832.00	885.49	820.56	768.34	821.25	C	898.21	950.94	C	960.67	932.42	C
8	851.71	895.73	C	775.00	815.19	C	897.35	954.69	928.58	963.99	C	933.70
9	850.09	C	C	785.92	805.80	860.67	897.27	C	934.73	958.96	C	934.04
10	858.96	C	818.94	791.47	C	863.99	885.92	C	938.48	950.68	933.79	916.21
11	858.53	889.59	826.45	791.55	C	872.70	891.13	964.08	941.30	C	944.03	908.45
12	C	898.98	819.54	C	805.20	872.61	C	952.39	936.52	C	964.93	917.15
13	C	903.84	809.56	C	816.89	876.37	C	949.23	C	959.90	982.42	C
14	863.57	893.77	811.69	784.90	819.62	C	905.55	962.63	C	962.20	986.35	C
15	868.60	884.98	C	783.36	822.53	C	901.54	966.72	937.63	972.44	C	911.60
16	865.19	C	C	771.25	826.88	877.73	904.44	C	945.90	958.70	C	918.09
17	863.57	C	788.65	768.86	C	879.27	915.10	C	961.26	956.14	986.26	928.50
18	867.15	C	801.62	763.40	C	881.91	923.98	948.63	956.48	C	997.95	930.20
19	C	876.02	800.94	C	830.89	870.90	C	939.85	963.74	C	991.04	937.20
20	C	886.86	789.08	C	832.51	869.71	C	945.31	C	960.84	1000.17	C
21	872.78	868.52	785.15	759.13	831.06	C	928.67	955.03	C	954.44	989.93	C
22	866.21	868.77	C	789.85	842.92	C	927.30	958.19	974.57	955.12	C	958.79
23	877.56	C	C	789.25	854.10	873.81	928.58	C	962.03	939.51	C	958.28
24	879.95	C	765.44	797.10	C	877.30	926.11	C	964.76	943.60	978.75	963.05
25	876.11	859.81	767.83	803.58	C	887.54	918.09	956.23	955.97	C	982.68	C
26	C	864.25	762.12	C	C	883.45	C	953.41	940.10	C	989.68	966.38
27	C	855.12	759.98	C	857.76	881.83	C	943.09	C	931.74	C	C
28	878.50	854.44	777.65	805.46	860.32	C	925.43	930.38	C	932.59	993.34	C
29	874.40	863.14	C	811.09	846.25	C	931.91	932.59	921.93	929.18	C	960.58
30	881.91		C	817.06	850.85	867.92	936.18	C	932.42	917.75	C	962.03
31	875.85		785.75		C		935.32	C		924.49		963.99
Close	875.85	863.14	785.75	817.06	850.85	867.92	935.32	932.59	932.42	924.49	993.34	963.99
Month Pt Change	37.11	−12.71	−77.39	31.31	33.79	17.07	67.40	−2.73	−0.17	−7.93	68.85	−29.35
Month % Change	4.4	−1.5	−9.0	4.0	4.1	2.0	7.8	−0.3	−0.02	−0.9	7.4	−3.0
QTR % Change			−6.3			10.5			7.4			3.4
Year % Change												14.9

HIGHLIGHTS

Election Year	Bull Market Begins 4/21	Best Six Months	7.9%	High Nov-20 1000.17
Carter	Recession Q1 - Q2	Worst Six Months	13.1%	Low Apr-21 759.13

DOW JONES INDUSTRIAL AVERAGE — 1981

Previous Month Close	Jan	Feb	Mar	Apr	May	Jun	Jul	Aug	Sep	Oct	Nov	Dec
	963.99	947.27	974.58	1003.87	997.75	991.75	976.88	952.34	881.47	849.98	852.55	888.98
1	C	C	C	1014.14	995.59	997.96	967.66	C	882.71	852.26	C	890.22
2	972.78	932.25	977.99	1009.01	C	987.48	959.19	C	884.23	860.73	866.82	882.61
3	C	941.38	966.02	1007.11	C	989.71	C	946.25	867.01	C	868.72	883.85
4	C	941.98	971.44	C	979.11	986.74	C	945.97	861.68	C	866.82	892.69
5	992.66	946.76	964.62	C	972.44	993.79	C	953.58	C	859.87	859.11	C
6	1004.69	952.30	964.62	994.24	973.34	C	949.30	952.91	C	856.26	852.45	C
7	980.89	C	C	992.89	978.39	C	954.15	942.54	C	868.72	C	886.99
8	965.70	C	C	993.43	976.40	995.64	953.48	C	851.12	878.14	C	881.75
9	968.69	947.18	976.42	998.83	C	994.44	959.00	C	853.88	873.00	855.21	888.22
10	C	948.63	972.66	1000.27	C	993.88	955.67	943.68	862.44	C	853.98	892.03
11	C	942.49	967.67	C	963.44	1007.42	C	949.30	872.81	C	857.12	886.51
12	968.77	936.60	989.82	C	970.82	1006.28	C	945.21	C	869.48	860.54	C
13	965.10	931.57	985.77	993.16	967.76	C	954.34	944.35	C	865.58	855.88	C
14	966.47	C	C	989.10	973.07	C	948.25	936.93	866.15	850.65	C	871.48
15	969.97	C	C	1001.71	985.95	1011.99	954.15	C	858.35	856.26	C	875.95
16	973.29	C	1002.79	1005.58	C	1003.33	955.48	C	851.60	851.69	845.03	868.72
17	C	939.68	992.53	C	C	1006.56	958.90	926.75	840.09	C	850.17	870.53
18	C	947.10	994.06	C	985.77	995.15	C	924.37	836.19	C	844.08	875.76
19	970.99	933.36	986.58	C	980.01	996.19	C	926.46	C	847.13	844.75	C
20	950.68	936.09	992.80	1015.94	976.86	C	949.54	928.37	C	851.88	852.93	C
21	946.25	C	C	1005.94	976.59	C	934.46	920.57	846.56	851.03	C	873.10
22	940.44	C	C	1007.02	971.72	994.20	924.66	C	845.70	848.27	C	871.96
23	940.19	945.23	1004.23	1010.27	C	1006.66	928.56	C	840.94	837.99	851.79	869.67
24	C	946.10	996.13	1020.35	C	999.33	936.74	900.11	835.14	C	870.24	873.38
25	C	954.40	1015.22	C	C	996.77	C	901.83	824.01	C	878.14	C
26	938.91	966.81	1005.76	C	983.96	992.87	C	899.26	C	830.96	C	C
27	949.49	974.58	994.78	1024.05	993.14	C	945.87	889.08	C	838.38	885.94	C
28	942.58	C	C	1016.93	994.25	C	939.40	892.22	842.56	837.61	C	870.34
29	948.89		C	1004.32	991.75	984.59	937.40	C	847.89	832.95	C	868.25
30	947.27		992.16	997.75	C	976.88	945.11	C	849.98	852.55	888.98	873.10
31	C		1003.87		C		952.34	881.47		C		875.00
Close	947.27	974.58	1003.87	997.75	991.75	976.88	952.34	881.47	849.98	852.55	888.98	875.00
Month Pt Change	−16.72	27.31	29.29	−6.12	−6.00	−14.87	−24.54	−70.87	−31.49	2.57	36.43	−13.98
Month % Change	−1.7	2.9	3.0	−0.6	−0.6	−1.5	−2.5	−7.4	−3.6	0.3	4.3	−1.6
QTR % Change			4.1			−2.7			−13.0			2.9
Year % Change												−9.2

Post Election Year	Bear Market Begins 4/27	Best Six Months −0.5%	High Apr-27	1024.05
Reagan (1st term)	Recession Begins Q3	Worst Six Months −14.6%	Low Sep-25	824.01

1982 — DOW JONES INDUSTRIAL AVERAGE

Previous Month Close	Jan	Feb	Mar	Apr	May	Jun	Jul	Aug	Sep	Oct	Nov	Dec
	875.00	871.10	824.39	822.77	848.36	819.54	811.93	808.60	901.31	896.25	991.72	1039.28
1	C	851.69	828.39	833.24	C	814.97	803.27	C	895.05	907.74	1005.70	1031.09
2	C	852.55	825.82	838.57	C	816.88	796.99	822.11	909.40	C	1022.08	1033.11
3	C	845.03	815.16	C	849.03	816.50	C	816.40	925.13	C	1065.49	1031.36
4	882.52	847.03	807.55	C	854.45	804.98	C	803.46	C	903.61	1050.22	C
5	865.30	851.03	807.36	835.33	854.45	C	C	795.85	C	907.19	1051.78	C
6	861.02	C	C	839.33	863.20	C	798.90	784.34	C	944.26	C	1055.65
7	861.78	C	C	836.85	869.20	804.03	799.66	C	914.28	965.97	C	1056.94
8	866.53	833.43	795.47	842.94	C	802.23	804.98	C	915.75	986.85	1037.44	1047.09
9	C	830.57	803.84	C	C	795.57	814.12	780.35	912.53	C	1060.25	1027.96
10	C	836.66	804.89	C	860.92	798.71	C	779.30	906.82	C	1044.52	1018.76
11	850.46	834.67	805.56	C	865.87	809.74	C	777.21	C	1012.79	1054.73	C
12	847.70	833.81	797.37	841.32	865.77	C	824.87	776.92	C	1003.68	1039.92	C
13	838.95	C	C	841.04	859.11	C	824.20	788.05	918.69	1015.18	C	1024.28
14	842.28	C	C	838.09	857.78	801.85	828.39	C	923.01	996.87	C	1009.38
15	847.60	C	800.99	839.61	C	801.27	827.34	C	930.46	993.10	1021.43	992.64
16	C	831.34	798.33	843.42	C	796.90	828.67	792.43	927.80	C	1008.00	990.25
17	C	827.63	795.85	C	845.32	791.48	C	831.24	916.94	C	1027.50	1011.50
18	855.12	828.96	805.27	C	840.85	788.62	C	829.43	C	1019.22	1032.10	C
19	847.41	824.30	805.65	846.08	835.90	C	826.10	838.57	C	1013.80	1021.25	C
20	845.89	C	C	840.56	832.48	C	833.43	869.29	916.30	1034.12	C	1004.51
21	848.27	C	C	843.42	835.90	789.95	832.19	C	934.79	1036.98	C	1030.26
22	845.03	811.26	819.54	853.12	C	799.66	832.00	C	927.61	1031.46	1000.00	1035.04
23	C	812.98	826.67	862.16	C	813.17	830.57	891.17	925.77	C	990.99	1045.07
24	C	826.77	823.34	C	836.38	810.41	C	874.90	919.52	C	1000.00	C
25	842.75	825.82	827.63	C	834.57	803.08	C	884.89	C	995.13	C	C
26	841.51	824.39	817.92	865.58	828.77	C	825.44	892.41	C	1006.07	1007.36	C
27	842.66	C	C	857.50	824.96	C	822.77	883.47	920.90	1006.35	C	1070.55
28	864.25	C	C	852.64	819.54	811.93	811.83	C	919.33	990.99	C	1058.87
29	871.10		823.82	844.94	C	812.21	812.21	C	906.27	991.72	1002.85	1059.60
30	C		824.49	848.36	C	811.93	808.60	893.30	896.25	C	1039.28	1047.37
31	C		822.77		C		C	901.31		C		1046.54
Close	871.10	824.39	822.77	848.36	819.54	811.93	808.60	901.31	896.25	991.72	1039.28	1046.54
Month Pt Change	-3.90	-46.71	-1.62	25.59	-28.82	-7.61	-3.33	92.71	-5.06	95.47	47.56	7.26
Month % Change	-0.4	-5.4	-0.2	3.1	-3.4	-0.9	-0.4	11.5	-0.6	10.7	4.8	0.7
QTR % Change			-6.0			-1.3			10.4			16.8
Year % Change												19.6

HIGHLIGHTS

Mid-Term Election Year	Bull Market Begins 8/12	Best Six Months 23.6%	High Dec-27	1070.55
Reagan (1st term)	Recession	Worst Six Months 16.9%	Low Aug-12	776.92

ALMANAC INVESTOR

DOW JONES INDUSTRIAL AVERAGE — 1983

Previous Month Close	Jan	Feb	Mar	Apr	May	Jun	Jul	Aug	Sep	Oct	Nov	Dec
	1046.54	1075.70	1112.62	1130.03	1226.20	1199.98	1221.96	1199.22	1216.16	1233.13	1225.20	1276.02
1	C	1059.79	1130.71	C	C	1202.21	1225.26	1194.21	1206.81	C	1229.27	1275.10
2	C	1062.64	1135.06	C	1204.33	1211.44	C	1188.00	1215.45	C	1237.30	1265.24
3	1027.04	1064.66	1138.06	C	1208.01	1213.04	C	1197.82	C	1231.30	1227.13	C
4	1046.08	1077.91	1140.96	1127.61	1212.65	C	C	1183.09	C	1236.69	1218.29	C
5	1044.89	C	C	1120.16	1219.72	C	1208.53	1183.29	C	1250.20	C	1270.53
6	1070.92	C	C	1113.49	1232.59	1214.24	1220.65	C	1238.72	1268.80	C	1269.31
7	1076.07	1087.10	1141.74	1117.65	C	1194.91	1210.44	C	1244.11	1272.15	1214.84	1273.78
8	C	1075.33	1119.78	1124.71	C	1185.50	1207.23	1163.06	1246.14	C	1214.94	1261.89
9	C	1067.42	1132.64	C	1228.23	1189.00	C	1168.27	1239.74	C	1232.52	1260.06
10	1092.35	1087.75	1120.94	C	1229.68	1196.11	C	1175.98	C	1284.65	1235.87	C
11	1083.79	1086.50	1117.74	1141.83	1219.72	C	1215.54	1174.39	C	1265.14	1250.20	C
12	1083.61	C	C	1145.32	1214.40	C	1198.52	1182.83	1229.07	1259.65	C	1261.59
13	1073.95	C	C	1156.64	1218.75	1220.55	1197.82	C	1224.09	1261.38	C	1255.89
14	1080.85	1097.10	1114.45	1165.25	C	1227.26	1204.33	C	1229.47	1263.52	1254.07	1246.65
15	C	1093.10	1124.52	1171.34	C	1237.28	1192.31	1193.50	1215.04	C	1247.97	1236.79
16	C	1087.43	1116.00	C	1202.98	1248.30	C	1190.45	1225.71	C	1251.32	1242.17
17	1084.81	1088.91	1116.97	C	1205.79	1242.19	C	1206.50	C	1268.70	1254.67	C
18	1079.65	1092.82	1117.74	1183.24	1203.56	C	1189.90	1192.48	C	1250.81	1251.02	C
19	1068.06	C	C	1174.54	1191.37	C	1197.12	1194.21	1233.94	1246.75	C	1244.61
20	1070.82	C	C	1191.47	1190.02	1239.18	1227.86	C	1249.19	1251.52	C	1241.97
21	1052.98	C	1125.29	1188.27	C	1247.40	1229.37	C	1243.29	1248.88	1268.80	1254.98
22	C	1080.40	1122.97	1196.30	C	1245.69	1231.17	1203.15	1257.52	C	1275.81	1253.66
23	C	1096.94	1140.87	C	1200.56	1241.79	C	1192.89	1255.59	C	1275.61	1250.51
24	1030.17	1121.81	1145.90	C	1219.04	1241.69	C	1184.25	C	1248.98	C	C
25	1042.03	1120.94	1140.09	1187.21	1229.01	C	1232.87	1185.06	C	1252.44	1277.44	C
26	1037.99	C	C	1209.46	1223.49	C	1243.69	1192.07	1260.77	1243.80	C	C
27	1063.65	C	C	1208.40	1216.14	1229.47	1230.47	C	1247.97	1242.07	C	1263.72
28	1064.75	1112.62	1133.32	1219.52	C	1209.23	1216.35	C	1241.97	1223.48	1269.82	1263.21
29	C		1131.19	1226.20	C	1213.84	1199.22	1194.11	1240.14	C	1287.20	1260.16
30	C		1143.29	C	C	1221.96	C	1196.04	1233.13	C	1276.02	1258.64
31	1075.70		1130.03		1199.98		C	1216.16		1225.20		C
Close	1075.70	1112.62	1130.03	1226.20	1199.98	1221.96	1199.22	1216.16	1233.13	1225.20	1276.02	1258.64
Month Pt Change	29.16	36.92	17.41	96.17	−26.22	21.98	−22.74	16.94	16.97	−7.93	50.82	−17.38
Month % Change	2.8	3.4	1.6	8.5	−2.1	1.8	−1.9	1.4	1.4	−0.6	4.1	−1.4
QTR % Change			8.0			8.1			0.9			2.1
Year % Change												20.3

HIGHLIGHTS

Pre-Election Year	Bear Market Begins 11/29	Best Six Months −4.4%	High Nov-29	1287.20
Reagan (1st term)	Expansion	Worst Six Months −0.1%	Low Jan-03	1027.04

1984 DOW JONES INDUSTRIAL AVERAGE

Previous Month Close	Jan	Feb	Mar	Apr	May	Jun	Jul	Aug	Sep	Oct	Nov	Dec
	1258.64	1220.58	1154.63	1164.89	1170.75	1104.85	1132.40	1115.28	1224.38	1206.71	1207.38	1188.94
1	C	1212.31	1159.44	C	1183.00	1124.35	C	1134.61	C	1198.98	1217.09	C
2	C	1213.88	1171.48	1153.16	1186.56	C	1130.08	1166.08	C	1191.36	1216.65	C
3	1252.74	1197.03	C	1148.76	1181.53	C	1134.28	1202.08	C	1182.86	C	1182.42
4	1269.05	C	C	1148.56	1165.31	1131.57	C	C	1212.35	1187.39	C	1185.07
5	1282.24	C	1165.20	1130.55	C	1124.89	1124.56	C	1209.03	1182.53	1229.24	1171.60
6	1286.64	1174.31	1152.53	1132.22	C	1133.84	1122.57	1202.96	1218.86	C	1244.15	1170.49
7	C	1180.49	1143.63	C	1166.56	1132.44	C	1204.62	1207.38	C	1233.22	1163.21
8	C	1156.30	1147.09	C	1176.30	1131.25	C	1196.11	C	1177.89	1228.69	C
9	1286.22	1152.74	1139.76	1133.90	1165.52	C	1134.05	1224.05	C	1175.13	1218.97	C
10	1278.48	1160.70	C	1138.30	1167.19	C	1126.88	1218.09	1202.52	1177.23	C	1172.26
11	1277.32	C	C	1130.97	1157.14	1115.61	1108.55	C	1197.99	1183.08	C	1178.33
12	1279.31	C	1155.36	1157.14	C	1110.53	1104.57	C	1200.31	1190.70	1219.19	1175.13
13	1270.10	1150.13	1164.78	1150.13	C	1110.53	1109.87	1220.08	1228.25	C	1206.60	1168.84
14	C	1163.84	1166.04	C	1151.07	1097.61	C	1214.11	1237.52	C	1206.93	1175.91
15	C	1158.71	1167.40	C	1150.86	1086.90	C	1198.98	C	1202.96	1206.16	C
16	1267.59	1154.94	1184.36	1160.28	1153.16	C	1116.83	1209.14	C	1197.77	1187.94	C
17	1271.46	1148.87	C	1164.57	1142.27	C	1122.90	1211.90	1237.08	1195.89	C	1176.79
18	1269.37	C	C	1156.51	1133.79	1109.65	1111.64	C	1226.26	1225.38	C	1211.57
19	1266.02	C	1171.38	1158.08	C	1115.83	1102.92	C	1213.01	1225.93	1185.29	1208.04
20	1259.11	C	1175.77	C	C	1131.63	1101.37	1216.98	1216.54	C	1195.12	1203.29
21	C	1139.34	1170.85	C	1125.31	1127.21	C	1239.73	1201.74	C	1201.52	1198.98
22	C	1134.21	1155.88	C	1116.62	1131.07	C	1231.78	C	1217.20	C	C
23	1244.45	1134.63	1154.84	1149.50	1113.80	C	1096.62	1232.44	C	1213.01	1220.30	C
24	1242.88	1165.10	C	1162.90	1103.43	C	1086.57	1236.53	1205.06	1216.43	C	1210.14
25	1231.89	C	C	1163.53	1107.10	1130.52	1096.95	C	1207.16	1211.02	C	C
26	1229.69	C	1152.95	1175.25	C	1122.79	1107.55	C	1212.12	1204.95	1212.35	1208.92
27	1230.00	1179.96	1154.31	1169.07	C	1116.72	1114.62	1227.92	1216.76	C	1220.19	1202.52
28	C	1157.14	1174.62	C	C	1126.55	C	1232.11	1206.71	C	1205.39	1204.17
29	C	1154.63	1170.75	C	1101.24	1132.40	C	1226.92	C	1201.41	1193.46	C
30	1221.52		1164.89	1170.75	1102.59	C	1109.98	1223.28	C	1217.31	1188.94	C
31	1220.58		C		1104.85		1115.28	1224.38		1207.38		1211.57
Close	1220.58	1154.63	1164.89	1170.75	1104.85	1132.40	1115.28	1224.38	1206.71	1207.38	1188.94	1211.57
Month Pt Change	-38.06	-65.95	10.26	5.86	-65.90	27.55	-17.12	109.10	-17.67	0.67	-18.44	22.63
Month % Change	-3.0	-5.4	0.9	0.5	-5.6	2.5	-1.5	9.8	-1.4	0.1	-1.5	1.9
QTR % Change			-7.4			-2.8			6.6			0.4
Year % Change												-3.7

DOW JONES INDUSTRIAL AVERAGE — 1985

Previous Month Close	Jan	Feb	Mar	Apr	May	Jun	Jul	Aug	Sep	Oct	Nov	Dec
	1211.57	1286.77	1284.01	1266.78	1258.06	1315.41	1335.46	1347.45	1334.01	1328.63	1374.31	1472.13
1	C	1277.72	1299.36	1272.75	1242.05	C	1337.14	1355.62	C	1340.95	1390.25	C
2	1198.87	C	C	1265.68	1242.27	C	1334.01	1353.05	C	1333.67	C	1457.91
3	1189.82	C	C	1258.06	1247.24	1310.93	1326.39	C	1329.19	1333.11	C	1459.06
4	1184.96	1290.08	1289.53	1259.05	C	1315.30	C	C	1326.72	1328.74	1389.68	1484.40
5	C	1285.23	1291.85	C	C	1320.56	1334.45	1346.89	1325.83	C	1396.67	1482.91
6	C	1280.59	1280.37	C	1247.79	1327.28	C	1325.16	1335.69	C	1403.44	1477.18
7	1190.59	1290.08	1271.53	C	1252.76	1316.42	C	1325.04	C	1324.37	1399.54	C
8	1191.70	1289.97	1269.66	1252.98	1249.78	C	1328.41	1329.86	C	1325.49	1404.36	C
9	1202.74	C	C	1253.86	1260.27	C	1321.91	1320.79	1339.27	1326.72	C	1497.02
10	1223.50	C	C	1259.94	1274.18	1318.44	1332.89	C	1333.45	1328.07	C	1499.20
11	1218.09	1276.06	1268.55	1263.69	C	1313.84	1337.70	C	1319.44	1339.94	1431.88	1511.70
12	C	1276.61	1271.75	1265.68	C	1306.34	1338.60	1314.29	1312.39	C	1433.60	1511.24
13	C	1297.92	1261.70	C	1277.50	1290.10	C	1315.30	1307.68	C	1427.75	1535.21
14	1234.54	1287.88	1260.05	C	1273.30	1300.96	C	1316.98	C	1354.73	1439.22	C
15	1230.79	1282.02	1247.35	1266.78	1273.52	C	1335.46	1317.76	C	1350.81	1435.09	C
16	1230.68	C	C	1269.55	1278.05	C	1347.89	1312.72	1309.14	1368.50	C	1553.10
17	1228.69	C	C	1272.31	1285.34	1298.39	1357.97	C	1298.16	1369.29	C	1544.50
18	1227.36	C	1249.67	1265.13	C	1304.77	1350.92	C	1300.40	1368.84	1440.02	1542.43
19	C	1280.59	1271.09	1266.56	C	1297.38	1359.54	1312.50	1306.79	C	1438.99	1543.92
20	C	1283.13	1265.24	C	1304.88	1299.73	C	1323.70	1297.94	C	1439.22	1543.00
21	1261.37	1279.04	1268.22	C	1309.70	1324.48	C	1329.53	C	1364.14	1462.27	C
22	1259.50	1275.84	1267.45	1266.56	1303.76	C	1357.64	1318.10	C	1364.36	1464.33	C
23	1274.73	C	C	1278.71	1296.71	C	1351.81	1318.32	1316.31	1367.16	C	1528.78
24	1270.43	C	C	1278.49	1301.97	1320.56	1348.90	C	1321.12	1362.34	C	1519.15
25	1276.06	1277.50	1259.94	1284.78	C	1323.03	1353.61	C	1312.05	1356.52	1456.65	C
26	C	1286.11	1259.72	1275.18	C	1323.81	1357.08	1317.65	1320.79	C	1456.77	1526.49
27	C	1281.03	1264.91	C	C	1332.21	C	1322.47	C	C	1475.69	1543.00
28	1277.83	1284.01	1260.71	C	1301.52	1335.46	C	1331.09	C	1359.99	C	C
29	1292.62		1266.78	1259.72	1302.98	C	1343.86	1335.13	C	1368.73	1472.13	C
30	1287.88		C	1258.06	1305.78	C	1346.10	1334.01	1328.63	1375.57	C	1550.46
31	1286.77		C		1315.41		1347.45	C		1374.31		1546.67
Close	1286.77	1284.01	1266.78	1258.06	1315.41	1335.46	1347.45	1334.01	1328.63	1374.31	1472.13	1546.67
Month Pt Change	75.20	−2.76	−17.23	−8.72	57.35	20.05	11.99	−13.44	−5.38	45.68	97.82	74.54
Month % Change	6.2	−0.2	−1.3	−0.7	4.6	1.5	0.9	−1.0	−0.4	3.4	7.1	5.1
QTR % Change			4.6			5.4			−0.5			16.4
Year % Change												27.7

HIGHLIGHTS

Post Election Year	Bull Market	Best Six Months 29.8%	High Dec-16	1553.10
Reagan (2nd Term)	Expansion	Worst Six Months 9.2%	Low Jan-04	1184.96

1986 — DOW JONES INDUSTRIAL AVERAGE

Previous Month Close	Jan	Feb	Mar	Apr	May	Jun	Jul	Aug	Sep	Oct	Nov	Dec
	1546.67	1570.99	1709.06	1818.61	1783.98	1876.71	1892.72	1775.31	1898.34	1767.58	1877.81	1914.23
1	C	C	C	1790.11	1777.78	C	1903.54	1763.64	C	1782.90	C	1912.68
2	1537.73	C	C	1795.26	1774.68	1861.95	1909.03	C	1870.36	1781.21	C	1955.57
3	1549.20	1594.27	1696.67	1766.40	C	1870.43	1900.87	C	1881.33	1774.18	1894.26	1947.27
4	C	1593.23	1686.42	1739.22	C	1863.29	C	1769.97	1919.71	C	1892.44	1939.68
5	C	1593.12	1686.66	C	1793.77	1879.44	C	1777.00	1899.75	C	1899.04	1925.06
6	1547.59	1600.69	1696.60	C	1787.95	1885.90	C	1779.53	C	1784.45	1891.59	C
7	1565.71	1613.42	1699.83	1735.51	1775.30	C	1839.00	1786.28	C	1784.45	1886.53	C
8	1526.61	C	C	1769.76	1786.21	C	1820.73	1782.62	1888.64	1803.85	C	1930.26
9	1518.23	C	C	1778.62	1789.43	1840.15	1826.07	C	1884.14	1796.82	C	1916.90
10	1513.53	1626.38	1702.95	1794.30	C	1837.19	1831.83	C	1879.50	1793.17	1892.29	1932.93
11	C	1622.82	1746.05	1790.18	C	1846.07	1821.43	1811.16	1792.89	C	1895.95	1923.65
12	C	1629.93	1745.45	C	1787.33	1838.13	C	1835.49	1758.72	C	1893.70	1912.26
13	1520.53	1645.07	1753.71	C	1785.34	1874.19	C	1844.49	C	1798.37	1862.20	C
14	1519.04	1664.45	1792.74	1805.31	1808.28	C	1793.45	1844.91	C	1800.20	1873.59	C
15	1527.29	C	C	1809.65	1774.68	C	1768.70	1855.60	1767.58	1831.69	C	1922.81
16	1541.63	C	C	1847.97	1759.80	1871.77	1774.18	C	1778.54	1836.19	C	1936.16
17	1536.70	C	1776.82	1855.03	C	1865.78	1781.78	C	1769.40	1837.04	1860.52	1918.31
18	C	1678.78	1789.87	1840.40	C	1868.94	1777.98	1869.52	1774.18	C	1817.21	1912.82
19	C	1658.26	1787.95	C	1758.18	1855.86	C	1862.91	1762.65	C	1826.63	1928.85
20	1529.13	1672.82	1804.24	C	1783.98	1879.54	C	1881.33	C	1811.02	1860.66	C
21	1514.45	1697.71	1768.56	1855.90	1775.17	C	1779.11	1881.19	C	1805.68	1893.56	C
22	1502.29	C	C	1830.98	1806.30	C	1795.13	1887.80	1793.45	1808.35	C	1926.18
23	1511.24	C	C	1829.61	1823.29	1864.26	1798.37	C	1797.81	1834.93	C	1914.37
24	1529.93	1698.28	1782.93	1831.72	C	1875.55	1791.62	C	1803.29	1832.26	1906.07	1926.88
25	C	1692.66	1778.50	1835.57	C	1885.05	1810.04	1871.77	1768.56	C	1912.12	C
26	C	1696.90	1810.70	C	C	1880.20	C	1904.25	1769.69	C	1916.76	1930.40
27	1537.61	1713.99	1821.72	C	1853.03	1885.26	C	1904.53	C	1841.82	C	C
28	1556.42	1709.06	C	1843.75	1878.28	C	1773.90	1900.17	C	1845.47	1914.23	C
29	1558.94		C	1825.89	1882.35	C	1766.87	1898.34	1755.20	1851.80	C	1912.12
30	1552.18		C	1783.98	1876.71	1892.72	1779.39	C	1767.58	1878.37	C	1908.61
31	1570.99		1818.61		C		1775.31	C		1877.81		1895.95
Close	1570.99	1709.06	1818.61	1783.98	1876.71	1892.72	1775.31	1898.34	1767.58	1877.81	1914.23	1895.95
Month Pt Change	24.32	138.07	109.55	-34.63	92.73	16.01	-117.41	123.03	-130.76	110.23	36.42	-18.28
Month % Change	1.6	8.8	6.4	-1.9	5.2	0.9	-6.2	6.9	-6.9	6.2	1.9	-1.0
QTR % Change			17.6			4.1			-6.6			7.3
Year % Change												22.6

HIGHLIGHTS

Mid-Term Election Year	Bull Market	Best Six Months	21.8%	High	Dec-02	1955.57
Reagan (2nd Term)	Expansion	Worst Six Months	5.3%	Low	Jan-22	1502.29

DOW JONES INDUSTRIAL AVERAGE 1987

Previous Month Close	Jan	Feb	Mar	Apr	May	Jun	Jul	Aug	Sep	Oct	Nov	Dec
	1895.95	2158.04	2223.99	2304.69	2286.36	2291.57	2418.53	2572.07	2662.95	2596.28	1993.53	1833.55
1	C	C	C	2316.05	2280.40	2288.23	2409.76	C	2610.97	2639.20	C	1842.34
2	1927.31	2179.42	2220.47	2320.45	C	2278.22	2436.70	C	2602.04	2640.99	2014.09	1848.97
3	C	2168.45	2226.52	2390.34	C	2320.69	C	2557.08	2599.49	C	1963.53	1776.53
4	C	2191.23	2257.45	C	2286.22	2337.08	C	2546.72	2561.38	C	1945.29	1766.74
5	1971.32	2201.49	2276.43	C	2338.07	2326.15	C	2566.65	C	2640.18	1985.41	C
6	1974.83	2186.87	2280.23	2405.54	2342.19	C	2429.53	2594.23	C	2548.63	1959.05	C
7	1993.95	C	C	2360.94	2334.66	C	2449.78	2592.00	C	2551.08	C	1812.17
8	2002.25	C	C	2372.16	2322.30	2351.64	2463.97	C	2545.12	2516.64	C	1868.37
9	2005.91	2176.74	2260.12	2339.20	C	2352.70	2451.21	C	2549.27	2482.21	1900.20	1902.52
10	C	2158.04	2280.09	2338.78	C	2353.61	2455.99	2635.84	2576.05	C	1878.15	1855.44
11	C	2171.96	2268.98	C	2307.30	2360.13	C	2680.48	2608.74	C	1899.20	1867.04
12	2009.42	2165.78	2267.34	C	2322.60	2377.73	C	2669.32	C	2471.44	1960.21	C
13	2012.94	2183.35	2258.66	2287.07	2329.68	C	2452.97	2691.49	C	2508.16	1935.01	C
14	2035.01	C	C	2252.98	2325.49	C	2481.35	2685.43	2613.04	2412.70	C	1932.86
15	2070.73	C	C	2282.95	2272.52	2391.54	2483.74	C	2566.58	2355.09	C	1941.48
16	2076.63	C	2248.44	2275.99	C	2407.35	2496.97	C	2530.19	2246.74	1949.10	1974.47
17	C	2237.49	2284.80	C	C	2407.35	2510.04	2700.57	2527.90	C	1922.25	1924.40
18	C	2237.63	2286.93	C	2258.66	2408.13	C	2654.66	2524.64	C	1939.16	1975.30
19	2102.50	2244.09	2299.57	C	2221.28	2420.85	C	2665.82	C	1738.74	1895.39	C
20	2104.47	2235.24	2333.52	2270.60	2215.87	C	2487.72	2706.79	C	1841.01	1913.63	C
21	2094.07	C	C	2337.07	2225.77	C	2467.95	2709.50	2492.82	2027.85	C	1990.38
22	2145.67	C	C	2285.94	2243.20	2445.51	2470.18	C	2568.05	1950.43	C	1978.45
23	2101.52	2216.54	2363.78	2280.97	C	2439.73	2471.94	C	2585.67	1950.76	1923.08	2005.64
24	C	2223.28	2369.18	2235.37	C	2428.41	2485.33	2697.07	2566.42	C	1963.53	1999.67
25	C	2226.24	2363.49	C	C	2451.05	C	2722.42	2570.17	C	1946.95	C
26	2107.28	2216.68	2372.59	C	2297.94	2436.86	C	2701.85	C	1793.93	C	C
27	2150.45	2223.99	2335.80	2230.54	2295.81	C	2493.94	2675.06	C	1846.49	1910.48	C
28	2163.39	C	C	2231.96	2310.68	C	2519.77	2639.35	2601.50	1846.82	C	1942.97
29	2160.01		C	2254.26	2291.57	2446.91	2539.54	C	2590.57	1938.33	C	1926.89
30	2158.04		2278.41	2286.36	C	2418.53	2567.44	C	2596.28	1993.53	1833.55	1950.10
31	C		2304.69		C		2572.07	2662.95		C		1938.83
Close	2158.04	2223.99	2304.69	2286.36	2291.57	2418.53	2572.07	2662.95	2596.28	1993.53	1833.55	1938.83
Month Pt Change	262.09	65.95	80.70	−18.33	5.21	126.96	153.54	90.88	−66.67	−602.75	−159.98	105.28
Month % Change	13.8	3.1	3.6	−0.8	0.2	5.5	6.3	3.5	−2.5	−23.2	−8.0	5.7
QTR % Change			21.6			4.9			7.3			−25.3
Year % Change												2.3

HIGHLIGHTS

Pre-Election Year	Bear Market 8/25 - 10/19	Best Six Months	1.9%	High Aug-25	2722.42
Reagan (2nd Term)	Expansion	Worst Six Months	-12.8%	Low Oct-19	1738.74

Data Bank

1988 DOW JONES INDUSTRIAL AVERAGE

Previous Month	Jan	Feb	Mar	Apr	May	Jun	Jul	Aug	Sep	Oct	Nov	Dec
Close	1938.83	1958.22	2071.62	1988.06	2032.33	2031.12	2141.71	2128.73	2031.65	2112.91	2148.65	2114.51
1	C	1944.63	2070.46	C	C	2064.01	2131.58	2130.51	2002.31	C	2150.96	2101.88
2	C	1952.92	2071.29	C	2043.27	2052.45	C	2131.22	2054.59	C	2156.83	2092.28
3	C	1924.57	2063.49	C	2058.36	2071.30	C	2134.07	C	2105.26	2170.34	C
4	2015.25	1923.57	2057.86	1980.60	2036.31	C	C	2126.60	C	2102.06	2145.80	C
5	2031.50	1910.48	C	1997.51	2020.23	C	2158.61	2119.13	C	2106.51	C	2123.76
6	2037.80	C	C	2061.67	2007.46	2075.21	2130.16	C	2065.26	2107.75	C	2149.36
7	2051.89	C	2056.37	2062.17	C	2054.59	2122.69	C	2065.79	2150.25	2124.64	2153.63
8	1911.31	1895.72	2081.07	2090.19	C	2102.95	2106.15	2107.40	2063.12	C	2127.49	2141.71
9	C	1914.46	2074.27	C	1997.35	2093.35	C	2079.13	2068.81	C	2118.24	2143.49
10	C	1962.04	2026.03	C	2003.65	2101.71	C	2034.14	C	2158.96	2114.69	C
11	1945.13	1961.54	2034.98	2095.99	1965.85	C	2111.31	2039.30	C	2156.47	2067.03	C
12	1928.55	1983.26	C	2110.08	1968.00	C	2092.64	2037.52	2072.37	2126.24	C	2139.58
13	1924.73	C	C	2107.10	1990.55	2099.40	2104.37	C	2083.04	2133.36	C	2143.49
14	1916.11	C	2050.07	2005.64	C	2124.47	2113.62	C	2100.64	2133.18	2065.08	2134.25
15	1956.07	C	2047.41	2013.93	C	2131.40	2129.45	2004.27	2092.28	C	2077.17	2133.00
16	C	2005.97	2064.32	C	2007.63	2094.24	C	2021.51	2098.15	C	2038.58	2150.71
17	C	2000.99	2086.04	C	1986.41	2104.02	C	2025.96	C	2140.47	2052.45	C
18	1963.86	1986.41	2087.37	2008.12	1951.09	C	2117.89	2027.03	C	2159.85	2062.41	C
19	1936.34	2014.59	C	1999.50	1958.72	C	2097.26	2016.00	2081.08	2137.27	C	2172.68
20	1879.14	C	C	1985.41	1952.59	2083.93	2110.60	C	2087.48	2181.19	C	2166.07
21	1879.31	C	2067.14	1987.40	C	2109.17	2086.59	C	2090.50	2183.50	2065.97	2164.64
22	1903.51	2040.29	2066.15	2015.09	C	2152.20	2060.99	1990.22	2080.01	C	2077.70	2160.36
23	C	2039.12	2067.64	C	1941.48	2148.29	C	1989.33	2090.68	C	2092.28	2168.93
24	C	2039.95	2023.87	C	1962.53	2142.96	C	2026.67	C	2170.34	C	C
25	1946.45	2017.57	1978.95	2035.97	1961.37	C	2071.83	2010.85	C	2173.36	2074.68	C
26	1920.59	2023.21	C	2044.76	1966.75	C	2073.97	2017.43	2085.17	2165.18	C	C
27	1911.14	C	C	2047.91	1956.44	2108.46	2053.70	C	2082.33	2140.83	C	2162.68
28	1930.04	C	1979.77	2041.28	C	2130.87	2082.33	C	2085.53	2149.89	2081.44	2166.43
29	1958.22	2071.62	1998.34	2032.33	C	2121.98	2128.73	2041.43	2119.31	C	2101.53	2182.68
30	C		1978.12	C	C	2141.71	C	2038.23	2112.91	C	2114.51	2168.57
31	C		1988.06		2031.12		C	2031.65		2148.65		C
Close	1958.22	2071.62	1988.06	2032.33	2031.12	2141.71	2128.73	2031.65	2112.91	2148.65	2114.51	2168.57
Month Pt Change	19.39	113.40	−83.56	44.27	−1.21	110.59	−12.98	−97.08	81.26	35.74	−34.14	54.06
Month % Change	1.0	5.8	−4.0	2.2	−0.1	5.4	−0.6	−4.6	4.0	1.7	−1.6	2.6
QTR % Change			2.5			7.7			−1.3			2.6
Year % Change												11.8

HIGHLIGHTS

Election Year	Bull Market	Best Six Months	12.6%	High Oct-21 2183.50
Reagan (2nd Term)	Expansion	Worst Six Months	5.7%	Low Jan-20 1879.14

DOW JONES INDUSTRIAL AVERAGE 1989

	Jan	Feb	Mar	Apr	May	Jun	Jul	Aug	Sep	Oct	Nov	Dec
Previous Month Close	2168.57	2342.32	2258.39	2293.62	2418.80	2480.15	2440.06	2660.66	2737.27	2692.82	2645.08	2706.27
1	C	2338.21	2243.04	C	2414.96	2490.63	C	2641.12	2752.09	C	2645.90	2747.65
2	C	2333.75	2265.71	C	2402.86	2517.83	C	2657.44	C	2713.72	2631.56	C
3	2144.64	2331.25	2274.29	2304.80	2393.70	C	2452.77	2661.61	C	2754.56	2629.51	C
4	2177.68	C	C	2298.20	2384.90	C	C	2653.45	C	2771.09	C	2753.63
5	2190.54	C	C	2304.80	2381.96	2480.70	2456.56	C	2744.68	2773.56	C	2741.68
6	2194.29	2321.07	2294.82	2291.97	C	2496.32	2462.44	C	2719.79	2785.52	2582.17	2736.77
7	C	2347.14	2290.71	2304.80	C	2512.32	2487.86	2694.99	2706.88	C	2597.13	2720.78
8	C	2343.21	2295.54	C	2376.47	2516.91	C	2699.17	2709.54	C	2623.36	2731.44
9	2199.46	2323.04	2291.43	C	2371.33	2513.42	C	2686.08	C	2791.41	2603.69	C
10	2193.21	2286.07	2282.14	2301.87	2374.45	C	2502.66	2712.63	C	2785.33	2625.61	C
11	2206.43	C	C	2311.58	2382.88	C	2514.61	2683.99	2704.41	2773.36	C	2728.24
12	2222.32	C	C	2319.65	2439.70	2518.84	2532.63	C	2707.26	2759.84	C	2752.13
13	2226.07	2282.50	2306.25	2296.00	C	2503.54	2538.32	C	2679.52	2569.26	2626.43	2761.09
14	C	2281.25	2306.25	2337.06	C	2503.36	2554.82	2677.92	2664.89	C	2610.25	2753.63
15	C	2303.93	2320.54	C	2463.89	2475.00	C	2687.78	2674.58	C	2632.58	2739.55
16	2224.64	2311.43	2340.71	C	2453.45	2486.38	C	2693.29	C	2657.38	2635.66	C
17	2214.64	2324.82	2292.14	2337.79	2462.43	C	2553.49	2679.63	C	2638.73	2652.66	C
18	2238.75	C	C	2379.40	2470.12	C	2544.76	2687.97	2687.50	2643.65	C	2697.53
19	2239.11	C	C	2386.91	2501.10	2479.89	2584.41	C	2687.31	2683.20	C	2695.61
20	2235.36	C	2262.50	2377.38	C	2472.88	2575.49	C	2683.89	2689.14	2632.04	2687.93
21	C	2326.43	2266.25	2409.46	C	2464.91	2607.36	2647.00	2680.28	C	2639.29	2691.13
22	C	2283.93	2263.21	C	2502.02	2482.17	C	2650.99	2681.61	C	2656.78	2711.39
23	2218.39	2289.46	2243.04	C	2478.01	2531.87	C	2678.11	C	2662.91	C	C
24	2256.43	2245.54	C	2402.68	2483.87	C	2584.98	2734.64	C	2659.22	2675.55	C
25	2265.89	C	C	2386.91	2482.59	C	2583.08	2732.36	2659.19	2653.28	C	C
26	2291.07	C	C	2389.11	2493.77	2511.38	2613.05	C	2663.94	2613.73	C	2709.26
27	2322.86	2250.36	2257.86	2418.99	C	2526.37	2635.43	C	2673.06	2596.72	2694.97	2724.40
28	C	2258.39	2275.54	2418.80	C	2504.74	2635.24	2743.36	2694.91	C	2702.01	2732.30
29	C		2281.52	C	C	2458.27	C	2726.63	2692.82	C	2688.78	2753.20
30	2324.11		2281.34	C	2475.55	2440.06	C	2728.15	C	2603.48	2706.27	C
31	2342.32		2293.62		2480.15		2660.66	2737.27		2645.08		C
Close	2342.32	2258.39	2293.62	2418.80	2480.15	2440.06	2660.66	2737.27	2692.82	2645.08	2706.27	2753.20
Month Pt Change	173.75	−83.93	35.23	125.18	61.35	−40.09	220.60	76.61	−44.45	−47.74	61.19	46.93
Month % Change	8.0	−3.6	1.6	5.5	2.5	−1.6	9.0	2.9	−1.6	−1.8	2.3	1.7
QTR % Change			5.8			6.4			10.4			2.2
Year % Change												27.0

HIGHLIGHTS

Post Election Year	Bull Market	Best Six Months	0.4%	High Oct-09	2791.41
GHW Bush	Expansion	Worst Six Months	9.4%	Low Jan-03	2144.64

1990 DOW JONES INDUSTRIAL AVERAGE

Previous Month Close	Jan	Feb	Mar	Apr	May	Jun	Jul	Aug	Sep	Oct	Nov	Dec
	2753.20	2590.54	2627.25	2707.21	2656.76	2876.66	2880.69	2905.20	2614.36	2452.48	2442.33	2559.65
1	C	2586.26	2635.59	C	2668.92	2900.97	C	2899.26	C	2515.84	2454.95	C
2	2810.15	2602.70	2660.36	2700.45	2689.64	C	2899.26	2864.60	C	2505.20	2490.84	C
3	2809.73	C	C	2736.71	2696.17	C	2911.63	2809.65	C	2489.36	C	2565.59
4	2796.08	C	C	2719.37	2710.36	2935.19	C	C	2613.37	2516.83	C	2579.70
5	2773.25	2622.52	2649.55	2721.17	C	2925.00	2879.21	C	2628.22	2510.64	2502.23	2610.40
6	C	2606.31	2676.80	2717.12	C	2911.65	2904.95	2716.34	2596.29	C	2485.15	2602.48
7	C	2640.09	2669.59	C	2721.62	2897.33	C	2710.64	2619.55	C	2440.84	2590.10
8	2794.37	2644.37	2696.17	C	2733.56	2862.38	C	2734.90	C	2523.76	2443.81	C
9	2766.00	2648.20	2683.33	2722.07	2732.88	C	2914.11	2758.91	C	2445.54	2488.61	C
10	2750.64	C	C	2731.08	2738.51	C	2890.84	2716.58	2615.59	2407.92	C	2596.78
11	2760.67	C	C	2729.73	2801.58	2892.57	2932.67	C	2612.62	2365.10	C	2586.14
12	2689.21	2619.14	2686.71	2751.80	C	2933.42	2969.80	C	2625.74	2398.02	2540.35	2622.28
13	C	2624.10	2674.55	C	C	2929.70	2980.20	2746.78	2582.67	C	2535.40	2614.36
14	C	2624.32	2687.84	C	2821.53	2928.22	C	2747.77	2564.11	C	2559.65	2593.81
15	2669.37	2649.55	2695.72	C	2822.45	2935.89	C	2748.27	C	2416.34	2545.05	C
16	2692.62	2635.59	2741.22	2763.06	2819.68	C	2999.75	2681.44	C	2381.19	2550.25	C
17	2659.13	C	C	2765.77	2831.71	C	2999.75	2644.80	2567.33	2387.87	C	2593.32
18	2666.38	C	C	2732.88	2819.91	2882.18	2981.68	C	2571.29	2452.72	C	2626.73
19	2677.90	C	2755.63	2711.94	C	2893.56	2993.81	C	2557.43	2520.79	2565.35	2626.73
20	C	2596.85	2738.74	2695.95	C	2895.30	2961.14	2656.44	2518.32	C	2530.20	2629.46
21	C	2583.56	2727.93	C	2844.68	2901.73	C	2603.96	2512.38	C	2539.36	2633.66
22	2600.45	2574.77	2695.72	C	2852.23	2857.18	C	2560.15	C	2516.09	C	C
23	2615.32	2564.19	2704.28	2666.67	2856.26	C	2904.70	2483.42	C	2494.06	2527.23	C
24	2604.50	C	C	2654.50	2855.55	C	2922.52	2532.92	2452.97	2504.21	C	2621.29
25	2561.04	C	C	2666.44	2820.92	2845.05	2930.94	C	2485.64	2484.16	C	C
26	2559.23	2602.48	2707.66	2676.58	C	2842.33	2920.79	C	2459.65	2436.14	2533.17	2637.13
27	C	2617.12	2736.94	2645.05	C	2862.13	2898.51	2611.63	2427.48	C	2543.81	2625.50
28	C	2627.25	2743.69	C	C	2878.71	C	2614.85	2452.48	C	2535.15	2629.21
29	2553.38		2727.70	C	2870.49	2880.69	C	2632.43	C	2430.20	2518.81	C
30	2543.24		2707.21	2656.76	2878.56	C	2917.33	2593.32	C	2448.02	2559.65	C
31	2590.54		C		2876.66		2905.20	2614.36		2442.33		2633.66
Close	2590.54	2627.25	2707.21	2656.76	2876.66	2880.69	2905.20	2614.36	2452.48	2442.33	2559.65	2633.66
Month Pt Change	−162.66	36.71	79.96	−50.45	219.90	4.03	24.51	−290.84	−161.88	−10.15	117.32	74.01
Month % Change	−5.9	1.4	3.0	−1.9	8.3	0.1	0.9	−10.0	−6.2	−0.4	4.8	2.9
QTR % Change			−1.7			6.4			−14.9			7.4
Year % Change												−4.3

HIGHLIGHTS

Mid-Term Election Year	Bear Market 7/16 - 10/11	Best Six Months	18.2%	High Jul-16 2999.75
GHW Bush	Recession Begins Q3	Worst Six Months	-8.1%	Low Oct-11 2365.10

DOW JONES INDUSTRIAL AVERAGE 1991

Previous Month Close	Jan	Feb	Mar	Apr	May	Jun	Jul	Aug	Sep	Oct	Nov	Dec
	2633.66	2736.39	2882.18	2913.86	2887.87	3027.50	2906.75	3024.82	3043.60	3016.77	3069.10	2894.68
1	C	2730.69	2909.90	2881.19	2930.20	C	2958.41	3017.67	C	3018.34	3056.35	C
2	2610.64	C	C	2945.05	2938.61	C	2972.72	3006.26	C	3012.52	C	2935.38
3	2573.51	C	C	2926.73	2938.86	3035.33	2934.70	C	3017.67	2984.79	C	2929.56
4	2566.09	2772.28	2914.11	2924.50	C	3027.95	C	C	3008.50	2961.76	3045.62	2911.67
5	C	2788.37	2972.52	2896.78	C	3005.37	2932.47	2989.04	3008.50	C	3031.31	2889.09
6	C	2830.94	2973.27	C	2941.64	2994.86	C	3027.28	3011.63	C	3038.46	2886.40
7	2522.77	2810.64	2963.37	C	2917.49	2976.74	C	3026.61	C	2942.75	3054.11	C
8	2509.41	2830.69	2955.20	2918.56	2930.90	C	2961.99	3013.86	C	2963.77	3045.62	C
9	2470.30	C	C	2873.02	2971.15	C	2947.23	2996.20	3007.16	2946.33	C	2871.65
10	2498.76	C	C	2874.50	2920.17	2975.40	2944.77	C	2982.56	2976.52	C	2863.82
11	2501.49	2902.23	2939.36	2905.45	C	2985.91	2959.75	C	2987.03	2983.68	3042.26	2865.38
12	C	2874.75	2922.52	2920.79	C	2961.99	2980.77	3001.34	3007.83	C	3054.11	2895.13
13	C	2909.16	2955.20	C	2924.42	2965.12	C	3008.72	2985.69	C	3065.30	2914.36
14	2483.91	2877.23	2952.23	C	2886.85	3000.45	C	3005.37	C	3019.45	3063.51	C
15	2490.59	2934.65	2948.27	2933.17	2865.38	C	2990.61	2998.43	C	3041.37	2943.20	C
16	2508.91	C	C	2986.88	2894.01	C	2983.90	2968.02	3015.21	3061.72	C	2919.05
17	2623.51	C	C	3004.46	2886.63	2993.96	2978.76	C	3013.19	3053.00	C	2902.28
18	2646.78	C	2929.95	2999.26	C	2986.81	3016.32	C	3017.89	3077.15	2972.72	2908.09
19	C	2932.18	2867.82	2965.59	C	2955.50	3016.32	2898.03	3024.37	C	2931.57	2914.36
20	C	2899.01	2872.03	C	2892.22	2953.94	C	2913.69	3019.23	C	2930.01	2934.48
21	2629.21	2891.83	2855.45	C	2906.08	2965.56	C	3001.79	C	3060.38	2932.69	C
22	2603.22	2889.36	2858.91	2927.72	2910.33	C	3012.97	3007.38	C	3039.80	2902.73	C
23	2619.06	C	C	2930.45	2900.04	C	2983.23	3040.25	3010.51	3040.92	C	3022.58
24	2643.07	C	C	2949.50	2913.91	2913.01	2966.23	C	3029.07	3016.32	C	3050.98
25	2659.41	2887.87	2865.84	2921.04	C	2910.11	2980.10	C	3021.02	3004.92	2902.06	C
26	C	2864.60	2914.85	2912.38	C	2913.01	2972.50	3039.36	3017.22	C	2916.14	3082.96
27	C	2889.11	2917.57	C	C	2934.93	C	3026.16	3006.04	C	2900.04	3101.52
28	2654.46	2882.18	2913.86	C	2958.86	2906.75	C	3055.23	C	3045.62	C	C
29	2662.62		C	2876.98	2969.59	C	2985.24	3049.64	C	3061.94	2894.68	C
30	2713.12		C	2887.87	3000.45	C	3016.32	3043.60	3016.77	3071.78	C	3163.91
31	2736.39		C		3027.50		3024.82	C		3069.10		3168.83
Close	2736.39	2882.18	2913.86	2887.87	3027.50	2906.75	3024.82	3043.60	3016.77	3069.10	2894.68	3168.83
Month Pt Change	102.73	145.79	31.68	−25.99	139.63	−120.75	118.07	18.78	−26.83	52.33	−174.42	274.15
Month % Change	3.9	5.3	1.1	−0.9	4.8	−4.0	4.1	0.6	−0.9	1.7	−5.7	9.5
QTR % Change			10.6			−0.2			3.8			5.0
Year % Change												20.3

HIGHLIGHTS

Pre-Election Year	Bull Market	Best Six Months	9.4%	High Dec-31	3168.83
GHW Bush	Expansion Begins Q2	Worst Six Months	6.3%	Low Jan-09	2470.30

1992 — DOW JONES INDUSTRIAL AVERAGE

Previous Month Close	Jan	Feb	Mar	Apr	May	Jun	Jul	Aug	Sep	Oct	Nov	Dec
	3168.83	3223.39	3267.67	3235.47	3359.12	3396.88	3318.52	3393.78	3257.35	3271.66	3226.28	3305.16
1	C	C	C	3249.33	3336.09	3413.21	3354.10	C	3266.26	3254.37	C	3294.36
2	3172.41	C	3275.27	3234.12	C	3396.10	3330.29	C	3290.31	3200.61	3262.21	3286.25
3	3201.48	3234.12	3290.25	3249.11	C	3406.99	C	3395.40	3292.20	C	3252.48	3276.53
4	C	3272.81	3268.56	C	3378.13	3399.73	C	3384.32	3281.93	C	3223.04	3288.68
5	C	3257.60	3241.50	C	3359.35	3398.69	C	3365.14	C	3179.00	3243.84	C
6	3200.13	3255.59	3221.60	3275.49	3369.41	C	3339.20	3340.56	C	3178.19	3240.06	C
7	3204.83	3225.40	C	3213.55	3363.37	C	3295.17	3332.18	C	3152.25	C	3307.33
8	3203.94	C	C	3181.35	3369.41	3404.13	3293.28	C	3260.59	3176.03	C	3322.18
9	3209.53	C	3215.12	3224.96	C	3369.92	3324.08	C	3271.39	3136.58	3240.87	3323.81
10	3199.46	3245.08	3230.99	3255.37	C	3343.22	3330.56	3337.58	3305.16	C	3225.47	3312.19
11	C	3251.57	3208.63	C	3397.58	3351.51	C	3331.10	3305.70	C	3240.33	3304.08
12	C	3276.83	3208.63	C	3385.12	3354.36	C	3320.83	C	3174.41	3239.79	C
13	3185.60	3246.65	3235.91	3269.90	3391.98	C	3337.31	3313.27	C	3201.42	3233.03	C
14	3246.20	3245.97	C	3306.13	3368.88	C	3358.39	3328.94	3376.22	3195.48	C	3292.20
15	3258.50	C	C	3353.76	3353.09	3354.90	3345.42	C	3327.32	3174.68	C	3284.36
16	3249.55	C	3236.36	3366.50	C	3329.49	3361.63	C	3319.21	3174.41	3205.74	3255.18
17	3264.98	C	3256.04	C	C	3287.76	3331.64	3324.89	3315.70	C	3193.32	3269.23
18	C	3224.73	3254.25	C	3376.03	3274.12	C	3329.48	3327.05	C	3207.37	3313.27
19	C	3230.32	3261.40	C	3397.99	3285.35	C	3307.06	C	3188.45	3209.53	C
20	3254.03	3280.64	3276.39	3336.31	3393.84	C	3303.00	3304.89	C	3186.02	3227.36	C
21	3223.39	3280.19	C	3343.25	3378.71	C	3308.41	3254.10	3320.83	3187.10	C	3312.46
22	3255.81	C	C	3338.77	3386.77	3280.80	3277.61	C	3280.85	3200.88	C	3321.10
23	3226.74	C	3272.14	3348.61	C	3285.62	3290.04	C	3278.69	3207.64	3223.04	3313.54
24	3232.78	3282.42	3260.96	3324.46	C	3290.70	3285.71	3228.17	3287.87	C	3248.70	3326.24
25	C	3257.83	3259.39	C	C	3284.01	C	3232.22	3250.32	C	3266.26	C
26	C	3283.32	3267.67	C	3364.21	3282.41	C	3246.81	C	3244.11	C	C
27	3240.61	3269.45	3231.44	3304.56	3370.44	C	3282.20	3254.64	C	3235.73	3282.20	C
28	3272.14	3267.67	C	3307.92	3398.43	C	3334.07	3267.61	3276.26	3251.40	C	3333.26
29	3224.96	C	C	3333.18	3396.88	3319.86	3379.19	C	3266.80	3246.27	C	3310.84
30	3244.86		3235.24	3359.12	C	3318.52	3391.89	C	3271.66	3226.28	3305.16	3321.10
31	3223.39		3235.47		C		3393.78	3257.35		C		3301.11
Close	**3223.39**	**3267.67**	**3235.47**	**3359.12**	**3396.88**	**3318.52**	**3393.78**	**3257.35**	**3271.66**	**3226.28**	**3305.16**	**3301.11**
Month Pt Change	54.56	44.28	−32.20	123.65	37.76	−78.36	75.26	−136.43	14.31	−45.38	78.88	−4.05
Month % Change	1.7	1.4	−1.0	3.8	1.1	−2.3	2.3	−4.0	0.4	−1.4	2.4	−0.1
QTR % Change			2.1			2.6			−1.4			0.9
Year % Change												4.2

HIGHLIGHTS

Election Year	Bull Market	Best Six Months	6.2%	High Jun-01	3413.21
GHW Bush	Expansion	Worst Six Months	−4.0%	Low Oct-09	3136.58

DOW JONES INDUSTRIAL AVERAGE   1993

Previous Month Close	Jan	Feb	Mar	Apr	May	Jun	Jul	Aug	Sep	Oct	Nov	Dec
	3301.11	3310.03	3370.81	3435.11	3427.55	3527.43	3516.08	3539.47	3651.25	3555.12	3680.59	3683.95
1	C	3332.18	3355.41	3439.44	C	3552.34	3510.54	C	3645.10	3581.11	3692.61	3697.08
2	C	3328.67	3400.53	3370.81	C	3553.45	3483.97	3560.99	3626.10	C	3697.64	3702.11
3	C	3373.79	3404.04	C	3446.46	3544.87	C	3561.27	3633.93	C	3661.87	3704.07
4	3309.22	3416.74	3398.91	C	3446.19	3545.14	C	3552.05	C	3577.76	3624.98	C
5	3307.87	3442.14	3404.58	3379.19	3449.10	C	C	3548.97	C	3587.26	3643.43	C
6	3305.16	C	C	3377.57	3441.90	C	3449.93	3560.43	C	3598.99	C	3710.21
7	3268.96	C	C	3397.02	3437.19	3532.13	3475.67	C	3607.10	3583.63	C	3718.88
8	3251.67	3437.54	3469.42	3396.48	C	3510.54	3514.42	C	3588.93	3584.74	3647.90	3734.53
9	C	3414.58	3472.12	C	C	3511.93	3521.06	3576.08	3589.49	C	3640.07	3729.78
10	C	3412.42	3478.34	C	3443.28	3491.72	C	3572.73	3621.63	C	3663.55	3740.67
11	3262.75	3422.69	3457.00	C	3468.75	3505.01	C	3583.35	C	3593.41	3662.43	C
12	3264.64	3392.43	3427.82	3428.09	3482.31	C	3524.38	3569.09	C	3593.13	3684.51	C
13	3263.56	C	C	3444.03	3447.99	C	3515.44	3569.65	3634.21	3603.19	C	3764.43
14	3267.88	C	C	3455.64	3443.01	3514.69	3542.55	C	3615.76	3621.63	C	3742.63
15	3271.12	C	3442.41	3455.92	C	3492.00	3550.93	C	3633.65	3629.73	3677.52	3716.92
16	C	3309.49	3442.95	3478.61	C	3511.65	3528.29	3579.15	3630.85	C	3710.77	3726.14
17	C	3312.19	3426.74	C	3449.93	3521.89	C	3586.98	3613.25	C	3704.35	3751.57
18	3274.91	3302.19	3465.64	C	3444.39	3494.77	C	3604.86	C	3642.31	3685.34	C
19	3255.99	3322.18	3471.58	3466.99	3500.03	C	3535.28	3612.13	C	3635.32	3694.01	C
20	3241.95	C	C	3443.49	3523.28	C	3544.78	3615.48	3575.80	3645.10	C	3755.21
21	3253.02	C	C	3439.44	3492.83	3510.82	3555.40	C	3537.24	3636.16	C	3745.15
22	3256.81	3342.99	3463.48	3429.17	C	3497.53	3525.22	C	3547.02	3649.30	3670.25	3762.19
23	C	3323.27	3461.86	3413.77	C	3466.81	3546.74	3605.98	3539.75	C	3674.17	3757.72
24	C	3356.50	3445.38	C	3507.78	3490.61	C	3638.96	3543.11	C	3687.58	C
25	3292.20	3365.14	3461.32	C	3516.63	3490.89	C	3652.09	C	3673.61	C	C
26	3298.95	3370.81	3439.98	3398.37	3540.16	C	3567.70	3648.18	C	3672.49	3683.95	C
27	3291.39	C	C	3415.93	3554.83	C	3565.46	3640.63	3567.70	3664.66	C	3792.93
28	3306.25	C	C	3413.50	3527.43	3530.20	3553.45	C	3566.02	3687.86	C	3793.77
29	3310.03		3455.10	3425.12	C	3518.85	3567.42	C	3566.30	3680.59	3677.80	3794.33
30	C		3457.27	3427.55	C	3516.08	3539.47	3643.99	3555.12	C	3683.95	3775.88
31	C		3435.11		C		C	3651.25		C		3754.09
Close	3310.03	3370.81	3435.11	3427.55	3527.43	3516.08	3539.47	3651.25	3555.12	3680.59	3683.95	3754.09
Month Pt Change	8.92	60.78	64.30	-7.56	99.88	-11.35	23.39	111.78	-96.13	125.47	3.36	70.14
Month % Change	0.3	1.8	1.9	-0.2	2.9	-0.3	0.7	3.2	-2.6	3.5	0.1	1.9
QTR % Change			4.1			2.4			1.1			5.6
Year % Change												13.7

HIGHLIGHTS

Post Election Year	Bull Market	Best Six Months	0.03%	High	Dec-29	3794.33
Clinton (1st Term)	Expansion	Worst Six Months	7.4%	Low	Jan-20	3241.95

1994   DOW JONES INDUSTRIAL AVERAGE

Previous Month Close	Jan 3754.09	Feb 3978.36	Mar 3832.02	Apr 3635.96	May 3681.69	Jun 3758.37	Jul 3624.96	Aug 3764.50	Sep 3913.42	Oct 3843.19	Nov 3908.12	Dec 3739.23
1	C	3964.01	3809.23	C	C	3760.83	3646.65	3798.17	3901.44	C	3863.37	3700.87
2	C	3975.54	3831.74	C	3701.02	3758.99	C	3796.22	3885.58	C	3837.13	3745.62
3	3756.60	3967.66	3824.42	C	3714.41	3772.22	C	3792.66	C	3846.89	3845.88	C
4	3783.90	3871.42	3832.30	3593.35	3697.75	C	C	3765.79	C	3801.13	3807.52	C
5	3798.82	C	C	3675.41	3695.97	C	3652.48	3747.02	C	3787.34	C	3741.92
6	3803.88	C	C	3679.73	3669.50	3768.52	3674.50	C	3898.70	3775.56	C	3745.95
7	3820.77	3906.32	3856.22	3693.26	C	3755.91	3688.42	C	3886.25	3797.43	3808.87	3735.52
8	C	3906.03	3851.72	3674.26	C	3749.45	3709.14	3753.81	3908.46	C	3830.74	3685.73
9	C	3931.92	3853.41	C	3629.04	3753.14	C	3755.76	3874.81	C	3831.75	3691.11
10	3865.51	3895.34	3830.62	C	3656.41	3773.45	C	3766.76	C	3821.32	3821.99	C
11	3850.31	3894.78	3862.70	3688.83	3629.04	C	3702.99	3750.90	C	3876.83	3801.47	C
12	3848.63	C	C	3681.69	3652.84	C	3702.66	3768.71	3860.34	3875.15	C	3718.37
13	3842.43	C	C	3661.47	3659.68	3783.12	3704.28	C	3879.86	3889.95	C	3715.34
14	3867.20	3904.06	3862.98	3663.25	C	3814.83	3739.25	C	3895.33	3910.47	3829.73	3746.29
15	C	3928.27	3849.59	3661.47	C	3790.41	3753.81	3760.29	3953.88	C	3826.36	3765.47
16	C	3937.27	3848.15	C	3671.50	3811.34	C	3784.57	3933.35	C	3845.20	3807.19
17	3870.29	3922.64	3865.14	C	3720.61	3776.78	C	3776.48	C	3923.93	3828.05	C
18	3870.29	3887.46	3895.65	3620.42	3732.89	C	3755.43	3755.43	C	3917.54	3815.26	C
19	3884.37	C	C	3619.82	3758.98	C	3748.31	3755.11	3936.72	3936.04	C	3790.70
20	3891.96	C	C	3598.71	3766.35	3741.90	3727.27	C	3869.09	3911.15	C	3767.15
21	3914.48	C	3864.85	3652.54	C	3707.97	3732.45	C	3851.60	3891.30	3769.51	3801.80
22	C	3911.66	3862.55	3648.68	C	3724.77	3735.04	3751.22	3837.13	C	3677.99	3814.92
23	C	3891.68	3869.46	C	3742.41	3699.09	C	3775.83	3831.75	C	3674.63	3833.43
24	3912.79	3839.90	3821.09	C	3745.17	3636.94	C	3846.73	C	3855.30	C	C
25	3895.34	3838.78	3774.73	3705.78	3755.30	C	3741.84	3829.89	C	3850.59	3708.27	C
26	3908.00	C	C	3699.54	3753.46	C	3735.68	3881.05	3849.24	3848.23	C	C
27	3926.30	C	C	C	3757.14	3685.50	3720.47	C	3863.04	3875.15	C	3861.69
28	3945.43	3832.02	3762.35	3668.31	C	3669.64	3730.83	C	3878.18	3930.66	3739.56	3839.49
29	C		3699.02	3681.69	C	3667.05	3764.50	3898.85	3854.63	C	3738.55	3833.43
30	C		3626.75	C	C	3624.96	C	3917.30	3843.19	C	3739.23	3834.44
31	3978.36		3635.96		3758.37		C	3913.42		3908.12		C
Close	**3978.36**	**3832.02**	**3635.96**	**3681.69**	**3758.37**	**3624.96**	**3764.50**	**3913.42**	**3843.19**	**3908.12**	**3739.23**	**3834.44**
Month Pt Change	224.27	−146.34	−196.06	45.73	76.68	−133.41	139.54	148.92	−70.23	64.93	−168.89	95.21
Month % Change	6.0	−3.7	−5.1	1.3	2.1	−3.5	3.8	4.0	−1.8	1.7	−4.3	2.5
QTR % Change			−3.1			−0.3			6.0			−0.2
Year % Change												2.1

HIGHLIGHTS

Mid-Term Election Year	Bull Market	Best Six Months 10.6%	High	Jan-31	3978.36
Clinton (1st Term)	Expansion	Worst Six Months 6.2%	Low	Apr-4	3593.35

	Jan	Feb	Mar	Apr	May	Jun	Jul	Aug	Sep	Oct	Nov	Dec
Previous Month Close	3834.44	3843.86	4011.05	4157.69	4321.27	4465.14	4556.10	4708.47	4610.56	4789.08	4755.48	5074.49
1	C	3847.56	3994.80	C	4316.08	4472.75	C	4700.37	4647.54	C	4766.68	5087.13
2	C	3870.77	3979.93	C	4328.88	4444.39	C	4690.15	C	4761.26	4808.59	C
3	3838.48	3928.64	3989.61	4168.41	4373.15	C	4585.15	4701.42	C	4749.70	4825.57	C
4	3857.65	C	C	4201.61	4359.66	C	C	4683.46	C	4740.67	C	5139.52
5	3850.92	C	C	4200.57	4343.40	4476.55	4615.23	C	4670.08	4762.71	C	5177.45
6	3867.41	3937.73	3997.56	4205.41	C	4485.20	4664.00	C	4683.81	4769.21	4814.01	5199.13
7	C	3937.39	3962.63	4192.62	C	4462.03	4702.73	4693.32	4669.72	C	4797.03	5159.39
8	C	3935.37	3979.23	C	4383.87	4458.57	C	4693.32	4700.72	C	4852.67	5156.86
9	3861.35	3932.68	3983.39	C	4390.78	4423.99	C	4671.49	C	4726.22	4864.23	C
10	3866.74	3939.07	4035.61	4198.15	4404.62	C	4702.39	4643.66	C	4720.80	4870.37	C
11	3862.03	C	C	4187.08	4411.19	C	4680.60	4618.30	4704.94	4735.25	C	5184.32
12	3859.00	C	C	4197.81	4430.56	4446.46	4727.29	C	4747.21	4764.88	C	5174.92
13	3908.46	3954.21	4025.23	4208.18	C	4484.51	4727.48	C	4765.52	4793.78	4872.90	5216.47
14	C	3958.25	4048.75	C	C	4491.08	4708.82	4659.86	4801.80	C	4871.81	5182.15
15	C	3986.17	4038.37	C	4437.47	4496.27	C	4640.84	4797.57	C	4922.75	5176.73
16	3932.34	3987.52	4069.15	C	4435.05	4510.79	C	4639.08	C	4784.38	4969.36	C
17	3930.66	3953.54	4073.65	4195.38	4422.60	C	4736.29	4630.63	C	4795.94	4989.95	C
18	3928.98	C	C	4179.13	4340.64	C	4686.28	4617.60	4780.41	4777.52	C	5075.21
19	3882.21	C	C	4207.49	4341.33	4553.68	4628.87	C	4767.04	4802.45	C	5109.89
20	3869.43	C	4083.68	4230.66	C	4550.56	4641.55	C	4792.69	4794.86	4983.09	5059.32
21	C	3963.97	4072.61	4270.09	C	4547.10	4641.55	4614.78	4767.40	C	5023.55	5096.53
22	C	3973.05	4082.99	C	4395.63	4589.64	C	4620.42	4764.15	C	5041.61	5097.97
23	3867.41	4003.33	4087.83	C	4436.44	4585.84	C	4584.85	C	4755.48	C	C
24	3862.70	4011.74	4138.67	4303.98	4438.16	C	4668.67	4580.62	C	4783.66	5048.84	C
25	3871.45	C	C	4300.17	4412.23	C	4714.45	4601.40	4769.93	4753.68	C	C
26	3870.44	C	C	4299.83	4369.00	4551.25	4707.06	C	4765.60	4703.82	C	5110.26
27	3857.99	3988.57	4157.34	4314.70	C	4542.61	4732.77	C	4762.35	4741.75	5070.88	5105.92
28	C	4011.05	4151.81	4321.27	C	4556.79	4715.51	4594.00	4787.64	C	5078.10	5095.80
29	C		4160.80	C	C	4550.56	C	4608.44	4789.08	C	5105.56	5117.12
30	3832.08		4172.56	C	4378.68	4556.10	C	4604.57	C	4756.57	5074.49	C
31	3843.86		4157.69		4465.14		4708.47	4610.56		4755.48		C
Close	3843.86	4011.05	4157.69	4321.27	4465.14	4556.10	4708.47	4610.56	4789.08	4755.48	5074.49	5117.12
Month Pt Change	9.42	167.19	146.64	163.58	143.87	90.96	152.37	−97.91	178.52	−33.60	319.01	42.63
Month % Change	0.2	4.3	3.7	3.9	3.3	2.0	3.3	−2.1	3.9	−0.7	6.7	0.8
QTR % Change			8.4			9.6			5.1			6.8
Year % Change												33.5

Pre-Election Year	Bull Market	Best Six Months 17.1%	High Dec-13 5216.47
Clinton (1st Term)	Expansion	Worst Six Months 10.0%	Low Jan-30 3832.08

1996   DOW JONES INDUSTRIAL AVERAGE

Previous Month Close	Jan	Feb	Mar	Apr	May	Jun	Jul	Aug	Sep	Oct	Nov	Dec
	5117.12	5395.30	5485.62	5587.14	5569.08	5643.18	5654.63	5528.91	5616.21	5882.17	6029.38	6521.70
1	C	5405.06	5536.56	5637.72	5575.22	C	5729.98	5594.75	C	5904.90	6021.93	C
2	5177.45	5373.99	C	5671.68	5498.27	C	5720.38	5679.83	C	5933.97	C	6521.70
3	5194.07	C	C	5689.74	5478.03	5624.71	5703.02	C	5648.39	5932.85	C	6442.69
4	5173.84	C	5600.15	5682.88	C	5665.71	C	C	5656.90	5992.86	6041.68	6422.94
5	5181.43	5407.59	5642.42	C	C	5697.48	5588.14	5674.28	5606.96	C	6081.18	6437.10
6	C	5459.61	5629.77	C	5464.31	5667.19	C	5696.11	5659.86	C	6177.71	6381.94
7	C	5492.12	5641.69	C	5420.95	5697.11	C	5718.67	C	5979.81	6206.04	C
8	5197.68	5539.45	5470.45	5594.37	5474.06	C	5550.83	5713.49	C	5966.77	6219.82	C
9	5130.13	5541.62	C	5560.41	5475.14	C	5581.86	5681.31	5733.84	5930.62	C	6463.94
10	5032.94	C	C	5485.98	5518.14	5687.87	5603.65	C	5727.18	5921.67	C	6473.25
11	5065.10	C	5581.00	5487.07	C	5668.66	5520.54	C	5754.92	5969.38	6255.60	6402.52
12	5061.12	5600.15	5583.89	5532.59	C	5668.29	5510.56	5704.98	5771.94	C	6266.04	6303.71
13	C	5601.23	5568.72	C	5582.60	5657.95	C	5647.28	5838.52	C	6274.24	6304.87
14	C	5579.55	5586.06	C	5624.71	5649.45	C	5666.88	C	6010.00	6313.00	C
15	5043.78	5551.37	5584.97	5592.92	5625.44	C	5349.51	5665.78	C	6004.78	6348.03	C
16	5088.22	5503.32	C	5620.02	5635.05	C	5358.76	5689.45	5889.20	6020.81	C	6268.35
17	5066.90	C	C	5549.93	5687.50	5652.78	5376.88	C	5888.83	6059.20	C	6308.33
18	5124.35	C	5683.60	5551.74	C	5628.03	5464.18	C	5877.36	6094.23	6346.91	6346.77
19	5184.68	C	5669.51	5535.48	C	5648.35	5426.82	5699.44	5867.74	C	6397.60	6473.64
20	C	5458.53	5655.42	C	5748.82	5659.43	C	5721.26	5888.46	C	6430.02	6484.40
21	C	5515.97	5626.88	C	5736.26	5705.23	C	5689.82	C	6090.87	6418.47	C
22	5219.36	5608.46	5636.64	5564.74	5778.00	C	5390.94	5733.47	C	6061.80	6471.76	C
23	5192.27	5630.49	C	5588.59	5762.12	C	5346.55	5722.74	5894.74	6036.46	C	6489.02
24	5242.84	C	C	5553.90	5762.86	5717.79	5354.69	C	5874.03	5992.48	C	6522.85
25	5216.83	C	5643.86	5566.91	C	5719.27	5422.01	C	5877.36	6007.02	6547.79	C
26	5271.75	5565.10	5670.60	5567.99	C	5682.70	5473.06	5693.89	5868.85	C	6528.41	6546.68
27	C	5549.21	5626.88	C	C	5677.53	C	5711.27	5872.92	C	6499.34	6560.91
28	C	5506.21	5630.85	C	5709.67	5654.63	C	5712.38	C	5972.73	C	C
29	5304.98	5485.62	5587.14	5573.41	5673.83	C	5434.59	5647.65	C	6007.02	6521.70	C
30	5381.21		C	5569.08	5693.41	C	5481.93	5616.21	5882.17	5993.23	C	6549.37
31	5395.30		C		5643.18		5528.91	C		6029.38		6448.27
Close	5395.30	5485.62	5587.14	5569.08	5643.18	5654.63	5528.91	5616.21	5882.17	6029.38	6521.70	6448.27
Month Pt Change	278.18	90.32	101.52	–18.06	74.10	11.45	–125.72	87.30	265.96	147.21	492.32	–73.43
Month % Change	5.4	1.7	1.9	–0.3	1.3	0.2	–2.2	1.6	4.7	2.5	8.2	–1.1
QTR % Change			9.2			1.2			4.0			9.6
Year % Change												26.0

HIGHLIGHTS

Election Year	Bull Market	Best Six Months	16.2%	High Dec-27 6560.91
Clinton (1st Term)	Expansion	Worst Six Months	8.3%	Low Jan-10 5032.94

DOW JONES INDUSTRIAL AVERAGE 1997

	Jan	Feb	Mar	Apr	May	Jun	Jul	Aug	Sep	Oct	Nov	Dec
Previous Month Close	6448.27	6813.09	6877.74	6583.48	7008.99	7331.04	7672.79	8222.61	7622.42	7945.26	7442.08	7823.13
1	C	C	C	6611.05	6976.48	C	7722.33	8194.04	C	8015.50	C	8013.11
2	6442.49	C	C	6517.01	7071.20	7289.40	7795.38	C	7879.78	8027.53	C	8018.83
3	6544.09	6806.16	6918.92	6477.35	C	7312.15	7895.81	C	7894.64	8038.58	7674.39	8032.01
4	C	6833.48	6852.72	6526.07	C	7269.66	C	8198.45	7867.24	C	7689.13	8050.16
5	C	6746.90	6945.85	C	7214.49	7305.29	C	8187.54	7822.41	C	7692.57	8149.13
6	6567.18	6773.06	6944.70	C	7225.32	7435.78	C	8259.31	C	8100.22	7683.24	C
7	6600.66	6855.80	7000.89	6555.91	7085.65	C	7858.49	8188.00	C	8178.31	7581.32	C
8	6549.48	C	C	6609.16	7136.62	C	7962.31	8031.22	7835.18	8095.06	C	8110.84
9	6625.67	C	C	6563.84	7169.53	7478.50	7842.43	C	7851.91	8061.42	C	8049.66
10	6703.79	6806.54	7079.39	6540.05	C	7539.27	7886.76	C	7719.28	8045.21	7552.59	7978.79
11	C	6858.11	7085.16	6391.69	C	7575.83	7921.82	8062.11	7660.98	C	7558.73	7848.99
12	C	6961.63	7039.37	C	7292.75	7711.47	C	7960.84	7742.97	C	7401.32	7838.30
13	6709.18	7022.44	6878.89	C	7274.21	7782.04	C	7928.32	C	8072.22	7487.76	C
14	6762.29	6988.96	6935.46	6451.90	7286.16	C	7922.98	7942.03	C	8096.29	7572.48	C
15	6726.88	C	C	6587.16	7333.55	C	7975.71	7694.66	7721.14	8057.98	C	7922.59
16	6765.37	C	C	6679.87	7194.67	7772.09	8038.88	C	7895.92	7938.88	C	7976.31
17	6833.10	C	6955.48	6658.60	C	7760.78	8020.77	C	7886.44	7847.03	7698.22	7957.41
18	C	7067.46	6896.56	6703.55	C	7718.71	7890.46	7803.36	7922.72	C	7650.82	7846.50
19	C	7020.13	6877.68	C	7228.88	7777.06	C	7918.10	7917.27	C	7724.74	7756.29
20	6843.87	6927.38	6820.28	C	7303.46	7796.51	C	8021.23	C	7921.44	7826.61	C
21	6883.90	6931.62	6804.79	6660.21	7290.69	C	7906.72	7893.95	C	8060.44	7881.07	C
22	6850.03	C	C	6833.59	7258.13	C	8061.65	7887.91	7996.83	8034.65	C	7819.31
23	6755.75	C	C	6812.72	7345.91	7604.26	8088.36	C	7970.06	7847.77	C	7691.77
24	6696.48	7008.20	6905.25	6792.25	C	7758.06	8116.93	C	7906.71	7715.41	7767.92	7660.13
25	C	7038.21	6876.17	6738.87	C	7689.98	8113.44	7859.57	7848.01	C	7808.95	C
26	C	6983.18	6880.70	C	C	7654.25	C	7782.22	7922.18	C	7794.78	7679.31
27	6660.69	6925.07	6740.59	C	7383.41	7687.72	C	7787.33	C	7161.15	C	C
28	6656.08	6877.74	C	6783.02	7357.23	C	8121.11	7694.43	C	7498.32	7823.13	C
29	6740.74		C	6962.03	7330.18	C	8174.53	7622.42	7991.43	7506.67	C	7792.41
30	6823.86		C	7008.99	7331.04	7672.79	8254.89	C	7945.26	7381.67	C	7915.97
31	6813.09		6583.48		C		8222.61	C		7442.08		7908.25
Close	6813.09	6877.74	6583.48	7008.99	7331.04	7672.79	8222.61	7622.42	7945.26	7442.08	7823.13	7908.25
Month Pt Change	364.82	64.65	−294.26	425.51	322.05	341.75	549.82	−600.19	322.84	−503.18	381.05	85.12
Month % Change	5.7	0.9	−4.3	6.5	4.6	4.7	7.2	−7.3	4.2	−6.3	5.1	1.1
QTR % Change			2.1			16.5			3.6			−0.5
Year % Change												22.6

HIGHLIGHTS

Post Election Year	Bull Market	Best Six Months 21.8%	High Aug-06	8259.31
Clinton (2nd Term)	Expansion	Worst Six Months 6.2%	Low Apr-11	6391.69

1998 — DOW JONES INDUSTRIAL AVERAGE

	Jan	Feb	Mar	Apr	May	Jun	Jul	Aug	Sep	Oct	Nov	Dec
Previous Month Close	7908.25	7906.50	8545.72	8799.81	9063.37	8899.95	8952.02	8883.29	7539.07	7842.62	8592.10	9116.55
1	C	C	C	8868.32	9147.07	8922.37	9048.67	C	7827.43	7632.53	C	9133.54
2	7965.04	8107.78	8550.45	8986.64	C	8891.24	9025.26	C	7782.37	7784.69	8706.15	9064.54
3	C	8160.35	8584.83	8983.41	C	8803.80	C	8786.74	7682.22	C	8706.15	8879.68
4	C	8129.71	8539.24	C	9192.66	8870.56	C	8487.31	7640.25	C	8783.14	9016.14
5	7978.99	8117.25	8444.33	C	9147.57	9037.71	C	8546.78	C	7726.24	8915.47	C
6	7906.25	8189.49	8569.39	9033.23	9054.65	C	9091.77	8577.68	C	7742.98	8975.46	C
7	7902.27	C	C	8956.50	8976.68	C	9085.04	8598.02	C	7741.69	C	9070.47
8	7802.62	C	C	8891.48	9055.15	9069.60	9174.97	C	8020.78	7731.91	C	9027.98
9	7580.42	8180.52	8567.14	8994.86	C	9049.92	9089.78	C	7865.02	7899.52	8897.96	9009.19
10	C	8295.61	8643.12	C	C	8971.70	9105.74	8574.85	7615.54	C	8863.98	8841.58
11	C	8314.55	8675.75	C	9091.52	8811.77	C	8462.85	7795.50	C	8823.82	8821.76
12	7647.18	8369.60	8659.56	C	9161.77	8834.94	C	8552.96	C	8001.47	8829.74	C
13	7732.13	8370.10	8602.52	9012.30	9211.84	C	9096.21	8459.50	C	7938.14	8919.59	C
14	7784.69	C	C	9110.20	9172.23	C	9245.54	8425.00	7945.35	7968.78	C	8695.60
15	7691.77	C	C	9162.27	9096.00	8627.93	9234.47	C	8024.39	8299.36	C	8823.30
16	7753.55	C	8718.85	9076.57	C	8665.29	9328.19	C	8089.78	8416.76	9011.25	8790.60
17	C	8398.50	8749.99	9167.50	C	8829.46	9337.97	8574.85	7873.77	C	8986.28	8875.82
18	C	8451.06	8775.40	C	9050.91	8813.01	C	8714.65	7895.66	C	9041.11	8903.63
19	C	8375.58	8803.05	C	9054.65	8712.87	C	8693.28	C	8466.45	9056.05	C
20	7873.12	8413.94	8906.43	9141.84	9171.48	C	9295.75	8611.41	C	8505.85	9159.55	C
21	7794.40	C	C	9184.94	9132.37	C	9190.19	8533.65	7933.25	8519.23	C	8988.85
22	7730.88	C	C	9176.72	9114.44	8711.13	9128.91	C	7897.20	8533.14	C	9044.46
23	7700.74	8410.20	8816.25	9143.33	C	8828.46	8932.98	C	8154.41	8452.29	9374.27	9202.03
24	C	8370.10	8904.44	9064.62	C	8923.87	8937.36	8566.61	8001.99	C	9301.15	9217.99
25	C	8457.78	8872.80	C	C	8935.58	C	8602.65	8028.77	C	9314.28	C
26	7712.94	8490.67	8846.89	C	8963.73	8944.54	C	8523.35	C	8432.21	C	C
27	7815.08	8545.72	8796.08	8917.64	8936.57	C	9028.24	8165.99	C	8366.04	9333.08	C
28	7915.47	C	C	8898.96	8970.20	C	8934.78	8051.68	8108.84	8371.97	C	9226.75
29	7973.02		C	8951.52	8899.95	8997.36	8914.96	C	8080.52	8495.03	C	9320.98
30	7906.50		8782.12	9063.37	C	8952.02	9026.95	C	7842.62	8592.10	9116.55	9274.64
31	C		8799.81		C		8883.29	7539.07		C		9181.43
Close	7906.50	8545.72	8799.81	9063.37	8899.95	8952.02	8883.29	7539.07	7842.62	8592.10	9116.55	9181.43
Month Pt Change	-1.75	639.22	254.09	263.56	-163.42	52.07	-68.73	-1344.22	303.55	749.48	524.45	64.88
Month % Change	-0.02	8.1	3.0	3.0	-1.8	0.6	-0.8	-15.1	4.0	9.6	6.1	0.7
QTR % Change			11.3			1.7			-12.4			17.1
Year % Change												16.1

HIGHLIGHTS

Mid-Term Election Year	Bull Market	Best Six Months	25.6%	High Nov-23	9374.27
Clinton (2nd Term)	Expansion	Worst Six Months	-5.2%	Low Aug-31	7539.07

ALMANAC INVESTOR

DOW JONES INDUSTRIAL AVERAGE — 1999

Previous Month Close	Jan	Feb	Mar	Apr	May	Jun	Jul	Aug	Sep	Oct	Nov	Dec
	9181.43	9358.83	9306.58	9786.16	10789.04	10559.74	10970.80	10655.15	10829.28	10336.95	10729.86	10877.81
1	C	9345.70	9324.78	9832.51	C	10596.26	11066.42	C	10937.88	10273.00	10648.51	10998.39
2	C	9274.12	9297.61	C	C	10577.89	11139.24	10645.96	10843.21	C	10581.84	11039.06
3	C	9366.81	9275.88	C	11014.69	10663.69	C	10677.31	11078.45	C	10609.06	11286.18
4	9184.27	9304.50	9467.40	C	10886.11	10799.84	C	10674.77	C	10401.23	10639.64	C
5	9311.19	9304.24	9736.08	10007.33	10955.41	C	C	10793.82	C	10400.59	10704.48	C
6	9544.97	C	C	9963.49	10946.82	C	11135.12	10714.03	C	10588.34	C	11225.01
7	9537.76	C	C	10085.31	11031.59	10909.38	11187.36	C	11034.13	10537.05	C	11106.65
8	9643.32	9291.11	9727.61	10197.70	C	10765.64	11126.89	C	11036.34	10649.76	10718.85	11068.12
9	C	9133.03	9693.76	10173.84	C	10690.29	11193.70	10707.70	11079.40	C	10617.32	11134.79
10	C	9177.31	9772.84	C	11007.25	10621.27	C	10655.15	11028.43	C	10597.74	11224.70
11	9619.89	9363.46	9897.44	C	11026.15	10490.51	C	10787.80	C	10648.18	10595.30	C
12	9474.68	9274.89	9876.35	10339.51	11000.37	C	11200.98	10789.39	C	10417.06	10769.32	C
13	9349.56	C	C	10395.01	11107.19	C	11175.02	10973.65	11030.33	10232.16	C	11192.59
14	9120.93	C	C	10411.66	10913.32	10563.33	11148.10	C	10910.33	10286.61	C	11160.17
15	9340.55	C	9958.77	10462.72	C	10594.99	11186.41	C	10801.42	10019.71	10760.75	11225.32
16	C	9297.03	9930.47	10493.89	C	10784.95	11209.84	11046.79	10737.46	C	10932.33	11244.89
17	C	9195.47	9879.41	C	10853.47	10841.63	C	11117.08	10803.63	C	10883.09	11257.43
18	C	9298.63	9997.62	C	10836.95	10855.56	C	10991.38	C	10116.28	11035.70	C
19	9355.22	9339.95	9903.55	10440.53	10887.39	C	11187.68	10963.84	C	10204.93	11003.89	C
20	9335.91	C	C	10448.55	10866.74	C	10996.13	11100.61	10823.90	10392.36	C	11144.27
21	9264.08	C	C	10581.42	10829.28	10815.98	11002.78	C	10598.47	10297.69	C	11200.54
22	9120.67	9552.68	9890.51	10727.18	C	10721.63	10969.22	C	10524.07	10470.25	11089.52	11203.60
23	C	9544.42	9671.83	10689.67	C	10666.86	10910.96	11299.76	10318.59	C	10995.63	11405.76
24	C	9399.67	9666.84	C	10654.67	10534.83	C	11283.30	10279.33	C	11008.17	C
25	9203.32	9366.34	9836.39	C	10531.09	10552.56	C	11326.04	C	10349.93	C	C
26	9324.58	9306.58	9822.24	10718.59	10702.16	C	10863.16	11198.45	C	10302.13	10988.91	C
27	9200.23	C	C	10831.71	10466.93	C	10979.04	11090.17	10303.39	10394.89	C	11391.08
28	9281.33	C	C	10845.45	10559.74	10655.15	10972.07	C	10275.53	10622.53	C	11476.71
29	9358.83		10006.78	10878.38	C	10815.35	10791.29	C	10213.48	10729.86	10947.92	11484.66
30	C		9913.26	10789.04	C	10970.80	10655.15	10914.13	10336.95	C	10877.81	11452.86
31	C		9786.16		C		C	10829.28		C		11497.12
Close	9358.83	9306.58	9786.16	10789.04	10559.74	10970.80	10655.15	10829.28	10336.95	10729.86	10877.81	11497.12
Month Pt Change	177.40	−52.25	479.58	1002.88	−229.30	411.06	−315.65	174.13	−492.33	392.91	147.95	619.31
Month % Change	1.9	−0.6	5.2	10.2	−2.1	3.9	−2.9	1.6	−4.5	3.8	1.4	5.7
QTR % Change			6.6			12.1			−5.8			11.2
Year % Change												25.2

HIGHLIGHTS

Pre-Election Year	Bull Market	Best Six Months	0.04%	High	Dec-31	11497.12
Clinton (2nd Term)	Expansion	Worst Six Months	-0.5%	Low	Jan-22	9120.67

2000   DOW JONES INDUSTRIAL AVERAGE

	Jan	Feb	Mar	Apr	May	Jun	Jul	Aug	Sep	Oct	Nov	Dec
Previous Month Close	11497.12	10940.53	10128.31	10921.92	10733.91	10522.33	10447.89	10521.98	11215.10	10650.92	10971.14	10414.49
1	C	11041.05	10137.93	C	10811.78	10652.20	C	10606.95	11238.78	C	10899.47	10373.54
2	C	11003.20	10164.92	C	10731.12	10794.76	C	10687.53	C	10700.13	10880.51	C
3	11357.51	11013.44	10367.20	11221.93	10480.13	C	10560.67	10706.58	C	10719.74	10817.95	C
4	10997.93	10963.80	C	11164.84	10412.49	C	10767.75	C	C	10784.48	C	10560.10
5	11122.65	C	C	11033.92	10577.86	10815.30	10483.60	C	11260.61	10724.92	C	10898.72
6	11253.26	C	10170.50	11114.27	C	10735.57	10481.47	C	11310.64	10596.54	10977.21	10664.38
7	11522.56	10905.79	9796.03	11111.48	C	10812.86	10635.98	10867.01	11259.87	C	10952.18	10617.36
8	C	10957.60	9856.53	C	10603.63	10668.72	C	10976.89	11220.65	C	10907.06	10712.91
9	C	10699.16	10010.73	C	10536.75	10614.06	C	10905.83	C	10568.43	10834.25	C
10	11572.20	10643.63	9928.82	11186.56	10367.78	C	10646.58	10908.76	C	10524.40	10602.95	C
11	11511.08	10425.21	C	11287.08	10545.97	C	10727.19	11027.80	11195.49	10413.79	C	10725.80
12	11551.10	C	C	11125.13	10609.37	10564.21	10783.41	C	11233.23	10034.58	C	10768.27
13	11582.43	C	9947.13	10923.55	C	10621.84	10788.71	C	11182.18	10192.18	10517.25	10794.44
14	11722.98	10519.84	9811.24	10305.77	C	10687.95	10812.75	11176.14	11087.47	C	10681.06	10674.99
15	C	10718.09	10131.41	C	10807.78	10714.82	C	11067.00	10927.00	C	10707.60	10434.96
16	C	10561.41	10630.60	C	10934.57	10449.30	C	11008.39	C	10238.80	10656.03	C
17	C	10514.57	10595.23	10582.51	10769.74	C	10804.27	11055.64	C	10089.71	10629.87	C
18	11560.72	10219.52	C	10767.42	10777.28	C	10739.92	11046.48	10808.52	9975.02	C	10645.42
19	11489.36	C	C	10674.96	10626.85	10557.84	10696.08	C	10789.29	10142.98	C	10584.37
20	11351.30	C	10680.24	10844.05	C	10435.16	10843.87	C	10687.92	10226.59	10462.65	10318.93
21	11251.71	C	10907.34	C	C	10497.74	10733.56	11079.81	10765.52	C	10494.50	10487.29
22	C	10304.84	10866.70	C	10542.55	10376.12	C	11139.15	10847.37	C	10399.32	10635.56
23	C	10225.73	11119.86	C	10422.27	10404.75	C	11144.65	C	10271.72	C	C
24	11008.17	10092.63	11112.72	10906.10	10535.35	C	10685.12	11182.74	C	10393.07	10470.23	C
25	11029.89	9862.12	C	11124.82	10323.92	C	10699.97	11192.63	10808.15	10326.48	C	C
26	11032.99	C	C	10945.50	10299.24	10542.99	10516.48	C	10631.32	10380.12	C	10692.44
27	11028.02	C	11025.85	10888.10	C	10504.46	10586.13	C	10628.36	10590.62	10546.07	10803.16
28	10738.87	10038.65	10936.11	10733.91	C	10527.79	10511.17	11252.84	10824.06	C	10507.58	10868.76
29	C	10128.31	11018.72	C	C	10398.04	C	11215.10	10650.92	C	10629.11	10786.85
30	C		10980.25	C	10527.13	10447.89	C	11103.01	C	10835.77	10414.49	C
31	10940.53		10921.92		10522.33		10521.98	11215.10		10971.14		C
Close	10940.53	10128.31	10921.92	10733.91	10522.33	10447.89	10521.98	11215.10	10650.92	10971.14	10414.49	10786.85
Month Pt Change	−556.59	−812.22	793.61	−188.01	−211.58	−74.44	74.09	693.12	−564.18	320.22	−556.65	372.36
Month % Change	−4.8	−7.4	7.8	−1.7	−2.0	−0.7	0.7	6.6	−5.0	3.0	−5.1	3.6
QTR % Change			−5.0			−4.3			1.9			1.3
Year % Change												−6.2

HIGHLIGHTS

Election Year	Bear Market Begins 1/14	Best Six Months	−2.2%	High Jan-14 11722.98
Clinton (2nd Term)	Expansion	Worst Six Months	2.2%	Low Mar-07 9796.03

DOW JONES INDUSTRIAL AVERAGE — 2001

	Jan	Feb	Mar	Apr	May	Jun	Jul	Aug	Sep	Oct	Nov	Dec
Previous Month Close	10786.85	10887.36	10495.28	9878.78	10734.97	10911.94	10502.40	10522.81	9949.75	8847.56	9075.14	9851.56
1	C	10983.63	10450.14	C	10898.34	10990.41	C	10510.01	C	8836.83	9263.90	C
2	10646.15	10864.10	10466.31	9777.93	10876.68	C	10593.72	10551.18	C	8950.59	9323.54	C
3	10945.75	C	C	9485.71	10796.65	C	10571.11	10512.78	C	9123.78	C	9763.96
4	10912.41	C	C	9515.42	10951.24	11061.52	C	C	9997.49	9060.88	C	9893.84
5	10662.01	10965.85	10562.30	9918.05	C	11175.84	10479.86	C	10033.27	9119.77	9441.03	10114.29
6	C	10957.42	10591.22	9791.09	C	11070.24	10252.68	10401.31	9840.84	C	9591.12	10099.14
7	C	10946.72	10729.60	C	10935.17	11090.74	C	10458.74	9605.85	C	9554.37	10049.46
8	10621.35	10880.55	10858.25	C	10883.51	10977.00	C	10293.50	C	9067.94	9587.52	C
9	10572.55	10781.45	10644.62	9845.15	10866.98	C	10299.40	10298.56	C	9052.44	9608.00	C
10	10604.27	C	C	10102.74	10910.44	C	10175.64	10416.25	9605.51	9240.86	C	9921.45
11	10609.55	C	C	10013.47	10821.31	10922.09	10241.02	C	C	9410.45	C	9888.37
12	10525.38	10946.77	10208.25	10126.94	C	10948.38	10478.99	C	C	9344.16	9554.37	9894.81
13	C	10903.32	10290.80	C	C	10871.62	10539.06	10415.91	C	C	9750.95	9766.45
14	C	10795.41	9973.46	C	10877.33	10690.13	C	10412.17	C	C	9823.61	9811.15
15	C	10891.02	10031.28	C	10872.97	10623.64	C	10345.95	C	9347.62	9872.39	C
16	10652.66	10799.82	9823.41	10158.56	11215.92	C	10472.12	10392.52	C	9384.23	9866.99	C
17	10584.34	C	C	10216.73	11248.58	C	10606.39	10240.78	8920.70	9232.97	C	9891.97
18	10678.28	C	C	10615.83	11301.74	10645.38	10569.83	C	8903.40	9163.22	C	9998.39
19	10587.59	C	9959.11	10693.71	C	10596.67	10610.00	C	8759.13	9204.11	9976.46	10070.49
20	C	10730.88	9720.76	10579.85	C	10647.33	10576.65	10320.07	8376.21	C	9901.38	9985.18
21	C	10526.58	9487.00	C	11337.92	10715.43	C	10174.14	8235.81	C	9834.68	10035.34
22	10578.24	10526.81	9389.48	C	11257.24	10604.59	C	10276.90	C	9377.03	C	C
23	10649.81	10441.90	9504.78	10532.23	11105.51	C	10424.42	10229.15	C	9340.08	9959.71	C
24	10646.97	C	C	10454.34	11122.42	C	10241.12	10423.17	8603.86	9345.62	C	10035.34
25	10729.52	C	C	10625.20	11005.37	10504.22	10405.67	C	8659.97	9462.90	C	C
26	10659.98	10642.53	9687.53	10692.35	C	10472.48	10455.63	C	8567.39	9545.17	9982.75	10088.14
27	C	10636.88	9947.54	10810.05	C	10434.84	10416.67	10382.35	8681.42	C	9872.60	10131.31
28	C	10495.28	9785.35	C	C	10566.21	C	10222.03	8847.56	C	9711.86	10136.99
29	10702.19		9799.06	C	11039.14	10502.40	C	10090.90	C	9269.50	9829.42	C
30	10881.20		9878.78	10734.97	10872.64	C	10401.72	9919.58	C	9121.98	9851.56	C
31	10887.36		C		10911.94		10522.81	9949.75		9075.14		10021.50
Close	10887.36	10495.28	9878.78	10734.97	10911.94	10502.40	10522.81	9949.75	8847.56	9075.14	9851.56	10021.50
Month Pt Change	100.51	–392.08	–616.50	856.19	176.97	–409.54	20.41	–573.06	–1102.19	227.58	776.42	169.94
Month % Change	0.9	–3.6	–5.9	8.7	1.6	–3.8	0.2	–5.4	–11.1	2.6	8.6	1.7
QTR % Change			–8.4			6.3			–15.8			13.3
Year % Change												–7.1

HIGHLIGHTS

Post Election Year	Bull Market Begins 9/21	Best Six Months	9.6%	High May-21 11337.92
GW Bush (1st Term)	Recession Begins Q2	Worst Six Months	-15.5%	Low Sep-21 8235.81

2002   DOW JONES INDUSTRIAL AVERAGE

Previous Month	Jan	Feb	Mar	Apr	May	Jun	Jul	Aug	Sep	Oct	Nov	Dec
Close	10021.50	9920.00	10106.13	10403.94	9946.22	9925.25	9243.26	8736.59	8663.50	7591.93	8397.03	8896.09
1	C	9907.26	10368.86	10362.70	10059.63	C	9109.79	8506.62	C	7938.79	8517.64	C
2	10073.40	C	C	10313.71	10091.87	C	9007.75	8313.13	C	7755.61	C	8862.57
3	10172.14	C	C	10198.29	10006.63	9709.79	9054.97	C	8308.05	7717.19	C	8742.93
4	10259.74	9687.09	10586.82	10235.17	C	9687.84	C	C	8425.12	7528.40	8571.60	8737.85
5	C	9685.43	10433.41	10271.64	C	9796.80	9379.50	8043.63	8283.70	C	8678.27	8623.28
6	C	9653.39	10574.29	C	9808.04	9624.64	C	8274.09	8427.20	C	8771.01	8645.77
7	10197.05	9625.44	10525.37	C	9836.55	9589.67	C	8456.15	C	7422.84	8586.24	C
8	10150.55	9744.24	10572.49	10249.08	10141.83	C	9274.90	8712.02	C	7501.49	8537.13	C
9	10094.09	C	C	10208.67	10037.42	C	9096.09	8745.45	8519.38	7286.27	C	8473.41
10	10067.86	C	C	10381.73	9939.92	9645.40	8813.50	C	8602.61	7533.95	C	8574.26
11	9987.53	9884.78	10611.24	10176.08	C	9517.26	8801.53	C	8581.17	7850.29	8358.95	8589.14
12	C	9863.74	10632.35	10190.82	C	9617.71	8684.53	8688.89	8379.41	C	8386.00	8538.40
13	C	9989.67	10501.85	C	10109.66	9502.80	C	8482.39	8312.69	C	8398.49	8433.71
14	9891.42	10001.99	10517.14	C	10298.14	9474.21	C	8743.31	C	7877.40	8542.13	C
15	9924.15	9903.04	10607.23	10093.67	10243.68	C	8639.19	8818.14	C	8255.68	8579.09	C
16	9712.27	C	C	10301.32	10289.21	C	8473.11	8778.06	8380.18	8036.03	C	8627.40
17	9850.04	C	C	10220.78	10353.08	9687.42	8542.48	C	8207.55	8275.04	C	8535.39
18	9771.85	C	10577.75	10205.28	C	9706.12	8409.49	C	8172.45	8322.40	8486.57	8447.35
19	C	9745.14	10635.25	10257.11	C	9561.57	8019.26	8990.79	7942.39	C	8474.78	8364.80
20	C	9941.17	10501.57	C	10229.50	9431.77	C	8872.07	7986.02	C	8623.01	8511.32
21	C	9834.68	10479.84	C	10105.71	9253.79	C	8957.23	C	8538.24	8845.15	C
22	9713.80	9968.15	10427.67	10136.43	10157.88	C	7784.58	9053.64	C	8450.16	8804.84	C
23	9730.96	C	C	10089.24	10216.08	C	7702.34	8872.96	7872.15	8494.27	C	8493.29
24	9796.07	C	C	10030.43	10104.26	9281.82	8191.29	C	7683.13	8317.34	C	8448.11
25	9840.08	10145.71	10281.67	10035.06	C	9126.82	8186.31	C	7841.82	8443.99	8849.40	C
26	C	10115.26	10353.36	9910.72	C	9120.11	8264.39	8919.01	7997.12	C	8676.42	8432.61
27	C	10127.58	10426.91	C	C	9269.92	C	8824.41	7701.45	C	8931.68	8303.78
28	9865.75	10106.13	10403.94	C	9981.58	9243.26	C	8694.09	C	8368.04	C	C
29	9618.24		C	9819.87	9923.04	C	8711.88	8670.99	C	8368.94	8896.09	C
30	9762.86		C	9946.22	9911.69	C	8680.03	8663.50	7591.93	8427.41	C	8332.85
31	9920.00		C		9925.25		8736.59	C		8397.03		8341.63
Close	9920.00	10106.13	10403.94	9946.22	9925.25	9243.26	8736.59	8663.50	7591.93	8397.03	8896.09	8341.63
Month Pt Change	-101.50	186.13	297.81	-457.72	-20.97	-681.99	-506.67	-73.09	-1071.57	805.10	499.06	-554.46
Month % Change	-1.0	1.9	2.9	-4.4	-0.2	-6.9	-5.5	-0.8	-12.4	10.6	5.9	-6.2
QTR % Change			3.8			-11.2			-17.9			9.9
Year % Change												-16.8

HIGHLIGHTS

Mid-Term Election Year	Bear Market 3/19 - 10/9	Best Six Months 1.0%	High Mar-19 10635.25
GW Bush (1st Term)	Expansion	Worst Six Months -15.6%	Low Oct-09 7286.27

DOW JONES INDUSTRIAL AVERAGE · 2003

Previous Month	Jan	Feb	Mar	Apr	May	Jun	Jul	Aug	Sep	Oct	Nov	Dec
Close	8341.63	8053.81	7891.08	7992.13	8480.09	8850.26	8985.44	9233.80	9415.82	9275.06	9801.12	9782.46
1	C	C	C	8069.86	8454.25	C	9040.95	9153.97	C	9469.20	C	9899.05
2	8607.52	C	C	8285.06	8582.68	8897.81	9142.84	C	9523.27	9487.80	C	9853.64
3	8601.69	8109.82	7837.86	8240.38	C	8922.95	9070.21	C	9568.46	9572.31	9858.46	9873.42
4	C	8013.29	7704.87	8277.15	C	9038.98	C	9186.04	9587.90	C	9838.83	9930.82
5	C	7985.18	7775.60	C	8531.57	9041.30	C	9036.32	9503.34	C	9820.83	9862.68
6	8773.57	7929.30	7673.99	C	8588.36	9062.79	C	9061.74	C	9594.98	9856.97	C
7	8740.59	7864.23	7740.03	8300.41	8560.63	C	9216.79	9126.45	C	9654.61	9809.79	C
8	8595.31	C	C	8298.92	8491.22	C	9223.09	9191.09	9586.29	9630.90	C	9965.27
9	8776.18	C	C	8197.94	8604.60	8980.00	9156.21	C	9507.20	9680.01	C	9923.42
10	8784.89	7920.11	7568.18	8221.33	C	9054.89	9036.04	C	9420.46	9674.68	9756.53	9921.86
11	C	7843.11	7524.06	8203.41	C	9183.22	9119.59	9217.35	9459.76	C	9737.79	10008.16
12	C	7758.17	7552.07	C	8726.73	9196.55	C	9310.06	9471.55	C	9848.83	10042.16
13	8785.98	7749.87	7821.75	C	8679.25	9117.12	C	9271.76	C	9764.38	9837.94	C
14	8842.62	7908.80	7859.71	8351.10	8647.82	C	9177.15	9310.56	C	9812.98	9768.68	C
15	8723.18	C	C	8402.36	8713.14	C	9128.97	9321.69	9448.81	9803.05	C	10022.82
16	8697.87	C	C	8257.61	8678.97	9318.96	9094.59	C	9567.34	9791.72	C	10129.56
17	8586.74	C	8141.92	8337.65	C	9323.02	9050.82	C	9545.65	9721.79	9710.83	10145.26
18	C	8041.15	8194.23	C	C	9293.80	9188.15	9412.45	9659.13	C	9624.16	10248.08
19	C	8000.60	8265.45	C	8493.39	9179.53	C	9428.90	9644.82	C	9690.46	10278.22
20	C	7914.96	8286.60	C	8491.36	9200.75	C	9397.51	C	9777.94	9619.42	C
21	8442.90	8018.11	8521.97	8328.90	8516.43	C	9096.69	9423.68	C	9747.64	9628.53	C
22	8318.73	C	C	8484.99	8594.02	C	9158.45	9348.87	9535.41	9598.24	C	10338.00
23	8369.47	C	C	8515.66	8601.38	9072.95	9194.24	C	9576.04	9613.13	C	10341.26
24	8131.01	7858.24	8214.68	8440.04	C	9109.85	9112.51	C	9425.51	9582.46	9747.79	10305.19
25	C	7909.50	8280.23	8306.35	C	9011.53	9284.57	9317.64	9343.96	C	9763.94	C
26	C	7806.98	8229.88	C	C	9079.04	C	9340.45	9313.08	C	9779.57	10324.67
27	7989.56	7884.99	8201.45	C	8781.35	8989.05	C	9333.79	C	9608.16	C	C
28	8088.84	7891.08	8145.77	8471.61	8793.12	C	9266.51	9374.21	C	9748.31	9782.46	C
29	8110.71		C	8502.99	8711.18	C	9204.46	9415.82	9380.24	9774.53	C	10450.00
30	7945.13		C	8480.09	8850.26	8985.44	9200.05	C	9275.06	9786.61	C	10425.04
31	8053.81		7992.13		C		9233.80	C		9801.12		10453.92
Close	8053.81	7891.08	7992.13	8480.09	8850.26	8985.44	9233.80	9415.82	9275.06	9801.12	9782.46	10453.92
Month Pt Change	−287.82	−162.73	101.05	487.96	370.17	135.18	248.36	182.02	−140.76	526.06	−18.66	671.46
Month % Change	−3.5	−2.0	1.3	6.1	4.4	1.5	2.8	2.0	−1.5	5.7	−0.2	6.9
QTR % Change			−4.2			12.4			3.2			12.7
Year % Change												25.3

HIGHLIGHTS

Pre-Election Year	Bull Market	Best Six Months	4.3%	High	Dec-31	10453.92
GW Bush (1st Term)	Expansion	Worst Six Months	15.6%	Low	Mar-11	7524.06

2004 DOW JONES INDUSTRIAL AVERAGE

Previous Month Close	Jan	Feb	Mar	Apr	May	Jun	Jul	Aug	Sep	Oct	Nov	Dec
Close	10453.92	10488.07	10583.92	10357.70	10225.57	10188.45	10435.48	10139.71	10173.92	10080.27	10027.47	10428.02
1	C	C	10678.14	10373.33	C	10202.65	10334.16	C	10168.46	10192.65	10054.39	10590.22
2	10409.85	10499.18	10591.48	10470.59	C	10262.97	10282.83	10179.16	10290.28	C	10035.73	10585.12
3	C	10505.18	10593.11	C	10314.00	10195.91	C	10120.24	10260.20	C	10137.05	10592.21
4	C	10470.74	10588.00	C	10317.20	10242.82	C	10126.51	C	10216.54	10314.76	C
5	10544.07	10495.55	10595.55	10558.37	10310.95	C	C	9963.03	C	10177.68	10387.54	C
6	10538.66	10593.03	C	10570.81	10241.26	C	10219.34	9815.33	C	10239.92	C	10547.06
7	10529.03	C	C	10480.15	10117.34	10391.08	10240.29	C	10342.79	10125.40	C	10440.58
8	10592.44	C	10529.48	10442.03	C	10432.52	10171.56	C	10313.36	10055.20	10391.31	10494.23
9	10458.89	10579.03	10456.96	C	C	10368.44	10213.22	9814.66	10289.10	C	10386.37	10552.82
10	C	10613.85	10296.89	C	9990.02	10410.10	C	9944.67	10313.07	C	10385.48	10543.22
11	C	10737.70	10128.38	C	10019.47	C	C	9938.32	C	10081.97	10469.84	C
12	10485.18	10694.07	10240.08	10515.56	10045.16	C	10238.22	9814.59	C	10077.18	10539.01	C
13	10427.18	10627.85	C	10381.28	10010.74	C	10247.59	9825.35	10314.76	10002.33	C	10638.32
14	10538.37	C	C	10377.95	10012.87	10334.73	10208.80	C	10318.16	9894.45	C	10676.45
15	10553.85	C	10102.89	10397.46	C	10380.43	10163.16	C	10231.36	9933.38	10550.24	10691.45
16	10600.51	C	10184.67	10451.97	C	10379.58	10139.78	9954.55	10244.49	C	10487.65	10705.64
17	C	10714.88	10300.30	C	9906.91	10377.52	C	9972.83	10284.46	C	10549.57	10649.92
18	C	10671.99	10295.78	C	9968.51	10416.41	C	10083.15	C	9956.32	10572.55	C
19	C	10664.73	10186.60	10437.85	9937.71	C	10094.06	10040.82	C	9897.62	10456.91	C
20	10528.66	10619.03	C	10314.50	9937.64	C	10149.07	10110.14	10204.89	9886.93	C	10661.60
21	10623.62	C	C	10317.27	9966.74	10371.47	10046.13	C	10244.93	9865.76	C	10759.43
22	10623.18	C	10064.75	10461.20	C	10395.07	10050.33	C	10109.18	9757.81	10489.42	10815.89
23	10568.29	10609.62	10063.64	10472.84	C	10479.57	9962.22	10073.05	10038.90	C	10492.60	10827.12
24	C	10566.37	10048.23	C	9958.43	10443.81	C	10098.63	10047.24	C	10520.31	C
25	C	10601.62	10218.82	C	10117.62	10371.84	C	10181.74	C	9749.99	C	C
26	10702.51	10580.14	10212.97	10444.73	10109.89	C	9961.92	10173.41	C	9888.48	10522.23	C
27	10609.92	10583.92	C	10478.16	10205.20	C	10085.14	10195.01	9988.54	10002.03	C	10776.13
28	10468.37	C	C	10342.60	10188.45	10357.09	10117.07	C	10077.40	10004.54	C	10854.54
29	10510.29	C	10329.63	10272.27	C	10413.43	10129.24	C	10136.24	10027.47	10475.90	10829.19
30	10488.07		10381.70	10225.57	C	10435.48	10139.71	10122.52	10080.27	C	10428.02	10800.30
31	C		10357.70		C		C	10173.92		C		10783.01
Close	10488.07	10583.92	10357.70	10225.57	10188.45	10435.48	10139.71	10173.92	10080.27	10027.47	10428.02	10783.01
Month Pt Change	34.15	95.85	−226.22	−132.13	−37.12	247.03	−295.77	34.21	−93.65	−52.80	400.55	354.99
Month % Change	0.3	0.9	−2.1	−1.3	−0.4	2.4	−2.8	0.3	−0.9	−0.5	4.0	3.4
QTR % Change			−0.9			0.8			−3.4			7.0
Year % Change												3.1

HIGHLIGHTS

Election Year	Bull Market	Best Six Months	1.6%	High	Dec-28	10854.54
GW Bush (1st Term)	Expansion	Worst Six Months	-1.9%	Low	Oct-25	9749.99

DOW JONES INDUSTRIAL AVERAGE 2005

Previous Month Close	Jan	Feb	Mar	Apr	May	Jun	Jul	Aug	Sep	Oct	Nov	Dec
	10783.01	10489.94	10766.23	10503.76	10192.51	10467.48						
1	C	10551.94	10830.00	10404.30	C	10549.87						
2	C	10596.79	10811.97	C	10251.70	10553.49						
3	10729.43	10593.10	10833.03	C	10256.95	10460.97						
4	10630.78	10716.13	10940.55	10421.14	10384.64	C						
5	10597.83	C	C	10458.46	10340.38	C						
6	10622.88	C	C	10486.02	10345.40	10467.03						
7	10603.96	10715.76	10936.86	10546.32	C	10483.07						
8	C	10724.63	10912.62	10461.34	C	10476.86						
9	C	10664.11	10805.62	C	10384.34	10503.02						
10	10621.03	10749.61	10851.51	C	10281.11	10512.63						
11	10556.22	10796.01	10774.36	10448.56	10300.25	C						
12	10617.78	C	C	10507.97	10189.48	C						
13	10505.83	C	C	10403.93	10140.12	10522.56						
14	10558.00	10791.13	10804.51	10278.75	C	10547.57						
15	C	10837.32	10745.10	10087.51	C	10566.37						
16	C	10834.88	10633.07	C	10252.29	10578.65						
17	C	10754.26	10626.35	C	10331.88	10623.07						
18	10628.79	10785.22	10629.67	10071.25	10464.45	C						
19	10539.97	C	C	10127.41	10493.19	C						
20	10471.47	C	C	10012.36	10471.91	10609.11						
21	10392.99	C	10565.39	10218.60	C	10599.67						
22	C	10611.20	10470.51	10157.71	C	10587.93						
23	C	10673.79	10456.02	C	10523.56	10421.44						
24	10368.61	10748.79	10442.87	C	10503.68	10297.84						
25	10461.56	10841.60	C	10242.47	10457.80	C						
26	10498.59	C	C	10151.13	10537.60	C						
27	10467.40	C	C	10198.80	10542.55	10290.78						
28	10427.20	10766.23	10485.65	10070.37	C	10405.63						
29	C		10405.70	10192.51	C	10374.48						
30	C		10540.93	C	C	10274.97						
31	10489.94		10503.76		10467.48								
Close	10489.94	10766.23	10503.76	10192.51	10467.48	10274.97						
Month Pt Change	−293.07	276.29	−262.47	−311.25	274.97	−192.51						
Month % Change	−2.7	2.6	−2.4	−3.0	2.7	−1.8						
QTR % Change			−2.6			−2.2							
Year % Change												

HIGHLIGHTS

Post Election Year	Bull Market	Best Six Months	1.6%	High	Mar-04	10940.55
GW Bush (2nd Term)	Expansion	Worst Six Months —		Low	Apr-20	10012.36

1950   STANDARD & POOR'S 500

Previous Month Close	Jan	Feb	Mar	Apr	May	Jun	Jul	Aug	Sep	Oct	Nov	Dec
	16.76	17.05	17.22	17.29	18.07	18.78	17.69	17.84	18.42	19.45	19.53	19.51
1	C	17.05	17.24	17.34	18.22	18.77	C	18.02	18.55	C	19.56	19.66
2	C	17.23	17.23	C	18.11	18.79	C	17.95	C	19.69	19.73	19.54
3	16.66	17.29	17.29	17.53	18.27	C	17.64	17.99	C	19.66	19.85	C
4	16.85	17.35	17.33	17.55	18.12	C	C	18.14	C	20.00	19.78	19.00
5	16.93	C	C	17.63	18.22	18.60	17.81	C	18.68	19.89	C	19.31
6	16.98	17.32	17.32	17.78	18.33	18.88	17.91	C	18.54	20.12	19.36	19.45
7	17.09	17.23	17.20	C	C	18.93	17.67	18.41	18.59	20.16	C	19.40
8	C	17.21	17.19	17.82	18.27	19.14	C	18.46	18.75	C	19.56	19.40
9	17.08	17.28	17.07	C	18.27	19.26	C	18.61	C	20.00	19.79	19.50
10	17.03	17.24	17.09	17.85	18.29	C	17.59	18.48	C	19.78	19.94	C
11	17.09	17.22	17.14	17.75	18.29	C	17.32	18.28	18.61	19.86	C	19.72
12	16.76	C	C	17.94	18.18	19.40	16.87	C	18.87	C	C	19.68
13	16.67	C	17.12	17.98	18.20	19.25	16.69	C	19.09	19.85	20.01	19.67
14	16.65	17.06	17.25	17.96	C	18.98	16.87	18.29	19.18	19.72	19.86	19.43
15	C	17.06	17.45	17.86	18.26	18.93	C	18.32	19.29	C	19.82	19.33
16	16.72	16.99	17.49	C	18.44	18.97	C	18.34	C	19.71	19.72	19.64
17	16.86	17.15	17.45	17.88	18.52	C	16.68	18.54	C	19.89	19.86	C
18	16.85	17.23	17.49	18.03	18.56	C	17.06	18.68	19.37	20.01	19.96	19.85
19	16.87	C	C	18.00	18.68	18.92	17.36	C	19.31	20.02	C	19.96
20	16.90	17.20	17.44	17.93	18.72	18.83	17.61	C	19.21	19.96	19.93	19.97
21	16.94	17.17	17.45	17.96	C	19.00	17.59	18.70	19.37	20.01	19.88	19.98
22	C	C	17.55	17.96	18.60	19.16	C	18.68	19.44	C	20.16	20.07
23	16.92	17.21	17.56	C	18.71	19.14	C	18.82	C	19.96	C	C
24	16.86	17.28	17.56	17.83	18.69	C	17.48	18.79	C	20.08	20.32	C
25	16.74	17.26	17.61	17.83	18.69	C	17.23	18.54	19.42	20.05	20.28	C
26	16.73	C	C	17.76	18.67	18.11	17.27	C	19.14	19.61	C	19.92
27	16.82	17.28	17.46	17.86	18.65	17.91	17.50	C	19.41	19.77	20.18	20.30
28	16.90	17.22	17.53	17.96	C	18.11	17.69	18.53	19.42	19.79	19.56	20.38
29	C		17.44	18.07	18.72	17.44	C	18.54	19.45	C	19.37	20.43
30	17.02		17.30	C	C	17.69	C	18.43	C	19.61	19.51	20.41
31	17.05		17.29		18.78		17.84	18.42		19.53		C
Close	17.05	17.22	17.29	18.07	18.78	17.69	17.84	18.42	19.45	19.53	19.51	20.41
Month Pt Change	0.29	0.17	0.07	0.78	0.71	−1.09	0.15	0.58	1.03	0.08	−0.02	0.90
Month % Change	1.7	1.0	0.4	4.5	3.9	−5.8	0.8	3.3	5.6	0.4	−0.1	4.6
QTR % Change			3.2			2.3			9.9			4.9
Year % Change												21.8

HIGHLIGHTS

Mid-Term Election Year	Bull Market	Best Six Months 14.8%	High Dec-29	20.43
Truman	Expansion	Worst Six Months 8.1%	Low Jan-14	16.65

STANDARD & POOR'S 500   1951

Previous Month Close	Jan	Feb	Mar	Apr	May	Jun	Jul	Aug	Sep	Oct	Nov	Dec
	20.41	21.66	21.80	21.40	22.43	21.52	20.96	22.40	23.28	23.26	22.94	22.88
1	C	21.77	21.85	C	22.53	21.48	C	22.51	C	23.47	23.10	22.94
2	20.77	21.96	21.93	21.32	22.62	C	21.10	22.82	C	23.64	22.93	C
3	20.69	22.08	21.94	21.26	22.81	C	21.23	22.85	C	23.79	22.74	23.01
4	20.87	C	C	21.40	22.77	21.24	C	C	23.28	23.72	C	23.14
5	20.87	22.20	21.79	21.69	22.69	21.33	21.64	C	23.42	23.78	22.82	23.07
6	20.88	22.12	21.79	21.72	C	21.48	21.64	23.01	23.47	23.77	C	23.34
7	C	21.99	21.86	21.68	22.63	21.56	C	23.03	23.53	C	22.49	23.37
8	21.00	22.09	21.95	C	22.61	21.49	C	22.93	C	23.75	22.47	23.41
9	21.12	22.17	21.95	21.68	22.64	C	21.73	22.84	C	23.65	22.75	C
10	20.85	22.21	21.91	21.65	22.51	C	21.63	22.79	23.62	23.61	22.89	23.42
11	21.19	C	C	21.64	22.33	21.61	21.68	C	23.50	23.70	C	23.30
12	21.11	C	21.70	21.83	22.22	21.52	21.80	C	23.60	C	C	23.37
13	21.10	22.18	21.41	22.09	C	21.55	21.98	22.80	23.71	23.80	22.79	23.39
14	C	22.12	21.25	22.20	22.18	21.84	C	22.70	23.69	C	22.85	23.37
15	21.30	22.00	21.29	C	21.76	22.04	C	22.79	C	23.85	22.84	23.36
16	21.46	22.13	21.64	22.04	21.69	C	21.73	22.87	C	23.77	22.82	C
17	21.55	22.15	21.67	22.09	21.91	C	21.92	22.94	23.62	23.69	22.84	23.41
18	21.40	C	C	22.13	21.51	22.05	21.88	C	23.59	23.67	C	23.49
19	21.36	21.83	21.56	22.04	21.55	22.02	21.84	C	23.59	23.32	22.73	23.57
20	21.41	21.79	21.52	22.04	C	21.91	21.88	22.93	23.57	23.13	22.68	23.57
21	C	21.86	21.64	22.05	21.46	21.78	C	22.83	23.40	C	22.64	23.51
22	21.18	C	21.73	C	21.36	21.55	C	22.75	C	22.75	C	23.53
23	21.26	21.92	C	22.05	21.16	C	22.10	22.90	C	22.84	22.40	C
24	21.16	21.96	21.47	21.96	21.05	C	22.44	22.88	23.30	23.03	22.30	23.54
25	21.03	C	C	21.97	21.03	21.29	22.32	C	23.38	22.96	C	C
26	21.26	21.93	21.53	22.16	21.08	21.30	22.47	C	23.40	22.81	22.43	23.44
27	21.53	21.76	21.51	22.39	C	21.37	22.53	22.85	23.27	22.45	22.66	23.65
28	C	21.80	21.26	22.43	21.21	21.10	C	22.90	23.26	C	22.61	23.69
29	21.67		21.33	C	21.35	20.96	C	23.08	C	22.69	22.67	23.69
30	21.74		21.48	22.43	C	C	22.63	23.24	C	22.66	22.88	C
31	21.66		21.40		21.52		22.40	23.28		22.94		23.77
Close	21.66	21.80	21.40	22.43	21.52	20.96	22.40	23.28	23.26	22.94	22.88	23.77
Month Pt Change	1.25	0.14	-0.40	1.03	-0.91	-0.56	1.44	0.88	-0.02	-0.32	-0.06	0.89
Month % Change	6.1	0.6	-1.8	4.8	-4.1	-2.6	6.9	3.9	-0.1	-1.4	-0.3	3.9
QTR % Change			4.9			-2.1			11.0			2.2
Year % Change												16.5

HIGHLIGHTS

Pre-Election Year	Bull Market	Best Six Months	1.7%	High Oct-15	23.85
Truman	Expansion	Worst Six Months	2.3%	Low Jan-03	20.69

Previous Month Close	Jan	Feb	Mar	Apr	May	Jun	Jul	Aug	Sep	Oct	Nov	Dec
	23.77	24.14	23.26	24.37	23.32	23.86	24.96	25.40	25.03	24.54	24.52	25.66
1	C	24.30	23.28	24.18	23.17	C	25.12	25.45	C	24.48	C	25.68
2	23.80	24.41	C	24.12	23.56	23.80	25.06	C	25.15	24.52	C	25.74
3	23.88	C	23.29	24.12	23.59	23.78	25.05	C	25.25	24.50	24.60	25.71
4	23.92	24.12	23.68	24.02	C	23.95	C	25.43	25.24	C	C	25.61
5	23.94	24.11	23.71	24.00	23.66	24.10	C	25.46	25.21	C	24.67	25.62
6	C	24.18	23.69	C	23.67	24.26	C	25.44	C	24.44	24.77	C
7	23.91	24.11	23.72	23.80	23.81	C	24.97	25.52	C	24.40	24.78	C
8	23.82	24.24	23.77	23.91	23.86	C	24.96	25.55	25.11	24.58	C	25.76
9	23.74	24.25	C	23.94	23.84	24.37	24.86	C	24.86	24.57	C	25.93
10	23.86	C	23.60	24.11	23.80	24.23	24.81	C	24.69	24.55	24.77	25.98
11	23.98	24.11	23.62	C	C	24.31	24.98	25.52	24.72	C	C	25.96
12	24.06	C	23.73	24.15	23.75	24.31	C	25.31	24.71	C	24.65	26.04
13	C	23.92	23.75	C	23.78	24.37	C	25.28	C	C	24.71	C
14	24.16	23.87	23.75	23.95	23.68	C	25.03	25.28	C	24.48	24.75	C
15	24.06	23.86	23.83	23.65	23.60	C	25.16	25.20	24.45	24.06	C	26.04
16	24.09	23.84	C	23.58	23.56	24.30	25.16	C	24.53	23.91	C	26.07
17	24.20	C	23.92	23.41	23.56	24.33	25.05	C	24.58	24.20	24.80	26.04
18	24.25	23.74	23.87	23.50	C	24.43	24.85	24.94	24.51	C	25.16	26.03
19	24.33	23.36	23.82	23.51	23.61	24.51	C	24.89	24.57	C	25.33	26.15
20	C	23.09	23.89	C	23.74	24.59	C	24.95	C	24.13	25.28	C
21	24.46	23.16	23.93	23.69	23.78	C	24.95	24.98	C	24.07	25.27	C
22	24.66	C	23.94	23.58	23.91	C	25.00	24.99	24.59	23.80	C	26.30
23	24.54	23.36	C	23.48	23.89	24.56	25.11	C	24.70	23.87	C	26.19
24	24.56	C	23.93	23.43	23.89	24.60	25.24	C	24.79	24.03	25.42	26.21
25	24.55	23.23	23.79	23.54	C	24.66	25.16	24.87	24.81	C	25.36	C
26	24.59	23.15	23.78	23.58	23.94	24.75	C	24.83	24.73	C	25.52	26.25
27	C	23.18	23.99	C	23.88	24.83	C	24.94	C	24.09	C	C
28	24.61	23.29	24.18	23.55	23.84	C	25.20	24.97	C	24.13	25.66	C
29	24.57	23.26	24.34	23.49	23.86	C	25.26	25.03	24.68	24.15	C	26.40
30	24.23		C	23.32	C	24.96	25.37	C	24.54	24.15	C	26.59
31	24.14		24.37		C		25.40	C		24.52		26.57
Close	24.14	23.26	24.37	23.32	23.86	24.96	25.40	25.03	24.54	24.52	25.66	26.57
Month Pt Change	0.37	–0.88	1.11	–1.05	0.54	1.10	0.44	–0.37	–0.49	–0.02	1.14	0.91
Month % Change	1.6	–3.6	4.8	–4.3	2.3	4.6	1.8	–1.5	–2.0	–0.1	4.6	3.5
QTR % Change			2.5			2.4			–1.7			8.3
Year % Change												11.8

STANDARD & POOR'S 500 — 1953

Previous Month Close	Jan	Feb	Mar	Apr	May	Jun	Jul	Aug	Sep	Oct	Nov	Dec
	26.57	26.38	25.90	25.29	24.62	24.54	24.14	24.75	23.32	23.35	24.54	24.76
1	C	C	C	25.25	24.73	24.15	24.24	C	23.42	23.49	C	24.78
2	26.54	26.51	25.93	25.23	C	24.22	24.31	C	23.56	23.59	24.66	24.95
3	C	26.54	26.00	C	C	24.18	24.36	24.84	23.51	C	C	24.97
4	C	26.42	25.78	C	25.00	24.03	C	24.78	23.57	C	24.51	24.98
5	26.66	26.15	25.79	C	25.03	24.09	C	24.68	C	23.48	24.64	C
6	26.48	25.81	25.84	24.61	25.00	C	24.38	24.80	C	23.39	24.61	C
7	26.37	C	C	24.71	24.90	C	24.51	24.78	C	23.58	C	24.95
8	26.22	C	C	24.93	24.97	24.02	24.51	C	23.61	23.61	C	24.88
9	26.08	25.69	25.83	24.88	C	23.60	24.43	C	23.65	23.66	24.66	24.84
10	C	25.62	25.91	24.82	C	23.54	24.41	24.75	23.41	C	24.37	24.78
11	C	25.64	26.12	C	24.91	23.75	C	24.72	23.14	C	C	24.76
12	25.86	C	26.13	C	24.74	23.82	C	24.78	C	C	24.46	C
13	26.02	25.74	26.18	24.77	24.73	C	24.17	24.73	C	23.57	24.54	C
14	26.08	C	C	24.86	24.85	C	24.08	24.62	22.71	23.68	C	24.69
15	26.13	C	C	24.96	24.84	23.62	24.15	C	22.90	23.95	C	24.71
16	26.02	25.65	26.22	24.91	C	23.55	24.18	C	23.01	24.14	24.38	24.96
17	C	25.50	26.33	24.62	C	23.85	24.35	24.56	23.07	C	24.25	24.94
18	C	25.48	26.24	C	24.75	23.84	C	24.46	22.95	C	24.29	24.99
19	26.01	25.57	26.22	C	24.70	23.84	C	24.31	C	24.16	24.40	C
20	26.14	25.63	26.18	24.73	24.93	C	24.22	24.29	C	24.17	24.44	C
21	26.09	C	C	24.67	25.06	C	24.16	24.35	22.88	24.19	C	24.95
22	26.12	C	C	24.46	25.03	23.96	24.19	C	23.20	24.30	C	24.76
23	26.07	C	26.02	24.19	C	24.12	24.23	C	23.23	24.35	24.36	24.69
24	C	25.75	26.17	24.20	C	24.09	24.23	24.09	23.24	C	24.50	24.80
25	C	25.91	26.10	C	24.99	24.19	C	23.93	23.30	C	24.52	C
26	26.02	25.95	25.95	C	24.87	24.21	C	23.86	C	24.31	C	C
27	26.05	25.90	25.99	24.34	24.64	C	24.07	23.79	C	24.26	24.66	C
28	26.13	C	C	24.52	24.46	C	24.11	23.74	23.45	24.29	C	24.71
29	26.20		C	24.68	24.54	24.14	24.26	C	23.49	24.58	C	24.55
30	26.38		25.61	24.62	C	24.14	24.49	C	23.35	24.54	24.76	24.76
31	C		25.29		C		24.75	23.32		C		24.81
Close	26.38	25.90	25.29	24.62	24.54	24.14	24.75	23.32	23.35	24.54	24.76	24.81
Month Pt Change	–0.19	–0.48	–0.61	–0.67	–0.08	–0.40	0.61	–1.43	0.03	1.19	0.22	0.05
Month % Change	–0.7	–1.8	–2.4	–2.6	–0.3	–1.6	2.5	–5.8	0.1	5.1	0.9	0.2
QTR % Change			–4.8			–4.5			–3.3			6.3
Year % Change												–6.6

HIGHLIGHTS

Post-Election Year	Bull Market	Best Six Months 15.2%	High Jan-05	26.66
Eisenhower (1st term)	Recession Begins Q3	Worst Six Months –0.3%	Low Sep-14	22.71

1954   STANDARD & POOR'S 500

Previous Month Close	Jan	Feb	Mar	Apr	May	Jun	Jul	Aug	Sep	Oct	Nov	Dec
	24.81	26.08	26.15	26.94	28.26	29.19	29.21	30.88	29.83	32.31	31.68	34.24
1	C	25.99	26.25	27.17	C	29.19	29.21	C	30.04	32.29	31.79	33.99
2	C	25.92	26.32	27.21	C	29.16	29.59	30.99	30.27	C	C	34.18
3	C	26.01	26.32	C	28.21	29.15	C	30.93	30.50	C	32.44	34.49
4	24.95	26.20	26.41	C	28.28	29.10	C	30.90	C	32.47	32.82	C
5	25.10	26.30	26.52	27.26	28.29	C	C	30.77	C	32.63	32.71	C
6	25.14	C	C	27.01	28.51	C	29.92	30.38	C	32.76	C	34.76
7	25.06	C	C	27.11	28.65	28.99	29.94	C	30.66	32.69	C	34.92
8	24.93	26.23	26.45	27.38	C	28.34	29.94	C	30.68	32.67	33.02	34.86
9	C	26.17	26.51	27.58	C	28.15	30.14	30.12	30.73	C	33.15	34.69
10	C	26.14	26.57	C	28.62	28.34	C	30.37	30.84	C	33.18	34.56
11	24.80	26.06	26.69	C	28.49	28.58	C	30.72	C	32.41	33.47	C
12	24.93	26.12	26.69	27.57	28.72	C	30.12	30.59	C	32.28	33.54	C
13	25.07	C	C	27.64	28.56	C	30.02	30.72	31.12	32.27	C	34.59
14	25.19	C	C	27.85	28.80	28.62	30.09	C	31.28	31.88	C	34.35
15	25.43	26.04	26.57	27.94	C	28.83	30.19	C	31.29	31.71	33.47	34.56
16	C	25.81	26.56	C	C	29.04	30.06	31.05	31.46	C	33.57	34.93
17	C	25.86	26.62	C	28.84	28.96	C	31.12	31.71	C	33.63	35.02
18	25.43	25.96	26.73	C	28.85	29.04	C	31.09	C	31.83	33.44	C
19	25.68	25.92	26.81	27.76	28.72	C	29.98	31.16	C	31.91	33.45	C
20	25.75	C	C	27.75	28.82	C	29.84	31.21	31.57	32.17	C	35.33
21	25.79	C	C	27.64	28.99	29.06	30.03	C	31.79	32.13	C	35.38
22	25.85	C	26.79	27.68	C	29.08	30.27	C	32.00	32.13	33.58	35.34
23	C	25.83	26.60	27.78	C	29.13	30.31	31.00	32.18	C	34.03	35.37
24	C	25.83	26.47	C	29.00	29.26	C	30.87	32.40	C	34.22	C
25	25.93	25.91	26.42	C	28.93	29.20	C	30.65	C	31.96	C	C
26	26.09	26.15	26.56	27.88	29.17	C	30.34	30.57	C	31.94	34.55	C
27	26.01	C	C	27.76	29.05	C	30.52	30.66	32.53	32.02	C	35.07
28	26.02	C	C	27.76	29.19	29.28	30.58	C	32.69	31.88	C	35.43
29	26.08		26.66	28.18	C	29.43	30.69	C	32.50	31.68	34.54	35.74
30	C		26.69	28.26	C	29.21	30.88	30.35	32.31	C	34.24	35.74
31	C		26.94		C		C	29.83		C		35.98
Close	26.08	26.15	26.94	28.26	29.19	29.21	30.88	29.83	32.31	31.68	34.24	35.98
Month Pt Change	1.27	0.07	0.79	1.32	0.93	0.02	1.67	−1.05	2.48	−0.63	2.56	1.74
Month % Change	5.1	0.3	3.0	4.9	3.3	0.1	5.7	−3.4	8.3	−1.9	8.1	5.1
QTR % Change			8.6			8.4			10.6			11.4
Year % Change												45.0

HIGHLIGHTS

Mid-Term Year	Bull Market	Best Six Months 19.8%	High Dec-31 35.98
Eisenhower (1st term)	Expansion Begins Q3	Worst Six Months 12.1%	Low Jan-11 24.80

STANDARD & POOR'S 500 — 1955

Previous Month Close	Jan	Feb	Mar	Apr	May	Jun	Jul	Aug	Sep	Oct	Nov	Dec
	35.98	36.63	36.76	36.58	37.96	37.91	41.03	43.52	43.18	43.67	42.34	45.51
1	C	36.72	36.83	36.95	C	37.96	41.19	42.93	43.37	C	42.28	45.35
2	C	36.61	37.15	C	38.04	38.09	C	43.03	43.60	C	42.35	45.44
3	36.75	36.44	37.29	C	37.70	38.37	C	43.09	C	42.49	43.24	C
4	36.42	36.96	37.52	36.83	37.64	C	C	42.36	C	42.82	43.96	C
5	35.52	C	C	37.08	37.82	C	41.69	42.56	C	42.99	C	45.70
6	35.04	C	C	37.17	37.89	38.69	43.18	C	43.86	42.70	C	45.70
7	35.33	36.96	37.28	37.34	C	38.96	42.58	C	43.85	42.38	44.15	45.55
8	C	36.46	36.58	C	C	39.22	42.64	42.31	43.88	C	C	45.82
9	C	36.75	36.22	C	37.93	39.01	C	41.75	43.89	C	44.61	45.89
10	35.79	37.08	36.45	C	37.85	39.25	C	41.74	C	41.15	44.72	C
11	35.68	37.15	35.82	37.44	37.42	C	42.75	42.13	C	40.80	45.24	C
12	35.58	C	C	37.66	37.20	C	42.75	42.21	44.19	41.52	C	45.42
13	35.43	C	C	37.71	37.00	39.62	42.24	C	44.80	41.39	C	45.45
14	35.28	36.89	34.96	37.79	C	39.57	42.25	C	44.99	41.22	46.41	45.07
15	C	36.89	35.71	37.96	C	39.89	42.40	42.17	44.75	C	46.21	45.06
16	C	36.77	35.98	C	37.02	39.96	C	41.86	45.09	C	45.91	45.13
17	34.58	36.84	36.12	C	36.97	40.10	C	41.90	C	41.35	45.59	C
18	34.80	36.89	36.18	38.27	37.28	C	42.36	41.84	C	41.65	45.54	C
19	34.96	C	C	38.22	37.49	C	42.10	42.02	45.16	42.07	C	45.02
20	35.13	C	C	38.28	37.74	40.14	42.23	C	45.13	42.59	C	44.95
21	35.44	36.85	35.95	38.32	C	40.51	42.64	C	45.39	42.59	45.22	45.34
22	C	C	36.17	38.01	C	40.60	43.00	41.98	45.39	C	45.66	45.41
23	C	36.82	36.64	C	37.48	40.75	C	42.55	45.63	C	45.72	45.50
24	35.52	36.62	36.93	C	37.46	40.96	C	42.61	C	42.91	C	C
25	35.51	36.57	36.96	38.11	37.60	C	43.48	42.80	C	42.63	45.68	C
26	35.95	C	C	38.31	37.85	C	43.58	42.99	42.61	42.29	C	C
27	35.99	C	C	38.11	37.93	40.99	43.76	C	43.58	42.14	C	45.22
28	36.19	36.76	36.83	37.68	C	40.77	43.50	C	44.31	42.37	45.38	45.05
29	C		36.85	37.96	C	40.79	43.52	42.96	44.03	C	45.56	45.15
30	C		36.52	C	C	41.03	C	42.92	43.67	C	45.51	45.48
31	36.63		36.58		37.91		C	43.18		42.34		C
Close	36.63	36.76	36.58	37.96	37.91	41.03	43.52	43.18	43.67	42.34	45.51	45.48
Month Pt Change	0.65	0.13	–0.18	1.38	–0.05	3.12	2.49	–0.34	0.49	–1.33	3.17	–0.03
Month % Change	1.8	0.4	–0.5	3.8	–0.1	8.2	6.1	–0.8	1.1	–3.0	7.5	–0.1
QTR % Change			1.7			12.2			6.4			4.1
Year % Change												26.4

HIGHLIGHTS

Pre-Election Year	Bull Market	Best Six Months 14.3%	High	Nov-14	46.41
Eisenhower (1st term)	Expansion	Worst Six Months 11.5%	Low	Jan-17	34.58

1956

STANDARD & POOR'S 500

Previous Month Close	Jan 45.48	Feb 43.82	Mar 45.34	Apr 48.48	May 48.38	Jun 45.20	Jul 46.97	Aug 49.39	Sep 47.51	Oct 45.35	Nov 45.58	Dec 45.08
1	C	44.03	45.54	C	48.16	45.58	C	49.42	C	44.70	46.52	C
2	C	44.22	45.81	48.70	48.17	C	46.93	49.74	C	45.52	46.98	C
3	45.16	44.78	C	48.53	48.34	C	47.32	49.64	C	46.28	C	45.98
4	45.00	C	C	48.80	48.51	45.85	C	C	47.89	46.29	C	45.84
5	44.95	C	46.06	48.57	C	45.86	47.80	C	48.02	46.00	47.60	46.39
6	45.14	44.81	46.04	48.85	C	45.63	48.04	48.86	48.10	C	C	46.81
7	C	44.60	46.01	C	48.22	45.99	C	49.16	47.81	C	47.11	47.04
8	C	44.16	46.12	C	48.02	45.14	C	49.36	C	46.43	46.73	C
9	44.51	43.66	46.70	48.61	47.94	C	48.25	49.32	C	46.20	46.34	C
10	44.16	43.64	C	47.93	47.16	C	48.54	49.09	47.56	46.84	C	46.80
11	44.38	C	C	48.31	47.12	45.71	48.69	C	47.38	46.81	C	46.48
12	44.75	C	47.13	48.02	C	46.36	48.58	C	47.05	47.00	46.49	46.13
13	44.67	43.58	47.06	47.95	C	46.42	48.72	48.58	46.99	C	46.27	46.50
14	C	43.42	47.53	C	46.86	46.31	C	48.90	47.21	C	46.01	46.54
15	C	44.04	47.99	C	46.37	46.37	C	48.99	C	46.86	45.72	C
16	44.14	43.82	48.14	47.96	46.05	C	49.14	48.88	C	46.62	45.74	C
17	44.47	44.52	C	47.93	46.61	C	49.31	48.82	47.19	46.26	C	46.54
18	44.17	C	C	47.74	46.39	46.17	49.30	C	46.79	46.34	C	46.54
19	43.72	C	48.59	47.57	C	46.22	49.32	C	46.24	46.24	45.29	46.43
20	43.22	44.45	48.87	47.76	C	46.41	49.35	48.25	46.21	C	44.89	46.07
21	C	44.56	48.23	C	45.99	46.73	C	47.89	46.58	C	44.67	46.37
22	C	C	48.72	C	45.26	46.59	C	47.42	C	46.23	C	C
23	43.11	44.95	48.83	47.65	45.02	C	49.33	48.00	C	46.12	45.14	C
24	43.65	45.32	C	47.26	44.60	C	49.33	47.95	46.40	45.93	C	C
25	43.72	C	C	47.09	44.62	46.41	49.44	C	45.75	45.85	C	C
26	43.46	C	48.62	47.49	C	46.72	49.48	C	45.82	46.27	44.87	46.39
27	43.35	45.27	48.25	47.99	C	47.07	49.08	47.66	45.60	C	44.91	46.35
28	C	45.43	48.51	C	44.10	47.13	C	47.57	45.35	C	44.43	46.56
29	C	45.34	48.48	C	45.11	46.97	C	47.36	C	46.40	44.38	C
30	43.50		C	48.38	C	C	49.00	46.94	C	46.37	45.08	C
31	43.82		C		45.20		49.39	47.51		45.58		46.67
Close	43.82	45.34	48.48	48.38	45.20	46.97	49.39	47.51	45.35	45.58	45.08	46.67
Month Pt Change	−1.66	1.52	3.14	−0.10	−3.18	1.77	2.42	−1.88	−2.16	0.23	−0.50	1.59
Month % Change	−3.6	3.5	6.9	−0.2	−6.6	3.9	5.2	−3.8	−4.5	0.5	−1.1	3.5
QTR % Change			6.6			−3.1			−3.4			2.9
Year % Change												2.6

HIGHLIGHTS

Election Year	Bear Market Begins 4/6/56	Best Six Months	0.4%	High Aug-02 49.74
Eisenhower (1st term)	Expansion	Worst Six Months	−5.8%	Low Jan-23 43.11

ALMANAC INVESTOR

Previous Month Close	Jan 46.67	Feb 44.72	Mar 43.26	Apr 44.11	May 45.74	Jun 47.43	Jul 47.37	Aug 47.91	Sep 45.22	Oct 42.42	Nov 41.06	Dec 41.72
1	C	44.62	43.74	44.14	46.02	C	47.43	47.79	C	42.76	40.44	C
2	46.20	C	C	44.42	46.39	C	47.90	47.68	C	43.10	C	41.36
3	46.60	C	C	44.54	46.34	47.37	48.46	C	45.44	43.14	C	41.37
4	46.66	44.53	44.06	44.44	C	47.28	C	C	45.05	42.79	40.37	41.54
5	C	43.89	44.22	44.49	C	47.27	48.69	47.26	44.82	C	C	41.52
6	C	43.82	44.33	C	46.27	47.60	C	46.67	44.68	C	40.43	41.31
7	46.42	43.62	44.21	C	46.13	47.65	C	47.03	C	42.22	40.67	C
8	46.25	43.32	44.07	44.39	46.31	C	48.90	46.90	C	41.95	40.19	C
9	46.16	C	C	44.79	46.36	C	48.72	46.92	44.28	41.99	C	40.92
10	46.27	C	C	44.98	46.59	47.40	49.05	C	43.87	40.96	C	40.56
11	46.18	42.57	43.78	44.94	C	47.94	48.86	C	44.26	40.94	40.18	40.51
12	C	42.39	43.75	45.04	C	48.05	49.08	46.33	44.82	C	39.60	40.55
13	C	43.04	44.04	C	46.88	48.14	C	46.30	44.80	C	39.55	40.73
14	45.86	42.99	44.07	C	46.67	48.15	C	45.73	C	41.24	39.44	C
15	45.18	43.51	44.05	44.95	46.83	C	49.13	45.75	C	41.67	40.37	C
16	45.23	C	C	45.02	47.02	C	48.88	45.83	44.58	41.33	C	40.12
17	45.22	C	C	45.08	47.15	48.24	48.58	C	44.64	40.65	C	39.42
18	44.64	43.46	43.85	45.41	C	48.04	48.53	C	44.69	40.33	40.04	39.38
19	C	43.49	44.04	C	C	47.72	48.58	44.91	44.40	C	39.81	39.80
20	C	43.63	44.10	C	47.27	47.43	C	45.29	43.69	C	39.92	39.48
21	44.40	43.48	44.11	C	47.33	47.15	C	45.49	C	39.15	40.48	C
22	44.53	C	44.06	45.48	47.14	C	48.47	45.16	C	38.98	40.87	C
23	44.87	C	C	45.65	47.15	C	48.56	44.51	42.69	40.73	C	39.48
24	45.03	C	C	45.72	47.21	46.78	48.61	C	42.98	40.71	C	39.52
25	44.82	43.38	43.88	45.56	C	47.15	48.61	C	42.46	40.59	41.18	C
26	C	43.45	43.91	45.50	C	47.09	48.45	43.89	42.57	C	40.09	39.92
27	C	43.41	44.09	C	46.78	47.26	C	44.61	42.55	C	41.25	39.78
28	44.49	43.26	44.18	C	46.69	47.37	C	44.64	C	40.42	C	C
29	44.71		44.11	45.73	47.11	C	47.92	44.46	C	40.69	41.72	C
30	44.91		C	45.74	C	C	47.92	45.22	42.42	41.02	C	39.58
31	44.72		C		47.43		47.91	C		41.06		39.99
Close	44.72	43.26	44.11	45.74	47.43	47.37	47.91	45.22	42.42	41.06	41.72	39.99
Month Pt Change	−1.95	−1.46	0.85	1.63	1.69	−0.06	0.54	−2.69	−2.80	−1.36	0.66	−1.73
Month % Change	−4.2	−3.3	2.0	3.7	3.7	−0.1	1.1	−5.6	−6.2	−3.2	1.6	−4.1
QTR % Change			−5.5			7.4			−10.4			−5.7
Year % Change												−14.3

HIGHLIGHTS

Post-Election Year	Bull Market Begins 10/22/57	Best Six Months	5.8%	High	Jul-15	49.13
Eisenhower (2nd term)	Recession Begins Q2	Worst Six Months	-10.2%	Low	Oct-22	38.98

1958

STANDARD & POOR'S 500

	Jan	Feb	Mar	Apr	May	Jun	Jul	Aug	Sep	Oct	Nov	Dec
Previous Month Close	39.99	41.70	40.84	42.10	43.44	44.09	45.24	47.19	47.75	50.06	51.33	52.48
1	C	C	C	41.93	43.54	C	45.28	47.49	C	49.98	C	52.69
2	40.33	C	C	41.60	43.69	44.31	45.32	C	48.00	50.17	C	52.46
3	40.87	42.04	41.13	41.48	C	44.46	45.47	C	48.18	50.37	51.56	52.53
4	C	42.46	41.35	C	C	44.50	C	47.94	48.10	C	C	52.55
5	C	42.19	41.47	C	43.79	44.55	C	47.75	47.97	C	52.03	52.46
6	40.68	42.10	42.00	C	44.01	44.64	C	47.46	C	50.68	52.45	C
7	41.00	41.73	42.07	41.33	43.93	C	45.62	47.77	C	50.97	52.26	C
8	40.99	C	C	41.63	43.99	C	45.40	48.05	48.13	51.06	C	52.52
9	40.75	C	C	41.65	44.00	44.57	45.25	C	48.46	51.05	C	52.82
10	40.37	41.48	42.21	41.70	C	44.48	45.42	C	48.31	51.39	52.57	53.46
11	C	41.11	42.51	41.74	C	44.49	45.72	48.18	48.64	C	52.98	53.35
12	C	40.93	42.41	C	43.75	44.75	C	47.73	48.53	C	53.05	53.22
13	40.49	40.94	42.46	C	43.62	45.02	C	47.81	C	51.62	52.83	C
14	40.67	41.33	42.33	42.00	43.12	C	45.14	47.91	C	51.26	53.09	C
15	40.99	C	C	42.43	43.34	C	45.11	47.50	48.96	50.58	C	53.37
16	41.06	C	C	42.10	43.36	45.18	45.25	C	49.35	50.94	C	53.57
17	41.10	41.11	42.04	42.25	C	44.94	45.55	C	49.33	51.46	53.24	53.92
18	C	41.17	41.89	42.71	C	45.34	45.77	47.22	49.08	C	53.13	54.15
19	C	41.15	42.09	C	43.24	44.61	C	47.30	49.40	C	53.20	54.07
20	41.35	40.91	42.11	C	43.61	44.85	C	47.32	C	51.27	53.21	C
21	41.30	40.88	42.42	42.93	43.55	C	46.33	47.63	C	51.27	52.70	C
22	41.20	C	C	42.80	43.78	C	46.41	47.73	49.20	51.07	C	53.71
23	41.36	C	C	42.80	43.87	44.69	46.40	C	49.56	50.97	C	53.42
24	41.71	40.65	42.58	43.14	C	44.52	46.65	C	49.78	50.81	51.33	54.11
25	C	40.61	42.44	43.36	C	44.63	46.97	47.74	49.57	C	51.02	C
26	C	40.92	42.30	C	43.85	44.84	C	47.90	49.66	C	51.90	C
27	41.59	40.68	42.17	C	43.79	44.90	C	47.91	C	50.42	C	C
28	41.63	40.84	42.20	43.22	43.85	C	47.15	47.66	C	50.61	52.48	C
29	41.88		C	43.00	44.09	C	46.96	47.75	49.87	51.19	C	54.74
30	41.68		C	43.44	C	45.24	47.09	C	50.06	51.27	C	54.93
31	41.70		42.10		C		47.19	C		51.33		55.21
Close	41.70	40.84	42.10	43.44	44.09	45.24	47.19	47.75	50.06	51.33	52.48	55.21
Month Pt Change	1.71	−0.86	1.26	1.34	0.65	1.15	1.95	0.56	2.31	1.27	1.15	2.73
Month % Change	4.3	−2.1	3.1	3.2	1.5	2.6	4.3	1.2	4.8	2.5	2.2	5.2
QTR % Change			5.3			7.5			10.7			10.3
Year % Change												38.1

HIGHLIGHTS

Mid-Term Year	Bull Market	Best Six Months	12.2%	High	Dec-31	55.21
Eisenhower (2nd term)	Expansion Begins Q3	Worst Six Months	18.2%	Low	Jan-02	40.33

STANDARD & POOR'S 500   1959

Previous Month Close	Jan	Feb	Mar	Apr	May	Jun	Jul	Aug	Sep	Oct	Nov	Dec
	55.21	55.42	55.41	55.44	57.59	58.68	58.47	60.51	59.60	56.88	57.52	58.28
1	C	C	C	55.69	57.65	58.63	58.97	C	58.87	56.94	C	58.70
2	55.44	55.21	55.73	56.00	C	58.23	59.28	C	58.92	57.20	57.41	58.60
3	C	55.28	56.25	56.44	C	58.25	C	60.71	58.26	C	C	58.73
4	C	55.06	56.35	C	57.65	57.63	C	60.61	58.54	C	57.26	58.85
5	55.66	54.81	56.43	C	57.75	57.51	C	60.30	C	57.14	57.32	C
6	55.59	54.37	56.21	56.60	57.61	C	59.65	60.24	C	57.09	57.60	C
7	54.89	C	C	56.48	56.88	C	60.01	59.87	C	56.94	C	58.96
8	55.40	C	C	56.21	57.32	56.76	60.03	C	57.70	56.81	C	59.34
9	55.77	53.58	56.15	56.17	C	56.36	59.97	C	57.29	57.00	57.50	58.97
10	C	54.32	56.31	56.22	C	57.19	59.91	58.62	56.99	C	57.48	59.02
11	C	54.35	56.35	C	57.56	57.25	C	59.39	57.41	C	57.49	58.88
12	55.78	54.00	56.60	C	57.65	57.29	C	59.25	C	57.32	57.17	C
13	55.47	54.42	56.67	56.43	57.97	C	59.41	59.15	C	57.16	56.85	C
14	55.62	C	C	56.71	58.37	C	59.55	59.29	56.99	56.71	C	59.04
15	55.83	C	C	56.96	58.16	56.99	59.59	C	56.68	56.87	C	58.90
16	55.81	54.50	56.06	57.43	C	56.56	59.41	C	56.72	57.33	56.22	58.97
17	C	54.29	56.52	57.92	C	57.09	59.16	59.17	56.41	C	56.38	58.86
18	C	54.50	56.39	C	58.15	57.05	C	58.62	56.09	C	56.99	59.14
19	55.68	55.02	56.34	C	58.32	57.13	C	58.27	C	57.01	56.94	C
20	55.72	55.52	56.39	58.17	58.09	C	58.91	59.14	C	56.66	56.97	C
21	56.04	C	C	58.11	58.14	C	59.41	59.08	55.27	56.55	C	59.24
22	55.97	C	C	57.73	58.33	57.13	59.61	C	55.14	56.00	C	59.14
23	56.00	C	55.87	57.60	C	57.12	59.67	C	55.82	56.56	57.08	58.96
24	C	55.48	55.96	57.96	C	57.41	59.65	58.87	56.78	C	57.35	59.00
25	C	55.24	55.88	C	58.18	57.73	C	58.99	56.73	C	57.44	C
26	55.77	55.34	55.76	C	58.09	57.98	C	59.07	C	56.94	C	C
27	55.78	55.41	C	58.14	58.19	C	60.02	59.64	C	57.42	57.70	C
28	55.16	C	C	57.92	58.39	C	60.32	59.49	57.15	57.46	C	58.98
29	55.20		C	57.69	58.68	58.37	60.62	C	57.51	57.41	C	59.30
30	55.42		55.45	57.59	C	58.47	60.50	C	56.88	57.52	58.28	59.77
31	C		55.44		C		60.51	59.60		C		59.89
Close	55.42	55.41	55.44	57.59	58.68	58.47	60.51	59.60	56.88	57.52	58.28	59.89
Month Pt Change	0.21	−0.01	0.03	2.15	1.09	−0.21	2.04	−0.91	−2.72	0.64	0.76	1.61
Month % Change	0.4	−0.02	0.1	3.9	1.9	−0.4	3.5	−1.5	−4.6	1.1	1.3	2.8
QTR % Change			0.4			5.5			−2.7			5.3
Year % Change												8.5

HIGHLIGHTS

Pre-Election Year	Bull Market	Best Six Months	-5.5%	High Aug-03	60.71
Eisnehower (2nd Term)	Expansion	Worst Six Monthhs	-0.1%	Low Feb-09	53.58

Data Bank

1960 STANDARD & POOR'S 500

Previous Month Close	Jan	Feb	Mar	Apr	May	Jun	Jul	Aug	Sep	Oct	Nov	Dec
	59.89	55.61	56.12	55.34	54.37	55.83	56.92	55.51	56.96	53.52	53.39	55.54
1	C	55.96	56.01	55.43	C	55.89	57.06	55.53	57.09	C	53.94	55.30
2	C	56.82	55.62	C	54.13	56.13	C	55.04	57.00	C	54.22	55.39
3	C	56.32	54.78	C	54.83	56.23	C	54.72	C	53.36	54.43	C
4	59.91	56.27	54.57	55.54	55.04	C	C	54.89	C	52.99	54.90	C
5	60.39	55.98	C	55.87	54.86	C	57.02	55.44	C	53.39	C	55.31
6	60.13	C	C	56.51	54.75	56.89	56.94	C	56.49	53.72	C	55.47
7	59.69	C	54.02	56.52	C	57.43	57.24	C	55.79	54.03	55.11	56.02
8	59.50	55.32	53.47	56.39	C	57.89	57.38	55.52	55.74	C	C	56.15
9	C	55.84	54.04	C	54.80	58.00	C	55.84	56.11	C	55.35	56.65
10	C	55.49	53.83	C	54.42	57.97	C	56.07	C	54.14	56.13	C
11	58.77	55.18	54.24	56.17	54.57	C	56.87	56.28	C	54.22	55.87	C
12	58.41	55.46	C	56.30	54.85	C	56.25	56.66	55.77	54.15	C	56.85
13	58.08	C	C	56.30	55.30	57.99	56.10	C	55.83	54.57	C	56.88
14	58.40	C	54.32	56.43	C	57.91	56.12	C	55.44	54.88	55.59	56.84
15	58.38	55.17	54.74	C	C	57.57	56.05	56.61	55.22	C	55.81	56.68
16	C	54.73	55.04	C	55.25	57.50	C	56.72	55.11	C	55.70	57.20
17	C	55.03	54.96	C	55.46	57.44	C	56.84	C	54.63	55.55	C
18	57.89	55.80	55.01	56.59	55.44	C	55.70	56.81	C	54.35	55.82	C
19	57.27	56.24	C	56.13	55.68	C	55.70	57.01	53.86	54.25	C	57.13
20	57.07	C	C	55.44	55.83	57.16	55.61	C	54.01	53.86	C	57.09
21	57.21	C	55.07	55.59	C	57.11	55.10	C	54.57	53.32	55.93	57.55
22	57.38	C	55.29	55.42	C	57.28	54.72	57.19	54.36	C	55.72	57.39
23	C	55.94	55.74	C	55.76	57.59	C	57.75	53.90	C	55.80	57.44
24	C	55.74	55.98	C	55.70	57.68	C	58.07	C	52.70	C	C
25	56.78	55.93	55.98	54.86	55.67	C	54.18	57.79	C	52.30	56.13	C
26	56.86	56.16	C	55.04	55.71	C	54.51	57.60	53.06	53.05	C	C
27	56.72	C	C	55.04	55.74	57.33	54.17	C	52.94	53.62	C	57.52
28	56.13	C	55.86	54.56	C	56.94	54.57	C	52.48	53.41	56.03	57.78
29	55.61	56.12	55.78	54.37	C	56.94	55.51	57.44	52.62	C	55.83	58.05
30	C		55.66	C	C	56.92	C	56.84	53.52	C	55.54	58.11
31	C		55.34		55.83		C	56.96		53.39		C
Close	55.61	56.12	55.34	54.37	55.83	56.92	55.51	56.96	53.52	53.39	55.54	58.11
Month Pt Change	−4.28	0.51	−0.78	−0.97	1.46	1.09	−1.41	1.45	−3.44	−0.13	2.15	2.57
Month % Change	−7.1	0.9	−1.4	−1.8	2.7	2.0	−2.5	2.6	−6.0	−0.20	4.0	4.6
QTR % Change			−7.6			2.9			−6.0			8.6
Year % Change												−3.0

HIGHLIGHTS

Election Year	Bear Market 1/5 to 10/25	Best Six Months 22.3%	High Jan-05	60.39
Eisnehower (2nd Term)	Recession Begins Q3	Worst Six Months −1.8%	Low Oct-25	52.30

STANDARD & POOR'S 500 — 1961

Previous Month	Jan	Feb	Mar	Apr	May	Jun	Jul	Aug	Sep	Oct	Nov	Dec
Close	58.11	61.78	63.44	65.06	65.31	66.56	64.64	66.76	68.07	66.73	68.62	71.32
1	C	61.90	63.43	C	65.17	66.56	C	67.37	68.19	C	68.73	71.78
2	C	62.30	63.85	C	65.64	66.73	C	66.94	C	66.77	69.11	C
3	57.57	62.22	63.95	65.60	66.18	C	65.21	67.29	C	66.73	69.47	C
4	58.36	C	C	65.66	66.44	C	C	67.68	C	67.18	C	72.01
5	58.57	C	C	65.46	66.52	67.08	65.63	C	67.96	67.77	C	71.93
6	58.48	61.76	64.05	65.61	C	66.89	65.81	C	68.46	67.97	70.01	71.99
7	C	61.65	63.47	65.96	C	66.64	65.77	67.67	68.35	C	C	71.70
8	C	62.21	63.44	C	66.41	66.67	C	67.82	67.88	C	70.87	72.04
9	58.81	62.02	63.50	C	66.47	66.66	C	67.74	C	67.94	70.77	C
10	58.97	61.50	63.48	66.53	66.41	C	65.71	67.95	C	68.11	71.07	C
11	59.14	C	C	66.62	66.39	C	65.69	68.06	67.28	68.17	C	72.39
12	59.32	C	C	66.31	66.45	66.15	65.32	C	67.96	68.16	C	72.64
13	59.60	61.14	63.66	66.26	C	65.80	64.86	C	68.01	68.04	71.27	72.53
14	C	61.41	63.38	66.37	C	65.98	65.28	67.72	67.53	C	71.66	71.98
15	C	61.92	63.57	C	66.83	65.69	C	67.55	67.65	C	71.67	72.01
16	59.58	62.30	64.21	C	67.08	65.18	C	67.73	C	67.85	71.62	C
17	59.34	62.10	64.60	66.68	67.39	C	64.79	68.11	C	67.87	71.62	C
18	59.68	C	C	66.20	66.99	C	64.41	68.29	67.21	68.21	C	71.76
19	59.77	C	C	65.81	67.27	64.58	64.70	C	66.68	68.45	C	71.26
20	59.96	62.32	64.86	65.82	C	65.15	64.71	C	66.96	68.48	71.72	71.12
21	C	62.36	64.74	65.77	C	65.14	64.86	68.43	66.99	C	71.78	70.86
22	C	C	64.70	C	66.85	64.90	C	68.44	66.72	C	71.70	70.91
23	60.29	62.59	64.53	C	66.68	65.16	C	67.98	C	68.06	C	C
24	60.45	62.84	64.42	64.40	66.26	C	64.87	67.59	C	67.98	71.84	C
25	60.53	C	C	65.30	66.01	C	65.23	67.67	65.77	68.34	C	C
26	60.62	C	C	65.55	66.43	64.47	65.84	C	65.78	68.46	C	71.02
27	61.24	63.30	64.35	65.46	C	64.47	66.61	C	66.47	68.34	71.85	71.65
28	C	63.44	64.38	65.31	C	64.59	66.71	67.70	66.58	C	71.75	71.69
29	C		64.93	C	C	64.52	C	67.55	66.73	C	71.70	71.55
30	61.97		65.06	C	C	64.64	C	67.81	C	68.42	71.32	C
31	61.78		C		66.56		66.76	68.07		68.62		C
Close	61.78	63.44	65.06	65.31	66.56	64.64	66.76	68.07	66.73	68.62	71.32	71.55
Month Pt Change	3.67	1.66	1.62	0.25	1.25	−1.92	2.12	1.31	−1.34	1.89	2.70	0.23
Month % Change	6.3	2.7	2.6	0.4	1.9	−2.9	3.3	2.0	−2.0	2.8	3.9	0.3
QTR % Change			12.0			−0.6			3.2			7.2
Year % Change												23.1

HIGHLIGHTS

Bear Market Begins 12/13/61	Bear Market Begins 12/13	Best Six Months -4.9%	High	Dec-12	72.64
Kennedy	Expansion Begins Q2	Worst Six Months 5.1%	Low	Jan-03	57.57

1962   STANDARD & POOR'S 500

Previous Month Close	Jan	Feb	Mar	Apr	May	Jun	Jul	Aug	Sep	Oct	Nov	Dec
	71.55	68.84	69.96	69.55	65.24	59.63	54.75	58.23	59.12	56.27	56.52	62.26
1	C	69.26	70.20	C	65.70	59.38	C	57.75	C	55.49	57.12	C
2	70.96	69.81	70.16	69.37	65.99	C	55.86	57.98	C	56.10	57.75	C
3	71.13	C	C	68.81	66.53	C	56.49	58.12	C	56.16	C	61.94
4	70.64	C	C	68.49	66.24	57.27	C	C	58.56	56.70	C	62.64
5	69.66	69.88	70.01	68.91	C	57.57	56.81	C	58.12	57.07	58.35	62.39
6	C	69.96	69.78	68.84	C	58.39	56.17	57.75	58.36	C	C	62.93
7	C	70.42	69.69	C	66.02	58.40	C	57.36	58.38	C	58.71	63.06
8	69.12	70.58	70.19	C	65.17	58.45	C	57.51	C	57.07	58.32	C
9	69.15	70.48	70.42	68.31	64.26	C	56.55	57.47	C	57.20	58.78	C
10	68.96	C	C	68.56	63.57	C	57.20	57.55	58.45	57.24	C	62.27
11	69.37	C	C	68.41	62.65	57.82	57.73	C	58.59	57.05	C	62.32
12	69.61	70.46	70.40	67.90	C	56.34	58.03	C	58.84	56.95	59.59	62.63
13	C	70.45	70.60	67.90	C	55.50	57.83	57.63	58.70	C	59.46	62.42
14	C	70.42	70.91	C	63.10	54.33	C	58.25	58.89	C	60.16	62.57
15	69.47	70.74	71.06	C	64.29	55.89	C	58.66	C	57.27	59.97	C
16	69.07	70.59	70.94	67.60	64.27	C	57.83	58.64	C	57.08	60.16	C
17	68.32	C	C	67.90	63.93	C	56.78	59.01	59.08	56.89	C	62.37
18	68.39	C	C	68.27	63.82	55.74	56.20	C	59.03	56.34	C	62.07
19	68.75	70.41	70.85	68.59	C	55.54	56.42	C	58.95	55.59	59.82	62.58
20	C	70.66	70.66	C	C	54.78	56.81	59.37	58.54	C	60.45	62.82
21	C	70.32	70.51	C	63.59	53.59	C	59.12	57.69	C	60.81	62.64
22	68.81	C	70.40	C	62.34	52.68	C	59.78	C	54.96	C	C
23	68.29	70.16	70.45	68.53	61.11	C	56.80	59.70	C	53.49	61.54	C
24	68.40	C	C	68.46	60.62	C	56.36	59.58	56.63	55.21	C	62.63
25	68.35	C	C	67.71	59.47	52.45	56.46	C	56.96	54.69	C	C
26	68.13	69.76	69.89	67.05	C	52.32	56.77	C	56.15	54.54	61.36	63.02
27	C	69.89	69.70	66.30	C	52.60	57.20	59.55	55.77	C	61.73	62.93
28	C	69.96	70.04	C	55.50	54.41	C	58.79	56.27	C	62.12	62.96
29	67.90		70.01	C	58.08	54.75	C	58.66	C	55.72	62.41	C
30	68.17		69.55	65.24	C	C	57.83	58.68	C	56.54	62.26	C
31	68.84		C		59.63		58.23	59.12		56.52		63.10
Close	68.84	69.96	69.55	65.24	59.63	54.75	58.23	59.12	56.27	56.52	62.26	63.10
Month Pt Change	-2.71	1.12	-0.41	-4.31	-5.61	-4.88	3.48	0.89	-2.85	0.25	5.74	0.84
Month % Change	-3.8	1.6	-0.6	-6.2	-8.6	-8.2	6.4	1.5	-4.8	0.4	10.2	1.3
QTR % Change			-2.8			-21.3			2.8			12.1
Year % Change												-11.8

HIGHLIGHTS

Mid-Term Election Year	Recession Q1 - Q2	Best Six Months	23.5%	High	Jan-03	71.13
Kennedy	Expansion	Worst Six Months	-13.4%	Low	Jun-26	52.32

STANDARD & POOR'S 500 — 1963

Previous Month Close	Jan	Feb	Mar	Apr	May	Jun	Jul	Aug	Sep	Oct	Nov	Dec
	63.10	66.20	64.29	66.57	69.80	70.80	69.37	69.13	72.50	71.70	74.01	73.23
1	C	66.31	64.10	66.85	69.97	C	68.86	69.07	C	72.22	73.83	C
2	62.69	C	C	66.84	70.17	C	69.46	69.30	C	72.30	C	73.66
3	63.72	C	C	67.36	70.03	70.69	69.94	C	72.66	72.83	C	73.62
4	64.13	66.17	64.72	67.85	C	70.70	C	C	72.64	72.85	73.45	73.80
5	C	66.11	64.74	68.28	C	70.53	70.22	69.71	73.00	C	C	74.28
6	C	66.40	64.85	C	69.53	70.58	C	70.17	72.84	C	72.81	74.00
7	64.12	66.17	65.26	C	69.44	70.41	C	69.96	C	72.70	73.06	C
8	64.74	66.17	65.33	68.52	70.01	C	69.74	70.02	C	72.60	73.36	C
9	64.59	C	C	68.45	70.35	C	70.04	70.48	72.58	72.18	C	73.96
10	64.71	C	C	68.29	70.52	69.94	69.89	C	72.99	72.20	C	73.99
11	64.85	65.76	65.51	68.77	C	70.03	69.76	C	73.20	72.27	73.52	73.90
12	C	65.83	65.67	C	C	70.41	69.64	70.59	73.15	C	73.23	73.91
13	C	66.15	65.91	C	70.48	70.23	C	70.79	73.17	C	73.29	74.06
14	65.20	66.35	65.60	C	70.21	70.25	C	71.07	C	72.30	72.95	C
15	65.11	66.41	65.93	69.09	70.43	C	69.20	71.38	C	72.40	72.35	C
16	64.67	C	C	69.14	70.25	C	69.14	71.49	73.07	72.97	C	74.30
17	65.13	C	C	68.92	70.29	69.94	68.93	C	73.12	73.26	C	74.74
18	65.18	66.52	65.61	68.89	C	70.02	68.49	C	72.80	73.32	71.83	74.63
19	C	66.20	65.47	69.23	C	70.09	68.35	71.44	73.22	C	71.90	74.40
20	C	65.83	65.95	C	69.96	70.01	C	71.38	73.30	C	72.56	74.28
21	65.28	65.92	65.85	C	70.14	70.25	C	71.29	C	73.38	71.62	C
22	65.44	C	66.19	69.30	70.14	C	67.90	71.54	C	72.96	69.61	C
23	65.62	C	C	69.53	70.10	C	67.91	71.76	72.96	73.00	C	73.81
24	65.75	C	C	69.72	70.02	70.20	68.28	C	73.30	73.28	C	73.97
25	65.92	65.46	66.21	69.76	C	70.04	68.26	C	72.89	74.01	C	C
26	C	65.47	66.40	69.70	C	69.41	68.54	71.91	72.27	C	72.38	74.32
27	C	65.01	66.68	C	69.87	69.07	C	71.52	72.13	C	72.25	74.44
28	66.24	64.29	66.58	C	70.01	69.37	C	72.04	C	74.48	C	C
29	66.23		66.57	69.65	70.33	C	68.67	72.16	C	74.46	73.23	C
30	65.85		C	69.80	C	C	69.24	72.50	71.70	73.80	C	74.56
31	66.20		C		70.80		69.13	C		74.01		75.02
Close	66.20	64.29	66.57	69.80	70.80	69.37	69.13	72.50	71.70	74.01	73.23	75.02
Month Pt Change	3.10	−1.91	2.28	3.23	1.00	−1.43	−0.24	3.37	−0.80	2.31	−0.78	1.79
Month % Change	4.9	−2.9	3.5	4.9	1.4	−2.0	−0.3	4.9	−1.1	3.2	−1.1	2.4
QTR % Change			5.5			4.2			3.4			4.6
Year % Change												18.9

Previous Month Close	Jan	Feb	Mar	Apr	May	Jun	Jul	Aug	Sep	Oct	Nov	Dec
	75.02	77.04	77.80	78.98	79.46	80.37	81.69	83.18	81.83	84.18	84.86	84.42
1	C	C	C	79.24	80.17	80.11	82.27	C	82.18	84.08	C	83.55
2	75.43	C	77.97	79.70	C	79.70	82.60	C	82.31	84.36	85.18	83.79
3	75.50	76.97	78.22	79.94	C	79.49	C	83.00	82.56	C	C	84.18
4	C	76.88	78.07	C	80.47	78.67	C	81.96	82.76	C	85.14	84.35
5	C	76.75	78.06	C	80.88	79.02	C	82.09	C	84.74	85.16	C
6	75.67	76.93	78.31	80.02	81.06	C	82.98	81.34	C	84.79	85.23	C
7	75.69	77.18	C	79.74	81.15	C	83.12	81.86	C	84.80	C	84.33
8	76.00	C	C	79.75	81.00	78.64	83.12	C	82.87	85.04	C	84.00
9	76.28	C	78.33	79.70	C	79.14	83.22	C	83.05	85.22	85.19	83.46
10	76.24	77.05	78.59	79.85	C	79.44	83.36	81.78	83.10	C	84.84	83.45
11	C	77.33	78.95	C	80.90	79.73	C	81.76	83.45	C	85.08	83.66
12	C	77.57	79.08	C	81.16	79.60	C	82.17	C	85.24	85.19	C
13	76.22	77.52	79.14	79.77	80.97	C	83.31	82.41	C	84.96	85.21	C
14	76.36	77.48	C	79.99	80.86	C	83.06	82.35	83.22	84.79	C	83.45
15	76.64	C	C	80.09	81.10	79.97	83.34	C	83.00	84.25	C	83.22
16	76.55	C	79.14	80.20	C	80.40	83.64	C	83.24	84.83	85.65	83.55
17	76.56	77.46	79.32	80.55	C	80.81	84.01	82.36	83.79	C	86.03	83.90
18	C	77.47	79.38	C	80.72	80.79	C	82.40	83.48	C	86.22	84.29
19	C	77.55	79.30	C	80.30	80.89	C	82.32	C	84.93	86.18	C
20	76.41	77.62	78.92	80.50	80.66	C	83.74	81.94	C	85.18	86.28	C
21	76.62	C	C	80.54	80.94	C	83.54	82.07	83.86	85.10	C	84.38
22	77.03	C	C	80.49	80.73	81.11	83.52	C	83.89	84.94	C	84.33
23	77.09	C	78.93	80.38	C	80.77	83.48	C	83.91	85.14	86.00	84.15
24	77.11	77.68	78.79	79.75	C	81.06	83.46	81.91	84.00	C	85.73	84.15
25	C	77.68	78.98	C	80.56	81.21	C	81.44	84.21	C	85.44	C
26	C	77.87	79.19	C	80.39	81.46	C	81.32	C	85.00	C	C
27	77.08	77.62	C	79.35	80.26	C	83.08	81.70	C	85.00	85.16	C
28	77.10	77.80	C	79.90	80.37	C	82.85	81.99	84.28	84.69	C	84.07
29	76.63	C	C	79.70	C	81.64	82.92	C	84.24	84.73	C	83.81
30	76.70		79.14	79.46	C	81.69	83.09	C	84.18	84.86	84.42	84.30
31	77.04		78.98		C		83.18	81.83		C		84.75
Close	77.04	77.80	78.98	79.46	80.37	81.69	83.18	81.83	84.18	84.86	84.42	84.75
Month Pt Change	2.02	0.76	1.18	0.48	0.91	1.32	1.49	−1.35	2.35	0.68	−0.44	0.33
Month % Change	2.7	1.0	1.5	0.6	1.1	1.6	1.8	−1.6	2.9	0.8	−0.5	0.4
QTR % Change			5.3			3.4			3.0			0.7
Year % Change												13.0

HIGHLIGHTS

Election Year	Bull Market	Best Six Months	5.0%	High	Nov-20	86.28
Johnson	Expansion	Worst Six Months	6.8%	Low	Jan-02	75.43

STANDARD & POOR'S 500 — 1965

Previous Month	Jan	Feb	Mar	Apr	May	Jun	Jul	Aug	Sep	Oct	Nov	Dec
Close	84.75	87.56	87.43	86.16	89.11	88.42	84.12	85.25	87.17	89.96	92.42	91.61
1	C	87.58	87.25	86.32	C	87.72	84.48	C	87.17	89.90	92.23	91.50
2	C	87.55	87.40	86.53	C	87.09	85.16	85.42	87.65	C	C	91.21
3	C	87.63	87.26	C	89.23	86.90	C	85.46	88.06	C	92.31	91.27
4	84.23	87.57	86.98	C	89.51	87.11	C	85.79	C	90.08	92.46	C
5	84.63	87.29	86.80	86.53	89.71	C	C	85.79	C	90.63	92.37	C
6	84.89	C	C	86.50	89.92	C	84.99	86.07	C	90.54	C	90.59
7	85.26	C	C	86.55	89.85	86.88	84.67	C	88.36	90.47	C	91.39
8	85.37	86.95	86.83	87.04	C	85.93	85.39	C	88.66	90.85	92.23	91.28
9	C	87.24	86.69	87.56	C	85.04	85.71	85.86	88.89	C	91.93	91.56
10	C	86.46	86.54	C	89.66	84.73	C	85.87	89.12	C	91.83	91.80
11	85.40	85.54	86.90	C	89.55	85.12	C	86.13	C	91.37	92.11	C
12	85.61	86.17	87.21	87.94	89.94	C	85.69	86.38	C	91.35	92.55	C
13	85.84	C	C	88.04	90.27	C	85.59	86.77	89.38	91.34	C	91.83
14	85.84	C	C	88.24	90.10	84.01	85.87	C	89.03	91.19	C	91.88
15	86.21	86.07	87.24	88.15	C	84.49	85.72	C	89.52	91.38	92.63	92.02
16	C	85.67	87.13	C	C	85.20	85.69	86.87	90.02	C	92.41	92.12
17	C	85.77	87.02	C	89.54	85.74	C	87.04	90.05	C	92.60	92.08
18	86.49	86.05	86.81	C	89.46	85.34	C	86.99	C	91.68	92.22	C
19	86.63	86.21	86.84	88.51	89.67	C	85.63	86.79	C	91.80	92.24	C
20	86.60	C	C	88.46	89.18	C	84.55	86.69	90.08	91.78	C	91.65
21	86.52	C	C	88.30	88.75	85.05	84.07	C	89.81	91.94	C	92.01
22	86.74	C	86.83	88.78	C	85.21	83.85	C	90.22	91.98	91.64	92.29
23	C	86.64	86.93	88.88	C	84.67	84.07	86.56	89.86	C	91.78	92.19
24	C	87.17	87.09	C	88.09	83.56	C	86.71	90.02	C	91.94	C
25	86.86	87.20	86.84	C	88.60	83.06	C	86.81	C	91.67	C	C
26	86.94	87.43	86.20	88.89	88.30	C	84.05	87.14	C	92.20	92.03	C
27	87.23	C	C	89.04	87.84	C	83.87	87.20	90.65	92.51	C	91.52
28	87.48	C	C	89.00	88.42	81.60	84.03	C	90.43	92.21	C	91.53
29	87.56		86.03	88.93	C	82.41	84.68	C	90.02	92.42	91.80	91.81
30	C		86.20	89.11	C	84.12	85.25	87.21	89.96	C	91.61	92.20
31	C		86.16		C		C	87.17		C		92.43
Close	87.56	87.43	86.16	89.11	88.42	84.12	85.25	87.17	89.96	92.42	91.61	92.43
Month Pt Change	2.81	−0.13	−1.27	2.95	−0.69	−4.30	1.13	1.92	2.79	2.46	−0.81	0.82
Month % Change	3.3	−0.1	−1.5	3.4	−0.8	−4.9	1.3	2.3	3.2	2.7	−0.9	0.9
QTR % Change			1.7			−2.4			6.9			2.7
Year % Change												9.1

HIGHLIGHTS

Post Election Year	Bull Market	Best Six Months	-1.5%	High Nov-15	92.63
Johnson	Expansion	Worst Six Months	3.7%	Low Jun-28	81.60

1966 — STANDARD & POOR'S 500

Previous Month Close	Jan	Feb	Mar	Apr	May	Jun	Jul	Aug	Sep	Oct	Nov	Dec
	92.43	92.88	91.22	89.23	91.06	86.13	84.74	83.60	77.10	76.56	80.20	80.45
1	C	92.16	90.06	89.94	C	86.10	85.61	82.31	77.70	C	80.81	80.08
2	C	92.53	89.15	C	90.90	85.96	C	82.33	77.42	C	80.88	80.13
3	92.18	92.65	89.47	C	89.85	86.06	C	83.15	C	74.90	80.56	C
4	92.26	93.26	89.24	90.76	89.39	C	C	83.93	C	75.10	80.81	C
5	92.85	C	C	91.31	87.93	C	85.82	84.00	C	74.69	C	80.24
6	93.06	C	C	91.56	87.84	85.42	87.06	C	76.96	74.05	C	80.84
7	93.14	93.59	88.04	91.76	C	84.83	87.38	C	76.37	73.20	80.73	81.72
8	C	93.55	88.18	C	C	84.93	87.61	83.75	76.05	C	C	82.05
9	C	94.06	88.96	C	86.32	85.50	C	83.49	76.29	C	81.38	82.14
10	93.33	93.83	88.96	C	87.08	86.44	C	83.11	C	74.53	81.89	C
11	93.41	93.81	88.85	91.79	87.23	C	87.45	83.02	C	74.91	81.94	C
12	93.19	C	C	91.45	86.23	C	86.88	83.17	77.91	77.04	C	83.00
13	93.36	C	C	91.54	85.47	86.83	86.30	C	78.32	76.89	C	82.73
14	93.50	93.53	87.85	91.87	C	87.07	86.82	C	79.13	76.60	81.37	82.64
15	C	93.17	87.35	91.99	C	86.73	87.08	82.74	80.08	C	81.69	81.64
16	C	93.16	87.86	C	84.41	86.47	C	81.63	79.99	C	82.37	81.58
17	93.77	92.66	88.17	C	83.63	86.51	C	81.18	C	77.47	81.80	C
18	93.95	92.41	88.53	91.58	85.12	C	86.99	80.16	C	78.68	81.26	C
19	93.69	C	C	91.57	85.02	C	86.33	79.62	79.59	78.05	C	81.27
20	93.36	C	C	92.08	85.43	86.48	85.51	C	79.04	77.84	C	80.96
21	93.47	91.87	89.20	92.42	C	86.71	85.52	C	77.71	78.19	80.09	81.38
22	C	C	89.46	92.27	C	86.85	85.41	78.24	77.94	C	79.67	81.69
23	C	91.48	89.13	C	86.20	86.50	C	78.11	77.67	C	80.21	81.47
24	93.71	90.89	89.29	C	86.77	86.58	C	79.07	C	78.42	C	C
25	93.85	91.14	89.54	92.08	87.07	C	83.83	78.06	C	78.90	80.85	C
26	93.70	C	C	91.99	87.07	C	83.70	76.41	77.86	79.58	C	C
27	93.67	C	C	91.76	87.33	86.08	84.10	C	78.10	80.23	C	81.00
28	93.31	91.22	89.62	91.13	C	85.67	83.77	C	77.11	80.24	80.71	80.61
29	C		89.27	91.06	C	84.86	83.60	74.53	76.31	C	80.42	80.37
30	C		88.78	C	C	84.74	C	75.86	76.56	C	80.45	80.33
31	92.88		89.23		86.13		C	77.10		80.20		C
Close	92.88	91.22	89.23	91.06	86.13	84.74	83.60	77.10	76.56	80.20	80.45	80.33
Month Pt Change	0.45	−1.66	−1.99	1.83	−4.93	−1.39	−1.14	−6.50	−0.54	3.64	0.25	−0.12
Month % Change	0.5	−1.8	−2.2	2.1	−5.4	−1.6	−1.3	−7.8	−0.7	4.8	0.3	−0.1
QTR % Change			−3.5			−5.0			−9.7			4.9
Year % Change												−13.1

HIGHLIGHTS

Mid-Term Election Year	Bear Market 2/9 - 10/7	Best Six Months 17.2%	High Feb-09 94.06
Johnson	Expansion	Worst Six Months-11.9%	Low Oct-07 73.20

Previous Month	Jan	Feb	Mar	Apr	May	Jun	Jul	Aug	Sep	Oct	Nov	Dec
Close	80.33	86.61	86.78	90.20	94.01	89.08	90.64	94.75	93.64	96.71	93.90	94.00
1	C	86.43	87.68	C	93.84	90.23	C	95.37	93.68	C	92.71	94.50
2	C	86.73	88.16	C	93.67	89.79	C	95.78	C	96.32	92.34	C
3	80.38	87.36	88.29	89.24	93.91	C	90.91	95.66	C	96.65	91.78	C
4	80.55	C	C	89.22	94.32	C	C	95.83	C	96.43	C	95.10
5	81.60	C	C	89.79	94.44	88.43	91.36	C	94.21	96.67	C	95.23
6	82.18	87.18	88.10	89.94	C	90.23	91.32	C	94.39	97.26	91.48	95.64
7	C	86.95	88.16	89.36	C	90.91	91.69	95.58	94.33	C	C	95.53
8	C	87.72	88.27	C	94.58	91.40	C	95.69	94.36	C	91.14	95.42
9	82.81	87.36	88.53	C	93.60	91.56	C	95.78	C	97.51	91.59	C
10	82.81	87.63	88.89	88.24	93.35	C	92.05	95.53	C	96.84	92.21	C
11	83.47	C	C	88.88	93.75	C	92.48	95.15	94.54	96.37	C	95.12
12	83.91	C	C	88.78	93.48	92.04	92.40	C	94.99	95.75	C	95.01
13	84.53	87.58	88.43	89.46	C	92.62	92.42	C	95.99	96.00	91.97	95.34
14	C	88.17	88.35	90.43	C	92.40	92.74	94.64	96.20	C	91.39	95.47
15	C	88.27	89.19	C	92.71	92.49	C	94.77	96.27	C	91.76	95.03
16	84.31	87.86	90.09	C	93.14	92.54	C	94.55	C	95.25	92.60	C
17	85.24	87.89	90.25	91.07	92.78	C	92.75	94.63	C	95.00	92.82	C
18	85.79	C	C	91.86	92.53	C	93.50	94.78	96.53	95.25	C	94.77
19	85.82	C	C	91.94	92.07	92.51	93.65	C	96.17	95.43	C	94.63
20	86.07	87.40	90.20	92.11	C	92.48	93.85	C	96.13	95.38	91.65	95.15
21	C	87.34	90.00	92.30	C	92.20	94.04	94.25	96.75	C	93.10	95.38
22	C	C	90.25	C	91.67	91.97	C	93.74	97.00	C	93.65	95.20
23	86.39	87.45	90.94	C	91.23	92.00	C	93.61	C	94.96	C	C
24	86.51	87.41	C	92.62	90.18	C	93.73	93.09	C	94.42	93.90	C
25	85.85	C	C	93.11	91.19	C	93.24	92.70	97.59	94.52	C	C
26	85.81	C	C	93.02	90.98	91.64	94.06	C	96.76	94.94	C	95.26
27	86.16	86.46	90.87	93.81	C	91.30	94.35	C	96.79	94.96	94.17	95.91
28	C	86.78	90.91	94.01	C	91.31	94.49	92.64	96.79	C	94.49	95.89
29	C		90.73	C	90.49	90.85	C	92.88	96.71	C	94.47	96.47
30	86.66		90.70	C	C	90.64	C	93.07	C	94.79	94.00	C
31	86.61		90.20		89.08		94.75	93.64		93.90		C
Close	86.61	86.78	90.20	94.01	89.08	90.64	94.75	93.64	96.71	93.90	94.00	96.47
Month Pt Change	6.28	0.17	3.42	3.81	-4.93	1.56	4.11	-1.11	3.07	-2.81	0.10	2.47
Month % Change	7.8	0.2	3.9	4.2	-5.2	1.8	4.5	-1.2	3.3	-2.9	0.1	2.6
QTR % Change			12.3			0.5			6.7			-0.2
Year % Change												20.1

1968   STANDARD & POOR'S 500

Previous Month Close	Jan	Feb	Mar	Apr	May	Jun	Jul	Aug	Sep	Oct	Nov	Dec
	96.47	92.24	89.36	90.20	97.59	98.68	99.58	97.74	98.86	102.67	103.41	108.37
1	C	92.56	89.11	92.48	97.97	C	99.40	97.28	C	102.86	103.06	C
2	96.11	92.27	C	92.64	98.59	C	99.74	96.63	C	C	C	108.12
3	95.67	C	C	93.47	98.66	99.99	100.91	C	99.32	103.22	C	108.02
4	95.36	C	87.92	93.84	C	100.38	C	C	100.02	103.71	103.10	C
5	95.94	91.87	87.72	93.29	C	99.89	C	96.85	100.74	C	C	107.67
6	C	91.90	89.26	C	98.35	100.65	C	97.25	101.20	C	103.27	107.93
7	C	92.06	89.10	C	98.90	101.27	C	C	C	103.70	103.50	C
8	96.62	90.90	89.03	94.95	98.91	C	101.94	97.04	C	103.74	103.95	C
9	96.50	89.86	C	C	98.39	C	102.23	97.01	101.23	C	C	107.66
10	96.52	C	C	95.67	98.50	101.41	C	C	100.73	103.29	C	107.39
11	96.62	C	90.13	96.53	C	101.66	102.39	C	C	103.18	C	C
12	96.72	C	90.23	C	C	C	102.34	98.01	100.52	C	104.62	107.32
13	C	89.07	90.03	C	98.19	101.25	C	98.53	100.86	C	105.13	107.58
14	C	90.14	88.32	C	98.12	101.13	C	C	C	103.32	105.20	C
15	96.42	90.30	89.10	96.59	98.07	C	102.26	98.07	C	103.53	105.78	C
16	95.82	89.96	C	96.62	97.60	C	101.70	98.68	101.24	C	C	107.10
17	95.64	C	C	96.81	96.90	100.13	C	C	101.50	104.01	C	106.66
18	95.56	C	89.59	97.08	C	99.99	101.44	C	C	104.82	105.92	C
19	95.24	90.31	88.99	95.85	C	C	100.46	99.00	101.59	C	106.14	106.97
20	C	91.24	88.98	C	96.45	101.51	C	98.96	101.66	C	C	106.34
21	C	91.24	88.33	C	96.93	100.66	C	C	C	104.99	105.97	C
22	94.03	C	88.42	95.32	97.18	C	99.33	98.70	C	104.57	106.30	C
23	93.66	90.89	C	96.48	96.97	C	99.21	98.69	102.24	C	C	105.21
24	93.17	C	C	96.62	97.15	100.39	C	C	102.59	103.84	C	105.04
25	93.30	C	88.33	96.92	C	100.08	97.94	C	C	104.20	106.48	C
26	93.45	90.18	88.93	97.20	C	C	98.34	98.94	102.36	C	107.26	105.15
27	C	90.53	89.66	C	96.99	99.98	C	98.81	102.31	C	107.76	104.74
28	C	90.08	89.57	C	97.62	99.58	C	C	C	103.90	C	C
29	93.35	89.36	90.20	97.46	97.92	C	97.65	98.74	C	103.30	108.37	C
30	92.89		C	97.59	C	C	97.74	98.86	102.67	C	C	103.80
31	92.24		C		98.68		C	C		103.41		103.86
Close	92.24	89.36	90.20	97.59	98.68	99.58	97.74	98.86	102.67	103.41	108.37	103.86
Month Pt Change	−4.23	−2.88	0.84	7.39	1.09	0.90	−1.84	1.12	3.81	0.74	4.96	−4.51
Month % Change	−4.4	−3.1	0.90	8.2	1.1	0.9	−1.8	1.1	3.9	0.7	4.8	−4.2
QTR % Change			−6.5			10.4			3.1			1.2
Year % Change												7.7

HIGHLIGHTS

Election Year	Bear Market Begins 12/3	Best Six Months	0.3%	High Nov-29	108.37
Johnson	Expansion	Worst Six Months	6.0%	Low Mar-05	87.72

STANDARD & POOR'S 500 · 1969

Previous Month Close	Jan	Feb	Mar	Apr	May	Jun	Jul	Aug	Sep	Oct	Nov	Dec
	103.86	103.01	98.13	101.51	103.69	103.46	97.71	91.83	95.51	93.12	97.24	93.81
1	C	C	C	101.42	103.51	C	98.08	93.47	C	92.52	C	93.22
2	103.93	C	C	100.78	104.00	102.94	98.94	C	95.54	93.24	C	92.65
3	103.99	102.89	98.38	100.68	C	102.63	99.61	C	94.98	93.19	97.15	91.65
4	C	102.92	99.32	C	C	102.59	C	92.99	94.20	C	97.21	91.95
5	C	103.20	99.71	C	104.37	102.76	C	93.41	93.64	C	97.64	91.73
6	102.47	103.54	98.70	C	104.86	102.12	C	93.92	C	93.38	97.67	C
7	101.22	103.53	98.65	99.89	104.67	C	99.03	93.99	C	93.09	98.26	C
8	100.80	C	C	100.14	105.10	C	97.63	93.94	92.70	92.67	C	90.84
9	101.22	C	C	101.02	105.05	101.20	96.88	C	93.38	93.03	C	90.55
10	100.93	C	98.99	101.55	C	100.42	95.38	C	94.95	93.56	98.33	90.48
11	C	103.65	99.32	101.65	C	99.05	95.77	93.36	94.22	C	98.07	90.52
12	C	103.63	99.05	C	104.89	98.26	C	92.63	94.13	C	97.89	90.81
13	100.44	103.71	98.39	C	105.34	98.65	C	92.70	C	94.55	97.42	C
14	101.13	103.61	98.00	101.57	106.16	C	94.55	93.34	C	95.70	97.07	C
15	101.62	C	C	101.53	105.85	C	94.24	94.00	94.87	95.72	C	90.54
16	102.18	C	C	100.63	105.94	98.32	95.18	C	94.95	96.37	C	89.72
17	102.03	102.44	98.25	100.78	C	97.95	95.76	C	94.76	96.26	96.41	89.20
18	C	101.40	98.49	101.24	C	97.81	94.95	94.57	94.90	C	96.39	90.61
19	C	100.65	99.21	C	104.97	97.24	C	95.07	95.19	C	95.90	91.38
20	101.69	99.79	99.84	C	104.04	96.67	C	95.07	C	96.46	94.91	C
21	101.63	C	99.63	100.56	104.47	C	C	95.35	C	97.20	94.32	C
22	101.98	C	C	100.78	104.60	C	93.52	95.92	95.63	97.83	C	90.58
23	102.43	C	C	100.80	104.59	96.23	93.12	C	95.63	97.46	C	90.23
24	102.38	98.60	99.50	101.27	C	97.32	92.80	C	95.50	98.12	93.24	91.18
25	C	97.98	99.66	101.72	C	97.01	92.06	94.93	94.77	C	92.94	C
26	C	98.45	100.39	C	104.36	97.25	C	94.30	94.16	C	93.27	91.89
27	102.40	98.14	101.10	C	103.57	97.33	C	94.49	C	97.94	C	C
28	102.41	98.13	101.51	102.03	103.26	C	90.21	94.89	C	97.66	93.81	C
29	102.51		C	102.79	103.46	C	89.48	95.51	93.41	96.81	C	91.25
30	102.55		C	103.69	C	97.71	89.93	C	93.12	96.93	C	91.60
31	103.01		C		C		91.83	C		97.24		92.06
Close	103.01	98.13	101.51	103.69	103.46	97.71	91.83	95.51	93.12	97.24	93.81	92.06
Month Pt Change	−0.85	−4.88	3.38	2.18	−0.23	−5.75	−5.88	3.68	−2.39	4.12	−3.43	−1.75
Month % Change	−0.8	−4.7	3.4	2.1	−0.2	−5.6	−6.0	4.0	−2.5	4.4	−3.5	−1.9
QTR % Change			−2.3			−3.7			−4.7			−1.1
Year % Change												−11.4

HIGHLIGHTS

Post Election Year	Bear Market	Best Six Months -16.2%	High May-14	106.16
Nixon (1st Term)	Expansion	Worst Six Months -6.2%	Low Dec-17	89.20

1970   STANDARD & POOR'S 500

Previous Month Close	Jan	Feb	Mar	Apr	May	Jun	Jul	Aug	Sep	Oct	Nov	Dec
	92.06	85.02	89.50	89.63	81.52	76.55	72.72	78.05	81.52	84.21	83.25	87.20
1	C	C	C	90.07	81.44	77.84	72.94	C	80.95	84.32	C	87.47
2	93.00	85.75	89.71	89.79	C	77.84	72.92	C	80.96	85.16	83.51	88.48
3	C	86.77	90.23	89.39	C	78.52	C	77.02	82.09	C	84.22	88.90
4	C	86.24	90.04	C	79.37	77.36	C	77.19	82.83	C	84.39	89.46
5	93.46	85.90	90.00	C	78.60	76.17	C	77.18	C	86.47	84.10	C
6	92.82	86.33	89.44	88.76	79.47	C	71.78	77.08	C	86.85	84.22	C
7	92.63	C	C	88.52	79.83	C	71.23	77.28	C	86.89	C	89.94
8	92.68	C	C	88.49	79.44	76.00	73.00	C	83.04	85.95	C	89.47
9	92.40	87.01	88.51	88.53	C	76.25	74.06	C	82.79	85.08	84.67	89.54
10	C	86.10	88.75	88.24	C	75.48	74.45	76.20	82.30	C	84.79	89.92
11	C	86.94	88.69	C	78.60	74.45	C	75.82	82.52	C	85.03	90.26
12	91.70	86.73	88.33	C	77.85	73.88	C	75.42	C	84.17	84.15	C
13	91.92	86.54	87.86	87.64	76.53	C	74.55	74.76	C	84.06	83.37	C
14	91.65	C	C	86.89	75.44	C	74.42	75.18	82.07	84.19	C	89.80
15	91.68	C	C	86.73	76.90	74.58	75.23	C	81.36	84.65	C	89.66
16	90.92	86.47	86.91	85.88	C	76.15	76.34	C	81.79	84.28	83.24	89.72
17	C	86.37	87.29	85.67	C	76.00	77.69	75.33	82.29	C	83.47	90.04
18	C	87.44	87.54	C	76.96	76.51	C	76.20	82.62	C	82.79	90.22
19	89.65	87.76	87.42	C	75.46	77.05	C	76.96	C	83.15	82.91	C
20	89.83	88.03	87.06	85.83	73.52	C	77.79	77.84	C	83.64	83.72	C
21	89.95	C	C	85.38	72.16	C	76.98	79.24	81.91	83.66	C	89.94
22	90.04	C	C	84.27	72.25	76.64	77.03	C	81.66	83.38	C	90.04
23	89.37	C	86.99	83.04	C	74.76	78.00	C	82.83	83.77	84.24	90.10
24	C	87.99	87.98	82.77	C	73.97	77.82	80.99	83.91	C	84.78	90.61
25	C	89.35	89.77	C	70.25	74.02	C	81.12	83.97	C	85.09	C
26	88.17	88.90	89.92	C	69.29	73.47	C	81.21	C	83.31	C	C
27	87.62	89.50	C	81.46	72.77	C	77.65	81.08	C	83.12	85.93	C
28	86.79	C	C	80.27	74.61	C	77.77	81.86	83.86	83.43	C	91.09
29	85.69		C	81.81	76.55	72.89	78.04	C	84.30	83.36	C	92.08
30	85.02		89.63	81.52	C	72.72	78.07	C	84.21	83.25	87.20	92.27
31	C		89.63		C		78.05	81.52		C		92.15
Close	85.02	89.50	89.63	81.52	76.55	72.72	78.05	81.52	84.21	83.25	87.20	92.15
Month Pt Change	−7.04	4.48	0.13	−8.11	−4.97	−3.83	5.33	3.47	2.69	−0.96	3.95	4.95
Month % Change	−7.6	5.3	0.1	−9.0	−6.1	−5.0	7.3	4.4	3.3	−1.1	4.7	5.7
QTR % Change			−2.6			−18.9			15.8			9.4
Year % Change												0.1

STANDARD & POOR'S 500 — 1971

Previous Month Close	Jan	Feb	Mar	Apr	May	Jun	Jul	Aug	Sep	Oct	Nov	Dec
	92.15	95.88	96.75	100.31	103.95	99.63	99.70	95.58	99.03	98.34	94.23	93.99
1	C	96.42	97.00	100.39	C	100.20	99.78	C	99.07	98.93	92.80	95.44
2	C	96.43	96.98	100.56	C	100.96	99.78	95.96	99.29	C	93.18	95.84
3	C	96.63	96.95	C	103.29	101.01	C	94.51	100.69	C	94.91	97.06
4	91.15	96.62	97.92	C	103.79	101.30	C	93.89	C	99.21	94.79	C
5	91.80	96.93	98.96	100.79	103.78	C	C	94.09	C	99.11	94.46	C
6	92.35	C	C	101.51	103.23	C	99.76	94.25	C	99.82	C	96.51
7	92.38	C	C	101.98	102.87	101.09	100.04	C	101.15	100.02	C	96.87
8	92.19	97.45	99.38	102.10	C	100.32	100.34	C	101.34	99.36	94.39	96.92
9	C	97.51	99.46	C	C	100.29	100.69	93.53	100.80	C	94.46	96.96
10	C	97.39	99.30	C	102.36	100.64	C	93.54	100.42	C	93.41	97.69
11	91.98	97.91	99.39	C	102.62	101.07	C	94.66	C	99.21	92.12	C
12	92.72	98.43	99.57	102.88	102.90	C	100.82	96.00	C	99.57	92.12	C
13	92.56	C	C	102.98	102.69	C	99.50	95.69	100.07	99.03	C	97.97
14	92.80	C	C	103.37	102.21	100.22	99.22	C	99.34	98.13	C	97.67
15	93.03	C	100.71	103.52	C	100.32	99.28	C	99.77	97.79	91.81	98.54
16	C	98.66	101.21	103.49	C	100.52	99.11	98.76	99.66	C	92.71	99.74
17	C	98.20	101.12	C	100.69	100.50	C	99.99	99.96	C	92.85	100.26
18	93.41	97.56	101.19	C	100.83	98.97	C	98.60	C	97.35	92.13	C
19	93.76	96.74	101.01	104.01	101.07	C	98.93	98.16	C	97.00	91.61	C
20	93.78	C	C	103.61	101.31	C	99.32	98.33	99.68	95.65	C	101.55
21	94.19	C	C	103.36	100.99	97.87	99.28	C	99.34	95.60	C	101.80
22	94.88	95.72	100.62	103.56	C	97.59	99.11	C	98.47	95.57	90.79	101.18
23	C	96.09	100.28	104.05	C	98.41	98.94	99.25	98.38	C	90.16	100.74
24	C	96.73	99.62	C	100.13	98.13	C	100.40	98.15	C	90.33	C
25	95.28	96.96	99.61	C	99.47	97.99	C	100.41	C	95.10	C	C
26	95.59	96.75	99.95	103.94	99.59	C	98.14	100.24	C	94.74	91.94	C
27	94.89	C	C	104.59	99.40	C	97.78	100.48	97.62	93.79	C	100.95
28	95.21	C	C	104.77	99.63	97.74	97.07	C	97.88	93.96	C	101.95
29	95.88		100.03	104.63	C	98.82	96.02	C	97.90	94.23	93.41	102.21
30	C		100.26	103.95	C	99.70	95.58	99.52	98.34	C	93.99	101.78
31	C		100.31		C		C	99.03		C		102.09
Close	95.88	96.75	100.31	103.95	99.63	99.70	95.58	99.03	98.34	94.23	93.99	102.09
Month Pt Change	3.73	0.87	3.56	3.64	-4.32	0.07	-4.12	3.45	-0.69	-4.11	-0.24	8.10
Month % Change	4.0	0.9	3.7	3.6	-4.2	0.1	-4.1	3.6	-0.7	-4.2	-0.3	8.6
QTR % Change			8.9			-0.6			-1.4			3.8
Year % Change												10.8

HIGHLIGHTS

Pre-Election Year	Bear Market 4/26 - 11/23	Best Six Months 14.3%	High Apr-28 104.77
Nixon (1st Term)	Expansion	Worst Six Months -9.4%	Low Nov-23 90.16

Previous Month	Jan	Feb	Mar	Apr	May	Jun	Jul	Aug	Sep	Oct	Nov	Dec
Close	102.09	103.94	106.57	107.20	107.67	109.53	107.14	107.39	111.09	110.55	111.58	116.67
1	C	104.01	107.35	C	106.69	109.69	C	108.40	111.51	C	112.67	117.38
2	C	104.68	107.32	C	106.08	109.73	C	109.29	C	110.16	113.23	C
3	101.67	104.64	107.94	107.48	105.99	C	107.49	110.14	C	110.30	114.22	C
4	102.09	104.86	C	108.12	106.25	C	C	110.43	C	110.09	C	117.77
5	103.06	C	C	109.00	106.63	108.82	108.10	C	111.23	108.89	C	117.58
6	103.51	C	108.77	109.42	C	108.21	109.04	C	110.55	109.62	113.98	118.01
7	103.47	104.54	108.87	109.62	C	107.65	108.69	110.61	110.29	C	C	118.60
8	C	104.74	108.96	C	106.14	107.28	C	110.69	110.15	C	113.35	118.86
9	C	105.55	108.94	C	104.74	106.86	C	110.86	C	109.90	113.50	C
10	103.32	105.59	108.38	109.45	105.42	C	108.11	111.05	C	109.99	113.73	C
11	103.65	105.08	C	109.76	105.77	C	107.32	111.95	109.51	109.50	C	119.12
12	103.59	C	C	110.18	106.38	107.01	106.89	C	108.47	108.60	C	118.66
13	102.99	C	107.33	109.91	C	107.55	106.28	C	108.90	107.92	113.90	118.56
14	103.39	104.59	107.61	109.84	C	108.39	106.80	112.55	108.93	C	114.95	118.24
15	C	105.03	107.75	C	106.86	108.44	C	112.06	108.81	C	114.50	118.26
16	C	105.62	107.50	C	106.66	108.36	C	111.66	C	106.77	115.13	C
17	103.70	105.59	107.92	109.51	106.89	C	105.88	111.34	C	107.50	115.49	C
18	104.05	105.28	C	109.77	107.94	C	105.83	111.76	108.61	108.19	C	116.90
19	103.88	C	C	109.20	108.98	108.11	106.14	C	108.55	108.05	C	116.34
20	103.88	C	107.59	109.04	C	108.56	105.81	C	108.60	109.24	115.53	115.95
21	103.65	C	106.69	108.89	C	108.79	106.66	111.72	108.43	C	116.21	115.11
22	C	105.29	106.84	C	109.69	108.68	C	112.41	108.52	C	116.90	115.83
23	C	105.38	107.75	C	109.78	108.27	C	112.26	C	110.35	C	C
24	102.57	105.45	107.52	108.19	110.31	C	107.92	111.02	C	110.81	117.27	C
25	102.78	106.18	C	107.12	110.46	C	107.60	110.67	108.05	110.72	C	C
26	102.50	C	C	106.89	110.66	107.48	107.53	C	108.12	110.99	C	116.30
27	103.50	C	107.30	107.05	C	107.37	107.28	C	109.66	110.62	116.72	116.93
28	104.16	106.19	107.17	107.67	C	107.02	107.38	110.23	110.35	C	116.47	C
29	C	106.57	106.49	C	C	106.82	C	110.41	110.55	C	116.52	118.05
30	C		107.20	C	110.35	107.14	C	110.57	C	110.59	116.67	C
31	103.94		C		109.53		107.39	111.09		111.58		C
Close	103.94	106.57	107.20	107.67	109.53	107.14	107.39	111.09	110.55	111.58	116.67	118.05
Month Pt Change	1.85	2.63	0.63	0.47	1.86	−2.39	0.25	3.70	−0.54	1.03	5.09	1.38
Month % Change	1.8	2.5	0.6	0.4	1.7	−2.2	0.2	3.4	−0.5	0.9	4.6	1.2
QTR % Change			5.0			−0.1			3.2			6.8
Year % Change												15.6

Election Year	Bull Market	Best Six Months	-4.1%	High Dec-11 119.12
Nixon (1st Term)	Expansion	Worst Six Months	3.6%	Low Jan-03 101.67

STANDARD & POOR'S 500 — 1973

Previous Month	Jan	Feb	Mar	Apr	May	Jun	Jul	Aug	Sep	Oct	Nov	Dec
Close	118.05	116.03	111.68	111.52	106.97	104.95	104.26	108.22	104.25	108.43	108.29	95.96
1	C	114.76	111.05	C	107.10	103.93	C	106.83	C	108.21	107.69	C
2	119.10	114.35	112.28	110.18	108.43	C	102.90	106.67	C	108.79	107.07	C
3	119.57	C	C	109.24	110.22	C	101.87	106.49	C	108.78	C	93.90
4	119.40	C	C	108.77	111.00	102.97	C	C	104.51	108.41	C	93.59
5	119.87	114.23	112.68	108.52	C	104.62	101.78	C	104.64	109.85	105.52	92.16
6	C	114.45	114.10	109.28	C	104.31	101.28	106.73	105.15	C	104.96	94.42
7	C	113.66	114.45	C	110.53	105.84	C	106.55	104.76	C	105.80	96.51
8	119.85	113.16	114.23	C	111.25	107.03	C	105.55	C	110.23	107.02	C
9	119.73	114.68	113.79	110.86	110.44	C	102.14	105.61	C	110.13	105.30	C
10	119.43	C	C	112.21	109.54	C	103.52	104.77	103.85	109.22	C	97.95
11	120.24	C	C	112.68	108.17	106.70	105.80	C	103.22	111.09	C	96.04
12	119.30	116.06	113.86	112.58	C	108.29	105.50	C	103.06	111.44	104.44	93.57
13	C	116.78	114.48	112.08	C	107.60	104.09	103.71	103.36	C	104.36	92.38
14	C	115.10	114.98	C	105.90	106.40	C	102.71	104.44	C	102.45	93.29
15	118.44	114.45	114.12	C	106.57	105.10	C	103.01	C	110.05	102.43	C
16	118.14	114.98	113.54	111.44	106.43	C	105.67	102.29	C	110.19	103.88	C
17	118.68	C	C	110.94	105.56	C	105.72	102.31	104.15	109.97	C	92.75
18	118.85	C	C	111.54	103.86	103.60	106.35	C	103.77	110.01	C	94.74
19	118.78	C	112.17	112.17	C	103.99	106.55	C	105.88	110.22	100.71	94.82
20	C	115.40	111.95	C	C	104.44	107.14	101.61	106.76	C	98.66	94.55
21	C	114.69	110.49	C	102.73	103.21	C	100.89	107.20	C	99.76	93.54
22	118.21	114.44	108.84	C	103.58	103.70	C	100.53	C	109.16	C	C
23	118.22	113.16	108.88	111.57	104.07	C	107.52	101.91	C	109.75	99.44	C
24	116.73	C	C	109.99	107.14	C	108.14	101.62	107.36	110.27	C	92.90
25	C	C	C	108.34	107.94	102.25	109.64	C	108.05	110.50	C	C
26	116.45	112.19	109.84	108.89	C	103.30	109.85	C	108.83	111.38	96.58	95.74
27	C	110.90	111.56	107.23	C	103.62	109.59	102.42	109.08	C	95.70	97.74
28	C	111.68	111.62	C	C	104.69	C	103.02	108.43	C	97.65	97.54
29	116.01		112.71	C	107.51	104.26	C	104.03	C	111.15	97.31	C
30	115.83		111.52	106.97	105.91	C	109.25	103.88	C	109.33	95.96	C
31	116.03		C		104.95		108.22	104.25		108.29		97.55
Close	116.03	111.68	111.52	106.97	104.95	104.26	108.22	104.25	108.43	108.29	95.96	97.55
Month Pt Change	-2.02	-4.35	-0.16	-4.55	-2.02	-0.69	3.96	-3.97	4.18	-0.14	-12.33	1.59
Month % Change	-1.7	-3.7	-0.1	-4.1	-1.9	-0.7	3.8	-3.7	4.0	-0.1	-11.4	1.7
QTR % Change			-5.5			-6.5			4.0			-10.0
Year % Change												-17.4

HIGHLIGHTS

Post Election Year	Bear Market Begins 1/11	Best Six Months -16.6%	High Jan-11	120.24
Nixon (2nd Term)	Expansion	Worst Six Months 1.2%	Low Dec-05	92.16

Previous Month	Jan	Feb	Mar	Apr	May	Jun	Jul	Aug	Sep	Oct	Nov	Dec
Close	97.55	96.57	96.22	93.98	90.31	87.28	86.00	79.31	72.15	63.54	73.90	69.97
1	C	95.32	95.53	93.25	92.22	C	86.02	78.75	C	63.39	73.88	C
2	97.68	C	C	93.35	92.09	C	84.30	78.59	C	63.38	C	68.11
3	99.80	C	C	94.33	91.29	89.10	84.25	C	70.52	62.28	C	67.17
4	98.90	93.29	95.53	94.33	C	90.14	C	C	68.69	62.34	73.08	67.41
5	C	93.00	97.32	93.01	C	90.31	83.66	79.29	70.87	C	75.11	66.13
6	C	93.26	97.98	C	91.12	91.96	C	80.52	71.42	C	74.75	65.01
7	98.07	93.30	96.94	C	91.46	92.55	C	82.65	C	64.95	75.21	C
8	96.12	92.33	97.78	92.03	91.64	C	81.09	81.57	C	64.84	74.91	C
9	93.42	C	C	92.61	92.96	C	81.48	80.86	69.72	67.82	C	65.60
10	92.39	C	C	92.40	91.47	93.10	79.99	C	69.24	69.79	C	67.28
11	93.66	90.66	98.88	92.12	C	92.28	79.89	C	68.55	71.14	75.15	67.67
12	C	90.94	99.15	C	C	92.06	83.15	79.75	66.71	C	73.67	67.45
13	C	90.98	99.74	C	90.66	92.34	C	78.49	65.20	C	73.35	67.07
14	93.42	90.95	99.65	C	90.69	91.30	C	76.73	C	72.74	73.06	C
15	94.23	92.27	99.28	92.05	90.45	C	83.78	76.30	C	71.44	71.91	C
16	95.67	C	C	93.66	89.72	C	82.81	75.67	66.26	70.33	C	66.46
17	97.30	C	C	94.36	88.21	90.04	83.70	C	67.38	71.17	C	67.58
18	95.56	C	98.05	94.78	C	89.45	83.78	C	67.72	72.28	69.27	67.90
19	C	92.12	97.23	93.75	C	88.84	83.54	74.57	70.09	C	68.20	67.65
20	C	93.44	97.57	C	87.86	88.21	C	74.95	70.14	C	67.90	66.91
21	95.40	94.71	97.34	C	87.91	87.46	C	73.51	C	73.50	68.18	C
22	96.55	95.39	97.27	93.38	87.09	C	83.81	72.80	C	73.13	68.90	C
23	97.07	C	C	91.81	87.29	C	84.65	71.55	69.42	71.03	C	65.96
24	96.82	C	C	90.30	88.58	87.69	84.99	C	68.02	70.22	C	66.88
25	96.63	95.03	97.64	89.57	C	88.98	83.98	C	67.57	70.12	68.83	C
26	C	96.00	97.95	90.18	C	87.61	82.40	72.16	66.46	C	69.47	67.44
27	C	96.40	96.59	C	C	86.31	C	70.94	64.94	C	69.94	67.14
28	96.09	96.22	94.82	C	88.37	86.00	C	70.76	C	70.09	C	C
29	96.01		93.98	90.00	86.89	C	80.94	69.99	C	72.83	69.97	C
30	97.06		C	90.31	87.43	C	80.50	72.15	63.54	74.31	C	67.16
31	96.57		C		87.28		79.31	C		73.90		68.56
Close	96.57	96.22	93.98	90.31	87.28	86.00	79.31	72.15	63.54	73.90	69.97	68.56
Month Pt Change	−0.98	−0.35	−2.24	−3.67	−3.03	−1.28	−6.69	−7.16	−8.61	10.36	−3.93	−1.41
Month % Change	−1.0	−0.4	−2.3	−3.9	−3.4	−1.50	−7.8	−9.0	−11.9	16.3	−5.3	−2.0
QTR % Change			−3.7			−8.5			−26.1			7.9
Year % Change												−29.7

HIGHLIGHTS

Mid-Term Election Year	Bull Market Begins 12/6	Best Six Months 18.1%	High Jan-03 99.80
Nixon (2nd Term) Ford 8/9/74 Recession		Worst Six Months -18.2%	Low Oct-03 62.28

STANDARD & POOR'S 500   1975

Previous Month	Jan	Feb	Mar	Apr	May	Jun	Jul	Aug	Sep	Oct	Nov	Dec
Close	68.56	76.98	81.59	83.36	87.30	91.15	95.19	88.75	86.88	83.87	89.04	91.24
1	C	C	C	82.64	88.10	C	94.85	87.99	C	82.93	C	90.67
2	70.23	C	C	82.43	89.22	92.58	94.18	C	85.48	83.82	C	89.33
3	70.71	77.82	83.03	81.51	C	92.89	94.36	C	86.03	85.95	88.09	87.60
4	C	77.61	83.56	80.88	C	92.60	C	87.15	86.20	C	88.51	87.84
5	C	78.95	83.90	C	90.08	92.69	C	86.23	85.62	C	89.15	86.82
6	71.07	78.56	83.69	C	88.64	92.48	C	86.25	C	86.88	89.55	C
7	71.02	78.63	84.30	80.35	89.08	C	93.54	86.30	C	86.77	89.33	C
8	70.04	C	C	80.99	89.56	C	93.39	86.02	85.89	87.94	C	87.07
9	71.17	C	C	82.84	90.53	91.21	94.80	C	84.60	88.37	C	87.30
10	72.61	78.36	84.95	83.77	C	90.44	94.81	C	83.79	88.21	89.34	88.08
11	C	78.58	84.36	84.18	C	90.55	94.66	86.55	83.45	C	89.87	87.80
12	C	79.92	83.59	C	90.61	90.08	C	87.12	83.30	C	91.19	87.83
13	72.31	81.01	83.74	C	91.58	90.52	C	85.97	C	89.46	91.04	C
14	71.68	81.50	84.76	85.60	92.27	C	95.19	85.60	C	89.28	90.97	C
15	72.14	C	C	86.30	91.41	C	95.61	86.36	82.88	89.23	C	88.09
16	72.05	C	C	86.60	90.43	91.46	94.61	C	82.09	89.37	C	88.93
17	70.96	C	86.01	87.25	C	90.58	93.63	C	82.37	88.86	91.46	89.15
18	C	80.93	85.13	86.30	C	90.39	93.20	86.20	84.06	C	91.00	89.43
19	C	81.44	84.34	C	90.53	92.02	C	84.95	85.88	C	89.98	88.80
20	71.08	82.21	83.61	C	90.07	92.61	C	83.22	C	89.82	89.64	C
21	70.70	82.62	83.39	87.23	89.06	C	92.44	83.07	C	90.56	89.53	C
22	71.74	C	C	87.09	89.39	C	91.45	84.28	85.07	90.71	C	88.14
23	72.07	C	C	86.12	90.58	93.62	90.18	C	84.94	91.24	C	88.73
24	72.98	81.44	81.42	86.04	C	94.19	90.07	C	85.74	89.83	89.70	89.46
25	C	79.53	82.06	86.62	C	94.62	89.29	85.06	85.64	C	90.71	C
26	C	80.37	83.59	C	C	94.81	C	83.96	86.19	C	90.94	90.25
27	75.37	80.77	83.85	C	90.34	94.81	C	84.43	C	89.73	C	C
28	76.03	81.59	C	86.23	89.71	C	88.69	86.40	C	90.51	91.24	C
29	77.26		C	85.64	89.68	C	88.19	86.88	85.03	89.39	C	90.13
30	76.21		C	87.30	91.15	95.19	88.83	C	83.87	89.31	C	89.77
31	76.98		83.36		C		88.75	C		89.04		90.19
Close	76.98	81.59	83.36	87.30	91.15	95.19	88.75	86.88	83.87	89.04	91.24	90.19
Month Pt Change	8.42	4.61	1.77	3.94	3.85	4.04	–6.44	–1.87	–3.01	5.17	2.20	–1.05
Month % Change	12.3	6.0	2.2	4.7	4.4	4.4	–6.8	–2.1	–3.5	6.2	2.5	–1.2
QTR % Change			21.6			14.2			–11.9			7.5
Year % Change												31.5

HIGHLIGHTS

Pre-Election Year	Bull Market	Best Six Months	14.2%	High Jul-15 95.61
Ford	Expansion Begins Q2	Worst Six Months	2.0%	Low Jan-08 70.04

1976 STANDARD & POOR'S 500

	Jan	Feb	Mar	Apr	May	Jun	Jul	Aug	Sep	Oct	Nov	Dec
Previous Month Close	90.19	100.86	99.71	102.77	101.64	100.18	104.28	103.44	102.91	105.24	102.90	102.10
1	C	C	100.02	102.24	C	99.85	103.59	C	104.06	104.17	103.10	102.49
2	90.90	100.87	100.58	102.25	C	100.22	104.11	103.19	103.92	C	C	102.12
3	C	101.18	99.98	C	100.92	100.13	C	104.14	104.30	C	101.92	102.76
4	C	101.91	98.92	C	101.46	99.15	C	104.43	C	104.03	102.41	C
5	92.58	100.39	99.11	103.51	100.88	C	C	103.85	C	103.23	100.82	C
6	93.53	99.46	C	103.36	101.16	C	103.54	103.79	C	102.97	C	103.56
7	93.95	C	C	102.21	101.88	98.63	103.83	C	105.03	103.54	C	103.49
8	94.58	C	100.19	101.28	C	98.80	103.98	C	104.94	102.56	99.60	104.08
9	94.95	99.62	100.58	100.35	C	98.74	104.98	103.49	104.40	C	99.32	104.51
10	C	100.47	100.94	C	103.10	99.56	C	104.41	104.65	C	98.81	104.70
11	C	100.77	101.89	C	102.95	100.92	C	104.06	C	101.64	99.64	C
12	96.33	100.25	100.86	100.20	102.77	C	105.90	104.22	C	100.81	99.24	C
13	95.57	99.67	C	101.05	102.16	C	105.67	104.25	104.29	102.12	C	104.63
14	97.13	C	C	100.31	101.34	101.95	105.95	C	103.94	100.85	C	105.07
15	96.61	C	99.80	100.67	C	101.46	105.20	C	104.25	100.88	99.90	105.14
16	97.00	C	100.92	C	C	102.01	104.68	104.43	105.34	C	100.04	104.80
17	C	99.05	100.86	C	101.09	103.61	C	104.80	106.27	C	100.61	104.26
18	C	99.85	100.45	C	101.26	103.76	C	104.56	C	101.47	101.89	C
19	98.32	101.41	100.58	101.44	101.18	C	104.29	103.39	C	101.45	101.92	C
20	98.86	102.10	C	102.87	102.00	C	103.72	102.37	106.32	101.74	C	103.65
21	98.24	C	C	103.32	101.26	104.28	103.82	C	107.83	100.77	C	104.22
22	98.04	C	100.71	102.98	C	103.47	103.93	C	107.46	99.96	102.59	104.71
23	99.21	101.61	102.24	102.29	C	103.25	104.06	101.96	106.92	C	101.96	104.84
24	C	102.03	103.42	C	99.44	103.79	C	101.27	106.80	C	102.41	C
25	C	101.69	102.85	C	99.49	103.72	C	102.03	C	100.07	C	C
26	99.68	100.11	102.85	102.43	99.34	C	104.07	101.32	C	101.06	103.15	C
27	99.07	99.71	C	101.86	99.38	C	103.48	101.48	107.27	101.76	C	106.06
28	98.53	C	C	102.13	100.18	103.43	103.05	C	105.92	101.61	C	106.77
29	100.11	C	102.41	102.13	C	103.86	102.93	C	105.37	102.90	102.44	106.34
30	100.86		102.01	101.64	C	104.28	103.44	102.07	105.24	C	102.10	106.88
31	C		102.77		C		C	102.91		C		107.46
Close	100.86	99.71	102.77	101.64	100.18	104.28	103.44	102.91	105.24	102.90	102.10	107.46
Month Pt Change	10.67	−1.15	3.06	−1.13	−1.46	4.10	−0.84	−0.53	2.33	−2.34	−0.80	5.36
Month % Change	11.8	−1.1	3.1	−1.1	−1.4	4.1	−0.8	−0.5	2.3	−2.2	−0.8	5.2
QTR % Change			13.9			1.5			0.9			2.1
Year % Change												19.1

HIGHLIGHTS

Election Year	Bear Market Begins 9/21	Best Six Months	−4.3%	High Sep-21	107.83
Ford	Expansion	Worst Six Months	1.2%	Low Jan-02	90.90

STANDARD & POOR'S 500   1977

Previous Month	Jan	Feb	Mar	Apr	May	Jun	Jul	Aug	Sep	Oct	Nov	Dec
Close	107.46	102.03	99.82	98.42	98.44	96.12	100.48	98.85	96.77	96.53	92.34	94.83
1	C	102.54	100.66	99.21	C	96.93	100.10	99.12	96.83	C	91.35	94.69
2	C	102.36	100.39	C	98.93	96.74	C	98.50	97.45	C	90.71	94.67
3	107.00	101.85	100.88	C	99.43	97.69	C	98.37	C	96.74	90.76	C
4	105.70	101.88	101.20	98.23	99.96	C	C	98.74	C	96.03	91.58	C
5	104.76	C	C	98.01	100.11	C	100.09	98.76	C	95.68	C	94.27
6	105.02	C	C	97.91	99.49	97.23	99.58	C	97.71	96.05	C	92.83
7	105.01	101.89	101.25	98.35	C	97.73	99.93	C	98.01	95.97	92.29	92.78
8	C	101.60	100.87	C	C	98.20	99.79	97.99	97.28	C	92.46	92.96
9	C	100.73	100.10	C	99.18	98.14	C	98.05	96.37	C	92.98	93.65
10	105.20	100.82	100.67	C	99.47	98.46	C	98.92	C	95.75	94.71	C
11	104.12	100.22	100.65	98.88	98.78	C	99.55	98.16	C	94.93	95.98	C
12	103.40	C	C	100.15	98.73	C	99.45	97.88	96.03	94.04	C	93.63
13	104.20	C	C	100.16	99.03	98.74	99.59	C	96.09	93.46	C	93.56
14	104.01	100.74	101.42	101.00	C	99.86	C	C	96.55	93.56	95.32	94.03
15	C	101.04	101.98	101.04	C	99.61	100.18	98.18	96.80	C	95.93	93.55
16	C	101.50	102.17	C	99.47	99.85	C	97.73	96.48	C	95.45	93.40
17	103.73	100.92	102.08	C	99.77	99.97	C	97.74	C	93.47	95.16	C
18	103.32	100.49	101.86	100.54	100.30	C	100.95	97.68	C	93.46	95.33	C
19	103.85	C	C	100.07	99.88	C	101.79	97.51	95.85	92.38	C	92.69
20	102.97	C	C	100.40	99.45	100.42	101.73	C	95.89	92.67	C	92.50
21	103.32	C	101.31	99.75	C	100.74	101.59	C	95.10	92.32	95.25	93.05
22	C	100.49	101.00	98.44	C	100.46	101.67	97.79	95.09	C	96.09	93.80
23	C	100.19	100.20	C	98.15	100.62	C	97.62	95.04	C	96.49	94.69
24	103.25	99.60	99.70	C	97.67	101.19	C	97.23	C	91.63	C	C
25	103.13	99.48	99.06	97.15	96.77	C	100.85	96.15	C	91.00	96.69	C
26	102.34	C	C	97.11	97.01	C	100.27	96.06	95.38	92.10	C	C
27	101.79	C	C	97.96	96.27	100.98	98.64	C	95.24	92.34	C	94.69
28	101.93	99.82	99.00	98.20	C	100.14	98.79	C	95.31	92.61	96.04	94.75
29	C		99.69	98.44	C	100.11	98.85	96.92	95.85	C	94.55	94.94
30	C		98.54	C	C	100.48	C	96.38	96.53	C	94.83	95.10
31	102.03		98.42		96.12		C	96.77		92.34		C
Close	102.03	99.82	98.42	98.44	96.12	100.48	98.85	96.77	96.53	92.34	94.83	95.10
Month Pt Change	−5.43	−2.21	−1.40	0.02	−2.32	4.36	−1.63	−2.08	−0.24	−4.19	2.49	0.27
Month % Change	−5.1	−2.2	−1.4	0.02	−2.4	4.5	−1.6	−2.1	−0.2	−4.3	2.7	0.3
QTR % Change			−8.4			2.1			−3.9			−1.5
Year % Change												−11.5

HIGHLIGHTS

Post Election Year	Bear Market	Best Six Months	4.9%	High	Jan-03	107.00
Carter	Expansion	Worst Six Months	-6.2%	Low	Nov-02	90.71

Data Bank

1978 STANDARD & POOR'S 500

Previous Month	Jan	Feb	Mar	Apr	May	Jun	Jul	Aug	Sep	Oct	Nov	Dec
Close	95.10	89.25	87.04	89.21	96.83	97.24	95.53	100.68	103.29	102.54	93.15	94.70
1	C	89.93	87.19	C	97.67	97.35	C	100.66	103.68	C	96.85	96.28
2	C	90.13	87.32	C	97.25	98.14	C	102.92	C	102.96	95.61	C
3	93.82	89.62	87.45	88.46	96.26	C	95.09	103.51	C	102.60	96.18	C
4	93.52	C	C	88.86	95.93	C	C	103.92	C	103.06	C	96.15
5	92.74	C	C	89.64	96.53	99.95	94.27	C	104.49	103.27	C	97.44
6	91.62	89.50	86.90	89.79	C	100.32	94.32	C	105.38	103.52	95.19	97.49
7	C	90.33	87.36	90.17	C	100.12	94.89	103.55	105.42	C	93.85	97.08
8	C	90.83	87.84	C	96.19	100.21	C	104.01	106.79	C	94.45	96.63
9	90.64	90.30	87.89	C	95.90	99.93	C	104.50	C	104.59	94.42	C
10	90.17	90.08	88.88	90.49	95.92	C	95.27	103.66	C	104.46	94.77	C
11	89.74	C	C	90.25	97.20	C	95.93	103.96	106.98	105.39	C	97.11
12	89.82	C	C	90.11	98.07	99.55	96.24	C	106.99	104.88	C	96.59
13	89.69	89.86	88.95	90.98	C	99.57	96.25	C	106.34	104.66	93.13	96.06
14	C	89.04	89.35	92.92	C	99.48	97.58	103.97	105.10	C	92.49	96.04
15	C	88.83	89.12	C	98.76	98.34	C	103.85	104.12	C	92.71	95.33
16	89.43	88.08	89.51	C	99.35	97.42	C	104.65	C	102.61	93.71	C
17	89.88	87.96	90.20	94.45	99.60	C	97.78	105.08	C	101.26	94.42	C
18	90.56	C	C	93.43	98.62	C	96.87	104.73	103.21	100.49	C	93.44
19	90.09	C	C	93.86	98.12	97.49	98.12	C	102.53	99.33	C	94.24
20	89.89	C	90.82	94.54	C	96.51	98.03	C	101.73	97.95	95.25	94.68
21	C	87.59	89.79	94.34	C	96.01	97.75	103.89	101.90	C	95.01	94.71
22	C	87.56	89.47	C	99.09	96.24	C	104.31	101.84	C	95.48	96.31
23	89.24	87.64	89.36	C	98.05	95.85	C	104.91	C	98.18	C	C
24	89.25	88.49	C	95.77	97.08	C	97.72	105.08	C	97.49	95.79	C
25	89.39	C	C	96.64	96.80	C	98.44	104.90	101.86	97.31	C	C
26	88.58	C	C	96.82	96.58	94.60	99.08	C	102.62	96.03	C	97.52
27	88.58	87.72	88.87	95.86	C	94.98	99.54	C	101.66	94.59	95.99	96.66
28	C	87.04	89.50	96.83	C	95.40	100.00	103.96	101.96	C	95.15	96.28
29	C		89.64	C	C	95.57	C	103.39	102.54	C	93.75	96.11
30	89.34		89.41	C	96.86	95.53	C	103.50	C	95.06	94.70	C
31	89.25		89.21		97.24		100.68	103.29		93.15		C
Close	89.25	87.04	89.21	96.83	97.24	95.53	100.68	103.29	102.54	93.15	94.70	96.11
Month Pt Change	−5.85	−2.21	2.17	7.62	0.41	−1.71	5.15	2.61	−0.75	−9.39	1.55	1.41
Month % Change	−6.2	−2.5	2.5	8.5	0.4	−1.8	5.4	2.6	−0.7	−9.2	1.7	1.5
QTR % Change			−6.2			7.1			7.3			−6.3
Year % Change												1.1

HIGHLIGHTS

Mid-Term Election Year	Bull Market 2/28 - 9/8	Best Six Months	9.2%	High Sep-12	106.99
Carter	Expansion	Worst Six Months	-3.8%	Low Mar-06	86.90

Previous Month	Jan	Feb	Mar	Apr	May	Jun	Jul	Aug	Sep	Oct	Nov	Dec
Close	96.11	99.93	96.28	101.59	101.76	99.08	102.91	103.81	109.32	109.32	101.82	106.16
1	C	99.96	96.90	C	101.68	99.17	C	104.17	C	108.56	102.57	C
2	96.73	99.50	96.97	100.90	101.72	C	101.99	104.10	C	109.59	102.51	C
3	97.80	C	C	102.40	101.81	C	102.09	104.04	C	109.59	C	105.83
4	98.58	C	C	102.65	100.69	99.32	C	C	107.44	110.17	C	106.79
5	99.13	98.09	98.06	103.26	C	100.62	102.43	C	106.40	111.27	101.82	107.25
6	C	98.05	97.87	103.18	C	101.30	103.62	104.30	106.85	C	101.20	108.00
7	C	97.16	98.44	C	99.02	101.79	C	105.65	107.66	C	99.87	107.52
8	98.80	97.65	99.58	C	99.17	101.49	C	105.98	C	109.88	100.30	C
9	99.33	97.87	99.54	102.87	99.46	C	104.47	105.49	C	106.63	101.51	C
10	98.77	C	C	103.34	98.52	C	104.20	106.40	108.17	105.30	C	107.67
11	99.10	C	C	102.31	98.52	101.91	103.64	C	107.51	105.05	C	107.49
12	99.93	98.20	99.67	102.00	C	102.85	102.69	C	107.82	104.49	103.51	107.52
13	C	98.93	99.84	C	C	102.31	102.32	107.42	107.85	C	102.94	107.67
14	C	98.87	99.71	C	98.06	102.20	C	107.52	108.76	C	103.39	108.92
15	100.69	98.73	99.86	C	98.14	102.09	C	108.25	C	103.36	104.13	C
16	99.46	98.67	100.69	101.12	98.42	C	102.74	108.09	C	103.19	103.79	C
17	99.48	C	C	101.24	99.94	C	101.83	108.30	108.84	103.39	C	109.33
18	99.72	C	C	101.70	99.93	101.56	101.69	C	108.00	103.61	C	108.30
19	99.75	C	101.06	101.28	C	101.58	101.61	C	108.28	101.60	104.23	108.20
20	C	99.42	100.50	101.23	C	101.63	101.82	108.83	110.51	C	103.69	108.26
21	C	99.07	101.25	C	100.14	102.09	C	108.91	110.47	C	103.89	107.59
22	99.90	98.33	101.67	C	100.51	102.64	C	108.99	C	100.71	C	C
23	100.60	97.78	101.60	101.57	99.89	C	101.59	108.63	C	100.28	104.67	C
24	100.16	C	C	102.20	99.93	C	101.97	108.60	109.61	100.44	C	107.66
25	101.19	C	C	102.50	100.22	102.09	103.08	C	109.68	100.00	C	C
26	101.86	97.67	101.04	102.01	C	101.66	103.10	C	109.96	100.57	106.80	107.78
27	C	96.13	102.48	101.80	C	102.27	103.10	109.14	110.21	C	106.38	107.96
28	C	96.28	102.12	C	C	102.80	C	109.02	109.32	C	106.77	107.84
29	101.55		102.03	C	100.05	102.91	C	109.02	C	100.71	106.81	C
30	101.05		101.59	101.76	99.11	C	103.15	109.02	C	102.67	106.16	C
31	99.93		C		99.08		103.81	109.32		101.82		107.94
Close	99.93	96.28	101.59	101.76	99.08	102.91	103.81	109.32	109.32	101.82	106.16	107.94
Month Pt Change	3.82	–3.65	5.31	0.17	–2.68	3.83	0.90	5.51	NC	–7.50	4.34	1.78
Month % Change	4.0	–3.7	5.5	0.2	–2.6	3.9	0.9	5.3	NC	–6.9	4.3	1.7
QTR % Change			5.7			1.3			6.2			–1.3
Year % Change												12.3

HIGHLIGHTS

Pre-Election Year	Bear Market	Best Six Months	4.4%	High Oct-05	111.27
Carter	Expansion	Worst Six Months	0.1%	Low Feb-27	96.13

	Jan	Feb	Mar	Apr	May	Jun	Jul	Aug	Sep	Oct	Nov	Dec
Previous Month Close	107.94	114.16	113.66	102.09	106.29	111.24	114.24	121.67	122.38	125.46	127.47	140.52
1	C	115.12	C	102.18	105.46	C	114.93	121.21	C	127.13	C	137.21
2	105.76	C	C	102.68	105.58	110.76	115.68	C	123.74	128.09	C	136.97
3	105.22	C	112.50	102.15	C	110.51	117.46	C	126.12	129.33	129.04	136.71
4	106.52	114.37	112.78	C	C	112.61	C	120.98	125.42	C	C	136.48
5	C	114.66	111.13	C	106.38	112.78	C	120.74	124.88	C	131.33	134.03
6	C	115.72	108.65	C	106.25	113.20	C	121.55	C	131.73	128.91	C
7	106.81	116.28	106.90	100.19	107.18	C	118.29	123.30	C	131.00	129.18	C
8	108.95	117.95	C	101.20	106.13	C	117.84	123.61	123.31	131.65	C	130.61
9	109.05	C	C	103.11	104.72	113.71	117.98	C	124.07	131.04	C	130.48
10	109.89	C	106.51	104.08	C	114.66	116.95	C	124.81	130.29	129.48	128.26
11	109.92	117.12	107.78	103.79	C	116.02	117.84	124.78	125.66	C	131.26	127.36
12	C	117.90	106.87	C	104.78	115.52	C	123.79	125.54	C	134.59	129.23
13	C	118.44	105.62	C	106.30	115.81	C	123.28	C	132.03	136.49	C
14	110.38	116.72	105.43	102.84	106.85	C	120.01	125.25	C	132.02	137.15	C
15	111.14	115.41	C	102.63	106.99	C	119.30	125.72	125.67	133.70	C	129.45
16	111.05	C	C	101.54	107.35	116.09	119.63	C	126.74	132.22	C	130.60
17	110.70	C	102.26	101.05	C	116.03	121.44	C	128.87	131.52	137.75	132.89
18	111.07	C	104.10	100.55	C	116.26	122.04	123.39	128.40	C	139.70	133.00
19	C	114.60	104.31	C	107.67	114.66	C	122.60	129.25	C	139.06	133.70
20	C	116.47	103.12	C	107.62	114.06	C	123.77	C	132.61	140.40	C
21	112.10	115.28	102.31	99.80	107.72	C	122.51	125.46	C	131.84	139.11	C
22	111.51	115.04	C	103.43	109.01	C	122.19	126.02	130.40	131.92	C	135.78
23	113.44	C	C	103.73	110.62	114.51	121.93	C	129.43	129.53	C	135.30
24	113.70	C	99.28	104.40	C	115.14	121.79	C	130.37	129.85	138.31	135.88
25	113.61	113.33	99.19	105.16	C	116.72	120.78	125.16	128.72	C	139.33	C
26	C	113.98	98.68	C	C	116.19	C	124.84	126.35	C	140.17	136.57
27	C	112.38	98.22	C	111.40	116.00	C	123.52	C	127.88	C	C
28	114.85	112.35	100.68	105.64	112.06	C	121.43	122.08	C	128.05	140.52	C
29	114.07	113.66	C	105.86	110.27	C	122.40	122.38	123.54	127.91	C	135.03
30	115.20		C	106.29	111.24	114.24	122.23	C	125.46	126.29	C	135.33
31	114.16		102.09		C		121.67	C		127.47		135.76
Close	114.16	113.66	102.09	106.29	111.24	114.24	121.67	122.38	125.46	127.47	140.52	135.76
Month Pt Change	6.22	−0.50	−11.57	4.20	4.95	3.00	7.43	0.71	3.08	2.01	13.05	−4.76
Month % Change	5.8	−0.4	−10.2	4.1	4.7	2.7	6.5	0.6	2.5	1.6	10.2	−3.4
QTR % Change			−5.4			11.9			9.8			8.2
Year % Change												25.8

HIGHLIGHTS

Election Year	Bull Market Begins 4/21	Best Six Months 4.2%	High Nov-28 140.52
Carter	Recession Q1 - Q2	Worst Six Months 19.9%	Low Mar-27 98.22

STANDARD & POOR'S 500   1981

Previous Month	Jan	Feb	Mar	Apr	May	Jun	Jul	Aug	Sep	Oct	Nov	Dec
Close	135.76	129.55	131.27	136.00	132.81	132.59	131.21	130.92	122.79	116.18	121.89	126.35
1	C	C	C	136.57	132.72	132.41	129.77	C	123.02	117.08	C	126.10
2	136.34	126.91	132.01	136.32	C	130.62	128.64	C	123.49	119.36	124.20	124.69
3	C	128.46	130.56	135.49	C	130.71	C	130.48	121.24	C	124.80	125.12
4	C	128.59	130.86	C	130.67	130.96	C	131.18	120.07	C	124.74	126.26
5	137.97	129.63	129.93	C	130.32	132.22	C	132.67	C	119.51	123.54	C
6	138.12	130.60	129.85	133.93	130.78	C	127.37	132.64	C	119.39	122.67	C
7	135.08	C	C	133.91	131.67	C	128.24	131.75	C	121.31	C	125.19
8	133.06	C	C	134.31	131.66	132.24	128.32	C	117.98	122.31	C	124.82
9	133.48	129.27	131.12	134.67	C	131.97	129.30	C	118.40	121.45	123.29	125.48
10	C	129.24	130.46	134.51	C	132.32	129.37	132.54	120.14	C	122.70	125.71
11	C	128.24	129.95	C	129.71	133.75	C	133.85	121.61	C	122.92	124.93
12	133.52	127.48	133.19	C	130.72	133.49	C	133.40	C	121.21	123.19	C
13	133.29	126.98	133.11	133.15	130.55	C	129.64	133.51	C	120.78	121.67	C
14	133.47	C	C	132.68	131.28	C	129.65	132.49	120.66	118.80	C	122.78
15	134.22	C	C	134.17	132.17	133.61	130.23	C	119.77	119.71	C	122.99
16	134.77	C	134.68	134.70	C	132.15	130.34	C	118.87	119.19	120.24	122.42
17	C	127.81	133.92	C	C	133.32	130.76	131.22	117.15	C	121.15	123.12
18	C	128.48	134.22	C	132.54	131.64	C	130.11	116.26	C	120.26	124.00
19	134.37	126.61	133.46	C	132.09	132.27	C	130.49	C	118.98	120.71	C
20	131.65	126.58	134.08	135.45	132.00	C	128.72	130.69	C	120.28	121.71	C
21	131.36	C	C	134.23	131.75	C	128.34	129.23	117.24	120.10	C	123.34
22	130.26	C	C	134.14	131.33	131.95	127.13	C	116.68	119.64	C	122.88
23	130.23	127.35	135.69	133.94	C	133.35	127.40	C	115.65	118.60	121.60	122.31
24	C	127.39	134.67	135.14	C	132.66	128.46	125.50	115.01	C	123.51	122.54
25	C	128.52	137.11	C	C	132.81	C	125.13	112.77	C	124.05	C
26	129.84	130.10	136.27	C	132.77	132.56	C	124.96	C	118.16	C	C
27	131.12	131.27	134.65	135.48	133.77	C	129.90	123.51	C	119.29	125.09	C
28	130.34	C	C	134.33	133.45	C	129.14	124.08	115.53	119.45	C	122.27
29	130.24		C	133.05	132.59	131.89	129.16	C	115.94	119.06	C	121.67
30	129.55		134.28	132.81	C	131.21	130.01	C	116.18	121.89	126.35	122.30
31	C		136.00		C		130.92	122.79		C		122.55
Close	129.55	131.27	136.00	132.81	132.59	131.21	130.92	122.79	116.18	121.89	126.35	122.55
Month Pt Change	–6.21	1.72	4.73	–3.19	–0.22	–1.38	–0.29	–8.13	–6.61	5.71	4.46	–3.80
Month % Change	–4.6	1.3	3.6	–2.3	–0.2	–1.0	–0.2	–6.2	–5.4	4.9	3.7	–3.0
QTR % Change			0.2			–3.5			–11.5			5.5
Year % Change												–9.7

1982   STANDARD & POOR'S 500

Previous Month Close	Jan	Feb	Mar	Apr	May	Jun	Jul	Aug	Sep	Oct	Nov	Dec
	122.55	120.40	113.11	111.96	116.44	111.88	109.61	107.09	119.51	120.42	133.71	138.54
1	C	117.78	113.31	113.79	C	111.68	108.71	C	118.25	121.97	135.47	138.72
2	C	118.01	112.68	115.12	C	112.04	107.65	108.98	120.28	C	137.49	138.82
3	C	116.48	110.92	C	116.81	111.86	C	107.83	122.68	C	142.87	138.69
4	122.74	116.42	109.88	C	117.46	110.09	C	106.14	C	121.51	141.85	C
5	120.05	117.26	109.34	114.73	117.67	C	C	105.16	C	121.98	142.16	C
6	119.18	C	C	115.36	118.68	C	107.29	103.71	C	125.97	C	141.77
7	118.93	C	C	115.46	119.47	110.12	107.22	C	121.37	128.80	C	142.72
8	119.55	114.63	107.34	116.22	C	109.63	107.53	C	122.20	131.05	140.44	141.81
9	C	113.68	108.83	C	C	108.99	108.83	103.08	121.97	C	143.02	140.00
10	C	114.66	109.41	C	118.38	109.61	C	102.84	120.97	C	141.16	139.57
11	116.78	114.43	109.36	C	119.42	111.24	C	102.60	C	134.47	141.76	C
12	116.30	114.38	108.61	116.00	119.17	C	109.57	102.42	C	134.44	139.53	C
13	114.88	C	C	115.99	118.22	C	109.45	103.85	122.24	136.71	C	139.95
14	115.54	C	C	115.83	118.01	109.96	110.44	C	123.10	134.57	C	137.39
15	116.33	C	109.45	116.35	C	109.69	110.47	C	124.29	133.57	137.03	135.24
16	C	114.06	109.28	116.81	C	108.87	111.07	104.09	123.77	C	135.42	135.30
17	C	113.69	109.08	C	116.71	107.60	C	109.04	122.55	C	137.93	137.49
18	117.22	113.82	110.30	C	115.84	107.28	C	108.53	C	136.73	138.34	C
19	115.97	113.22	110.61	116.70	114.89	C	110.73	109.16	C	136.58	137.02	C
20	115.27	C	C	115.44	114.59	C	111.54	113.02	122.51	139.23	C	136.26
21	115.75	C	C	115.72	114.89	107.20	111.42	C	124.88	139.06	C	138.61
22	115.38	111.59	112.77	117.19	C	108.30	111.47	C	123.99	138.83	134.22	138.83
23	C	111.51	113.55	118.64	C	110.14	111.17	116.11	123.81	C	132.93	139.72
24	C	113.47	112.97	C	114.79	109.83	C	115.34	123.32	C	133.88	C
25	115.41	113.21	113.21	C	114.40	109.14	C	117.58	C	133.32	C	C
26	115.19	113.11	111.94	119.26	113.11	C	110.36	118.55	C	134.48	134.88	C
27	115.74	C	C	118.00	112.66	C	109.43	117.11	123.62	135.28	C	142.18
28	118.92	C	C	117.26	111.88	110.26	107.73	C	123.24	133.59	C	140.77
29	120.40		112.30	116.13	C	110.21	107.72	C	121.63	133.71	134.20	141.24
30	C		112.27	116.44	C	109.61	107.09	117.66	120.42	C	138.54	140.33
31	C		111.96		C		C	119.51		C		140.64
Close	120.40	113.11	111.96	116.44	111.88	109.61	107.09	119.51	120.42	133.71	138.54	140.64
Month Pt Change	-2.15	-7.29	-1.15	4.48	-4.56	-2.27	-2.52	12.42	0.91	13.29	4.83	2.10
Month % Change	-1.8	-6.1	-1.0	4.0	-3.9	-2.0	-2.3	11.6	0.8	11.0	3.6	1.5
QTR % Change			-8.6			-2.1			9.9			16.8
Year % Change												14.8

HIGHLIGHTS

Mid-Term Election Year	Bull Market Begins 8/12	Best Six Months	23.0%	High Nov-09	143.02
Reagan (1st term)	Recession	Worst Six Months	14.8%	Low Aug-12	102.42

STANDARD & POOR'S 500 — 1983

Previous Month Close	Jan	Feb	Mar	Apr	May	Jun	Jul	Aug	Sep	Oct	Nov	Dec
	140.64	145.30	148.06	152.96	164.42	162.39	168.11	162.56	164.40	166.07	163.55	166.40
1	C	142.96	150.88	C	C	162.55	168.91	162.04	164.23	C	163.64	166.49
2	C	143.23	152.30	C	162.11	163.98	C	162.01	165.00	C	164.84	165.44
3	138.34	144.26	153.48	C	162.34	164.42	C	163.44	C	165.80	163.45	C
4	141.35	146.14	153.67	153.02	163.31	C	C	161.33	C	166.27	162.44	C
5	141.96	C	C	151.89	164.28	C	166.60	161.74	C	167.74	C	165.77
6	145.27	C	C	151.04	166.10	164.83	168.48	C	167.89	170.28	C	165.47
7	145.18	146.93	153.67	151.76	C	162.77	167.56	C	167.96	170.80	161.91	165.91
8	C	145.70	151.26	152.85	C	161.36	167.08	159.18	167.77	C	161.76	165.20
9	C	145.00	152.87	C	165.81	161.83	C	160.13	166.92	C	163.97	165.09
10	146.78	147.50	151.80	C	165.95	162.68	C	161.54	C	172.65	164.41	C
11	145.78	147.63	151.24	155.14	164.96	C	168.11	161.55	C	170.34	166.29	C
12	146.69	C	C	155.82	164.25	C	165.53	162.16	165.48	169.63	C	165.62
13	145.72	C	C	156.77	164.90	164.84	165.46	C	164.80	169.88	C	164.93
14	146.65	148.92	150.83	158.11	C	165.53	166.01	C	165.35	169.86	166.58	163.33
15	C	148.30	151.36	158.75	C	167.12	164.29	163.71	164.38	C	165.36	161.67
16	C	147.43	149.80	C	163.40	169.14	C	163.41	166.24	C	166.08	162.39
17	146.71	147.44	149.59	C	163.71	169.13	C	165.29	C	170.43	166.13	C
18	146.40	148.00	149.90	159.74	163.27	C	163.95	163.55	C	167.81	165.09	C
19	145.27	C	C	158.71	161.99	C	164.83	163.98	167.62	166.73	C	162.32
20	146.29	C	C	160.71	162.14	169.02	169.29	C	169.25	166.98	C	162.00
21	143.85	C	151.19	160.05	C	170.53	169.06	C	168.41	165.95	166.05	163.56
22	C	145.48	150.66	160.42	C	170.99	168.89	164.34	169.76	C	166.84	163.27
23	C	146.79	152.81	C	163.43	170.57	C	162.77	169.51	C	166.96	163.22
24	139.97	149.60	153.37	C	165.54	170.40	C	161.25	C	165.99	C	C
25	141.75	149.74	152.67	158.81	166.21	C	169.53	160.84	C	166.47	167.18	C
26	141.54	C	C	161.81	165.48	C	170.35	162.14	170.07	165.38	C	C
27	144.27	C	C	161.44	164.46	168.46	167.59	C	168.43	164.84	C	164.76
28	144.51	148.06	151.85	162.95	C	165.68	165.04	C	168.01	163.37	166.54	165.34
29	C		151.59	164.42	C	166.64	162.56	162.25	167.23	C	167.91	164.86
30	C		153.39	C	C	168.11	C	162.58	166.07	C	166.40	164.93
31	145.30		152.96		162.39		C	164.40		163.55		C
Close	145.30	148.06	152.96	164.42	162.39	168.11	162.56	164.40	166.07	163.55	166.40	164.93
Month Pt Change	4.66	2.76	4.90	11.46	−2.03	5.72	−5.55	1.84	1.67	−2.52	2.85	−1.47
Month % Change	3.3	1.9	3.3	7.5	−1.2	3.5	−3.3	1.1	1.0	−1.5	1.7	−0.9
QTR % Change			8.8			9.9			−1.2			−0.7
Year % Change												17.3

HIGHLIGHTS

Pre-Election Year	Bear Market Begins 11/29	Best Six Months -2.1%	High Oct-10	172.65
Reagan (1st term)	Expansion	Worst Six Months -0.5%	Low Jan-03	138.34

1984 STANDARD & POOR'S 500

Previous Month Close	Jan	Feb	Mar	Apr	May	Jun	Jul	Aug	Sep	Oct	Nov	Dec
	164.93	163.41	157.06	159.18	160.05	150.55	153.18	150.66	166.68	166.10	166.09	163.58
1	C	162.74	158.19	C	161.68	153.24	C	154.08	C	164.62	167.49	C
2	C	163.36	159.24	157.98	161.90	C	153.20	157.99	C	163.59	167.42	C
3	164.04	160.91	C	157.66	161.20	C	153.70	162.35	C	162.44	C	162.82
4	166.78	C	C	157.54	159.11	154.34	C	C	164.88	162.92	C	163.38
5	168.81	C	157.89	155.04	C	153.65	152.76	C	164.29	162.68	168.58	162.10
6	169.28	158.08	156.25	155.48	C	155.01	152.24	162.60	165.65	C	170.41	162.76
7	C	158.74	154.57	C	159.47	154.92	C	162.71	164.37	C	169.17	162.26
8	C	155.85	155.19	C	160.52	155.17	C	161.75	C	162.13	168.68	C
9	168.90	155.42	154.35	155.45	160.11	C	153.36	165.54	C	161.67	167.60	C
10	167.95	156.30	C	155.87	160.00	C	152.89	165.42	164.26	162.11	C	162.83
11	167.79	C	C	155.00	158.49	153.06	150.56	C	164.45	162.78	C	163.07
12	167.75	C	156.34	157.73	C	152.19	150.03	C	164.68	164.18	167.36	162.63
13	167.02	154.95	156.78	157.31	C	152.13	150.88	165.43	167.94	C	165.97	161.81
14	C	156.61	156.77	C	157.50	150.39	C	164.42	168.78	C	165.99	162.69
15	C	156.25	157.41	C	158.00	149.03	C	162.80	C	165.77	165.89	C
16	167.18	156.13	159.27	158.32	157.99	C	151.60	163.77	C	164.78	164.10	C
17	167.83	155.74	C	158.97	156.57	C	152.38	164.14	168.87	164.14	C	163.61
18	167.55	C	C	157.90	155.78	151.73	151.40	C	167.65	168.10	C	168.11
19	167.04	C	157.78	158.02	C	152.61	150.37	C	166.94	167.96	163.10	167.16
20	166.21	C	158.86	C	C	154.84	149.55	164.94	167.47	C	164.18	166.38
21	C	154.64	158.66	C	154.73	154.51	C	167.83	165.67	C	164.52	165.51
22	C	154.31	156.69	C	153.88	154.46	C	167.06	C	167.36	C	C
23	164.87	154.29	156.86	156.80	153.15	C	148.95	167.12	C	167.09	166.92	C
24	165.94	157.51	C	158.07	151.23	C	147.82	167.51	165.28	167.20	C	166.76
25	164.84	C	C	158.65	151.62	153.97	148.83	C	165.62	166.31	C	C
26	164.24	C	156.67	160.30	C	152.71	150.08	C	166.28	165.29	165.55	166.47
27	163.94	159.30	157.30	159.89	C	151.64	151.19	166.44	166.96	C	166.29	165.75
28	C	156.82	159.88	C	C	152.84	C	167.40	166.10	C	165.02	166.26
29	C	157.06	159.52	C	150.29	153.18	C	167.10	C	164.78	163.91	C
30	162.87		159.18	160.05	150.35	C	150.19	166.60	C	166.84	163.58	C
31	163.41		C		150.55		150.66	166.68		166.09		167.24
Close	163.41	157.06	159.18	160.05	150.55	153.18	150.66	166.68	166.10	166.09	163.58	167.24
Month Pt Change	-1.52	-6.35	2.12	0.87	-9.50	2.63	-2.52	16.02	-0.58	-0.01	-2.51	3.66
Month % Change	-0.9	-3.9	1.3	0.5	-5.9	1.7	-1.6	10.6	-0.3	-0.01	-1.5	2.2
QTR % Change			-3.5			-3.8			8.4			0.7
Year % Change												1.4

HIGHLIGHTS

Election Year	Bull Market Begins 7/24	Best Six Months 8.3%	High Nov-06 170.41
Reagan (1st term)	Expansion	Worst Six Months 3.8%	Low Jul-24 147.82

ALMANAC INVESTOR

STANDARD & POOR'S 500 — 1985

Previous Month Close	Jan	Feb	Mar	Apr	May	Jun	Jul	Aug	Sep	Oct	Nov	Dec
	167.24	179.63	181.18	180.66	179.83	189.55	191.85	190.92	188.63	182.08	189.82	202.17
1	C	178.63	183.23	181.27	178.37	C	192.43	192.11	C	185.07	191.53	C
2	165.37	C	C	180.53	179.01	C	192.01	191.48	C	184.06	C	200.46
3	164.57	C	C	179.11	180.08	189.32	191.45	C	187.91	184.36	C	200.86
4	163.68	180.35	182.06	179.03	C	190.04	C	C	187.37	183.22	191.25	204.23
5	C	180.61	182.23	C	C	190.16	192.52	190.62	187.27	C	192.37	203.88
6	C	180.43	180.65	C	179.99	191.06	C	187.93	188.24	C	192.76	202.99
7	164.24	181.82	179.51	C	180.76	189.68	C	187.68	C	181.87	192.62	C
8	163.99	182.19	179.10	178.03	180.62	C	191.93	188.95	C	181.87	193.72	C
9	165.18	C	C	178.21	181.92	C	191.05	188.32	188.25	182.52	C	204.25
10	168.31	C	C	179.42	184.28	189.51	192.37	C	186.90	182.78	C	204.39
11	167.91	180.51	178.79	180.19	C	189.04	192.94	C	185.03	184.28	197.29	206.31
12	C	180.56	179.66	180.54	C	187.61	193.29	187.63	183.69	C	198.08	206.73
13	C	183.35	178.19	C	184.61	185.33	C	187.30	182.91	C	197.10	209.94
14	170.51	182.41	177.84	C	183.87	187.10	C	187.41	C	186.37	199.06	C
15	170.81	181.60	176.53	180.92	184.54	C	192.72	187.26	C	186.08	198.11	C
16	171.19	C	C	181.20	185.66	C	194.72	186.10	182.88	187.98	C	212.02
17	170.73	C	C	181.68	187.42	186.53	195.65	C	181.36	187.66	C	210.65
18	171.32	C	176.88	180.84	C	187.34	194.38	C	181.71	187.04	198.71	209.81
19	C	181.33	179.54	181.11	C	186.63	195.13	186.38	183.39	C	198.67	210.02
20	C	181.18	179.08	C	189.72	186.73	C	188.08	182.05	C	198.99	210.94
21	175.23	180.19	179.35	C	189.64	189.61	C	189.16	C	186.96	201.41	C
22	175.48	179.36	179.04	180.70	188.56	C	194.35	187.36	C	188.04	201.52	C
23	177.30	C	C	181.88	187.60	C	192.55	187.17	184.30	189.09	C	208.57
24	176.71	C	C	182.26	188.29	189.15	191.58	C	182.62	188.50	C	207.14
25	177.35	179.23	177.97	183.43	C	189.74	192.06	C	180.66	187.52	200.35	C
26	C	181.17	178.43	182.18	C	190.06	192.40	187.31	181.29	C	200.67	207.65
27	C	180.71	179.55	C	C	191.23	C	188.10	C	C	202.54	209.61
28	177.40	181.18	179.54	C	187.86	191.85	C	188.83	C	187.76	C	C
29	179.18		180.66	180.63	187.68	C	189.60	188.93	C	189.23	202.17	C
30	179.39		C	179.83	187.75	C	189.93	188.63	182.08	190.07	C	210.68
31	179.63		C		189.55		190.92	C		189.82		211.28
Close	179.63	181.18	180.66	179.83	189.55	191.85	190.92	188.63	182.08	189.82	202.17	211.28
Month Pt Change	12.39	1.55	−0.52	−0.83	9.72	2.30	−0.93	−2.29	−6.55	7.74	12.35	9.11
Month % Change	7.4	0.9	−0.3	−0.5	5.4	1.2	−0.5	−1.2	−3.5	4.3	6.5	4.5
QTR % Change			8.0			6.2			−5.1			16.0
Year % Change												26.3

HIGHLIGHTS

Post Election Year	Bull Market	Best Six Months 24.1%	High	Dec-16	212.02
Reagan (2nd Term)	Expansion	Worst Six Months 5.6%	Low	Jan-04	163.68

1986

STANDARD & POOR'S 500

Previous Month Close	Jan	Feb	Mar	Apr	May	Jun	Jul	Aug	Sep	Oct	Nov	Dec
	211.28	211.78	226.92	238.90	235.52	247.35	250.84	236.12	252.93	231.32	243.98	249.22
1	C	C	C	235.14	235.16	C	252.04	234.91	C	233.60	C	249.05
2	209.59	C	C	235.71	234.79	245.04	252.70	C	248.52	233.92	C	254.00
3	210.88	213.96	225.42	232.47	C	245.51	251.79	C	250.08	233.71	245.80	253.85
4	C	212.79	224.38	228.69	C	243.94	C	235.99	253.83	C	246.20	253.04
5	C	212.96	224.34	C	237.73	245.65	C	237.03	250.47	C	246.58	251.17
6	210.65	213.47	225.13	C	237.24	245.67	C	236.84	C	234.78	245.87	C
7	213.80	214.56	225.57	228.63	236.08	C	244.05	237.04	C	234.41	245.77	C
8	207.97	C	C	233.52	237.13	C	241.59	236.88	248.14	236.68	C	251.16
9	206.11	C	C	233.75	237.85	239.96	242.82	C	247.67	235.85	C	249.28
10	205.96	216.24	226.58	236.44	C	239.58	243.01	C	247.06	235.48	246.13	250.96
11	C	215.92	231.69	235.97	C	241.13	242.22	240.68	235.18	C	247.08	248.17
12	C	215.97	232.54	C	237.58	241.49	C	243.34	230.67	C	246.64	247.35
13	206.72	217.40	233.19	C	236.41	245.73	C	245.67	C	235.91	243.02	C
14	206.64	219.76	236.55	237.28	237.54	C	238.11	246.25	C	235.37	244.50	C
15	208.26	C	C	237.73	234.43	C	233.66	247.15	231.94	238.80	C	248.21
16	209.17	C	C	242.22	232.76	246.13	235.01	C	231.72	239.53	C	250.04
17	208.43	C	234.67	243.03	C	244.35	236.07	C	231.68	238.84	243.21	247.56
18	C	222.45	235.78	242.38	C	244.99	236.36	247.38	232.31	C	236.78	246.78
19	C	219.76	235.60	C	233.20	244.06	C	246.51	232.21	C	237.66	249.73
20	207.53	222.22	236.54	C	236.11	247.58	C	249.77	C	235.97	242.05	C
21	205.79	224.62	233.34	244.74	235.45	C	236.24	249.67	C	235.88	245.86	C
22	203.49	C	C	242.42	240.12	C	238.18	250.19	234.93	236.26	C	248.75
23	204.25	C	C	241.75	241.35	245.26	238.67	C	235.67	239.28	C	246.34
24	206.43	224.34	235.33	242.02	C	247.03	237.95	C	236.28	238.26	247.45	246.75
25	C	223.79	234.72	242.29	C	248.93	240.22	247.81	231.83	C	248.17	C
26	C	224.04	237.30	C	C	248.74	C	252.84	232.23	C	248.77	246.92
27	207.39	226.77	238.97	C	244.75	249.60	C	253.30	C	238.77	C	C
28	209.81	226.92	C	243.08	246.63	C	236.01	252.84	C	239.26	249.22	C
29	210.29		C	240.51	247.98	C	234.55	252.93	229.91	240.94	C	244.67
30	209.33		C	235.52	247.35	250.84	236.59	C	231.32	243.71	C	243.37
31	211.78		238.90		C		236.12	C		243.98		242.17
Close	211.78	226.92	238.90	235.52	247.35	250.84	236.12	252.93	231.32	243.98	249.22	242.17
Month Pt Change	0.50	15.14	11.98	–3.38	11.83	3.49	–14.72	16.81	–21.61	12.66	5.24	–7.05
Month % Change	0.2	7.1	5.3	–1.4	5.0	1.4	–5.9	7.1	–8.5	5.5	2.1	–2.8
QTR % Change			13.1			5.0			–7.8			4.7
Year % Change												14.6

HIGHLIGHTS

Mid-Term Election Year	Bull Market	Best Six Months 18.2%	High	Dec-02	254.00
Reagan (2nd Term)	Expansion	Worst Six Months 3.6%	Low	Jan-22	203.49

ALMANAC INVESTOR

STANDARD & POOR'S 500 — 1987

Previous Month Close	Jan	Feb	Mar	Apr	May	Jun	Jul	Aug	Sep	Oct	Nov	Dec
	242.17	274.08	284.20	291.70	288.36	290.10	304.00	318.66	329.80	321.83	251.79	230.30
1	C	C	C	292.39	288.03	289.83	302.94	C	323.40	327.33	C	232.00
2	246.45	276.45	283.00	293.63	C	288.46	305.63	C	321.68	328.07	255.75	233.45
3	C	275.99	284.12	300.41	C	293.47	C	317.57	320.21	C	250.82	225.21
4	C	279.64	288.62	C	289.36	295.09	C	316.23	316.70	C	248.96	223.92
5	252.19	281.16	290.52	C	295.34	293.45	C	318.45	C	328.08	254.48	C
6	252.78	280.04	290.66	301.95	295.47	C	304.92	322.09	C	319.22	250.41	C
7	255.33	C	C	296.69	294.71	C	307.40	323.00	C	318.52	C	228.76
8	257.28	C	C	297.26	293.37	296.72	308.29	C	313.56	314.16	C	234.91
9	258.73	278.16	288.30	292.86	C	297.28	307.52	C	313.92	311.07	243.17	238.89
10	C	275.07	290.86	292.49	C	297.47	308.37	328.00	317.13	C	239.00	233.57
11	C	277.54	290.31	C	291.57	298.73	C	333.33	321.98	C	241.90	235.32
12	260.30	275.62	291.22	C	293.30	301.62	C	332.39	C	309.39	248.52	C
13	259.95	279.70	289.89	285.62	293.98	C	307.63	334.65	C	314.52	245.64	C
14	262.64	C	C	279.16	294.24	C	310.68	333.99	323.08	305.23	C	242.19
15	265.49	C	C	284.44	287.43	302.69	310.42	C	317.74	298.08	C	242.80
16	266.28	C	288.23	286.91	C	304.76	312.70	C	314.86	282.70	246.76	248.08
17	C	285.49	292.47	C	C	304.81	314.59	334.11	314.93	C	243.04	242.98
18	C	285.42	292.78	C	286.65	305.69	C	329.25	314.86	C	245.55	249.16
19	269.34	285.57	294.08	C	279.62	306.97	C	329.83	C	224.84	240.05	C
20	269.04	285.48	298.17	286.09	278.21	C	311.39	334.84	C	236.83	242.00	C
21	267.84	C	C	293.07	280.17	C	308.55	335.90	310.54	258.38	C	249.54
22	273.91	C	C	287.19	282.16	309.65	308.47	C	319.50	248.25	C	249.95
23	270.10	282.38	301.16	286.82	C	308.43	307.81	C	321.19	248.22	242.99	253.16
24	C	282.88	301.64	281.52	C	306.86	309.27	333.33	319.72	C	246.39	252.02
25	C	284.00	300.38	C	C	308.96	C	336.77	320.16	C	244.10	C
26	269.61	282.96	300.93	C	289.11	307.16	C	334.57	C	227.67	C	C
27	273.75	284.20	296.13	281.83	288.73	C	310.65	331.38	C	233.19	240.34	C
28	275.40	C	C	282.51	290.76	C	312.33	327.04	323.20	233.28	C	245.57
29	274.24		C	284.57	290.10	307.90	315.65	C	321.69	244.77	C	244.59
30	274.08		289.20	288.36	C	304.00	318.05	C	321.83	251.79	230.30	247.86
31	C		291.70		C		318.66	329.80		C		247.08
Close	274.08	284.20	291.70	288.36	290.10	304.00	318.66	329.80	321.83	251.79	230.30	247.08
Month Pt Change	31.91	10.12	7.50	-3.34	1.74	13.90	14.66	11.14	-7.97	-70.04	-21.49	16.78
Month % Change	13.2	3.7	2.6	-1.1	0.6	4.8	4.8	3.5	-2.4	-21.8	-8.5	7.3
QTR % Change			20.5			4.2			5.9			-23.2
Year % Change												2.0

HIGHLIGHTS

Pre-Election Year	Bear Market 8/25 - 10/19	Best Six Months	3.8%	High Aug-25	336.77
Reagan (2nd Term)	Expansion	Worst Six Months	-12.7%	Low Dec-04	223.92

Data Bank

1988   STANDARD & POOR'S 500

Previous Month Close	Jan	Feb	Mar	Apr	May	Jun	Jul	Aug	Sep	Oct	Nov	Dec
	247.08	257.07	267.82	258.89	261.33	262.16	273.50	272.02	261.52	271.91	278.97	273.70
1	C	255.04	267.22	C	C	266.69	271.78	272.21	258.35	C	279.06	272.49
2	C	255.57	267.98	C	261.56	265.33	C	272.06	264.48	C	279.06	271.81
3	C	252.21	267.88	C	263.00	266.45	C	272.98	C	271.38	279.20	C
4	255.94	252.21	267.30	256.09	260.32	C	C	271.93	C	270.62	276.31	C
5	258.63	250.96	C	258.51	258.79	C	275.81	271.15	C	271.86	C	274.93
6	258.89	C	C	265.49	257.48	267.05	272.02	C	265.59	272.39	C	277.59
7	261.07	C	267.38	266.16	C	265.17	271.78	C	265.87	278.07	273.93	278.13
8	243.40	249.10	269.43	269.43	C	271.52	270.02	269.98	265.88	C	275.15	276.57
9	C	251.72	269.06	C	256.54	270.20	C	266.49	266.84	C	273.33	277.03
10	C	256.66	263.84	C	257.62	271.26	C	261.90	C	278.24	273.69	C
11	247.49	255.95	264.94	270.16	253.31	C	270.55	262.75	C	277.93	267.92	C
12	245.42	257.63	C	271.37	253.85	C	267.85	262.55	266.47	273.98	C	276.52
13	245.81	C	C	271.57	256.78	271.43	269.32	C	267.43	275.22	C	276.31
14	245.88	C	266.37	259.75	C	274.30	270.26	C	269.31	275.50	267.72	275.31
15	252.05	C	266.13	259.77	C	274.45	272.05	258.69	268.13	C	268.34	274.28
16	C	259.83	268.65	C	258.71	269.77	C	260.56	270.65	C	263.82	276.29
17	C	259.21	271.22	C	255.39	270.68	C	260.77	C	276.41	264.60	C
18	251.88	257.91	271.12	259.21	251.35	C	270.51	261.03	C	279.38	266.47	C
19	249.32	261.61	C	257.92	252.57	C	268.47	260.24	268.82	276.97	C	278.91
20	242.63	C	C	256.13	253.02	268.94	270.00	C	269.73	282.88	C	277.47
21	243.14	C	268.74	256.42	C	271.67	266.66	C	270.16	283.66	266.22	277.38
22	246.50	265.64	268.84	260.14	C	275.66	263.50	256.98	269.18	C	267.21	276.87
23	C	265.02	268.91	C	250.83	274.82	C	257.09	269.76	C	269.00	277.87
24	C	264.43	263.35	C	253.51	273.78	C	261.13	C	282.28	C	C
25	252.17	261.58	258.51	262.46	253.76	C	264.68	259.18	C	282.38	267.23	C
26	249.57	262.46	C	263.93	254.63	C	265.19	259.68	268.88	281.38	C	C
27	249.38	C	C	263.80	253.42	269.06	262.50	C	268.26	277.28	C	276.83
28	253.29	C	258.06	262.61	C	272.31	266.02	C	269.08	278.53	268.64	277.08
29	257.07	267.82	260.07	261.33	C	270.98	272.02	262.33	272.59	C	270.91	279.40
30	C		258.07	C	C	273.50	C	262.51	271.91	C	273.70	277.72
31	C		258.89		262.16		C	261.52		278.97		C
Close	257.07	267.82	258.89	261.33	262.16	273.50	272.02	261.52	271.91	278.97	273.70	277.72
Month Pt Change	9.99	10.75	−8.93	2.44	0.83	11.34	−1.48	−10.50	10.39	7.06	−5.27	4.02
Month % Change	4.0	4.2	−3.3	0.9	0.3	4.3	−0.5	−3.9	4.0	2.6	−1.9	1.5
QTR % Change			4.8			5.6			−0.6			2.1
Year % Change												12.4

HIGHLIGHTS

Election Year	Bull Market	Best Six Months 11.0%	High	Oct-21 283.66
Reagan (2nd Term)	Expansion	Worst Six Months 6.8%	Low	Jan-20 242.63

STANDARD & POOR'S 500 — 1989

	Jan	Feb	Mar	Apr	May	Jun	Jul	Aug	Sep	Oct	Nov	Dec
Previous Month Close	277.72	297.47	288.86	294.87	309.64	320.52	317.98	346.08	351.45	349.15	340.36	345.99
1	C	297.09	287.11	C	309.12	321.97	C	343.75	353.73	C	341.20	350.63
2	C	296.84	289.95	C	308.12	325.52	C	344.34	C	350.87	338.48	C
3	275.31	296.97	291.18	296.39	308.16	C	319.23	344.74	C	354.71	337.62	C
4	279.43	C	C	295.31	307.77	C	C	343.92	C	356.94	C	351.41
5	280.01	C	C	296.24	307.61	322.03	320.64	C	352.56	356.97	C	349.58
6	280.67	296.04	294.81	295.29	C	324.24	321.55	C	349.24	358.78	332.61	348.55
7	C	299.63	293.87	297.16	C	326.95	324.91	349.41	348.35	C	334.81	347.59
8	C	298.65	294.08	C	306.00	326.75	C	349.35	348.76	C	338.15	348.69
9	280.98	296.06	293.93	C	305.19	326.69	C	346.94	C	359.80	336.57	C
10	280.38	292.02	292.88	297.11	305.80	C	327.07	348.25	C	359.13	339.10	C
11	282.01	C	C	298.49	306.95	C	328.78	344.74	347.66	356.99	C	348.56
12	283.17	C	C	298.99	313.84	326.24	329.81	C	348.70	355.39	C	351.73
13	283.87	292.54	295.32	296.40	C	323.91	329.95	C	345.46	333.65	339.55	352.75
14	C	291.81	295.14	301.36	C	323.83	331.84	343.06	343.16	C	337.99	350.93
15	C	294.24	296.67	C	316.16	320.08	C	344.71	345.06	C	340.54	350.14
16	284.14	294.81	299.44	C	315.28	321.35	C	345.66	C	342.85	340.58	C
17	283.55	296.76	292.69	301.72	317.48	C	332.44	344.45	C	341.16	341.61	C
18	286.53	C	C	306.02	317.97	C	331.35	346.03	346.73	341.76	C	343.69
19	286.90	C	C	307.15	321.24	321.89	335.73	C	346.55	347.13	C	342.46
20	286.63	C	289.92	306.19	C	321.25	333.51	C	346.47	347.16	339.35	342.84
21	C	295.98	291.33	309.61	C	320.48	335.90	340.67	345.70	C	339.59	344.78
22	C	290.91	290.49	C	321.98	322.32	C	341.19	347.05	C	341.91	347.42
23	284.50	292.05	288.98	C	318.32	328.00	C	344.70	C	344.83	C	C
24	288.49	287.13	C	308.69	319.14	C	333.67	351.52	C	343.70	343.97	C
25	289.14	C	C	306.75	319.17	C	333.88	350.52	344.23	342.50	C	C
26	291.69	C	C	306.93	321.59	326.60	338.05	C	344.33	337.93	C	346.81
27	293.82	287.82	290.57	309.58	C	328.44	341.99	C	345.10	335.06	345.61	348.81
28	C	288.86	291.59	309.64	C	325.81	342.15	352.09	348.60	C	345.77	350.67
29	C		292.35	C	C	319.68	C	349.84	349.15	C	343.60	353.40
30	294.99		292.52	C	319.05	317.98	C	350.65	C	335.07	345.99	C
31	297.47		294.87		320.52		346.08	351.45		340.36		C
Close	297.47	288.86	294.87	309.64	320.52	317.98	346.08	351.45	349.15	340.36	345.99	353.40
Month Pt Change	19.75	-8.61	6.01	14.77	10.88	-2.54	28.10	5.37	-2.30	-8.79	5.63	7.41
Month % Change	7.1	-2.9	2.1	5.0	3.5	-0.8	8.8	1.6	-0.7	-2.5	1.7	2.1
QTR % Change			6.2			7.8			9.8			1.2
Year % Change												27.3

HIGHLIGHTS

Post Election Year	Bull Market	Best Six Months	-2.8%	High Oct-09	359.80
GHW Bush	Expansion	Worst Six Months	9.9%	Low Jan-03	275.31

1990 — STANDARD & POOR'S 500

Previous Month Close	Jan	Feb	Mar	Apr	May	Jun	Jul	Aug	Sep	Oct	Nov	Dec
	353.40	329.08	331.89	339.94	330.80	361.23	358.02	356.15	322.56	306.05	304.00	322.22
1	C	328.79	332.74	C	332.25	363.16	C	355.52	C	314.94	307.02	C
2	359.69	330.92	335.54	338.70	334.48	C	359.54	351.48	C	315.21	311.85	C
3	358.76	C	C	343.64	335.57	C	360.16	344.86	C	311.40	C	324.10
4	355.67	C	C	341.09	338.39	367.40	C	C	323.09	312.69	C	326.35
5	352.20	331.85	333.74	340.73	C	366.64	355.68	C	324.39	311.50	314.59	329.92
6	C	329.66	337.93	340.08	C	364.96	358.42	334.43	320.46	C	311.62	329.07
7	C	333.75	336.95	C	340.53	363.15	C	334.83	323.40	C	306.01	327.75
8	353.79	332.96	340.27	C	342.01	358.71	C	338.35	C	313.48	307.61	C
9	349.62	333.62	337.93	341.37	342.86	C	359.52	339.94	C	305.10	313.74	C
10	347.31	C	C	342.07	343.82	C	356.49	335.52	321.63	300.39	C	328.89
11	348.53	C	C	341.92	352.00	361.63	361.23	C	321.04	295.46	C	326.44
12	339.93	330.08	338.67	344.34	C	366.25	365.44	C	322.54	300.03	319.48	330.19
13	C	331.02	336.00	C	C	364.90	367.31	338.84	318.65	C	317.67	329.34
14	C	332.01	336.87	C	354.75	362.90	C	339.39	316.83	C	320.40	326.82
15	337.00	334.89	338.07	C	354.28	362.91	C	340.06	C	303.23	317.02	C
16	340.75	332.72	341.91	344.74	354.00	C	368.95	332.39	C	298.92	317.12	C
17	337.40	C	C	344.68	354.47	C	367.52	327.83	317.77	298.76	C	326.02
18	338.19	C	C	340.72	354.64	356.88	364.22	C	318.60	305.74	C	330.05
19	339.15	C	343.53	338.09	C	358.47	365.32	C	316.60	312.48	319.34	330.20
20	C	327.99	341.57	335.12	C	359.10	361.61	328.51	311.48	C	315.31	330.12
21	C	327.67	339.74	C	358.00	360.47	C	321.86	311.32	C	316.03	331.75
22	330.38	325.70	335.69	C	358.43	355.43	C	316.55	C	314.76	C	C
23	331.61	324.15	337.22	331.05	359.29	C	355.31	307.06	C	312.36	315.10	C
24	330.26	C	C	330.36	358.41	C	355.79	311.51	304.59	312.60	C	329.90
25	326.08	C	C	332.03	354.58	352.31	357.09	C	308.26	310.17	C	C
26	325.80	328.67	337.63	332.92	C	352.06	355.91	C	305.06	304.71	316.51	330.85
27	C	330.26	341.50	329.11	C	355.14	353.44	321.44	300.97	C	318.10	328.29
28	C	331.89	342.00	C	C	357.63	C	321.34	306.05	C	317.95	328.72
29	325.20		340.79	C	360.65	358.02	C	324.19	C	301.88	316.42	C
30	322.98		339.94	330.80	360.86	C	355.55	318.71	C	304.06	322.22	C
31	329.08		C		361.23		356.15	322.56		304.00		330.22
Close	329.08	331.89	339.94	330.80	361.23	358.02	356.15	322.56	306.05	304.00	322.22	330.22
Month Pt Change	−24.32	2.81	8.05	−9.14	30.43	−3.21	−1.87	−33.59	−16.51	−2.05	18.22	8.00
Month % Change	−6.9	0.9	2.4	−2.7	9.2	−0.9	−0.5	−9.4	−5.1	−0.7	6.0	2.5
QTR % Change			−3.8			5.3			−14.5			7.9
Year % Change												−6.6

HIGHLIGHTS

Mid-Term Election Year	Bear Market 7/16 - 10/11	Best Six Months 23.5%	High Jul-16	368.95
GHW Bush	Recession Begins Q3	Worst Six Months -8.1%	Low Oct-11	295.46

STANDARD & POOR'S 500   1991

Previous Month Close	Jan	Feb	Mar	Apr	May	Jun	Jul	Aug	Sep	Oct	Nov	Dec
	330.22	343.93	367.07	375.22	375.35	389.83	371.16	387.81	395.43	387.86	392.46	375.22
1	C	343.05	370.47	371.30	380.29	C	377.92	387.12	C	389.20	391.32	C
2	326.45	C	C	379.50	380.52	C	377.47	387.18	C	388.26	C	381.40
3	321.91	C	C	378.94	380.80	388.06	373.33	C	392.15	384.47	C	380.96
4	321.00	348.34	369.33	379.77	C	387.74	C	C	389.97	381.24	390.28	380.07
5	C	351.26	376.72	375.36	C	385.09	374.08	385.06	389.14	C	388.71	377.40
6	C	358.07	376.17	C	380.08	383.63	C	390.62	389.10	C	389.97	379.10
7	315.44	356.52	375.91	C	377.32	379.43	C	390.56	C	379.50	393.72	C
8	314.90	359.35	374.95	378.66	378.51	C	377.94	389.32	C	380.67	392.89	C
9	311.49	C	C	373.56	383.25	C	376.11	387.12	388.57	376.80	C	378.26
10	314.53	C	C	373.15	375.74	378.57	375.74	C	384.56	380.55	C	377.90
11	315.23	368.58	372.96	377.63	C	381.05	376.97	C	385.09	381.45	393.12	377.70
12	C	365.50	370.03	380.40	C	376.65	380.25	388.02	387.34	C	396.74	381.55
13	C	369.02	374.57	C	376.76	377.63	C	389.62	383.59	C	397.41	384.47
14	312.49	364.22	373.50	C	371.62	382.29	C	389.90	C	386.47	397.15	C
15	313.73	369.06	373.59	381.19	368.57	C	382.39	389.33	C	391.01	382.62	C
16	316.17	C	C	387.62	372.19	C	381.54	385.58	385.78	392.80	C	384.46
17	327.97	C	C	390.45	372.39	380.13	381.18	C	385.50	391.92	C	382.74
18	332.23	C	372.11	388.46	C	378.59	385.37	C	386.94	392.50	385.24	383.48
19	C	369.39	366.59	384.20	C	375.09	384.22	376.47	387.56	C	379.43	382.52
20	C	365.14	367.92	C	372.28	375.42	C	379.43	387.92	C	378.53	387.04
21	331.06	364.97	366.58	C	375.35	377.75	C	390.59	C	390.02	380.06	C
22	328.31	365.65	367.48	380.95	376.19	C	382.88	391.33	C	387.83	376.14	C
23	330.21	C	C	381.76	374.96	C	379.42	394.17	385.92	387.94	C	396.82
24	334.78	C	C	382.76	377.49	370.94	378.64	C	387.71	385.07	C	399.33
25	336.07	367.26	369.83	379.25	C	370.65	380.96	C	386.88	384.20	375.34	C
26	C	362.81	376.30	379.02	C	371.59	380.93	393.85	386.49	C	377.96	404.84
27	C	367.74	375.35	C	C	374.40	C	393.06	385.90	C	376.55	406.46
28	336.03	367.07	375.22	C	381.94	371.16	C	396.64	C	389.52	C	C
29	335.84		C	373.66	382.79	C	383.15	396.47	C	391.48	375.22	C
30	340.91		C	375.35	386.96	C	386.69	395.43	387.86	392.96	C	415.14
31	343.93		C		389.83		387.81	C		392.46		417.09
Close	343.93	367.07	375.22	375.35	389.83	371.16	387.81	395.43	387.86	392.46	375.22	417.09
Month Pt Change	13.71	23.14	8.15	0.13	14.48	−18.67	16.65	7.62	−7.57	4.60	−17.24	41.87
Month % Change	4.2	6.7	2.2	0.03	3.9	−4.8	4.5	2.0	−1.9	1.2	−4.4	11.2
QTR % Change			13.6			−1.1			4.5			7.5
Year % Change												26.3

HIGHLIGHTS

Pre-Election Year	Bulll Market	Best Six Months	5.7%	High Dec-31	417.09
GHW Bush	Expansion Begins Q2	Worst Six Months	4.6%	Low Jan-09	311.49

Previous Month Close	Jan 417.09	Feb 408.79	Mar 412.70	Apr 403.69	May 414.95	Jun 415.35	Jul 408.14	Aug 424.21	Sep 414.03	Oct 417.80	Nov 418.68	Dec 431.35
1	C	C	C	404.23	412.53	417.30	412.88	C	416.07	416.29	C	430.78
2	417.26	C	412.45	400.50	C	413.50	411.77	C	417.98	410.47	422.75	429.89
3	419.34	409.53	412.85	401.55	C	414.59	C	425.09	417.98	C	419.92	429.91
4	C	413.85	409.33	C	416.91	413.26	C	424.36	417.08	C	417.11	432.06
5	C	413.84	406.51	C	416.84	413.48	C	422.19	C	407.57	418.34	C
6	417.96	413.82	404.44	405.59	416.79	C	413.84	420.59	C	407.18	417.58	C
7	417.40	411.09	C	398.06	415.85	C	409.16	418.88	C	404.25	C	435.31
8	418.10	C	C	394.50	416.05	413.36	410.28	C	414.44	407.75	C	436.99
9	417.61	C	405.21	400.64	C	410.06	414.23	C	416.36	402.66	418.59	435.65
10	415.10	413.77	406.89	404.29	C	407.25	414.62	419.42	419.95	C	418.62	434.64
11	C	413.76	404.03	C	418.49	409.05	C	418.90	419.58	C	422.20	433.73
12	C	417.13	403.89	C	416.29	409.76	C	417.78	C	407.44	422.87	C
13	414.34	413.69	405.84	406.08	416.45	C	414.87	417.73	C	409.30	422.43	C
14	420.44	412.48	C	412.39	413.14	C	417.68	419.91	425.27	409.37	C	432.84
15	420.77	C	C	416.28	410.09	410.29	417.10	C	419.77	409.60	C	432.57
16	418.21	C	406.39	416.05	C	408.32	417.54	C	419.92	411.73	420.68	431.52
17	418.86	C	409.58	C	C	402.26	415.62	420.74	419.93	C	419.27	435.43
18	C	407.38	409.15	C	412.81	400.96	C	421.34	422.93	C	422.85	441.28
19	C	408.26	409.80	C	416.37	403.67	C	418.19	C	414.98	423.61	C
20	416.36	413.90	411.30	410.16	415.39	C	413.75	418.26	C	415.48	426.65	C
21	412.64	411.46	C	410.26	412.60	C	413.76	414.85	422.14	415.67	C	440.70
22	418.13	C	C	409.81	414.02	403.40	410.93	C	417.14	414.90	C	440.31
23	414.96	C	409.91	411.60	C	404.04	412.08	C	417.44	414.10	425.12	439.03
24	415.48	412.27	408.88	409.02	C	403.84	411.60	410.72	418.47	C	427.59	439.77
25	C	410.45	407.52	C	C	403.12	C	411.61	414.35	C	429.19	C
26	C	415.35	407.86	C	411.41	403.45	C	413.51	C	418.16	C	C
27	414.99	413.86	403.50	408.45	412.17	C	411.54	413.53	C	418.49	430.16	C
28	414.96	412.70	C	409.11	416.74	C	417.52	414.84	416.62	420.13	C	439.15
29	410.34	C	C	412.02	415.35	408.94	422.23	C	416.80	420.86	C	437.98
30	411.62		403.00	414.95	C	408.14	423.92	C	417.80	418.68	431.35	438.82
31	408.79		403.69		C		424.21	414.03		C		435.71
Close	408.79	412.70	403.69	414.95	415.35	408.14	424.21	414.03	417.80	418.68	431.35	435.71
Month Pt Change	−8.30	3.91	−9.01	11.26	0.40	−7.21	16.07	−10.18	3.77	0.88	12.67	4.36
Month % Change	−2.0	1.0	−2.2	2.8	0.1	−1.7	3.9	−2.4	0.9	0.2	3.0	1.0
QTR % Change			−3.2			1.1			2.4			4.3
Year % Change												4.5

HIGHLIGHTS

Election Year	Bull Market	Best Six Months	5.1%	High	Dec-18	441.28
GHW Bush	Expansion	Worst Six Months	0.9%	Low	Apr-08	394.50

Previous Month Close	Jan	Feb	Mar	Apr	May	Jun	Jul	Aug	Sep	Oct	Nov	Dec
	435.71	438.78	443.38	451.67	440.19	450.19	450.53	448.13	463.56	458.93	467.83	461.79
1	C	442.52	442.01	450.30	C	453.83	449.02	C	463.15	461.29	469.10	461.89
2	C	442.56	447.90	441.39	C	453.85	445.84	450.15	461.30	C	468.44	463.11
3	C	447.20	449.26	C	442.46	452.49	C	449.27	461.34	C	463.02	464.89
4	435.38	449.56	447.34	C	444.05	450.06	C	448.54	C	461.34	457.49	C
5	434.34	448.93	446.11	442.29	444.52	C	C	448.13	C	461.20	459.57	C
6	434.52	C	C	441.16	443.26	C	441.43	448.68	C	460.74	C	466.43
7	430.73	C	C	442.73	442.31	447.69	442.83	C	458.52	459.18	C	466.76
8	429.05	447.85	454.71	441.84	C	444.71	448.64	C	456.65	460.31	460.21	466.29
9	C	445.33	454.40	C	C	445.78	448.13	450.72	457.50	C	460.33	464.18
10	C	446.23	456.33	C	442.80	445.38	C	449.45	461.72	C	463.72	463.93
11	430.95	447.66	453.72	C	444.36	447.26	C	450.46	C	460.88	462.64	C
12	431.04	444.58	449.83	448.37	444.80	C	448.98	448.96	C	461.12	465.39	C
13	433.03	C	C	449.22	439.23	C	448.09	450.14	462.06	461.49	C	465.70
14	435.94	C	C	448.66	439.56	447.71	450.08	C	459.90	466.83	C	463.06
15	437.15	C	451.43	448.40	C	446.27	449.22	C	461.60	469.50	463.75	461.84
16	C	433.91	451.37	448.94	C	447.43	445.75	452.38	459.43	C	466.74	463.34
17	C	433.30	448.31	C	440.37	448.54	C	453.13	458.83	C	464.81	466.38
18	436.84	431.90	451.89	C	440.32	443.68	C	456.04	C	468.45	463.62	C
19	435.13	434.22	450.18	447.46	447.57	C	446.03	456.43	C	466.21	462.60	C
20	433.37	C	C	445.10	450.59	C	447.31	456.16	455.05	466.07	C	465.85
21	435.49	C	C	443.63	445.84	446.22	447.18	C	452.95	465.36	C	465.30
22	436.11	435.24	448.88	439.46	C	445.93	444.51	C	456.20	463.27	459.13	467.32
23	C	434.80	448.76	437.03	C	443.19	447.10	455.23	457.74	C	461.03	467.38
24	C	440.87	448.07	C	448.00	446.62	C	459.77	457.63	C	462.36	C
25	440.01	442.34	450.88	C	448.85	447.60	C	460.13	C	464.20	C	C
26	439.95	443.38	447.78	433.54	453.44	C	449.09	461.04	C	464.30	463.06	C
27	438.11	C	C	438.01	452.41	C	448.24	460.54	461.80	464.61	C	470.54
28	438.66	C	C	438.02	450.19	451.85	447.19	C	461.53	467.73	C	470.94
29	438.78		450.77	438.89	C	450.69	450.24	C	460.11	467.83	461.90	470.58
30	C		451.97	440.19	C	450.53	448.13	461.90	458.93	C	461.79	468.64
31	C		451.67		C		C	463.56		C		466.45
Close	438.78	443.38	451.67	440.19	450.19	450.53	448.13	463.56	458.93	467.83	461.79	466.45
Month Pt Change	3.07	4.60	8.29	−11.48	10.00	0.34	−2.40	15.43	−4.63	8.90	−6.04	4.66
Month % Change	0.7	1.0	1.9	−2.5	2.3	0.1	−0.5	3.4	−1.0	1.9	−1.3	1.0
QTR % Change			3.7			−0.3			1.9			1.6
Year % Change												7.1

		HIGHLIGHTS			
Post Election Year	Bull Market	Best Six Months -3.6%	High	Dec-28	470.94
Clinton (1st Term)	Expansion	Worst Six Months 6.3%	Low	Jan-08	429.05

1994 STANDARD & POOR'S 500

Previous Month Close	Jan 466.45	Feb 481.61	Mar 467.14	Apr 445.77	May 450.91	Jun 456.50	Jul 444.27	Aug 458.26	Sep 475.49	Oct 462.69	Nov 472.35	Dec 453.69
1	C	479.62	464.44	C	C	457.63	446.20	461.01	473.17	C	468.42	448.92
2	C	482.00	464.81	C	453.02	457.65	C	460.56	470.99	C	466.50	453.30
3	465.44	480.71	463.01	C	453.03	460.13	C	461.45	C	461.74	467.91	C
4	466.89	469.81	464.74	438.92	451.72	C	C	458.40	C	454.59	462.28	C
5	467.55	C	C	448.29	451.38	C	446.37	457.09	C	453.52	C	453.32
6	467.12	C	C	448.05	447.82	458.88	446.13	C	471.86	452.36	C	453.11
7	469.90	471.76	466.91	450.88	C	458.21	448.38	C	470.96	455.10	463.07	451.23
8	C	471.05	465.88	447.10	C	457.06	449.55	457.89	473.14	C	465.65	445.45
9	C	472.77	467.06	C	442.32	457.86	C	457.93	468.18	C	465.40	446.96
10	475.27	468.93	463.90	C	446.01	458.67	C	460.30	C	459.04	464.37	C
11	474.13	470.18	466.44	449.87	441.49	C	448.06	458.88	C	465.79	462.35	C
12	474.17	C	C	447.57	443.75	C	447.95	461.94	466.21	465.47	C	449.47
13	472.47	C	C	446.26	444.14	459.10	448.73	C	467.51	467.77	C	450.15
14	474.91	470.23	467.39	446.38	C	462.37	453.41	C	468.80	469.10	466.04	454.97
15	C	472.52	467.01	446.18	C	460.61	454.16	461.23	474.81	C	465.03	455.34
16	C	472.79	469.42	C	444.49	461.93	C	465.01	471.19	C	465.60	458.80
17	473.30	470.34	470.90	C	449.37	458.45	C	465.17	C	468.96	463.56	C
18	474.25	467.69	471.06	442.46	453.69	C	455.22	463.17	C	467.66	461.47	C
19	474.30	C	C	442.54	456.48	C	453.86	463.68	470.85	470.28	C	457.91
20	474.98	C	C	441.96	454.92	455.48	451.60	C	463.36	466.85	C	457.10
21	474.72	C	468.54	448.73	C	451.34	452.61	C	461.46	464.89	458.30	459.61
22	C	471.46	468.80	447.63	C	453.09	453.11	462.32	461.27	C	450.09	459.67
23	C	470.69	468.54	C	453.20	449.63	C	464.51	459.67	C	449.93	459.83
24	471.97	464.26	464.35	C	454.81	442.80	C	469.03	C	460.83	C	C
25	470.92	466.07	460.58	452.71	456.34	C	454.25	468.08	C	461.53	452.29	C
26	473.20	C	C	451.87	457.06	C	453.36	473.80	460.82	462.62	C	C
27	477.05	C	C	C	457.33	447.31	452.57	C	462.05	465.85	C	462.47
28	478.70	467.14	460.00	449.10	C	446.07	454.23	C	464.84	473.77	454.16	460.86
29	C		452.48	450.91	C	447.63	458.26	474.59	462.24	C	455.17	461.16
30	C		445.55	C	C	444.27	C	476.07	462.69	C	453.69	459.27
31	481.61		445.77		456.50		C	475.49		472.35		C
Close	481.61	467.14	445.77	450.91	456.50	444.27	458.26	475.49	462.69	472.35	453.69	459.27
Month Pt Change	15.16	−14.47	−21.37	5.14	5.59	−12.23	13.99	17.23	−12.80	9.66	−18.66	5.58
Month % Change	3.3	−3.0	−4.6	1.2	1.2	−2.7	3.1	3.8	−2.7	2.1	−4.0	1.2
QTR % Change			−4.4			−0.3			4.1			−0.7
Year % Change												−1.5

HIGHLIGHTS

Mid-Term Election Year	Bull Market	Best Six Months 9.0%	High Feb-02	482.00
Clinton (1st Term)	Expansion	Worst Six Months 4.8%	Low Apr-04	438.92

STANDARD & POOR'S 500 — 1995

Previous Month Close	Jan	Feb	Mar	Apr	May	Jun	Jul	Aug	Sep	Oct	Nov	Dec
	459.27	470.42	487.39	500.71	514.71	533.40	544.75	562.06	561.88	584.41	581.50	605.37
1	C	470.40	485.65	C	514.26	533.49	C	559.64	563.84	C	584.22	606.98
2	C	472.78	485.13	C	514.86	532.51	C	558.80	C	581.72	589.72	C
3	459.11	478.64	485.42	501.85	520.48	C	547.09	558.75	C	582.34	590.57	C
4	460.71	C	C	505.24	520.54	C	C	558.94	C	581.47	C	613.68
5	460.34	C	C	505.57	520.12	535.60	547.26	C	569.17	582.63	C	617.68
6	460.68	481.14	485.63	506.08	C	535.55	553.99	C	570.17	582.49	588.46	620.18
7	C	480.81	482.12	506.42	C	533.13	556.37	560.03	570.29	C	586.32	616.17
8	C	481.19	483.14	C	523.96	532.35	C	560.39	572.68	C	591.71	617.48
9	460.83	480.19	483.16	C	523.56	527.94	C	559.71	C	578.37	593.26	C
10	461.68	481.46	489.57	507.01	524.36	C	557.19	557.45	C	577.52	592.72	C
11	461.66	C	C	505.53	524.37	C	554.78	555.11	573.91	579.46	C	619.52
12	461.64	C	C	507.17	525.55	530.88	560.89	C	576.51	583.10	C	618.78
13	465.97	481.65	490.05	509.23	C	536.05	561.00	C	578.77	584.50	592.30	621.69
14	C	482.55	492.89	C	C	536.47	559.89	559.74	583.61	C	589.29	616.92
15	C	484.54	491.88	C	527.74	537.12	C	558.57	583.35	C	593.96	616.34
16	469.38	485.22	495.41	C	528.19	539.83	C	559.97	C	583.03	597.34	C
17	470.05	481.97	495.52	506.13	527.07	C	562.72	559.04	C	586.78	600.07	C
18	469.72	C	C	505.37	519.58	C	558.46	559.21	582.77	587.44	C	606.81
19	466.95	C	C	504.92	519.19	545.22	550.98	C	584.20	590.65	C	611.93
20	464.78	C	496.15	505.29	C	544.98	553.54	C	586.77	587.46	596.85	605.94
21	C	482.74	495.07	508.49	C	543.98	553.62	558.11	583.00	C	600.24	610.49
22	C	485.07	495.67	C	523.65	551.07	C	559.52	581.73	C	598.40	611.96
23	465.81	486.91	495.95	C	528.59	549.71	C	557.14	C	585.06	C	C
24	465.86	488.11	500.97	512.89	528.61	C	556.63	557.46	C	586.54	599.97	C
25	467.44	C	C	512.10	528.59	C	561.10	560.10	581.81	582.47	C	C
26	468.32	C	C	512.66	523.65	544.13	561.61	C	581.41	576.72	C	614.30
27	470.39	483.81	503.20	513.55	C	542.43	565.22	C	581.04	579.70	601.32	614.53
28	C	487.39	503.90	514.71	C	544.73	562.93	559.05	585.87	C	606.45	614.12
29	C		503.12	C	C	543.87	C	560.00	584.41	C	607.64	615.93
30	468.51		502.22	C	523.58	544.75	C	560.92	C	583.25	605.37	C
31	470.42		500.71		533.40		562.06	561.88		581.50		C
Close	470.42	487.39	500.71	514.71	533.40	544.75	562.06	561.88	584.41	581.50	605.37	615.93
Month Pt Change	11.15	16.97	13.32	14.00	18.69	11.35	17.31	–0.18	22.53	–2.91	23.87	10.56
Month % Change	2.4	3.6	2.7	2.8	3.6	2.1	3.2	–0.03	4.0	–0.5	4.1	1.7
QTR % Change			9.0			8.8			7.3			5.4
Year % Change												34.1

HIGHLIGHTS

Pre-Election Year	Bull Market	Best Six Months 12.5%	High Dec-13	621.69
Clinton (1st Term)	Expansion	Worst Six Months 13.0%	Low Jan-03	459.11

1996 — STANDARD & POOR'S 500

Previous Month Close	Jan	Feb	Mar	Apr	May	Jun	Jul	Aug	Sep	Oct	Nov	Dec
	615.93	636.02	640.43	645.50	654.17	669.12	670.63	639.95	651.99	687.31	705.27	757.02
1	C	638.46	644.37	653.73	654.58	C	675.88	650.02	C	689.08	703.77	C
2	620.73	635.84	C	655.26	643.38	C	673.61	662.49	C	694.01	C	756.56
3	621.32	C	C	655.88	641.63	667.68	672.40	C	654.72	692.78	C	748.28
4	617.70	C	650.81	655.86	C	672.56	C	C	655.61	701.46	706.73	745.10
5	616.71	641.43	655.79	C	C	678.44	657.44	660.23	649.44	C	714.14	744.38
6	C	646.33	652.00	C	640.81	673.03	C	662.38	655.68	C	724.59	739.60
7	C	649.93	653.65	C	638.26	673.31	C	664.16	C	703.34	727.65	C
8	618.46	656.07	633.50	644.24	644.78	C	652.54	662.59	C	700.64	730.82	C
9	609.45	656.37	C	642.19	645.44	C	654.75	662.10	663.76	696.74	C	749.81
10	598.48	C	C	633.50	652.09	672.16	656.06	C	663.81	694.61	C	747.54
11	602.69	C	640.02	631.18	C	670.97	645.67	C	667.28	700.66	731.87	740.73
12	601.81	661.45	637.09	636.71	C	669.04	646.19	665.77	671.15	C	729.56	729.33
13	C	660.51	638.55	C	661.51	667.92	C	660.20	680.54	C	731.13	728.64
14	C	655.58	640.87	C	665.60	665.85	C	662.05	C	703.54	735.88	C
15	599.82	651.32	641.43	642.49	665.42	C	629.80	662.28	C	702.57	737.62	C
16	608.44	647.98	C	645.00	664.85	C	628.37	665.21	683.98	704.41	C	720.98
17	606.37	C	C	641.61	668.91	665.16	634.07	C	682.94	706.99	C	726.04
18	608.24	C	652.65	643.61	C	662.06	643.56	C	681.47	710.82	737.02	731.54
19	611.83	C	651.69	645.07	C	661.96	638.73	666.58	683.00	C	742.16	745.76
20	C	640.65	649.98	C	673.15	662.10	C	665.69	687.02	C	743.95	748.87
21	C	648.10	649.19	C	672.76	666.84	C	665.07	C	709.85	742.75	C
22	613.40	658.86	650.62	647.89	678.42	C	633.77	670.68	C	706.57	748.73	C
23	612.79	659.08	C	651.58	676.00	C	626.87	667.03	686.48	707.27	C	746.92
24	619.96	C	C	650.17	678.51	668.85	626.65	C	685.61	702.29	C	751.03
25	617.03	C	650.04	652.87	C	668.48	631.17	C	685.83	700.92	757.03	C
26	621.62	650.46	652.97	653.46	C	664.39	635.90	663.88	685.86	C	755.96	755.82
27	C	647.24	648.91	C	C	668.55	C	666.40	686.19	C	755.00	756.79
28	C	644.75	648.94	C	672.23	670.63	C	664.81	C	697.26	C	C
29	624.22	640.43	645.50	654.16	667.93	C	630.91	657.40	C	701.50	757.02	C
30	630.15		C	654.17	671.70	C	635.26	651.99	687.31	700.90	C	753.85
31	636.02		C		669.12		639.95	C		705.27		740.74
Close	636.02	640.43	645.50	654.17	669.12	670.63	639.95	651.99	687.31	705.27	757.02	740.74
Month Pt Change	20.09	4.41	5.07	8.67	14.95	1.51	−30.68	12.04	35.32	17.96	51.75	−16.28
Month % Change	3.3	0.7	0.8	1.3	2.3	0.2	−4.6	1.9	5.4	2.6	7.3	−2.2
QTR % Change			4.8			3.9			2.5			7.8
Year % Change												20.3

HIGHLIGHTS

Election Year	Bull Market	Best Six Months 13.6%	High	Nov-25	757.03
Clinton (1st Term)	Expansion	Worst Six Months 7.8%	Low	Jan-10	598.48

STANDARD & POOR'S 500 — 1997

	Jan	Feb	Mar	Apr	May	Jun	Jul	Aug	Sep	Oct	Nov	Dec
Previous Month Close	740.74	786.16	790.82	757.12	801.34	848.28	885.14	954.29	899.47	947.28	914.62	955.40
1	C	C	C	759.64	798.53	C	891.03	947.14	C	955.41	C	974.77
2	737.01	C	C	750.11	812.97	846.36	904.03	C	927.58	960.46	C	971.68
3	748.03	786.73	795.31	750.32	C	845.48	916.92	C	927.86	965.03	938.99	976.77
4	C	789.26	790.95	757.90	C	840.11	C	950.30	930.87	C	940.76	973.10
5	C	778.28	801.99	C	830.29	843.43	C	952.37	929.05	C	942.76	983.79
6	747.65	780.15	798.56	C	827.76	858.01	C	960.32	C	972.69	938.03	C
7	753.23	789.56	804.97	762.13	815.62	C	912.20	951.19	C	983.12	927.51	C
8	748.41	C	C	766.12	820.26	C	918.75	933.54	931.20	973.84	C	982.37
9	754.85	C	C	760.60	824.78	862.91	907.54	C	933.62	970.62	C	975.78
10	759.50	785.43	813.65	758.34	C	865.27	913.78	C	919.03	966.98	921.13	969.79
11	C	789.59	811.34	737.65	C	869.57	916.68	937.00	912.59	C	923.78	954.94
12	C	802.77	804.26	C	837.66	883.48	C	926.53	923.91	C	905.96	953.39
13	759.51	811.82	789.56	C	833.13	893.27	C	922.02	C	968.10	916.66	C
14	768.86	808.48	793.17	743.73	836.04	C	918.38	924.77	C	970.28	928.35	C
15	767.20	C	C	754.72	841.88	C	925.76	900.81	919.77	965.72	C	963.39
16	769.75	C	C	763.53	829.75	893.90	936.59	C	945.64	955.25	C	968.04
17	776.17	C	795.71	761.77	C	894.42	931.61	C	943.00	944.16	946.20	965.54
18	C	816.29	789.66	766.34	C	889.06	915.30	912.49	947.29	C	938.23	955.30
19	C	812.49	785.77	C	833.27	897.99	C	926.01	950.51	C	944.59	946.78
20	776.70	802.80	782.65	C	841.66	898.70	C	939.35	C	955.61	958.98	C
21	782.72	801.77	784.10	760.37	839.35	C	912.94	925.05	C	972.28	963.09	C
22	786.23	C	C	774.61	835.66	C	933.98	923.54	955.43	968.49	C	953.70
23	777.56	C	C	773.64	847.03	878.62	936.56	C	951.93	950.69	C	939.13
24	770.52	810.28	790.89	771.18	C	896.34	940.28	C	944.48	941.64	946.67	932.70
25	C	812.10	789.07	765.37	C	888.99	938.79	920.16	937.91	C	950.82	C
26	C	805.68	790.50	C	C	883.68	C	913.02	945.22	C	951.64	936.46
27	765.02	795.07	773.88	C	849.71	887.30	C	913.70	C	876.99	C	C
28	765.02	790.82	C	772.96	847.21	C	936.45	903.67	C	921.85	955.40	C
29	772.50		C	794.05	844.08	C	942.29	899.47	953.34	919.16	C	953.35
30	784.17		C	801.34	848.28	885.14	952.29	C	947.28	903.68	C	970.84
31	786.16		757.12		C		954.29	C		914.62		970.43
Close	786.16	790.82	757.12	801.34	848.28	885.14	954.29	899.47	947.28	914.62	955.40	970.43
Month Pt Change	45.42	4.66	-33.70	44.22	46.94	36.86	69.15	-54.82	47.81	-32.66	40.78	15.03
Month % Change	6.1	0.6	-4.3	5.8	5.9	4.3	7.8	-5.7	5.3	-3.4	4.5	1.6
QTR % Change			2.2			16.9			7.0			2.4
Year % Change												31.0

HIGHLIGHTS

Post Election Year	Bull Market	Best Six Months 21.6%	High Dec-05	983.79
Clinton (2nd Term)	Expansion	Worst Six Months 14.1%	Low Jan-02	737.01

Previous Month Close	Jan	Feb	Mar	Apr	May	Jun	Jul	Aug	Sep	Oct	Nov	Dec
	970.43	980.28	1049.34	1101.75	1111.75	1090.82	1133.84	1120.67	957.28	1017.01	1098.67	1163.63
1	C	C	C	1108.15	1121.00	1090.98	1148.56	C	994.26	986.39	C	1175.28
2	975.04	1001.27	1047.70	1120.01	C	1093.22	1146.42	C	990.47	1002.60	1111.60	1171.25
3	C	1006.00	1052.02	1122.70	C	1082.73	C	1112.44	982.26	C	1110.84	1150.14
4	C	1006.90	1047.33	C	1122.07	1094.83	C	1072.12	973.89	C	1118.67	1176.74
5	977.07	1003.54	1035.05	C	1115.50	1113.86	C	1081.43	C	988.56	1133.68	C
6	966.58	1012.46	1055.69	1121.38	1104.92	C	1157.31	1089.63	C	984.59	1141.01	C
7	964.00	C	C	1109.55	1095.14	C	1154.66	1089.45	C	970.68	C	1187.70
8	956.05	C	C	1101.65	1108.14	1115.72	1166.37	C	1023.46	959.44	C	1181.38
9	927.69	1010.74	1052.31	1110.67	C	1118.41	1158.56	C	1006.20	984.32	1130.20	1183.49
10	C	1019.01	1064.25	C	C	1112.28	1164.33	1083.14	980.19	C	1128.26	1165.02
11	C	1020.01	1068.47	C	1106.64	1094.58	C	1068.98	1009.06	C	1120.97	1166.46
12	939.21	1024.14	1069.92	C	1115.79	1098.84	C	1084.22	C	997.71	1117.69	C
13	952.12	1020.09	1068.61	1109.69	1118.86	C	1165.19	1074.91	C	994.80	1125.72	C
14	957.94	C	C	1115.75	1117.37	C	1177.58	1062.75	1029.72	1005.53	C	1141.20
15	950.73	C	C	1119.32	1108.73	1077.01	1174.81	C	1037.68	1047.49	C	1162.83
16	961.51	C	1079.27	1108.17	C	1087.59	1183.99	C	1045.48	1056.42	1135.86	1161.94
17	C	1022.76	1080.45	1122.72	C	1107.11	1186.75	1083.67	1018.87	C	1139.32	1179.98
18	C	1032.08	1085.52	C	1105.82	1106.37	C	1101.20	1020.09	C	1144.48	1188.03
19	C	1028.28	1089.74	C	1109.52	1100.65	C	1098.06	C	1062.39	1152.61	C
20	978.60	1034.21	1099.16	1123.65	1119.06	C	1184.10	1091.60	C	1063.93	1163.55	C
21	970.81	C	C	1126.67	1114.64	C	1165.07	1081.18	1023.89	1069.92	C	1202.84
22	963.04	C	C	1130.54	1110.47	1103.24	1164.08	C	1029.80	1078.48	C	1203.57
23	957.59	1038.14	1095.55	1119.58	C	1119.49	1139.75	C	1066.09	1070.67	1188.21	1228.54
24	C	1030.56	1105.65	1107.90	C	1132.88	1140.80	1088.14	1042.72	C	1182.99	1226.27
25	C	1042.90	1101.93	C	C	1129.28	C	1092.85	1044.75	C	1186.87	C
26	956.95	1048.67	1100.80	C	1094.02	1133.20	C	1084.19	C	1072.32	C	C
27	969.02	1049.34	1095.44	1086.54	1092.23	C	1147.27	1042.59	C	1065.34	1192.33	C
28	977.46	C	C	1085.11	1097.60	C	1130.24	1027.14	1048.69	1068.09	C	1225.49
29	985.49		C	1094.63	1090.82	1138.49	1125.21	C	1049.02	1085.93	C	1241.81
30	980.28		1093.55	1111.75	C	1133.84	1142.95	C	1017.01	1098.67	1163.63	1231.93
31	C		1101.75		C		1120.67	957.28		C		1229.23
Close	980.28	1049.34	1101.75	1111.75	1090.82	1133.84	1120.67	957.28	1017.01	1098.67	1163.63	1229.23
Month Pt Change	9.85	69.06	52.41	10.00	−20.93	43.02	−13.17	−163.39	59.73	81.66	64.96	65.60
Month % Change	1.0	7.0	5.0	0.9	−1.9	3.9	−1.2	−14.6	6.2	8.0	5.9	5.6
QTR % Change			13.5			2.9			−10.3			20.9
Year % Change												26.7

HIGHLIGHTS

Mid-Term Election Year	Bull Market	Best Six Months 21.5%	High Dec-29	1241.81
Clinton (2nd Term)	Expansion	Worst Six Months -1.2%	Low Jan-09	927.69

Previous Month Close	Jan	Feb	Mar	Apr	May	Jun	Jul	Aug	Sep	Oct	Nov	Dec
	1229.23	1279.64	1238.33	1286.37	1335.18	1301.84	1372.71	1328.72	1320.41	1282.71	1362.93	1388.91
1	C	1273.00	1236.16	1293.72	C	1294.26	1380.96	C	1331.07	1282.81	1354.12	1397.72
2	C	1261.99	1225.50	C	C	1294.81	1391.22	1328.05	1319.11	C	1347.74	1409.04
3	C	1272.07	1227.70	C	1354.63	1299.54	C	1322.18	1357.24	C	1354.93	1433.30
4	1228.10	1248.49	1246.64	C	1332.00	1327.75	C	1305.33	C	1304.60	1362.64	C
5	1244.78	1239.40	1275.47	1321.12	1347.31	C	C	1313.71	C	1301.35	1370.23	C
6	1272.34	C	C	1317.89	1332.05	C	1388.12	1300.29	C	1325.40	C	1423.33
7	1269.73	C	C	1326.89	1345.00	1334.52	1395.86	C	1350.45	1317.64	C	1409.17
8	1275.09	1243.77	1282.73	1343.98	C	1317.33	1394.42	C	1344.15	1336.02	1377.01	1403.88
9	C	1216.14	1279.84	1348.35	C	1318.64	1403.28	1297.80	1347.66	C	1365.28	1408.11
10	C	1223.55	1286.84	C	1340.30	1302.82	C	1281.43	1351.66	C	1373.46	1417.04
11	1263.88	1254.04	1297.68	C	1355.61	1293.64	C	1301.93	C	1335.21	1381.46	C
12	1239.51	1230.13	1294.59	1358.64	1364.00	C	1399.10	1298.16	C	1313.04	1396.06	C
13	1234.40	C	C	1349.82	1367.56	C	1393.56	1327.68	1344.13	1285.55	C	1415.22
14	1212.19	C	C	1328.44	1337.80	1294.00	1398.17	C	1336.29	1283.42	C	1403.17
15	1243.26	C	1307.26	1322.86	C	1301.16	1409.62	C	1317.97	1247.41	1394.39	1413.32
16	C	1241.87	1306.38	1319.00	C	1330.41	1418.78	1330.77	1318.48	C	1420.07	1418.78
17	C	1224.03	1297.82	C	1339.49	1339.90	C	1344.16	1335.42	C	1410.71	1421.03
18	C	1237.28	1316.55	C	1333.32	1342.84	C	1332.85	C	1254.13	1424.94	C
19	1252.00	1239.19	1299.29	1289.48	1344.23	C	1407.65	1323.59	C	1261.32	1422.00	C
20	1256.62	C	C	1306.17	1338.83	C	1377.10	1336.61	1335.53	1289.43	C	1418.09
21	1235.16	C	C	1336.12	1330.29	1349.00	1379.29	C	1307.58	1283.61	C	1433.43
22	1225.19	1272.14	1297.01	1358.82	C	1335.88	1360.97	C	1310.51	1301.65	1420.94	1436.13
23	C	1271.18	1262.14	1356.85	C	1333.06	1356.94	1360.22	1280.41	C	1404.64	1458.34
24	C	1253.41	1268.59	C	1306.65	1315.78	C	1363.50	1277.36	C	1417.08	C
25	1233.98	1245.02	1289.99	C	1284.40	1315.31	C	1381.79	C	1293.63	C	C
26	1252.31	1238.33	1282.80	1360.04	1304.76	C	1347.76	1362.01	C	1281.91	1416.62	C
27	1243.17	C	C	1362.80	1281.41	C	1362.84	1348.27	1283.31	1296.71	C	1457.10
28	1265.37	C	C	1350.91	1301.84	1331.35	1365.40	C	1282.20	1342.44	C	1457.66
29	1279.64		1310.17	1342.83	C	1351.45	1341.03	C	1268.37	1362.93	1407.83	1463.46
30	C		1300.75	1335.18	C	1372.71	1328.72	1324.02	1282.71	C	1388.91	1464.47
31	C		1286.37		C		C	1320.41		C		1469.25
Close	1279.64	1238.33	1286.37	1335.18	1301.84	1372.71	1328.72	1320.41	1282.71	1362.93	1388.91	1469.25
Month Pt Change	50.41	−41.31	48.04	48.81	−33.34	70.87	−43.99	−8.31	−37.70	80.22	25.98	80.34
Month % Change	4.1	−3.2	3.9	3.8	−2.5	5.4	−3.2	−0.6	−2.9	6.3	1.9	5.8
QTR % Change			4.6			6.7			−6.6			14.5
Year % Change												19.5

2000 STANDARD & POOR'S 500

Previous Month Close	Jan	Feb	Mar	Apr	May	Jun	Jul	Aug	Sep	Oct	Nov	Dec
	1469.25	1394.46	1366.42	1498.58	1452.43	1420.60	1454.60	1430.83	1517.68	1436.51	1429.40	1314.95
1	C	1409.28	1379.19	C	1468.25	1448.81	C	1438.10	1520.77	C	1421.22	1315.23
2	C	1409.12	1381.76	C	1446.29	1477.26	C	1438.70	C	1436.23	1428.32	C
3	1455.22	1424.97	1409.17	1505.97	1415.10	C	1469.54	1452.56	C	1426.46	1426.69	C
4	1399.42	1424.37	C	1494.73	1409.57	C	C	1462.93	C	1434.32	C	1324.97
5	1402.11	C	C	1487.37	1432.63	1467.63	1446.23	C	1507.08	1436.28	C	1376.54
6	1403.45	C	1391.28	1501.34	C	1457.84	1456.67	C	1492.25	1408.99	1432.19	1351.46
7	1441.47	1424.24	1355.62	1516.35	C	1471.36	1478.90	1479.32	1502.51	C	1431.87	1343.55
8	C	1441.72	1366.70	C	1424.17	1461.67	C	1482.80	1494.50	C	1409.28	1369.89
9	C	1411.70	1401.69	C	1412.14	1456.95	C	1472.87	C	1402.03	1400.14	C
10	1457.60	1416.83	1395.07	1504.46	1383.05	C	1475.62	1460.25	C	1387.02	1365.98	C
11	1438.56	1387.12	C	1500.59	1407.81	C	1480.88	1471.84	1489.26	1364.59	C	1380.20
12	1432.25	C	C	1467.17	1420.96	1446.00	1492.92	C	1481.99	1329.78	C	1371.18
13	1449.68	C	1383.62	1440.51	C	1469.44	1495.84	C	1484.91	1374.17	1351.26	1359.99
14	1465.15	1389.94	1359.15	1356.56	C	1470.54	1509.98	1491.56	1480.87	C	1382.95	1340.93
15	C	1402.05	1392.15	C	1452.36	1478.73	C	1484.43	1465.81	C	1389.81	1312.15
16	C	1387.67	1458.47	C	1466.04	1464.46	C	1479.85	C	1374.62	1372.32	C
17	C	1388.26	1464.47	1401.44	1447.80	C	1510.49	1496.07	C	1349.97	1367.72	C
18	1455.14	1346.09	C	1441.61	1437.21	C	1493.74	1491.72	1444.51	1342.13	C	1322.74
19	1455.90	C	C	1427.47	1406.95	1486.00	1481.96	C	1459.90	1388.76	C	1305.60
20	1445.57	C	1456.63	1434.54	C	1475.95	1495.57	C	1451.34	1396.93	1342.62	1264.74
21	1441.36	C	1493.87	C	C	1479.13	1480.19	1499.48	1449.05	C	1347.35	1274.86
22	C	1352.17	1500.64	C	1400.72	1452.18	C	1498.13	1448.72	C	1322.36	1305.97
23	C	1360.69	1527.35	C	1373.86	1441.48	C	1505.97	C	1395.78	C	C
24	1401.53	1353.43	1527.46	1429.86	1399.05	C	1464.29	1508.31	C	1398.13	1341.77	C
25	1410.03	1333.36	C	1477.44	1381.52	C	1474.47	1506.45	1439.03	1364.90	C	C
26	1404.09	C	C	1460.99	1378.02	1455.31	1452.42	C	1427.21	1364.44	C	1315.19
27	1398.56	C	1523.86	1464.92	C	1450.55	1449.62	C	1426.57	1379.58	1348.97	1328.92
28	1360.16	1348.05	1507.73	1452.43	C	1454.82	1419.89	1514.09	1458.29	C	1336.09	1334.22
29	C	1366.42	1508.52	C	C	1442.39	C	1509.84	1436.51	C	1341.91	1320.28
30	C		1487.92	C	1422.45	1454.60	C	1502.59	C	1398.66	1314.95	C
31	1394.46		1498.58		1420.60		1430.83	1517.68		1429.40		C
Close	1394.46	1366.42	1498.58	1452.43	1420.60	1454.60	1430.83	1517.68	1436.51	1429.40	1314.95	1320.28
Month Pt Change	-74.79	-28.04	132.16	-46.15	-31.83	34.00	-23.77	86.85	-81.17	-7.11	-114.45	5.33
Month % Change	-5.1	-2.0	9.7	-3.1	-2.2	2.4	-1.6	6.1	-5.3	-0.5	-8.0	0.4
QTR % Change			2.0			-2.9			-1.2			-8.1
Year % Change												-10.1

HIGHLIGHTS

Election Year	Bear Market Begins 1/14	Best Six Months -12.6%	High Mar-24 1527.46
Clinton (2nd Term)	Expansion	Worst Six Months -1.6%	Low Dec-20 1264.74

Previous Month Close	Jan 1320.28	Feb 1366.01	Mar 1239.94	Apr 1160.33	May 1249.46	Jun 1255.82	Jul 1224.42	Aug 1211.23	Sep 1133.58	Oct 1040.94	Nov 1059.78	Dec 1139.45
1	C	1373.47	1241.23	C	1266.44	1260.67	C	1215.93	C	1038.55	1084.10	C
2	1283.27	1349.47	1234.18	1145.87	1267.43	C	1236.71	1220.75	C	1051.33	1087.20	C
3	1347.56	C	C	1106.46	1248.58	C	1234.45	1214.35	C	1072.28	C	1129.90
4	1333.34	C	C	1103.25	1266.61	1267.11	C	C	1132.94	1069.63	C	1144.80
5	1298.35	1354.31	1241.41	1151.44	C	1283.57	1219.24	C	1131.74	1071.38	1102.84	1170.35
6	C	1352.26	1253.80	1128.43	C	1270.03	1190.59	1200.48	1106.40	C	1118.86	1167.10
7	C	1340.89	1261.89	C	1263.51	1276.96	C	1204.40	1085.78	C	1115.80	1158.31
8	1295.86	1332.53	1264.74	C	1261.20	1264.96	C	1183.53	C	1062.44	1118.54	C
9	1300.80	1314.76	1233.42	1137.59	1255.54	C	1198.78	1183.43	C	1056.75	1120.31	C
10	1313.27	C	C	1168.38	1255.18	C	1181.52	1190.16	1092.54	1080.99	C	1139.93
11	1326.82	C	C	1165.89	1245.67	1254.39	1180.18	C	C	1097.43	C	1136.76
12	1318.32	1330.31	1180.16	1183.50	C	1255.85	1208.14	C	C	1091.65	1118.33	1137.07
13	C	1318.80	1197.66	C	C	1241.60	1215.68	1191.29	C	C	1139.09	1119.38
14	C	1315.92	1166.71	C	1248.92	1219.87	C	1186.73	C	C	1141.21	1123.09
15	C	1326.61	1173.56	C	1249.44	1214.36	C	1178.02	C	1089.98	1142.24	C
16	1326.65	1301.53	1150.53	1179.68	1284.99	C	1202.45	1181.66	C	1097.54	1138.65	C
17	1329.47	C	C	1191.81	1288.49	C	1214.44	1161.97	1038.77	1077.09	C	1134.36
18	1347.97	C	C	1238.16	1291.96	1208.43	1207.71	C	1032.74	1068.61	C	1142.92
19	1342.54	C	1170.81	1253.70	C	1212.58	1215.02	C	1016.10	1073.48	1151.06	1149.56
20	C	1278.94	1142.62	1242.98	C	1223.14	1210.85	1171.41	984.54	C	1142.66	1139.93
21	C	1255.27	1122.14	C	1312.83	1237.04	C	1157.26	965.80	C	1137.03	1144.89
22	1342.90	1252.82	1117.58	C	1309.38	1225.35	C	1165.31	C	1089.90	C	C
23	1360.40	1245.86	1139.83	1224.36	1289.05	C	1191.03	1162.09	C	1084.78	1150.34	C
24	1364.30	C	C	1209.47	1293.17	C	1171.65	1184.93	1003.45	1085.20	C	1144.65
25	1357.51	C	C	1228.75	1277.89	1218.60	1190.49	C	1012.27	1100.09	C	C
26	1354.95	1267.65	1152.69	1234.52	C	1216.76	1202.93	C	1007.04	1104.61	1157.42	1149.37
27	C	1257.94	1182.17	1253.05	C	1211.07	1205.82	1179.21	1018.61	C	1149.50	1157.13
28	C	1239.94	1153.29	C	C	1226.20	C	1161.51	1040.94	C	1128.52	1161.02
29	1364.17		1147.95	C	1267.93	1224.42	C	1148.60	C	1078.30	1140.20	C
30	1364.30		1160.33	1249.46	1248.08	C	1204.52	1129.03	C	1059.79	1139.45	C
31	1366.01		C		1255.82		1211.23	1133.58		1059.78		1148.08
Close	1366.01	1239.94	1160.33	1249.46	1255.82	1224.42	1211.23	1133.58	1040.94	1059.78	1139.45	1148.08
Month Pt Change	45.73	−126.07	−79.61	89.13	6.36	−31.40	−13.19	−77.65	−92.64	18.84	79.67	8.63
Month % Change	3.5	−9.2	−6.4	7.7	0.5	−2.5	−1.1	−6.4	−8.2	1.8	7.5	0.8
QTR % Change			−12.1			5.5			−15.0			10.3
Year % Change												−13.0

2002 STANDARD & POOR'S 500

Previous Month Close	Jan	Feb	Mar	Apr	May	Jun	Jul	Aug	Sep	Oct	Nov	Dec
	1148.08	1130.20	1106.73	1147.39	1076.92	1067.14	989.82	911.62	916.07	815.28	885.76	936.31
1	C	1122.20	1131.78	1146.54	1086.46	C	968.65	884.66	C	847.91	900.96	C
2	1154.67	C	C	1136.76	1084.56	C	948.09	864.24	C	827.91	C	934.53
3	1165.27	C	C	1125.40	1073.43	1040.68	953.99	C	878.02	818.95	C	920.75
4	1172.51	1094.44	1153.84	1126.34	C	1040.69	C	C	893.40	800.58	908.35	917.57
5	C	1090.02	1146.14	1122.73	C	1049.90	989.03	834.60	879.15	C	915.39	906.55
6	C	1083.51	1162.77	C	1052.67	1029.15	C	859.57	893.92	C	923.76	912.23
7	1164.89	1080.17	1157.54	C	1049.49	1027.53	C	876.77	C	785.28	902.65	C
8	1160.71	1096.22	1164.31	1125.29	1088.85	C	976.98	905.46	C	798.55	894.74	C
9	1155.14	C	C	1117.80	1073.01	C	952.83	908.64	902.96	776.76	C	892.00
10	1156.55	C	C	1130.47	1054.99	1030.74	920.47	C	909.58	803.92	C	904.45
11	1145.60	1111.94	1168.26	1103.69	C	1013.60	927.37	C	909.45	835.32	876.19	904.96
12	C	1107.50	1165.58	1111.01	C	1020.26	921.39	903.80	886.91	C	882.95	901.59
13	C	1118.51	1154.09	C	1074.56	1009.56	C	884.21	889.81	C	882.53	889.48
14	1138.41	1116.48	1153.04	C	1097.28	1007.27	C	919.62	C	841.44	904.27	C
15	1146.19	1104.18	1166.16	1102.55	1091.07	C	917.93	930.25	C	881.27	909.83	C
16	1127.57	C	C	1128.37	1098.23	C	901.05	928.77	891.10	860.02	C	910.40
17	1138.88	C	C	1126.07	1106.59	1036.17	906.04	C	873.52	879.20	C	902.99
18	1127.58	C	1165.55	1124.47	C	1037.14	881.56	C	869.46	884.39	900.36	891.12
19	C	1083.34	1170.29	1125.17	C	1019.99	847.76	950.72	843.32	C	896.74	884.25
20	C	1097.98	1151.85	C	1091.88	1006.29	C	937.43	845.39	C	914.15	895.75
21	C	1080.95	1153.59	C	1079.88	989.14	C	949.36	C	899.72	933.76	C
22	1119.31	1089.84	1148.70	1107.83	1086.02	C	819.85	962.70	C	890.16	930.55	C
23	1128.18	C	C	1100.96	1097.08	C	797.70	940.86	833.70	896.14	C	897.38
24	1132.15	C	C	1093.14	1083.82	992.72	843.42	C	819.29	882.50	C	892.47
25	1133.28	1109.43	1131.87	1091.48	C	976.14	838.68	C	839.66	897.65	932.88	C
26	C	1109.38	1138.49	1076.32	C	973.53	852.84	947.95	854.95	C	913.31	889.66
27	C	1109.89	1144.58	C	C	990.64	C	934.82	827.37	C	938.87	875.40
28	1133.06	1106.73	1147.39	C	1074.55	989.82	C	917.87	C	890.23	C	C
29	1100.64		C	1065.45	1067.66	C	898.96	917.80	C	882.15	936.31	C
30	1113.57		C	1076.92	1064.66	C	902.78	916.07	815.28	890.71	C	879.39
31	1130.20		C		1067.14		911.62	C		885.76		879.82
Close	1130.20	1106.73	1147.39	1076.92	1067.14	989.82	911.62	916.07	815.28	885.76	936.31	879.82
Month Pt Change	-17.88	-23.47	40.66	-70.47	-9.78	-77.32	-78.20	4.45	-100.79	70.48	50.55	-56.49
Month % Change	-1.6	-2.1	3.7	-6.1	-0.9	-7.2	-7.9	0.5	-11.0	8.6	5.7	-6.0
QTR % Change			-0.1			-13.7			-17.6			7.9
Year % Change												-23.4

HIGHLIGHTS

Mid-Term Election Year	Bear Market 3/19 - 10/9	Best Six Months	3.5%	High Jan-04	1172.51
GW Bush (1st Term)	Expansion	Worst Six Months	-17.8%	Low Oct-09	776.76

Previous Month Close	Jan 879.82	Feb 855.70	Mar 841.15	Apr 849.18	May 916.92	Jun 963.59	Jul 974.50	Aug 990.31	Sep 1008.01	Oct 995.97	Nov 1050.71	Dec 1058.20
1	C	C	C	858.48	916.30	C	982.32	980.15	C	1018.22	C	1070.12
2	909.03	C	C	880.90	930.08	967.00	993.75	C	1021.99	1020.24	C	1066.62
3	908.59	860.32	834.81	876.45	C	971.56	985.70	C	1026.27	1029.85	1059.02	1064.73
4	C	848.20	821.99	878.85	C	986.24	C	982.82	1027.97	C	1053.25	1069.72
5	C	843.59	829.85	C	926.55	990.14	C	965.46	1021.39	C	1051.81	1061.50
6	929.01	838.15	822.10	C	934.39	987.76	C	967.08	C	1034.35	1058.05	C
7	922.93	829.69	828.89	879.93	929.62	C	1004.42	974.12	C	1039.25	1053.21	C
8	909.93	C	C	878.29	920.27	C	1007.84	977.59	1031.64	1033.78	C	1069.30
9	927.58	C	C	865.99	933.41	975.93	1002.21	C	1023.17	1038.73	C	1060.18
10	927.57	835.97	807.48	871.58	C	984.84	988.70	C	1010.92	1038.06	1047.11	1059.05
11	C	829.20	800.73	868.30	C	997.48	998.14	980.59	1016.42	C	1046.57	1071.21
12	C	818.68	804.19	C	945.11	998.51	C	990.35	1018.63	C	1058.56	1074.14
13	926.26	817.37	831.90	C	942.30	988.61	C	984.03	C	1045.35	1058.41	C
14	931.66	834.89	833.27	885.23	939.28	C	1003.86	990.51	C	1049.48	1050.35	C
15	918.22	C	C	890.81	946.67	C	1000.42	990.67	1014.81	1046.76	C	1068.04
16	914.60	C	C	879.91	944.30	1010.74	994.00	C	1029.32	1050.07	C	1075.13
17	901.78	C	862.79	893.58	C	1011.66	981.73	C	1025.97	1039.32	1043.63	1076.48
18	C	851.17	866.45	C	C	1010.09	993.32	999.74	1039.58	C	1034.15	1089.18
19	C	845.13	874.02	C	920.77	994.70	C	1002.35	1036.30	C	1042.44	1088.67
20	C	837.10	875.67	C	919.73	995.69	C	1000.30	C	1044.68	1033.65	C
21	887.62	848.17	895.79	892.01	923.42	C	978.80	1003.27	C	1046.03	1035.28	C
22	878.36	C	C	911.37	931.87	C	988.11	993.06	1022.82	1030.36	C	1092.94
23	887.34	C	C	919.02	933.22	981.64	988.61	C	1029.03	1033.77	C	1096.02
24	861.40	832.58	864.23	911.43	C	983.45	981.60	C	1009.38	1028.91	1052.08	1094.04
25	C	838.57	874.74	898.81	C	975.32	998.68	993.71	1003.27	C	1053.89	C
26	C	827.55	869.95	C	C	985.82	C	996.73	996.85	C	1058.45	1095.89
27	847.48	837.28	868.52	C	951.48	976.22	C	996.79	C	1031.13	C	C
28	858.54	841.15	863.50	914.84	953.22	C	996.52	1002.84	C	1046.79	1058.20	C
29	864.36		C	917.84	949.64	C	989.28	1008.01	1006.58	1048.11	C	1109.48
30	844.61		C	916.92	963.59	974.50	987.49	C	995.97	1046.94	C	1109.64
31	855.70		849.18		C		990.31	C		1050.71		1111.92
Close	855.70	841.15	849.18	916.92	963.59	974.50	990.31	1008.01	995.97	1050.71	1058.20	1111.92
Month Pt Change	−24.12	−14.55	8.03	67.74	46.67	10.91	15.81	17.70	−12.04	54.74	7.49	53.72
Month % Change	−2.7	−1.7	1.0	8.0	5.1	1.1	1.6	1.8	−1.2	5.5	0.7	5.1
QTR % Change			−3.5			14.8			2.2			11.6
Year % Change												26.4

HIGHLIGHTS

Pre-Election Year	Bull Market	Best Six Months	5.4%	High Dec-31	1111.92
GW Bush (1st Term)	Expansion	Worst Six Months	14.6%	Low Mar-11	800.73

2004 STANDARD & POOR'S 500

Previous Month Close	Jan	Feb	Mar	Apr	May	Jun	Jul	Aug	Sep	Oct	Nov	Dec
	1111.92	1131.13	1144.94	1126.21	1107.30	1120.68	1140.84	1101.72	1104.24	1114.58	1130.20	1173.82
1	C	C	1155.96	1132.17	C	1121.20	1128.94	C	1105.91	1131.50	1130.51	1191.37
2	1108.48	1135.26	1149.10	1141.81	C	1124.99	1125.38	1106.62	1118.31	C	1130.54	1190.33
3	C	1136.03	1151.04	C	1117.49	1116.64	C	1099.69	1113.63	C	1143.20	1191.17
4	C	1126.52	1154.88	C	1119.55	1122.50	C	1098.63	C	1135.17	1161.67	C
5	1122.22	1128.59	1156.87	1150.57	1121.53	C	C	1080.70	C	1134.48	1166.17	C
6	1123.67	1142.76	C	1148.16	1113.99	C	1116.21	1063.97	C	1142.05	C	1190.25
7	1126.33	C	C	1140.53	1098.70	1140.42	1118.33	C	1121.30	1130.65	C	1177.07
8	1131.92	C	1147.21	1139.32	C	1142.18	1109.11	C	1116.27	1122.14	1164.89	1182.81
9	1121.86	1139.81	1140.58	C	C	1131.33	1112.81	1065.22	1118.38	C	1164.08	1189.24
10	C	1145.54	1123.89	C	1087.12	1136.47	C	1079.04	1123.92	C	1162.91	1188.00
11	C	1157.76	1106.78	C	1095.45	C	C	1075.79	C	1124.39	1173.48	C
12	1127.23	1152.11	1120.57	1145.20	1097.28	C	1114.35	1063.23	C	1121.84	1184.17	C
13	1121.22	1145.81	C	1129.44	1096.44	C	1115.14	1064.80	1125.82	1113.65	C	1198.68
14	1130.52	C	C	1128.17	1095.70	1125.29	1111.47	C	1128.33	1103.29	C	1203.38
15	1132.05	C	1104.49	1128.84	C	1132.01	1106.69	C	1120.37	1108.20	1183.81	1205.72
16	1139.83	C	1110.70	1134.61	C	1133.56	1101.39	1079.34	1123.50	C	1175.43	1203.21
17	C	1156.99	1123.75	C	1084.10	1132.05	C	1081.71	1128.55	C	1181.94	1194.22
18	C	1151.82	1122.32	C	1091.49	1135.02	C	1095.17	C	1114.02	1183.55	C
19	C	1147.06	1109.78	1135.82	1088.68	C	1100.90	1091.23	C	1103.23	1170.34	C
20	1138.77	1144.11	C	1118.15	1089.19	C	1108.67	1098.35	1122.20	1103.66	C	1194.65
21	1147.62	C	C	1124.09	1093.56	1130.30	1093.88	C	1129.30	1106.49	C	1205.45
22	1143.94	C	1095.40	1139.93	C	1134.41	1096.84	C	1113.56	1095.74	1177.24	1209.57
23	1141.55	1140.99	1093.95	1140.60	C	1144.06	1086.20	1095.68	1108.36	C	1176.94	1210.13
24	C	1139.09	1091.33	C	1095.41	1140.65	C	1096.19	1110.11	C	1181.76	C
25	C	1143.67	1109.19	C	1113.05	1134.43	C	1104.96	C	1094.81	C	C
26	1155.37	1144.91	1108.06	1135.53	1114.94	C	1084.07	1105.09	C	1111.09	1182.65	C
27	1144.05	1144.94	C	1138.11	1121.28	C	1094.83	1107.77	1103.52	1125.40	C	1204.92
28	1128.48	C	C	1122.41	1120.68	1133.35	1095.42	C	1110.06	1127.44	C	1213.54
29	1134.11	C	1122.47	1113.89	C	1136.20	1100.43	C	1114.80	1130.20	1178.57	1213.45
30	1131.13		1127.00	1107.30	C	1140.84	1101.72	1099.15	1114.58	C	1173.82	1213.55
31	C		1126.21		C		C	1104.24		C		1211.92
Close	1131.13	1144.94	1126.21	1107.30	1120.68	1140.84	1101.72	1104.24	1114.58	1130.20	1173.82	1211.92
Month Pt Change	19.21	13.81	−18.73	−18.91	13.38	20.16	−39.12	2.52	10.34	15.62	43.62	38.10
Month % Change	1.7	1.2	−1.6	−1.7	1.2	1.8	−3.4	0.2	0.9	1.4	3.9	3.2
QTR % Change			1.3			1.3			−2.3			8.7
Year % Change												9.0

HIGHLIGHTS

Election Year	Bull Market	Best Six Months	2.4%	High Dec-30 1213.55
GW Bush (1st Term)	Expansion	Worst Six Months	2.1%	Low Aug-12 1063.23

STANDARD & POOR'S 500 — 2005

	Jan	Feb	Mar	Apr	May	Jun	Jul	Aug	Sep	Oct	Nov	Dec
Previous Month Close	1211.92	1181.27	1203.60	1180.59	1156.85	1191.50						
1	C	1189.41	1210.41	1172.92	C	1202.27						
2	C	1193.19	1210.08	C	1162.16	1204.29						
3	1202.08	1189.89	1210.47	C	1161.17	1196.02						
4	1188.05	1203.03	1222.12	1176.12	1175.65	C						
5	1183.74	C	C	1181.39	1172.63	C						
6	1187.89	C	C	1184.07	1171.35	1197.51						
7	1186.19	1201.72	1225.31	1191.14	C	1197.26						
8	C	1202.30	1219.43	1181.20	C	1194.67						
9	C	1191.99	1207.01	C	1178.84	1200.93						
10	1190.25	1197.01	1209.25	C	1166.22	1198.11						
11	1182.99	1205.30	1200.08	1181.21	1171.11	C						
12	1187.70	C	C	1187.76	1159.36	C						
13	1177.45	C	C	1173.79	1154.05	1200.82						
14	1184.52	1206.14	1206.83	1162.05	C	1203.91						
15	C	1210.12	1197.75	1142.62	C	1206.58						
16	C	1210.34	1188.07	C	1165.69	1210.96						
17	C	1200.75	1190.21	C	1173.80	1216.96						
18	1195.98	1201.59	1189.65	1145.98	1185.56	C						
19	1184.63	C	C	1152.78	1191.08	C						
20	1175.41	C	C	1137.50	1189.28	1216.10						
21	1167.87	C	1183.78	1159.95	C	1213.61						
22	C	1184.16	1171.71	1152.12	C	1213.88						
23	C	1190.80	1172.53	C	1193.86	1200.73						
24	1163.75	1200.20	1171.42	C	1194.07	1191.57						
25	1168.41	1211.37	C	1162.10	1190.01	C						
26	1174.07	C	C	1151.74	1197.62	C						
27	1174.55	C	C	1156.38	1198.78	1190.69						
28	1171.36	1203.60	1174.28	1143.22	C	1201.57						
29	C		1165.36	1156.85	C	1199.85						
30	C		1181.41	C	C	1191.33						
31	1181.27		1180.59		1191.50							
Close	1181.27	1203.60	1180.59	1156.85	1191.50	1191.33						
Month Pt Change	-30.65	22.33	-23.01	-23.74	34.65	-0.17						
Month % Change	-2.5	1.9	-1.9	-2.0	3.0	-0.01						
QTR % Change			-2.6			0.9						
Year % Change												

HIGHLIGHTS

Post Election Year	Bull Market	Best Six Months 2.4%	High Mar-07	1225.31
GW Bush (2nd Term)	Expansion	Worst Six Months—	Low Apr-20	1137.50

NASDAQ COMPOSITE 1971

Previous Month Close	Jan	Feb	Mar	Apr	May	Jun	Jul	Aug	Sep	Oct	Nov	Dec
Close	89.61	98.77	101.34	105.97	112.30	108.25	107.80	105.27	108.42	109.03	105.10	103.97
1	C	99.06	101.78	106.34	C	108.87	108.47	C	108.65	109.58	103.69	105.85
2	C	99.55	101.84	106.86	C	109.56	108.77	105.59	108.96	C	103.54	106.15
3	C	99.62	102.07	C	111.35	110.22	C	104.41	109.98	C	105.01	107.26
4	89.85	100.14	102.78	C	111.77	110.66	C	103.26	C	109.96	105.56	C
5	89.06	100.00	103.51	107.17	111.68	C	C	103.11	C	109.99	105.46	C
6	89.83	C	C	107.56	111.06	C	109.23	103.78	C	110.68	C	106.92
7	90.81	C	C	108.06	110.66	110.76	110.01	C	110.53	110.98	C	107.26
8	91.23	100.84	104.23	108.38	C	110.02	110.42	C	110.58	110.74	105.43	107.71
9	C	100.76	104.41	C	C	109.79	110.91	103.18	110.55	C	105.72	107.97
10	C	100.69	104.14	C	110.15	110.06	C	103.04	110.42	C	104.86	108.81
11	92.14	101.45	104.26	C	110.33	110.20	C	104.08	C	110.71	103.74	C
12	92.72	102.05	104.50	108.87	110.37	C	111.24	105.21	C	110.91	103.91	C
13	94.31	C	C	108.85	110.55	C	110.76	105.44	110.22	110.69	C	109.16
14	94.27	C	C	109.08	110.74	109.57	110.34	C	109.77	109.87	C	109.07
15	95.05	C	105.13	109.69	C	109.36	110.27	C	109.79	109.60	103.44	109.45
16	C	102.19	105.56	109.96	C	109.44	109.98	107.86	109.78	C	103.71	110.01
17	C	101.74	105.50	C	109.15	109.44	C	108.93	110.10	C	103.64	110.52
18	95.22	101.42	105.88	C	108.40	108.16	C	108.39	C	109.06	103.44	C
19	94.92	100.70	105.77	110.16	108.33	C	109.37	108.01	C	107.99	102.95	C
20	95.00	C	C	109.53	108.72	C	109.79	107.89	109.99	106.58	C	111.50
21	96.07	C	C	109.52	108.85	106.50	109.74	C	109.82	106.61	C	111.73
22	97.89	99.68	105.37	109.99	C	105.49	109.54	C	108.99	106.80	101.79	111.97
23	C	99.72	105.11	110.69	C	105.99	109.63	108.26	108.80	C	100.31	111.94
24	C	100.64	104.70	C	108.42	106.37	C	108.60	108.88	C	100.40	C
25	98.27	101.23	104.60	C	107.50	106.56	C	108.85	C	106.29	C	C
26	98.47	101.34	105.07	111.13	107.53	C	109.35	108.97	C	105.69	101.64	C
27	98.25	C	C	111.69	107.60	C	108.57	109.30	108.18	104.28	C	111.70
28	97.82	C	C	112.37	108.25	106.45	107.45	C	108.38	104.50	C	111.93
29	98.77		105.20	112.46	C	107.22	105.81	C	108.60	105.10	103.08	112.57
30	C		105.44	112.30	C	107.80	105.27	108.71	109.03	C	103.97	112.97
31	C		105.97		C		C	108.42		C		114.12
Close	98.77	101.34	105.97	112.30	108.25	107.80	105.27	108.42	109.03	105.10	103.97	114.12
Month Pt Change	9.16	2.57	4.63	6.33	–4.05	–0.45	–2.53	3.15	0.61	–3.93	–1.13	10.15
Month % Change	10.2	2.6	4.6	6.0	–3.6	–0.4	–2.3	3.0	0.6	–3.6	–1.1	9.8
QTR % Change			18.3			1.7			1.1			4.7
Year % Change												27.4

1972

NASDAQ COMPOSITE

Previous Month Close	Jan	Feb	Mar	Apr	May	Jun	Jul	Aug	Sep	Oct	Nov	Dec
	114.12	118.87	125.38	128.14	131.33	132.53	130.08	127.75	129.95	129.61	130.24	132.96
1	C	119.58	126.29	C	130.16	133.13	C	128.45	130.70	C	131.59	133.94
2	C	120.47	126.58	C	129.34	133.52	C	129.39	C	129.30	132.12	C
3	113.65	120.66	127.19	128.06	128.77	C	130.59	130.31	C	129.48	133.34	C
4	113.93	121.24	C	128.78	128.92	C	C	130.94	C	129.29	C	134.14
5	114.83	C	C	130.00	129.43	132.74	131.28	C	130.33	128.01	C	134.28
6	115.72	C	127.88	130.92	C	132.00	131.86	C	129.63	128.13	133.58	134.68
7	116.05	121.14	127.83	131.80	C	131.00	131.50	130.97	129.21	C	C	135.06
8	C	121.35	128.40	C	128.62	131.07	C	130.61	129.13	C	133.06	135.15
9	C	122.16	128.85	C	125.78	130.57	C	130.75	C	128.51	132.82	C
10	116.10	122.71	128.55	131.76	126.77	C	130.85	130.84	C	129.02	133.12	C
11	116.64	122.86	C	132.47	127.95	C	130.47	131.68	128.26	128.57	C	134.83
12	116.90	C	C	133.17	129.44	130.38	130.11	C	127.18	127.87	C	134.27
13	116.42	C	127.34	133.06	C	130.78	129.03	C	127.51	127.19	132.77	133.66
14	116.74	122.26	127.73	133.88	C	131.45	129.38	131.70	127.58	C	132.90	133.33
15	C	122.61	128.14	C	130.34	131.29	C	131.48	127.67	C	132.45	133.53
16	C	123.35	127.77	C	130.36	131.28	C	131.46	C	125.87	132.26	C
17	116.93	123.44	128.01	133.74	129.76	C	128.40	130.89	C	126.43	132.33	C
18	117.66	123.40	C	134.10	130.82	C	127.54	131.43	127.61	127.05	C	132.54
19	117.45	C	C	132.68	132.16	130.76	127.78	C	127.42	126.91	C	132.39
20	117.32	C	127.53	132.86	C	131.07	127.09	C	127.51	128.00	132.12	131.93
21	117.21	C	125.73	133.01	C	131.38	127.63	131.29	127.30	C	132.19	131.08
22	C	123.30	126.36	C	132.38	130.79	C	131.29	127.46	C	132.49	131.28
23	C	123.61	127.38	C	132.52	130.22	C	131.10	C	128.66	C	C
24	116.49	124.00	127.55	131.90	133.47	C	128.77	130.40	C	128.91	133.02	C
25	116.30	124.83	C	130.84	133.80	C	128.47	130.31	126.82	128.89	C	C
26	116.39	C	C	130.92	133.95	129.31	128.65	C	127.07	129.37	C	131.18
27	117.37	C	127.56	131.01	C	129.79	128.36	C	128.55	129.53	132.57	131.93
28	118.44	124.94	127.72	131.33	C	129.58	128.15	129.77	129.13	C	132.71	C
29	C	125.38	127.53	C	C	129.35	C	129.44	129.61	C	132.73	133.73
30	C		128.14	C	133.45	130.08	C	129.78	C	129.46	132.96	C
31	118.87		C		132.53		127.75	129.95		130.24		C
Close	118.87	125.38	128.14	131.33	132.53	130.08	127.75	129.95	129.61	130.24	132.96	133.73
Month Pt Change	4.75	6.51	2.76	3.19	1.20	–2.45	–2.33	2.20	–0.34	0.63	2.72	0.77
Month % Change	4.2	5.5	2.2	2.5	0.9	–1.8	–1.8	1.7	–0.3	0.5	2.1	0.6
QTR % Change			12.3			1.5			–0.4			3.2
Year % Change												17.2

HIGHLIGHTS

Election Year	Bull Market	Best Eight Months -22.5%	High	Dec-08	135.15
Nixon (1st Term)	Expansion	Worst Four Months 0.1%	Low	Jan-03	113.65

NASDAQ COMPOSITE   1973

Previous Month	Jan	Feb	Mar	Apr	May	Jun	Jul	Aug	Sep	Oct	Nov	Dec
Close	133.73	128.40	120.41	117.46	107.85	102.64	100.98	108.64	104.87	111.20	110.17	93.51
1	C	126.94	119.53	C	107.96	102.30	C	107.13	C	110.97	109.62	C
2	134.63	126.48	120.11	115.79	109.05	C	100.15	106.98	C	111.76	108.93	C
3	135.38	C	C	114.47	109.81	C	99.45	106.82	C	112.13	C	91.97
4	135.44	C	C	112.89	110.89	100.77	C	C	105.50	111.51	C	91.56
5	135.91	126.00	120.55	112.02	C	101.71	99.39	C	106.03	112.56	107.12	89.73
6	C	126.27	121.91	113.27	C	101.70	99.48	107.21	106.36	C	106.29	91.27
7	C	124.99	122.28	C	110.48	102.57	C	107.30	107.02	C	106.72	92.32
8	136.02	123.97	122.11	C	110.67	103.72	C	106.13	C	113.17	107.31	C
9	135.99	125.86	121.99	114.01	110.54	C	100.01	106.15	C	113.07	105.77	C
10	136.06	C	C	114.81	110.32	C	101.18	105.32	106.25	112.17	C	93.54
11	136.84	C	C	115.29	109.10	103.04	102.69	C	105.77	113.56	C	92.20
12	136.01	126.88	121.86	115.59	C	104.79	103.17	C	105.33	114.10	105.08	90.81
13	C	127.19	122.09	115.22	C	104.33	103.03	104.35	105.60	C	104.74	89.12
14	C	125.42	122.10	C	106.46	103.56	C	103.59	106.07	C	101.98	89.63
15	134.60	124.43	121.60	C	106.14	102.26	C	103.35	C	113.13	101.63	C
16	134.03	124.55	121.22	114.55	106.10	C	103.97	103.31	C	113.14	101.38	C
17	134.07	C	C	113.64	105.19	C	104.64	103.71	106.27	112.66	C	89.13
18	134.34	C	C	113.71	102.89	100.77	105.77	C	106.30	112.82	C	90.56
19	133.87	C	119.94	114.15	C	100.96	106.52	C	107.91	113.25	99.00	90.24
20	C	125.01	119.26	C	C	101.19	107.68	102.67	108.76	C	96.58	90.27
21	C	123.95	117.89	C	100.76	100.40	C	102.12	109.46	C	97.32	89.52
22	133.15	123.68	115.69	C	101.59	100.99	C	101.34	C	112.29	C	C
23	132.44	122.34	115.47	113.02	102.09	C	107.75	102.53	C	111.81	97.30	C
24	130.49	C	C	111.23	104.27	C	108.29	102.40	109.69	112.13	C	88.67
25	C	C	C	109.37	105.17	99.43	109.19	C	109.80	112.31	C	C
26	129.76	121.27	115.54	109.72	C	99.96	109.17	C	110.62	112.79	94.13	90.19
27	C	119.80	116.89	108.40	C	100.22	109.36	102.91	111.27	C	93.07	91.25
28	C	120.41	117.14	C	C	101.16	C	102.99	111.20	C	94.94	91.68
29	128.46		118.19	C	104.85	100.98	C	103.79	C	112.09	94.62	C
30	128.22		117.46	107.85	103.19	C	108.88	103.99	C	110.63	93.51	C
31	128.40		C		102.64		108.64	104.87		110.17		92.19
Close	128.40	120.41	117.46	107.85	102.64	100.98	108.64	104.87	111.20	110.17	93.51	92.19
Month Pt Change	−5.33	−7.99	−2.95	−9.61	−5.21	−1.66	7.66	−3.77	6.33	−1.03	−16.66	−1.32
Month % Change	−4.0	−6.2	−2.4	−8.2	−4.8	−1.6	7.6	−3.5	6.0	−0.9	−15.1	−1.4
QTR % Change			−12.2			−14.0			10.1			−17.1
Year % Change												−31.1

HIGHLIGHTS

Post Election Year	Bear Market Begins 1/11	Best Eight Months -31.1%	High Jan-11	136.84
Nixon (2nd Term)	Expansion	Worst Four Months 9.1%	Low Dec-24	88.67

1974 NASDAQ COMPOSITE

Previous Month Close	Jan	Feb	Mar	Apr	May	Jun	Jul	Aug	Sep	Oct	Nov	Dec
	92.19	94.93	94.35	92.27	86.86	80.20	75.96	69.99	62.37	55.67	65.23	62.95
1	C	94.15	94.05	91.90	87.63	C	75.39	69.63	C	55.48	65.06	C
2	92.53	C	C	92.03	87.97	C	73.81	69.40	C	55.67	C	61.66
3	94.18	C	C	92.13	87.47	81.08	73.66	C	60.88	54.87	C	60.50
4	94.10	92.89	93.80	91.88	C	81.77	C	C	58.95	55.16	64.62	60.41
5	C	92.46	94.71	90.70	C	82.21	73.57	69.67	60.22	C	65.99	58.92
6	C	92.74	95.12	C	87.31	83.20	C	70.53	60.70	C	66.11	58.21
7	94.47	92.81	94.53	C	86.66	83.71	C	71.68	C	56.57	66.64	C
8	94.02	92.20	95.17	89.92	85.74	C	70.96	70.66	C	56.13	66.51	C
9	92.20	C	C	90.18	85.81	C	70.59	70.69	59.37	57.57	C	57.91
10	91.42	C	C	89.87	84.30	83.92	69.82	C	58.97	59.13	C	58.76
11	92.23	91.13	95.87	89.79	C	83.34	69.65	C	58.96	60.42	66.72	59.27
12	C	90.50	95.80	C	C	83.10	71.68	70.36	57.71	C	65.36	59.36
13	C	90.08	96.33	C	83.18	83.24	C	68.82	56.66	C	64.98	59.22
14	92.40	90.21	96.51	C	83.16	82.76	C	67.25	C	61.73	65.04	C
15	93.07	90.98	96.53	89.42	83.51	C	71.98	66.88	C	61.40	64.41	C
16	94.49	C	C	90.33	83.50	C	71.63	65.86	57.24	61.19	C	58.85
17	95.95	C	C	90.72	81.93	81.54	72.71	C	57.72	62.04	C	59.18
18	95.32	C	95.37	90.90	C	81.25	72.81	C	58.12	62.75	62.09	59.63
19	C	90.82	94.75	90.31	C	80.66	73.40	65.13	59.52	C	60.93	59.46
20	C	91.56	94.95	C	81.43	79.85	C	65.72	59.90	C	60.75	58.67
21	94.48	92.17	95.36	C	81.29	79.11	C	64.92	C	63.82	61.49	C
22	95.29	92.93	95.45	90.27	80.72	C	73.42	63.59	C	64.14	62.07	C
23	95.76	C	C	88.47	80.55	C	74.44	62.57	59.66	63.40	C	57.86
24	95.61	C	C	86.95	81.45	78.88	74.63	C	58.84	62.60	C	58.30
25	95.40	92.72	95.35	86.04	C	79.35	73.51	C	58.76	62.88	61.68	C
26	C	93.11	95.27	86.24	C	78.27	72.83	62.94	57.87	C	62.65	58.88
27	C	94.06	94.21	C	C	76.83	C	62.34	57.12	C	62.80	58.74
28	95.02	94.35	92.87	C	81.06	75.96	C	62.43	C	62.50	C	C
29	94.56		92.27	86.46	79.78	C	71.49	61.37	C	63.67	62.95	C
30	95.17		C	86.86	80.09	C	71.30	62.37	55.67	64.88	C	58.78
31	94.93		C		80.20		69.99	C		65.23		59.82
Close	94.93	94.35	92.27	86.86	80.20	75.96	69.99	62.37	55.67	65.23	62.95	59.82
Month Pt Change	2.74	-0.58	-2.08	-5.41	-6.66	-4.24	-5.97	-7.62	-6.70	9.56	-2.28	-3.13
Month % Change	3.0	-0.6	-2.2	-5.9	-7.7	-5.30	-7.9	-10.9	-10.7	17.2	-3.5	-5.0
QTR % Change			0.1			-17.7			-26.7			7.5
Year % Change												-35.1

HIGHLIGHTS

Mid-Term Election Year	Bull Market Begins 12/6	Best Eight Months 33.4%	High Mar-15 96.53
Nixon (2nd Term) Ford 8/9/74 Recession		Worst Four Months -14.1%	Low Oct-03 54.87

NASDAQ COMPOSITE 1975

Previous Month	Jan	Feb	Mar	Apr	May	Jun	Jul	Aug	Sep	Oct	Nov	Dec
Close	59.82	69.78	73.00	75.66	78.54	83.10	87.02	83.19	79.01	74.33	76.99	78.80
1	C	C	C	75.42	79.27	C	86.33	81.82	C	73.80	C	78.66
2	60.70	C	C	75.62	80.25	83.88	85.64	C	77.89	74.16	C	77.33
3	61.23	70.73	73.83	74.95	C	84.14	86.20	C	78.08	75.50	76.62	75.67
4	C	70.13	74.21	74.73	C	84.08	C	80.98	78.13	C	76.86	75.20
5	C	71.07	73.90	C	81.14	84.24	C	80.17	77.78	C	77.30	74.72
6	61.74	71.46	74.02	C	80.81	84.77	C	80.24	C	76.03	77.39	C
7	61.89	71.12	74.40	74.34	81.31	C	85.60	79.59	C	75.88	77.21	C
8	61.50	C	C	74.53	82.12	C	85.39	79.55	77.46	76.61	C	74.92
9	62.37	C	C	75.40	82.82	84.01	86.50	C	76.60	76.87	C	74.52
10	63.69	70.82	74.88	75.76	C	83.40	86.83	C	75.24	76.96	77.46	75.25
11	C	70.83	75.04	76.31	C	83.60	87.20	79.45	74.85	C	78.00	75.08
12	C	71.59	74.13	C	82.30	82.99	C	79.60	74.72	C	79.27	74.91
13	63.34	72.88	74.68	C	82.35	83.43	C	79.09	C	77.70	79.22	C
14	63.11	73.26	76.07	77.33	82.91	C	87.58	78.45	C	78.19	78.98	C
15	63.87	C	C	77.51	82.79	C	88.00	78.58	74.47	78.20	C	74.54
16	64.80	C	C	78.00	82.44	84.01	87.39	C	73.78	78.22	C	75.19
17	64.40	C	76.27	78.26	C	83.43	87.13	C	73.87	77.63	79.10	75.80
18	C	72.47	76.18	78.08	C	83.47	87.02	78.03	74.78	C	78.62	76.07
19	C	72.87	75.67	C	81.99	84.55	C	76.65	76.39	C	77.87	75.92
20	64.44	73.58	75.78	C	81.82	85.24	C	75.52	C	78.13	77.67	C
21	64.18	73.79	75.92	79.08	80.95	C	86.77	75.90	C	78.43	77.74	C
22	64.12	C	C	78.54	81.56	C	85.72	76.45	75.86	78.91	C	75.59
23	64.49	C	C	78.24	82.62	85.77	84.62	C	75.94	79.06	C	75.88
24	65.38	73.14	74.42	78.07	C	86.23	84.14	C	76.43	78.62	77.92	76.37
25	C	72.07	74.33	78.64	C	86.30	83.60	76.84	76.10	C	78.18	C
26	C	72.24	75.56	C	C	86.45	C	76.21	76.14	C	78.56	77.13
27	67.04	72.53	76.18	C	82.49	86.50	C	76.57	C	78.29	C	C
28	67.92	73.00	C	78.28	81.98	C	83.09	78.06	C	78.73	78.80	C
29	69.08		C	77.82	81.78	C	82.67	79.01	75.37	77.58	C	76.94
30	68.99		C	78.54	83.10	87.02	83.03	C	74.33	77.45	C	76.67
31	69.78		75.66		C		83.19	C		76.99		77.62
Close	69.78	73.00	75.66	78.54	83.10	87.02	83.19	79.01	74.33	76.99	78.80	77.62
Month Pt Change	9.96	3.22	2.66	2.88	4.56	3.92	–3.83	–4.18	–4.68	2.66	1.81	–1.18
Month % Change	16.6	4.6	3.6	3.8	5.8	4.7	–4.4	–5.0	–5.9	3.6	2.4	–1.5
QTR % Change			26.5			15.0			–14.6			4.4
Year % Change												29.8

HIGHLIGHTS

Pre-Election Year	Bull Market	Best Eight Months 17.3%	High Jul-15	88.00
Ford	Expansion Begins Q2	Worst Four Months -11.5%	Low Jan-02	60.70

1976 NASDAQ COMPOSITE

Previous Month Close	Jan	Feb	Mar	Apr	May	Jun	Jul	Aug	Sep	Oct	Nov	Dec
	77.62	87.05	90.26	90.62	90.08	88.04	90.32	91.29	89.70	91.26	90.35	91.12
1	C	C	90.25	90.44	C	87.81	90.28	C	90.59	90.44	90.39	91.83
2	78.06	87.28	90.54	90.63	C	88.16	90.88	91.27	90.68	C	C	91.84
3	C	87.38	90.17	C	89.05	88.26	C	92.01	91.02	C	89.38	92.31
4	C	88.45	89.65	C	89.24	87.75	C	91.87	C	90.46	90.06	C
5	78.76	88.02	89.47	91.43	89.24	C	C	91.48	C	89.75	89.47	C
6	80.27	87.25	C	91.55	89.42	C	90.62	91.64	C	89.03	C	92.63
7	80.99	C	C	90.80	90.02	87.22	90.60	C	91.21	89.63	C	93.01
8	81.65	C	89.97	90.04	C	87.12	90.79	C	91.26	89.38	88.74	93.37
9	82.31	87.83	89.98	88.89	C	86.95	91.48	91.33	90.86	C	88.08	94.10
10	C	87.95	90.20	C	90.55	87.31	C	91.89	91.19	C	87.82	94.62
11	C	88.69	91.21	C	90.59	87.71	C	91.81	C	89.02	88.15	C
12	82.71	88.88	90.99	88.60	90.64	C	91.94	91.89	C	88.76	88.10	C
13	82.42	88.96	C	88.66	90.22	C	91.97	91.81	90.96	89.30	C	94.62
14	83.62	C	C	88.75	89.78	88.40	92.44	C	90.53	88.73	C	94.65
15	83.73	C	89.72	89.17	C	88.45	92.52	C	90.63	89.06	88.13	94.92
16	84.30	C	89.86	C	C	88.93	92.40	91.77	91.04	C	88.52	94.93
17	C	88.82	90.11	C	89.49	89.72	C	92.01	91.61	C	89.01	94.64
18	C	89.23	89.55	C	89.53	90.05	C	91.85	C	89.46	89.81	C
19	84.73	90.14	89.54	89.59	89.25	C	92.08	90.74	C	89.45	89.97	C
20	84.90	91.02	C	90.61	89.53	C	91.68	90.19	91.89	89.63	C	94.47
21	84.95	C	C	90.77	89.39	90.15	91.53	C	92.42	89.49	C	94.68
22	84.62	C	89.69	90.96	C	89.54	91.66	C	92.44	89.26	90.47	95.18
23	85.26	91.31	90.36	90.60	C	89.19	91.60	89.60	92.27	C	90.22	95.22
24	C	91.73	90.93	C	88.15	89.80	C	89.13	92.31	C	90.69	C
25	C	92.09	90.67	C	87.81	90.05	C	89.55	C	89.37	C	C
26	85.05	91.45	90.89	90.57	88.10	C	91.48	89.20	C	89.42	91.42	C
27	84.76	90.26	C	89.98	87.78	C	91.30	89.14	92.44	89.62	C	95.68
28	84.63	C	C	90.30	88.04	89.87	91.01	C	91.64	89.85	C	96.22
29	86.15	C	90.69	90.55	C	90.11	90.85	C	91.27	90.35	91.08	96.29
30	87.05		90.49	90.08	C	90.32	91.29	89.28	91.26	C	91.12	97.05
31	C		90.62		C		C	89.70		C		97.88
Close	87.05	90.26	90.62	90.08	88.04	90.32	91.29	89.70	91.26	90.35	91.12	97.88
Month Pt Change	9.43	3.21	0.36	-0.54	-2.04	2.28	0.97	-1.59	1.56	-0.91	0.77	6.76
Month % Change	12.1	3.7	0.4	-0.6	-2.3	2.6	1.1	-1.7	1.7	-1.0	0.9	7.4
QTR % Change			16.7			-0.3			1.0			7.3
Year % Change												26.1

HIGHLIGHTS

Election Year	Bear Market Begins 9/21	Best Eight Months 10.4%	High Dec-31 97.88
Ford	Expansion	Worst Four Months 0.03%	Low Jan-02 78.06

Previous Month Close	Jan	Feb	Mar	Apr	May	Jun	Jul	Aug	Sep	Oct	Nov	Dec
	97.88	95.54	94.57	94.13	95.48	95.59	99.73	100.65	100.10	100.85	97.52	103.15
1	C	96.30	95.14	94.54	C	95.86	99.90	100.76	100.40	C	96.74	103.68
2	C	96.46	95.19	C	95.83	95.80	C	100.40	100.83	C	96.51	104.10
3	97.69	96.33	95.53	C	96.21	96.19	C	100.02	C	101.16	96.49	C
4	97.22	96.74	96.07	93.90	96.63	C	C	100.39	C	100.81	97.21	C
5	96.89	C	C	93.66	96.89	C	100.12	100.86	C	100.82	C	104.15
6	97.29	C	C	93.89	96.90	96.11	99.96	C	100.78	101.31	C	102.97
7	97.53	96.61	96.17	94.03	C	96.17	100.28	C	101.16	101.62	97.85	102.85
8	C	96.59	96.23	C	C	96.59	100.81	100.55	101.28	C	98.21	103.06
9	C	95.99	95.75	C	96.76	96.63	C	100.52	100.91	C	98.70	103.57
10	97.31	96.29	95.94	C	97.16	97.07	C	100.81	C	101.69	99.98	C
11	96.41	96.09	96.07	94.37	96.92	C	100.85	100.94	C	101.23	100.94	C
12	96.02	C	C	95.06	96.96	C	100.75	100.76	100.60	99.83	C	103.89
13	96.84	C	C	95.10	97.41	97.28	100.93	C	100.46	99.03	C	104.10
14	97.20	96.13	96.19	96.00	C	97.70	C	C	100.61	99.05	100.98	103.96
15	C	96.41	96.39	96.26	C	97.67	101.41	100.89	100.97	C	101.52	103.89
16	C	96.62	96.58	C	97.79	98.22	C	100.65	100.74	C	101.56	104.05
17	97.14	96.56	96.42	C	97.90	98.61	C	100.72	C	99.14	101.86	C
18	97.13	96.38	96.44	96.17	98.47	C	102.01	100.86	C	99.25	102.22	C
19	97.55	C	C	96.10	98.36	C	102.38	100.85	100.35	98.45	C	103.30
20	97.08	C	C	96.36	98.00	98.72	102.43	C	100.23	98.60	C	102.50
21	97.32	C	96.26	95.82	C	98.83	102.70	C	99.76	98.54	102.35	103.03
22	C	96.14	96.05	95.12	C	98.78	103.11	101.05	99.47	C	102.93	103.41
23	C	95.76	95.76	C	97.15	99.17	C	100.94	99.57	C	103.74	103.94
24	97.37	94.84	95.54	C	96.66	99.66	C	100.75	C	97.89	C	C
25	97.06	94.90	95.28	94.26	96.18	C	103.01	100.14	C	96.83	104.33	C
26	96.51	C	C	94.12	96.17	C	102.40	99.89	99.74	96.86	C	C
27	96.04	C	C	94.79	95.90	99.63	101.25	C	99.74	97.07	C	103.96
28	95.72	94.57	94.85	95.06	C	99.28	100.68	C	99.96	97.49	104.06	104.04
29	C		94.92	95.48	C	99.34	100.65	100.37	100.27	C	103.20	104.42
30	C		94.23	C	C	99.73	C	100.11	100.85	C	103.15	105.05
31	95.54		94.13		95.59		C	100.10		97.52		C
Close	95.54	94.57	94.13	95.48	95.59	99.73	100.65	100.10	100.85	97.52	103.15	105.05
Month Pt Change	-2.34	-0.97	-0.44	1.35	0.11	4.14	0.92	-0.55	0.75	-3.33	5.63	1.90
Month % Change	-2.4	-1.0	-0.5	1.4	0.1	4.3	0.9	-0.5	0.7	-3.3	5.8	1.8
QTR % Change			-3.8			5.9			1.1			4.2
Year % Change												7.3

HIGHLIGHTS

Post Election Year	Bear Market	Best Eight Months	23.4%	High	Dec-30	105.05
Carter	Expansion	Worst Four Months	-2.2%	Low	Apr-05	93.66

1978 NASDAQ COMPOSITE

Previous Month Close	Jan	Feb	Mar	Apr	May	Jun	Jul	Aug	Sep	Oct	Nov	Dec
Close	105.05	100.84	101.47	106.20	115.18	120.24	120.30	126.32	135.01	132.89	111.12	114.69
1	C	101.54	101.47	C	115.96	120.34	C	126.81	135.35	C	114.65	116.19
2	C	101.94	101.71	C	116.12	121.03	C	128.16	C	133.30	114.63	C
3	104.00	102.22	101.95	105.89	116.21	C	120.15	129.02	C	133.11	115.49	C
4	103.66	C	C	106.20	116.48	C	C	129.71	C	133.10	C	116.57
5	103.21	C	C	106.95	117.27	122.10	119.22	C	135.46	133.54	C	117.67
6	101.66	102.27	101.74	107.47	C	122.85	118.82	C	136.48	134.00	115.08	118.45
7	C	102.75	102.02	108.23	C	123.10	119.16	130.21	137.09	C	112.83	118.55
8	C	103.18	102.41	C	117.14	123.99	C	130.49	138.36	C	112.99	118.77
9	100.20	103.20	102.82	C	117.05	124.41	C	131.64	C	134.64	113.88	C
10	99.58	103.58	103.42	108.53	117.55	C	119.38	131.58	C	134.93	114.84	C
11	99.09	C	C	108.44	118.25	C	119.83	132.00	138.95	135.27	C	119.15
12	99.54	C	C	108.87	119.40	124.29	120.28	C	139.24	135.57	C	118.50
13	99.77	103.34	103.53	109.99	C	124.24	120.43	C	139.25	135.58	113.00	118.13
14	C	102.78	103.66	111.29	C	124.51	121.58	132.11	138.34	C	110.88	118.15
15	C	102.56	103.80	C	119.80	124.19	C	131.95	137.36	C	111.44	117.41
16	99.36	102.17	104.38	C	120.78	123.69	C	132.77	C	133.94	112.21	C
17	99.98	102.25	104.94	111.91	121.84	C	122.36	134.14	C	130.96	113.69	C
18	100.42	C	C	111.43	121.66	C	122.09	134.71	135.65	128.92	C	114.33
19	100.58	C	C	111.64	121.57	122.92	122.80	C	134.06	127.22	C	114.73
20	100.63	C	105.36	112.86	C	122.03	123.75	C	132.66	123.82	114.51	115.33
21	C	101.99	105.02	113.32	C	120.63	123.60	133.77	132.10	C	114.56	115.85
22	C	102.13	105.16	C	121.93	120.68	C	133.87	132.30	C	115.37	116.93
23	100.34	102.16	105.39	C	120.97	120.74	C	134.73	C	121.94	C	C
24	100.54	102.70	C	113.60	119.80	C	123.59	135.28	C	121.14	116.17	C
25	100.87	C	C	114.28	119.82	C	123.79	135.84	132.11	121.16	C	C
26	100.53	C	C	114.70	119.86	119.54	124.48	C	132.92	118.00	C	117.68
27	100.62	102.22	105.30	114.59	C	119.18	125.13	C	132.01	115.25	115.97	117.33
28	C	101.47	105.68	115.18	C	119.52	125.62	135.24	132.11	C	115.60	117.30
29	C		106.08	C	C	119.98	C	134.63	132.89	C	114.09	117.98
30	100.97		106.18	C	120.00	120.30	C	134.75	C	112.40	114.69	C
31	100.84		106.20		120.24		126.32	135.01		111.12		C
Close	100.84	101.47	106.20	115.18	120.24	120.30	126.32	135.01	132.89	111.12	114.69	117.98
Month Pt Change	−4.21	0.63	4.73	8.98	5.06	0.06	6.02	8.69	−2.12	−21.77	3.57	3.29
Month % Change	−4.0	0.6	4.7	8.5	4.4	0.1	5.0	6.9	−1.6	−16.4	3.2	2.9
QTR % Change			1.1			13.3			10.5			−11.2
Year % Change												12.3

Previous Month Close	Jan	Feb	Mar	Apr	May	Jun	Jul	Aug	Sep	Oct	Nov	Dec
Close	117.98	125.82	122.56	131.76	133.82	131.42	138.13	141.33	150.44	149.98	135.53	144.26
1	C	125.76	123.33	C	133.79	131.76	C	141.90	C	149.59	136.42	C
2	117.84	125.82	123.67	131.36	133.99	C	136.98	142.54	C	150.01	136.88	C
3	119.11	C	C	132.33	134.20	C	137.03	142.63	C	150.51	C	143.86
4	120.66	C	C	132.75	133.72	131.95	C	C	148.49	151.42	C	144.80
5	122.05	124.34	124.72	133.37	C	133.02	137.79	C	146.03	152.29	136.11	145.92
6	C	124.31	124.43	133.75	C	133.62	138.64	142.41	146.87	C	135.66	147.04
7	C	122.80	125.61	C	130.60	134.55	C	143.30	148.07	C	134.14	147.49
8	121.92	123.41	127.05	C	129.60	134.96	C	144.06	C	150.98	134.77	C
9	122.66	123.76	127.25	133.74	130.34	C	139.15	144.27	C	145.20	135.86	C
10	122.28	C	C	134.22	129.71	C	138.97	145.07	148.91	139.31	C	147.97
11	122.76	C	C	133.57	129.69	135.04	138.85	C	148.39	140.09	C	147.83
12	123.74	124.05	127.19	133.54	C	135.92	138.68	C	148.66	140.71	137.05	148.51
13	C	124.89	127.69	C	C	136.01	138.52	146.07	149.33	C	137.14	148.97
14	C	124.61	127.59	C	128.99	136.02	C	146.30	150.56	C	137.76	150.03
15	124.47	124.93	127.85	C	129.01	136.25	C	147.14	C	138.39	138.92	C
16	123.74	125.57	128.55	132.48	129.35	C	138.89	147.44	C	138.34	139.07	C
17	123.59	C	C	132.26	130.44	C	137.86	147.84	150.46	139.04	C	150.56
18	124.31	C	C	132.91	131.01	135.85	137.26	C	149.19	139.46	C	149.72
19	124.65	C	129.14	133.18	C	136.05	137.57	C	149.44	136.59	139.98	149.65
20	C	125.83	128.79	133.67	C	136.45	137.98	147.95	150.20	C	139.50	150.27
21	C	125.76	129.44	C	131.16	136.71	C	147.99	150.65	C	138.88	150.17
22	124.66	125.45	130.08	C	131.90	137.24	C	148.74	C	133.16	C	C
23	125.46	125.04	130.58	133.87	132.12	C	137.57	149.13	C	132.61	139.85	C
24	125.34	C	C	134.29	132.10	C	138.02	149.40	150.12	133.02	C	149.97
25	126.42	C	C	134.78	132.68	136.89	138.97	C	149.27	132.73	C	C
26	127.04	124.90	130.11	134.64	C	136.53	139.52	C	149.88	133.75	141.95	150.01
27	C	122.64	130.78	134.37	C	137.40	140.02	149.51	150.37	C	142.55	150.23
28	C	122.56	130.87	C	C	138.08	C	149.54	149.98	C	143.53	150.83
29	126.77		131.29	C	132.46	138.13	C	150.04	C	133.91	144.16	C
30	126.51		131.76	133.82	131.39	C	140.54	150.06	C	135.48	144.26	C
31	125.82		C		131.42		141.33	150.44		135.53		151.14
Close	125.82	122.56	131.76	133.82	131.42	138.13	141.33	150.44	149.98	135.53	144.26	151.14
Month Pt Change	7.84	–3.26	9.20	2.06	–2.40	6.71	3.20	9.11	–0.46	–14.45	8.73	6.88
Month % Change	6.6	–2.6	7.5	1.6	–1.8	5.1	2.3	6.4	–0.3	–9.6	6.4	4.8
QTR % Change			11.7			4.8			8.6			0.8
Year % Change												28.1

HIGHLIGHTS

Pre-Election Year	Bear Market	Best Eight Months 16.4%	High Oct-05	152.29
Carter	Expansion	Worst Four Months -1.9%	Low Jan-02	117.84

	Jan	Feb	Mar	Apr	May	Jun	Jul	Aug	Sep	Oct	Nov	Dec
Previous Month Close	151.14	161.75	158.03	131.00	139.99	150.45	157.78	171.81	181.52	187.76	192.78	208.15
1	C	162.30	C	133.14	139.68	C	158.17	172.49	C	189.62	C	204.91
2	148.17	C	C	135.80	140.25	150.17	159.18	C	182.34	190.81	C	203.71
3	145.97	C	156.87	136.01	C	149.92	160.87	C	184.53	193.43	193.15	204.90
4	148.02	162.02	155.39	C	C	151.21	C	171.89	185.05	C	C	206.19
5	C	162.20	152.94	C	141.04	152.21	C	172.52	185.61	C	196.03	203.02
6	C	162.99	148.64	C	142.23	152.68	C	173.45	C	196.01	193.96	C
7	148.62	163.77	146.19	133.40	143.58	C	163.63	175.24	C	196.17	193.51	C
8	150.68	165.25	C	134.47	143.26	C	163.58	175.88	184.45	197.18	C	195.87
9	151.60	C	C	136.04	143.06	153.00	164.09	C	184.84	197.53	C	195.07
10	153.12	C	143.75	137.28	C	154.15	163.84	C	186.31	197.79	193.10	193.58
11	153.87	164.46	144.56	137.75	C	155.22	164.82	177.11	188.16	C	195.02	188.75
12	C	164.57	144.63	C	142.96	155.31	C	176.62	189.58	C	197.78	191.22
13	C	164.98	144.97	C	144.10	156.59	C	177.02	C	198.87	200.25	C
14	154.40	163.54	144.44	136.67	145.66	C	166.52	178.76	C	199.02	201.76	C
15	154.96	162.56	C	136.39	146.62	C	167.05	179.89	189.59	199.43	C	191.83
16	155.99	C	C	135.76	147.24	156.79	167.10	C	191.31	197.95	C	191.88
17	155.81	C	139.70	134.55	C	156.98	168.67	C	193.95	197.24	201.59	194.02
18	156.14	C	138.92	134.66	C	157.19	169.99	177.24	193.61	C	203.76	196.01
19	C	161.06	139.97	C	147.24	156.73	C	176.28	195.33	C	205.02	197.91
20	C	162.10	139.64	C	146.93	156.51	C	177.68	C	197.15	206.50	C
21	157.35	161.31	138.80	133.08	146.75	C	170.48	179.91	C	196.46	206.07	C
22	156.92	160.08	C	135.71	147.96	C	169.79	181.70	195.94	197.90	C	199.79
23	158.50	C	C	136.92	149.48	156.99	169.82	C	195.05	195.81	C	199.86
24	159.24	C	134.61	138.69	C	157.66	169.92	C	195.18	196.17	204.22	200.14
25	159.70	157.97	132.52	137.92	C	158.74	169.63	181.58	194.05	C	205.41	C
26	C	158.50	132.22	C	C	159.00	C	182.39	190.77	C	207.06	201.28
27	C	157.73	124.09	C	150.10	159.18	C	182.15	C	194.35	C	C
28	160.70	157.46	129.25	138.54	150.70	C	170.02	180.99	C	193.76	208.15	C
29	160.29	158.03	C	139.35	150.09	C	171.06	181.52	185.79	194.49	C	199.84
30	161.30		C	139.99	150.45	157.78	172.33	C	187.76	192.51	C	200.46
31	161.75		131.00		C		171.81	C		192.78		202.34
Close	161.75	158.03	131.00	139.99	150.45	157.78	171.81	181.52	187.76	192.78	208.15	202.34
Month Pt Change	10.61	−3.72	−27.03	8.99	10.46	7.33	14.03	9.71	6.24	5.02	15.37	−5.81
Month % Change	7.0	−2.3	−17.1	6.9	7.5	4.9	8.9	5.7	3.4	2.7	8.0	−2.8
QTR % Change			−13.3			20.4			19.0			7.8
Year % Change												33.9

NASDAQ COMPOSITE 1981

Previous Month	Jan	Feb	Mar	Apr	May	Jun	Jul	Aug	Sep	Oct	Nov	Dec
Close	202.34	197.81	198.01	210.18	216.74	223.47	215.75	211.63	195.75	180.03	195.24	201.37
1	C	C	C	211.34	216.68	223.02	214.63	C	195.17	181.09	C	201.13
2	203.55	193.09	199.06	211.96	C	219.59	212.80	C	195.39	184.37	197.25	200.35
3	C	193.56	198.35	212.65	C	218.89	C	210.40	191.99	C	198.78	199.90
4	C	194.57	198.75	C	213.32	219.68	C	210.09	189.63	C	199.73	200.88
5	204.17	196.29	199.05	C	211.55	221.30	C	211.03	C	185.91	200.02	C
6	204.07	197.87	199.89	211.27	211.98	C	209.10	211.67	C	185.87	199.97	C
7	197.35	C	C	211.76	213.66	C	208.01	211.36	C	188.78	C	199.71
8	195.89	C	C	212.80	214.84	220.84	208.44	C	184.79	191.01	C	198.13
9	197.66	196.93	200.14	213.91	C	220.01	210.03	C	184.77	191.27	199.92	198.29
10	C	196.70	199.03	215.15	C	220.40	210.54	210.84	187.55	C	199.90	198.92
11	C	195.81	198.16	C	212.79	222.34	C	211.67	189.81	C	200.05	198.64
12	198.44	194.61	200.67	C	213.12	222.76	C	211.95	C	191.28	200.99	C
13	198.05	193.89	202.17	214.33	213.78	C	210.86	212.36	C	191.92	200.16	C
14	199.08	C	C	213.39	215.18	C	209.88	212.12	189.62	189.43	C	195.67
15	199.85	C	C	214.98	216.51	222.96	210.84	C	189.56	189.85	C	195.16
16	201.13	C	203.44	216.64	C	220.58	212.02	C	187.82	190.24	197.16	195.09
17	C	193.98	203.19	C	C	220.61	212.76	209.65	185.71	C	197.68	195.70
18	C	194.73	204.00	C	216.94	218.71	C	207.01	184.27	C	197.60	197.01
19	201.58	192.74	204.45	C	216.12	219.56	C	207.22	C	189.77	197.32	C
20	198.72	192.29	206.29	217.55	217.63	C	209.27	207.97	C	191.23	198.60	C
21	198.09	C	C	216.73	218.35	C	207.17	206.76	184.41	192.38	C	196.37
22	197.12	C	C	217.19	219.23	218.60	206.16	C	183.26	192.43	C	195.64
23	197.52	193.06	207.62	218.02	C	219.23	206.41	C	179.99	191.91	198.01	195.45
24	C	193.94	207.70	219.56	C	218.77	208.00	200.76	180.39	C	199.04	195.70
25	C	193.99	209.31	C	C	219.31	C	197.78	175.12	C	200.01	C
26	196.13	196.13	209.53	C	220.24	219.76	C	197.81	C	191.01	C	C
27	197.18	198.01	208.82	219.88	222.17	C	209.42	196.82	C	192.61	201.02	C
28	197.37	C	C	217.63	223.31	C	208.91	197.55	175.03	193.75	C	195.14
29	197.88		C	216.22	223.47	218.22	208.95	C	178.51	193.08	C	193.91
30	197.81		208.96	216.74	C	215.75	210.03	C	180.03	195.24	201.37	194.66
31	C		210.18		C		211.63	195.75		C		195.84
Close	197.81	198.01	210.18	216.74	223.47	215.75	211.63	195.75	180.03	195.24	201.37	195.84
Month Pt Change	-4.53	0.20	12.17	6.56	6.73	-7.72	-4.12	-15.88	-15.72	15.21	6.13	-5.53
Month % Change	-2.2	0.1	6.1	3.1	3.1	-3.5	-1.9	-7.5	-8.0	8.4	3.1	-2.7
QTR % Change			3.9			2.7			-16.6			8.8
Year % Change												-3.2

HIGHLIGHTS

Post Election Year	Bear Market Begins 4/27	Best Eight Months-12.3%	High May-29	223.47
Reagan (1st term)	Recession Begins Q3	Worst Four Months-9.5%	Low Sep-28	175.03

1982 NASDAQ COMPOSITE

Previous Month Close	Jan	Feb	Mar	Apr	May	Jun	Jul	Aug	Sep	Oct	Nov	Dec
Close	195.84	188.39	179.43	175.65	184.70	178.54	171.30	167.35	177.71	187.65	212.63	232.31
1	C	186.82	180.13	177.31	C	177.36	170.60	C	177.30	188.70	214.52	235.59
2	C	187.46	180.14	178.56	C	177.82	170.05	168.37	179.50	C	217.65	236.18
3	C	187.43	178.01	C	184.97	177.10	C	167.97	182.05	C	222.77	237.16
4	195.53	187.14	176.29	C	185.95	174.82	C	166.56	C	188.02	225.01	C
5	192.33	188.21	173.97	178.21	185.88	C	C	165.15	C	188.77	227.03	C
6	191.15	C	C	178.68	187.27	C	169.22	163.59	C	191.98	C	239.29
7	191.02	C	C	179.91	188.13	173.84	168.08	C	180.88	195.59	C	240.65
8	192.05	184.63	171.03	181.15	C	173.28	166.80	C	181.79	198.89	226.74	240.70
9	C	182.51	169.71	C	C	170.94	168.07	161.38	182.77	C	230.19	237.24
10	C	182.97	170.42	C	187.57	171.37	C	161.32	182.47	C	230.41	233.85
11	188.80	182.25	170.09	C	188.19	173.55	C	160.77	C	202.31	231.52	C
12	187.32	182.52	168.23	180.89	188.06	C	168.85	159.84	C	202.16	232.61	C
13	185.73	C	C	180.76	187.66	C	169.35	159.14	182.90	205.17	C	233.33
14	185.89	C	C	180.41	188.22	172.15	169.21	C	184.60	204.85	C	231.33
15	187.32	C	167.92	181.12	C	171.19	169.61	C	186.31	204.46	229.34	225.69
16	C	180.71	168.28	182.25	C	171.44	170.18	159.68	186.80	C	224.97	225.60
17	C	181.25	168.20	C	186.90	169.85	C	162.28	186.61	C	227.75	228.93
18	187.21	181.38	170.13	C	185.81	168.50	C	164.99	C	206.61	229.28	C
19	186.16	180.65	171.76	182.37	183.91	C	170.09	164.92	C	207.48	229.41	C
20	185.72	C	C	181.94	182.72	C	170.83	166.96	186.00	210.70	C	227.88
21	186.40	C	C	182.32	182.40	168.00	171.54	C	187.91	214.28	C	228.52
22	185.83	179.07	173.83	183.66	C	169.05	172.06	C	188.62	215.29	225.79	231.04
23	C	177.49	174.95	184.93	C	170.86	172.11	169.88	188.15	C	225.17	232.33
24	C	178.58	174.84	C	181.71	171.12	C	172.23	188.61	C	226.88	C
25	183.52	179.44	175.83	C	181.12	170.48	C	174.93	C	210.89	C	C
26	183.41	179.43	175.20	185.80	178.76	C	171.45	178.17	C	209.92	228.64	C
27	183.57	C	C	184.72	178.37	C	170.71	177.60	188.64	212.20	C	233.20
28	186.22	C	C	184.89	178.54	171.07	168.37	C	189.04	211.87	C	232.20
29	188.39		175.50	184.15	C	170.53	167.60	C	188.26	212.63	228.39	232.27
30	C		175.42	184.70	C	171.30	167.35	176.36	187.65	C	232.31	231.28
31	C		175.65		C		C	177.71		C		232.41
Close	188.39	179.43	175.65	184.70	178.54	171.30	167.35	177.71	187.65	212.63	232.31	232.41
Month Pt Change	−7.45	−8.96	−3.78	9.05	−6.16	−7.24	−3.95	10.36	9.94	24.98	19.68	0.10
Month % Change	−3.8	−4.8	−2.1	5.2	−3.3	−4.1	−2.3	6.2	5.6	13.3	9.3	0.04
QTR % Change			−10.3			−2.5			9.5			23.9
Year % Change												18.7

HIGHLIGHTS

Mid-Term Election Year	Bull Market Begins 8/12	Best Eight Months 49.9%	High Dec-08	240.70
Reagan (1st term)	Recession	Worst Four Months 24.1%	Low Aug-13	159.14

NASDAQ COMPOSITE   1983

Previous Month Close	Jan 232.41	Feb 248.35	Mar 260.67	Apr 270.80	May 293.06	Jun 308.73	Jul 318.70	Aug 303.96	Sep 292.42	Oct 296.65	Nov 274.55	Dec 285.67
1	C	248.15	261.82	C	C	307.95	321.58	302.08	294.55	C	273.04	286.07
2	C	248.28	263.40	C	290.54	310.45	C	303.18	297.85	C	275.18	283.91
3	230.59	249.44	265.21	C	289.65	313.85	C	303.86	C	294.64	274.86	C
4	231.64	251.65	265.94	268.73	293.21	C	C	299.70	C	294.81	273.17	C
5	232.73	C	C	268.83	297.32	C	317.15	300.20	C	294.57	C	282.49
6	236.61	C	C	266.47	301.64	315.48	319.14	C	301.23	295.78	C	282.05
7	238.60	252.02	265.39	266.74	C	314.17	320.03	C	300.76	297.36	271.12	282.15
8	C	251.10	263.16	268.10	C	312.49	319.57	294.93	301.79	C	269.57	280.57
9	C	251.38	265.06	C	302.65	312.74	C	294.26	302.23	C	271.00	280.51
10	240.94	254.77	266.08	C	304.34	315.24	C	296.65	C	297.42	273.08	C
11	240.85	256.64	266.18	270.81	302.89	C	320.38	297.56	C	295.41	277.13	C
12	242.91	C	C	272.73	302.15	C	316.93	299.58	300.76	291.59	C	279.94
13	243.48	C	C	275.93	303.94	318.05	314.59	C	297.93	290.44	C	278.92
14	245.63	258.67	264.34	278.81	C	320.04	315.49	C	298.34	290.04	279.51	276.42
15	C	259.06	264.25	281.60	C	322.04	312.87	301.78	297.19	C	278.92	275.35
16	C	259.07	264.66	C	299.60	326.50	C	299.85	298.27	C	279.94	276.01
17	247.14	259.00	264.01	C	301.02	326.11	C	300.84	C	289.69	281.26	C
18	246.65	261.29	265.01	282.83	303.51	C	310.29	299.78	C	283.62	281.28	C
19	245.20	C	C	281.86	302.82	C	311.17	299.10	301.83	279.85	C	275.58
20	245.99	C	C	284.81	303.56	324.63	316.76	C	303.36	281.25	C	274.51
21	243.97	C	266.33	286.84	C	325.96	319.29	C	303.26	279.49	283.05	275.63
22	C	259.18	267.52	288.55	C	328.19	320.71	298.76	304.56	C	284.55	276.21
23	C	259.99	269.26	C	303.86	327.33	C	293.66	303.61	C	284.69	276.54
24	236.73	262.31	270.37	C	307.36	328.91	C	290.86	C	276.81	C	C
25	239.19	262.44	270.89	286.58	309.16	C	320.84	289.53	C	278.60	285.49	C
26	241.43	C	C	288.11	311.39	C	320.38	290.31	303.77	277.85	C	C
27	245.44	C	C	288.93	312.05	324.34	315.04	C	300.78	277.50	C	276.68
28	246.93	260.67	269.15	290.84	C	315.87	308.45	C	299.76	276.14	284.47	276.57
29	C		268.77	293.06	C	316.24	303.96	289.36	299.29	C	285.62	277.06
30	C		270.78	C	C	318.70	C	289.86	296.65	C	285.67	278.60
31	248.35		270.80		308.73		C	292.42		274.55		C
Close	248.35	260.67	270.80	293.06	308.73	318.70	303.96	292.42	296.65	274.55	285.67	278.60
Month Pt Change	15.94	12.32	10.13	22.26	15.67	9.97	–14.74	–11.54	4.23	–22.10	11.12	–7.07
Month % Change	6.9	5.0	3.9	8.2	5.3	3.2	–4.6	–3.8	1.4	–7.4	4.1	–2.5
QTR % Change			16.5			17.7			–6.9			–6.1
Year % Change												19.9

1984 — NASDAQ COMPOSITE

Previous Month Close	Jan	Feb	Mar	Apr	May	Jun	Jul	Aug	Sep	Oct	Nov	Dec
	278.60	268.43	252.57	250.78	247.44	232.82	239.65	229.70	254.64	249.94	247.03	242.53
1	C	266.43	253.50	C	250.26	235.90	C	233.35	C	247.86	247.97	C
2	C	266.16	255.54	249.80	253.01	C	237.91	238.87	C	246.10	247.92	C
3	277.63	264.01	C	248.88	252.55	C	238.29	246.24	C	244.81	C	240.90
4	280.97	C	C	248.51	250.89	238.75	C	C	251.39	245.20	C	240.96
5	284.45	C	253.86	245.74	C	238.43	237.83	C	250.61	245.46	248.41	238.78
6	287.90	258.64	252.24	243.94	C	239.49	236.72	249.27	252.22	C	250.54	239.07
7	C	257.81	249.16	C	251.35	239.89	C	249.09	251.68	C	249.75	238.94
8	C	253.96	249.66	C	252.42	240.35	C	248.02	C	244.56	249.50	C
9	287.27	251.69	249.01	242.84	252.60	C	236.99	250.33	C	244.09	249.50	C
10	287.63	254.04	C	243.45	252.91	C	236.25	252.43	250.53	243.29	C	238.50
11	287.68	C	C	241.79	250.57	238.12	234.82	C	251.80	244.73	C	238.79
12	287.63	C	249.74	242.56	C	237.04	234.22	C	251.45	246.11	249.26	238.67
13	286.85	250.57	250.67	244.01	C	237.78	234.67	251.35	253.34	C	247.84	238.08
14	C	252.43	250.25	C	248.87	235.62	C	250.63	255.60	C	246.98	239.04
15	C	252.73	251.05	C	249.00	235.64	C	249.70	C	247.67	246.01	C
16	286.29	251.84	253.37	243.88	248.68	C	233.69	250.33	C	247.27	245.12	C
17	286.86	251.33	C	245.59	246.12	C	233.50	250.37	255.39	247.09	C	238.46
18	287.21	C	C	245.48	244.61	236.82	232.23	C	253.99	249.76	C	243.44
19	286.49	C	251.65	245.51	C	237.87	230.89	C	253.01	251.18	242.88	244.88
20	284.41	C	252.74	C	C	238.35	229.37	250.22	253.13	C	243.04	244.49
21	C	249.96	252.49	C	243.15	239.75	C	253.33	252.68	C	243.01	244.28
22	C	249.16	250.77	C	240.80	241.11	C	253.86	C	250.56	C	C
23	280.20	247.09	249.98	243.93	239.58	C	227.06	254.12	C	250.61	245.45	C
24	278.82	251.44	C	244.06	235.39	C	225.73	254.78	250.80	250.83	C	245.82
25	277.35	C	C	243.90	235.23	240.85	225.30	C	250.01	249.00	C	C
26	275.61	C	249.30	245.93	C	238.88	227.06	C	250.23	247.38	244.90	246.06
27	273.18	254.32	249.10	246.90	C	237.20	229.30	253.29	250.29	C	245.41	245.65
28	C	251.55	251.01	C	C	238.32	C	254.37	249.94	C	245.04	246.08
29	C	252.57	251.63	C	232.61	239.65	C	254.81	C	246.50	243.30	C
30	269.23		250.78	247.44	231.93	C	228.95	254.56	C	247.45	242.53	C
31	268.43		C		232.82		229.70	254.64		247.03		247.35
Close	268.43	252.57	250.78	247.44	232.82	239.65	229.70	254.64	249.94	247.03	242.53	247.35
Month Pt Change	–10.17	–15.86	–1.79	–3.34	–14.62	6.83	–9.95	24.94	–4.70	–2.91	–4.50	4.82
Month % Change	–3.7	–5.9	–0.7	–1.3	–5.9	2.9	–4.2	10.9	–1.8	–1.2	–1.8	2.0
QTR % Change			–10.0			–4.4			4.3			–1.0
Year % Change												–11.2

HIGHLIGHTS

Election Year	Bull Market Begins 7/24	Best Eight Months	19.9%	High	Jan-06 287.90
Reagan (1st term)	Expansion	Worst Four Months	3.1%	Low	Jul-25 225.30

NASDAQ COMPOSITE 1985

Previous Month Close	Jan	Feb	Mar	Apr	May	Jun	Jul	Aug	Sep	Oct	Nov	Dec
	247.35	278.70	284.17	279.20	280.56	290.80	296.20	301.29	297.71	280.33	292.54	313.95
1	C	278.43	287.16	280.32	279.63	C	296.48	304.01	C	281.77	294.11	C
2	245.91	C	C	279.74	279.01	C	296.91	304.53	C	281.15	C	312.95
3	246.41	C	C	277.86	280.31	290.59	297.33	C	296.56	281.41	C	313.14
4	246.19	280.77	287.06	277.44	C	290.99	C	C	295.58	280.46	294.23	316.68
5	C	282.72	287.10	C	C	291.77	298.58	302.14	295.28	C	295.25	318.19
6	C	284.46	285.45	C	279.85	291.85	C	300.21	296.19	C	296.74	316.59
7	246.04	287.20	283.19	C	280.89	291.03	C	298.20	C	278.30	297.47	C
8	246.00	288.35	282.37	276.45	281.07	C	297.80	298.72	C	276.95	300.02	C
9	247.34	C	C	276.63	283.27	C	297.15	299.14	296.06	278.28	C	316.88
10	250.65	C	C	278.76	287.46	290.70	298.51	C	294.50	279.41	C	317.29
11	252.16	287.43	281.20	280.12	C	290.54	300.52	C	291.43	281.75	302.31	318.86
12	C	286.57	281.42	280.63	C	289.66	302.39	298.31	289.93	C	304.41	320.58
13	C	288.32	278.21	C	288.14	286.93	C	297.02	287.21	C	303.85	323.99
14	255.46	288.35	277.46	C	287.72	287.95	C	297.64	C	284.25	305.21	C
15	257.78	287.72	277.97	281.07	288.33	C	303.04	297.61	C	284.97	306.17	C
16	260.24	C	C	282.28	289.75	C	305.17	296.46	285.38	286.68	C	325.16
17	261.16	C	C	283.33	291.70	287.38	307.77	C	281.07	288.25	C	323.25
18	263.05	C	277.14	283.11	C	287.92	306.88	C	281.04	288.38	306.10	322.48
19	C	286.91	278.85	282.81	C	288.15	307.76	295.63	283.59	C	306.85	322.67
20	C	287.27	278.78	C	294.48	287.37	C	296.36	284.35	C	307.01	323.12
21	266.41	286.99	279.03	C	293.94	288.71	C	297.65	C	287.72	309.27	C
22	268.42	286.18	278.91	281.82	293.03	C	306.83	296.85	C	288.54	310.80	C
23	270.72	C	C	282.57	292.15	C	306.23	296.68	286.09	289.81	C	321.58
24	272.34	C	C	283.07	292.14	289.97	303.71	C	284.12	290.58	C	320.37
25	274.00	283.95	276.26	283.97	C	292.30	304.44	C	281.82	289.49	309.77	C
26	C	285.00	276.18	284.14	C	293.40	304.62	296.29	280.20	C	310.50	320.29
27	C	284.11	277.56	C	C	295.34	C	295.98	280.01	C	313.01	322.75
28	275.03	284.17	278.17	C	290.88	296.20	C	296.99	C	289.17	C	C
29	276.17		279.20	282.11	290.64	C	300.94	297.31	C	291.12	313.95	C
30	278.58		C	280.56	289.94	C	300.59	297.71	280.33	292.26	C	323.13
31	278.70		C		290.80		301.29	C		292.54		324.93
Close	278.70	284.17	279.20	280.56	290.80	296.20	301.29	297.71	280.33	292.54	313.95	324.93
Month Pt Change	31.35	5.47	-4.97	1.36	10.24	5.40	5.09	-3.58	-17.38	12.21	21.41	10.98
Month % Change	12.7	2.0	-1.7	0.5	3.6	1.9	1.7	-1.2	-5.8	4.4	7.3	3.5
QTR % Change			12.9			6.1			-5.4			15.9
Year % Change												31.4

Data Bank

1986   NASDAQ COMPOSITE

Previous Month Close	Jan	Feb	Mar	Apr	May	Jun	Jul	Aug	Sep	Oct	Nov	Dec
	324.93	335.77	359.53	374.72	383.24	400.16	405.51	371.37	382.86	350.67	360.77	359.57
1	C	C	C	374.15	381.67	C	407.61	370.66	C	352.34	C	357.87
2	324.99	C	C	374.13	383.18	399.35	409.48	C	380.14	352.59	C	360.71
3	325.72	337.46	359.78	374.51	C	399.48	411.16	C	378.88	352.75	361.14	363.04
4	C	337.88	361.01	372.23	C	399.05	C	366.66	381.03	C	361.89	364.07
5	C	338.85	359.84	C	386.00	400.03	C	366.75	378.36	C	362.08	362.96
6	325.99	340.76	361.50	C	386.28	400.25	C	364.73	C	353.20	361.23	C
7	329.74	342.20	362.24	369.07	385.33	C	400.96	365.05	C	352.38	360.99	C
8	328.09	C	C	373.09	387.40	C	390.65	365.87	372.78	352.90	C	361.01
9	323.01	C	C	374.16	389.10	394.73	393.39	C	369.55	353.06	C	359.03
10	324.14	344.04	363.93	377.17	C	392.83	392.03	C	366.80	353.53	359.98	359.05
11	C	344.91	367.36	378.91	C	395.44	391.55	369.94	353.34	C	361.31	357.73
12	C	346.27	369.69	C	388.07	396.53	C	373.29	346.78	C	361.19	355.93
13	324.19	347.88	370.35	C	386.66	399.59	C	376.92	C	354.05	358.00	C
14	324.79	350.21	371.83	380.84	387.34	C	384.80	379.52	C	353.77	358.59	C
15	328.19	C	C	381.71	385.75	C	378.70	380.18	345.86	355.65	C	353.32
16	330.01	C	C	387.64	384.67	398.54	379.73	C	343.67	356.23	C	353.77
17	330.72	C	370.01	389.96	C	396.28	381.59	C	346.90	355.72	357.07	352.29
18	C	352.36	371.52	390.06	C	395.24	381.07	379.27	348.60	C	352.62	351.38
19	C	352.09	371.69	C	383.74	396.40	C	378.82	349.43	C	349.80	352.24
20	329.51	353.11	372.71	C	385.28	396.88	C	380.93	C	353.51	352.19	C
21	328.52	355.65	372.59	391.04	386.05	C	379.46	381.15	C	353.10	354.65	C
22	326.76	C	C	390.48	389.62	C	379.87	381.52	352.55	353.92	C	351.30
23	326.69	C	C	389.05	391.91	396.83	379.85	C	353.37	356.20	C	348.76
24	328.85	355.49	370.67	391.52	C	398.92	378.74	C	354.52	356.66	356.10	349.62
25	C	354.88	369.28	392.34	C	402.22	379.83	379.26	351.49	C	356.95	C
26	C	355.27	370.60	C	C	402.87	C	380.49	351.61	C	358.15	350.01
27	330.20	358.06	373.31	C	394.89	403.53	C	381.69	C	356.58	C	C
28	332.64	359.53	C	391.43	397.16	C	374.78	382.40	C	357.20	359.57	C
29	334.72		C	389.18	397.97	C	372.03	382.86	347.83	358.45	C	348.03
30	334.32		C	383.24	400.16	405.51	370.83	C	350.67	361.05	C	347.32
31	335.77		374.72		C		371.37	C		360.77		349.33
Close	335.77	359.53	374.72	383.24	400.16	405.51	371.37	382.86	350.67	360.77	359.57	349.33
Month Pt Change	10.84	23.76	15.19	8.52	16.92	5.35	-34.14	11.49	-32.19	10.10	-1.20	-10.24
Month % Change	3.3	7.1	4.2	2.3	4.4	1.3	-8.4	3.1	-8.4	2.9	-0.3	-2.8
QTR % Change			15.3			8.2			-13.5			-0.4
Year % Change												7.5

HIGHLIGHTS

Mid-Term Election Year	Bull Market	Best Eight Months	17.7%	High	Jul-03	411.16
Reagan (2nd Term)	Expansion	Worst Four Months	-11.0%	Low	Jan-09	323.01

NASDAQ COMPOSITE — 1987

	Jan	Feb	Mar	Apr	May	Jun	Jul	Aug	Sep	Oct	Nov	Dec
Previous Month Close	349.33	392.06	424.97	430.05	417.81	416.54	424.67	434.93	454.97	444.29	323.30	305.16
1	C	C	C	428.34	418.44	415.01	424.46	C	452.50	448.45	C	305.24
2	353.26	397.18	423.91	432.07	C	413.60	425.88	C	448.93	451.61	328.33	305.22
3	C	399.38	423.56	437.36	C	415.90	C	433.13	448.36	C	320.66	298.75
4	C	403.12	426.74	C	418.45	417.41	C	432.77	446.48	C	320.13	292.92
5	361.19	405.70	429.00	C	422.43	417.82	C	436.26	C	453.63	326.18	C
6	366.02	406.91	429.45	437.78	422.38	C	425.10	440.80	C	447.51	326.39	C
7	372.49	C	C	434.01	422.63	C	424.55	443.58	C	444.64	C	294.77
8	377.54	C	C	434.91	423.17	419.41	424.93	C	437.60	440.03	C	297.96
9	380.65	405.78	426.79	431.99	C	421.67	425.58	C	439.19	438.43	320.43	301.95
10	C	403.50	429.39	430.93	C	422.81	426.00	446.27	443.48	C	315.19	300.81
11	C	408.25	431.43	C	422.16	423.37	C	449.36	446.17	C	317.80	302.57
12	385.46	409.18	432.48	C	420.53	425.38	C	449.23	C	433.04	324.00	C
13	386.40	412.48	431.97	423.71	421.91	C	426.53	451.55	C	434.81	322.97	C
14	389.95	C	C	413.20	422.65	C	431.14	451.61	445.49	428.28	C	309.36
15	392.57	C	C	416.32	418.88	425.39	431.21	C	441.94	422.51	C	312.68
16	389.87	C	430.86	419.46	C	427.53	433.21	C	440.85	406.33	322.37	319.25
17	C	418.18	434.79	C	C	428.44	434.08	451.65	440.75	C	316.75	319.51
18	C	417.09	435.16	C	413.54	428.97	C	446.76	440.86	C	318.22	326.91
19	392.59	417.03	437.00	C	408.15	429.08	C	447.95	C	360.21	313.93	C
20	392.06	417.24	439.64	417.73	406.57	C	431.51	452.75	C	327.79	312.49	C
21	389.55	C	C	418.56	408.47	C	429.37	455.20	436.01	351.86	C	328.67
22	393.17	C	C	418.16	407.40	429.25	429.30	C	437.90	336.13	C	327.30
23	392.19	415.22	438.04	417.43	C	427.98	427.63	C	440.70	328.45	313.13	331.48
24	C	417.39	438.13	412.62	C	427.26	429.13	453.80	441.24	C	316.68	333.19
25	C	421.01	437.48	C	C	427.20	C	455.10	441.88	C	317.78	C
26	387.98	422.93	438.71	C	411.44	426.68	C	455.26	C	298.90	C	C
27	390.75	424.97	436.85	409.67	412.59	C	428.87	454.79	C	296.34	316.47	C
28	392.04	C	C	411.94	414.35	C	429.97	453.29	442.29	291.88	C	325.60
29	390.98		C	414.20	416.54	426.48	431.20	C	441.86	307.05	C	325.53
30	392.06		427.07	417.81	C	424.67	433.57	C	444.29	323.30	305.16	329.70
31	C		430.05		C		434.93	454.97		C		330.47
Close	392.06	424.97	430.05	417.81	416.54	424.67	434.93	454.97	444.29	323.30	305.16	330.47
Month Pt Change	42.73	32.91	5.08	−12.24	−1.27	8.13	10.26	20.04	−10.68	−120.99	−18.14	25.31
Month % Change	12.2	8.4	1.2	−2.8	−0.3	2.0	2.4	4.6	−2.3	−27.2	−5.6	8.3
QTR % Change			23.1			−1.3			4.6			−25.6
Year % Change												−5.4

HIGHLIGHTS

Pre-Election Year	Bear Market 8/25 - 10/19	Best Eight Months	22.1%	High Aug-26	455.26
Reagan (2nd Term)	Expansion	Worst Four Months	-23.9%	Low Oct-28	291.88

Previous Month Close	Jan	Feb	Mar	Apr	May	Jun	Jul	Aug	Sep	Oct	Nov	Dec
	330.47	344.66	366.95	374.64	379.23	370.34	394.66	387.33	376.55	387.71	382.46	371.45
1	C	346.20	367.32	C	C	374.81	394.69	388.00	372.96	C	382.35	373.87
2	C	347.19	370.38	C	379.74	374.65	C	387.80	376.51	C	381.78	373.91
3	C	343.71	372.01	C	382.23	376.86	C	388.52	C	384.48	382.77	C
4	338.48	344.66	373.36	371.89	381.62	C	C	388.86	C	384.20	381.02	C
5	344.07	345.75	C	373.41	379.51	C	396.11	387.71	C	384.52	C	375.41
6	346.72	C	C	377.74	379.42	379.35	395.45	C	377.33	385.15	C	377.00
7	349.66	C	374.54	378.88	C	379.32	395.43	C	377.96	385.67	376.51	376.36
8	338.47	344.52	376.93	381.83	C	383.41	394.33	387.66	379.73	C	378.84	375.22
9	C	344.97	380.28	C	376.27	384.60	C	384.23	381.60	C	377.74	375.20
10	C	349.32	376.76	C	375.43	386.25	C	378.51	C	385.49	378.40	C
11	336.20	351.04	375.48	382.52	369.24	C	394.15	379.11	C	385.28	373.76	C
12	331.97	353.27	C	383.38	370.23	C	393.52	378.95	382.07	382.55	C	374.20
13	332.68	C	C	383.41	372.48	386.81	393.56	C	382.38	383.46	C	372.98
14	334.23	C	376.67	374.52	C	388.53	394.67	C	383.85	384.59	372.36	372.77
15	340.14	C	376.57	373.90	C	389.08	394.59	374.07	382.70	C	372.13	373.01
16	C	354.74	378.54	C	373.35	387.10	C	375.66	383.91	C	367.79	375.80
17	C	355.28	380.70	C	372.27	386.92	C	376.22	C	385.01	367.43	C
18	340.53	355.63	381.58	375.11	366.99	C	394.77	377.22	C	386.25	367.58	C
19	340.36	357.12	C	376.86	366.25	C	391.28	377.42	383.44	385.76	C	376.39
20	333.68	C	C	374.24	366.03	385.99	391.63	C	384.10	388.62	C	376.05
21	334.25	C	378.57	373.20	C	387.75	388.86	C	384.91	388.59	365.07	375.60
22	337.59	359.98	379.76	374.04	C	390.53	387.35	373.73	384.86	C	365.36	376.50
23	C	361.08	380.09	C	363.26	391.03	C	373.53	384.97	C	367.76	377.34
24	C	363.14	375.60	C	365.16	391.62	C	376.03	C	387.23	C	C
25	340.51	363.62	372.54	375.27	365.73	C	387.12	374.04	C	386.12	366.38	C
26	339.22	363.40	C	377.84	367.29	C	385.79	374.43	382.75	385.19	C	C
27	339.80	C	C	378.67	366.66	389.00	383.32	C	382.22	381.77	C	376.64
28	342.36	C	370.42	378.77	C	391.67	384.08	C	383.28	382.79	366.09	376.76
29	344.66	366.95	372.96	379.23	C	391.66	387.33	376.21	386.05	C	368.15	379.05
30	C		371.78	C	C	394.66	C	376.49	387.71	C	371.45	381.38
31	C		374.64		370.34			C	376.55		382.46	C
Close	344.66	366.95	374.64	379.23	370.34	394.66	387.33	376.55	387.71	382.46	371.45	381.38
Month Pt Change	14.19	22.29	7.69	4.59	−8.89	24.32	−7.33	−10.78	11.16	−5.25	−11.01	9.93
Month % Change	4.3	6.5	2.1	1.2	−2.3	6.6	−1.9	−2.8	3.0	−1.4	−2.9	2.7
QTR % Change			13.4			5.3			−1.8			−1.6
Year % Change												15.4

HIGHLIGHTS

Election Year	Bull Market	Best Eight Months 13.8%	High Jul-05	396.11
Reagan (2nd Term)	Expansion	Worst Four Months -3.1%	Low Jan-12	331.97

NASDAQ COMPOSITE — 1989

Previous Month	Jan	Feb	Mar	Apr	May	Jun	Jul	Aug	Sep	Oct	Nov	Dec
Close	381.38	401.30	399.71	406.73	427.55	446.17	435.29	453.84	469.33	472.92	455.63	456.09
1	C	403.23	399.80	C	427.47	448.32	C	453.29	471.34	C	456.64	457.10
2	C	405.16	402.53	C	428.03	451.63	C	454.08	C	475.19	453.14	C
3	378.56	406.35	403.99	407.65	428.84	C	436.00	456.93	C	477.28	452.97	C
4	382.76	C	C	407.18	429.23	C	C	457.42	C	479.32	C	458.28
5	383.79	C	C	408.30	430.74	447.84	436.94	C	471.42	480.66	C	458.55
6	384.74	406.00	406.26	408.20	C	447.96	439.57	C	469.25	483.64	448.02	456.67
7	C	409.19	406.18	410.71	C	452.20	442.42	461.73	469.68	C	449.40	456.31
8	C	407.97	406.40	C	429.32	453.99	C	463.30	471.31	C	454.05	456.22
9	385.28	406.39	405.67	C	428.97	453.65	C	462.41	C	485.73	454.07	C
10	384.59	402.37	405.90	411.14	429.64	C	442.69	463.55	C	484.14	456.19	C
11	385.31	C	C	413.54	430.63	C	444.50	462.48	470.42	482.16	C	452.42
12	387.01	C	C	415.68	434.83	453.39	446.81	C	471.86	482.19	C	450.43
13	387.09	401.27	406.56	413.86	C	450.73	447.89	C	471.83	467.29	455.94	451.14
14	C	402.02	406.01	417.68	C	450.64	448.90	459.99	468.78	C	454.03	447.48
15	C	404.17	406.98	C	436.21	447.10	C	460.91	467.57	C	455.84	443.84
16	387.36	405.70	409.51	C	435.66	447.21	C	460.79	C	460.98	455.28	C
17	386.05	407.19	402.19	417.76	438.52	C	449.88	460.83	C	459.93	456.72	C
18	388.88	C	C	420.72	439.81	C	447.86	461.97	466.89	463.28	C	436.03
19	391.08	C	C	421.91	442.05	446.09	451.23	C	467.05	470.80	C	434.35
20	391.66	C	398.50	421.51	C	444.58	449.24	C	466.72	470.67	455.71	436.94
21	C	406.38	401.77	423.76	C	443.86	449.29	458.33	467.00	C	454.14	441.09
22	C	402.49	400.57	C	441.78	445.33	C	458.36	468.07	C	455.14	444.57
23	389.99	403.07	400.94	C	440.15	448.36	C	461.68	C	467.22	C	C
24	391.99	399.96	C	423.18	441.49	C	445.98	465.88	C	461.70	456.63	C
25	394.03	C	C	422.71	442.89	C	446.47	466.75	466.71	462.89	C	C
26	397.09	C	C	423.38	445.21	447.29	449.12	C	467.84	458.15	C	445.26
27	397.96	398.94	400.56	426.18	C	448.55	452.48	C	467.77	452.76	456.17	448.81
28	C	399.71	402.60	427.55	C	444.90	452.82	467.19	471.14	C	456.66	449.98
29	C		403.70	C	C	437.91	C	466.57	472.92	C	455.81	454.82
30	399.22		404.56	C	444.21	435.29	C	468.27	C	451.37	456.09	C
31	401.30		406.73		446.17		453.84	469.33		455.63		C
Close	401.30	399.71	406.73	427.55	446.17	435.29	453.84	469.33	472.92	455.63	456.09	454.82
Month Pt Change	19.92	−1.59	7.02	20.82	18.62	−10.88	18.55	15.49	3.59	−17.29	0.46	−1.27
Month % Change	5.2	−0.4	1.8	5.1	4.4	−2.4	4.3	3.4	0.8	−3.7	0.1	−0.3
QTR % Change			6.6			7.0			8.6			−3.8
Year % Change												19.3

HIGHLIGHTS

Post Election Year	Bull Market	Best Eight Months	1.5%	High Oct-09	485.73
GHW Bush	Expansion	Worst Four Months	4.7%	Low Jan-03	378.56

1990 NASDAQ COMPOSITE

Previous Month Close	Jan 454.82	Feb 415.81	Mar 425.83	Apr 435.54	May 420.07	Jun 458.97	Jul 462.29	Aug 438.24	Sep 381.21	Oct 344.51	Nov 329.84	Dec 359.06
1	C	417.76	427.21	C	421.85	462.13	C	435.91	C	354.65	330.60	C
2	459.33	422.21	431.02	433.18	423.58	C	462.04	428.89	C	356.39	336.45	C
3	460.90	C	C	437.65	425.44	C	461.76	417.46	C	351.45	C	361.32
4	459.39	C	C	435.42	428.61	465.61	C	C	381.67	349.89	C	364.11
5	458.22	424.73	430.15	433.42	C	464.61	459.19	C	382.44	347.36	340.76	370.87
6	C	423.99	432.33	430.90	C	464.96	460.53	400.04	378.78	C	340.53	372.29
7	C	426.79	432.47	C	431.23	464.09	C	402.08	380.38	C	336.80	371.54
8	458.71	427.32	436.50	C	431.84	460.87	C	407.73	C	348.14	336.37	C
9	456.77	428.84	436.76	430.18	431.34	C	461.68	412.98	C	339.11	341.95	C
10	450.70	C	C	431.90	433.20	C	460.97	408.03	381.73	333.25	C	371.47
11	448.86	C	C	433.53	438.10	462.79	463.90	C	379.49	325.61	C	367.99
12	439.72	426.38	436.56	436.31	C	466.56	467.17	C	380.32	327.55	351.46	370.42
13	C	425.75	434.58	C	C	468.86	468.44	408.30	376.18	C	352.87	371.50
14	C	426.56	436.15	C	441.61	467.10	C	410.33	374.42	C	356.87	368.83
15	436.64	429.61	438.06	C	442.50	467.55	C	411.45	C	329.54	354.46	C
16	440.16	429.01	442.16	436.70	442.93	C	469.60	402.27	C	325.44	350.85	C
17	438.68	C	C	435.42	445.74	C	464.48	393.49	374.11	326.78	C	365.72
18	437.52	C	C	431.52	448.31	460.79	460.82	C	372.21	334.03	C	370.17
19	440.88	C	442.91	429.00	C	460.53	458.17	C	371.68	337.36	352.73	371.22
20	C	423.83	440.08	425.79	C	460.80	455.27	388.59	364.43	C	348.29	372.30
21	C	421.52	439.30	C	452.89	461.27	C	379.68	362.25	C	348.77	373.60
22	431.94	422.75	434.51	C	453.89	459.33	C	374.84	C	341.12	C	C
23	430.42	419.52	437.25	420.08	456.87	C	444.64	360.22	C	341.09	349.04	C
24	425.66	C	C	419.19	458.29	C	442.56	367.33	352.16	340.98	C	372.41
25	425.24	C	C	420.56	453.69	455.64	445.45	C	354.78	339.74	C	C
26	421.33	420.95	438.84	421.06	C	455.38	445.43	C	350.03	334.36	348.86	372.40
27	C	422.61	439.50	417.98	C	456.89	442.59	381.27	341.19	C	354.05	371.05
28	C	425.83	436.69	C	C	460.38	C	382.86	344.51	C	355.06	371.20
29	418.11		435.42	C	457.51	462.29	C	381.78	C	330.80	355.75	C
30	410.72		435.54	420.07	458.77	C	439.38	378.68	C	329.83	359.06	C
31	415.81		C		458.97		438.24	381.21		329.84		373.84
Close	415.81	425.83	435.54	420.07	458.97	462.29	438.24	381.21	344.51	329.84	359.06	373.84
Month Pt Change	−39.01	10.02	9.71	−15.47	38.90	3.32	−24.05	−57.03	−36.70	−14.67	29.22	14.78
Month % Change	−8.6	2.4	2.3	−3.6	9.3	0.7	−5.2	−13.0	−9.6	−4.3	8.9	4.1
QTR % Change			−4.2			6.1			−25.5			8.5
Year % Change												−17.8

HIGHLIGHTS

Mid-Term Election Year	Bear Market 7/16 - 10/11	Best Eight Months	44.3%	High Jul-16	469.60
GHW Bush	Recession Begins Q3	Worst Four Months	-28.7%	Low Oct-16	325.44

NASDAQ COMPOSITE 1991

Previous Month	Jan	Feb	Mar	Apr	May	Jun	Jul	Aug	Sep	Oct	Nov	Dec
Close	373.84	414.20	453.05	482.30	484.72	506.11	475.92	502.04	525.68	526.88	542.98	523.90
1	C	417.69	456.73	480.86	487.85	C	481.31	504.15	C	528.51	540.93	C
2	372.19	C	C	491.20	491.13	C	478.78	505.67	C	526.33	C	530.91
3	367.51	C	C	495.05	492.10	507.10	474.32	C	520.91	520.51	C	533.34
4	367.24	424.80	461.13	497.57	C	507.25	C	C	517.92	520.40	537.50	535.28
5	C	432.20	473.05	495.79	C	505.20	474.05	502.61	516.93	C	538.82	534.03
6	C	439.24	473.80	C	491.48	502.94	C	505.20	516.94	C	539.48	536.30
7	360.24	435.01	475.74	C	491.51	498.54	C	507.46	C	516.20	545.28	C
8	359.00	436.80	475.11	495.65	492.51	C	479.51	509.39	C	517.25	548.08	C
9	357.45	C	C	492.46	497.81	C	483.64	508.31	518.07	513.81	C	535.35
10	361.92	C	C	490.76	493.42	495.85	487.17	C	511.28	515.94	C	534.23
11	361.80	444.10	467.15	499.31	C	496.62	488.37	C	514.76	519.05	550.71	531.64
12	C	443.98	461.40	501.62	C	491.05	492.71	510.00	521.13	C	555.68	536.02
13	C	447.97	468.18	C	493.93	491.14	C	514.40	516.71	C	556.17	540.90
14	355.75	444.31	467.79	C	488.79	495.07	C	517.68	C	525.66	554.84	C
15	357.30	448.71	466.29	500.84	478.08	C	496.19	515.67	C	534.11	531.29	C
16	365.20	C	C	506.75	481.77	C	493.60	512.47	515.68	540.94	C	543.73
17	375.81	C	C	511.31	481.38	494.32	493.42	C	515.17	536.27	C	539.70
18	376.99	C	466.27	506.62	C	491.59	496.80	C	518.55	538.90	534.73	539.84
19	C	450.32	462.81	501.19	C	485.36	497.55	497.64	522.67	C	523.47	534.53
20	C	446.02	466.09	C	480.10	485.88	C	502.05	527.19	C	526.12	535.76
21	379.70	446.38	464.60	C	483.60	485.82	C	517.97	C	536.96	530.33	C
22	379.03	448.95	464.15	494.38	487.29	C	494.99	518.30	C	537.14	526.46	C
23	383.91	C	C	496.08	489.60	C	489.65	521.06	524.69	535.17	C	543.90
24	391.33	C	C	498.45	492.67	475.23	487.42	C	526.47	528.75	C	549.56
25	394.28	451.09	468.49	496.03	C	473.30	490.28	C	527.82	525.13	522.88	C
26	C	447.71	478.57	494.64	C	473.08	492.69	521.38	526.94	C	522.23	559.30
27	C	450.82	482.37	C	C	476.24	C	521.75	524.48	C	522.78	565.71
28	396.80	453.05	482.30	C	497.17	475.92	C	526.29	C	529.41	C	C
29	400.61		C	487.74	499.05	C	493.35	526.39	C	534.51	523.90	C
30	408.53		C	484.72	503.19	C	498.27	525.68	526.88	541.32	C	579.75
31	414.20		C		506.11		502.04	C		542.98		586.34
Close	414.20	453.05	482.30	484.72	506.11	475.92	502.04	525.68	526.88	542.98	523.90	586.34
Month Pt Change	40.36	38.85	29.25	2.42	21.39	–30.19	26.12	23.64	1.20	16.10	–19.08	62.44
Month % Change	10.8	9.4	6.5	0.5	4.4	–6.0	5.5	4.7	0.2	3.1	–3.5	11.9
QTR % Change			29.0			–1.3			10.7			11.3
Year % Change												56.8

HIGHLIGHTS

Pre-Election Year	Bulll Market	Best Eight Months	3.8%	High	Dec-31	586.34
GHW Bush	Expansion Begins Q2	Worst Four Months	14.1%	Low	Jan-14	355.75

Previous Month Close	Jan	Feb	Mar	Apr	May	Jun	Jul	Aug	Sep	Oct	Nov	Dec
	586.34	620.21	633.47	603.77	578.68	585.31	563.60	580.83	563.12	583.27	605.17	652.73
1	C	C	C	602.09	578.14	588.37	568.99	C	565.61	578.33	C	653.95
2	586.45	C	635.47	593.82	C	589.18	563.35	C	571.25	571.63	607.57	652.91
3	592.65	623.43	634.25	590.01	C	589.93	C	582.36	574.88	C	604.58	656.36
4	C	631.00	630.29	C	583.54	588.26	C	581.32	573.44	C	605.52	661.60
5	C	636.97	621.97	C	588.07	585.43	C	576.87	C	565.21	614.08	C
6	597.90	637.67	615.95	596.29	589.36	C	563.17	574.02	C	570.55	616.82	C
7	602.29	634.95	C	581.61	587.16	C	557.41	573.74	C	569.20	C	666.53
8	610.32	C	C	573.68	585.76	582.01	557.57	C	571.17	573.88	C	667.12
9	619.80	C	615.82	586.75	C	573.80	564.75	C	574.89	570.52	622.05	663.92
10	615.70	634.13	623.46	584.24	C	569.71	567.80	573.14	581.24	C	627.76	658.93
11	C	633.37	617.14	C	587.13	567.68	C	571.60	583.01	C	634.92	655.79
12	C	644.92	615.92	C	583.96	569.52	C	570.85	C	573.84	634.37	C
13	617.63	639.10	618.62	588.15	582.38	C	570.22	570.99	C	576.44	637.16	C
14	625.75	636.43	C	594.81	576.46	C	575.21	573.18	594.21	576.22	C	654.73
15	630.82	C	C	600.03	574.43	569.01	575.47	C	587.86	578.64	C	650.75
16	627.34	C	617.94	591.81	C	564.07	576.19	C	585.89	582.61	634.01	649.63
17	626.85	C	623.27	C	C	553.24	570.52	572.47	587.82	C	627.07	658.46
18	C	626.41	624.94	C	576.53	549.17	C	570.87	589.12	C	634.86	661.29
19	C	622.41	625.96	C	578.05	554.20	C	567.61	C	590.67	638.57	C
20	619.38	632.23	624.28	577.20	580.29	C	564.28	567.86	C	592.70	642.60	C
21	604.87	629.75	C	575.05	579.10	C	568.63	563.70	588.58	597.15	C	662.46
22	620.68	C	C	578.23	580.30	549.72	563.88	C	583.00	597.12	C	660.84
23	622.86	C	621.83	576.05	C	553.36	565.24	C	582.96	597.30	638.84	662.96
24	624.68	624.93	618.68	572.89	C	551.39	565.61	555.39	585.93	C	645.94	665.88
25	C	621.40	619.48	C	C	548.20	C	554.22	577.20	C	648.33	C
26	C	632.40	615.40	C	575.65	547.84	C	558.80	C	598.92	C	C
27	621.00	633.95	604.67	566.94	577.35	C	564.73	563.27	C	596.95	649.49	C
28	621.29	633.47	C	560.33	580.49	C	571.63	563.56	575.34	601.39	C	666.25
29	616.31	C	C	569.94	585.31	558.80	577.49	C	577.63	605.82	C	669.01
30	621.37		602.07	578.68	C	563.60	578.80	C	583.27	605.17	652.73	671.85
31	620.21		603.77		C		580.83	563.12		C		676.95
Close	620.21	633.47	603.77	578.68	585.31	563.60	580.83	563.12	583.27	605.17	652.73	676.95
Month Pt Change	33.87	13.26	−29.70	−25.09	6.63	−21.71	17.23	−17.71	20.15	21.90	47.56	24.22
Month % Change	5.8	2.1	−4.7	−4.2	1.1	−3.7	3.1	−3.0	3.6	3.8	7.9	3.7
QTR % Change			3.0			−6.7			3.5			16.1
Year % Change												15.5

HIGHLIGHTS

Election Year	Bull Market	Best Eight Months	16.3%	High	Dec-31	676.95
GHW Bush	Expansion	Worst Four Months	7.4%	Low	Jun-26	547.84

NASDAQ COMPOSITE 1993

Previous Month Close	Jan	Feb	Mar	Apr	May	Jun	Jul	Aug	Sep	Oct	Nov	Dec
	676.95	696.34	670.77	690.13	661.42	700.53	703.95	704.70	742.84	762.78	779.26	754.39
1	C	701.77	669.51	686.64	C	704.28	703.59	C	746.15	763.23	783.77	763.81
2	C	705.12	677.72	669.85	C	705.86	704.49	707.66	748.65	C	785.66	766.73
3	C	708.67	683.92	C	666.71	706.22	C	709.01	749.71	C	772.95	772.22
4	671.80	708.85	680.73	C	678.16	702.01	C	713.79	C	764.84	757.26	C
5	674.34	700.98	681.37	670.71	683.26	C	C	715.50	C	762.27	762.99	C
6	681.85	C	C	664.14	680.04	C	702.22	718.08	C	764.77	C	771.09
7	678.21	C	C	668.88	681.44	694.61	698.79	C	739.35	762.49	C	769.35
8	677.21	698.44	687.23	666.33	C	687.74	702.71	C	730.73	764.27	766.21	767.89
9	C	692.21	688.96	C	C	689.24	705.81	718.49	737.71	C	769.84	761.49
10	C	695.02	692.87	C	682.82	688.05	C	717.08	744.31	C	776.50	760.74
11	682.40	695.88	694.28	C	683.06	693.19	C	718.77	C	767.65	778.98	C
12	679.45	690.54	692.78	673.12	681.69	C	707.67	717.12	C	772.46	779.32	C
13	686.78	C	C	673.83	675.64	C	708.47	718.26	740.32	778.97	C	759.72
14	695.70	C	C	673.94	676.37	696.41	712.49	C	732.64	785.41	C	751.47
15	697.15	C	695.21	670.32	C	697.34	708.69	C	739.55	787.42	772.45	752.97
16	C	665.39	695.47	666.78	C	696.25	699.73	726.89	739.80	C	771.69	755.53
17	C	659.43	687.40	C	677.96	695.94	C	731.01	740.11	C	762.36	759.23
18	698.13	662.45	687.41	C	680.78	689.59	C	734.83	C	782.91	754.34	C
19	696.81	663.61	682.72	663.03	690.43	C	695.83	730.48	C	768.71	751.56	C
20	697.44	C	C	661.97	697.43	C	701.90	730.96	740.21	768.25	C	760.15
21	700.77	C	C	664.04	694.29	688.74	700.08	C	733.56	771.28	C	755.63
22	701.63	652.42	676.62	663.51	C	686.77	695.52	C	745.54	772.68	738.13	756.07
23	C	651.56	675.04	658.41	C	684.79	700.24	730.86	752.26	C	746.82	758.70
24	C	662.46	674.36	C	694.69	688.72	C	735.14	754.65	C	753.18	C
25	706.95	667.07	681.01	C	695.04	694.81	C	733.66	C	769.75	C	C
26	707.16	670.77	681.54	645.87	704.09	C	704.54	731.39	C	765.46	754.87	C
27	697.90	C	C	652.52	704.59	C	701.00	734.07	759.95	771.88	C	761.06
28	694.67	C	C	658.16	700.53	702.84	705.59	C	763.66	773.49	C	764.56
29	696.34		680.76	658.45	C	701.07	707.24	C	763.17	779.26	751.54	768.48
30	C		686.25	661.42	C	703.95	704.70	737.38	762.78	C	754.39	771.08
31	C		690.13		C		C	742.84		C		776.80
Close	696.34	670.77	690.13	661.42	700.53	703.95	704.70	742.84	762.78	779.26	754.39	776.80
Month Pt Change	19.39	−25.57	19.36	−28.71	39.11	3.42	0.75	38.14	19.94	16.48	−24.87	22.41
Month % Change	2.9	−3.7	2.9	−4.2	5.9	0.5	0.1	5.4	2.7	2.2	−3.2	3.0
QTR % Change			1.9			2.0			8.4			1.8
Year % Change												14.7

HIGHLIGHTS

Post Election Year	Bull Market	Best Eight Months	-9.4%	High Oct-15	787.42
Clinton (1st Term)	Expansion	Worst Four Months	10.7%	Low Apr-26	645.87

1994 NASDAQ COMPOSITE

Previous Month Close	Jan	Feb	Mar	Apr	May	Jun	Jul	Aug	Sep	Oct	Nov	Dec
Close	776.80	800.47	792.50	743.46	733.84	735.19	705.96	722.16	765.62	764.29	777.49	750.32
1	C	797.24	788.64	C	C	735.52	706.85	724.85	758.95	C	772.19	741.19
2	C	799.57	783.47	C	740.68	739.50	C	724.80	759.23	C	771.82	745.02
3	770.76	797.79	784.58	C	739.37	742.38	C	723.69	C	760.88	772.10	C
4	774.28	777.28	790.55	727.41	740.30	C	C	720.18	C	747.30	766.08	C
5	778.05	C	C	750.95	740.55	C	703.59	718.67	C	746.28	C	745.71
6	780.41	C	C	750.72	732.86	743.43	701.00	C	759.48	744.19	C	741.23
7	782.94	779.20	795.05	755.17	C	739.30	706.53	C	764.28	749.96	762.31	734.27
8	C	782.70	792.12	748.71	C	729.79	707.46	720.47	769.30	C	767.54	719.12
9	C	786.53	793.05	C	722.96	728.88	C	722.61	763.73	C	767.25	719.05
10	786.69	783.42	789.09	C	725.00	734.25	C	728.20	C	756.81	764.38	C
11	785.52	781.39	789.20	748.11	717.00	C	706.83	728.20	C	765.57	762.12	C
12	786.87	C	C	739.22	719.61	C	709.59	731.61	760.01	767.00	C	719.12
13	787.81	C	C	727.38	716.92	731.70	719.35	C	765.83	767.89	C	719.49
14	792.31	785.45	792.80	727.31	C	735.98	721.56	C	768.61	767.08	768.14	725.67
15	C	790.12	793.52	727.97	C	735.84	721.36	732.89	778.66	C	769.02	730.68
16	C	792.62	798.99	C	711.91	734.97	C	735.51	777.91	C	769.64	729.07
17	792.18	790.24	803.85	C	711.52	729.35	C	742.66	C	765.78	765.84	C
18	793.02	788.85	803.93	720.45	721.90	C	722.62	742.17	C	764.81	764.67	C
19	789.28	C	C	712.85	727.31	C	719.32	742.43	776.72	770.62	C	727.89
20	793.02	C	C	705.52	726.70	718.85	712.77	C	766.74	768.24	C	728.51
21	794.28	C	797.30	718.74	C	708.79	715.03	C	760.71	765.38	757.74	737.12
22	C	791.15	796.34	722.56	C	712.74	716.68	742.29	760.44	C	741.21	739.34
23	C	789.11	797.51	C	724.95	700.85	C	747.98	757.46	C	736.70	742.19
24	790.65	779.44	786.68	C	731.47	693.79	C	751.72	C	761.21	C	C
25	786.39	783.78	783.45	730.80	732.07	C	716.88	754.80	C	758.26	742.52	C
26	788.80	C	C	734.21	731.64	C	715.66	762.94	755.63	763.24	C	C
27	792.88	C	C	C	733.14	702.68	712.13	C	755.37	767.47	C	746.19
28	796.53	792.50	772.50	731.69	C	702.05	712.43	C	760.01	776.15	745.73	742.46
29	C		755.29	733.84	C	704.01	722.16	763.21	759.34	C	751.48	749.53
30	C		744.91	C	C	705.96	C	766.46	764.29	C	750.32	751.96
31	800.47		743.46		735.19		C	765.62		777.49		C
Close	800.47	792.50	743.46	733.84	735.19	705.96	722.16	765.62	764.29	777.49	750.32	751.96
Month Pt Change	23.67	–7.97	–49.04	–9.62	1.35	–29.23	16.20	43.46	–1.33	13.20	–27.17	1.64
Month % Change	3.0	–1.0	–6.2	–1.3	0.2	–4.0	2.3	6.0	–0.2	1.7	–3.5	0.2
QTR % Change			–4.3			–5.0			8.3			–1.6
Year % Change												–3.2

HIGHLIGHTS

Mid-Term Election Year	Bull Market	Best Eight Months 20.1%	High Mar-18	803.93
Clinton (1st Term)	Expansion	Worst Four Months 10.1%	Low Jun-24	693.79

NASDAQ COMPOSITE   1995

Previous Month Close	Jan	Feb	Mar	Apr	May	Jun	Jul	Aug	Sep	Oct	Nov	Dec
	751.96	755.20	793.73	817.21	843.98	864.58	933.45	1001.21	1020.11	1043.54	1036.06	1059.20
1	C	758.31	791.87	C	841.63	868.82	C	991.11	1019.47	C	1040.50	1055.31
2	C	763.64	793.68	C	841.79	872.97	C	983.75	C	1027.57	1057.32	C
3	743.58	772.06	798.79	818.05	850.26	C	934.53	982.70	C	1020.45	1065.66	C
4	745.84	C	C	813.72	846.75	C	C	991.09	C	1002.27	C	1069.79
5	745.66	C	C	816.32	843.53	882.85	941.82	C	1039.30	1014.20	C	1065.89
6	749.69	778.85	797.77	813.80	C	879.40	952.93	C	1044.28	1012.04	1062.14	1061.73
7	C	778.97	791.33	814.69	C	881.58	969.76	995.22	1051.08	C	1043.90	1053.17
8	C	783.77	795.81	C	849.29	886.13	C	997.12	1060.03	C	1047.94	1062.41
9	752.09	785.44	796.24	C	848.17	884.38	C	1005.10	C	984.74	1065.59	C
10	756.52	790.43	802.22	821.26	847.62	C	976.63	1000.61	C	983.47	1063.87	C
11	755.74	C	C	824.83	853.83	C	970.22	1004.11	1066.56	1001.57	C	1061.50
12	756.51	C	C	828.53	858.94	887.98	988.63	C	1065.00	1015.63	C	1052.07
13	762.16	789.42	802.31	832.64	C	894.23	994.15	C	1067.40	1018.38	1058.46	1056.54
14	C	790.62	808.24	C	C	895.72	999.33	1012.44	1066.96	C	1040.62	1038.19
15	C	795.63	807.38	C	863.06	902.68	C	1012.37	1051.10	C	1041.85	1030.48
16	768.16	793.31	809.34	C	868.25	908.65	C	1025.75	C	1018.13	1044.48	C
17	772.14	786.97	808.33	830.82	871.93	C	1005.89	1029.24	C	1035.44	1045.03	C
18	772.38	C	C	825.74	864.06	C	988.53	1031.28	1050.18	1045.13	C	1002.56
19	768.55	C	C	816.55	864.57	922.09	952.87	C	1060.32	1046.97	C	1026.41
20	762.05	C	810.49	819.01	C	929.83	960.57	C	1065.09	1039.53	1029.47	1025.27
21	C	784.62	809.78	823.44	C	929.19	961.77	1019.70	1058.51	C	1024.99	1040.64
22	C	787.93	809.10	C	871.18	940.09	C	1025.29	1053.39	C	1021.24	1046.89
23	759.51	791.35	811.39	C	879.64	938.87	C	1028.19	C	1036.92	C	C
24	763.20	791.08	818.66	828.91	877.98	C	978.57	1020.93	C	1039.24	1030.17	C
25	760.98	C	C	831.28	877.32	C	993.75	1019.97	1046.15	1026.47	C	C
26	757.56	C	C	836.91	871.87	926.98	1000.18	C	1038.05	1017.57	C	1049.37
27	758.91	784.50	822.63	840.95	C	919.56	1010.66	C	1026.54	1025.55	1029.32	1048.13
28	C	793.73	826.14	843.98	C	920.52	1005.28	1008.15	1047.05	C	1050.05	1042.22
29	C		819.16	C	C	926.81	C	1003.64	1043.54	C	1057.57	1052.13
30	751.83		816.86	C	858.70	933.45	C	1012.61	C	1039.69	1059.20	C
31	755.20		817.21		864.58		1001.21	1020.11		1036.06		C
Close	755.20	793.73	817.21	843.98	864.58	933.45	1001.21	1020.11	1043.54	1036.06	1059.20	1052.13
Month Pt Change	3.24	38.53	23.48	26.77	20.60	68.87	67.76	18.90	23.43	−7.48	23.14	−7.07
Month % Change	0.4	5.1	3.0	3.3	2.4	8.0	7.3	1.9	2.3	−0.7	2.2	−0.7
QTR % Change			8.7			14.2			11.8			0.8
Year % Change												39.9

HIGHLIGHTS

Pre-Election Year	Bull Market	Best Eight Months 14.4%	High Dec-04	1069.79
Clinton (1st Term)	Expansion	Worst Four Months 11.0%	Low Jan-03	743.58

Data Bank   459

Previous Month Close	Jan 1052.13	Feb 1059.79	Mar 1100.05	Apr 1101.40	May 1190.52	Jun 1243.43	Jul 1185.02	Aug 1080.59	Sep 1141.50	Oct 1226.92	Nov 1221.51	Dec 1292.61
1	C	1069.46	1086.08	1106.57	1199.66	C	1197.45	1098.85	C	1221.51	1221.78	C
2	1058.65	1072.11	C	1111.29	1178.33	C	1191.15	1124.92	C	1236.11	C	1299.82
3	1046.26	C	C	1115.85	1184.60	1238.73	1181.60	C	1142.29	1233.09	C	1300.37
4	1029.82	C	1084.88	1118.21	C	1243.68	C	C	1143.82	1247.56	1220.48	1297.02
5	1033.47	1083.34	1096.81	C	C	1249.15	1158.35	1120.53	1125.66	C	1229.07	1300.12
6	C	1089.08	1091.82	C	1186.31	1232.52	C	1128.87	1139.39	C	1245.49	1287.68
7	C	1084.88	1093.12	C	1182.67	1229.76	C	1141.11	C	1250.87	1254.14	C
8	1032.37	1093.17	1063.73	1105.66	1183.43	C	1148.82	1137.51	C	1240.15	1257.51	C
9	998.81	1094.60	C	1109.15	1187.82	C	1153.59	1137.27	1148.71	1237.98	C	1316.27
10	990.21	C	C	1105.28	1202.76	1230.04	1141.19	C	1149.43	1236.97	C	1312.55
11	1011.10	C	1080.50	1097.14	C	1230.76	1106.36	C	1153.95	1248.27	1262.67	1309.12
12	1008.23	1095.38	1073.05	1100.94	C	1235.47	1103.49	1138.27	1165.81	C	1256.53	1298.33
13	C	1087.22	1088.64	C	1221.87	1225.65	C	1126.15	1188.67	C	1260.72	1284.91
14	C	1088.03	1091.07	C	1234.49	1213.18	C	1133.51	C	1256.36	1270.36	C
15	988.57	1090.54	1099.59	1110.44	1233.56	C	1060.19	1134.69	C	1258.10	1261.80	C
16	995.87	1090.71	C	1124.92	1239.31	C	1053.47	1133.65	1193.96	1250.99	C	1260.98
17	998.30	C	C	1120.87	1241.88	1207.64	1086.65	C	1203.31	1241.96	C	1266.32
18	1007.24	C	1114.42	1136.30	C	1183.08	1109.82	C	1205.71	1242.48	1254.57	1285.38
19	1018.45	C	1112.50	1138.70	C	1179.27	1097.68	1130.91	1212.09	C	1262.62	1295.86
20	C	1083.24	1101.82	C	1248.11	1167.34	C	1124.67	1219.69	C	1264.94	1288.56
21	C	1096.85	1099.79	C	1244.42	1175.44	C	1126.84	C	1236.41	1258.08	C
22	1029.44	1117.11	1102.22	1153.50	1247.38	C	1081.39	1143.96	C	1220.00	1274.36	C
23	1028.04	1117.79	C	1166.76	1248.65	C	1049.07	1143.05	1211.47	1227.88	C	1279.52
24	1043.46	C	C	1176.83	1247.80	1182.90	1042.37	C	1215.27	1227.00	C	1287.63
25	1035.95	C	1087.09	1184.17	C	1172.58	1062.39	C	1224.66	1222.60	1280.37	C
26	1040.96	1113.05	1088.35	1186.89	C	1153.29	1079.44	1139.22	1227.98	C	1281.20	1294.57
27	C	1106.17	1093.88	C	C	1166.01	C	1149.02	1230.05	C	1287.32	1291.38
28	C	1107.55	1094.83	C	1236.30	1185.02	C	1153.88	C	1215.89	C	C
29	1042.51	1100.05	1101.40	1188.20	1225.63	C	1066.47	1145.03	C	1203.05	1292.61	C
30	1051.30		C	1190.52	1233.48	C	1071.95	1141.50	1226.92	1206.23	C	1287.75
31	1059.79		C		1243.43		1080.59	C		1221.51		1291.03
Close	1059.79	1100.05	1101.40	1190.52	1243.43	1185.02	1080.59	1141.50	1226.92	1221.51	1292.61	1291.03
Month Pt Change	7.66	40.26	1.35	89.12	52.91	−58.41	−104.43	60.91	85.42	−5.41	71.10	−1.58
Month % Change	0.7	3.8	0.1	8.1	4.4	−4.7	−8.8	5.6	7.5	−0.4	5.8	−0.1
QTR % Change			4.7			7.6			3.5			5.2
Year % Change												22.7

HIGHLIGHTS

Election Year	Bull Market	Best Eight Months	18.1%	High	Dec-09	1316.27
Clinton (1st Term)	Expansion	Worst Four Months	3.1%	Low	Jan-15	988.57

ALMANAC INVESTOR

NASDAQ COMPOSITE — 1997

Previous Month Close	Jan	Feb	Mar	Apr	May	Jun	Jul	Aug	Sep	Oct	Nov	Dec
	1291.03	1379.85	1309.00	1221.70	1260.76	1400.32	1442.07	1593.81	1587.32	1685.69	1593.61	1600.55
1	C	C	C	1216.93	1270.50	C	1438.25	1594.33	C	1690.30	C	1630.72
2	1280.70	C	C	1201.00	1305.33	1404.79	1455.61	C	1618.09	1702.41	C	1606.37
3	1310.68	1376.05	1311.18	1213.76	C	1384.91	1467.61	C	1618.24	1715.87	1629.98	1615.13
4	C	1373.75	1317.37	1236.73	C	1379.67	C	1605.45	1624.63	C	1631.15	1613.42
5	C	1348.44	1329.09	C	1339.24	1390.05	C	1621.53	1635.77	C	1637.33	1633.90
6	1316.40	1346.40	1315.43	C	1328.30	1404.84	C	1630.44	C	1721.91	1623.44	C
7	1327.73	1357.71	1311.80	1251.35	1322.91	C	1470.74	1624.18	C	1737.27	1602.40	C
8	1320.35	C	C	1257.37	1330.83	C	1485.10	1598.52	1645.35	1741.77	C	1651.54
9	1326.20	C	C	1249.43	1335.05	1412.17	1486.63	C	1656.22	1745.85	C	1620.55
10	1332.02	1335.34	1322.72	1235.77	C	1401.69	1490.93	C	1639.25	1739.03	1590.72	1596.61
11	C	1331.51	1316.76	1206.90	C	1407.85	1502.62	1586.74	1639.86	C	1584.86	1558.54
12	C	1358.96	1304.13	C	1344.19	1411.32	C	1576.24	1649.33	C	1541.72	1536.58
13	1330.91	1370.81	1293.28	C	1333.59	1423.03	C	1583.40	C	1742.12	1557.74	C
14	1346.36	1367.19	1292.97	1216.41	1335.55	C	1523.88	1586.69	C	1732.79	1583.51	C
15	1333.53	C	C	1212.88	1353.58	C	1542.11	1562.03	1634.92	1723.37	C	1536.56
16	1340.58	C	C	1210.27	1340.73	1431.95	1580.63	C	1668.60	1699.66	C	1553.00
17	1349.05	C	1279.43	1217.07	C	1443.11	1568.85	C	1666.47	1666.85	1614.11	1547.37
18	C	1365.79	1269.34	1222.57	C	1432.43	1547.99	1569.52	1670.02	C	1600.44	1523.19
19	C	1365.58	1249.29	C	1341.24	1447.14	C	1600.71	1680.36	C	1601.22	1524.74
20	1364.28	1347.40	1259.26	C	1363.88	1447.10	C	1628.70	C	1685.45	1626.56	C
21	1376.97	1334.32	1254.07	1203.95	1373.75	C	1536.23	1607.36	C	1712.54	1620.75	C
22	1388.06	C	C	1212.74	1372.60	C	1563.86	1598.69	1689.45	1708.08	C	1532.06
23	1378.37	C	C	1227.14	1389.72	1434.32	1567.65	C	1697.36	1671.25	C	1509.91
24	1363.83	1345.08	1242.64	1228.10	C	1452.43	1569.13	C	1687.41	1650.92	1586.99	1499.53
25	C	1347.69	1248.06	1209.29	C	1446.24	1569.58	1601.57	1678.89	C	1589.04	C
26	C	1340.55	1269.08	C	C	1436.38	C	1591.30	1682.24	C	1594.50	1511.38
27	1352.81	1312.66	1249.51	C	1409.21	1438.15	C	1595.54	C	1535.09	C	C
28	1354.37	1309.00	C	1217.03	1410.18	C	1563.53	1581.32	C	1603.02	1600.55	C
29	1355.17		C	1242.63	1403.04	C	1572.32	1587.32	1694.98	1602.75	C	1537.45
30	1371.02		C	1260.76	1400.32	1442.07	1588.05	C	1685.69	1570.41	C	1565.03
31	1379.85		1221.70		C		1593.81	C		1593.61		1570.35
Close	1379.85	1309.00	1221.70	1260.76	1400.32	1442.07	1593.81	1587.32	1685.69	1593.61	1600.55	1570.35
Month Pt Change	88.82	−70.85	−87.30	39.06	139.56	41.75	151.74	−6.49	98.37	−92.08	6.94	−30.20
Month % Change	6.9	−5.1	−6.7	3.2	11.1	3.0	10.5	−0.4	6.2	−5.5	0.4	−1.9
QTR % Change			−5.4			18.0			16.9			−6.8
Year % Change												21.6

HIGHLIGHTS

Post Election Year	Bull Market	Best Eight Months 18.9%	High Oct-09	1745.85
Clinton (2nd Term)	Expansion	Worst Four Months 10.5%	Low Apr-02	1201.00

1998   NASDAQ COMPOSITE

Previous Month Close	Jan	Feb	Mar	Apr	May	Jun	Jul	Aug	Sep	Oct	Nov	Dec
	1570.35	1619.36	1770.51	1835.68	1868.41	1778.87	1894.74	1872.39	1499.25	1693.84	1771.39	1949.54
1	C	C	C	1847.66	1873.44	1746.82	1914.46	C	1575.09	1612.33	C	2003.75
2	1581.53	1652.89	1758.54	1852.96	C	1761.79	1894.00	C	1592.85	1614.98	1800.91	1995.21
3	C	1666.34	1757.14	1855.40	C	1742.31	C	1851.10	1571.86	C	1788.43	1954.33
4	C	1680.44	1759.70	C	1878.86	1769.95	C	1785.64	1566.52	C	1823.57	2003.16
5	1594.12	1676.90	1711.92	C	1864.91	1782.92	C	1788.20	C	1536.69	1837.10	C
6	1580.14	1694.35	1753.49	1829.14	1856.68	C	1909.47	1829.51	C	1510.89	1856.56	C
7	1561.70	C	C	1798.71	1835.14	C	1908.11	1846.77	C	1462.61	C	2040.64
8	1555.54	C	C	1807.01	1864.37	1787.77	1935.39	C	1660.86	1419.12	C	2034.75
9	1503.22	1690.43	1725.16	1820.24	C	1800.76	1939.82	C	1624.55	1492.49	1861.05	2050.42
10	C	1709.04	1748.51	C	C	1773.25	1943.04	1839.21	1585.33	C	1865.62	2015.96
11	C	1708.55	1756.85	C	1848.07	1749.75	C	1792.70	1641.64	C	1862.11	2029.31
12	1507.58	1714.34	1764.06	C	1860.16	1745.05	C	1825.53	C	1546.08	1851.06	C
13	1541.63	1710.42	1771.66	1824.95	1866.18	C	1965.53	1802.54	C	1509.45	1847.99	C
14	1548.76	C	C	1843.03	1865.36	C	1968.41	1790.19	1665.69	1540.97	C	1966.92
15	1547.06	C	C	1863.26	1846.77	1715.75	1994.54	C	1678.11	1611.01	C	2012.60
16	1562.88	C	1788.18	1858.24	C	1753.12	2000.56	C	1689.91	1620.95	1861.68	2009.36
17	C	1703.43	1779.30	1866.60	C	1776.40	2008.76	1818.04	1646.25	C	1878.52	2043.88
18	C	1715.73	1788.28	C	1831.62	1772.70	C	1855.12	1663.77	C	1897.44	2086.14
19	C	1727.01	1799.98	C	1845.87	1781.29	C	1842.69	C	1648.73	1919.68	C
20	1590.14	1728.13	1789.16	1887.14	1831.75	C	2014.25	1832.45	C	1639.19	1928.21	C
21	1587.92	C	C	1903.87	1820.99	C	1979.14	1797.61	1680.43	1674.75	C	2138.03
22	1576.51	C	C	1917.61	1805.00	1805.82	1969.75	C	1697.80	1702.64	C	2120.98
23	1575.93	1751.76	1792.51	1881.39	C	1844.57	1935.22	C	1760.27	1693.86	1977.42	2172.54
24	C	1738.71	1812.44	1868.96	C	1877.76	1930.99	1790.82	1720.34	C	1965.88	2163.03
25	C	1766.48	1824.51	C	C	1863.25	C	1798.17	1743.59	C	1985.21	C
26	1561.46	1777.11	1828.54	C	1778.09	1869.53	C	1768.13	C	1724.98	C	C
27	1578.90	1770.51	1823.62	1820.31	1781.10	C	1933.26	1686.41	C	1717.63	2016.44	C
28	1610.82	C	C	1831.77	1794.62	C	1896.53	1639.68	1739.22	1737.35	C	2180.30
29	1619.49		C	1851.64	1778.87	1891.08	1881.49	C	1734.05	1757.19	C	2181.77
30	1619.36		1818.70	1868.41	C	1894.74	1919.58	C	1693.84	1771.39	1949.54	2166.95
31	C		1835.68		C		1872.39	1499.25		C		2192.69
Close	1619.36	1770.51	1835.68	1868.41	1778.87	1894.74	1872.39	1499.25	1693.84	1771.39	1949.54	2192.69
Month Pt Change	49.01	151.15	65.17	32.73	−89.54	115.87	−22.35	−373.14	194.59	77.55	178.15	243.15
Month % Change	3.1	9.3	3.7	1.8	−4.8	6.5	−1.2	−19.9	13.0	4.6	10.1	12.5
QTR % Change			16.9			3.2			−10.6			29.5
Year % Change												39.6

HIGHLIGHTS

Mid-Term Election Year	Bull Market	Best Eight Months 51.6%	High Dec-31	2192.69
Clinton (2nd Term)	Expansion	Worst Four Months -6.5%	Low Oct-08	1419.12

                                 ALMANAC INVESTOR

NASDAQ COMPOSITE 1999

Previous Month Close	Jan	Feb	Mar	Apr	May	Jun	Jul	Aug	Sep	Oct	Nov	Dec
Close	2192.69	2505.89	2288.03	2461.40	2542.85	2470.52	2686.12	2638.49	2739.35	2746.16	2966.43	3336.16
1	C	2510.09	2295.18	2493.37	C	2412.03	2706.18	C	2750.80	2736.85	2967.65	3353.71
2	C	2463.42	2259.03	C	C	2432.41	2741.02	2623.63	2734.24	C	2981.63	3452.78
3	C	2493.41	2265.20	C	2535.58	2403.32	C	2587.99	2843.11	C	3028.51	3520.63
4	2208.05	2410.07	2292.89	C	2485.12	2478.34	C	2540.00	C	2795.97	3055.95	C
5	2251.27	2373.62	2337.11	2560.06	2534.45	C	C	2565.83	C	2799.67	3102.29	C
6	2320.86	C	C	2563.17	2472.28	C	2736.78	2547.97	C	2857.21	C	3546.01
7	2326.09	C	C	2544.43	2503.62	2524.21	2743.04	C	2837.26	2860.70	C	3586.92
8	2344.41	2404.92	2397.62	2573.39	C	2474.56	2771.86	C	2808.74	2886.57	3143.97	3586.08
9	C	2310.79	2392.94	2593.05	C	2519.35	2793.07	2518.98	2852.02	C	3125.04	3594.17
10	C	2309.50	2406.00	C	2526.39	2484.62	C	2490.11	2887.06	C	3155.96	3620.24
11	2384.59	2405.55	2412.25	C	2566.68	2447.88	C	2564.98	C	2915.95	3197.29	C
12	2320.75	2321.89	2381.53	2598.81	2606.54	C	2790.44	2549.49	C	2872.43	3221.15	C
13	2316.81	C	C	2583.50	2582.00	C	2778.23	2637.81	2844.77	2801.27	C	3658.17
14	2276.82	C	C	2507.28	2527.86	2398.31	2818.13	C	2868.29	2806.84	C	3571.66
15	2348.20	C	2431.44	2521.77	C	2414.67	2839.37	C	2814.17	2731.83	3219.54	3621.95
16	C	2313.87	2439.27	2484.04	C	2517.83	2864.48	2645.28	2806.72	C	3295.52	3715.06
17	C	2248.91	2428.97	C	2561.84	2544.15	C	2671.22	2869.62	C	3269.39	3753.06
18	C	2260.55	2462.96	C	2558.36	2563.44	C	2657.73	C	2689.15	3347.11	C
19	2408.17	2283.60	2421.27	2345.61	2577.40	C	2830.29	2621.43	C	2688.18	3369.25	C
20	2415.49	C	C	2409.64	2542.23	C	2732.18	2648.33	2886.15	2788.13	C	3783.87
21	2344.72	C	C	2489.08	2520.14	2630.28	2761.77	C	2821.10	2801.95	C	3911.15
22	2338.88	2342.01	2395.94	2561.61	C	2580.26	2684.44	C	2858.16	2816.52	3392.56	3937.30
23	C	2376.35	2322.84	2590.69	C	2598.12	2692.40	2719.57	2749.83	C	3342.87	3969.44
24	C	2339.38	2365.28	C	2453.66	2553.99	C	2752.37	2740.41	C	3420.50	C
25	2369.31	2326.82	2434.80	C	2380.90	2552.65	C	2805.60	C	2815.95	C	C
26	2433.41	2288.03	2419.17	2652.05	2427.18	C	2619.19	2774.62	C	2811.47	3447.81	C
27	2407.14	C	C	2602.41	2419.15	C	2679.33	2758.90	2761.75	2802.52	C	3975.38
28	2477.34	C	C	2550.37	2470.52	2602.44	2705.84	C	2756.25	2875.22	C	3972.11
29	2505.89		2492.84	2528.44	C	2642.11	2640.01	C	2730.27	2966.43	3421.37	4041.46
30	C		2480.29	2542.85	C	2686.12	2638.49	2712.69	2746.16	C	3336.16	4036.87
31	C		2461.40		C		C	2739.35		C		4069.31
Close	2505.89	2288.03	2461.40	2542.85	2470.52	2686.12	2638.49	2739.35	2746.16	2966.43	3336.16	4069.31
Month Pt Change	313.20	–217.86	173.37	81.45	–72.33	215.60	–47.63	100.86	6.81	220.27	369.73	733.15
Month % Change	14.3	–8.7	7.6	3.3	–2.8	8.7	–1.8	3.8	0.2	8.0	12.5	22.0
QTR % Change			12.3			9.1			2.2			48.2
Year % Change												85.6

HIGHLIGHTS

Pre-Election Year	Bull Market	Best Eight Months	33.7%	High Dec-31 4069.31
Clinton (2nd Term)	Expansion	Worst Four Months	10.4%	Low Jan-04 2208.05

2000 — NASDAQ COMPOSITE

Previous Month Close	Jan	Feb	Mar	Apr	May	Jun	Jul	Aug	Sep	Oct	Nov	Dec
	4069.31	3940.35	4696.69	4572.83	3860.66	3400.91	3966.11	3766.99	4206.35	3672.82	3369.63	2597.93
1	C	4051.98	4784.08	C	3958.08	3582.50	C	3685.52	4234.33	C	3333.39	2645.29
2	C	4073.96	4754.51	C	3785.45	3813.38	C	3658.46	C	3568.90	3429.02	C
3	4131.15	4210.98	4914.79	4223.68	3707.31	C	3991.93	3759.88	C	3455.83	3451.58	C
4	3901.69	4244.14	C	4148.89	3720.24	C	C	3787.36	C	3523.10	C	2615.75
5	3877.54	C	C	4169.22	3816.82	3821.76	3863.10	C	4143.18	3472.10	C	2889.80
6	3727.13	C	4904.85	4267.56	C	3756.37	3960.57	C	4013.34	3361.01	3416.21	2796.50
7	3882.62	4321.77	4847.84	4446.45	C	3839.26	4023.20	3862.99	4098.35	C	3415.79	2752.66
8	C	4427.50	4897.26	C	3669.38	3825.56	C	3848.55	3978.41	C	3231.70	2917.43
9	C	4363.24	5046.86	C	3585.01	3874.84	C	3853.50	C	3355.56	3200.35	C
10	4049.67	4485.63	5048.62	4188.20	3384.73	C	3980.29	3759.99	C	3240.54	3028.99	C
11	3921.19	4395.45	C	4055.90	3499.58	C	3956.42	3789.47	3896.35	3168.49	C	3015.10
12	3850.02	C	C	3769.63	3529.06	3767.91	4099.59	C	3849.51	3074.68	C	2931.77
13	3957.21	C	4907.24	3676.78	C	3851.06	4174.86	C	3893.89	3316.77	2966.72	2822.77
14	4064.27	4418.55	4706.63	3321.29	C	3797.41	4246.18	3849.69	3913.86	C	3138.27	2728.51
15	C	4420.77	4582.62	C	3607.65	3845.74	C	3851.66	3835.23	C	3165.49	2653.27
16	C	4427.65	4717.39	C	3717.57	3860.56	C	3861.20	C	3290.68	3031.88	C
17	C	4548.92	4798.13	3539.16	3644.96	C	4274.67	3940.87	C	3213.96	3027.19	C
18	4130.81	4411.74	C	3793.57	3538.71	C	4177.17	3930.34	3726.52	3171.56	C	2624.52
19	4151.29	C	C	3706.41	3390.40	3989.83	4055.63	C	3865.64	3418.60	C	2511.71
20	4189.51	C	4610.00	3643.88	C	4013.36	4184.56	C	3897.44	3483.14	2875.64	2332.78
21	4235.40	C	4711.68	C	C	4064.01	4094.45	3953.15	3828.87	C	2871.45	2340.12
22	C	4382.12	4864.75	C	3364.21	3936.84	C	3958.21	3803.76	C	2755.34	2517.02
23	C	4550.33	4940.61	C	3164.55	3845.34	C	4011.01	C	3468.69	C	C
24	4096.08	4617.65	4963.03	3482.48	3270.61	C	3981.57	4053.28	C	3419.79	2904.38	C
25	4167.41	4590.50	C	3711.23	3205.35	C	4029.57	4042.68	3741.22	3229.57	C	C
26	4069.91	C	C	3630.09	3205.11	3912.12	3987.72	C	3689.10	3272.18	C	2493.52
27	4039.56	C	4958.56	3774.03	C	3858.96	3842.23	C	3656.30	3278.36	2880.49	2539.35
28	3887.07	4577.85	4833.89	3860.66	C	3940.34	3663.00	4070.59	3778.32	C	2734.98	2557.76
29	C	4696.69	4644.67	C	C	3877.23	C	4082.17	3672.82	C	2706.93	2470.52
30	C		4457.89	C	3459.48	3966.11	C	4103.81	C	3191.40	2597.93	C
31	3940.35		4572.83		3400.91		3766.99	4206.35		3369.63		C
Close	3940.35	4696.69	4572.83	3860.66	3400.91	3966.11	3766.99	4206.35	3672.82	3369.63	2597.93	2470.52
Month Pt Change	-128.96	756.34	-123.86	-712.17	-459.75	565.20	-199.12	439.36	-533.53	-303.19	-771.70	-127.41
Month % Change	-3.2	19.2	-2.6	-15.6	-11.9	16.6	-5.0	11.7	-12.7	-8.3	-22.9	-4.9
QTR % Change			12.4			-13.3			-7.4			-32.7
Year % Change												-39.3

HIGHLIGHTS

Election Year	Bear Market Begins 1/14	Best Eight Months -35.9%	High Mar-10	5048.62
Clinton (2nd Term)	Expansion	Worst Four Months -15.0%	Low Dec-20	2332.78

NASDAQ COMPOSITE   2001

Previous Month Close	Jan	Feb	Mar	Apr	May	Jun	Jul	Aug	Sep	Oct	Nov	Dec
	2470.52	2772.73	2151.83	1840.26	2116.24	2110.49	2160.54	2027.13	1805.43	1498.80	1690.20	1930.58
1	C	2782.79	2183.37	C	2168.24	2149.44	C	2068.38	C	1480.46	1746.30	C
2	2291.86	2660.50	2117.63	1782.97	2220.60	C	2148.72	2087.38	C	1492.33	1745.73	C
3	2616.69	C	C	1673.00	2146.20	C	2140.80	2066.33	C	1580.81	C	1904.90
4	2566.83	C	C	1638.80	2191.53	2155.93	C	C	1770.78	1597.31	C	1963.10
5	2407.65	2643.21	2142.92	1785.00	C	2233.66	2080.11	C	1759.01	1605.30	1793.65	2046.84
6	C	2664.49	2204.43	1720.36	C	2217.73	2004.16	2034.26	1705.64	C	1835.08	2054.27
7	C	2607.82	2223.92	C	2173.57	2264.00	C	2027.79	1687.70	C	1837.53	2021.26
8	2395.92	2562.06	2168.73	C	2198.77	2215.10	C	1966.36	C	1605.95	1827.77	C
9	2441.30	2470.97	2052.78	1745.71	2156.63	C	2026.71	1963.32	C	1570.19	1828.48	C
10	2524.18	C	C	1852.03	2128.86	C	1962.79	1956.47	1695.38	1626.26	C	1992.12
11	2640.57	C	C	1898.95	2107.43	2170.78	1972.04	C	C	1701.47	C	2001.93
12	2626.50	2489.66	1923.38	1961.43	C	2169.95	2075.74	C	C	1703.40	1840.13	2011.38
13	C	2427.72	2014.78	C	C	2121.66	2084.79	1982.55	C	C	1892.11	1946.51
14	C	2491.40	1972.09	C	2081.92	2044.07	C	1964.53	C	C	1903.19	1953.17
15	C	2552.91	1940.71	C	2085.58	2028.43	C	1918.89	C	1696.31	1900.57	C
16	2618.55	2425.38	1890.91	1909.57	2166.44	C	2029.12	1930.32	C	1722.07	1898.58	C
17	2682.78	C	C	1923.22	2193.68	C	2067.32	1867.01	1579.55	1646.34	C	1987.45
18	2768.49	C	C	2079.44	2198.88	1988.63	2016.17	C	1555.08	1652.72	C	2004.76
19	2770.38	C	1951.18	2182.14	C	1992.66	2046.59	C	1527.80	1671.31	1934.42	1982.89
20	C	2318.35	1857.44	2163.41	C	2031.24	2029.37	1881.35	1470.93	C	1880.51	1918.54
21	C	2268.94	1830.23	C	2305.59	2058.76	C	1831.30	1423.19	C	1875.05	1945.83
22	2757.91	2244.96	1897.70	C	2313.85	2034.84	C	1860.01	C	1708.08	C	C
23	2840.39	2262.51	1928.68	2059.32	2243.48	C	1988.56	1842.97	C	1704.44	1903.20	C
24	2859.15	C	C	2016.61	2282.02	C	1959.24	1916.80	1499.40	1731.54	C	1944.48
25	2754.28	C	C	2059.80	2251.03	2050.87	1984.32	C	1501.64	1775.47	C	C
26	2781.30	2308.50	1918.49	2034.88	C	2064.62	2022.96	C	1464.04	1768.96	1941.23	1960.70
27	C	2207.82	1972.26	2075.68	C	2074.74	2029.07	1912.41	1460.71	C	1935.97	1976.42
28	C	2151.83	1854.13	C	C	2125.46	C	1864.98	1498.80	C	1887.97	1987.26
29	2838.34		1820.57	C	2175.54	2160.54	C	1843.17	C	1699.52	1933.26	C
30	2838.35		1840.26	2116.24	2084.50	C	2017.84	1791.68	C	1667.41	1930.58	C
31	2772.73		C		2110.49		2027.13	1805.43		1690.20		1950.40
Close	2772.73	2151.83	1840.26	2116.24	2110.49	2160.54	2027.13	1805.43	1498.80	1690.20	1930.58	1950.40
Month Pt Change	302.21	−620.90	−311.57	275.98	−5.75	50.05	−133.41	−221.70	−306.63	191.40	240.38	19.82
Month % Change	12.2	−22.4	−14.5	15.0	−0.3	2.4	−6.2	−10.9	−17.0	12.8	14.2	1.0
QTR % Change			−25.5			17.4			−30.6			30.1
Year % Change												−21.1

HIGHLIGHTS

Post Election Year	Bull Market Begins 9/21	Best Eight Months	−13.4%	High Jan-24 2859.15
GW Bush (1st Term)	Recession Begins Q2	Worst Four Months	−21.8%	Low Sep-21 1423.19

2002   NASDAQ COMPOSITE

Previous Month Close	Jan	Feb	Mar	Apr	May	Jun	Jul	Aug	Sep	Oct	Nov	Dec
	1950.40	1934.03	1731.49	1845.35	1688.23	1615.73	1463.21	1328.26	1314.85	1172.06	1329.75	1478.78
1	C	1911.24	1802.74	1862.62	1677.53	C	1403.80	1280.00	C	1213.72	1360.70	C
2	1979.25	C	C	1804.40	1644.82	C	1357.82	1247.92	C	1187.30	C	1484.78
3	2044.27	C	C	1784.35	1613.03	1562.56	1380.17	C	1263.84	1165.56	C	1448.96
4	2059.38	1855.53	1859.32	1789.75	C	1578.12	C	C	1292.31	1139.90	1396.54	1430.35
5	C	1838.52	1866.29	1770.03	C	1595.26	1448.36	1206.01	1251.00	C	1401.17	1410.75
6	C	1812.71	1890.40	C	1578.48	1554.88	C	1259.55	1295.30	C	1418.99	1422.44
7	2037.10	1782.11	1881.63	C	1573.82	1535.48	C	1280.90	C	1119.40	1376.71	C
8	2055.74	1818.88	1929.67	1785.87	1696.29	· C	1405.61	1316.52	C	1129.21	1359.28	C
9	2044.89	C	C	1742.57	1650.49	C	1381.12	1306.12	1304.60	1114.11	C	1367.14
10	2047.24	C	C	1767.07	1600.85	1530.69	1346.01	C	1320.09	1163.37	C	1390.76
11	2022.46	1846.66	1929.49	1725.24	C	1497.18	1374.43	C	1315.45	1210.47	1319.19	1396.59
12	C	1834.21	1897.12	1756.19	C	1519.12	1373.50	1306.84	1279.68	C	1349.56	1399.55
13	C	1859.16	1862.03	C	1652.54	1496.86	C	1269.28	1291.40	C	1361.34	1362.42
14	1990.74	1843.37	1854.14	C	1719.05	1504.74	C	1334.30	C	1220.53	1411.52	C
15	2000.91	1805.20	1868.30	1753.78	1725.56	C	1382.62	1345.01	C	1282.44	1411.14	C
16	1944.44	C	C	1816.79	1730.44	C	1375.26	1361.01	1275.88	1232.42	C	1400.33
17	1985.82	C	C	1810.67	1741.39	1553.29	1397.25	C	1259.94	1272.29	C	1392.05
18	1930.34	C	1877.06	1802.43	C	1542.96	1356.95	C	1252.13	1287.86	1393.69	1361.51
19	C	1750.61	1880.87	1796.83	C	1496.83	1319.15	1394.54	1216.45	C	1374.51	1354.10
20	C	1775.57	1832.87	C	1701.59	1464.75	C	1376.59	1221.09	C	1419.35	1363.07
21	C	1716.24	1868.83	C	1664.18	1440.96	C	1409.25	C	1309.67	1467.55	C
22	1882.53	1724.54	1851.39	1758.68	1673.45	C	1282.65	1422.95	C	1292.80	1468.74	C
23	1922.38	C	C	1730.29	1697.63	C	1229.05	1380.62	1184.93	1320.23	C	1381.69
24	1942.58	C	C	1713.34	1661.49	1460.34	1290.23	C	1182.17	1298.71	C	1372.47
25	1937.70	1769.88	1812.49	1713.70	C	1423.99	1240.08	C	1222.29	1331.13	1481.90	C
26	C	1766.86	1824.17	1663.89	C	1429.33	1262.12	1391.74	1221.61	C	1444.43	1367.89
27	C	1751.88	1826.75	C	C	1459.20	C	1347.78	1199.16	C	1487.94	1348.31
28	1943.91	1731.49	1845.35	C	1652.17	1463.21	C	1314.38	C	1315.83	C	C
29	1892.99		C	1656.93	1624.39	C	1335.25	1335.77	C	1300.54	1478.78	C
30	1913.44		C	1688.23	1631.92	C	1344.19	1314.85	1172.06	1326.73	C	1339.54
31	1934.03		C		1615.73		1328.26	C		1329.75		1335.51
Close	1934.03	1731.49	1845.35	1688.23	1615.73	1463.21	1328.26	1314.85	1172.06	1329.75	1478.78	1335.51
Month Pt Change	−16.37	−202.54	113.86	−157.12	−72.50	−152.52	−134.95	−13.41	−142.79	157.69	149.03	−143.27
Month % Change	−0.8	−10.5	6.6	−8.5	−4.3	−9.4	−9.2	−1.0	−10.9	13.5	11.2	−9.7
QTR % Change			−5.4			−20.7			−19.9			13.9
Year % Change												−31.5

Previous Month Close	Jan	Feb	Mar	Apr	May	Jun	Jul	Aug	Sep	Oct	Nov	Dec
	1335.51	1320.91	1337.52	1341.17	1464.31	1595.91	1622.80	1735.02	1810.45	1786.94	1932.21	1960.26
1	C	C	C	1348.30	1472.56	C	1640.13	1715.62	C	1832.25	C	1989.82
2	1384.85	C	C	1396.72	1502.88	1590.75	1678.73	C	1841.48	1836.22	C	1980.07
3	1387.08	1323.79	1320.29	1396.58	C	1603.56	1663.46	C	1852.90	1880.57	1967.70	1960.25
4	C	1306.15	1307.77	1383.51	C	1634.65	C	1714.06	1868.97	C	1957.96	1968.80
5	C	1301.50	1314.40	C	1504.04	1646.01	C	1673.50	1858.24	C	1959.37	1937.82
6	1421.32	1301.73	1302.89	C	1523.71	1627.42	C	1652.68	C	1893.46	1976.37	C
7	1431.57	1282.47	1305.29	1389.51	1506.76	C	1720.71	1652.18	C	1907.85	1970.74	C
8	1401.07	C	C	1382.94	1489.69	C	1746.46	1644.03	1888.62	1893.78	C	1948.85
9	1438.46	C	C	1356.74	1520.15	1603.97	1747.46	C	1873.43	1911.90	C	1908.32
10	1447.72	1296.68	1278.37	1365.61	C	1627.67	1715.86	C	1823.81	1915.31	1941.64	1904.65
11	C	1295.46	1271.47	1358.85	C	1646.02	1733.93	1661.51	1846.09	C	1930.75	1942.32
12	C	1278.97	1279.24	C	1541.40	1653.62	C	1687.01	1855.03	C	1973.11	1949.00
13	1446.04	1277.44	1340.77	C	1539.68	1626.49	C	1686.61	C	1933.53	1967.35	C
14	1460.99	1310.17	1340.33	1384.95	1534.90	C	1754.82	1700.34	C	1943.19	1930.26	C
15	1438.80	C	C	1391.01	1551.38	C	1753.21	1702.01	1845.70	1939.10	C	1918.26
16	1423.75	C	C	1394.72	1538.53	1666.58	1747.97	C	1887.25	1950.14	C	1924.29
17	1376.19	C	1392.27	1425.50	C	1668.44	1698.02	C	1883.10	1912.36	1909.61	1921.33
18	C	1346.54	1400.55	C	C	1677.14	1708.50	1739.49	1909.55	C	1881.75	1956.18
19	C	1334.32	1397.07	C	1492.77	1648.64	C	1761.11	1905.70	C	1899.65	1951.02
20	C	1331.23	1402.77	C	1491.09	1644.72	C	1760.54	C	1925.14	1881.92	C
21	1364.25	1349.02	1421.84	1424.37	1489.87	C	1681.41	1777.55	C	1940.90	1893.88	C
22	1359.48	C	C	1451.36	1507.55	C	1706.10	1765.32	1874.62	1898.07	C	1955.80
23	1388.27	C	C	1466.16	1510.09	1610.75	1719.18	C	1901.72	1885.51	C	1974.78
24	1342.14	1322.38	1369.78	1457.23	C	1605.61	1701.42	C	1843.70	1865.59	1947.14	1969.23
25	C	1328.98	1391.01	1434.54	C	1602.66	1730.70	1764.31	1817.24	C	1943.04	C
26	C	1303.68	1387.45	C	C	1634.01	C	1770.65	1792.07	C	1953.31	1973.14
27	1325.27	1323.94	1384.25	C	1556.69	1625.26	C	1782.13	C	1882.91	C	C
28	1342.18	1337.52	1369.60	1462.24	1563.24	C	1735.36	1800.18	C	1932.26	1960.26	C
29	1358.06		C	1471.30	1574.95	C	1731.37	1810.45	1824.56	1936.56	C	2006.48
30	1322.35		C	1464.31	1595.91	1622.80	1720.91	C	1786.94	1932.69	C	2009.88
31	1320.91		1341.17		C		1735.02	C		1932.21		2003.37
Close	1320.91	1337.52	1341.17	1464.31	1595.91	1622.80	1735.02	1810.45	1786.94	1932.21	1960.26	2003.37
Month Pt Change	−14.60	16.61	3.65	123.14	131.60	26.89	112.22	75.43	−23.51	145.27	28.05	43.11
Month % Change	−1.1	1.3	0.3	9.2	9.0	1.7	6.9	4.3	−1.3	8.1	1.5	2.2
QTR % Change			0.4			21.0			10.1			12.1
Year % Change												50.0

HIGHLIGHTS

Pre-Election Year	Bull Market	Best Eight Months	6.0%	High	Dec-30	2009.88
GW Bush (1st Term)	Expansion	Worst Four Months	19.1%	Low	Mar-11	1271.47

2004 NASDAQ COMPOSITE

Previous Month Close	Jan	Feb	Mar	Apr	May	Jun	Jul	Aug	Sep	Oct	Nov	Dec
	2003.37	2066.15	2029.82	1994.22	1920.15	1986.74	2047.79	1887.36	1838.10	1896.84	1974.99	2096.81
1	C	C	2057.80	2015.01	C	1990.77	2015.55	C	1850.41	1942.20	1979.87	2138.23
2	2006.68	2063.15	2039.65	2057.17	C	1988.98	2006.66	1892.09	1873.43	C	1984.79	2143.57
3	C	2066.21	2033.36	C	1938.72	1960.26	C	1859.42	1844.48	C	2004.33	2147.96
4	C	2014.14	2055.11	C	1950.48	1978.62	C	1855.06	C	1952.40	2023.63	C
5	2047.36	2019.56	2047.63	2079.12	1957.26	C	C	1821.63	C	1955.50	2038.94	C
6	2057.37	2064.01	C	2059.90	1937.74	C	1963.43	1776.89	C	1971.03	C	2151.25
7	2077.68	C	C	2050.24	1917.96	2020.62	1966.08	C	1858.56	1948.52	C	2114.66
8	2100.25	C	2008.78	2052.88	C	2023.53	1935.32	C	1850.64	1919.97	2039.25	2126.11
9	2086.92	2060.57	1995.16	C	C	1990.61	1946.33	1774.64	1869.65	C	2043.33	2129.01
10	C	2075.33	1964.15	C	1896.07	1999.87	C	1808.70	1894.31	C	2034.56	2128.07
11	C	2089.66	1943.89	C	1931.35	C	C	1782.42	C	1928.76	2061.27	C
12	2111.78	2073.61	1984.73	2065.48	1925.59	C	1936.92	1752.49	C	1925.17	2085.34	C
13	2096.44	2053.56	C	2030.08	1926.03	C	1931.66	1757.22	1910.38	1920.53	C	2148.50
14	2111.13	C	C	2024.85	1904.25	1969.99	1914.88	C	1915.40	1903.02	C	2159.84
15	2109.08	C	1939.20	2002.17	C	1995.60	1912.71	C	1896.52	1911.50	2094.09	2162.55
16	2140.46	C	1943.09	1995.74	C	1998.23	1883.15	1782.84	1904.08	C	2078.62	2146.15
17	C	2080.35	1976.76	C	1876.64	1983.67	C	1795.25	1910.09	C	2099.68	2135.20
18	C	2076.47	1962.44	C	1897.82	1986.73	C	1831.37	C	1936.52	2104.28	C
19	C	2045.96	1940.47	2020.43	1898.17	C	1883.83	1819.89	C	1922.90	2070.63	C
20	2147.98	2037.93	C	1978.63	1896.59	C	1917.07	1838.02	1908.07	1932.97	C	2127.85
21	2142.45	C	C	1995.63	1912.09	1974.38	1874.37	C	1921.18	1953.62	C	2150.91
22	2119.01	C	1909.90	2032.91	C	1994.15	1889.06	C	1885.71	1915.14	2085.19	2157.03
23	2123.87	2007.52	1901.80	2049.77	C	2020.98	1849.09	1838.70	1886.43	C	2084.28	2160.62
24	C	2005.44	1909.48	C	1922.98	2015.57	C	1836.89	1879.48	C	2102.54	C
25	C	2022.98	1967.17	C	1964.65	2025.47	C	1860.72	C	1914.04	C	C
26	2153.83	2032.57	1960.02	2036.77	1976.15	C	1839.02	1852.92	C	1928.79	2101.97	C
27	2116.04	2029.82	C	2032.53	1984.50	C	1869.10	1862.09	1859.88	1969.99	C	2154.22
28	2077.37	C	C	1989.54	1986.74	2019.82	1858.26	C	1869.87	1975.74	C	2177.19
29	2068.23	C	1992.57	1958.78	C	2034.93	1881.06	C	1893.94	1974.99	2106.87	2177.00
30	2066.15		2000.63	1920.15	C	2047.79	1887.36	1836.49	1896.84	C	2096.81	2178.34
31	C		1994.22		C		C	1838.10		C		2175.44
Close	2066.15	2029.82	1994.22	1920.15	1986.74	2047.79	1887.36	1838.10	1896.84	1974.99	2096.81	2175.44
Month Pt Change	62.78	–36.33	–35.60	–74.07	66.59	61.05	–160.43	–49.26	58.74	78.15	121.82	78.63
Month % Change	3.1	–1.8	–1.8	–3.7	3.5	3.1	–7.8	–2.6	3.2	4.1	6.2	3.7
QTR % Change			–0.5			2.7			–7.4			14.7
Year % Change												8.6

HIGHLIGHTS

Election Year	Bull Market	Best Eight Months	4.2%	High Dec-30	2178.34
GW Bush (1st Term)	Expansion	Worst Four Months	-3.6%	Low Aug-12	1752.49

Previous Month	Jan	Feb	Mar	Apr	May	Jun	Jul	Aug	Sep	Oct	Nov	Dec
Close	2175.44	2062.41	2051.72	1999.23	1921.65	2068.22						
1	C	2068.70	2071.25	1984.81	C	2087.86						
2	C	2075.06	2067.50	C	1928.65	2097.80						
3	2152.15	2057.64	2058.40	C	1933.07	2071.43						
4	2107.86	2086.66	2070.61	1991.07	1962.23	C						
5	2091.24	C	C	1999.32	1961.80	C						
6	2090.00	C	C	1999.14	1967.35	2075.76						
7	2088.61	2082.03	2090.21	2018.79	C	2067.16						
8	C	2086.68	2073.55	1999.35	C	2060.18						
9	C	2052.55	2061.29	C	1979.67	2076.91						
10	2097.04	2053.10	2059.72	C	1962.77	2063.00						
11	2079.62	2076.66	2041.60	1992.12	1971.55	C						
12	2092.53	C	C	2005.40	1963.88	C						
13	2070.56	C	C	1974.37	1976.78	2068.96						
14	2087.91	2082.92	2051.04	1946.71	C	2069.04						
15	C	2089.21	2034.98	1908.15	C	2074.92						
16	C	2087.43	2015.75	C	1994.43	2089.15						
17	C	2061.34	2016.42	C	2004.15	2090.11						
18	2106.04	2058.62	2007.79	1912.92	2030.65	C						
19	2073.59	C	C	1932.36	2042.58	C						
20	2045.88	C	C	1913.76	2046.42	2088.13						
21	2034.27	C	2007.51	1962.41	C	2091.07						
22	C	2030.32	1989.34	1932.19	C	2092.03						
23	C	2031.25	1990.22	C	2056.65	2070.66						
24	2008.70	2051.70	1991.06	C	2061.62	2053.27						
25	2019.95	2065.40	C	1950.78	2050.12	C						
26	2046.09	C	C	1927.44	2071.24	C						
27	2047.15	C	C	1930.43	2075.73	2045.20						
28	2035.83	2051.72	1992.52	1904.18	C	2069.89						
29	C		1973.88	1921.65	C	2068.89						
30	C		2005.67	C	C	2056.96						
31	2062.41		1999.23		2068.22							
Close	2062.41	2051.72	1999.23	1921.65	2068.22	2056.96						
Month Pt Change	−113.03	−10.69	−52.49	−77.58	146.57	−11.26						
Month % Change	−5.2	−0.5	−2.6	−3.9	7.6	−0.5						
QTR % Change			−8.1			2.9						
Year % Change												

HIGHLIGHTS

Post Election Year	Bull Market	Best Eight Months	4.2%	High	Jan-03	2152.15
GW Bush (2nd Term)	Expansion	Worst Four Months	—	Low	Apr-28	1904.18

RUSSELL 1000 INDEX — 1979

Previous Month Close	Jan	Feb	Mar	Apr	May	Jun	Jul	Aug	Sep	Oct	Nov	Dec
Close	**51.58**	**53.76**	**51.88**	**54.97**	**55.15**	**53.92**	**56.25**	**56.86**	**60.04**	**60.05**	**55.78**	**58.65**
1	C	53.78	52.24	C	55.15	53.98	C	57.05	C	59.69	56.25	C
2	51.89	53.58	52.30	54.59	55.16	C	55.76	57.08	C	60.20	56.25	C
3	52.45	C	C	55.34	55.19	C	55.84	57.04	C	60.27	C	58.47
4	52.91	C	C	55.51	54.61	54.08	C	C	59.08	60.63	C	58.99
5	53.23	52.83	52.88	55.84	C	54.74	56.06	C	58.44	61.18	55.91	59.27
6	C	52.86	52.76	55.81	C	55.12	56.66	57.14	58.73	C	55.58	59.68
7	C	52.36	53.11	C	53.66	55.44	C	57.82	59.20	C	54.88	59.45
8	53.11	52.63	53.67	C	53.69	55.32	C	57.99	C	60.46	55.13	C
9	53.37	52.76	53.68	55.66	53.86	C	57.13	57.80	C	58.50	55.82	C
10	53.08	C	C	55.90	53.38	C	56.96	58.30	59.49	57.61	C	59.55
11	53.34	C	C	55.40	53.42	55.46	56.61	C	59.09	57.55	C	59.44
12	53.75	52.93	53.75	55.26	C	55.99	56.16	C	59.31	57.32	56.84	59.48
13	C	53.33	53.87	C	C	55.78	55.96	58.79	59.32	C	56.63	59.59
14	C	53.27	53.85	C	53.15	55.68	C	58.86	59.88	C	56.87	60.23
15	54.11	53.23	53.97	C	53.19	55.72	C	59.29	C	56.65	57.31	C
16	53.49	53.23	54.40	54.81	53.32	C	56.21	59.20	C	56.55	57.19	C
17	53.48	C	C	54.80	54.13	C	55.70	59.37	59.85	56.71	C	60.53
18	53.70	C	C	55.10	54.17	55.39	55.61	C	59.38	56.82	C	59.98
19	53.67	C	54.61	54.89	C	55.44	55.60	C	59.54	55.68	57.43	59.92
20	C	53.64	54.31	54.90	C	55.51	55.75	59.67	60.66	C	57.13	60.01
21	C	53.49	54.69	C	54.29	55.76	C	59.72	60.64	C	57.22	59.66
22	53.72	53.06	54.92	C	54.52	56.04	C	59.83	C	55.02	C	C
23	54.07	52.75	54.90	55.07	54.25	C	55.60	59.64	C	54.83	57.70	C
24	53.88	C	C	55.36	54.29	C	55.79	59.65	60.17	54.95	C	59.69
25	54.41	C	C	55.55	54.47	55.78	56.40	C	60.22	54.76	C	C
26	54.76	52.68	54.63	55.29	C	55.55	56.44	C	60.39	55.09	58.88	59.75
27	C	51.83	55.39	55.16	C	55.89	56.49	59.92	60.48	C	58.67	59.83
28	C	51.88	55.20	C	C	56.20	C	59.84	60.05	C	58.89	59.84
29	54.60		55.18	C	54.41	56.25	C	59.84	C	55.19	58.91	C
30	54.38		54.97	55.15	53.91	C	56.53	59.85	C	56.16	58.65	C
31	53.76		C		53.92		56.86	60.04		55.78		59.87
Close	**53.76**	**51.88**	**54.97**	**55.15**	**53.92**	**56.25**	**56.86**	**60.04**	**60.05**	**55.78**	**58.65**	**59.87**
Month Pt Change	2.18	−1.88	3.09	0.18	−1.23	2.33	0.61	3.18	0.01	−4.27	2.87	1.22
Month % Change	4.2	−3.5	6.0	0.3	−2.2	4.3	1.1	5.6	0.02	−7.1	5.1	2.1
QTR % Change			6.6			2.3			6.8			−0.3
Year % Change												16.1

HIGHLIGHTS

Election Year	Bull Market Begins 4/21	Best Nine Months	5.4%	High Oct-05	61.18
Carter	Recession Q1 - Q2	Worst Three Months	6.8%	Low Feb-27	51.83

1980 RUSSELL 1000 INDEX

Previous Month Close	Jan	Feb	Mar	Apr	May	Jun	Jul	Aug	Sep	Oct	Nov	Dec
	59.87	63.40	63.07	55.79	58.38	61.31	63.27	67.30	68.05	69.84	71.08	78.26
1	C	63.85	C	55.95	58.01	C	63.65	67.13	C	70.84	C	76.52
2	58.64	C	C	56.38	58.09	61.12	64.08	C	68.76	71.40	C	76.30
3	58.31	C	62.51	56.15	C	61.01	64.99	C	70.09	72.14	71.88	76.20
4	59.06	63.43	62.54	C	C	62.11	C	66.86	69.78	C	C	76.03
5	C	63.58	61.63	C	58.51	62.26	C	66.83	69.54	C	73.10	74.50
6	C	64.12	60.22	C	58.52	62.55	C	67.26	C	73.37	71.76	C
7	59.26	64.38	59.19	55.07	58.94	C	65.51	68.22	C	72.98	71.86	C
8	60.41	65.27	C	55.67	58.47	C	65.33	68.40	68.70	73.35	C	72.59
9	60.45	C	C	56.78	57.73	62.81	65.39	C	69.11	73.07	C	72.44
10	60.96	C	58.81	57.25	C	63.31	64.86	C	69.58	72.72	72.05	71.24
11	61.07	64.84	59.54	57.14	C	64.04	65.33	69.05	70.07	C	73.00	70.54
12	C	65.28	59.09	C	57.72	63.85	C	68.52	70.09	C	74.77	71.59
13	C	65.47	58.46	C	58.54	64.02	C	68.32	C	73.66	75.85	C
14	61.25	64.49	58.27	56.58	58.93	C	66.46	69.38	C	73.68	76.22	C
15	61.61	63.91	C	56.45	58.99	C	66.13	69.62	70.14	74.69	C	71.68
16	61.62	C	C	55.86	59.21	64.15	66.27	C	70.73	73.84	C	72.29
17	61.48	C	56.41	55.59	C	64.11	67.22	C	71.79	73.53	76.58	73.53
18	61.59	C	57.33	55.37	C	64.22	67.41	68.34	71.55	C	77.74	73.76
19	C	63.52	57.56	C	59.35	63.36	C	67.94	71.91	C	77.38	74.25
20	C	64.49	56.95	C	59.31	63.09	C	68.56	C	74.11	78.10	C
21	62.15	63.91	56.54	54.94	59.38	C	67.68	69.58	C	73.68	77.41	C
22	61.75	63.64	C	56.81	60.10	C	67.53	69.95	72.56	73.80	C	75.27
23	62.71	C	C	57.01	60.95	63.34	67.45	C	72.15	72.44	C	75.01
24	62.88	C	54.83	57.46	C	63.71	67.40	C	72.64	72.59	76.90	75.29
25	62.84	62.69	54.65	57.81	C	64.52	66.84	69.51	71.64	C	77.50	C
26	C	63.05	54.36	C	C	64.28	C	69.39	70.37	C	77.97	75.64
27	C	62.25	53.68	C	61.40	64.20	C	68.70	C	71.54	C	C
28	63.50	62.26	55.15	58.06	61.81	C	67.14	67.91	C	71.60	78.26	C
29	63.13	63.07	C	58.20	60.87	C	67.64	68.05	68.75	71.47	C	74.81
30	63.80		C	58.38	61.31	63.27	67.61	C	69.84	70.40	C	74.97
31	63.40		55.79		C		67.30	C		71.08		75.20
Close	63.40	63.07	55.79	58.38	61.31	63.27	67.30	68.05	69.84	71.08	78.26	75.20
Month Pt Change	3.53	–0.33	–7.28	2.59	2.93	1.96	4.03	0.75	1.79	1.24	7.18	–3.06
Month % Change	5.9	–0.5	–11.5	4.6	5.0	3.2	6.4	1.1	2.6	1.8	10.1	–3.9
QTR % Change			–6.8			13.4			10.4			7.7
Year % Change												25.6

HIGHLIGHTS

Election Year	Bull Market Begins 4/21	Best Nine Months	4.5%	High Nov-28	78.26
Carter	Recession Q1 - Q2	Worst Three Months	10.4%	Low Mar-27	53.68

RUSSELL 1000 INDEX
1981

Previous Month Close	Jan 75.20	Feb 71.75	Mar 72.49	Apr 75.21	May 73.77	Jun 73.90	Jul 73.01	Aug 72.92	Sep 68.42	Oct 64.06	Nov 67.54	Dec 70.23
1	C	C	C	75.54	73.68	73.69	72.36	C	68.59	64.61	C	70.04
2	75.60	70.15	72.81	75.51	C	72.63	71.66	C	68.81	65.93	68.90	69.29
3	C	70.96	72.08	75.10	C	72.70	C	72.69	67.37	C	69.23	69.57
4	C	71.10	72.20	C	72.51	72.80	C	73.10	66.72	C	69.25	70.08
5	76.30	71.73	71.78	C	72.28	73.52	C	74.07	C	66.07	68.66	C
6	76.34	72.22	71.69	74.25	72.55	C	70.86	74.08	C	66.04	68.28	C
7	74.51	C	C	74.12	73.11	C	71.28	73.66	C	67.08	C	69.53
8	73.47	C	C	74.56	73.15	73.50	71.40	C	65.38	67.64	C	69.22
9	73.72	71.51	72.29	74.83	C	73.26	71.95	C	65.59	67.26	68.58	69.58
10	C	71.46	71.90	74.82	C	73.49	72.04	73.98	66.68	C	68.30	69.72
11	C	70.93	71.64	C	72.07	74.27	C	74.71	67.44	C	68.45	69.29
12	73.74	70.51	73.34	C	72.64	74.22	C	74.51	C	67.09	68.62	C
13	73.58	70.31	73.33	73.99	72.63	C	72.12	74.64	C	66.94	67.75	C
14	73.80	C	C	73.64	73.07	C	72.15	74.11	66.85	65.86	C	68.17
15	74.26	C	C	74.43	73.59	74.27	72.48	C	66.38	66.32	C	68.24
16	74.60	C	74.18	74.74	C	73.42	72.64	C	65.81	66.06	66.88	67.97
17	C	70.68	73.84	C	C	74.06	72.90	73.40	64.80	C	67.33	68.26
18	C	71.04	74.02	C	73.74	73.18	C	72.67	64.25	C	66.97	68.73
19	74.40	69.98	73.61	C	73.48	73.53	C	72.87	C	65.95	67.34	C
20	72.97	69.92	74.08	75.14	73.57	C	71.75	72.92	C	66.66	67.95	C
21	72.78	C	C	74.44	73.48	C	71.56	72.18	64.68	66.58	C	68.35
22	72.17	C	C	74.42	73.34	73.41	70.92	C	64.39	66.37	C	68.09
23	72.16	70.29	74.93	74.38	C	74.19	71.08	C	63.71	65.84	67.83	67.81
24	C	70.39	74.50	74.93	C	73.75	71.73	70.00	63.47	C	68.77	67.96
25	C	70.96	75.68	C	C	73.88	C	69.73	62.03	C	69.03	C
26	71.84	71.82	75.33	C	74.07	73.80	C	69.66	C	65.59	C	C
27	72.60	72.49	74.53	75.10	74.52	C	72.37	68.82	C	66.19	69.60	C
28	72.19	C	C	74.39	74.31	C	71.96	69.18	63.47	66.31	C	67.79
29	72.14		C	73.72	73.90	73.41	71.98	C	63.89	66.04	C	67.44
30	71.75		74.33	73.77	C	73.01	72.37	C	64.06	67.54	70.23	67.74
31	C		75.21		C		72.92	68.42		C		67.93
Close	71.75	72.49	75.21	73.77	73.90	73.01	72.92	68.42	64.06	67.54	70.23	67.93
Month Pt Change	−3.45	0.74	2.72	−1.44	0.13	−0.89	−0.09	−4.50	−4.36	3.48	2.69	−2.30
Month % Change	−4.6	1.0	3.8	−1.9	0.2	−1.2	−0.1	−6.2	−6.4	5.4	4.0	−3.3
QTR % Change			0.0			−2.9			−12.3			6.0
Year % Change												−9.7

HIGHLIGHTS

Post Election Year	Bear Market Begins 4/27	Best Nine Months	−6.5%	High Jan-06	76.34
Reagan (1st term)	Recession Begins Q3	Worst Three Months	−12.3%	Low Sep-25	62.03

1982 RUSSELL 1000 INDEX

Previous Month Close	Jan	Feb	Mar	Apr	May	Jun	Jul	Aug	Sep	Oct	Nov	Dec
	67.93	66.12	62.21	61.43	63.85	61.53	59.92	58.54	65.14	65.89	73.34	76.28
1	C	64.78	62.38	62.38	C	61.31	59.42	C	64.56	66.65	74.25	76.45
2	C	64.94	62.08	63.08	C	61.49	58.93	59.43	65.60	C	75.41	76.45
3	C	64.23	61.15	C	64.09	61.34	C	58.92	66.85	C	78.21	76.41
4	68.02	64.11	60.53	C	64.44	60.41	C	58.04	C	66.43	77.78	C
5	66.58	64.59	60.20	62.90	64.52	C	C	57.53	C	66.71	78.01	C
6	66.07	C	C	63.25	65.04	C	58.70	56.82	C	68.75	C	77.88
7	65.88	C	C	63.33	65.50	60.34	58.62	C	66.17	70.25	C	78.38
8	66.14	63.15	59.16	63.73	C	60.07	58.70	C	66.60	71.55	77.17	77.96
9	C	62.62	59.72	C	C	59.67	59.40	56.39	66.56	C	78.47	77.04
10	C	63.05	60.05	C	64.97	59.96	C	56.28	66.03	C	77.60	76.70
11	64.64	62.96	59.99	C	65.56	60.91	C	56.12	C	73.27	77.93	C
12	64.35	62.93	59.50	63.61	65.37	C	59.81	55.98	C	73.30	76.94	C
13	63.53	C	C	63.60	64.97	C	59.77	56.68	66.63	74.61	C	76.86
14	63.88	C	C	63.51	64.91	60.19	60.20	C	67.15	73.50	C	75.60
15	64.30	C	59.86	63.74	C	60.00	60.22	C	67.69	72.98	75.61	74.42
16	C	62.71	59.79	64.04	C	59.60	60.53	56.83	67.55	C	74.66	74.39
17	C	62.58	59.69	C	64.18	58.97	C	59.34	66.91	C	75.94	75.51
18	64.73	62.67	60.42	C	63.67	58.69	C	59.35	C	74.56	76.23	C
19	64.08	62.38	60.59	64.01	63.18	C	60.39	59.53	C	74.54	75.65	C
20	63.69	C	C	63.40	62.97	C	60.76	61.51	66.85	75.96	C	74.89
21	63.89	C	C	63.53	63.12	58.66	60.77	C	68.05	75.90	C	76.01
22	63.63	61.48	61.77	64.26	C	59.20	60.82	C	67.69	75.88	74.17	76.21
23	C	61.39	62.14	65.00	C	60.17	60.69	63.13	67.57	C	73.48	76.68
24	C	62.38	61.84	C	63.04	60.00	C	62.92	67.34	C	73.98	C
25	63.50	62.32	62.00	C	62.83	59.60	C	64.12	C	73.03	C	C
26	63.34	62.21	61.41	65.31	62.08	C	60.26	64.71	C	73.52	74.48	C
27	63.64	C	C	64.71	61.82	C	59.76	63.97	67.47	74.08	C	77.88
28	65.37	C	C	64.33	61.53	60.09	58.83	C	67.30	73.25	C	77.22
29	66.12		61.51	63.76	C	60.09	58.79	C	66.48	73.34	74.08	77.48
30	C		61.55	63.85	C	59.92	58.54	64.20	65.89	C	76.28	77.12
31	C		61.43		C		C	65.14		C		77.24
Close	66.12	62.21	61.43	63.85	61.53	59.92	58.54	65.14	65.89	73.34	76.28	77.24
Month Pt Change	−1.81	−3.91	−0.78	2.42	−2.32	−1.61	−1.38	6.60	0.75	7.45	2.94	0.96
Month % Change	−2.7	−5.9	−1.3	3.9	−3.6	−2.6	−2.3	11.3	1.2	11.3	4.0	1.3
QTR % Change			−9.6			−2.5			10.0			17.2
Year % Change												13.7

HIGHLIGHTS

Mid-Term Election Year	Bull Market Begins 8/12	Best Nine Months	41.4%	High Nov-09 78.47
Reagan (1st term)	Recession	Worst Three Months	10.0%	Low Aug-12 55.98

RUSSELL 1000 INDEX 1983

	Jan	Feb	Mar	Apr	May	Jun	Jul	Aug	Sep	Oct	Nov	Dec
Previous Month Close	77.24	79.75	81.45	84.06	90.04	89.89	93.18	90.18	90.65	91.85	89.69	91.50
1	C	78.64	82.84	C	C	89.91	93.68	89.78	90.64	C	89.73	91.53
2	C	78.66	83.61	C	88.98	90.59	C	89.75	91.19	C	90.44	90.93
3	76.04	79.21	84.27	C	89.01	90.87	C	90.36	C	91.60	89.82	C
4	77.45	80.19	84.41	84.02	89.57	C	C	89.25	C	91.89	89.25	C
5	77.87	C	C	83.54	90.24	C	92.46	89.43	C	92.63	C	90.96
6	79.71	C	C	83.02	91.25	91.12	93.47	C	92.59	93.96	C	90.79
7	79.70	80.64	84.40	83.29	C	90.18	93.04	C	92.61	94.24	88.91	91.03
8	C	80.06	83.19	83.86	C	89.43	92.80	88.13	92.59	C	88.77	90.64
9	C	79.73	83.99	C	91.08	89.67	C	88.49	92.37	C	89.85	90.66
10	80.56	80.98	83.51	C	91.21	90.30	C	89.27	C	95.07	90.11	C
11	80.11	81.10	83.22	84.94	90.74	C	93.28	89.41	C	93.89	91.18	C
12	80.56	C	C	85.32	90.43	C	91.92	89.91	91.56	93.38	C	90.83
13	80.11	C	C	85.90	90.81	91.43	91.72	C	91.09	93.41	C	90.46
14	80.60	81.82	82.92	86.54	C	91.75	92.06	C	91.50	93.44	91.45	89.58
15	C	81.65	83.15	86.98	C	92.56	91.09	90.68	91.04	C	90.86	88.78
16	C	81.23	82.43	C	89.94	93.64	C	90.45	91.91	C	91.24	89.09
17	80.69	81.18	82.27	C	90.19	93.71	C	91.42	C	93.62	91.26	C
18	80.53	81.49	82.41	87.48	90.13	C	90.79	90.65	C	92.13	90.80	C
19	79.93	C	C	86.93	89.48	C	91.27	90.84	92.88	91.50	C	89.08
20	80.38	C	C	87.94	89.52	93.68	93.61	C	93.60	91.69	C	88.91
21	79.11	C	83.00	87.71	C	94.42	93.64	C	93.20	91.04	91.28	89.69
22	C	80.18	82.82	87.90	C	94.78	93.60	90.91	93.91	C	91.68	89.50
23	C	80.81	83.90	C	90.09	94.56	C	89.99	93.86	C	91.70	89.42
24	76.94	82.29	84.22	C	91.21	94.61	C	89.17	C	91.05	C	C
25	77.82	82.38	83.91	87.10	91.63	C	93.92	88.93	C	91.35	91.88	C
26	77.78	C	C	88.53	91.35	C	94.30	89.55	93.98	90.80	C	C
27	79.20	C	C	88.43	90.96	93.59	92.90	C	93.15	90.50	C	90.14
28	79.35	81.45	83.43	89.05	C	91.98	91.42	C	92.91	89.78	91.53	90.41
29	C		83.32	90.04	C	92.43	90.18	89.54	92.53	C	92.23	90.22
30	C		84.20	C	C	93.18	C	89.71	91.85	C	91.50	90.38
31	79.75		84.06		89.89		C	90.65		89.69		C
Close	79.75	81.45	84.06	90.04	89.89	93.18	90.18	90.65	91.85	89.69	91.50	90.38
Month Pt Change	2.51	1.70	2.61	5.98	–0.15	3.29	–3.00	0.47	1.20	–2.16	1.81	–1.12
Month % Change	3.2	2.1	3.2	7.1	–0.2	3.7	–3.2	0.5	1.3	–2.4	2.0	–1.2
QTR % Change			8.8			10.8			–1.4			–1.6
Year % Change												17.0

HIGHLIGHTS

Pre-Election Year	Bear Market Begins 11/29	Best Nine Months	–10.1%	High Oct-10	95.07
Reagan (1st term)	Expansion	Worst Three Months	–1.4%	Low Jan-03	76.04

1984 — RUSSELL 1000 INDEX

Previous Month	Jan	Feb	Mar	Apr	May	Jun	Jul	Aug	Sep	Oct	Nov	Dec
Close	90.38	88.69	84.76	85.73	86.00	80.94	82.61	81.13	89.87	89.67	89.62	88.36
1	C	88.31	85.35	C	86.84	82.34	C	82.87	C	88.88	90.32	C
2	C	88.59	85.93	85.13	87.09	C	82.51	84.97	C	88.31	90.37	C
3	89.92	87.28	C	84.85	86.78	C	82.79	87.43	C	87.73	C	87.96
4	91.31	C	C	84.80	85.75	83.03	C	C	89.03	87.92	C	88.16
5	92.47	C	85.21	83.45	C	82.68	82.34	C	88.69	87.84	91.00	87.51
6	92.80	85.78	84.29	83.55	C	83.30	82.06	87.65	89.37	C	91.95	87.81
7	C	86.02	83.38	C	85.86	83.30	C	87.65	88.79	C	91.32	87.64
8	C	84.49	83.65	C	86.44	83.44	C	87.19	C	87.53	91.08	C
9	92.62	84.14	83.21	83.57	86.23	C	82.59	89.05	C	87.34	90.61	C
10	92.16	84.55	C	83.79	86.13	C	82.37	89.21	88.70	87.55	C	87.87
11	92.08	C	C	83.33	85.36	82.38	81.20	C	88.87	87.92	C	88.04
12	92.02	C	84.19	84.64	C	81.99	80.91	C	88.91	88.70	90.48	87.83
13	91.68	83.80	84.52	84.53	C	81.94	81.32	89.13	90.50	C	89.79	87.43
14	C	84.60	84.51	C	84.79	81.04	C	88.64	91.05	C	89.74	87.88
15	C	84.46	84.92	C	85.05	80.49	C	87.90	C	89.47	89.67	C
16	91.67	84.32	85.85	85.02	85.02	C	81.57	88.40	C	89.04	88.80	C
17	91.94	84.07	C	85.43	84.18	C	81.92	88.50	91.10	88.73	C	88.37
18	91.77	C	C	84.90	83.70	81.78	81.46	C	90.55	90.62	C	90.62
19	91.49	C	85.04	84.93	C	82.31	80.91	C	90.19	90.69	88.16	90.27
20	90.93	C	85.55	C	C	83.34	80.48	88.82	90.48	C	88.65	89.92
21	C	83.47	85.43	C	83.19	83.27	C	90.33	89.67	C	88.88	89.56
22	C	83.24	84.48	C	82.65	83.31	C	90.02	C	90.38	C	C
23	90.12	83.14	84.45	84.35	82.27	C	80.04	90.12	C	90.26	90.10	C
24	90.43	84.80	C	84.87	81.16	C	79.49	90.29	89.33	90.31	C	90.12
25	89.83	C	C	85.16	81.32	83.07	79.96	C	89.43	89.83	C	C
26	89.43	C	84.33	86.06	C	82.39	80.65	C	89.74	89.25	89.43	90.00
27	89.26	85.81	84.60	85.96	C	81.81	81.30	89.75	90.08	C	89.84	89.63
28	C	84.59	85.93	C	C	82.40	C	90.19	89.67	C	89.19	89.89
29	C	84.76	85.86	C	80.67	82.61	C	90.12	C	88.96	88.60	C
30	88.52		85.73	86.00	80.69	C	80.88	89.84	C	89.97	88.36	C
31	88.69		C		80.94		81.13	89.87		89.62		90.31
Close	88.69	84.76	85.73	86.00	80.94	82.61	81.13	89.87	89.67	89.62	88.36	90.31
Month Pt Change	−1.69	−3.93	0.97	0.27	−5.06	1.67	−1.48	8.74	−0.20	−0.05	−1.26	1.95
Month % Change	−1.9	−4.4	1.1	0.3	−5.9	2.1	−1.8	10.8	−0.2	−0.1	−1.4	2.2
QTR % Change			−5.1			−3.6			8.5			0.7
Year % Change												−0.1

HIGHLIGHTS

Election Year	Bull Market Begins 7/24	Best Nine Months	16.7%	High Jan-06	92.80
Reagan (1st term)	Expansion	Worst Three Months	8.5%	Low Jul-24	79.49

ALMANAC INVESTOR

RUSSELL 1000 INDEX — 1985

Previous Month Close	Jan	Feb	Mar	Apr	May	Jun	Jul	Aug	Sep	Oct	Nov	Dec
	90.31	97.31	98.38	98.03	97.72	103.02	104.65	103.78	102.76	98.75	103.16	109.91
1	C	96.84	99.45	98.36	97.04	C	104.95	104.50	C	100.24	103.96	C
2	89.39	C	C	98.01	97.25	C	104.81	104.21	C	99.84	C	108.98
3	89.05	C	C	97.26	97.84	103.05	104.56	C	102.37	99.96	C	109.23
4	88.61	97.77	98.88	97.21	C	103.49	C	C	102.01	99.39	103.92	110.89
5	C	98.02	98.94	C	C	103.64	105.12	103.65	102.01	C	104.55	110.79
6	C	97.99	98.13	C	97.85	104.12	C	102.39	102.48	C	104.78	110.26
7	88.85	98.75	97.56	C	98.25	103.46	C	102.11	C	98.74	104.76	C
8	88.83	98.95	97.33	96.79	98.26	C	104.79	102.85	C	98.66	105.44	C
9	89.40	C	C	96.88	99.00	C	104.42	102.55	102.58	99.03	C	110.95
10	91.02	C	C	97.51	100.31	103.36	105.08	C	101.79	99.27	C	111.06
11	90.95	98.08	97.13	97.96	C	103.11	105.43	C	100.76	100.08	107.20	112.11
12	C	98.07	97.52	98.15	C	102.45	105.65	102.20	100.00	C	107.69	112.35
13	C	99.49	96.71	C	100.42	101.28	C	102.01	99.50	C	107.20	113.97
14	92.24	99.15	96.57	C	100.10	102.11	C	102.11	C	101.17	108.16	C
15	92.46	98.69	96.10	98.38	100.44	C	105.47	102.03	C	101.05	107.76	C
16	92.82	C	C	98.56	101.03	C	106.52	101.46	99.42	101.95	C	114.97
17	92.64	C	C	98.78	102.03	101.85	106.90	C	98.58	101.94	C	114.32
18	92.90	C	96.06	98.32	C	102.27	106.25	C	98.72	101.69	108.01	113.86
19	C	98.58	97.35	98.46	C	102.05	106.55	101.60	99.62	C	108.02	113.90
20	C	98.60	97.19	C	103.10	102.02	C	102.39	99.11	C	108.16	114.35
21	94.84	98.07	97.36	C	103.08	103.20	C	102.91	C	101.64	109.40	C
22	95.01	97.70	97.19	98.21	102.50	C	106.08	102.09	C	102.24	109.52	C
23	96.00	C	C	98.84	102.00	C	105.10	101.97	100.09	102.76	C	113.11
24	95.82	C	C	99.05	102.32	103.19	104.46	C	99.24	102.51	C	112.39
25	96.23	97.46	96.58	99.62	C	103.53	104.56	C	98.23	101.94	108.89	C
26	C	98.37	96.77	99.05	C	103.72	104.69	102.12	98.43	C	109.02	112.61
27	C	98.19	97.35	C	C	104.36	C	102.46	C	C	109.95	113.64
28	96.33	98.38	97.45	C	102.23	104.65	C	102.80	C	102.03	C	C
29	97.18		98.03	98.22	102.16	C	103.15	102.87	C	102.78	109.91	C
30	97.36		C	97.72	102.18	C	103.23	102.76	98.75	103.25	C	114.15
31	97.31		C		103.02		103.78	C		103.16		114.39
Close	97.31	98.38	98.03	97.72	103.02	104.65	103.78	102.76	98.75	103.16	109.91	114.39
Month Pt Change	7.00	1.07	−0.35	−0.31	5.30	1.63	−0.87	−1.02	−4.01	4.41	6.75	4.48
Month % Change	7.8	1.1	−0.4	−0.3	5.4	1.6	−0.8	−1.0	−3.9	4.5	6.5	4.1
QTR % Change			8.5			6.8			−5.6			15.8
Year % Change												26.7

HIGHLIGHTS

Post Election Year	Bull Market	Best Nine Months 38.5%	High Dec-16	114.97
Reagan (2nd Term)	Expansion	Worst Three Months -5.6%	Low Jan-04	88.61

Previous Month Close	Jan	Feb	Mar	Apr	May	Jun	Jul	Aug	Sep	Oct	Nov	Dec
	114.39	115.39	123.71	130.07	128.44	134.82	136.75	128.74	137.43	125.70	132.11	133.97
1	C	C	C	128.45	128.36	C	137.35	128.17	C	126.79	C	133.79
2	113.57	C	C	128.65	128.25	133.69	137.87	C	135.33	126.89	C	136.25
3	114.24	116.53	123.14	127.22	C	133.83	137.50	C	135.80	126.81	132.99	136.38
4	C	116.15	122.76	125.20	C	133.11	C	128.47	137.59	C	133.22	136.07
5	C	116.22	122.59	C	129.74	133.78	C	128.85	135.82	C	133.42	135.11
6	114.22	116.53	123.06	C	129.55	133.79	C	128.72	C	127.30	133.06	C
7	115.87	117.03	123.23	124.87	128.97	C	133.45	128.96	C	127.10	132.99	C
8	113.21	C	C	127.42	129.59	C	131.63	128.96	134.31	128.20	C	135.04
9	112.01	C	C	127.72	129.92	130.99	132.47	C	133.92	127.85	C	134.07
10	111.99	117.84	123.75	129.09	C	130.69	132.54	C	133.37	127.69	133.12	134.86
11	C	117.84	126.25	128.93	C	131.53	132.37	130.96	127.34	C	133.59	133.53
12	C	117.97	126.83	C	129.70	131.76	C	132.44	124.95	C	133.30	132.99
13	112.33	118.67	127.15	C	129.19	133.83	C	133.74	C	127.88	131.50	C
14	112.31	119.74	128.61	129.62	129.76	C	130.21	134.21	C	127.63	132.13	C
15	113.22	C	C	129.83	128.27	C	128.03	134.54	125.39	129.31	C	133.25
16	113.76	C	C	132.09	127.49	133.93	128.54	C	125.27	129.73	C	134.21
17	113.49	C	127.67	132.63	C	133.16	129.15	C	125.65	129.34	131.38	133.02
18	C	121.21	128.31	132.47	C	133.35	129.31	134.65	125.83	C	128.23	132.53
19	C	120.01	128.11	C	127.63	133.10	C	134.30	125.67	C	128.35	133.67
20	113.05	121.07	128.64	C	129.07	134.34	C	135.92	C	127.99	130.52	C
21	112.24	122.35	127.38	133.60	128.82	C	129.17	135.88	C	127.95	132.36	C
22	111.14	C	C	132.48	131.04	C	130.28	136.11	127.07	128.15	C	133.32
23	111.46	C	C	131.90	131.76	133.58	130.47	C	127.67	129.65	C	131.99
24	112.60	122.19	127.96	132.10	C	134.59	130.15	C	128.13	129.28	133.11	132.32
25	C	121.93	127.70	132.08	C	135.60	131.27	134.96	126.06	C	133.49	C
26	C	122.07	129.07	C	C	135.56	C	137.26	126.12	C	133.70	132.55
27	113.14	123.54	130.02	C	133.57	136.01	C	137.53	C	129.54	C	C
28	114.32	123.71	C	132.37	134.59	C	129.01	137.39	C	129.82	133.97	C
29	114.67		C	131.01	135.08	C	128.15	137.43	124.86	130.66	C	131.36
30	114.24		C	128.44	134.82	136.75	128.94	C	125.70	132.07	C	130.64
31	115.39		130.07		C		128.74	C		132.11		130.00
Close	115.39	123.71	130.07	128.44	134.82	136.75	128.74	137.43	125.70	132.11	133.97	130.00
Month Pt Change	1.00	8.32	6.36	−1.63	6.38	1.93	−8.01	8.69	−11.73	6.41	1.86	−3.97
Month % Change	0.9	7.2	5.1	−1.3	5.0	1.4	−5.9	6.8	−8.5	5.1	1.4	−3.0
QTR % Change			13.7			5.1			−8.1			3.4
Year % Change												13.6

HIGHLIGHTS

Mid-Term Election Year	Bull Market	Best Nine Months	27.2%	High	Jul-02	137.87
Reagan (2nd Term)	Expansion	Worst Three Months	-8.1%	Low	Jan-22	111.14

RUSSELL 1000 INDEX

1987

Previous Month Close	Jan	Feb	Mar	Apr	May	Jun	Jul	Aug	Sep	Oct	Nov	Dec
	130.00	146.48	152.29	155.20	152.39	152.94	159.84	166.57	172.95	168.83	131.89	121.28
1	C	C	C	155.26	152.20	152.88	159.34	C	169.92	171.58	C	122.04
2	132.26	147.80	151.84	155.89	C	152.15	160.52	C	168.86	172.10	133.68	122.69
3	C	147.68	152.28	159.04	C	154.46	C	165.87	168.09	C	131.20	118.73
4	C	149.48	154.36	C	152.74	155.27	C	165.32	166.42	C	130.35	117.65
5	135.44	150.39	155.32	C	155.67	154.66	C	166.57	C	172.15	133.11	C
6	135.94	149.93	155.30	159.70	155.66	C	160.09	168.47	C	167.98	131.37	C
7	137.42	C	C	157.20	155.27	C	161.08	169.08	C	167.50	C	119.83
8	138.51	C	C	157.44	154.67	156.23	161.51	C	164.48	165.33	C	122.81
9	139.28	148.91	154.17	155.23	C	156.53	161.25	C	164.74	163.86	127.89	124.92
10	C	147.34	155.45	154.82	C	156.68	161.65	171.51	166.41	C	125.69	122.59
11	C	148.60	155.22	C	153.80	157.37	C	174.08	168.81	C	127.01	123.33
12	140.13	147.82	155.63	C	154.40	158.91	C	173.70	C	162.83	130.25	C
13	139.95	149.70	154.99	151.39	154.74	C	161.36	174.91	C	165.25	128.99	C
14	141.27	C	C	147.86	154.80	C	162.89	174.76	169.29	160.83	C	126.72
15	142.68	C	C	150.38	151.49	159.67	162.74	C	166.83	157.25	C	127.11
16	142.77	C	154.08	151.77	C	160.45	163.74	C	165.45	149.44	129.44	129.79
17	C	152.48	155.99	C	C	160.54	164.60	174.96	165.41	C	127.55	127.65
18	C	152.48	156.11	C	150.66	160.91	C	172.45	165.26	C	128.79	130.69
19	144.30	152.66	156.79	C	147.33	161.47	C	172.68	C	121.04	126.12	C
20	144.25	152.71	158.71	151.34	146.61	C	163.07	175.18	C	124.70	126.88	C
21	143.52	C	C	154.48	147.66	C	161.68	175.77	163.14	135.85	C	131.03
22	146.42	C	C	151.89	148.49	162.67	161.64	C	167.13	130.59	C	131.06
23	144.66	151.23	159.93	151.57	C	162.11	161.23	C	168.16	130.19	127.41	132.73
24	C	151.57	160.15	148.95	C	161.34	161.89	174.62	167.59	C	129.10	132.22
25	C	152.23	159.63	C	C	162.32	C	176.22	167.84	C	128.16	C
26	144.17	151.75	159.86	C	152.03	161.46	C	175.33	C	119.45	C	C
27	146.21	152.29	157.56	148.92	152.08	C	162.59	173.72	C	121.86	126.44	C
28	147.04	C	C	149.47	153.06	C	163.36	171.65	169.23	121.83	C	129.04
29	146.50		C	150.56	152.94	161.68	164.99	C	168.64	127.74	C	128.58
30	146.48		153.98	152.39	C	159.84	166.27	C	168.83	131.89	121.28	130.25
31	C		155.20		C		166.57	172.95		C		130.02
Close	146.48	152.29	155.20	152.39	152.94	159.84	166.57	172.95	168.83	131.89	121.28	130.02
Month Pt Change	16.48	5.81	2.91	-2.81	0.55	6.90	6.73	6.38	-4.12	-36.94	-10.61	8.74
Month % Change	12.7	4.0	1.9	-1.8	0.4	4.5	4.2	3.8	-2.4	-21.9	-8.0	7.2
QTR % Change			19.4			3.0			5.6			-23.0
Year % Change												0.02

HIGHLIGHTS

Pre-Election Year	Bear Market 8/25 - 10/19	Best Nine Months-13.9%	High Aug-25	176.22
Reagan (2nd Term)	Expansion	Worst Three Months5.6%	Low Dec-04	117.65

1988 — RUSSELL 1000 INDEX

Previous Month Close	Jan	Feb	Mar	Apr	May	Jun	Jul	Aug	Sep	Oct	Nov	Dec
	130.02	135.55	141.54	137.45	138.37	138.66	145.31	143.99	139.26	144.68	147.55	144.59
1	C	134.90	141.32	C	C	141.03	144.62	144.17	137.70	C	147.58	144.17
2	C	135.16	141.86	C	138.43	140.38	C	144.16	140.56	C	147.54	143.86
3	C	133.60	141.95	C	139.14	141.00	C	144.66	C	144.30	147.66	C
4	134.34	133.49	141.69	136.06	137.95	C	C	144.24	C	143.99	146.37	C
5	135.86	133.05	C	137.13	137.20	C	146.39	143.80	C	144.61	C	145.25
6	136.14	C	C	140.39	136.58	141.32	144.66	C	141.56	144.89	C	146.52
7	137.13	C	141.71	140.83	C	140.52	144.49	C	141.28	147.52	145.05	146.83
8	128.80	132.12	142.70	142.47	C	143.55	143.69	143.27	141.43	C	145.68	146.07
9	C	133.27	142.58	C	135.99	143.04	C	141.49	141.94	C	144.79	146.29
10	C	135.75	140.03	C	136.40	143.57	C	139.14	C	147.60	144.96	C
11	130.39	135.51	140.38	142.87	134.25	C	143.90	139.53	C	147.45	142.16	C
12	129.27	136.28	C	143.48	134.59	C	142.62	139.40	141.78	145.49	C	146.06
13	129.54	C	C	143.52	136.02	143.66	143.26	C	142.21	146.05	C	145.94
14	129.61	C	141.04	137.77	C	145.10	143.71	C	143.14	146.17	141.96	145.41
15	132.69	C	140.96	137.64	C	145.23	144.48	137.50	142.59	C	142.22	144.95
16	C	137.26	142.20	C	136.90	143.10	C	138.45	143.78	C	139.93	145.91
17	C	137.49	143.54	C	135.48	143.45	C	138.61	C	146.57	140.22	C
18	132.75	136.45	143.47	137.32	133.45	C	143.76	138.80	C	147.91	141.10	C
19	131.65	138.18	C	136.80	133.91	C	142.66	138.50	142.96	146.80	C	147.07
20	128.35	C	C	135.81	134.12	142.62	143.28	C	143.44	149.58	C	146.50
21	128.67	C	142.28	135.88	C	143.91	141.67	C	143.71	149.94	140.87	146.43
22	130.32	140.06	142.39	137.57	C	145.91	140.16	136.94	143.25	C	141.30	146.25
23	C	139.92	142.52	C	133.04	145.66	C	136.98	143.52	C	142.23	146.78
24	C	139.82	139.80	C	134.33	145.26	C	138.85	C	149.39	C	C
25	133.06	138.63	137.49	138.65	134.58	C	140.65	137.95	C	149.35	141.36	C
26	131.91	138.99	C	139.42	135.07	C	140.88	138.20	143.08	148.84	C	C
27	131.82	C	C	139.41	134.54	143.10	139.58	C	142.80	146.77	C	146.31
28	133.70	C	137.03	138.85	C	144.59	141.19	C	143.18	147.37	142.00	146.55
29	135.55	141.54	138.05	138.37	C	144.01	143.99	139.52	144.87	C	143.17	147.61
30	C		137.09	C	C	145.31	C	139.65	144.68	C	144.59	146.99
31	C		137.45		138.66		C	139.26		147.55		C
Close	135.55	141.54	137.45	138.37	138.66	145.31	143.99	139.26	144.68	147.55	144.59	146.99
Month Pt Change	5.53	5.99	−4.09	0.92	0.29	6.65	−1.32	−4.73	5.42	2.87	−2.96	2.40
Month % Change	4.3	4.4	−2.9	0.7	0.2	4.8	−0.9	−3.3	3.9	2.0	−2.0	1.7
QTR % Change			5.7			5.7			−0.4			1.6
Year % Change												13.1

HIGHLIGHTS

Election Year	Bull Market	Best Nine Months	16.5%	High Oct-21	149.94
Reagan (2nd Term)	Expansion	Worst Three Months	−0.4%	Low Jan-20	128.35

RUSSELL 1000 INDEX — 1989

	Jan	Feb	Mar	Apr	May	Jun	Jul	Aug	Sep	Oct	Nov	Dec
Previous Month Close	146.99	156.93	152.98	155.99	163.63	169.85	168.49	182.27	185.33	184.40	179.17	181.85
1	C	156.87	152.29	C	163.43	170.66	C	181.26	186.49	C	179.75	184.02
2	C	156.83	153.67	C	163.03	172.45	C	181.58	C	185.33	178.46	C
3	145.78	156.92	154.27	156.80	163.10	C	169.07	181.93	C	187.21	178.06	C
4	147.77	C	C	156.32	162.96	C	C	181.55	C	188.36	C	184.50
5	148.07	C	C	156.81	162.96	170.84	169.68	C	185.99	188.50	C	183.71
6	148.46	156.53	155.89	156.42	C	171.77	170.25	C	184.33	189.45	175.56	183.17
7	C	158.35	155.56	157.34	C	173.26	171.94	184.08	183.94	C	176.52	182.67
8	C	157.93	155.68	C	162.14	173.27	C	184.13	184.16	C	178.30	183.11
9	148.69	156.43	155.55	C	161.73	173.22	C	183.11	C	189.93	177.67	C
10	148.42	154.36	155.11	157.32	162.03	C	172.99	183.84	C	189.62	178.80	C
11	149.14	C	C	158.00	162.58	C	173.90	182.28	183.61	188.50	C	182.85
12	149.70	C	C	158.28	165.88	172.99	174.44	C	184.21	187.70	C	184.15
13	150.01	154.52	156.24	157.04	C	171.82	174.63	C	182.68	176.82	179.05	184.67
14	C	154.30	156.15	159.32	C	171.74	175.40	181.38	181.40	C	178.30	183.73
15	C	155.54	156.83	C	167.04	169.88	C	182.06	182.02	C	179.54	183.13
16	150.22	155.89	158.22	C	166.72	170.43	C	182.51	C	180.65	179.54	C
17	149.88	156.81	154.80	159.52	167.87	C	175.72	182.00	C	179.81	180.03	C
18	151.31	C	C	161.51	168.19	C	175.19	182.72	182.79	180.27	C	179.88
19	151.60	C	C	162.13	169.74	170.58	177.31	C	182.84	183.08	C	179.19
20	151.45	C	153.37	161.73	C	170.30	176.23	C	182.78	183.05	178.90	179.38
21	C	156.44	154.06	163.25	C	169.98	177.19	180.14	182.54	C	178.88	180.44
22	C	154.03	153.64	C	170.17	170.79	C	180.26	183.12	C	179.97	181.89
23	150.42	154.53	152.98	C	168.51	173.46	C	181.95	C	181.84	C	C
24	152.24	152.25	C	162.85	168.88	C	176.05	185.30	C	180.97	180.98	C
25	152.64	C	C	162.04	168.97	C	176.17	184.91	181.72	180.49	C	C
26	153.94	C	C	162.20	170.19	172.83	178.13	C	181.89	178.31	C	181.69
27	155.07	152.50	153.64	163.49	C	173.75	180.15	C	182.23	176.66	181.72	182.75
28	C	152.98	154.19	163.63	C	172.42	180.34	185.58	183.96	C	181.88	183.70
29	C		154.60	C	C	169.37	C	184.56	184.40	C	180.87	185.11
30	155.69		154.78	C	169.13	168.49	C	184.99	C	176.61	181.85	C
31	156.93		155.99		169.85		182.27	185.33		179.17		C
Close	156.93	152.98	155.99	163.63	169.85	168.49	182.27	185.33	184.40	179.17	181.85	185.11
Month Pt Change	9.94	–3.95	3.01	7.64	6.22	–1.36	13.78	3.06	–0.93	–5.23	2.68	3.26
Month % Change	6.8	–2.5	2.0	4.9	3.8	–0.8	8.2	1.7	–0.5	–2.8	1.5	1.8
QTR % Change			6.1			8.0			9.4			0.4
Year % Change												25.9

HIGHLIGHTS

Post Election Year	Bull Market	Best Nine Months 1.0%	High	Oct-09	189.93
GHW Bush	Expansion	Worst Three Months 9.4%	Low	Jan-03	145.78

1990 RUSSELL 1000 INDEX

Previous Month Close	Jan	Feb	Mar	Apr	May	Jun	Jul	Aug	Sep	Oct	Nov	Dec
	185.11	171.44	173.43	177.28	172.32	187.66	186.29	184.32	166.69	157.83	156.62	166.69
1	C	171.45	173.91	C	173.06	188.78	C	184.03	C	162.45	158.08	C
2	188.03	172.73	175.44	176.63	174.09	C	186.96	181.81	C	162.74	160.57	C
3	187.75	C	C	179.02	174.67	C	187.27	178.33	C	160.76	C	167.78
4	186.25	C	C	177.84	176.03	190.97	C	C	166.92	161.26	C	168.98
5	184.57	173.26	174.62	177.56	C	190.74	185.20	C	167.59	160.62	161.99	171.04
6	C	172.22	176.50	177.10	C	190.02	186.51	172.68	165.73	C	160.76	170.58
7	C	174.12	176.10	C	177.11	189.09	C	172.96	167.19	C	158.03	169.90
8	185.25	173.89	177.70	C	177.80	186.95	C	174.90	C	161.60	158.77	C
9	183.23	174.29	176.67	177.74	178.12	C	186.99	175.87	C	157.39	161.80	C
10	181.85	C	C	178.11	178.73	C	185.56	173.70	166.53	154.95	C	170.45
11	182.22	C	C	178.16	182.68	188.33	187.78	C	166.19	152.36	C	169.33
12	178.03	172.58	177.01	179.43	C	190.60	189.87	C	166.87	154.63	164.96	171.07
13	C	172.90	175.76	C	C	190.05	190.76	173.74	164.92	C	164.26	170.81
14	C	173.35	176.13	C	184.16	188.99	C	175.53	163.94	C	165.71	169.42
15	176.43	174.81	176.63	C	183.98	188.85	C	175.97	C	156.23	164.15	C
16	178.23	173.83	178.39	179.66	183.82	C	191.56	172.06	C	154.05	164.16	C
17	176.70	C	C	179.59	184.11	C	190.77	169.49	164.34	154.05	C	168.93
18	176.92	C	C	177.62	184.21	185.95	189.07	C	164.62	157.58	C	171.02
19	177.50	C	179.16	176.26	C	186.62	189.43	C	163.73	160.76	165.16	171.20
20	C	171.46	178.20	174.75	C	186.81	187.59	169.59	161.06	C	163.20	171.29
21	C	171.16	177.37	C	186.02	187.46	C	166.19	160.87	C	163.44	171.95
22	173.20	170.39	175.27	C	186.32	185.27	C	163.48	C	161.97	C	C
23	173.49	169.54	176.04	172.64	186.83	C	184.28	158.41	C	160.92	163.00	C
24	172.65	C	C	172.23	186.58	C	184.40	160.78	157.32	160.97	C	171.09
25	170.74	C	C	173.05	184.74	183.60	185.08	C	159.14	159.83	C	C
26	170.29	171.53	176.28	173.38	C	183.41	184.58	C	157.52	157.07	163.62	171.59
27	C	172.47	178.04	171.52	C	184.78	183.33	166.04	155.27	C	164.54	170.46
28	C	173.43	178.19	C	C	186.03	C	166.04	157.83	C	164.62	170.56
29	169.80		177.57	C	187.50	186.29	C	167.43	C	155.61	163.91	C
30	168.38		177.28	172.32	187.56	C	184.08	164.96	C	156.54	166.69	C
31	171.44		C		187.66		184.32	166.69		156.62		171.22
Close	171.44	173.43	177.28	172.32	187.66	186.29	184.32	166.69	157.83	156.62	166.69	171.22
Month Pt Change	-13.67	1.99	3.85	-4.96	15.34	-1.37	-1.97	-17.63	-8.86	-1.21	10.07	4.53
Month % Change	-7.4	1.2	2.2	-2.8	8.9	-0.7	-1.1	-9.6	-5.3	-0.8	6.4	2.7
QTR % Change			-4.2			5.1			-15.3			8.5
Year % Change												-7.5

HIGHLIGHTS

Mid-Term Election Year	Bear Market 7/16 - 10/11	Best Nine Months 22.8%	High Jul-16 191.56
GHW Bush	Recession Begins Q3	Worst Three Months -15.3%	Low Oct-11 152.36

RUSSELL 1000 INDEX — 1991

	Jan	Feb	Mar	Apr	May	Jun	Jul	Aug	Sep	Oct	Nov	Dec
Previous Month Close	171.22	179.00	191.34	196.15	195.94	203.32	193.78	202.67	207.18	204.02	206.96	198.46
1	C	178.81	193.05	194.27	195.94	C	197.15	202.37	C	204.73	206.40	C
2	169.40	C	C	198.35	198.70	C	196.93	202.55	C	204.21	C	201.53
3	167.15	C	C	198.33	198.91	202.54	194.89	C	205.51	202.26	C	201.47
4	166.78	181.86	192.69	198.72	C	202.45	C	C	204.32	200.79	205.68	201.10
5	C	183.38	196.44	196.66	C	201.23	195.27	201.41	203.85	C	204.99	199.87
6	C	186.66	196.18	C	198.53	200.49	C	204.03	203.79	C	205.58	200.75
7	163.87	185.82	196.06	C	197.19	198.51	C	204.16	C	199.71	207.48	C
8	163.48	187.11	195.54	198.07	197.67	C	197.19	203.72	C	200.36	207.24	C
9	161.94	C	C	195.69	199.97	C	196.59	202.67	203.53	198.51	C	200.29
10	163.47	C	C	195.36	196.45	197.92	196.50	C	201.42	200.23	C	200.08
11	163.84	191.72	194.51	197.67	C	198.99	197.15	C	201.84	200.67	207.58	199.86
12	C	190.32	192.86	198.94	C	196.81	198.69	203.13	203.09	C	209.46	201.85
13	C	192.05	195.11	C	196.88	197.28	C	204.03	201.18	C	209.79	203.33
14	162.25	189.75	194.74	C	194.36	199.59	C	204.37	C	203.24	209.57	C
15	162.86	192.14	194.60	199.28	192.49	C	199.87	204.12	C	205.78	202.10	C
16	164.38	C	C	202.47	194.31	C	199.50	202.29	202.20	206.92	C	203.49
17	170.28	C	C	204.06	194.44	198.62	199.32	C	202.12	206.28	C	202.51
18	172.16	C	193.96	203.05	C	197.88	201.31	C	202.92	206.60	203.29	202.77
19	C	192.34	191.31	200.94	C	196.00	200.77	197.60	203.48	C	200.24	202.17
20	C	190.22	191.92	C	194.31	196.13	C	199.02	203.85	C	199.90	204.49
21	171.81	190.14	191.39	C	195.79	197.13	C	204.65	C	205.32	200.76	C
22	170.54	190.57	191.73	199.15	196.35	C	200.04	205.06	C	204.36	198.80	C
23	171.55	C	C	199.41	195.97	C	198.25	206.42	202.91	204.33	C	209.48
24	173.97	C	C	199.87	197.17	193.66	197.72	C	203.79	202.80	C	210.97
25	174.68	191.30	193.07	198.25	C	193.34	198.95	C	203.48	202.27	198.23	C
26	C	189.09	196.42	198.05	C	193.67	199.04	206.26	203.37	C	199.47	214.02
27	C	191.48	196.25	C	C	195.18	C	205.90	202.94	C	198.99	215.09
28	174.76	191.34	196.15	C	199.32	193.78	C	207.72	C	204.87	C	C
29	174.78		C	195.36	199.88	C	200.12	207.62	C	206.02	198.46	C
30	177.42		C	195.94	201.97	C	201.91	207.18	204.02	207.05	C	219.47
31	179.00		C		203.32		202.67	C		206.96		220.61
Close	179.00	191.34	196.15	195.94	203.32	193.78	202.67	207.18	204.02	206.96	198.46	220.61
Month Pt Change	7.78	12.34	4.81	−0.21	7.38	−9.54	8.89	4.51	−3.16	2.94	−8.50	22.15
Month % Change	4.5	6.9	2.5	−0.1	3.8	−4.7	4.6	2.2	−1.5	1.4	−4.1	11.2
QTR % Change			14.6			−1.2			5.3			8.1
Year % Change												28.8

HIGHLIGHTS

Pre-Election Year	Bull Market	Best Nine Months	5.7%	High Dec-31	220.61
GHW Bush	Expansion Begins Q2	Worst Three Months	5.3%	Low Jan-09	161.94

1992 RUSSELL 1000 INDEX

	Jan	Feb	Mar	Apr	May	Jun	Jul	Aug	Sep	Oct	Nov	Dec
Previous Month Close	220.61	217.52	219.50	214.29	219.13	219.71	215.60	224.37	218.86	221.15	222.65	230.44
1	C	C	C	214.49	217.96	220.71	218.14	C	219.96	220.33	C	230.23
2	218.62	C	219.53	212.49	C	218.93	217.58	C	221.02	217.37	224.58	229.69
3	221.65	217.93	219.61	212.76	C	219.36	C	224.90	221.13	C	223.24	229.77
4	C	220.20	217.87	C	220.23	218.63	C	224.55	220.70	C	221.96	230.89
5	C	220.46	216.05	C	220.44	218.63	C	223.32	C	215.75	222.80	C
6	221.26	220.44	214.93	214.73	220.49	C	218.55	222.44	C	215.86	222.64	C
7	221.19	219.01	C	210.91	219.97	C	216.29	221.70	C	214.55	C	232.45
8	221.75	C	C	208.87	219.98	218.35	216.78	C	219.31	216.35	C	233.28
9	221.85	C	215.34	212.23	C	216.49	218.90	C	220.28	213.85	223.31	232.50
10	220.52	220.18	216.42	213.99	C	215.04	219.28	221.82	222.08	C	223.54	231.93
11	C	220.23	214.93	C	221.18	215.78	C	221.57	222.14	C	225.52	231.52
12	C	222.14	214.77	C	220.09	216.29	C	221.10	C	216.09	225.73	C
13	219.99	220.31	215.78	215.05	220.11	C	219.50	221.04	C	217.20	225.67	C
14	223.06	219.67	C	218.25	218.31	C	220.92	222.14	225.32	217.24	C	231.07
15	223.57	C	C	220.12	216.94	216.36	220.54	C	222.57	217.42	C	230.89
16	222.12	C	216.00	219.79	C	215.39	220.71	C	222.52	218.45	224.80	230.17
17	222.28	C	217.65	C	C	212.26	219.58	222.56	222.48	C	223.93	232.23
18	C	217.02	217.48	C	218.16	211.54	C	222.85	223.82	C	225.79	235.06
19	C	217.24	217.83	C	219.95	212.98	C	221.24	C	220.30	226.25	C
20	220.77	220.10	218.47	216.51	219.73	C	218.61	221.28	C	220.58	227.81	·C
21	218.55	218.94	C	216.41	218.31	C	218.85	219.50	223.50	220.74	C	234.94
22	221.57	C	C	216.41	218.89	212.64	217.39	C	221.02	220.29	C	234.94
23	220.30	C	217.78	217.13	C	213.18	217.96	C	221.08	219.98	227.03	234.37
24	220.55	218.98	217.19	215.89	C	213.01	217.84	217.08	221.70	C	228.41	234.69
25	C	218.05	216.70	C	C	212.62	C	217.32	219.39	C	229.30	C
26	C	220.69	216.69	C	217.32	212.75	C	218.39	C	221.94	C	C
27	220.24	220.12	214.34	215.61	217.85	C	217.87	218.76	C	222.00	229.81	C
28	220.26	219.50	C	215.68	219.97	C	220.91	219.27	220.22	222.91	C	234.55
29	218.01	C	C	217.43	219.71	215.73	223.29	C	220.46	223.55	C	234.22
30	218.77		213.99	219.13	C	215.60	224.16	C	221.15	222.65	230.44	234.64
31	217.52		214.29		C		224.37	218.86		C		233.59
Close	217.52	219.50	214.29	219.13	219.71	215.60	224.37	218.86	221.15	222.65	230.44	233.59
Month Pt Change	-3.09	1.98	-5.21	4.84	0.58	-4.11	8.77	-5.51	2.29	1.50	7.79	3.15
Month % Change	-1.4	0.9	-2.4	2.3	0.3	-1.9	4.1	-2.5	1.0	0.7	3.5	1.4
QTR % Change			-2.9			0.6			2.6			5.6
Year % Change												5.9

HIGHLIGHTS

Election Year	Bull Market	Best Nine Months	9.3%	High Dec-18	235.06
GHW Bush	Expansion	Worst Three Months	2.6%	Low Apr-08	208.87

	Jan	Feb	Mar	Apr	May	Jun	Jul	Aug	Sep	Oct	Nov	Dec
Previous Month Close	233.59	235.25	236.67	241.80	235.13	240.80	241.78	240.78	249.20	247.95	250.97	246.70
1	C	237.25	236.22	240.95	C	242.61	241.17	C	249.17	248.97	251.71	247.27
2	C	237.41	239.04	236.00	C	242.60	239.67	241.78	248.47	C	251.32	247.95
3	C	239.76	240.03	C	236.52	241.97	C	241.51	248.52	C	247.96	248.97
4	233.13	241.14	238.99	C	237.50	240.51	C	241.37	C	248.96	244.53	C
5	232.50	240.51	238.39	236.46	237.96	C	C	241.20	C	248.66	245.84	C
6	232.71	C	C	235.74	237.14	C	237.59	241.51	C	248.34	C	249.73
7	230.79	C	C	236.67	236.67	238.93	238.10	C	246.83	247.42	C	249.91
8	229.91	239.87	242.47	236.08	C	237.25	240.94	C	245.51	247.87	246.30	249.61
9	C	238.44	242.54	C	C	237.88	240.87	242.63	246.16	C	246.54	248.43
10	C	239.01	243.75	C	237.11	237.63	C	242.16	248.44	C	248.23	248.37
11	230.99	239.68	242.61	C	237.94	238.70	C	242.48	C	248.24	247.90	C
12	231.01	238.13	240.70	239.40	237.95	C	241.27	241.69	C	248.71	249.30	C
13	232.20	C	C	240.19	234.89	C	241.00	242.15	248.56	249.06	C	249.11
14	233.85	C	C	240.05	234.83	239.01	242.02	C	247.25	251.63	C	247.76
15	234.58	C	241.48	239.78	C	238.46	241.55	C	248.12	252.77	248.23	247.09
16	C	232.06	241.41	239.94	C	239.10	239.75	243.30	247.33	C	249.54	247.80
17	C	231.37	239.67	C	235.20	239.64	C	244.03	247.04	C	248.21	249.42
18	234.54	230.76	241.38	C	235.26	237.23	C	245.43	C	251.78	247.39	C
19	233.80	231.83	240.41	239.09	239.02	C	239.57	245.47	C	250.09	246.77	C
20	232.94	C	C	237.81	240.70	C	240.25	245.40	245.27	249.85	C	249.33
21	234.06	C	C	237.15	238.45	238.50	240.06	C	244.02	249.66	C	248.94
22	234.39	231.91	239.60	235.00	C	238.38	238.65	C	245.93	248.82	244.43	249.90
23	C	231.84	239.48	233.55	C	237.19	239.95	245.02	246.93	C	245.76	250.19
24	C	235.23	239.09	C	239.36	238.93	C	247.29	246.98	C	246.78	C
25	236.24	236.15	240.65	C	239.86	239.62	C	247.43	C	248.94	C	C
26	236.07	236.67	239.44	231.31	242.38	C	241.20	247.80	C	248.75	247.42	C
27	234.90	C	C	233.70	241.82	C	240.66	247.52	249.10	249.19	C	251.75
28	235.06	C	C	233.89	240.80	242.24	240.32	C	249.18	250.66	C	252.26
29	235.25		240.75	234.28	C	241.73	241.75	C	248.56	250.97	246.95	252.28
30	C		241.64	235.13	C	241.78	240.78	248.23	247.95	C	246.70	251.45
31	C		241.80		C		C	249.20		C		250.71
Close	235.25	236.67	241.80	235.13	240.80	241.78	240.78	249.20	247.95	250.97	246.70	250.71
Month Pt Change	1.66	1.42	5.13	–6.67	5.67	0.98	–1.00	8.42	–1.25	3.02	–4.27	4.01
Month % Change	0.7	0.6	2.2	–2.8	2.4	0.4	–0.4	3.5	–0.5	1.2	–1.7	1.6
QTR % Change			3.5			–0.0			2.6			1.1
Year % Change												7.3

Post Election Year	Bull Market	Best Nine Months	–4.4%	High	Oct-15	252.77
Clinton (1st Term)	Expansion	Worst Three Months	2.6%	Low	Jan-08	229.91

Previous Month Close	Jan	Feb	Mar	Apr	May	Jun	Jul	Aug	Sep	Oct	Nov	Dec
	250.71	258.08	250.52	239.19	241.71	244.13	237.11	244.44	254.04	247.49	251.62	241.82
1	C	258.31	249.28	C	C	244.94	238.17	245.91	252.72	C	249.67	239.31
2	C	258.31	249.07	C	243.06	245.14	C	245.85	251.62	C	248.95	241.32
3	249.92	257.70	248.27	C	243.01	246.36	C	246.15	C	246.91	249.65	C
4	250.41	251.77	249.30	235.38	242.53	C	C	244.71	C	243.12	246.97	C
5	250.61	C	C	240.78	242.24	C	238.14	243.92	C	242.38	C	241.52
6	250.34	C	C	240.80	240.05	246.13	238.08	C	251.88	241.76	C	241.21
7	251.77	252.63	250.60	242.20	C	245.62	239.26	C	251.63	243.29	247.06	240.08
8	C	252.49	250.00	240.11	C	244.68	239.86	244.46	252.72	C	248.40	236.89
9	C	253.51	250.34	C	236.85	244.58	C	244.56	250.13	C	248.27	237.52
10	254.32	251.67	248.90	C	238.59	245.38	C	245.92	C	245.26	247.64	C
11	253.80	252.03	250.24	241.34	236.09	C	239.12	245.20	C	248.72	246.59	C
12	253.89	C	C	239.98	237.11	C	239.17	246.60	248.97	248.58	C	238.60
13	253.26	C	C	238.97	237.23	245.60	239.94	C	249.57	249.61	C	239.16
14	254.50	252.19	250.89	239.10	C	247.02	242.42	C	250.33	250.17	248.47	241.81
15	C	253.39	250.83	239.23	C	246.21	242.69	246.39	253.57	C	248.13	242.31
16	C	253.38	252.22	C	237.24	246.92	C	248.21	251.83	C	248.26	243.77
17	253.68	252.08	253.07	C	239.58	245.01	C	248.54	C	249.99	247.10	C
18	254.00	250.72	253.29	237.34	242.41	C	243.15	247.54	C	249.42	245.95	C
19	253.79	C	C	237.15	243.84	C	242.39	247.84	251.66	250.80	C	243.27
20	254.25	C	C	236.70	243.19	243.08	241.04	C	247.82	248.95	C	243.05
21	254.16	C	251.91	240.36	C	240.70	241.52	C	246.59	247.90	244.08	244.40
22	C	252.53	251.83	239.91	C	241.58	241.80	247.27	246.38	C	239.65	244.42
23	C	252.12	251.83	C	242.28	239.60	C	248.51	245.52	C	239.61	244.69
24	252.79	248.89	249.45	C	243.43	236.12	C	250.57	C	245.84	C	C
25	252.14	249.85	247.61	242.42	243.99	C	242.36	250.26	C	246.00	241.07	C
26	253.34	C	C	242.09	244.47	C	241.87	253.13	246.15	246.70	C	C
27	255.57	C	C	C	244.62	238.43	241.38	C	246.65	248.37	C	246.01
28	256.63	250.52	246.99	240.53	C	237.88	242.20	C	248.26	252.38	241.91	245.06
29	C		242.86	241.71	C	238.72	244.44	253.52	247.12	C	242.53	245.52
30	C		239.21	C	C	237.11	C	254.38	247.49	C	241.82	244.65
31	258.08		239.19		244.13		C	254.04		251.62		C
Close	258.08	250.52	239.19	241.71	244.13	237.11	244.44	254.04	247.49	251.62	241.82	244.65
Month Pt Change	7.37	−7.56	−11.33	2.52	2.42	−7.02	7.33	9.60	−6.55	4.13	−9.80	2.83
Month % Change	2.9	−2.9	−4.5	1.1	1.0	−2.9	3.1	3.9	−2.6	1.7	−3.9	1.2
QTR % Change			−4.6			−0.9			4.4			−1.1
Year % Change												−2.4

HIGHLIGHTS

Mid-Term Election Year	Bull Market	Best Nine Months	16.9%	High Feb-01	258.31
Clinton (1st Term)	Expansion	Worst Three Months	4.4%	Low Apr-04	235.38

RUSSELL 1000 INDEX — 1995

	Jan	Feb	Mar	Apr	May	Jun	Jul	Aug	Sep	Oct	Nov	Dec
Previous Month Close	244.65	250.52	260.08	266.11	272.81	282.48	289.29	299.98	301.40	313.28	311.37	324.36
1	C	250.72	259.04	C	272.46	282.79	C	298.55	302.35	C	312.99	324.78
2	C	251.99	258.65	C	272.72	282.66	C	297.95	C	311.73	316.15	C
3	244.41	255.29	258.86	266.64	275.59	C	290.49	297.72	C	311.79	316.95	C
4	245.32	C	C	268.21	275.53	C	C	297.96	C	310.86	C	328.38
5	245.15	C	C	268.39	275.43	284.42	290.90	C	305.34	311.74	C	330.14
6	245.49	256.79	258.70	268.62	C	284.34	294.41	C	306.15	311.78	315.95	330.98
7	C	256.60	256.65	268.84	C	283.10	297.15	298.72	306.18	C	314.44	328.77
8	C	256.78	257.20	C	277.39	282.64	C	298.95	307.60	C	317.04	329.41
9	245.63	256.37	257.31	C	277.58	280.29	C	298.76	C	309.02	318.16	C
10	246.06	257.06	260.57	269.35	278.07	C	296.47	297.52	C	308.50	317.84	C
11	245.96	C	C	268.74	278.34	C	295.20	296.61	308.21	310.20	C	330.42
12	245.98	C	C	269.68	278.98	281.81	298.54	C	309.36	312.47	C	329.61
13	248.26	257.08	260.85	270.68	C	284.57	298.68	C	310.56	313.45	317.51	331.18
14	C	257.43	262.34	C	C	284.73	298.81	299.06	312.90	C	315.64	328.17
15	C	258.60	261.84	C	280.10	285.19	C	298.61	312.61	C	317.68	327.71
16	250.32	258.73	263.53	C	280.33	286.58	C	299.80	C	312.74	319.64	C
17	250.78	256.96	263.41	268.84	279.65	C	299.27	299.56	C	314.95	320.99	C
18	250.51	C	C	268.17	275.72	C	297.08	299.66	312.36	315.49	C	322.36
19	248.97	C	C	267.66	275.56	289.38	292.60	C	313.40	316.80	C	325.51
20	247.77	C	263.59	267.96	C	289.49	294.12	C	314.84	314.96	318.92	322.87
21	C	257.10	263.15	269.55	C	289.19	294.34	298.91	312.81	C	320.23	325.28
22	C	258.33	263.37	C	277.83	292.91	C	299.69	312.03	C	319.40	326.12
23	248.08	259.60	263.52	C	280.38	292.05	C	298.69	C	313.81	C	C
24	248.38	260.10	266.25	271.65	280.37	C	296.19	298.67	C	314.35	320.44	C
25	249.00	C	C	271.36	280.34	C	298.66	299.99	311.77	311.81	C	C
26	249.35	C	C	271.68	277.93	289.08	299.19	C	311.61	308.79	C	327.43
27	250.45	257.90	267.48	272.22	C	288.00	301.36	C	311.19	310.34	321.09	327.68
28	C	260.08	267.80	272.81	C	289.13	300.32	299.40	313.96	C	323.87	327.58
29	C		267.33	C	C	288.85	C	299.81	313.28	C	324.90	328.89
30	249.44		267.00	C	277.74	289.29	C	300.66	C	312.38	324.36	C
31	250.52		266.11		282.48		299.98	301.40		311.37		C
Close	250.52	260.08	266.11	272.81	282.48	289.29	299.98	301.40	313.28	311.37	324.36	328.89
Month Pt Change	5.87	9.56	6.03	6.70	9.67	6.81	10.69	1.42	11.88	−1.91	12.99	4.53
Month % Change	2.4	3.8	2.3	2.5	3.5	2.4	3.7	0.5	3.9	−0.6	4.2	1.4
QTR % Change			8.8			8.7			8.3			5.0
Year % Change												34.4

HIGHLIGHTS

Pre-Election Year	Bull Market	Best Nine Months 14.0%	High Dec-13	331.18
Clinton (1st Term)	Expansion	Worst Three Months 8.3%	Low Jan-03	244.41

1996 RUSSELL 1000 INDEX

	Jan	Feb	Mar	Apr	May	Jun	Jul	Aug	Sep	Oct	Nov	Dec
Previous Month Close	328.89	338.97	342.56	345.01	349.84	357.35	357.10	339.44	347.79	366.77	374.38	401.05
1	C	340.25	344.00	349.17	350.31	C	360.14	345.13	C	367.48	373.94	C
2	331.08	338.99	C	349.97	344.40	C	358.89	351.98	C	370.21	C	401.21
3	331.18	C	C	350.28	343.78	356.57	357.93	C	348.62	369.60	C	397.46
4	328.91	C	347.47	350.20	C	359.25	C	C	349.14	374.18	375.38	395.79
5	328.21	341.91	350.02	C	C	362.23	350.21	350.67	345.73	C	379.30	395.28
6	C	344.49	348.27	C	343.11	359.38	C	351.93	349.18	C	384.94	392.72
7	C	346.19	349.03	C	341.54	359.18	C	353.11	C	375.01	386.60	C
8	329.06	349.30	338.52	343.88	344.50	C	347.29	352.27	C	373.39	388.03	C
9	324.03	349.52	C	343.08	344.96	C	348.61	351.81	353.00	371.40	C	398.14
10	318.24	C	C	338.52	348.68	358.72	348.70	C	353.15	370.31	C	396.88
11	320.87	C	341.63	336.69	C	358.16	342.82	C	354.89	373.37	388.62	393.24
12	320.60	351.81	339.97	339.80	C	357.49	343.08	353.53	357.12	C	387.60	387.45
13	C	351.15	340.84	C	353.51	356.74	C	350.55	362.09	C	388.45	386.72
14	C	348.95	342.03	C	355.78	355.56	C	351.86	C	375.02	390.99	C
15	319.27	347.49	342.63	342.82	355.65	C	333.97	352.09	C	374.43	391.52	C
16	323.39	345.73	C	344.38	355.75	C	332.84	353.40	363.82	375.12	C	382.40
17	322.97	C	C	342.50	357.80	355.12	336.69	C	363.47	376.31	C	384.84
18	324.04	C	348.34	343.82	C	353.29	342.04	C	362.71	378.08	390.99	388.02
19	326.07	C	347.72	344.58	C	353.20	339.24	353.89	363.56	C	393.39	395.01
20	C	342.00	346.82	C	359.85	352.85	C	353.26	365.68	C	394.42	396.42
21	C	345.76	346.45	C	359.56	355.05	C	353.03	C	377.24	393.61	C
22	327.08	351.44	347.15	346.25	362.13	C	336.38	356.25	C	375.11	396.67	C
23	326.83	351.61	C	348.26	360.94	C	332.37	354.62	365.24	375.33	C	395.21
24	330.61	C	C	347.84	362.05	356.05	331.94	C	364.98	373.11	C	397.46
25	329.09	C	346.44	349.28	C	355.71	334.72	C	365.50	372.36	401.02	C
26	331.48	347.48	347.74	349.53	C	353.21	337.80	353.11	366.04	C	400.41	399.75
27	C	345.81	346.16	C	C	355.48	C	354.55	366.19	C	400.15	400.50
28	C	344.91	346.29	C	358.85	357.10	C	354.11	C	370.19	C	C
29	332.72	342.56	345.01	349.90	356.55	C	335.01	350.42	C	371.96	401.05	C
30	335.96		C	349.84	358.58	C	337.12	347.79	366.77	371.92	C	399.42
31	338.97		C		357.35		339.44	C		374.38		393.75
Close	338.97	342.56	345.01	349.84	357.35	357.10	339.44	347.79	366.77	374.38	401.05	393.75
Month Pt Change	10.08	3.59	2.45	4.83	7.51	−0.25	−17.66	8.35	18.98	7.61	26.67	−7.30
Month % Change	3.1	1.1	0.7	1.4	2.1	−0.1	−4.9	2.5	5.5	2.1	7.1	−1.8
QTR % Change			4.9			3.5			2.7			7.4
Year % Change												19.7

HIGHLIGHTS

Election Year	Bull Market	Best Nine Months 26.2%	High Dec-02	401.21
Clinton (1st Term)	Expansion	Worst Three Months 2.7%	Low Jan-10	318.24

RUSSELL 1000 INDEX — 1997

Previous Month Close	Jan	Feb	Mar	Apr	May	Jun	Jul	Aug	Sep	Oct	Nov	Dec
	393.75	416.77	417.46	398.19	419.15	445.06	462.95	499.89	475.33	500.78	483.86	504.25
1	C	C	C	399.43	418.11	C	466.36	496.66	C	504.47	C	514.34
2	391.09	C	C	394.65	426.12	444.30	472.80	C	488.27	507.31	C	512.85
3	396.94	416.97	419.69	394.86	C	443.73	479.10	C	488.95	509.84	496.06	515.66
4	C	417.87	418.01	399.23	C	441.20	C	498.11	490.45	C	497.31	514.34
5	C	412.09	423.29	C	435.42	442.91	C	499.65	490.12	C	498.88	519.72
6	397.07	413.28	421.82	C	433.88	449.85	C	503.65	C	513.72	496.42	C
7	399.96	417.88	425.01	401.98	427.94	C	477.19	499.00	C	518.94	490.58	C
8	397.67	C	C	403.88	430.16	C	480.64	489.85	491.37	514.80	C	519.15
9	400.93	C	C	401.11	432.32	452.24	475.41	C	492.68	513.57	C	515.68
10	403.33	415.49	429.23	399.57	C	453.19	478.35	C	485.90	511.85	487.46	512.25
11	C	417.21	428.15	389.03	C	455.36	480.12	491.15	482.65	C	488.35	504.30
12	C	424.21	424.49	C	438.62	462.19	C	486.37	488.45	C	479.00	503.00
13	403.19	428.86	416.82	C	436.29	467.13	C	484.59	C	512.43	483.94	C
14	408.23	427.50	418.30	391.86	437.93	C	481.07	486.22	C	513.12	490.03	C
15	407.27	C	C	397.21	440.97	C	484.72	474.96	486.76	511.16	C	507.62
16	408.68	C	C	401.30	435.05	467.39	490.29	C	499.00	505.95	C	510.39
17	412.11	C	418.85	400.71	C	468.00	487.54	C	498.38	499.75	499.35	509.57
18	C	431.09	415.73	402.41	C	465.74	480.02	479.88	500.54	C	495.41	504.42
19	C	429.52	413.29	C	436.54	470.37	C	486.59	502.06	C	498.36	500.69
20	412.86	424.32	412.31	C	440.81	470.49	C	493.39	C	505.55	505.71	C
21	415.76	423.34	412.84	398.62	439.82	C	478.52	486.56	C	514.31	507.60	C
22	417.65	C	C	405.46	437.91	C	488.85	485.56	504.71	512.91	C	503.85
23	413.60	C	C	405.22	443.83	460.68	490.48	C	503.00	503.41	C	497.03
24	409.44	427.55	416.01	404.11	C	469.01	492.22	C	499.46	498.40	499.39	493.97
25	C	428.64	415.45	400.37	C	465.33	491.58	484.44	495.96	C	501.69	C
26	C	425.47	416.17	C	C	462.57	C	481.12	499.54	C	502.43	495.87
27	406.38	419.74	407.65	C	445.27	464.52	C	481.50	C	465.44	C	C
28	406.54	417.46	C	404.31	444.22	C	490.25	476.88	C	486.93	504.25	C
29	409.82		C	415.27	442.59	C	493.28	475.33	503.69	486.29	C	504.26
30	415.69		C	419.15	445.06	462.95	498.85	C	500.78	478.16	C	513.41
31	416.77		398.19		C		499.89	C		483.86		513.79
Close	416.77	417.46	398.19	419.15	445.06	462.95	499.89	475.33	500.78	483.86	504.25	513.79
Month Pt Change	23.02	0.69	−19.27	20.96	25.91	17.89	36.94	−24.56	25.45	−16.92	20.39	9.54
Month % Change	5.8	0.2	−4.6	5.3	6.2	4.0	8.0	−4.9	5.4	−3.4	4.2	1.9
QTR % Change			1.1			16.3			8.2			2.6
Year % Change												30.5

1998   RUSSELL 1000 INDEX

Previous Month Close	Jan	Feb	Mar	Apr	May	Jun	Jul	Aug	Sep	Oct	Nov	Dec
	513.79	517.02	553.14	580.31	585.46	572.16	592.57	584.97	496.66	529.11	570.63	605.31
1	C	C	C	583.59	589.83	571.50	599.94	C	514.73	512.34	C	611.08
2	515.37	528.23	552.44	589.47	C	572.57	599.09	C	513.70	520.57	578.28	609.81
3	C	530.62	554.22	590.88	C	567.44	C	580.60	508.92	C	577.65	599.83
4	C	531.15	552.11	C	590.65	573.49	C	559.48	504.44	C	582.31	612.84
5	516.63	529.52	545.62	C	587.33	582.86	C	563.23	C	511.85	589.99	C
6	510.99	533.88	556.25	589.83	581.94	C	604.61	568.48	C	509.29	593.73	C
7	509.16	C	C	584.00	576.94	C	603.65	569.74	C	501.51	C	618.39
8	505.11	C	C	580.07	583.50	584.28	609.75	C	529.84	494.35	C	615.24
9	490.26	533.11	554.55	584.63	C	585.78	606.20	C	521.17	507.64	588.15	615.58
10	C	537.51	560.85	C	C	582.20	608.68	566.47	507.55	C	587.05	605.81
11	C	538.28	563.47	C	582.44	573.42	C	558.12	522.01	C	583.14	605.86
12	495.10	540.51	564.17	C	586.44	574.86	C	566.42	C	515.31	581.75	C
13	502.27	538.73	563.49	584.57	587.73	C	609.26	561.76	C	513.40	585.58	C
14	505.65	C	C	587.90	587.03	C	615.01	555.88	532.92	519.28	C	592.96
15	502.17	C	C	589.84	582.28	563.90	614.17	C	537.32	540.93	C	603.86
16	507.49	C	568.81	584.08	C	569.15	618.58	C	541.98	546.09	590.69	603.36
17	C	539.93	569.72	591.41	C	578.89	620.15	565.68	528.87	C	592.86	612.96
18	C	544.77	572.42	C	580.77	578.54	C	574.63	530.36	C	595.95	617.12
19	C	543.17	574.61	C	582.78	575.47	C	572.58	C	549.95	600.03	C
20	516.29	545.71	578.81	592.04	586.83	C	619.22	568.72	C	551.44	605.35	C
21	512.54	C	C	593.36	584.61	C	609.55	562.75	531.98	554.32	C	625.33
22	508.62	C	C	595.18	582.09	577.20	608.27	C	535.37	558.61	C	625.38
23	505.69	547.82	576.66	589.30	C	585.30	596.05	C	553.54	554.99	617.76	637.74
24	C	543.51	582.07	583.29	C	591.77	595.85	565.83	541.72	C	615.20	636.89
25	C	549.85	580.20	C	C	590.05	C	567.82	542.45	C	617.30	C
26	504.78	552.93	579.79	C	573.70	591.78	C	562.62	C	556.41	C	C
27	510.38	553.14	576.96	571.42	572.22	C	598.43	540.61	C	552.98	619.96	C
28	515.19	C	C	571.53	575.11	C	589.58	532.43	544.62	554.49	C	637.63
29	519.41		C	576.64	572.16	594.92	587.03	C	544.64	563.64	C	645.36
30	517.02		575.97	585.46	C	592.57	596.13	C	529.11	570.63	605.31	641.86
31	C		580.31		C		584.97	496.66		C		642.87
Close	517.02	553.14	580.31	585.46	572.16	592.57	584.97	496.66	529.11	570.63	605.31	642.87
Month Pt Change	3.23	36.12	27.17	5.15	-13.30	20.41	-7.60	-88.31	32.45	41.52	34.68	37.56
Month % Change	0.6	7.0	4.9	0.9	-2.3	3.6	-1.3	-15.1	6.5	7.8	6.1	6.2
QTR % Change			12.9			2.1			-10.7			21.5
Year % Change												25.1

HIGHLIGHTS

Mid-Term Election Year	Bull Market	Best Nine Months	34.9%	High Dec-29 645.36
Clinton (2nd Term)	Expansion	Worst Three Months	-10.7%	Low Jan-09 490.26

RUSSELL 1000 INDEX — 1999

Previous Month Close	Jan	Feb	Mar	Apr	May	Jun	Jul	Aug	Sep	Oct	Nov	Dec
	642.87	665.64	643.67	667.49	695.25	679.10	713.61	690.51	683.27	663.83	707.19	724.66
1	C	662.57	643.20	670.89	C	674.75	717.87	C	689.12	663.48	703.15	729.04
2	C	656.95	638.30	C	C	675.57	723.25	689.80	683.04	C	700.27	736.11
3	C	662.57	638.82	C	704.96	677.43	C	685.77	702.87	C	704.16	748.90
4	641.78	650.17	648.14	C	694.00	691.58	C	676.51	C	674.55	708.99	C
5	649.75	644.77	662.39	684.46	701.65	C	C	680.92	C	673.59	713.91	C
6	663.67	C	C	682.72	693.32	C	721.93	673.78	C	686.19	C	744.22
7	662.72	C	C	686.59	700.05	695.50	724.84	C	699.74	682.45	C	738.69
8	665.64	646.70	666.23	695.37	C	686.48	724.43	C	696.07	690.68	717.64	736.34
9	C	632.53	664.56	697.67	C	687.10	728.61	671.65	697.78	C	711.31	738.83
10	C	635.46	667.95	C	698.24	678.82	C	662.91	700.12	C	715.61	742.70
11	660.93	651.49	673.17	C	706.20	673.96	C	673.60	C	691.46	718.87	C
12	648.69	639.16	671.37	702.89	711.09	C	726.52	672.15	C	679.53	727.31	C
13	645.68	C	C	699.22	713.04	C	723.75	687.38	695.92	665.67	C	740.89
14	633.91	C	C	689.38	697.45	673.35	726.49	C	692.25	665.19	C	733.10
15	649.45	C	677.65	686.33	C	677.35	732.51	C	682.95	646.79	726.27	737.32
16	C	644.88	677.15	684.94	C	692.28	736.69	689.17	682.63	C	739.42	740.29
17	C	635.79	673.05	C	698.55	697.36	C	696.08	691.36	C	734.93	741.87
18	C	642.75	682.01	C	695.02	698.40	C	690.52	C	649.15	742.62	C
19	654.18	644.11	672.70	669.88	701.05	C	730.76	685.19	C	653.74	741.39	C
20	655.86	C	C	678.89	698.38	C	715.01	691.97	691.14	667.39	C	741.11
21	644.51	C	C	694.77	694.19	701.81	716.87	C	677.03	664.23	C	749.68
22	639.62	660.77	671.25	705.85	C	695.07	707.67	C	678.74	673.36	741.24	751.73
23	C	660.56	653.85	704.98	C	694.11	705.96	704.25	662.92	C	732.28	762.54
24	C	651.89	657.63	C	681.64	684.93	C	705.25	661.71	C	738.48	C
25	643.60	647.12	668.38	C	669.84	684.45	C	713.97	C	669.78	C	C
26	652.64	643.67	664.70	706.68	680.00	C	700.10	704.90	C	664.17	738.94	C
27	647.68	C	C	708.13	669.13	C	708.14	697.58	664.50	671.76	C	760.09
28	658.93	C	C	702.36	679.10	692.76	709.07	C	663.67	695.45	C	761.42
29	665.64		678.57	698.76	C	703.11	696.27	C	657.38	707.19	733.95	765.32
30	C		673.80	695.25	C	713.61	690.51	685.09	663.83	C	724.66	765.66
31	C		667.49		C		C	683.27		C		767.97
Close	665.64	643.67	667.49	695.25	679.10	713.61	690.51	683.27	663.83	707.19	724.66	767.97
Month Pt Change	22.77	-21.97	23.82	27.76	-16.15	34.51	-23.10	-7.24	-19.44	43.36	17.47	43.31
Month % Change	3.5	-3.3	3.7	4.2	-2.3	5.1	-3.2	-1.0	-2.8	6.5	2.5	6.0
QTR % Change			3.8			6.9			-7.0			15.7
Year % Change												19.5

HIGHLIGHTS

Pre-Election Year	Bull Market	Best Nine Months	15.9%	High Dec-31	767.97
Clinton (2nd Term)	Expansion	Worst Three Months	-7.0%	Low Feb-09	632.53

2000 — RUSSELL 1000 INDEX

Previous Month Close	Jan 767.97	Feb 736.08	Mar 733.04	Apr 797.99	May 771.58	Jun 750.98	Jul 769.68	Aug 755.57	Sep 811.17	Oct 772.60	Nov 763.06	Dec 692.40
1	C	744.71	740.33	C	779.52	767.55	C	758.66	813.71	C	758.99	694.16
2	C	744.72	740.66	C	765.83	785.02	C	758.62	C	769.84	765.34	C
3	761.52	753.55	756.41	797.25	750.04	C	777.32	767.21	C	761.95	764.91	C
4	731.95	752.57	C	790.45	748.69	C	C	773.19	C	766.99	C	698.08
5	733.24	C	C	788.23	760.32	779.58	764.34	C	805.47	766.63	C	728.44
6	733.27	C	748.41	796.70	C	773.15	770.86	C	796.27	751.58	767.15	715.51
7	753.14	753.76	729.60	805.59	C	780.58	782.61	781.81	803.18	C	766.43	712.07
8	C	762.73	734.76	C	755.31	775.62	C	782.55	798.08	C	752.13	729.83
9	C	747.06	752.88	C	748.63	773.97	C	778.13	C	748.51	745.96	C
10	764.10	749.97	749.67	796.41	731.09	C	781.28	771.62	C	737.85	727.48	C
11	753.06	735.19	C	793.14	744.84	C	782.80	778.37	794.34	726.05	C	737.22
12	750.26	C	C	774.98	751.25	767.08	790.85	C	791.38	706.69	C	730.76
13	761.07	C	741.51	760.94	C	779.07	794.23	C	793.53	732.70	717.67	723.83
14	769.96	736.42	727.08	715.20	C	778.98	802.15	788.59	792.69	C	736.16	711.86
15	C	742.24	741.26	C	767.84	783.31	C	785.22	784.00	C	740.41	697.35
16	C	735.82	777.86	C	775.80	776.20	C	783.69	C	734.06	729.68	C
17	C	737.18	781.64	740.14	765.61	C	802.92	792.56	C	720.78	726.23	C
18	764.91	716.05	C	762.30	758.97	C	792.44	790.55	771.35	715.59	C	702.41
19	766.78	C	C	754.49	742.61	788.47	784.55	C	781.00	740.73	C	692.35
20	762.48	C	774.79	757.32	C	784.55	794.56	C	777.91	746.41	710.32	668.75
21	761.52	C	794.06	C	C	786.11	785.50	794.60	775.47	C	711.84	672.50
22	C	719.29	800.06	C	739.31	771.89	C	794.62	776.85	C	697.66	691.55
23	C	726.07	813.49	C	724.78	765.32	C	799.83	C	746.67	C	C
24	741.03	725.03	813.56	754.56	737.38	C	775.95	802.10	C	746.21	710.55	C
25	745.04	714.86	C	780.72	728.38	C	780.47	801.39	772.78	728.97	C	C
26	741.78	C	C	771.68	727.09	771.45	769.23	C	766.29	728.77	C	695.98
27	739.47	C	811.29	775.37	C	767.76	765.04	C	766.41	736.44	713.29	704.19
28	719.67	721.72	802.37	771.58	C	771.25	748.29	805.56	784.09	C	704.02	708.24
29	C	733.04	799.63	C	C	765.35	C	804.38	772.60	C	706.46	700.09
30	C		789.03	C	752.39	769.68	C	802.30	C	743.87	692.40	C
31	736.08		797.99		750.98		755.57	811.17		763.06		C
Close	736.08	733.04	797.99	771.58	750.98	769.68	755.57	811.17	772.60	763.06	692.40	700.09
Month Pt Change	−31.89	−3.04	64.95	−26.41	−20.60	18.70	−14.11	55.60	−38.57	−9.54	−70.66	7.69
Month % Change	−4.2	−0.4	8.9	−3.3	−2.7	2.5	−1.8	7.4	−4.8	−1.2	−9.3	1.1
QTR % Change			3.9			−3.5			0.4			−9.4
Year % Change												−8.8

HIGHLIGHTS

Election Year	Bear Market Begins 1/14	Best Nine Months −16.3%	High Sep-01 813.71
Clinton (2nd Term)	Expansion	Worst Three Months 0.4%	Low Dec-20 668.75

RUSSELL 1000 INDEX — 2001

Previous Month Close	Jan	Feb	Mar	Apr	May	Jun	Jul	Aug	Sep	Oct	Nov	Dec
Close	700.09	722.55	654.25	610.36	658.90	662.39	646.64	637.43	597.67	546.46	557.29	599.32
1	C	725.81	655.05	C	667.86	665.55	C	640.37	C	544.84	569.49	C
2	676.89	712.44	651.83	601.68	669.52	C	652.85	642.90	C	551.13	570.69	C
3	712.63	C	C	580.11	658.96	C	651.49	639.86	C	562.75	C	594.13
4	703.72	C	C	577.85	668.51	668.77	C	C	597.52	561.66	C	602.40
5	683.83	714.56	655.84	604.16	C	678.22	643.31	C	596.10	561.82	578.96	615.84
6	C	714.29	662.54	591.50	C	671.33	628.20	632.49	583.18	C	587.46	614.64
7	C	707.12	666.13	C	666.54	675.11	C	634.28	572.54	C	586.17	609.94
8	681.95	702.82	666.33	C	665.50	668.40	C	623.29	C	557.39	587.06	C
9	684.96	693.76	649.59	596.49	662.29	C	631.98	622.91	C	554.61	587.63	C
10	693.86	C	C	613.53	661.49	C	622.77	626.37	575.57	567.39	C	600.66
11	702.21	C	C	612.81	656.44	662.45	621.65	C	C	576.97	C	599.11
12	698.40	701.65	621.35	622.42	C	662.74	636.43	C	C	573.63	586.90	599.06
13	C	695.06	631.71	C	C	655.25	640.17	627.60	C	C	598.10	589.82
14	C	694.41	615.67	C	657.87	643.14	C	625.34	C	C	599.60	591.51
15	C	700.92	618.33	C	658.31	640.39	C	620.49	C	572.77	600.02	C
16	702.67	688.47	605.71	620.01	677.47	C	632.86	621.82	C	577.15	598.24	C
17	704.78	C	C	626.79	679.93	C	639.39	611.65	547.04	565.80	C	597.25
18	713.73	C	C	651.24	681.62	637.23	635.62	C	543.04	561.36	C	602.16
19	709.92	C	616.95	660.41	C	638.98	638.92	C	534.26	564.10	605.12	605.38
20	C	675.52	601.60	654.76	C	645.38	636.86	616.18	517.85	C	600.18	600.13
21	C	663.05	590.60	C	693.69	652.27	C	609.05	507.98	C	597.42	602.70
22	710.26	661.03	588.01	C	692.12	646.07	C	613.37	C	572.73	C	C
23	720.44	658.41	599.86	643.88	680.72	C	626.91	611.87	C	569.86	604.45	C
24	722.68	C	C	635.98	683.16	C	616.29	623.26	527.29	570.23	C	602.69
25	717.67	C	C	646.55	675.46	642.40	625.29	C	531.59	578.28	C	C
26	716.93	670.44	606.73	649.37	C	641.31	632.63	C	528.38	580.57	608.77	605.26
27	C	663.92	622.10	659.49	C	638.78	634.44	620.62	534.59	C	605.05	609.38
28	C	654.25	606.77	C	C	647.21	C	611.48	546.46	C	593.74	611.71
29	722.44		603.73	C	669.09	646.64	C	604.95	C	566.89	600.08	C
30	727.35		610.36	658.90	657.82	C	633.88	595.06	C	557.03	599.32	C
31	722.55		C		662.39		637.43	597.67		557.29		604.94
Close	722.55	654.25	610.36	658.90	662.39	646.64	637.43	597.67	546.46	557.29	599.32	604.94
Month Pt Change	22.46	−68.30	−43.89	48.54	3.49	−15.75	−9.21	−39.76	−51.21	10.83	42.03	5.62
Month % Change	3.2	−9.5	−6.7	8.0	0.5	−2.4	−1.4	−6.2	−8.6	2.0	7.5	0.9
QTR % Change			−12.8			5.9			−15.5			10.7
Year % Change												−13.6

HIGHLIGHTS

Post Election Year	Bull Market Begins 9/21	Best Nine Months	-4.2%	High	Jan-30 727.35
GW Bush (1st Term)	Recession Begins Q2	Worst Three Months	-15.5%	Low	Sep-21 507.98

2002   RUSSELL 1000 INDEX

Previous Month Close	Jan	Feb	Mar	Apr	May	Jun	Jul	Aug	Sep	Oct	Nov	Dec
	604.94	596.66	583.88	607.35	572.04	566.18	523.72	484.39	486.08	433.22	468.51	495.00
1	C	592.51	597.38	607.12	576.63	C	511.71	470.30	C	449.66	476.57	C
2	608.26	C	C	601.59	575.25	C	500.62	459.41	C	438.90	C	494.14
3	614.07	C	C	595.53	569.30	552.61	503.00	C	466.31	433.83	C	486.72
4	618.38	578.26	609.50	596.05	C	552.21	C	C	474.48	423.77	480.31	484.94
5	C	576.59	606.01	594.26	C	556.79	521.47	443.70	466.98	C	483.79	479.54
6	C	572.37	614.60	C	558.71	545.87	C	456.97	474.97	C	488.28	482.49
7	614.26	570.18	611.73	C	556.81	545.71	C	465.84	C	415.53	477.13	C
8	612.17	579.00	615.55	595.76	577.64	C	515.02	480.75	C	422.01	472.63	C
9	609.35	C	C	591.71	569.31	C	501.82	482.33	479.53	410.52	C	471.93
10	609.85	C	C	598.52	560.04	547.09	485.95	C	482.66	425.11	C	478.40
11	604.57	587.10	617.31	584.66	C	537.40	489.33	C	482.57	441.45	462.88	478.78
12	C	585.06	615.85	588.69	C	540.65	486.77	479.96	470.59	C	466.56	477.15
13	C	590.80	609.95	C	569.99	534.94	C	469.43	472.10	C	466.05	470.94
14	600.09	589.81	609.47	C	582.38	534.11	C	487.40	C	444.90	477.44	C
15	604.25	582.97	616.42	584.55	579.36	C	484.93	493.12	C	465.68	480.59	C
16	594.71	C	C	598.05	582.17	C	477.40	492.87	472.61	454.24	C	481.70
17	600.73	C	C	596.80	586.62	549.16	480.53	C	463.27	465.12	C	477.89
18	594.73	C	616.42	596.14	C	549.57	467.28	C	461.18	467.44	475.79	471.65
19	C	571.83	618.74	596.40	C	540.58	450.64	504.04	447.38	C	473.67	468.10
20	C	579.52	608.93	C	578.97	532.69	C	497.25	448.21	C	482.75	474.24
21	C	570.58	610.29	C	572.61	523.71	C	503.71	C	475.47	493.34	C
22	589.93	575.00	607.91	587.25	575.41	C	436.00	510.52	C	470.19	491.88	C
23	595.08	C	C	583.78	581.45	C	424.18	498.90	442.31	473.28	C	475.24
24	597.26	C	C	579.95	574.63	525.06	448.05	C	434.77	466.10	C	472.66
25	598.06	585.17	598.93	579.38	C	516.18	445.89	C	445.48	474.23	493.43	C
26	C	585.30	602.42	571.32	C	514.61	452.92	502.83	453.36	C	483.06	471.38
27	C	585.56	605.68	C	C	523.47	C	495.52	439.18	C	496.39	463.91
28	598.23	583.88	607.35	C	570.12	523.72	C	486.67	C	470.48	C	C
29	582.17		C	565.67	566.50	C	477.61	487.14	C	465.89	495.00	C
30	588.48		C	572.04	565.00	C	479.79	486.08	433.22	470.73	C	465.77
31	596.66		C		566.18		484.39	C		468.51		466.18
Close	596.66	583.88	607.35	572.04	566.18	523.72	484.39	486.08	433.22	468.51	495.00	466.18
Month Pt Change	−8.28	−12.78	23.47	−35.31	−5.86	−42.46	−39.33	1.69	−52.86	35.29	26.49	−28.82
Month % Change	−1.4	−2.1	4.0	−5.8	−1.0	−7.5	−7.5	0.3	−10.9	8.1	5.7	−5.8
QTR % Change			0.4			−13.8			−17.3			7.6
Year % Change												−22.9

HIGHLIGHTS

Mid-Term Election Year	Bear Market 3/19 - 10/9	Best Nine Months	19.8%	High Mar-19	618.74
GW Bush (1st Term)	Expansion	Worst Three Months	−17.3%	Low Oct-09	410.52

RUSSELL 1000 INDEX   2003

Previous Month	Jan	Feb	Mar	Apr	May	Jun	Jul	Aug	Sep	Oct	Nov	Dec
Close	466.18	454.30	446.37	450.35	486.09	512.92	518.94	528.53	538.40	532.15	562.51	568.32
1	C	C	C	455.63	485.82	C	522.95	523.06	C	543.71	C	574.90
2	481.37	C	C	467.24	493.26	514.89	529.23	C	545.75	545.07	C	573.27
3	481.15	456.37	443.18	464.74	C	517.08	525.23	C	547.97	550.27	567.21	571.73
4	C	450.16	436.53	465.76	C	524.92	C	524.17	549.03	C	564.20	573.73
5	C	447.77	440.42	C	491.87	527.31	C	515.03	545.70	C	563.75	569.16
6	492.07	444.88	436.50	C	495.83	526.12	C	515.49	C	552.73	567.10	C
7	488.67	440.42	439.94	466.35	493.48	C	535.18	518.86	C	555.42	564.80	C
8	481.81	C	C	465.13	488.60	C	537.15	520.61	551.32	552.62	C	573.27
9	490.83	C	C	458.90	495.38	519.32	534.63	C	547.02	555.31	C	567.97
10	490.93	443.64	428.91	461.47	C	524.09	527.37	C	539.84	555.03	561.26	566.88
11	C	440.15	425.31	460.03	C	530.73	532.28	522.26	542.80	C	560.62	573.68
12	C	434.35	426.69	C	501.59	531.35	C	527.44	544.07	C	567.49	575.16
13	490.27	433.41	441.22	C	500.19	526.00	C	524.27	C	559.13	567.84	C
14	493.06	442.03	441.89	468.87	498.81	C	535.76	527.59	C	561.27	563.48	C
15	486.15	C	C	471.79	502.55	C	533.72	527.92	542.04	559.46	C	571.71
16	484.25	C	C	466.28	501.57	537.58	530.28	C	549.55	561.28	C	575.01
17	477.61	C	457.12	473.30	C	538.11	523.37	C	548.01	555.47	559.84	575.80
18	C	450.85	459.14	C	C	537.13	529.28	532.83	555.06	C	554.80	582.61
19	C	447.75	462.72	C	489.30	529.09	C	534.34	553.38	C	558.98	582.31
20	C	443.78	463.95	C	488.69	529.52	C	533.44	C	558.11	554.40	C
21	470.29	449.67	474.58	472.65	490.86	C	521.78	535.44	C	559.05	555.43	C
22	465.67	C	C	482.64	495.47	C	526.65	530.02	546.28	550.75	C	584.42
23	470.38	C	C	486.80	496.65	521.81	527.18	C	549.63	552.44	C	586.19
24	456.95	441.61	458.18	482.84	C	522.63	523.63	C	539.39	550.24	564.51	585.26
25	C	444.80	463.80	476.26	C	519.00	532.06	529.98	535.75	C	565.73	C
26	C	439.08	461.27	C	C	524.57	C	531.51	532.11	C	568.12	586.22
27	449.48	444.25	460.53	C	506.21	519.93	C	531.99	C	551.85	C	C
28	455.27	446.37	458.17	484.60	506.95	C	531.31	535.51	C	560.18	568.32	C
29	458.29		C	486.26	505.15	C	527.95	538.40	537.32	561.13	C	593.44
30	448.23		C	486.09	512.92	518.94	527.12	C	532.15	560.51	C	593.64
31	454.30		450.35		C		528.53	C		562.51		594.56
Close	454.30	446.37	450.35	486.09	512.92	518.94	528.53	538.40	532.15	562.51	568.32	594.56
Month Pt Change	−11.88	−7.93	3.98	35.74	26.83	6.02	9.59	9.87	−6.25	30.36	5.81	26.24
Month % Change	−2.5	−1.7	0.9	7.9	5.5	1.2	1.8	1.9	−1.2	5.7	1.0	4.6
QTR % Change			−3.4			15.2			2.5			11.7
Year % Change												27.5

HIGHLIGHTS

Pre-Election Year	Bull Market	Best Nine Months	14.5%	High	Dec-31	594.56
GW Bush (1st Term)	Expansion	Worst Three Months	2.5%	Low	Mar-11	425.31

2004 — RUSSELL 1000 INDEX

	Jan	Feb	Mar	Apr	May	Jun	Jul	Aug	Sep	Oct	Nov	Dec
Previous Month Close	594.56	605.21	612.58	603.42	591.83	599.40	609.31	587.21	589.09	595.66	604.51	629.26
1	C	C	618.68	607.11	C	599.76	602.94	C	590.37	604.52	604.69	638.69
2	592.94	607.21	615.16	611.88	C	601.68	601.19	589.76	596.70	C	604.57	638.03
3	C	607.34	615.99	C	597.34	596.85	C	585.94	594.16	C	611.51	638.66
4	C	602.10	618.16	C	598.46	600.05	C	585.01	C	606.58	621.06	C
5	599.93	603.01	619.67	616.29	599.88	C	C	575.48	C	606.14	623.35	C
6	600.77	610.90	C	614.58	595.65	C	595.98	566.69	C	610.11	C	638.23
7	602.29	C	C	610.98	587.20	609.48	597.24	C	598.33	603.90	C	631.13
8	605.18	C	614.55	610.12	C	610.13	592.05	C	595.61	599.44	622.61	633.99
9	600.39	609.67	610.78	C	C	604.19	593.95	567.25	596.92	C	622.22	637.42
10	C	612.74	601.91	C	580.36	606.63	C	574.66	599.88	C	621.81	637.09
11	C	619.18	593.01	C	585.20	C	C	572.97	C	600.71	627.45	C
12	603.31	616.20	600.48	612.72	585.85	C	594.49	566.26	C	599.48	633.44	C
13	600.02	612.96	C	604.19	585.54	C	594.80	566.06	601.17	595.15	C	642.51
14	604.79	C	C	603.15	584.91	600.45	592.98	C	602.36	589.86	C	645.09
15	605.64	C	591.80	603.50	C	604.19	590.86	C	598.21	592.37	633.47	646.82
16	609.95	C	594.89	606.38	C	605.16	587.99	574.66	600.22	C	629.22	645.26
17	C	618.62	601.78	C	578.67	604.32	C	576.27	602.66	C	632.67	641.06
18	C	616.05	600.81	C	582.79	605.76	C	583.63	C	595.56	633.38	C
19	C	613.25	594.36	607.40	581.27	C	587.64	581.36	C	590.06	626.24	C
20	609.78	611.45	C	598.02	581.59	C	592.09	585.68	599.34	590.26	C	640.85
21	614.31	C	C	601.32	583.93	603.36	583.67	C	603.27	592.20	C	646.65
22	612.51	C	586.51	609.79	C	605.60	585.01	C	595.06	586.63	629.97	648.94
23	611.13	609.36	585.86	609.82	C	610.81	579.24	584.18	592.27	C	630.19	649.27
24	C	608.32	584.30	C	585.17	609.44	C	584.49	593.23	C	632.97	C
25	C	611.14	593.91	C	594.75	605.86	C	589.08	C	586.08	C	C
26	618.34	612.29	593.39	607.56	596.16	C	577.44	589.19	C	594.35	633.53	C
27	612.50	612.58	C	608.67	599.34	C	583.18	590.87	589.54	602.23	C	646.53
28	604.08	C	C	600.27	599.40	605.13	583.13	C	592.90	603.07	C	651.41
29	606.40	C	601.03	595.36	C	606.59	586.30	C	595.46	604.51	631.65	651.44
30	605.21		603.54	591.83	C	609.31	587.21	586.18	595.66	C	629.26	651.76
31	C		603.42		C		C	589.09		C		650.99
Close	605.21	612.58	603.42	591.83	599.40	609.31	587.21	589.09	595.66	604.51	629.26	650.99
Month Pt Change	10.65	7.37	−9.16	−11.59	7.57	9.91	−22.10	1.88	6.57	8.85	24.75	21.73
Month % Change	1.8	1.2	−1.5	−1.9	1.3	1.7	−3.6	0.3	1.1	1.5	4.1	3.5
QTR % Change			1.5			1.0			−2.2			9.3
Year % Change												9.5

HIGHLIGHTS

Election Year	Bull Market	Best Nine Months	8.4%	High Dec-30	651.76
GW Bush (1st Term)	Expansion	Worst Three Months	-2.2%	Low Aug-13	566.06

RUSSELL 1000 INDEX 2005

Previous Month Close	Jan	Feb	Mar	Apr	May	Jun	Jul	Aug	Sep	Oct	Nov	Dec
	650.99	633.99	646.93	635.78	623.32	644.28						
1	C	638.58	650.75	631.94	C	650.03						
2	C	640.68	650.56	C	626.18	651.41						
3	645.13	638.94	650.46	C	625.87	647.16						
4	637.09	646.25	656.68	633.47	633.57	C						
5	634.21	C	C	636.21	632.33	C						
6	636.41	C	C	637.55	631.81	648.02						
7	635.58	645.52	658.76	641.43	C	647.85						
8	C	645.92	655.49	636.14	C	646.39						
9	C	640.25	648.75	C	635.83	649.84						
10	638.09	642.78	649.79	C	629.51	648.32						
11	634.08	647.33	645.39	636.04	632.12	C						
12	636.49	C	C	639.52	625.84	C						
13	631.57	C	C	632.10	622.82	649.85						
14	635.52	647.99	649.55	625.73	C	651.52						
15	C	650.01	644.95	615.69	C	652.93						
16	C	650.26	639.45	C	629.23	655.54						
17	C	645.31	640.57	C	633.65	658.56						
18	641.60	645.61	640.19	617.47	640.31	C						
19	635.50	C	C	621.66	643.34	C						
20	630.82	C	C	613.37	642.62	658.20						
21	626.90	C	637.41	624.95	C	656.85						
22	C	636.17	631.12	620.77	C	657.01						
23	C	639.64	631.29	C	645.10	650.19						
24	624.33	644.88	630.95	C	645.11	645.03						
25	626.49	651.08	C	626.45	642.53	C						
26	629.77	C	C	621.14	646.85	C						
27	630.09	C	C	623.48	647.69	644.73						
28	628.46	646.93	632.13	616.32	C	650.75						
29	C		627.27	623.32	C	650.04						
30	C		635.83	C	C	645.92						
31	633.99		635.78		644.28							
Close	633.99	646.93	635.78	623.32	644.28	645.92						
Month Pt Change	−17.00	12.94	−11.15	−12.46	20.96	1.64						
Month % Change	−2.6	2.0	−1.7	−2.0	3.4	0.3						
QTR % Change			−2.3			1.6							
Year % Change												

HIGHLIGHTS

Post Election Year	Bull Market	Best Nine Months 8.4%	High	Mar-07	658.76
GW Bush (2nd Term)	Expansion	Worst Three Months—	Low	Apr-20	613.37

RUSSELL 2000 INDEX — 1979

Previous Month Close	Jan	Feb	Mar	Apr	May	Jun	Jul	Aug	Sep	Oct	Nov	Dec
Close	40.52	44.18	42.78	46.94	48.00	47.13	49.62	51.08	55.05	54.68	48.51	52.43
1	C	44.13	43.09	C	48.03	47.26	C	51.33	C	54.51	48.86	C
2	40.81	44.17	43.28	46.67	48.09	C	49.17	51.51	C	54.83	49.06	C
3	41.54	C	C	47.20	48.15	C	49.30	51.54	C	55.09	C	52.31
4	42.16	C	C	47.44	47.82	47.28	C	C	54.07	55.42	C	52.65
5	42.72	43.54	43.63	47.69	C	47.76	49.55	C	53.01	55.85	48.74	53.00
6	C	43.51	43.58	47.70	C	48.06	49.98	51.55	53.41	C	48.56	53.50
7	C	42.98	43.95	C	46.58	48.36	C	51.96	53.84	C	47.95	53.69
8	42.60	43.21	44.41	C	46.27	48.49	C	52.16	C	55.14	48.	C
9	42.97	43.43	44.47	47.61	46.48	C	50.22	52.25	C	52.53	48.74	C
10	42.87	C	C	47.81	46.14	C	50.15	52.62	54.04	50.13	C	53.91
11	43.07	C	C	47.54	46.21	48.59	50.05	C	53.70	50.52	C	53.94
12	43.55	43.45	44.61	47.64	C	49.03	49.93	C	53.92	50.76	49.31	54.24
13	C	43.85	44.84	C	C	49.06	49.83	52.95	54.11	C	49.30	54.45
14	C	43.84	44.88	C	45.99	48.99	C	53.11	54.63	C	49.51	54.91
15	43.80	43.94	45.10	C	46.03	49.10	C	53.51	C	49.87	49.93	C
16	43.43	44.11	45.48	47.20	46.05	C	49.99	53.44	C	49.76	49.85	C
17	43.34	C	C	47.16	46.62	C	49.45	53.60	54.58	50.03	C	55.24
18	43.74	C	C	47.49	46.83	48.90	49.19	C	54.18	50.13	C	54.91
19	43.90	C	45.66	47.48	C	48.93	49.44	C	54.30	48.99	50.07	54.89
20	C	44.27	45.52	47.58	C	49.11	49.61	53.74	54.69	C	50.00	55.15
21	C	44.25	45.80	C	46.99	49.36	C	53.83	54.80	C	49.91	55.10
22	43.86	44.12	46.04	C	47.26	49.58	C	54.06	C	47.50	C	C
23	44.17	43.91	46.32	47.74	47.28	C	49.49	54.13	C	47.23	50.35	C
24	44.07	C	C	48.01	47.41	C	49.68	54.13	54.47	47.44	C	55.16
25	44.36	C	C	48.19	47.66	49.25	50.12	C	54.36	47.37	C	C
26	44.62	43.83	46.11	48.13	C	49.10	50.35	C	54.63	47.81	51.35	55.30
27	C	42.85	46.54	48.06	C	49.34	50.62	54.26	54.81	C	51.68	55.42
28	C	42.78	46.53	C	C	49.58	C	54.24	54.68	C	52.08	55.65
29	44.58	46.78	C	47.63	49.62	C	54.41	C	47.92	52.39	C	
30	44.51	46.94	48.00	47.14	C	50.77	54.58	C	48.59	52.43	C	
31	44.18		C		47.13		51.08	55.05		48.51		55.91
Close	44.18	42.78	46.94	48.00	47.13	49.62	51.08	55.05	54.68	48.51	52.43	55.91
Month Pt Change	3.66	-1.40	4.16	1.06	-0.87	2.49	1.46	3.97	-0.37	-6.17	3.92	3.48
Month % Change	9.0	-3.2	9.7	2.3	-1.8	5.3	2.9	7.8	-0.7	-11.3	8.1	6.6
QTR % Change		15.8		5.7		10.2		2.2				
Year % Change						38.0						

HIGHLIGHTS

Election Year	Bull Market Begins 4/21	Best Eight Months 18.5%	High Dec-31 55.91
Carter	Recession Q1 - Q2	Worst Four Months -2.2%	Low Jan-02 40.81

1980 — RUSSELL 2000 INDEX

Previous Month Close	Jan	Feb	Mar	Apr	May	Jun	Jul	Aug	Sep	Oct	Nov	Dec
	55.91	**60.50**	**59.22**	**48.27**	**51.18**	**55.26**	**57.47**	**63.81**	**67.97**	**69.94**	**72.64**	**77.70**
1	C	60.81	C	48.80	51.03	C	57.72	64.17	C	70.57	C	76.51
2	54.92	C	C	49.43	51.20	55.23	58.11	C	68.60	71.02	C	76.11
3	54.11	C	58.81	49.36	C	55.25	58.78	C	69.65	72.08	73.04	76.54
4	55.08	60.78	58.22	C	C	55.83	C	63.96	69.79	C	C	76.89
5	C	61.02	57.24	C	51.50	56.05	C	64.24	70.09	C	73.98	75.78
6	C	61.30	55.68	C	51.81	56.30	C	64.73	C	73.25	72.91	C
7	55.42	61.53	54.70	48.29	52.33	C	59.47	65.47	C	73.11	72.67	C
8	56.32	61.92	C	48.55	52.33	C	59.45	65.70	69.63	73.63	C	73.08
9	56.70	C	C	49.16	52.12	56.42	59.66	C	69.86	73.82	C	72.58
10	57.39	C	53.56	49.83	C	56.66	59.61	C	70.51	73.83	72.70	71.70
11	57.74	61.57	53.99	50.09	C	56.97	60.10	66.15	71.26	C	73.47	69.89
12	C	61.68	53.95	C	52.10	56.89	C	65.78	71.72	C	74.54	70.89
13	C	61.75	53.76	C	52.58	57.31	C	65.96	C	74.40	75.45	C
14	58.27	61.13	53.55	49.59	53.06	C	60.95	66.91	C	74.45	75.85	C
15	58.45	60.77	C	49.45	53.39	C	61.04	67.26	71.85	74.86	C	71.07
16	58.59	C	C	49.12	53.72	57.31	61.42	C	72.56	74.20	C	71.14
17	58.75	C	51.62	48.71	C	57.43	62.19	C	73.43	73.93	75.74	71.91
18	58.88	C	51.47	48.69	C	57.39	62.62	66.11	73.28	C	76.32	72.51
19	C	60.25	51.93	C	53.86	57.05	C	65.76	73.91	C	76.47	73.21
20	C	60.66	51.71	C	53.88	57.00	C	66.35	C	74.11	77.10	C
21	59.30	60.28	51.43	48.06	53.88	C	62.84	67.42	C	73.83	76.81	C
22	58.91	59.81	C	49.46	54.38	C	62.68	68.08	74.02	74.35	C	73.98
23	59.45	C	C	49.93	55.00	57.17	62.69	C	73.12	73.44	C	73.97
24	59.74	C	49.65	50.54	C	57.44	62.82	C	73.12	73.73	76.27	74.16
25	59.86	59.11	48.72	50.40	C	57.96	62.56	68.04	72.62	C	76.92	C
26	C	59.21	48.56	C	C	57.93	C	68.25	71.16	C	77.34	74.48
27	C	58.93	45.36	C	55.21	58.02	C	68.04	C	73.04	C	C
28	60.30	58.94	47.54	50.62	55.40	C	62.68	67.41	C	72.93	77.70	C
29	59.98	59.22	C	50.91	55.01	C	63.24	67.97	68.88	73.01	C	73.90
30	60.47		C	51.18	55.26	57.47	63.80	C	69.94	72.34	C	74.05
31	60.50		48.27		C		63.81	C		72.64		74.80
Close	**60.50**	**59.22**	**48.27**	**51.18**	**55.26**	**57.47**	**63.81**	**67.97**	**69.94**	**72.64**	**77.70**	**74.80**
Month Pt Change	4.59	−1.28	−10.95	2.91	4.08	2.21	6.34	4.16	1.97	2.70	5.06	−2.90
Month % Change	8.2	−2.1	−18.5	6.0	8.0	4.0	11.0	6.5	2.9	3.9	7.0	−3.7
QTR % Change			−13.7			19.1			21.7			6.9
Year % Change												33.8

HIGHLIGHTS

Election Year	Bull Market Begins 4/21	Best Eight Months	13.7%	High Nov-28	77.70
Carter	Recession Q1 - Q2	Worst Four Months	26.4%	Low Mar-27	45.36

RUSSELL 2000 INDEX   1981

Previous Month	Jan	Feb	Mar	Apr	May	Jun	Jul	Aug	Sep	Oct	Nov	Dec
Close	74.80	74.33	74.52	80.25	82.25	84.72	82.56	80.41	73.94	67.55	73.06	75.14
1	C	C	C	80.79	82.13	84.73	81.94	C	73.68	68.04	C	75.05
2	75.49	72.40	74.87	81.04	C	83.67	81.24	C	73.95	69.43	74.11	74.71
3	C	72.55	74.76	81.21	C	83.54	C	79.92	72.72	C	74.60	74.74
4	C	73.03	74.97	C	80.63	83.75	C	79.86	71.85	C	74.80	75.22
5	76.28	73.75	75.12	C	80.07	84.11	C	80.31	C	70.04	74.70	C
6	76.58	74.39	75.42	80.58	80.33	C	79.94	80.57	C	70.22	74.59	C
7	73.77	C	C	80.86	80.84	C	79.58	80.40	C	71.40	C	74.67
8	73.28	C	C	81.16	81.25	84.05	79.58	C	69.88	72.34	C	74.09
9	73.97	74.21	75.73	81.62	C	83.67	80.06	C	69.96	72.45	74.53	74.11
10	C	74.13	75.48	81.98	C	83.82	80.41	80.15	71.08	C	74.49	74.34
11	C	73.92	75.33	C	80.42	84.62	C	80.49	72.08	C	74.54	74.24
12	74.24	73.55	76.28	C	80.56	84.92	C	80.59	C	72.53	74.81	C
13	74.09	73.32	76.64	81.56	80.89	C	80.44	80.69	C	72.70	74.47	C
14	74.47	C	C	81.27	81.46	C	80.02	80.55	71.94	71.73	C	73.11
15	74.76	C	C	81.96	81.96	85.16	80.42	C	71.84	71.89	C	73.19
16	75.07	C	77.17	82.67	C	84.26	80.66	C	71.21	71.87	73.23	73.15
17	C	73.21	77.15	C	C	84.29	80.93	79.71	70.23	C	73.26	73.34
18	C	73.32	77.55	C	82.04	83.64	C	78.76	69.50	C	73.27	73.82
19	75.14	72.62	77.86	C	81.84	83.87	C	78.85	C	71.58	73.13	C
20	74.18	72.57	78.58	82.97	82.23	C	79.74	79.07	C	72.10	73.74	C
21	73.99	C	C	82.55	82.50	C	78.98	78.58	69.41	72.36	C	73.59
22	73.65	C	C	82.65	82.77	83.67	78.65	C	69.18	72.12	C	73.50
23	73.77	72.70	78.99	82.92	C	83.98	78.52	C	67.74	71.75	73.56	73.43
24	C	72.95	78.91	83.44	C	83.79	79.06	76.25	67.63	C	73.94	73.57
25	C	72.92	79.69	C	C	83.82	C	75.10	65.37	C	74.35	C
26	73.36	73.79	79.78	C	83.26	83.79	C	75.03	C	71.30	C	C
27	73.80	74.52	79.49	83.60	83.94	C	79.51	74.53	C	71.94	74.81	C
28	73.89	C	C	82.70	84.51	C	79.37	74.80	65.56	72.33	C	73.32
29	74.40		C	82.07	84.72	83.18	79.46	C	67.08	72.14	C	72.86
30	74.33		79.46	82.25	C	82.56	79.91	C	67.55	73.06	75.14	73.08
31	C		80.25		C		80.41	73.94		C		73.67
Close	74.33	74.52	80.25	82.25	84.72	82.56	80.41	73.94	67.55	73.06	75.14	73.67
Month Pt Change	-0.47	0.19	5.73	2.00	2.47	-2.16	-2.15	-6.47	-6.39	5.51	2.08	-1.47
Month % Change	-0.6	0.3	7.7	2.5	3.0	-2.5	-2.6	-8.0	-8.6	8.2	2.8	-2.0
QTR % Change			7.3			2.9			-18.2			9.1
Year % Change												-1.5

HIGHLIGHTS

Post Election Year	Bear Market Begins 4/27	Best Eight Months -11.5%	High	Jun-15	85.16
Reagan (1st term)	Recession Begins Q3	Worst Four Months -11.5%	Low	Sep-25	65.37

1982   RUSSELL 2000 INDEX

Previous Month Close	Jan	Feb	Mar	Apr	May	Jun	Jul	Aug	Sep	Oct	Nov	Dec
	73.67	70.96	67.21	66.21	69.59	67.39	64.67	63.59	68.38	70.84	80.86	87.96
1	C	70.24	67.45	66.83	C	66.94	64.35	C	68.12	71.29	81.43	89.08
2	C	70.40	67.37	67.35	C	67.09	64.13	63.99	69.03	C	82.79	89.16
3	C	70.30	66.37	C	69.71	66.90	C	63.79	69.75	C	84.92	89.26
4	73.88	70.11	65.63	C	70.14	66.04	C	63.19	C	71.04	85.32	C
5	72.78	70.62	64.87	67.32	70.06	C	C	62.60	C	71.46	86.17	C
6	72.29	C	C	67.58	70.56	C	63.92	62.05	C	72.76	C	90.02
7	72.29	C	C	67.89	71.02	65.61	63.79	C	69.50	74.04	C	90.89
8	72.73	69.19	63.71	68.26	C	65.32	63.46	C	70.01	74.97	86.17	91.01
9	C	68.33	63.33	C	C	64.63	64.13	60.97	70.31	C	87.58	90.06
10	C	68.52	63.68	C	70.65	64.81	C	60.88	70.07	C	87.45	89.14
11	71.26	68.33	63.60	C	71.06	65.69	C	60.55	C	76.27	87.83	C
12	70.66	68.43	63.13	68.15	71.03	C	64.55	60.33	C	76.37	88.17	C
13	69.97	C	C	68.27	70.87	C	64.55	60.35	70.18	78.08	C	88.96
14	70.06	C	C	68.13	70.98	65.07	64.52	C	70.75	78.18	C	88.01
15	70.51	C	62.98	68.42	C	64.79	64.65	C	71.10	78.19	86.77	86.10
16	C	67.87	63.17	68.78	C	64.73	64.80	60.79	71.29	C	85.08	85.83
17	C	68.01	63.18	C	70.35	64.08	C	61.97	71.02	C	86.30	86.87
18	70.52	68.00	63.86	C	69.88	63.61	C	62.86	C	79.14	86.96	C
19	70.23	67.67	64.34	68.87	69.44	C	64.84	62.80	C	79.23	86.96	C
20	70.03	C	C	68.60	68.93	C	65.08	63.83	70.70	80.42	C	86.39
21	70.14	C	C	68.85	68.83	63.66	65.28	C	71.50	80.80	C	86.88
22	69.94	67.08	65.44	69.35	C	63.97	65.46	C	71.74	81.69	85.71	87.36
23	C	66.53	65.85	69.91	C	64.72	65.51	64.98	71.49	C	85.36	87.90
24	C	66.95	65.90	C	68.52	64.82	C	65.57	71.60	C	85.95	C
25	68.97	67.28	66.33	C	68.38	64.50	C	66.90	C	79.74	C	C
26	68.82	67.21	66.09	70.19	67.51	C	65.22	67.99	C	79.32	86.67	C
27	68.82	C	C	69.77	67.17	C	64.95	67.75	71.54	80.58	C	88.45
28	70.15	C	C	69.75	67.39	64.64	64.00	C	71.67	80.57	C	88.07
29	70.96		66.15	69.45	C	64.44	63.61	C	71.03	80.86	86.49	88.28
30	C		66.18	69.59	C	64.67	63.59	67.79	70.84	C	87.96	88.18
31	C		66.21		C		C	68.38		C		88.90
Close	70.96	67.21	66.21	69.59	67.39	64.67	63.59	68.38	70.84	80.86	87.96	88.90
Month Pt Change	−2.71	−3.75	−1.00	3.38	−2.20	−2.72	−1.08	4.79	2.46	10.02	7.10	0.94
Month % Change	−3.7	−5.3	−1.5	5.1	−3.2	−4.0	−1.7	7.5	3.6	14.1	8.8	1.1
QTR % Change			−10.1			−2.3			9.5			25.5
Year % Change												20.7

HIGHLIGHTS

Mid-Term Election Year	Bull Market Begins 8/12	Best Eight Months 53.6%	High Dec-08 91.01
Reagan (1st term)	Recession	Worst Four Months 25.0%	Low Aug-12 60.33

	Jan	Feb	Mar	Apr	May	Jun	Jul	Aug	Sep	Oct	Nov	Dec
Previous Month Close	88.90	95.53	101.23	103.77	111.20	118.94	124.17	120.43	115.60	117.43	109.17	114.66
1	C	95.32	101.82	C	C	118.77	125.26	119.13	116.04	C	108.57	114.71
2	C	95.56	102.64	C	110.51	119.77	C	118.87	116.76	C	109.27	114.23
3	88.29	96.21	103.47	C	110.48	120.81	C	118.86	C	116.74	109.16	C
4	89.08	97.31	103.77	103.31	111.50	C	C	117.48	C	116.74	108.69	C
5	89.88	C	C	103.26	113.01	C	123.90	117.90	C	116.96	C	113.83
6	91.89	C	C	102.43	114.56	121.28	124.96	C	118.06	117.57	C	113.68
7	92.64	97.74	104.08	102.54	C	120.94	125.18	C	118.33	117.96	108.13	113.82
8	C	97.58	103.29	103.00	C	119.97	124.98	116.01	118.72	C	107.76	113.26
9	C	97.82	103.98	C	115.06	120.21	C	115.43	118.96	C	108.24	113.19
10	93.76	99.04	104.14	C	115.93	121.26	C	116.10	C	118.08	108.94	C
11	93.55	99.33	104.01	103.65	115.60	C	125.26	116.38	C	117.40	110.37	C
12	94.23	C	C	104.31	115.60	C	123.83	117.00	118.49	116.39	C	113.02
13	94.21	C	C	105.24	116.55	122.31	123.13	C	117.57	116.00	C	112.70
14	95.11	99.99	103.29	106.33	C	123.12	123.53	C	117.70	115.91	111.30	111.88
15	C	100.18	103.10	107.09	C	124.06	122.57	117.77	117.38	C	111.63	111.39
16	C	100.10	103.03	C	115.14	125.37	C	117.23	117.74	C	111.76	111.49
17	95.83	100.04	102.65	C	115.96	125.55	C	117.81	C	115.71	112.27	C
18	95.89	100.61	102.98	107.75	116.72	C	121.50	117.61	C	113.84	112.50	C
19	95.31	C	C	107.44	116.26	C	121.88	117.65	118.91	112.14	C	111.20
20	95.63	C	C	108.45	116.37	125.40	123.73	C	119.33	112.49	C	110.75
21	94.68	C	101.82	108.73	C	125.98	124.49	C	119.14	111.86	113.00	111.11
22	C	99.51	102.09	109.30	C	126.60	125.02	117.72	119.54	C	113.40	111.32
23	C	99.80	102.91	C	116.59	126.48	C	116.80	119.43	C	113.59	111.39
24	91.68	100.68	103.55	C	118.20	126.99	C	115.88	C	110.87	C	C
25	92.47	100.62	103.58	108.55	119.09	C	125.15	115.12	C	110.99	113.97	C
26	93.13	C	C	109.35	119.53	C	125.71	115.27	119.53	110.64	C	C
27	94.47	C	C	109.54	119.90	125.40	124.03	C	118.47	110.27	C	111.39
28	94.98	101.23	103.00	110.33	C	122.67	122.22	C	118.19	109.72	113.84	111.33
29	C		102.81	111.20	C	122.84	120.43	114.73	118.02	C	114.62	111.50
30	C		103.49	C	C	124.17	C	115.03	117.43	C	114.66	112.27
31	95.53		103.77		118.94		C	115.60		109.17		C
Close	95.53	101.23	103.77	111.20	118.94	124.17	120.43	115.60	117.43	109.17	114.66	112.27
Month Pt Change	6.63	5.70	2.54	7.43	7.74	5.23	−3.74	−4.83	1.83	−8.26	5.49	−2.39
Month % Change	7.5	6.0	2.5	7.2	7.0	4.4	−3.0	−4.0	1.6	−7.0	5.0	−2.1
QTR % Change			16.7			19.7			−5.4			−4.4
Year % Change												26.3

HIGHLIGHTS

Pre-Election Year	Bear Market Begins 11/29	Best Eight Months	−8.1%	High Jun-24 126.99
Reagan (1st term)	Expansion	Worst Four Months	−12.1%	Low Jan-03 88.29

1984 — RUSSELL 2000 INDEX

Previous Month Close	Jan	Feb	Mar	Apr	May	Jun	Jul	Aug	Sep	Oct	Nov	Dec
	112.27	110.21	103.72	104.10	103.34	97.75	100.30	95.25	106.21	105.17	103.07	100.11
1	C	109.61	104.24	C	104.34	98.97	C	96.69	C	104.39	103.42	C
2	C	109.56	105.17	103.72	105.42	C	99.79	98.96	C	103.86	103.54	C
3	112.38	108.66	C	103.35	105.75	C	100.06	102.02	C	103.19	C	99.48
4	113.66	C	C	103.22	105.23	99.97	C	C	105.51	103.31	C	99.47
5	115.18	C	104.75	102.12	C	99.87	99.76	C	105.23	103.43	103.81	98.65
6	116.19	106.50	104.20	101.45	C	100.26	99.37	103.31	105.75	C	104.47	98.59
7	C	105.78	103.11	C	105.32	100.49	C	103.30	105.51	C	104.08	98.61
8	C	104.43	103.34	C	105.70	100.60	C	102.84	C	103.09	103.99	C
9	116.25	103.17	102.93	101.00	105.47	C	99.16	104.08	C	102.82	104.05	C
10	116.37	103.68	C	101.05	105.46	C	99.23	104.76	105.12	102.54	C	98.62
11	116.47	C	C	100.63	104.65	99.72	98.57	C	105.46	102.96	C	98.66
12	116.69	C	103.20	101.10	C	99.36	97.94	C	105.32	103.49	103.77	98.72
13	116.42	102.39	103.85	101.61	C	99.45	98.13	104.39	106.07	C	103.26	98.55
14	C	102.96	103.78	C	104.03	98.86	C	104.27	106.82	C	102.94	98.82
15	C	103.08	104.13	C	103.95	98.63	C	103.80	C	103.80	102.61	C
16	116.32	102.75	105.01	101.66	104.02	C	97.76	104.12	C	103.74	102.04	C
17	116.52	102.58	C	102.24	103.02	C	97.83	104.24	106.71	103.65	C	98.70
18	116.55	C	C	102.14	102.34	99.09	97.31	C	106.45	104.50	C	100.23
19	116.40	C	104.10	102.15	C	99.58	96.80	C	106.18	104.88	101.10	100.71
20	115.76	C	104.44	C	C	99.68	96.12	104.12	106.19	C	101.01	100.57
21	C	101.95	104.53	C	101.61	100.09	C	105.21	106.13	C	100.92	100.35
22	C	101.91	103.86	C	100.63	100.49	C	105.40	C	104.74	C	C
23	114.36	101.26	103.56	101.71	100.23	C	94.94	105.58	C	104.73	101.73	C
24	114.07	102.90	C	101.90	98.62	C	94.21	105.93	105.58	104.59	C	100.88
25	113.69	C	C	102.12	98.53	100.46	93.95	C	105.18	104.06	C	C
26	113.14	C	103.28	102.90	C	99.80	94.45	C	105.21	103.41	101.44	100.83
27	112.37	104.16	103.12	103.20	C	99.28	95.31	105.42	105.27	C	101.41	100.61
28	C	103.35	103.74	C	C	99.75	C	105.77	105.17	C	101.00	100.81
29	C	103.72	104.00	C	97.67	100.30	C	105.97	C	102.99	100.45	C
30	110.73		104.10	103.34	97.41	C	95.07	106.00	C	103.33	100.11	C
31	110.21		C		97.75		95.25	106.21		103.07		101.49
Close	110.21	103.72	104.10	103.34	97.75	100.30	95.25	106.21	105.17	103.07	100.11	101.49
Month Pt Change	-2.06	-6.49	0.38	-0.76	-5.59	2.55	-5.05	10.96	-1.04	-2.10	-2.96	1.38
Month % Change	-1.8	-5.9	0.4	-0.7	-5.4	2.6	-5.0	11.5	-1.0	-2.0	-2.9	1.4
QTR % Change			-7.3			-3.7			4.9			-3.5
Year % Change												-9.6

HIGHLIGHTS

Election Year	Bull Market Begins 7/24	Best Eight Months 14.9%	High Jan-12 116.69
Reagan (1st term)	Expansion	Worst Four Months 2.8%	Low Jul-25 93.95

RUSSELL 2000 INDEX — 1985

Previous Month	Jan	Feb	Mar	Apr	May	Jun	Jul	Aug	Sep	Oct	Nov	Dec
Close	101.49	114.77	117.54	114.92	113.35	117.26	118.38	121.56	120.10	112.65	116.73	124.62
1	C	114.62	118.68	115.09	113.02	C	118.64	122.32	C	113.26	117.33	C
2	101.21	C	C	114.85	112.73	C	118.86	122.49	C	113.13	C	124.34
3	101.27	C	C	114.19	113.11	117.28	118.87	C	119.42	113.16	C	124.73
4	101.24	115.42	118.46	114.02	C	117.46	C	C	118.87	112.87	117.32	126.34
5	C	116.25	118.53	C	C	117.76	119.58	121.56	118.76	C	117.76	126.83
6	C	116.98	117.98	C	113.08	117.75	C	120.36	119.13	C	118.20	125.97
7	101.55	118.22	117.37	C	113.32	117.39	C	119.68	C	112.23	118.37	C
8	101.76	118.85	117.01	113.64	113.31	C	119.26	120.15	C	111.81	119.27	C
9	102.34	C	C	113.51	114.06	C	119.03	120.06	118.99	112.17	C	126.09
10	103.63	C	C	114.06	115.46	116.86	119.69	C	118.21	112.57	C	126.06
11	104.10	118.44	116.36	114.51	C	116.71	120.39	C	117.07	113.29	120.15	126.73
12	C	118.43	116.20	114.58	C	116.47	120.86	119.49	116.17	C	121.23	127.43
13	C	119.37	115.07	C	115.63	115.50	C	119.07	114.96	C	120.83	128.82
14	105.72	119.32	114.95	C	115.39	115.89	C	119.24	C	114.05	121.64	C
15	106.48	118.95	114.96	114.71	115.56	C	121.00	119.43	C	114.24	121.93	C
16	107.32	C	C	114.97	115.87	C	122.20	118.79	114.40	115.00	C	129.04
17	107.79	C	C	115.35	116.76	115.60	123.02	C	112.88	115.48	C	128.12
18	108.47	C	114.33	115.18	C	115.72	122.78	C	112.74	115.52	121.74	127.63
19	C	118.63	114.88	115.02	C	115.71	123.60	118.57	113.88	C	122.48	127.84
20	C	118.89	114.70	C	117.71	115.57	C	118.90	114.12	C	122.30	128.71
21	110.08	118.46	114.81	C	117.70	116.06	C	119.44	C	115.23	123.33	C
22	110.55	117.92	114.52	114.68	117.39	C	123.25	119.00	C	115.56	123.96	C
23	111.50	C	C	114.76	117.09	C	123.10	119.10	114.69	115.99	C	128.25
24	111.86	C	C	114.76	117.20	116.29	122.65	C	114.07	116.23	C	127.71
25	112.35	116.96	113.63	114.88	C	117.05	122.84	C	113.24	115.88	123.35	C
26	C	117.42	113.64	114.74	C	117.25	122.95	118.93	112.61	C	123.42	128.00
27	C	117.32	114.12	C	C	117.91	C	119.22	C	C	124.17	128.92
28	113.00	117.54	114.46	C	116.95	118.38	C	119.51	C	115.60	C	C
29	113.61		114.92	113.97	116.92	C	121.61	119.72	C	116.14	124.62	C
30	114.46		C	113.35	116.87	C	121.31	120.10	112.65	116.53	C	129.15
31	114.77		C		117.26		121.56	C		116.73		129.87
Close	114.77	117.54	114.92	113.35	117.26	118.38	121.56	120.10	112.65	116.73	124.62	129.87
Month Pt Change	13.28	2.77	–2.62	–1.57	3.91	1.12	3.18	–1.46	–7.45	4.08	7.89	5.25
Month % Change	13.1	2.4	–2.2	–1.4	3.4	1.0	2.7	–1.2	–6.2	3.6	6.8	4.2
QTR % Change			13.2			3.0			–4.8			15.3
Year % Change												28.0

HIGHLIGHTS

Post Election Year	Bull Market	Best Eight Months 32.1%	High Dec-31	129.87
Reagan (2nd Term)	Expansion	Worst Four Months -1.4%	Low Jan-02	101.21

1986 RUSSELL 2000 INDEX

Previous Month Close	Jan 129.87	Feb 131.78	Mar 141.00	Apr 147.63	May 149.66	Jun 154.61	Jul 154.23	Aug 139.65	Sep 143.83	Oct 134.73	Nov 139.95	Dec 139.26
1	C	C	C	146.78	149.03	C	154.89	139.39	C	135.53	C	138.57
2	130.19	C	C	146.55	149.41	154.09	155.28	C	142.94	135.74	C	139.93
3	130.88	132.36	141.26	146.10	C	154.46	155.30	C	142.59	135.43	140.02	140.17
4	C	132.11	141.91	145.07	C	154.26	C	138.04	144.14	C	140.35	140.42
5	C	132.20	141.28	C	150.42	154.35	C	138.42	143.24	C	140.85	139.98
6	130.74	132.90	142.25	C	150.56	154.60	C	137.77	C	135.43	140.49	C
7	131.99	133.86	142.55	144.08	150.22	C	151.21	138.03	C	135.19	140.74	C
8	130.62	C	C	145.77	151.06	C	147.47	138.27	141.93	135.50	C	139.31
9	128.23	C	C	146.15	151.80	152.54	148.57	C	141.27	135.55	C	138.75
10	128.46	134.46	143.01	147.20	C	152.39	148.41	C	140.47	135.56	140.67	138.82
11	C	134.76	144.38	147.72	C	153.23	148.59	139.54	135.39	C	140.94	138.01
12	C	135.25	145.27	C	151.39	153.57	C	140.85	133.25	C	140.75	137.20
13	128.84	135.80	145.46	C	150.93	154.67	C	141.92	C	135.64	139.93	C
14	129.35	136.56	145.92	148.59	151.13	C	145.86	142.75	C	135.53	140.23	C
15	130.23	C	C	148.74	150.27	C	143.11	143.27	132.89	136.82	C	136.58
16	130.73	C	C	150.73	150.03	154.25	143.60	C	132.07	136.92	C	136.73
17	131.05	C	144.82	151.71	C	153.58	144.08	C	132.67	136.91	139.34	136.19
18	C	137.50	145.70	152.01	C	152.90	143.88	143.12	132.66	C	137.37	135.86
19	C	137.21	145.74	C	149.69	153.15	C	142.87	133.07	C	136.05	136.89
20	130.72	137.85	146.27	C	150.06	152.47	C	143.56	C	136.19	137.33	C
21	130.14	139.09	147.16	152.66	150.28	C	143.18	143.54	C	136.32	137.98	C
22	129.54	C	C	152.26	151.64	C	143.33	143.58	134.26	136.42	C	136.06
23	129.57	C	C	151.73	152.40	152.35	143.45	C	135.09	137.26	C	134.77
24	130.53	138.86	146.05	152.64	C	153.14	142.79	C	135.68	137.48	138.13	135.45
25	C	138.76	145.58	152.95	C	153.74	142.98	142.72	134.63	C	138.49	C
26	C	139.05	146.36	C	C	153.78	C	143.18	135.00	C	138.60	135.70
27	130.74	140.23	147.39	C	153.35	153.73	C	143.43	C	137.61	C	C
28	131.39	141.00	C	152.67	154.10	C	141.15	143.63	C	137.96	139.26	C
29	130.89		C	151.75	154.29	C	139.94	143.83	133.86	138.70	C	134.76
30	131.11		C	149.66	154.61	154.23	139.59	C	134.73	139.48	C	134.23
31	131.78		147.63		C		139.65	C		139.95		135.00
Close	131.78	141.00	147.63	149.66	154.61	154.23	139.65	143.83	134.73	139.95	139.26	135.00
Month Pt Change	1.91	9.22	6.63	2.03	4.95	–0.38	–14.58	4.18	–9.10	5.22	–0.69	–4.26
Month % Change	1.5	7.0	4.7	1.4	3.3	–0.2	–9.5	3.0	–6.3	3.9	–0.5	–3.1
QTR % Change			13.7			4.5			–12.6			0.2
Year % Change												4.0

HIGHLIGHTS

Mid-Term Election Year	Bull Market	Best Eight Months	17.7%	High	Jul-03	155.30
Reagan (2nd Term)	Expansion	Worst Four Months	-9.3%	Low	Jan-09	128.23

RUSSELL 2000 INDEX 1987

Previous Month Close	Jan	Feb	Mar	Apr	May	Jun	Jul	Aug	Sep	Oct	Nov	Dec
	135.00	150.48	162.84	166.79	161.82	161.02	164.75	169.42	174.25	170.81	118.26	111.70
1	C	C	C	165.93	161.58	160.90	164.39	C	172.95	171.40	C	111.27
2	137.25	152.29	162.74	167.33	C	160.40	164.97	C	171.65	172.08	120.21	111.27
3	C	153.36	162.81	169.55	C	161.25	C	169.07	171.45	C	117.72	111.11
4	C	155.65	164.02	C	161.40	161.77	C	168.80	170.60	C	117.19	108.94
5	140.76	157.29	164.68	C	162.87	162.09	C	169.72	C	172.54	118.94	C
6	142.04	157.74	164.82	169.77	163.11	C	164.61	170.94	C	170.21	119.33	C
7	144.23	C	C	168.59	163.41	C	165.37	171.67	C	168.87	C	106.49
8	145.86	C	C	168.45	163.52	162.53	165.87	C	166.78	167.06	C	106.44
9	146.85	157.27	164.13	167.14	C	162.92	166.21	C	167.44	166.12	117.62	107.24
10	C	156.60	165.26	166.86	C	163.29	166.38	172.37	168.97	C	115.56	108.89
11	C	158.50	165.98	C	163.71	163.35	C	173.01	170.54	C	116.25	108.63
12	148.57	158.86	166.95	C	163.21	164.19	C	172.73	C	163.86	118.35	C
13	148.86	159.78	166.82	164.51	163.63	C	166.35	173.20	C	164.14	118.31	C
14	150.45	C	C	159.74	164.04	C	167.61	173.26	170.43	161.79	C	109.31
15	151.72	C	C	161.07	162.38	164.03	168.04	C	169.20	159.66	C	112.07
16	150.29	C	165.86	162.65	C	164.57	168.86	C	168.92	152.74	118.27	114.36
17	C	161.81	167.06	C	C	164.99	169.49	172.96	168.82	C	116.30	116.82
18	C	161.33	167.02	C	160.36	165.08	C	171.34	168.75	C	116.69	116.94
19	151.03	161.22	167.52	C	158.37	165.62	C	171.95	C	133.60	115.11	C
20	150.98	161.24	168.65	162.20	157.06	C	168.81	173.74	C	121.39	114.45	C
21	149.77	C	C	162.09	157.87	C	167.37	174.33	167.40	130.65	C	119.45
22	150.96	C	C	162.11	157.83	165.76	167.10	C	167.56	124.57	C	119.31
23	149.85	160.09	168.44	161.87	C	165.16	166.76	C	168.65	121.59	114.47	120.80
24	C	160.55	168.34	160.28	C	164.93	167.18	173.96	168.72	C	115.58	121.59
25	C	161.46	168.33	C	C	165.27	C	174.44	168.85	C	115.97	C
26	148.82	161.89	169.00	C	159.28	164.94	C	174.27	C	110.33	C	C
27	149.82	162.84	168.46	158.57	159.74	C	167.16	173.98	C	108.51	115.61	C
28	150.45	C	C	159.33	160.02	C	167.53	173.31	169.52	106.08	C	119.00
29	150.43		C	160.34	161.02	164.97	168.13	C	169.06	110.80	C	118.30
30	150.48		165.04	161.82	C	164.75	168.97	C	170.81	118.26	111.70	119.50
31	C		166.79		C		169.42	174.25		C		120.42
Close	150.48	162.84	166.79	161.82	161.02	164.75	169.42	174.25	170.81	118.26	111.70	120.42
Month Pt Change	15.48	12.36	3.95	–4.97	–0.80	3.73	4.67	4.83	–3.44	–52.55	–6.56	8.72
Month % Change	11.5	8.2	2.4	–3.0	–0.5	2.3	2.8	2.9	–2.0	–30.8	–5.5	7.8
QTR % Change			23.5			–1.2			3.7			–29.5
Year % Change												–10.8

HIGHLIGHTS

Pre-Election Year	Bear Market 8/25 - 10/19	Best Eight Months	27.9%	High Aug-25	174.44
Reagan (2nd Term)	Expansion	Worst Four Months	-28.2%	Low Oct-28	106.08

Data Bank

1988   RUSSELL 2000 INDEX

Previous Month Close	Jan	Feb	Mar	Apr	May	Jun	Jul	Aug	Sep	Oct	Nov	Dec
	120.42	125.24	136.10	142.15	145.01	141.37	151.30	149.89	145.74	149.08	147.25	142.01
1	C	125.72	136.26	C	C	142.87	151.03	150.50	144.56	C	147.21	142.56
2	C	125.94	137.36	C	144.73	142.80	C	150.63	145.48	C	146.97	142.77
3	C	125.38	137.77	C	145.31	143.50	C	150.67	C	147.80	147.13	C
4	123.50	125.51	138.06	140.41	145.22	C	C	150.65	C	147.77	146.25	C
5	126.13	125.77	C	140.72	144.79	C	151.29	150.31	C	148.08	C	143.45
6	127.00	C	C	142.11	144.64	144.18	151.01	C	145.73	148.25	C	143.93
7	128.03	C	139.06	142.88	C	144.21	151.15	C	146.07	148.60	144.76	144.00
8	123.84	125.26	140.36	144.11	C	145.73	151.16	150.11	146.65	C	145.27	143.75
9	C	125.52	141.64	C	143.71	146.54	C	148.93	147.23	C	144.80	143.86
10	C	127.16	140.51	C	143.34	147.09	C	146.86	C	148.61	145.01	C
11	122.52	128.03	140.59	144.67	140.97	C	151.11	146.68	C	148.50	143.67	C
12	121.23	129.21	C	145.32	141.29	C	150.73	146.95	147.25	147.95	C	143.45
13	121.30	C	C	145.21	142.17	147.33	150.68	C	147.38	147.97	C	143.17
14	121.78	C	140.84	141.67	C	147.89	151.15	C	147.82	148.20	142.91	143.18
15	123.67	C	140.94	141.14	C	148.13	151.42	145.36	147.74	C	143.00	143.17
16	C	129.90	141.91	C	142.18	147.37	C	145.57	148.03	C	141.31	144.34
17	C	130.22	142.69	C	141.75	147.16	C	145.38	C	148.15	140.71	C
18	124.05	130.57	142.47	142.08	139.93	C	151.42	145.50	C	147.91	140.86	C
19	124.44	131.23	C	142.55	139.60	C	150.69	145.68	147.85	148.61	C	144.53
20	121.76	C	C	141.70	140.15	147.24	151.10	C	147.95	149.15	C	144.48
21	121.63	C	141.96	141.26	C	147.61	150.36	C	147.83	148.95	139.95	144.20
22	122.79	132.37	142.35	141.69	C	148.63	149.52	144.26	147.62	C	139.87	144.51
23	C	132.52	143.07	C	139.20	148.95	C	144.00	147.83	C	140.41	144.88
24	C	133.42	141.43	C	139.46	149.23	C	144.95	C	148.66	C	C
25	123.68	134.00	140.38	142.25	139.79	C	149.44	144.24	C	148.45	140.14	C
26	123.25	134.17	C	143.12	140.27	C	149.61	144.45	147.13	148.14	C	C
27	123.37	C	C	143.65	140.09	148.74	148.77	C	146.78	146.67	C	144.67
28	124.31	C	139.21	144.07	C	149.49	148.96	C	146.99	147.17	140.09	144.94
29	125.24	136.10	140.36	145.01	C	149.56	149.89	144.89	148.00	C	140.65	145.70
30	C		140.03	C	C	151.30	C	145.14	149.08	C	142.01	147.37
31	C		142.15		141.37		C	145.74		147.25		C
Close	125.24	136.10	142.15	145.01	141.37	151.30	149.89	145.74	149.08	147.25	142.01	147.37
Month Pt Change	4.82	10.86	6.05	2.86	−3.64	9.93	−1.41	−4.15	3.34	−1.83	−5.24	5.36
Month % Change	4.0	8.7	4.4	2.0	−2.5	7.0	−0.9	−2.8	2.3	−1.2	−3.6	3.8
QTR % Change			18.0			6.4			−1.5			−1.1
Year % Change												22.4

HIGHLIGHTS

Election Year	Bull Market	Best Eight Months 13.7%	High Jul-15	151.42
Reagan (2nd Term)	Expansion	Worst Four Months -2.7%	Low Jan-12	121.23

RUSSELL 2000 INDEX   1989

Previous Month Close	Jan	Feb	Mar	Apr	May	Jun	Jul	Aug	Sep	Oct	Nov	Dec
	147.37	153.84	154.56	157.89	164.68	171.53	167.42	174.50	178.20	178.21	167.47	168.17
1	C	154.38	154.67	C	164.30	172.40	C	174.22	178.71	C	167.82	168.51
2	C	154.94	155.68	C	164.55	173.41	C	174.38	C	178.83	167.25	C
3	146.79	155.69	156.32	158.29	164.78	C	167.60	175.36	C	179.37	167.39	C
4	148.39	C	C	157.97	165.17	C	C	175.38	C	179.39	C	168.59
5	148.75	C	C	158.52	165.72	172.37	167.95	C	178.82	179.92	C	168.43
6	149.82	155.58	157.24	158.40	C	172.17	168.64	C	178.13	180.45	165.77	168.87
7	C	156.84	157.53	159.27	C	172.94	170.16	176.59	178.43	C	165.79	168.59
8	C	157.00	157.90	C	165.23	173.23	C	176.66	179.16	C	167.21	168.77
9	149.60	156.56	157.80	C	165.31	173.37	C	176.73	C	180.78	167.07	C
10	149.23	155.07	157.75	159.46	165.64	C	170.74	177.06	C	180.27	167.63	C
11	149.27	C	C	160.33	166.05	C	171.18	176.56	178.29	179.71	C	168.02
12	149.81	C	C	161.21	167.12	173.32	171.93	C	178.77	179.53	C	168.05
13	149.93	154.70	157.98	160.53	C	172.62	172.28	C	178.81	172.84	167.52	168.36
14	C	154.98	157.73	161.63	C	172.38	172.47	175.69	177.56	C	167.28	167.26
15	C	155.56	158.33	C	167.32	171.03	C	175.82	176.69	C	167.66	166.52
16	149.95	156.29	159.26	C	167.25	171.45	C	175.87	C	170.28	167.58	C
17	149.70	157.07	156.72	161.45	168.27	C	172.99	175.65	C	169.98	168.26	C
18	150.83	C	C	162.29	168.99	C	172.86	175.94	176.38	170.97	C	163.94
19	151.29	C	C	162.46	169.64	171.05	174.09	C	176.35	173.35	C	162.82
20	151.40	C	155.30	162.59	C	170.69	173.88	C	176.19	173.26	167.29	163.02
21	C	156.76	156.16	163.31	C	170.25	173.91	174.64	176.42	C	166.62	163.94
22	C	155.39	156.03	C	169.52	170.62	C	174.48	176.80	C	167.18	165.19
23	150.95	155.41	156.01	C	169.06	171.44	C	175.67	C	172.10	C	C
24	151.45	154.25	C	163.29	169.48	C	172.91	177.01	C	169.77	167.90	C
25	151.78	C	C	163.28	170.12	C	172.79	177.10	175.99	170.23	C	C
26	152.52	C	C	163.60	171.01	171.16	173.40	C	176.55	168.81	C	165.41
27	152.92	153.96	155.88	164.28	C	171.79	174.23	C	176.23	166.98	168.20	166.02
28	C	154.56	156.58	164.68	C	170.81	174.12	177.09	177.37	C	168.48	166.27
29	C		156.80	C	C	168.07	C	176.85	178.21	C	168.06	168.30
30	153.02		156.76	C	170.58	167.42	C	177.44	C	166.32	168.17	C
31	153.84		157.89		171.53		174.50	178.20		167.47		C
Close	153.84	154.56	157.89	164.68	171.53	167.42	174.50	178.20	178.21	167.47	168.17	168.30
Month Pt Change	6.47	0.72	3.33	6.79	6.85	−4.11	7.08	3.70	0.01	−10.74	0.70	0.13
Month % Change	4.4	0.5	2.2	4.3	4.2	−2.4	4.2	2.1	0.01	−6.0	0.4	0.1
QTR % Change			7.1			6.0			6.4			−5.6
Year % Change												14.2

HIGHLIGHTS

Post Election Year	Bull Market	Best Eight Months	0.9%	High	Oct-09	180.78
GHW Bush	Expansion	Worst Four Months	0.03%	Low	Jan-03	146.79

Previous Month Close	Jan	Feb	Mar	Apr	May	Jun	Jul	Aug	Sep	Oct	Nov	Dec
	168.30	153.27	157.72	163.63	158.09	168.91	169.04	161.51	139.52	126.70	118.83	127.50
1	C	154.36	158.04	C	158.49	169.70	C	160.76	C	128.43	118.91	C
2	169.95	156.00	159.19	162.34	159.13	C	169.00	158.58	C	129.07	120.36	C
3	170.79	C	C	163.40	159.72	C	168.94	154.35	C	128.06	C	128.15
4	170.09	C	C	162.84	160.39	170.62	C	C	139.11	127.72	C	128.69
5	169.65	156.89	159.29	162.78	C	170.23	168.02	C	140.02	126.84	121.29	130.70
6	C	156.90	160.40	162.38	C	169.91	168.20	149.01	139.34	C	121.30	131.13
7	C	158.25	160.40	C	160.73	169.80	C	149.20	140.11	C	120.35	130.95
8	169.55	158.59	162.07	C	160.89	168.93	C	151.12	C	126.89	120.15	C
9	169.30	159.13	162.08	161.46	161.08	C	168.11	152.54	C	124.36	121.30	C
10	167.94	C	C	161.91	161.67	C	167.69	150.84	140.34	122.77	C	130.70
11	168.01	C	C	162.17	163.12	169.09	168.66	C	139.78	120.02	C	129.87
12	164.37	158.50	162.23	162.58	C	170.03	169.43	C	139.89	120.38	123.23	130.57
13	C	158.19	162.06	C	C	170.87	170.04	150.12	138.71	C	123.65	130.96
14	C	158.22	162.78	C	163.84	170.63	C	151.14	137.89	C	124.74	130.18
15	162.93	159.20	163.26	C	163.66	170.90	C	151.30	C	120.44	124.31	C
16	163.30	159.30	164.21	162.52	163.86	C	169.97	148.47	C	119.32	124.25	C
17	163.51	C	C	162.24	164.81	C	168.89	145.63	137.46	119.48	C	129.12
18	162.76	C	C	161.40	165.44	168.72	167.86	C	136.90	120.95	C	129.96
19	163.57	C	164.38	160.76	C	168.38	167.02	C	136.76	122.12	124.73	130.57
20	C	157.86	164.24	160.06	C	168.12	166.82	144.16	134.72	C	124.13	130.73
21	C	157.05	164.24	C	166.65	168.44	C	140.78	133.74	C	124.04	130.86
22	161.13	157.80	162.74	C	167.22	168.01	C	139.01	C	121.61	C	C
23	160.41	156.64	163.62	158.48	167.80	C	162.87	132.91	C	122.29	124.26	C
24	158.16	C	C	158.36	167.94	C	163.24	134.22	130.37	122.25	C	130.46
25	157.99	C	C	158.62	167.29	167.13	163.69	C	130.52	122.39	C	C
26	156.61	156.35	163.82	158.73	C	166.89	164.08	C	128.65	120.87	123.99	130.82
27	C	156.84	164.07	157.82	C	167.24	163.17	138.67	126.18	C	125.24	130.62
28	C	157.72	163.80	C	C	168.41	C	139.58	126.70	C	125.99	130.46
29	154.94		163.41	C	168.20	169.04	C	140.05	C	119.69	126.10	C
30	152.62		163.63	158.09	168.67	C	161.95	139.31	C	118.82	127.50	C
31	153.27		C		168.91		161.51	139.52		118.83		132.16
Close	153.27	157.72	163.63	158.09	168.91	169.04	161.51	139.52	126.70	118.83	127.50	132.16
Month Pt Change	−15.03	4.45	5.91	−5.54	10.82	0.13	−7.53	−21.99	−12.82	−7.87	8.67	4.66
Month % Change	−8.9	2.9	3.7	−3.4	6.8	0.1	−4.5	−13.6	−9.2	−6.2	7.3	3.7
QTR % Change			−2.8			3.3			−25.0			4.3
Year % Change												−21.5

RUSSELL 2000 INDEX 1991

	Jan	Feb	Mar	Apr	May	Jun	Jul	Aug	Sep	Oct	Nov	Dec
Previous Month Close	132.16	144.17	160.00	171.01	170.61	178.34	167.61	172.76	179.11	180.16	185.00	176.37
1	C	145.50	161.26	170.31	172.20	C	168.47	172.75	C	180.08	184.62	C
2	131.65	C	C	172.61	173.64	C	168.22	173.05	C	179.79	C	176.65
3	130.35	C	C	173.75	173.96	178.52	167.05	C	177.98	178.22	C	177.40
4	130.21	148.16	163.49	174.52	C	178.54	C	C	177.34	178.37	183.84	177.82
5	C	150.20	166.78	173.89	C	178.51	167.01	172.49	177.35	C	183.96	177.23
6	C	152.29	167.03	C	173.78	178.40	C	172.91	177.45	C	184.34	177.54
7	128.20	151.08	167.66	C	173.96	177.15	C	173.07	C	176.67	185.80	C
8	127.57	151.72	167.96	174.03	174.61	C	167.46	173.21	C	177.08	186.30	C
9	126.71	C	C	173.12	175.79	C	168.13	173.32	177.47	176.27	C	176.70
10	127.56	C	C	173.13	174.27	176.57	169.04	C	175.71	176.43	C	175.78
11	127.62	154.17	166.45	174.79	C	176.63	169.04	C	176.09	176.97	186.79	174.70
12	C	154.21	164.87	175.78	C	174.66	170.05	173.55	177.04	C	188.02	175.79
13	C	155.88	166.08	C	174.37	174.71	C	174.44	176.74	C	188.04	177.50
14	125.39	155.32	166.23	C	172.60	175.60	C	174.87	C	178.48	187.82	C
15	125.25	156.83	165.36	175.74	169.47	C	171.08	174.72	C	180.59	181.72	C
16	126.80	C	C	177.31	170.72	C	171.14	174.09	176.42	182.84	C	178.55
17	130.25	C	C	178.71	170.61	175.26	171.31	C	176.24	182.83	C	177.66
18	129.84	C	165.37	177.58	C	174.68	177.27	C	176.91	183.42	181.66	177.37
19	C	156.76	164.09	176.42	C	172.93	172.87	169.17	178.23	C	177.55	176.20
20	C	155.44	165.51	C	170.36	172.52	C	170.73	179.34	C	178.14	176.07
21	130.34	156.36	165.78	C	171.44	172.45	C	174.96	C	182.98	178.75	C
22	131.08	157.41	165.80	173.69	171.80	C	172.43	175.54	C	183.00	177.37	C
23	132.63	C	C	174.05	172.41	C	171.24	176.21	178.80	182.96	C	177.90
24	135.04	C	C	175.00	173.22	169.27	170.18	C	179.04	180.86	C	179.55
25	136.49	158.44	166.72	174.60	C	168.28	170.57	C	178.96	179.94	176.12	C
26	C	157.13	168.64	173.82	C	167.63	170.65	176.58	179.13	C	175.50	182.35
27	C	158.44	169.82	C	C	168.22	C	176.74	178.68	C	175.52	184.23
28	137.80	160.00	171.01	C	174.32	167.61	C	178.20	C	180.74	C	C
29	139.22		C	172.06	175.17	C	170.66	178.54	C	181.90	176.37	C
30	142.03		C	170.61	176.82	C	171.54	179.11	180.16	183.35	C	187.84
31	144.17		C		178.34		172.76	C		185.00		189.94
Close	144.17	160.00	171.01	170.61	178.34	167.61	172.76	179.11	180.16	185.00	176.37	189.94
Month Pt Change	12.01	15.83	11.01	-0.40	7.73	-10.73	5.15	6.35	1.05	4.84	-8.63	13.57
Month % Change	9.1	11.0	6.9	-0.2	4.5	-6.0	3.1	3.7	0.6	2.7	-4.7	7.7
QTR % Change			29.4			-2.0			7.5			5.4
Year % Change												43.7

HIGHLIGHTS

Pre-Election Year	Bull Market	Best Eight Months	2.0%	High	Dec-31	189.94
GHW Bush	Expansion Begins Q2	Worst Four Months	10.4%	Low	Jan-15	125.25

Previous Month Close	Jan	Feb	Mar	Apr	May	Jun	Jul	Aug	Sep	Oct	Nov	Dec
	189.94	205.16	211.15	203.69	196.25	198.52	188.64	194.74	188.79	192.92	198.90	213.81
1	C	C	C	202.38	196.55	199.38	189.60	C	189.23	191.35	C	213.80
2	188.75	C	211.79	200.49	C	199.94	188.32	C	190.69	189.49	199.90	214.21
3	192.09	205.87	212.09	199.04	C	199.97	C	195.35	191.47	C	199.63	214.78
4	C	207.82	211.27	C	197.76	199.82	C	195.40	191.32	C	199.55	215.91
5	C	209.34	208.69	C	198.48	199.14	C	194.47	C	186.50	200.76	C
6	194.33	210.26	207.24	199.58	199.14	C	187.78	193.43	C	187.82	201.56	C
7	195.77	210.08	C	195.99	198.95	C	186.55	193.43	C	187.98	C	217.42
8	198.08	C	C	193.03	198.91	198.60	185.81	C	190.19	189.26	C	217.76
9	200.57	C	206.86	196.23	C	196.49	187.67	C	190.61	188.21	203.17	216.89
10	199.31	210.53	208.20	197.12	C	195.03	188.85	192.73	192.12	C	204.60	215.45
11	C	210.71	206.87	C	199.67	194.04	C	192.57	192.79	C	206.91	215.25
12	C	212.61	205.98	C	199.23	194.44	C	192.39	C	188.74	206.76	C
13	199.86	211.54	206.76	197.06	199.08	C	189.52	192.11	C	190.04	207.43	C
14	202.35	211.56	C	198.91	197.57	C	190.83	192.61	194.72	190.36	C	214.93
15	204.30	C	C	199.68	196.93	193.90	191.14	C	193.19	189.13	C	213.71
16	204.39	C	206.09	198.42	C	192.84	191.23	C	192.75	191.61	207.29	212.72
17	205.06	C	207.21	C	C	189.30	190.42	192.81	193.04	C	206.13	214.21
18	C	210.08	208.16	C	197.19	187.62	C	192.55	193.22	C	207.82	215.55
19	C	208.36	208.47	C	197.21	188.27	C	191.54	C	193.62	208.69	C
20	204.30	210.89	208.35	195.17	197.42	C	189.03	190.94	C	194.42	209.78	C
21	200.94	210.40	C	194.71	197.28	C	189.77	190.01	193.40	195.53	C	214.99
22	203.71	C	C	195.00	198.09	186.46	188.91	C	192.36	195.24	C	214.80
23	204.66	C	207.76	194.71	C	186.94	189.25	C	192.23	195.88	209.72	215.26
24	205.42	208.89	206.91	194.56	C	186.38	189.60	187.48	192.92	C	210.79	216.26
25	C	207.58	206.91	C	C	185.94	C	186.63	190.89	C	211.94	C
26	C	210.20	206.24	C	196.67	186.01	C	187.29	C	196.65	C	C
27	205.06	211.01	203.83	193.18	196.96	C	189.73	188.37	C	196.53	212.50	C
28	204.98	211.15	C	191.62	197.43	C	191.48	188.82	190.50	197.80	C	215.89
29	203.87	C	C	193.56	198.52	187.13	192.99	C	190.71	198.26	C	216.85
30	204.87		202.95	196.25	C	188.64	193.82	C	192.92	198.90	213.81	218.42
31	205.16		203.69		C		194.74	188.79		C		221.01
Close	205.16	211.15	203.69	196.25	198.52	188.64	194.74	188.79	192.92	198.90	213.81	221.01
Month Pt Change	15.22	5.99	–7.46	–7.44	2.27	–9.88	6.10	–5.95	4.13	5.98	14.91	7.20
Month % Change	8.0	2.9	–3.5	–3.7	1.2	–5.0	3.2	–3.1	2.2	3.1	7.5	3.4
QTR % Change			7.2			–7.4			2.3			14.6
Year % Change												16.4

HIGHLIGHTS

Election Year	Bull Market	Best Eight Months	17.3%	High	Dec-31	221.01
GHW Bush	Expansion	Worst Four Months	5.4%	Low	Jul-08	185.81

RUSSELL 2000 INDEX   1993

	Jan	Feb	Mar	Apr	May	Jun	Jul	Aug	Sep	Oct	Nov	Dec
Previous Month Close	221.01	228.10	222.41	229.21	222.68	232.19	233.35	236.46	246.19	252.95	259.18	250.41
1	C	229.03	222.43	228.66	C	233.09	234.13	C	247.11	253.00	259.50	252.61
2	C	229.70	224.11	224.74	C	233.88	234.23	237.16	248.07	C	260.17	252.91
3	C	231.96	225.71	C	223.66	234.32	C	237.79	248.67	C	257.11	253.86
4	219.76	232.36	225.61	C	226.17	233.39	C	238.52	C	253.54	253.11	C
5	220.08	230.49	226.22	224.04	227.73	C	C	238.22	C	253.07	253.11	C
6	221.62	C	C	222.55	227.95	C	233.92	238.72	C	254.34	C	253.98
7	221.12	C	C	222.96	227.97	231.60	233.19	C	246.12	254.06	C	254.03
8	220.12	230.42	227.95	222.83	C	229.37	234.13	C	243.00	253.96	254.57	254.37
9	C	228.63	228.70	C	C	229.79	234.97	239.23	244.62	C	255.78	253.40
10	C	228.68	229.91	C	228.15	229.10	C	239.63	246.56	C	256.98	252.81
11	221.16	229.74	230.40	C	228.80	229.56	C	239.96	C	255.03	257.53	C
12	220.42	228.71	229.53	223.88	228.90	C	235.89	239.49	C	256.50	257.94	C
13	221.49	C	C	225.32	227.54	C	236.35	239.70	246.44	257.89	C	252.23
14	223.79	C	C	225.26	227.48	229.82	237.84	C	244.46	259.03	C	249.89
15	225.24	C	230.80	224.60	C	230.46	237.54	C	245.32	259.98	256.47	249.84
16	C	221.20	230.19	224.43	C	230.12	236.16	240.18	245.68	C	255.42	250.58
17	C	218.55	228.75	C	227.42	229.96	C	241.25	245.95	C	253.73	252.25
18	225.23	219.84	228.93	C	227.92	229.02	C	242.82	C	259.57	252.00	C
19	225.50	220.91	227.84	223.42	229.31	C	234.86	242.59	C	255.95	250.99	C
20	225.96	C	C	222.62	230.30	C	234.98	242.95	245.84	255.02	C	251.92
21	226.55	C	C	223.37	229.93	228.32	234.91	C	243.67	255.21	C	250.50
22	227.53	218.10	225.87	223.62	C	228.09	233.76	C	246.48	255.79	246.85	250.38
23	C	217.55	225.34	222.69	C	227.72	234.31	242.95	247.94	C	248.12	251.32
24	C	219.61	224.93	C	229.89	228.33	C	244.16	248.74	C	249.82	C
25	229.35	220.76	226.45	C	230.49	229.53	C	244.37	C	255.52	C	C
26	230.55	222.41	226.94	219.48	232.14	C	235.62	243.80	C	254.82	250.15	C
27	227.98	C	C	219.53	232.66	C	235.15	244.08	249.99	255.96	C	252.43
28	227.19	C	C	220.43	232.19	231.29	235.99	C	250.69	256.88	C	253.74
29	228.10		227.13	221.33	C	231.72	236.52	C	251.51	259.18	250.14	256.01
30	C		227.68	222.68	C	233.35	236.46	244.82	252.95	C	250.41	256.19
31	C		229.21		C		C	246.19		C		258.59
Close	228.10	222.41	229.21	222.68	232.19	233.35	236.46	246.19	252.95	259.18	250.41	258.59
Month Pt Change	7.09	−5.69	6.80	−6.53	9.51	1.16	3.11	9.73	6.76	6.23	−8.77	8.18
Month % Change	3.2	−2.5	3.1	−2.8	4.3	0.5	1.3	4.1	2.7	2.5	−3.4	3.3
QTR % Change			3.7			1.8			8.4			2.2
Year % Change												17.0

HIGHLIGHTS

Post Election Year	Bull Market	Best Eight Months	−7.3%	High Nov-02	260.17
Clinton (1st Term)	Expansion	Worst Four Months	11.1%	Low Feb-23	217.55

Previous Month Close	Jan 258.59	Feb 266.52	Mar 265.53	Apr 251.06	May 252.55	Jun 249.28	Jul 240.29	Aug 244.06	Sep 257.32	Oct 256.12	Nov 255.02	Dec 244.25
1	C	266.50	264.34	C	C	250.08	241.12	245.06	256.06	C	253.48	242.03
2	C	267.62	262.80	C	254.04	251.99	C	245.66	256.19	C	253.75	242.81
3	256.53	267.57	263.15	C	254.50	252.10	C	245.76	C	254.78	254.15	C
4	256.97	261.67	264.71	247.04	254.46	C	C	244.81	C	251.35	252.75	C
5	258.02	C	C	253.96	254.10	C	240.73	244.19	C	249.37	C	242.93
6	258.33	C	C	254.53	251.65	252.74	240.68	C	255.80	249.53	C	242.21
7	259.19	261.68	266.69	255.95	C	251.67	241.72	C	256.81	250.71	251.84	240.17
8	C	263.39	266.56	254.68	C	249.92	241.92	244.61	258.15	C	252.12	236.09
9	C	265.22	266.44	C	248.30	249.24	C	244.95	256.76	C	251.69	235.16
10	259.75	264.14	265.42	C	248.54	250.58	C	246.44	C	252.48	250.59	C
11	259.63	262.89	265.49	254.74	245.61	C	241.66	246.29	C	254.43	249.38	C
12	260.23	C	C	252.73	246.29	C	242.13	247.11	255.87	254.91	C	235.49
13	260.64	C	C	249.62	245.60	250.35	243.62	C	256.96	255.12	C	235.84
14	261.27	263.19	266.19	250.08	C	251.13	245.76	C	257.55	254.87	250.39	237.88
15	C	264.53	266.86	250.15	C	251.26	245.62	247.82	259.78	C	250.86	241.20
16	C	265.96	269.11	C	244.16	251.73	C	248.18	259.79	C	250.52	241.00
17	261.89	264.88	269.79	C	243.95	250.39	C	249.31	C	254.97	249.58	C
18	262.40	264.05	271.08	248.40	246.79	C	245.59	249.21	C	254.02	248.58	C
19	262.60	C	C	245.62	248.65	C	245.26	249.69	259.03	254.80	C	240.44
20	263.37	C	C	242.14	248.28	247.08	243.65	C	256.50	253.61	C	240.61
21	263.80	C	268.99	245.32	C	244.11	243.91	C	254.42	252.86	246.79	243.31
22	C	265.05	269.56	246.55	C	245.28	243.33	249.74	254.38	C	242.26	243.61
23	C	264.92	270.20	C	247.78	242.50	C	251.49	253.65	C	240.61	244.73
24	262.89	262.21	267.07	C	248.36	239.39	C	252.66	C	251.60	C	C
25	262.05	263.00	266.45	249.32	248.24	C	243.35	253.16	C	250.57	242.03	C
26	262.84	C	C	250.95	248.94	C	242.97	254.59	253.22	250.82	C	C
27	263.66	C	C	C	249.46	240.29	242.03	C	253.08	252.26	C	245.93
28	265.03	265.53	262.51	251.31	C	238.96	241.75	C	254.40	255.00	242.69	245.27
29	C		257.04	252.55	C	240.18	244.06	255.16	254.18	C	243.69	246.89
30	C		252.45	C	C	240.29	C	256.14	256.12	C	244.25	250.36
31	266.52		251.06		249.28		C	257.32		255.02		C
Close	266.52	265.53	251.06	252.55	249.28	240.29	244.06	257.32	256.12	255.02	244.25	250.36
Month Pt Change	7.93	-0.99	-14.47	1.49	-3.27	-8.99	3.77	13.26	-1.20	-1.10	-10.77	6.11
Month % Change	3.1	-0.4	-5.4	0.6	-1.3	-3.6	1.6	5.4	-0.5	-0.4	-4.2	2.5
QTR % Change			-2.9			-4.3			6.6			-2.2
Year % Change												-3.2

RUSSELL 2000 INDEX   1995

	Jan	Feb	Mar	Apr	May	Jun	Jul	Aug	Sep	Oct	Nov	Dec
Previous Month Close	250.36	246.85	256.57	260.77	266.17	270.25	283.63	299.72	305.31	310.38	296.25	308.58
1	C	247.50	256.05	C	265.94	271.48	C	298.33	306.17	C	297.70	309.74
2	C	248.62	256.16	C	265.90	272.27	C	297.83	C	306.99	300.99	C
3	247.24	250.78	256.90	260.81	266.84	C	283.74	297.37	C	304.00	302.79	C
4	247.65	C	C	260.75	265.66	C	C	298.27	C	300.82	C	312.51
5	247.46	C	C	261.21	265.62	274.22	284.77	C	308.31	301.21	C	313.11
6	248.08	252.44	255.81	261.23	C	274.69	286.35	C	310.55	301.82	302.94	312.67
7	C	252.97	254.13	260.02	C	274.81	289.35	299.14	312.13	C	301.45	310.96
8	C	253.79	254.87	C	267.01	275.73	C	298.81	314.42	C	302.30	311.55
9	248.37	254.28	254.79	C	266.56	275.21	C	299.58	C	296.64	303.96	C
10	248.98	255.42	256.01	261.61	267.77	C	290.67	299.24	C	294.61	304.32	C
11	248.16	C	C	262.53	268.94	C	291.05	299.08	314.90	297.91	C	312.07
12	248.27	C	C	262.96	269.85	276.45	293.77	C	315.56	300.62	C	311.56
13	249.95	255.53	256.18	263.98	C	278.23	294.67	C	315.97	302.07	303.60	312.59
14	C	255.24	257.26	C	C	278.85	294.88	300.27	316.12	C	301.52	312.53
15	C	257.47	257.39	C	270.93	280.29	C	300.67	314.29	C	301.46	310.42
16	251.72	255.93	258.18	C	272.17	280.81	C	302.35	C	302.20	302.80	C
17	252.92	254.71	257.32	263.96	272.79	C	295.96	303.65	C	302.70	303.84	C
18	252.31	C	C	262.80	270.95	C	293.59	304.30	313.34	304.05	C	303.72
19	251.01	C	C	260.60	270.55	282.23	287.07	C	313.87	303.42	C	306.00
20	249.64	C	257.83	261.25	C	282.54	289.42	C	314.81	302.82	302.22	308.83
21	C	253.86	257.15	262.51	C	282.75	290.53	305.48	313.60	C	301.12	310.67
22	C	253.94	256.79	C	271.58	284.37	C	304.32	312.05	C	301.24	312.31
23	248.07	254.95	257.53	C	272.93	284.02	C	304.51	C	301.10	C	C
24	248.94	255.47	258.85	263.70	272.44	C	293.39	303.72	C	300.85	302.26	C
25	248.80	C	C	263.97	271.96	C	294.70	304.36	310.16	297.84	C	C
26	248.08	C	C	264.89	270.57	281.31	296.10	C	308.96	294.63	C	312.83
27	248.47	253.86	259.85	265.70	C	280.29	298.75	C	305.85	294.55	303.23	314.07
28	C	256.57	260.27	266.17	C	279.94	299.23	303.32	308.46	C	304.62	313.99
29	C		259.90	C	C	281.08	C	301.50	310.38	C	306.72	315.97
30	246.56		260.28	C	269.15	283.63	C	303.26	C	296.24	308.58	C
31	246.85		260.77		270.25		299.72	305.31		296.25		C
Close	246.85	256.57	260.77	266.17	270.25	283.63	299.72	305.31	310.38	296.25	308.58	315.97
Month Pt Change	-3.51	9.72	4.20	5.40	4.08	13.38	16.09	5.59	5.07	-14.13	12.33	7.39
Month % Change	-1.4	3.9	1.6	2.1	1.5	5.0	5.7	1.9	1.7	-4.6	4.2	2.4
QTR % Change			4.2			8.8			9.4			1.8
Year % Change												26.2

HIGHLIGHTS

Pre-Election Year	Bull Market	Best Eight Months	17.0%	High	Sep-14	316.12
Clinton (1st Term)	Expansion	Worst Four Months	4.4%	Low	Jan-30	246.56

Data Bank

Previous Month Close	Jan 315.97	Feb 315.38	Mar 324.93	Apr 330.77	May 348.28	Jun 361.85	Jul 346.61	Aug 316.00	Sep 333.88	Oct 346.39	Nov 340.57	Dec 354.11
1	C	317.32	324.10	332.44	350.28	C	347.72	319.42	C	345.33	339.76	C
2	316.81	317.72	C	333.23	345.94	C	346.94	324.41	C	348.19	C	355.34
3	315.21	C	C	334.07	346.85	361.44	344.80	C	333.38	347.24	C	357.83
4	310.77	C	325.56	334.79	C	362.66	C	C	334.56	349.30	339.90	358.10
5	312.19	318.46	326.85	C	C	363.59	339.78	324.74	331.59	C	339.86	359.05
6	C	320.15	327.11	C	346.87	361.19	C	325.30	334.10	C	342.43	355.50
7	C	319.41	327.42	C	345.66	358.84	C	327.55	C	348.83	344.29	C
8	312.39	320.47	319.21	330.71	345.19	C	336.68	327.35	C	347.36	344.56	C
9	307.40	321.12	C	332.43	347.63	C	336.44	327.44	335.63	346.10	C	360.49
10	302.91	C	C	331.03	351.15	359.74	332.71	C	336.28	346.64	C	361.30
11	305.72	C	322.07	329.47	C	359.41	324.58	C	336.70	347.89	345.69	357.70
12	305.14	321.41	321.02	331.18	C	359.65	323.69	327.37	338.14	C	346.12	356.38
13	C	319.82	323.46	C	354.50	357.40	C	325.63	340.79	C	346.11	354.18
14	C	321.07	325.08	C	357.46	355.08	C	326.72	C	349.00	347.26	C
15	302.13	320.75	325.08	333.52	358.11	C	314.72	327.68	C	349.01	346.52	C
16	301.75	321.59	C	335.57	358.76	C	310.12	328.91	342.29	348.36	C	350.48
17	302.62	C	C	334.85	360.63	353.93	318.19	C	342.25	348.20	C	350.13
18	304.01	C	328.67	337.46	C	349.05	322.92	C	341.58	347.85	345.93	353.08
19	305.28	C	328.93	338.51	C	347.20	321.54	329.34	341.33	C	346.94	356.10
20	C	318.91	328.34	C	363.07	344.16	C	329.20	342.82	C	347.53	356.71
21	C	321.34	328.87	C	363.04	345.21	C	328.94	C	346.10	347.17	C
22	307.17	325.14	329.48	340.99	364.61	C	317.65	331.41	C	342.82	349.91	C
23	308.31	325.76	C	343.52	364.39	C	311.72	331.77	341.59	342.93	C	355.42
24	310.43	C	C	344.64	364.59	346.82	307.77	C	342.66	343.08	C	355.87
25	310.56	C	327.72	346.24	C	344.44	311.58	C	343.72	342.97	352.29	C
26	311.22	325.30	327.71	347.83	C	339.81	314.57	331.52	345.00	C	351.37	357.72
27	C	324.85	328.49	C	C	341.95	C	333.75	345.52	C	352.66	359.17
28	C	325.26	328.82	C	361.57	346.61	C	335.61	C	340.10	C	C
29	311.82	324.93	330.77	348.22	359.11	C	313.12	334.51	C	338.05	354.11	C
30	313.38		C	348.28	360.34	C	313.54	333.88	346.39	338.18	C	359.99
31	315.38		C		361.85		316.00	C		340.57		362.61
Close	315.38	324.93	330.77	348.28	361.85	346.61	316.00	333.88	346.39	340.57	354.11	362.61
Month Pt Change	−0.59	9.55	5.84	17.51	13.57	−15.24	−30.61	17.88	12.51	−5.82	13.54	8.50
Month % Change	−0.2	3.0	1.8	5.3	3.9	−4.2	−8.8	5.7	3.7	−1.7	4.0	2.4
QTR % Change			4.7			4.8			−0.1			4.7
Year % Change												14.8

Election Year	Bull Market	Best Eight Months 16.4%	High May-22 364.61
Clinton (1st Term)	Expansion	Worst Four Months -1.7%	Low Jan-16 301.75

RUSSELL 2000 INDEX — 1997

	Jan	Feb	Mar	Apr	May	Jun	Jul	Aug	Sep	Oct	Nov	Dec
Previous Month Close	362.61	369.45	360.05	342.56	343.00	380.76	396.37	414.48	423.43	453.82	433.26	429.92
1	C	C	C	340.88	345.66	C	394.13	414.21	C	454.69	C	434.16
2	358.96	C	C	337.79	353.98	383.52	394.72	C	428.05	456.94	C	432.48
3	361.85	369.53	360.49	336.38	C	383.28	396.17	C	428.79	459.52	440.98	433.81
4	C	368.32	361.91	340.84	C	382.67	C	415.63	429.71	C	442.31	434.91
5	C	365.49	363.93	C	362.43	384.99	C	418.32	433.04	C	444.76	438.06
6	362.31	365.48	363.80	C	361.73	387.14	C	420.73	C	461.70	442.83	C
7	364.16	366.75	365.46	344.91	360.22	C	396.26	420.12	C	463.78	435.22	C
8	364.17	C	C	345.97	360.10	C	398.28	414.19	435.99	463.66	C	442.03
9	365.59	C	C	346.73	361.42	387.90	397.40	C	437.75	464.55	C	438.16
10	366.09	364.15	367.09	345.16	C	387.31	399.15	C	436.90	465.03	435.40	432.81
11	C	362.75	367.87	339.25	C	387.62	402.26	412.64	435.93	C	433.43	424.70
12	C	365.40	364.40	C	363.76	389.54	C	411.42	440.09	C	423.44	422.63
13	365.85	368.18	360.06	C	363.56	392.07	C	411.64	C	465.21	423.39	C
14	367.52	369.13	361.04	338.61	364.48	C	403.85	411.87	C	463.97	428.41	C
15	367.19	C	C	340.78	365.91	C	406.39	408.58	440.17	462.74	C	420.76
16	366.92	C	C	340.24	365.28	392.20	410.22	C	445.18	457.16	C	425.34
17	367.88	C	357.37	340.43	C	392.55	408.11	C	446.15	449.29	435.65	426.44
18	C	370.05	354.93	341.74	C	392.46	405.89	408.73	446.50	C	432.13	420.35
19	C	370.17	351.79	C	366.57	396.49	C	413.79	447.17	C	430.69	420.03
20	369.35	367.56	352.31	C	368.20	393.60	C	419.07	C	453.85	435.70	C
21	370.32	366.37	351.73	338.27	370.06	C	403.44	417.04	C	458.93	435.05	C
22	370.65	C	C	338.09	371.46	C	406.16	415.73	448.98	458.25	C	422.88
23	370.46	C	C	338.40	375.67	390.82	407.64	C	449.42	449.36	C	422.03
24	368.14	366.45	349.48	338.52	C	393.30	408.19	C	448.58	447.53	427.83	421.04
25	C	366.79	350.70	335.85	C	391.22	408.54	418.09	447.92	C	426.91	C
26	C	363.85	352.31	C	C	390.27	C	418.31	448.88	C	428.16	421.49
27	365.52	361.15	348.95	C	376.74	392.53	C	420.84	C	420.13	C	C
28	366.47	360.05	C	336.10	377.79	C	408.68	421.59	C	429.89	429.92	C
29	366.25		C	340.58	378.43	C	409.88	423.43	451.31	434.87	C	426.67
30	368.29		C	343.00	380.76	396.37	413.44	C	453.82	428.66	C	434.01
31	369.45		342.56		C		414.48	C		433.26		437.02
Close	369.45	360.05	342.56	343.00	380.76	396.37	414.48	423.43	453.82	433.26	429.92	437.02
Month Pt Change	6.84	-9.40	-17.49	0.44	37.76	15.61	18.11	8.95	30.39	-20.56	-3.34	7.10
Month % Change	1.9	-2.5	-4.9	0.1	11.0	4.1	4.6	2.2	7.2	-4.5	-0.8	1.7
QTR % Change			-5.5			15.7			14.5			-3.7
Year % Change												20.5

HIGHLIGHTS

Post Election Year	Bull Market	Best Eight Months	-3.1%	High	Oct-13	465.21
Clinton (2nd Term)	Expansion	Worst Four Months	9.3%	Low	Apr-25	335.85

1998 RUSSELL 2000 INDEX

	Jan	Feb	Mar	Apr	May	Jun	Jul	Aug	Sep	Oct	Nov	Dec
Previous Month Close	437.02	430.05	461.83	480.68	482.89	456.62	457.39	419.75	337.95	363.59	378.16	397.75
1	C	C	C	484.93	484.94	451.17	459.85	C	348.10	350.04	C	398.74
2	436.52	434.42	461.54	486.43	C	449.70	458.31	C	352.65	349.71	386.82	397.49
3	C	437.80	462.42	485.79	C	449.16	C	413.36	346.29	C	387.56	395.00
4	C	441.84	462.13	C	485.46	451.74	C	401.63	347.07	C	392.96	398.37
5	437.06	444.06	456.82	C	481.74	454.24	C	398.69	C	336.80	396.79	C
6	433.10	445.50	463.72	481.88	479.37	C	459.97	406.62	C	332.55	400.32	C
7	429.79	C	C	475.15	475.96	C	459.04	415.80	C	322.23	C	401.17
8	425.71	C	C	475.33	479.51	456.34	459.97	C	361.93	310.28	C	401.48
9	412.95	447.28	461.12	480.04	C	456.74	460.00	C	352.69	318.40	398.43	401.96
10	C	451.19	464.62	C	C	451.08	458.43	411.64	344.97	C	396.86	396.50
11	C	452.02	467.12	C	476.90	444.35	C	400.60	353.62	C	393.47	395.37
12	410.88	452.40	467.77	C	476.13	441.59	C	408.55	C	325.62	392.20	C
13	418.44	454.29	468.77	479.56	477.48	C	458.75	403.83	C	320.33	389.36	C
14	421.93	C	C	484.85	475.55	C	459.43	402.79	357.72	324.98	C	387.94
15	421.75	C	C	487.12	472.44	433.86	461.98	C	357.73	334.81	C	389.57
16	426.25	C	471.76	484.41	C	438.37	463.64	C	359.85	342.87	390.42	389.85
17	C	453.19	471.11	487.01	C	444.08	462.36	403.96	355.29	C	389.43	393.78
18	C	454.69	472.18	C	467.61	439.79	C	411.29	363.26	C	392.12	397.42
19	C	454.21	474.30	C	470.86	438.47	C	405.84	C	352.45	394.37	C
20	431.31	453.99	474.25	488.81	468.54	C	461.92	401.73	C	358.31	394.29	C
21	429.89	C	C	491.41	467.19	C	456.14	395.64	362.64	359.94	C	401.83
22	426.20	C	C	491.14	462.99	441.65	450.93	C	368.24	366.40	C	400.24
23	424.81	456.29	473.96	484.95	C	447.42	442.33	C	376.00	367.05	398.15	404.79
24	C	454.30	476.26	480.32	C	451.31	438.58	393.70	370.25	C	396.60	405.56
25	C	458.49	477.14	C	C	450.16	C	389.76	369.02	C	399.32	C
26	421.01	461.54	477.81	C	455.08	450.27	C	380.42	C	372.07	C	C
27	422.53	461.83	477.15	468.50	450.26	C	433.16	366.10	C	371.50	402.09	C
28	428.60	C	C	472.54	455.81	C	427.54	358.54	368.01	371.47	C	408.28
29	431.99		C	476.98	456.62	453.83	426.19	C	365.80	374.48	C	410.41
30	430.05		476.24	482.89	C	457.39	429.50	C	363.59	378.16	397.75	411.91
31	C		480.68		C		419.75	337.95		C		421.96
Close	430.05	461.83	480.68	482.89	456.62	457.39	419.75	337.95	363.59	378.16	397.75	421.96
Month Pt Change	−6.97	31.78	18.85	2.21	−26.27	0.77	−37.64	−81.80	25.64	14.57	19.59	24.21
Month % Change	−1.6	7.4	4.1	0.5	−5.4	0.2	−8.2	−19.5	7.6	4.0	5.2	6.1
QTR % Change			10.0			−4.8			−20.5			16.1
Year % Change												−3.4

HIGHLIGHTS

Mid-Term Election Year	Bull Market	Best Eight Months 21.0%	High Apr-21 491.41
Clinton (2nd Term)	Expansion	Worst Four Months -17.3%	Low Oct-08 310.28

RUSSELL 2000 INDEX — 1999

Previous Month Close	Jan	Feb	Mar	Apr	May	Jun	Jul	Aug	Sep	Oct	Nov	Dec
	421.96	427.22	392.26	397.63	432.81	438.68	457.68	444.77	427.83	427.30	428.64	454.08
1	C	426.08	394.39	398.74	C	437.46	454.31	C	430.99	423.53	431.82	453.67
2	C	421.73	394.43	C	C	436.74	456.51	442.63	427.42	C	432.39	460.44
3	C	423.74	391.95	C	433.28	435.98	C	436.28	435.97	C	438.46	464.58
4	421.26	417.79	394.02	C	432.59	442.33	C	429.70	C	426.61	439.90	C
5	422.09	412.72	398.01	402.29	434.27	C	C	429.75	C	426.01	442.41	C
6	427.79	C	C	401.08	433.38	C	456.55	428.04	C	429.76	C	465.75
7	427.83	C	C	397.77	436.11	446.65	452.69	C	438.24	428.11	C	465.70
8	431.23	411.33	400.06	399.89	C	443.76	454.75	C	435.90	427.71	445.07	468.84
9	C	403.13	399.20	405.86	C	445.19	457.98	425.89	437.77	C	446.28	464.90
10	C	397.96	401.12	C	441.85	442.27	C	422.82	441.19	C	448.72	466.71
11	433.13	406.16	401.08	C	446.81	438.01	C	428.19	C	430.19	447.49	C
12	427.36	398.44	398.38	412.32	449.26	C	459.30	428.82	C	424.68	449.69	C
13	424.86	C	C	417.24	450.84	C	458.11	434.05	439.65	419.32	C	470.38
14	420.10	C	C	417.39	443.13	431.53	461.46	C	438.24	419.31	C	462.75
15	427.05	C	400.84	417.77	C	434.01	465.80	C	436.33	414.70	452.97	461.32
16	C	396.40	399.17	421.58	C	441.20	465.26	433.82	430.25	C	456.88	465.26
17	C	389.54	398.43	C	441.35	443.38	C	436.00	434.45	C	457.07	466.21
18	C	391.09	399.55	C	442.45	445.05	C	433.10	C	408.90	462.04	C
19	430.89	392.30	396.58	412.41	446.14	C	461.37	432.77	C	410.93	461.27	C
20	430.62	C	C	415.34	448.02	C	453.55	434.38	433.20	413.94	C	467.19
21	424.05	C	C	426.57	449.14	449.44	454.63	C	426.50	414.27	C	475.79
22	422.44	397.82	393.20	428.85	C	447.33	451.49	C	427.53	418.69	460.77	477.94
23	C	399.01	383.37	431.73	C	447.04	448.38	437.25	420.21	C	454.45	482.43
24	C	395.26	384.40	C	440.39	443.16	C	437.12	417.09	C	455.93	C
25	422.11	392.69	392.99	C	434.45	443.11	C	437.86	C	417.76	C	C
26	425.33	392.26	393.92	434.97	435.41	C	442.87	436.02	C	415.79	458.94	C
27	421.12	C	C	435.16	432.92	C	446.48	432.45	421.86	416.77	C	484.46
28	423.97	C	C	433.53	438.68	448.61	446.61	C	418.49	422.81	C	488.48
29	427.22		399.76	432.85	C	454.08	441.58	C	421.52	428.64	456.95	497.01
30	C		398.78	432.81	C	457.68	444.77	427.36	427.30	C	454.08	496.59
31	C		397.63		C		C	427.83		C		504.75
Close	427.22	392.26	397.63	432.81	438.68	457.68	444.77	427.83	427.30	428.64	454.08	504.75
Month Pt Change	5.26	−34.96	5.37	35.18	5.87	19.00	−12.91	−16.94	−0.53	1.34	25.44	50.67
Month % Change	1.2	−8.2	1.4	8.8	1.4	4.3	−2.8	−3.8	−0.1	0.3	5.9	11.2
QTR % Change			−5.8			15.1			−6.6			18.1
Year % Change												19.6

HIGHLIGHTS

Pre-Election Year	Bull Market	Best Eight Months	20.7%	High Dec-31	504.75
Clinton (2nd Term)	Expansion	Worst Four Months	-6.3%	Low Mar-23	383.37

2000 — RUSSELL 2000 INDEX

Previous Month Close	Jan	Feb	Mar	Apr	May	Jun	Jul	Aug	Sep	Oct	Nov	Dec
	504.75	496.23	577.71	539.09	506.25	476.18	517.23	500.64	537.89	521.37	497.68	445.94
1	C	503.75	588.35	C	518.93	492.47	C	497.77	541.91	C	495.18	456.84
2	C	509.89	584.04	C	505.35	513.03	C	500.22	C	511.67	506.97	C
3	496.42	521.63	597.88	516.04	495.56	C	524.04	499.45	C	504.67	507.75	C
4	478.38	525.52	C	506.12	501.91	C	C	503.63	C	507.49	C	450.39
5	478.83	C	C	518.04	512.84	513.30	518.25	C	539.02	502.67	C	471.17
6	475.34	C	601.64	532.50	C	511.65	523.32	C	536.32	491.02	503.96	463.54
7	488.31	532.39	595.47	542.99	C	516.54	528.22	509.87	542.82	C	506.01	461.10
8	C	537.49	594.68	C	500.08	514.54	C	508.72	535.69	C	500.68	479.07
9	C	536.00	606.05	C	490.86	523.06	C	507.50	C	489.53	495.33	C
10	501.89	542.21	603.81	518.66	474.28	C	530.83	501.65	C	481.63	480.90	C
11	492.61	537.10	C	510.13	489.39	C	529.74	510.27	533.62	474.74	C	487.23
12	490.04	C	C	493.44	490.94	508.51	540.25	C	532.43	462.97	C	477.76
13	501.19	C	590.14	489.22	C	513.75	542.76	C	534.00	480.39	476.55	469.91
14	507.56	539.94	572.99	453.72	C	509.67	542.63	514.48	539.21	C	486.91	461.82
15	C	540.24	558.87	C	497.81	512.25	C	509.93	530.88	C	491.79	458.03
16	C	547.76	574.24	C	505.98	513.74	C	512.74	C	481.75	481.64	C
17	C	558.42	574.77	459.26	499.66	C	545.18	516.46	C	470.88	482.61	C
18	513.46	545.68	C	486.09	490.95	C	536.28	515.51	516.68	466.21	C	463.25
19	520.02	C	C	486.23	479.70	522.79	527.86	C	523.31	481.30	C	458.78
20	527.28	C	549.20	481.84	C	525.69	534.75	C	521.43	487.45	470.24	443.80
21	533.94	C	552.79	C	C	527.61	522.70	516.45	514.36	C	466.79	447.03
22	C	540.95	571.19	C	471.67	515.01	C	517.46	518.82	C	457.90	462.99
23	C	549.91	573.79	C	459.01	510.41	C	517.88	C	489.96	C	C
24	522.95	554.04	574.01	468.54	461.74	C	514.25	523.30	C	487.85	471.87	C
25	521.59	556.74	C	489.03	456.17	C	514.33	525.11	515.38	475.21	C	C
26	521.04	C	C	484.24	457.37	516.36	513.81	C	509.89	479.76	C	466.63
27	517.02	C	573.65	494.58	C	508.08	501.61	C	508.13	479.85	471.70	479.30
28	504.62	557.68	559.04	506.25	C	520.99	490.22	526.48	523.81	C	459.02	494.03
29	C	577.71	543.00	C	C	512.58	C	529.63	521.37	C	454.60	483.53
30	C		531.57	C	476.70	517.23	C	532.33	C	482.72	445.94	C
31	496.23		539.09		476.18		500.64	537.89		497.68		C
Close	496.23	577.71	539.09	506.25	476.18	517.23	500.64	537.89	521.37	497.68	445.94	483.53
Month Pt Change	-8.52	81.48	-38.62	-32.84	-30.07	41.05	-16.59	37.25	-16.52	-23.69	-51.74	37.59
Month % Change	-1.7	16.4	-6.7	-6.1	-5.9	8.6	-3.2	7.4	-3.1	-4.5	-10.4	8.4
QTR % Change			6.8			-4.1			0.8			-7.3
Year % Change												-4.2

HIGHLIGHTS

Election Year	Bear Market Begins 1/14	Best Eight Months	3.0%	High Mar-09	606.05
Clinton (2nd Term)	Expansion	Worst Four Months	-3.8%	Low Dec-20	443.80

RUSSELL 2000 INDEX — 2001

Previous Month Close	Jan	Feb	Mar	Apr	May	Jun	Jul	Aug	Sep	Oct	Nov	Dec
	483.53	508.34	474.37	450.53	485.32	496.50	512.64	484.78	468.56	404.87	428.17	460.78
1	C	508.94	473.30	C	490.47	501.72	C	489.24	C	397.60	434.88	C
2	462.49	501.50	476.88	439.76	491.64	C	498.39	488.99	C	401.79	433.07	C
3	484.39	C	C	426.96	485.65	C	496.83	487.15	C	413.22	C	457.03
4	477.20	C	C	425.74	492.89	507.32	C	C	466.96	417.04	C	467.84
5	463.14	500.74	475.79	444.73	C	516.48	492.73	C	462.51	414.97	437.54	479.42
6	C	505.76	481.13	434.66	C	512.58	483.26	480.96	453.39	C	442.78	482.23
7	C	507.08	484.84	C	489.64	514.77	C	480.33	445.19	C	440.80	481.21
8	461.64	502.89	481.49	C	491.77	511.64	C	472.62	C	412.18	439.06	C
9	463.95	497.05	473.65	441.67	490.18	C	485.98	474.17	C	408.68	438.10	C
10	475.45	C	C	451.84	490.58	C	478.14	475.52	440.73	421.66	C	474.18
11	483.86	C	C	449.25	487.36	506.93	475.83	C	C	431.04	C	474.77
12	485.75	505.35	458.40	455.02	C	506.93	489.04	C	C	428.59	440.48	475.31
13	C	502.57	462.26	C	C	505.12	490.71	477.60	C	C	448.34	468.67
14	C	503.49	453.69	C	486.64	495.38	C	480.19	C	C	452.82	471.29
15	C	508.85	452.16	C	489.63	495.13	C	478.95	C	430.09	449.39	C
16	493.28	499.28	441.80	450.90	497.21	C	483.80	481.68	C	434.53	451.31	C
17	493.46	C	C	455.58	504.76	C	490.57	475.65	417.67	424.49	C	479.94
18	494.63	C	C	466.51	506.28	490.53	483.62	C	411.66	421.06	C	485.49
19	488.09	C	451.27	472.40	C	488.73	487.54	C	403.20	425.70	457.71	482.07
20	C	491.14	444.48	466.71	C	495.86	487.93	478.87	387.65	C	453.90	474.08
21	C	483.51	435.74	C	515.91	497.82	C	472.24	378.89	C	452.31	484.02
22	490.15	477.26	432.80	C	517.23	488.65	C	477.18	C	430.50	C	C
23	502.06	477.45	443.27	461.07	507.36	C	482.70	473.42	C	427.37	458.42	C
24	502.25	C	C	462.35	510.40	C	474.26	480.81	393.79	427.65	C	485.81
25	499.00	C	C	472.74	508.62	484.19	476.99	C	396.18	435.96	C	C
26	498.68	488.31	447.38	477.56	C	490.82	485.07	C	389.79	438.65	461.22	490.19
27	C	478.75	452.88	483.97	C	495.58	485.01	478.93	392.96	C	460.71	492.62
28	C	474.37	442.20	C	C	502.99	C	474.20	404.87	C	453.70	493.62
29	507.91		441.53	C	502.37	512.64	C	473.34	C	429.41	463.33	C
30	511.66		450.53	485.32	493.96	C	484.71	468.06	C	422.83	460.78	C
31	508.34		C		496.50		484.78	468.56		428.17		488.50
Close	508.34	474.37	450.53	485.32	496.50	512.64	484.78	468.56	404.87	428.17	460.78	488.50
Month Pt Change	24.81	−33.97	−23.84	34.79	11.18	16.14	−27.86	−16.22	−63.69	23.30	32.61	27.72
Month % Change	5.1	−6.7	−5.0	7.7	2.3	3.3	−5.4	−3.3	−13.6	5.8	7.6	6.0
QTR % Change			−6.8			13.8			−21.0			20.7
Year % Change												1.0

Data Bank

Previous Month Close	Jan	Feb	Mar	Apr	May	Jun	Jul	Aug	Sep	Oct	Nov	Dec
	488.50	483.10	469.36	506.46	510.67	487.47	462.64	392.42	390.96	362.27	373.50	406.35
1	C	480.04	478.34	504.50	510.83	C	447.73	389.21	C	368.09	383.45	C
2	487.19	C	C	500.49	513.37	C	432.84	376.45	C	360.22	C	408.54
3	495.51	C	C	496.60	512.32	474.39	429.47	C	379.13	356.85	C	400.83
4	499.30	470.09	488.00	498.37	C	473.76	C	C	389.75	347.98	386.97	397.53
5	C	468.82	487.59	497.76	C	475.04	440.92	367.12	381.06	C	386.07	394.45
6	C	462.41	494.80	C	502.91	465.29	C	380.79	391.57	C	392.73	396.72
7	493.18	458.40	494.92	C	498.98	470.51	C	383.47	C	338.29	383.15	C
8	497.90	466.67	499.85	503.01	509.75	C	433.61	389.84	C	340.32	379.00	C
9	494.74	C	C	503.01	501.39	C	429.25	388.45	392.47	327.04	C	386.29
10	495.31	C	C	511.30	492.73	469.29	419.78	C	394.16	336.18	C	393.47
11	489.94	471.32	500.75	503.73	C	462.78	416.68	C	393.37	344.93	369.14	393.88
12	C	472.01	498.90	515.46	C	462.99	413.28	388.56	386.27	C	374.69	395.36
13	C	476.33	495.45	C	499.72	455.98	C	377.76	389.99	C	376.11	387.98
14	483.01	470.75	497.76	C	511.72	459.07	C	389.41	C	346.53	386.24	C
15	485.00	469.25	499.12	512.74	513.54	C	409.08	390.73	C	360.52	385.92	C
16	476.42	C	C	522.95	507.40	C	407.27	395.97	386.13	350.85	C	394.90
17	482.39	C	C	518.77	508.94	470.74	409.69	C	379.31	362.57	C	391.25
18	474.37	C	502.80	518.57	C	469.71	396.71	C	376.75	363.37	382.58	383.93
19	C	459.98	504.73	517.40	C	462.92	386.20	401.29	365.54	C	379.57	383.41
20	C	467.25	499.04	C	503.17	460.25	C	397.84	367.28	C	388.59	386.88
21	C	458.44	505.44	C	495.46	461.07	C	406.79	C	368.63	397.68	C
22	469.43	465.07	502.39	510.93	493.91	C	379.65	409.67	C	362.66	400.00	C
23	477.45	C	C	510.29	501.24	C	363.99	400.13	358.68	368.95	C	389.73
24	479.73	C	C	507.32	493.64	459.09	378.56	C	356.58	366.02	C	388.12
25	479.35	468.19	496.39	508.85	C	452.45	378.11	C	365.14	372.64	404.85	C
26	C	471.29	501.66	501.50	C	452.97	382.26	407.73	370.69	C	398.32	389.40
27	C	472.61	505.85	C	C	458.72	C	397.45	361.78	C	410.24	384.16
28	481.28	469.36	506.46	C	492.41	462.64	C	389.38	C	369.01	C	C
29	473.98		C	500.54	487.60	C	400.81	394.40	C	368.63	406.35	C
30	479.72		C	510.67	487.83	C	400.91	390.96	362.27	374.17	C	382.23
31	483.10		C		487.47		392.42	C		373.50		383.09
Close	483.10	469.36	506.46	510.67	487.47	462.64	392.42	390.96	362.27	373.50	406.35	383.09
Month Pt Change	−5.40	−13.74	37.10	4.21	−23.20	−24.83	−70.22	−1.46	−28.69	11.23	32.85	−23.26
Month % Change	−1.1	−2.8	7.9	0.8	−4.5	−5.1	−15.2	−0.4	−7.3	3.1	8.8	−5.7
QTR % Change			3.7			−8.7			−21.7			5.7
Year % Change												−21.6

HIGHLIGHTS

Mid-Term Election Year	Bear Market 3/19 - 10/9	Best Eight Months	20.0%	High Apr-16	522.95
GW Bush (1st Term)	Expansion	Worst Four Months	-19.3%	Low Oct-09	327.04

RUSSELL 2000 INDEX   2003

Previous Month Close	Jan	Feb	Mar	Apr	May	Jun	Jul	Aug	Sep	Oct	Nov	Dec
	383.09	372.17	360.52	364.54	398.68	441.00	448.37	476.02	497.42	487.68	528.22	546.51
1	C	C	C	368.69	398.83	C	449.17	468.08	C	500.32	C	554.59
2	392.58	C	C	376.30	407.67	442.63	458.89	C	507.50	503.20	C	553.60
3	390.31	370.25	359.31	375.22	C	443.87	456.35	C	510.71	512.28	537.84	545.19
4	C	368.72	356.51	373.28	C	451.23	C	464.77	512.56	C	538.87	544.15
5	C	366.99	356.54	C	409.80	456.69	C	457.45	508.87	C	538.91	539.01
6	397.00	364.74	353.84	C	412.75	453.94	C	453.91	C	516.72	542.94	C
7	393.95	358.78	354.18	376.57	410.23	C	465.71	453.77	C	520.77	542.96	C
8	389.07	C	C	374.66	407.68	C	473.97	453.94	517.13	515.68	C	543.04
9	395.94	C	C	372.28	413.53	444.79	476.99	C	513.57	521.34	C	534.54
10	396.44	362.10	348.01	372.69	C	450.96	469.03	C	501.76	519.06	533.21	528.49
11	C	359.96	347.03	371.30	C	455.50	473.77	459.27	507.43	C	528.57	542.92
12	C	355.38	345.94	C	418.20	456.74	C	466.95	509.06	C	540.66	547.59
13	396.18	354.77	355.44	C	419.23	449.71	C	467.47	C	527.57	541.20	C
14	398.45	358.50	354.39	377.61	419.44	C	479.03	471.22	C	531.84	532.96	C
15	395.53	C	C	379.60	422.05	C	476.93	471.92	507.64	527.35	C	535.25
16	394.88	C	C	377.73	414.69	457.47	473.68	C	515.66	529.64	C	537.74
17	388.10	C	365.40	383.70	C	458.01	459.93	C	515.10	520.36	526.21	538.72
18	C	364.53	368.00	C	C	457.51	464.76	480.92	519.46	C	521.68	546.90
19	C	360.28	368.51	C	408.32	450.33	C	488.70	520.20	C	525.62	546.88
20	C	359.74	370.49	C	409.03	449.56	C	489.46	C	521.44	523.08	C
21	383.17	364.36	376.23	385.30	410.73	C	457.17	494.82	C	525.53	525.93	C
22	380.53	C	C	391.16	415.09	C	464.00	485.51	513.65	513.15	C	549.37
23	383.71	C	C	394.97	418.40	439.41	466.14	C	519.36	510.49	C	555.03
24	375.06	358.22	367.25	392.27	C	440.89	465.26	C	507.86	506.43	539.51	552.35
25	C	361.20	371.79	388.50	C	443.21	468.88	483.87	495.06	C	543.18	C
26	C	357.97	368.18	C	C	449.90	C	486.51	485.29	C	545.31	554.90
27	368.58	361.43	369.50	C	427.71	448.75	C	490.92	C	515.35	C	C
28	373.17	360.52	368.70	395.20	430.48	C	473.83	495.81	C	525.85	546.51	C
29	374.84		C	395.78	432.64	C	473.60	497.42	492.71	531.81	C	563.88
30	367.62		C	398.68	441.00	448.37	472.80	C	487.68	530.37	C	565.47
31	372.17		364.54		C		476.02	C		528.22		556.91
Close	372.17	360.52	364.54	398.68	441.00	448.37	476.02	497.42	487.68	528.22	546.51	556.91
Month Pt Change	−10.92	−11.65	4.02	34.14	42.32	7.37	27.65	21.40	−9.74	40.54	18.29	10.40
Month % Change	−2.9	−3.1	1.1	9.4	10.6	1.7	6.2	4.5	−2.0	8.3	3.5	1.9
QTR % Change			−4.8			23.0			8.8			14.2
Year % Change												45.4

HIGHLIGHTS

Pre-Election Year	Bull Market	Best Eight Months	12.0%	High	Dec-30	565.47
GW Bush (1st Term)	Expansion	Worst Four Months	17.8%	Low	Mar-12	345.94

	Jan	Feb	Mar	Apr	May	Jun	Jul	Aug	Sep	Oct	Nov	Dec
Previous Month Close	556.91	580.76	585.56	590.31	559.80	568.28	591.52	551.29	547.93	572.94	583.79	633.77
1	C	C	594.77	595.32	C	572.49	582.43	C	552.46	585.03	587.00	643.68
2	560.85	580.54	591.06	603.45	C	573.56	582.72	551.93	559.78	C	585.44	642.51
3	C	579.15	591.32	C	565.48	562.44	C	543.63	556.24	C	595.33	642.21
4	C	564.03	598.38	C	569.64	567.75	C	542.67	C	589.09	602.13	C
5	568.92	569.54	599.54	606.39	570.06	C	C	532.36	C	587.34	604.29	C
6	569.89	584.07	C	599.33	563.09	C	572.41	519.65	C	592.66	C	639.03
7	574.62	C	C	601.64	548.56	578.90	572.03	C	562.93	582.60	C	625.50
8	579.62	C	592.51	597.88	C	577.91	560.71	C	557.79	575.65	602.08	631.15
9	575.20	585.49	585.95	C	C	568.58	563.73	518.38	566.18	C	606.64	629.19
10	C	592.83	575.01	C	537.86	569.12	C	529.83	569.91	C	609.61	632.24
11	C	597.07	568.74	C	548.67	C	C	526.63	C	577.56	616.30	C
12	583.01	592.75	582.84	599.65	548.99	C	562.24	517.10	C	576.71	621.98	C
13	581.16	585.14	C	585.83	547.17	C	562.69	517.39	573.10	569.42	C	638.03
14	586.12	C	C	582.02	543.76	557.67	559.74	C	570.96	564.88	C	643.54
15	586.36	C	566.95	580.30	C	567.92	562.16	C	568.52	569.42	623.86	648.61
16	590.41	C	566.64	583.37	C	570.07	555.48	528.06	574.54	C	617.89	642.23
17	C	594.48	578.57	C	535.34	569.57	C	530.00	573.17	C	622.97	642.08
18	C	591.48	574.55	C	542.56	570.54	C	541.61	C	572.03	622.06	C
19	C	582.59	570.74	586.95	540.86	C	554.73	537.44	C	566.67	613.44	C
20	597.98	579.89	C	575.81	540.75	C	564.19	547.92	570.74	570.13	C	638.05
21	597.48	C	C	583.22	545.81	568.74	548.57	C	576.92	576.66	C	646.20
22	591.73	C	558.99	593.24	C	571.89	546.52	C	565.89	567.78	621.52	648.46
23	596.14	570.20	560.92	590.71	C	580.15	539.23	543.47	565.80	C	624.53	649.37
24	C	571.87	557.63	C	551.72	579.05	C	545.01	565.97	C	629.50	C
25	C	579.04	571.53	C	565.39	587.70	C	550.14	C	571.67	C	C
26	601.50	583.86	572.92	589.45	567.77	C	533.49	547.25	C	577.61	631.16	C
27	595.17	585.56	C	590.76	568.56	C	544.61	551.67	558.36	587.18	C	644.34
28	583.91	C	C	577.06	568.28	584.10	541.20	C	565.66	585.63	C	654.57
29	579.86	C	583.39	567.25	C	587.83	549.83	C	571.07	583.79	634.46	653.34
30	580.76		589.40	559.80	C	591.52	551.29	544.56	572.94	C	633.77	653.06
31	C		590.31		C		C	547.93		C		651.57
Close	580.76	585.56	590.31	559.80	568.28	591.52	551.29	547.93	572.94	583.79	633.77	651.57
Month Pt Change	23.85	4.80	4.75	−30.51	8.48	23.24	−40.23	−3.36	25.01	10.85	49.98	17.80
Month % Change	4.3	0.8	0.8	−5.2	1.5	4.1	−6.8	−0.6	4.6	1.9	8.6	2.8
QTR % Change			6.0			0.2			−3.1			13.7
Year % Change												17.0

HIGHLIGHTS

Election Year	Bull Market	Best Eight Months	9.6%	High	Dec-28	654.57
GW Bush (1st Term)	Expansion	Worst Four Months	-1.3%	Low	Aug-12	517.10

RUSSELL 2000 INDEX   2005

Previous Month	Jan	Feb	Mar	Apr	May	Jun	Jul	Aug	Sep	Oct	Nov	Dec
Close	651.57	624.02	634.06	615.07	579.38	616.71						
1	C	628.14	638.53	611.55	C	623.76						
2	C	631.98	637.33	C	585.86	625.24						
3	640.44	629.32	638.29	C	584.48	620.31						
4	628.54	637.44	644.95	613.76	595.22	C						
5	617.48	C	C	614.50	595.64	C						
6	619.82	C	C	616.21	596.52	622.94						
7	613.21	636.62	643.86	619.76	C	623.78						
8	C	638.72	637.98	610.75	C	620.47						
9	C	625.71	631.08	C	602.91	626.23						
10	617.74	626.81	626.94	C	595.04	626.33						
11	611.53	634.76	626.84	607.17	595.57	C						
12	613.19	C	C	613.03	586.89	C						
13	610.13	C	C	602.54	582.02	629.02						
14	617.48	635.02	630.30	591.94	C	634.39						
15	C	634.94	626.82	580.78	C	637.19						
16	C	638.85	622.92	C	591.71	644.03						
17	C	631.14	625.46	C	595.27	644.19						
18	624.87	630.13	622.57	585.33	607.88	C						
19	617.91	C	C	594.94	610.46	C						
20	612.34	C	C	584.96	609.41	641.84						
21	611.08	C	621.57	598.98	C	641.04						
22	C	617.93	618.58	589.53	C	643.45						
23	C	620.54	612.06	C	612.87	634.12						
24	604.53	627.56	615.27	C	612.95	630.41						
25	606.50	637.53	C	596.44	606.40	C						
26	616.57	C	C	587.66	614.70	C						
27	616.90	C	C	587.14	616.90	628.31						
28	613.00	634.06	615.12	575.02	C	641.48						
29	C		604.63	579.38	C	642.76						
30	C		614.90	C	C	639.66						
31	624.02		615.07		616.71							
Close	624.02	634.06	615.07	579.38	616.71	639.66						
Month Pt Change	−27.55	10.04	−18.99	−35.69	37.33	22.95						
Month % Change	−4.2	1.6	−3.0	−5.8	6.4	3.7						
QTR % Change			−5.6			4.0						
Year % Change												

HIGHLIGHTS

Post Election Year	Bull Market	Best Eight Months	9.8%	High	Mar-04	644.95
GW Bush (2nd Term)	Expansion	Worst Four Months	—	Low	Apr-28	575.02

Data Bank   525